JANUARY 1971
VOLUME XIII—NO. 1

JOURNAL OF INTER-AMERICAN STUDIES and WORLD AFFAIRS

JOURNAL OF INTER-AMERICAN STUDIES and WORLD AFFAIRS

Vol. XIII, No. 1 JANUARY 1971

The Movement for Regional Arms Control in Latin America	HUGH B. STINSON AND JAMES D. COCHRANE	1
Rural Unrest and Agrarian Policy in Argentina, 1912–1930	CARL SOLBERG	18
La Virgen de las Mercedes en la Isla de Santo Domingo	RAMÓN LUGO LOVATÓN	53
A Profile of Amazonia	FRANCES M. FOLAND	62
Student Political Activism in Guatemala	JOHN H. PETERSEN	78
Interpersonal Relationship and *Caudillismo* in Paraguay	FREDERIC HICKS	89
The Functional Elites of Quito	EMILY M. NETT	112
Contemporáneos in Mexican Intellectual History, 1928–1931	EDWARD J. MULLEN	121
Units of One and the Visible Event	URSULA LAMB	131
Nuevas Corrientes		136
Center Notes		139
Books		141

Published Quarterly for the

CENTER FOR ADVANCED INTERNATIONAL STUDIES

by the

UNIVERSITY OF MIAMI PRESS

Coral Gables, Florida

CONTRIBUTORS

JAMES D. COCHRANE, who specializes in Latin American politics, is the author of *The Politics of Regional Integration: The Central American Case* (1969) * * * HUGH B. STINSON teaches political science at the University of Southwestern Louisiana; a former NDEA Fellow, he is a Ph. D. candidate at Tulane University * * * CARL E. SOLBERG, author of *Immigration and Nationalism: Argentina and Chile, 1890–1914,* has concentrated his research on social, economic, and intellectual histories of Argentina, Uruguay, and Chile from 1880 to 1930 * * * RAMÓN LUGO LOVATÓN, professor of history of Santo Domingo at the University of Santo Domingo, has published many biographies and monographs. Formerly director of the National Archives, he is now director of the National Museum * * * FRANCES M. FOLAND, who is completing her Ph.D. at Columbia University in political science, derived much data for this article from a two-month stay in Amazônia which included trips from Rodônia to the interior of Pará * * * JOHN H. PETERSEN studies the student movements throughout Latin America. This article shows the results of field research in Guatemala * * * FREDERIC HICKS taught for three years at the Universidad Nacional de Asunción, is now chairman of the Department of Anthropology at the University of Louisville * * * EMILY M. NETT, who moved from Texas Southern University to the University of Evansville in 1969, did preliminary research for this study during a stay in Ecuador from 1963 to 1965 * * * EDWARD J. MULLEN teaches courses in contemporary Latin American literature and has published articles on various members of the Mexican literary generation "Contemporáneos" *** URSULA LAMB is a Senior Lecturer in Latin American history at Yale University. Her most recent book, *A Navigator's Universe* (University of Chicago Press) is due to be out this Spring.

All correspondence concerning manuscripts or exchange information should be directed to the Editor, *Journal of Inter-American Studies and World Affairs,* Box 8134, University of Miami, Coral Gables, Florida 33124. Correspondence regarding book reviews should be sent to the Book Review Editor, *Journal of Inter-American Studies and World Affairs,* Box 8123, University of Miami, Coral Gables, Florida 33124. Subscriptions and business correspondence should be addressed to *Journal of Inter-American Studies and World Affairs,* University of Miami Press, Drawer 9088, Coral Gables, Florida 33124. Annual subscription, $8.00; students, $6.50. Single issues available; please inquire concerning prices.

The *Journal of Inter-American Studies and World Affairs* is indexed in *Public Affairs Information Service, Historical Abstracts, Social Sciences and Humanities Index, Indice Bibliográfico, Current Contents: Behavioral, Social, and Management,* and others.

PRINTED IN THE UNITED STATES OF AMERICA

Hugh B. Stinson
and
James D. Cochrane
Department of Political Science
Tulane University at New Orleans

THE MOVEMENT FOR REGIONAL ARMS CONTROL IN LATIN AMERICA

The post-World War II period in Latin America, as elsewhere, has been marked by the presence of two somewhat contradictory phenomena in the field of armaments. On the one hand, most of the countries have continued their long-standing tradition of devoting a substantial portion of their national budgets to the military and have expanded their arsenals of weapons and stocks of military equipment.[1] On the other hand, several governments have suggested various arms control measures for the Latin American countries. The aim of some of these suggestions has been a reduction in the level of armaments, equipment, and force size; the aim of other suggestions has been more modest—to freeze armaments and forces at existing levels; and the aim of still other suggestions has been to ban nuclear weapons from the region.

Most of the arms control proposals have received little if any attention. Three of them, however—the Costa Rican proposal of 1958, the

[1] The tradition in nearly all Latin American countries of devoting sizeable portions of national budgets to the military, arms and equipment purchases, force sizes, U.S. military assistance programs to the countries south of the Rio Grande, and the political role of the armed forces in the Latin American countries are subjects thoroughly dealt with in a number of studies. See, for example: John J. Johnson, *The Military and Society in Latin America* (Stanford: Stanford University Press, 1964); Edwin Lieuwen, *Arms and Politics in Latin America*, rev. ed. (New York: Praeger, 1961); Joseph E. Loftus, *Latin American Defense Expenditures, 1938–1965* (Santa Monica, Calif.: The Rand Corporation, January, 1968); and U.S. Congress, Senate, Committee on Foreign Relations, Subcommittee on American Republics Affairs, *Survey of the Alliance for Progress: The Latin American Military*, 90th Cong., 1st sess., 1967 (a study prepared by Edwin Lieuwen).

Chilean proposal of 1960, and the Five Presidents' Declaration of 1963—did receive at least a measure of consideration from the other Latin American governments. The Costa Rican and Chilean measures, which aimed at reducing or freezing force sizes and the stock of weapons and equipment and cutting military expenditures, came to naught. The same is not true of the Five Presidents' Declaration, which called for a banning of nuclear weapons from Latin America. That proposal led ultimately to the 1967 Treaty of Tlatelolco.

The subject of this paper is arms control in Latin America. The objective of the paper is threefold: to describe the three proposals noted above; to explore at some length subsequent efforts to ban nuclear weapons from Latin America; and to identify the factors that (a) retarded general arms control efforts and (b) promoted the effort to exclude nuclear weapons from Latin America. The paper provides at most an introduction to the subject of arms control in Latin America. It is not, nor is it intended to be, a comprehensive and definitive exploration of the subject.

THE COSTA RICAN AND CHILEAN PROPOSALS

The Costa Rican and Chilean proposals were calls for general arms control or arms limitation on the part of all Latin American countries. They mounted attacks, direct and indirect, against the entire range of subjects under the armaments heading—arms purchases of all types, force size, equipment, and general military expenditures.

The Costa Rican Proposal

The Costa Rican proposal was first put forward on 20 November 1957, when Gonzalo Facio, the Costa Rican Ambassador to the Organization of American States (OAS), addressed the Overseas Press Club in New York. In his speech, he urged that the military expenditures of all Latin American governments be subjected to "substantial reduction." The ambassador went on to call for the establishment of a special OAS committee to prepare a treaty, to be signed by all Latin American states, renouncing weapons acquisitions "in excess of security requirements." The ambassador cited as the principal benefit of his government's proposal the fact that by reducing expenditures on armaments additional funds could be devoted to economic and social development in the region.[2]

Two crucial terms were left undefined. The ambassador did not spell out what he meant by a "substantial reduction" of expenditures nor did he indicate what would constitute "weapons acquisitions in excess of security

---

2 *Hispanic American Report*, January 1958, p. 19.

requirements." Apparently, definition of these terms was to be made by the special OAS committee.

The Costa Rican proposal was formally presented to the Organization of American States during March 1958. In his statement to the OAS Council, the ambassador argued that the arms expenditures of the Latin American countries were without purpose. The Latin American armed forces as equipped were not, he held, capable of playing a meaningful part in hemispheric defense; moreover, the arms and equipment purchases being made by the Latin American governments were not of a nature to make the forces capable of a significant role in that defense. Therefore, the Costa Rican proposal stated, the Latin American countries should openly face the fact that they were militarily dependent on the United States and leave hemispheric security to Washington. By abandoning the claim to a role in regional defense, the governments could greatly reduce their military expenditures, and the economic resources thus freed could be channelled into economic development. In addition, the proposal urged the Latin American government to put their military personnel to work on various economic development projects. As in his New York speech, the ambassador called for the creation of a special OAS committee to draft an arms control convention or treaty.[3]

The Costa Rican proposal received a chilly reception from virtually all OAS members. The very blunt statements regarding the ability of the Latin American armed forces to contribute to hemispheric security was responsible for much of the unfriendly reception accorded the proposal. While the armed forces of the Latin American countries are not in a position to play any meaningful role in regional defense (and while there is perhaps private or silent recognition of this fact on the part of at least some political and military leaders in Latin America), few military officers or government officials are prepared to acknowledge their military impotence openly and, in turn, to admit their dependence on the United States. The United States was no more enthusiastic about the proposal than were the Latin American countries, but for different reasons. Washington had "reservations" about the proposal because it was at variance with prevailing U.S. military policy toward Latin America—a policy of aiding the Latin American armed forces to participate in hemispheric defense.[4]

The proposal, however, was not rejected outright. Instead, the

---

[3] *Hispanic American Report*, March 1958, p. 141; *The New York Times*, 6 March 1958, p. 4.

[4] The U.S. policy is described and subjected to analysis in Lieuwen, *Arms and Politics*, pp. 196–244.

council of the OAS voted to refer it to the foreign ministers of the member-countries for study.[5] This maneuver might be described as the typical or normal way by which the council disposes of difficult or unpopular issues. Describing the operations of the council, Slater writes:

> A . . . function of the Council has been to delay or bury issues that were not at the time susceptible of actual settlement. In this capacity, the Council plays a role analogous to an interagency committee in a pluralistic political system. By creating the impression that something is being done, the Council helps to reduce domestic pressures on harassed governments and spread the responsibility for unpopular actions or non-actions.[6]

As was intended, the Costa Rican proposal was not heard of again.

The Chilean Proposal

In his 1959 Christmas message to other Latin American chief executives, President Jorge Alessandri of Chile called for a halt to the purchase of new offensive weapons by all Latin American countries. The immediate impetus for the Alessandri call was the acquisition of a new cruiser by Chile's traditional rival, Peru, and in his message Alessandri was openly and sharply critical of the Peruvian action.[7] The Alessandri initiative produced virtually no response. Despite this, the Chilean government did not drop the matter. Its next move was to make an even broader proposal —a call for general arms control in Latin America. As part of his campaign for arms control, Alessandri raised the issue during his February 1960 conference with President Eisenhower during the latter's visit to Santiago. In the communique that followed the Alessandri-Eisenhower meeting, President Eisenhower expressed support for the principle of arms control in Latin America after an equilibrium in military strength had been reached among the countries of the region.[8] The U. S. president also endorsed the idea in an address to the Chilean legislature.[9]

Shortly after the Alessandri-Eisenhower meeting, the Chilean ambassador to the Organization of American States, Walter Muller, presented his government's proposal to the council of the organization. The proposal called for creation of a study group to explore the entire question of hemispheric arms limitation and to submit a detailed report with

---

[5] *Hispanic American Report*, March 1958, p. 133.

[6] Jerome Slater, *The OAS and United States Foreign Policy* (Columbus: Ohio State University Press, 1967), p. 45 .

[7] The *New York Times*, 20 December 1959, p. 32.

[8] Ibid., 2 March 1960, p. 16.

[9] Dwight D. Eisenhower, *The White House Years: Waging Peace, 1956–1961* (Garden City: Doubleday, 1965), p. 532.

specific recommendations to the Eleventh Inter-American Conference scheduled to meet in Quito later in 1960. The Chilean ambassador discussed the economic consequences of arms purchases but made no specific or concrete suggestions beyond recommending that all future arms acquisitions be publicized. In brief, the proposal as put forward by Chile in the OAS was extremely general (one might even say vague), amounting to little more than a statement that arms control was desirable or good and that the Latin American countries should take steps to reduce their armaments. Colombia and Peru endorsed the Chilean proposal; Ecuador did the same and went on to suggest that some type of inter-American security force be a part of any arms control arrangement.[10] The Chilean proposal received sufficient support from the other members of the OAS for the council to set up the called-for study group. However, the Quito meeting at which the group was to present its report was not held, and no report or set of specific proposals or recommendations was ever forthcoming. The Chilean proposal entered into oblivion, just as the Costa Rican one before it had done.

One generalization can be made. The fate that befell the two proposals is not merely due to the bluntness of the Costa Rican proposal or to the fact that the Quito meeting was not held. Rather, the outcome of the proposals is attributable to the fact that arms control or arms limitation—when aimed at affecting conventional armaments and armaments policy in Latin America—evoked relatively little interest and received only limited political support. The reasons for the lack of interest and support are taken up in the concluding section of the paper.

THE FIVE PRESIDENTS' DECLARATION

On 29 April 1963 President Goulart of Brazil issued a statement, later termed the Five Presidents' Declaration, which had been prepared jointly with the presidents of Bolivia, Chile, Ecuador, and Mexico. In the Declaration the five presidents announced that they were prepared to sign a multilateral agreement "whereby their countries would undertake not to manufacture, receive, store, or test nuclear weapons or nuclear launching devices," and they went on to express the hope that other Latin American countries would do the same.[11] Brazil had advocated denuclearization of Latin America since 1961. In 1962 the Brazilian delegate to the United Nations had presented to the General Assembly a draft

---

10 "Arms and the Hemisphere," *Americas* 12 (February 1960): 2.

11 The statement is reproduced in Alfonso García Robles, *The Denuclearization of Latin America* (New York: Carnegie Endowment for International Peace, 1967), pp. 69–70.

resolution calling on all Latin American states to pledge not to acquire any nuclear weapons or delivery vehicles.[12] But it was not until the Five Presidents' Declaration that the idea of a denuclearized Latin America attracted wide attention or enthusiasm in the region.

The Declaration was placed before the General Assembly in resolution form during May 1963 and referred to the First Committee for consideration. In the committee the resolution was greeted with expressions of support and approval from a host of countries. All of the Latin American countries, except Cuba, indicated their approval. A number of Afro-Asian countries as well as Australia, New Zealand, and some European states did the same. However, First Committee consideration of the resolution was not confined to general statements of approval and praise. Several Latin American countries addressed themselves to substantive issues. The question of the geographical area to be covered by the ban was raised by at least three countries. Colombia and Ecuador urged emphatically that all Caribbean countries and colonies be covered by the ban. What the two countries were insisting upon, although they did not spell it out, was the inclusion of Cuba in the agreement. Panama expressed the view that all territory in Latin America *including the Canal Zone* should be covered by the resolution. The question of the peaceful use of nuclear explosives was also raised. Mexico maintained that a treaty banning nuclear weapons should make specific allowance for nuclear explosions for peaceful purposes.[13]

Cold war politics, too, entered into the discussion. Charges and countercharges were exchanged by the United States and Cuba. Cuba announced that it would not support the denuclearization resolution unless the United States agreed to dismantle its bases in the Caribbean. The United States, in rejecting the Cuban demand, questioned for the first, but not the last, time the wisdom of an agreement to ban nuclear weapons from Latin America if Cuba was not included.

The First Committee approved the resolution by a vote of 89-0, with fourteen abstentions (mostly by Communist countries, including Cuba). A short time later, the General Assembly approved the resolution by a vote of 91-0, with fifteen abstentions. Among those abstaining on the General Assembly vote was Venezuela. That country abstained on the ground that without Cuban adherence a treaty would be both meaningless and potentially dangerous to hemispheric security. Adoption of the Five

---

12 See E. Bradford Burns, "Tradition and Variation in Brazilian Foreign Policy," *Journal of Inter-American Studies* 9 (April 1967): 203; and Janio Quadros, "Brazil's New Foreign Policy," *Foreign Affairs* 40 (October 1961): 26.

13 The *New York Times,* 30 October 1962, p. 16; 9 November 1962, p. 2.

Presidents' Declaration by the General Assembly accomplished nothing of substance. It was merely an endorsement or expression of support and encouragement. Nevertheless, the United Nations action had considerable symbolic value for the cause of Latin American arms control.

THE TREATY OF TLATELOLCO

For nearly a year no action was taken to pursue the goal laid down by the General Assembly resolution. The inaction is accounted for in the main by political events in Brazil. That country, under President Goulart, had provided the leadership for the denuclearization effort. Apparently the other Latin American governments expected Brazil to continue in that role and to initiate steps toward a denuclearization treaty. In the month immediately following the General Assembly action, the Goulart government was preoccupied with domestic matters. Then, in April 1964, a military coup removed Goulart from office and replaced him with a regime backed by the armed forces. The new government expressed support for banning nuclear weapons from Latin America but offered no leadership to the effort. In time, Mexico assumed the leadership position.

Mexico's first action was to invite all Latin American governments to send delegates to the Preliminary Meeting on the Denuclearization of Latin America. That meeting, held in Mexico City on 23 November 1964, established the Preparatory Commission for the Denuclearization of Latin America and charged the newly-created body with a broad range of tasks: defining the geographical area to be covered by the nuclear ban; studying methods of verification and control; exploring the possibility or probability of compliance with a ban by the nuclear powers and nations having colonial and other possessions in the region covered by the treaty; and, finally, drafting the preliminary version of a treaty banning nuclear weapons from Latin America. The commission held a total of four sessions in its effort to produce a treaty, an end that it reached early in 1967.

The First Session

The First Session, which met 15-22 March 1965, was devoted to organizational and procedural matters. Three working groups were set up. Group A[14] was charged with defining the geographical area to be covered by the ban, securing the participation of those Latin American states not taking part in the First Session of the Preparatory Commission,[15] and

[14] Group A was composed of Argentina, Chile, Costa Rica, Ecuador, Panama, and Uruguay.

[15] At the First Session, Guatemala sent an observer instead of a fully accredited delegate. Cuba sent neither a delegate nor an observer.

obtaining the promise of those countries (France, the Netherlands, the United Kingdom, and the United States) holding colonies or other territory in Latin America that they would observe the provisions of the treaty by not placing or allowing nuclear weapons in the territory under their jurisdiction. Group B[16] was instructed to study methods of verification, inspection, and control in the enforcement of a nuclear ban. Group C[17] was assigned the task of securing commitments from the nuclear powers (China, France, the Soviet Union, the United Kingdom, and the United States) that they would respect the treaty by pledging not to place their nuclear weapons in Latin America, either directly or through transfer of such weapons to any state in the region.[18]

The Second Session

The Preparatory Commission convened again in the late summer of 1965, meeting from 23 August to 2 September. All of the Latin American states except Cuba participated. (Cuba had indicated that it would not participate in or cooperate in any way with the denuclearization effort.) Additionally, a number of non-Latin American observers, including a representative of the U.S. government, attended.

The Second Session was devoted to receiving the reports of the working groups. Groups A and C had little of a positive or encouraging nature to report concerning their efforts to persuade the nuclear powers and states holding territory in Latin America to respect the treaty. The United States and the Soviet Union had expressed support and encouragement but had refrained from committing themselves. The United Kingdom and France had not replied to the inquiries directed to them.[19] While not encouraged by the reports of the two working groups, the commission did not look upon the situation as hopeless. Instead of abandoning its attempt to obtain compliance by the relevant non-Latin American states, the commission chose to increase its efforts. It did so by creating a Negotiating Committee that was charged with obtaining the desired pledges of compliance during the forthcoming Twentieth Session of the U.N. General Assembly.[20]

The report of Group B consisted of drafts of various articles of the

---

[16] Group B was composed of El Salvador, Haiti, Honduras, Mexico, Paraguay, and Peru.

[17] Group C was composed of Bolivia, Brazil, Colombia, the Dominican Republic, Nicaragua, and Venezuela.

[18] García Robles, *Denuclearization*, pp. 82–84. All references to this work refer to official Acts of the Preparatory Commission, which are reproduced therein.

[19] The *New York Times*, 19 July 1965, p. 8.

[20] García Robles, *Denuclearization*, pp. 92–93.

treaty. One draft article stated that the treaty would prohibit the testing, use, acquisition, receipt, or storage of nuclear weapons or launching devices by any signatory. Another draft article defined "nuclear weapons" as all weapons using any type of fissionable material together with any accessories designed to be used with such weapons. Still another draft article defined the territory to be covered by the ban as, in effect, the entire western hemisphere south of the continental United States.[21]

Before the session concluded, the participants were requested to submit opinions and suggestions concerning points to be covered in the treaty to the Co-ordinating Committee, which had been established to prepare a preliminary draft of the final treaty. That draft, it was agreed, would be taken up at the Third Session of the Preparatory Commission.

Two Draft Treaties—and Disagreement

The Co-ordinating Committee met through January and February 1966. Two draft treaties emerged: the majority (or Mexican) draft and the minority (or Brazilian-Colombian) draft. The two had identical wording on most of their twenty-six articles and differed only slightly on all but one other article.[22] The principal difference between the two drafts centered around the question of when the treaty would enter into force. The Mexican draft called for the treaty to enter into force among the states that had ratified it as soon as eleven had done so. The Brazilian-Colombian draft was more stringent. It provided that the treaty would enter into force only when *all* Latin American states had ratified it, when *all* nuclear powers had signed Protocol II to the treaty (stating that they would not place nuclear weapons in the area covered by the treaty), and when *all* colonial and other countries holding territory within the area covered by the treaty had signed Protocol I (agreeing not to place nuclear weapons in the territory they controlled).[23] The objective of the Brazilian-Colombian draft was to gain Cuban and Soviet compliance before the Latin American states committed themselves.

The Third Session

By the time the Third Session of the Preparatory Commission met, 19 April–4 May 1966, debate over the two drafts had become vigorous. Two subjects were before the commission at the Third Session: the report of the Negotiating Committee and the two treaty drafts. The report

21 Ibid., pp. 96–106.

22 Ibid., pp. 117–130.

23 Ibid., pp. 128–29. Also, see "Issues before the 21st General Assembly," *International Conciliation*, no. 559 (September 1966), pp. 34–36, for a general statement of the similarities and differences in the two drafts.

of the Negotiating Committee was gloomy. The committee had been unable to establish any contact with Peking; the other nuclear powers had made no definite commitment to respect the ban on nuclear weapons, although by the same token none had stated that it would not do so. Similarly, those states having colonies or other possessions in Latin America had not committed themselves. The commission concluded that beyond the issuance of appeals, there was little or nothing more that could be done to obtain compliance.[24]

The second subject before the commission, the treaty drafts, was the main one. During the meeting many of the minor differences between the two drafts were reconciled. However, the troublesome issue of when the treaty would go into effect remained. On that point Brazil refused to compromise. The Brazilian delegate stated that his country would not participate in a treaty banning nuclear weapons from Latin America if that treaty did not include Cuba, for that country was, he held, the one most likely to acquire nuclear weapons. Argentina and Venezuela expressed agreement with the Brazilian stand—as did the United States through its ambassador in Mexico City.[25] The majority, supporting the Mexican draft, also refused to compromise. The Third Session ended in an air of discord and indecision, with final action on a draft treaty being postponed. At this point it seemed more than a slight possibility that the denuclearization effort would falter, although none of the participants was prepared to admit that this might happen.

The Fourth Session—Part I

The Fourth Session was scheduled to convene on 31 August 1966. As that date approached several participants urged postponement, for the basic disagreement that marked the Third Session still prevailed. The commission was convened on schedule but only to vote to delay for five months the remainder of the Fourth Session. This time period was to be used for resolving the dispute that existed. Discussions were carried on through the fall and early winter of 1966, and the impasse was finally broken by the García Robles compromise that was worked out during the Christmas holiday period. The compromise was that (a) the treaty would contain a provision requiring ratification by all Latin American states and signature of the protocols by all appropriate outside powers before it could become effective, but (b) the treaty would also contain a provision allowing states to waive the requirement of complete ratification and compliance. If

[24] García Robles, *Denuclearization*, p. 113.

[25] The *New York Times*, 17 April 1966, p. 28.

eleven states ratified the treaty and made the necessary waiver, the treaty would be in force for them regardless of what other states did or did not do.

The Fourth Session—Part II

The Fourth Session reconvened on 31 January 1967. The Latin American governments had been requested to send delegates empowered to sign the treaty, and all did so. After two weeks of detailed discussion, during which the document was carefully scrutinized, the final draft of the Treaty of Tlatelolco[26] was approved by unanimous vote on 12 February. It was formally signed two days later. Of the agreement one observer has remarked: "The treaty, as in the case of all previous ones in the field of arms control, bears the hallmark of the 'attainable' rather than of 'ideal.' " [27]

THE FOLLOW-UP

The signing of the treaty did not complete the effort to ban nuclear weapons from Latin America. Two hurdles remained—ratification of the Treaty of Tlatelolco by the signatories, and compliance by the nuclear powers and the states holding territory in Latin America.

Ratification has proceeded at a fairly slow pace. But by the end of May 1969, thirteen states—more than half the signatories—had deposited instruments of ratification. Twelve of the ratifying states waived the requirement of universal ratification and compliance and the treaty is in force for them. The states are: Mexico, El Salvador, the Dominican Republic, Uruguay, Honduras, Nicaragua, Ecuador, Bolivia, Haiti, Peru, Barbados, and Paraguay. The other state to have ratified, Brazil, did not make the waiver.

Compliance by the outside states has been slow in coming and is still limited or partial. The Soviet Union has not signed the protocol prohibiting nuclear powers from selling or delivering nuclear weapons to Latin America. Publicly, Moscow has questioned the use, permitted by the treaty, of nuclear explosions for peaceful purposes.[28] However, the

[26] The name of the treaty derives from the area of Mexico City where the Preparatory Commission met and the treaty was signed. The full text of the treaty with protocols is reproduced in William B. Bader, *The United States and the Spread of Nuclear Weapons* (New York: Pegasus, 1968), pp. 146–165. For the complete texts of the rival drafts that were reconciled by the compromise, see García Robles, *Denuclearization*, pp. 117–130.

[27] Hallowell Bowser, "Denuclearization in Latin America," *Saturday Review* (20 May 1967), p. 32.

[28] *The New York Times*, 13 February 1967, p. 1. At the same time, Moscow has indicated a conditional willingness to undertake the obligations contained in Protocol II, the condition being that other nuclear powers do the same. In reporting

Soviet inaction is probably in part explained by the refusal of its Western Hemisphere ally, Cuba, to adhere to the treaty. China has refused to sign the protocol for nuclear powers despite the fact that it has, in the past, called for creation of denuclearized or nuclear-free zones and in doing so identified Latin America as a region where such a zone might be established.[29] Peking explained its refusal, in the main, on the ground that the Treaty of Tlatelolco was a United Nations-sponsored agreement and therefore unacceptable to it.[30] (Legally the Preparatory Commission was a U.N. agency, but it functioned completely apart from the global organization.)

France, too, declined—without actually refusing—to give the pledges sought from it. Noting the status of the islands of Guadeloupe and Martinique as integral parts of metropolitan France and its sovereignty over French Guiana, Paris declared itself reluctant to make a commitment never to place nuclear weapons in these territories.[31]

The United Kingdom, after first expressing reservations about signing either protocol because of its responsibilities for defending its Caribbean possessions, later agreed to sign both. The Netherlands, too, first expressed reservations and then agreed to sign Protocol I[32] on the condition that a "substantial number" of Latin American states ratified the treaty. The United States signed Protocol II, agreeing not to supply nuclear weapons to any Latin American nation, but refused to sign Protocol I on the ground that that protocol would prevent Washington from using Puerto

---

this Soviet position, the Chairman of the Preparatory Commission stressed that "the statement did not say *all* nuclear powers, but *other* nuclear powers must adhere if the Soviet Union were to do likewise. The implication was clear to the delegates that the Russians would not insist upon Chinese ratification of the protocol before accepting it themselves." (*The Denuclearization of Latin America: Implications for Arms Control*, a study prepared for the U.S. Arms Control and Disarmament Agency [Los Angeles: Security Studies Project, University of California, 30 June 1968], pp. 49–50. Hereafter this work is cited as: *Denuclearization: Implications for Arms Control.*)

29 See Morton H. Halperin and Dwight H. Perkins, *Communist China and Arms Control* (New York: Praeger, 1965), p. 119.

30 The *New York Times,* 2 October 1966. The Chinese government stated that "while China would never 'at any time and under any circumstances be the first to use nuclear weapons,' Peking could not support a treaty which was so clearly the end result of General Assembly activities, for the UN 'has violated all the rights of the People's Republic of China in the world organization'; furthermore, 'the denuclearization of zones bordering on the United States . . . will serve no purpose if the latter continues to maintain nuclear weapons in its territory and in its Latin American bases.' " (*Denuclearization: Implications for Arms Control,* p. 50.)

31 See "Issues Before the 22nd General Assembly," *International Conciliation,* no. 564 (September 1967), p. 43.

32 The *New York Times,* 27 October 1967, p. 13.

Rico, the Virgin Islands, or the Canal Zone for storage or transport of nuclear weapons.

RETARDING AND PROMOTING FACTORS IN ARMS CONTROL

Several questions stem from or are raised by the foregoing review of arms control proposals in Latin America and the action taken with regard to them. Why did the two efforts at general arms control fail? Put somewhat differently, what factors worked against the Costa Rican and Chilean proposals? Conversely, what factors promoted the effort to ban nuclear weapons from Latin America? What is the prospect for future efforts at arms control or arms limitation among the Latin American countries?

Factors Retarding General Arms Control

It was noted earlier that the Costa Rican and Chilean proposals did not evoke much interest and did not have the political support necessary for adoption. Several factors appear to be responsible: security concerns, U.S. policy, the attitude of the Latin American armed forces, and prestige considerations.

Security. Whitaker and Jordan maintain that national defense and security have not been major concerns of the Latin American countries, given the fact that they have not been subject to any serious external military threat since early in the nineteenth century. Their present military weakness has left the burden of hemispheric defense—statements to the contrary notwithstanding—to the United States.[33] Whitaker and Jordan are correct as far as they go. They err, however, in ignoring the fact that a number of Latin American states perceive threats to their security, threats emanating from within Latin America. Disputes over territory exist between a number of the countries of Latin America. In addition, various jealousies, tensions, and fears not connected with territorial questions mark relations between several pairs of countries. And, as Burr notes, the Latin American states involved in these various conflicts regard them as "fighting matters." [34]

In short, fear of military attack does exist in many Latin American states, and such fears are an inducement to maintain armed forces at existing levels and to purchase new weapons. The frequent arms races among states in the region can be traced in part to genuine concern for

---

[33] Arthur P. Whitaker and David C. Jordan, *Nationalism in Contemporary Latin America* (New York: The Free Press, 1966), p. 188.

[34] Robert N. Burr, *Our Troubled Hemisphere: Perspectives on United States-Latin American Relations* (Washington: The Brookings Institution, 1967), p. 79.

national security on the part of political leaders. These attitudes have not encouraged efforts at general arms control in Latin America.

The United States. During most of the post-World War II period, U.S. military policy toward Latin America worked against arms limitation among its southern neighbors. Until the early 1960s U.S. policy stressed regional or collective defense, calling upon the Latin American states to join with the United States in preparing to deter or repel outside attack on the hemisphere and providing training, equipment, and weapons to the Latin American armed forces. In short, the U.S. policy emphasized building up the armed forces of the Latin American countries, not holding them at existing levels and certainly not reducing them. Seemingly, arms control in Latin America was seen by Washington as something that might adversely affect not only the security of Latin America but the security of the United States as well.[35]

Beginning in the late 1950s, however, Washington began to reassess its military policy toward Latin America. From that reassessment came a shift in policy, a shift away from an objective of preparing the Latin American armed forces to participate in hemispheric defense to one of preparing them to deal with internal security threats.[36] While the new policy may not have viewed Latin American arms control as a threat to the security of the hemisphere, it did not openly advocate or push such arms control. With reference to the two general arms control proposals, the United States took a somewhat ambivalent position. The United States did not support the Costa Rican proposal, although it did not reject it either. The United States endorsed the Chilean proposal but did so without any real enthusiasm.

The Latin American armed forces. Although there is scant hard evidence on the matter, it appears that the armed forces of most Latin American countries opposed the two arms control proposals. This might be termed "expected." Pye, in his examination of the military in developing countries, argues that military officers are continually comparing the strength of their forces with those of other countries, and that they are sensitive to real or perceived deficiencies in their own organizations.[37]

---

[35] This argument is made in Edward Bernard Glick, "The Feasibility of Arms Control and Disarmament in Latin America," *Orbis* 9 (Fall 1965): 757.

[36] The revised U.S. military policy toward Latin America is dealt with in Edwin Lieuwen, *Generals vs. Presidents: Neo-Militarism in Latin America* (New York: Praeger, 1964), especially pp. 124–126. See also James F. Lacy, "United States Military Policy Toward Latin America: An Analysis of a Change" (unpublished M.A. thesis, Tulane University, 1968).

[37] Lucian Pye, "Armies in the process of Political Modernization," in John J. Johnson, ed., *The Role of the Military in Underdeveloped Countries* (Princeton: Princeton University Press, 1962), pp. 78–80.

Given this concern, it is natural for officers to look with anything but enthusiasm on measures that would limit or reduce force size and weapons arsenals or that would preclude obtaining new weapons or equipment. Further arms control measures such as those called for by Costa Rica and Chile could easily be interpreted by the armed forces as threatening the many privileges which they have traditionally enjoyed, since the portion of government funds going to the military in each country would be reduced. In view of the very considerable political influence possessed by the armed forces in most Latin American countries, their opposition to limitations on conventional armaments must be regarded as a major obstacle to such action.

Prestige. Traditionally the possession of military strength has been viewed as a source of international prestige and acquisition of additional weapons has been seen as a means of enhancing prestige. As Schelling puts it: "The harm that people can do, or that nations can do, is impressive." [38] Kemp argues that the primary reason for weapons purchases by developing nations is a symbolic one: weapons are the most respected indices of national power and prestige.[39] Evidence suggests that the Latin American states, like most other states, see a link between prestige and armaments. Schmitt and Burks report that there is in Latin America a distinct tendency on the part of the populace to look with pride on a large modern military and to regard any attempt to reduce the strength of the armed forces as an attack on national security and prestige.[40] Johnson, referring to the widely held Brazilian notion that an impressive military establishment is required for international prestige, states: "This explains why some intellectuals who might normally oppose the military in general, and heavy military expenditures in particular, accept them as 'the price of future world prestige.' " [41] Given such attitudes, it may be argued that prestige considerations have acted as a distinct hindrance to the progress of general arms control in Latin America.

Factors Promoting Denuclearization

Just as several factors worked against general arms control or arms limitation, a combination of factors promoted the effort to ban nuclear weapons from Latin America.

---

[38] Thomas C. Schelling, *Arms and Influence* (New Haven: Yale University Press, 1966), p. v.

[39] Geoffrey Kemp, "Arms Sales and Arms Control in Developing Countries," *The World Today* 22 (September 1966): 391.

[40] Karl M. Schmitt and David D. Burks, *Evolution or Chaos: Dynamics of Latin American Government and Politics* (New York: Praeger, 1963), pp. 37–38.

[41] Johnson, *Military and Society*, p. 239.

Security. While security considerations appear to have worked against general arms control, they have seemingly promoted the ban on nuclear weapons into the region as a threat to their security. If one nation or a few nations obtained them, the existing regional balance of power—and the security that derives from the balance—would be upset.

Prestige. Although the view that armaments are a source of prestige is widely accepted and acted on, it is not the only view that can be, or is, taken. Just as prestige may derive from armaments, there is a prestige factor in arms control efforts. The essence of prestige, to quote Van Dyke, is found in a "reputation for distinctive success in meeting whatever tests are thought to be significant." [42] Padelford and Lincoln take a similar view, holding that prestige stems from a nation's reputation for success.[43] Achievement is the primary element of prestige, especially achievement in a field of activity that is valued or regarded as significant and difficult in the international system. Unquestionably, arms control is such a field. Moreover, the prestige factor was used by those advocating a denuclearized Latin America. Time and again the proponents of the ban argued that adoption of the Five Presidents' Declaration would make Latin America a "model" for the rest of the world. García Robles used similar arguments at the Mexico City meetings.

Acquiescence by the armed forces. The Latin American armed forces acquiesced in denuclearization. Undoubtedly they did so because banning nuclear weapons from the region did not alter the existing military situation in the region or pose a threat to the status of the armed forces.

The United States and the Nuclear Ban

Although the United States indicated its approval of the principle of a nuclear-free Latin America, it did not actively support or seek to advance the effort to ban nuclear weapons from the countries south of the Rio Grande. At least one author has been critical of the U.S. position. Bader, who has held a situation as consultant to the Senate Foreign Relations Committee, declares: "The same urgency that moved the United States . . . to agree to a nuclear free zone in Antarctica and outer space should be there in responding to nuclear free zones in Africa and Latin America." He continues: "We [the United States] obviously cannot take the lead in the formation of such an arrangement, but we can

---

[42] Vernon Van Dyke, *International Politics*, 2nd ed. (New York: Appleton-Century-Crofts, 1966), p. 163.

[43] Norman J. Padelford and George A. Lincoln, *The Dynamics of International Politics*, 2nd ed. (New York: Macmillan, 1967), p. 15.

encourage the process. . . ." [44] (Bader's criticism could be applied also to the position taken by other nuclear powers.) Although it is admittedly conjecture, it seems plausible to think that Washington's attitude and actions might have been very different if Cuba had agreed to adhere to the treaty and if the Soviet Union had done the same.

The Treaty of Tlatelolco and the Future of Arms Control

The Treaty of Tlatelolco constitutes the first successful effort at arms control or arms limitation in Latin America during the period since the end of World War II. While the treaty is a limited step, it is not an entirely insignificant one. As the U.N. secretary general, U Thant, has put it: "The Treaty for the Prohibition of Nuclear Weapons in Latin America marks an important milestone in the long and difficult search for disarmament. . . . It provides the statute for the creation, for the first time in history, of a nuclear-free zone for an inhabited portion of the earth." [45]

No evidence exists, however, to suggest that the treaty is a prelude to further action in the field of arms control. The various factors that have retarded or doomed arms control in the past still exist and make future action unlikely. An indication that the outlook is not bright is the record of achievement, or non-achievement, that has followed the agreement by the Latin American governments to eliminate unnecessary military expenditures, an agreement made during the meeting of presidents in Punta del Este, Uruguay. No concrete action has been taken to give effect to the agreement, and there is no evidence to suggest that any such action will be taken in the foreseeable future.[46]

---

[44] Bader, *Spread of Nuclear Weapons*, p. 116.

[45] Quoted in Alfonso García Robles, "The Treaty of Tlatelolco: Origin, Purposes and Scope of the Prohibition of Nuclear Weapons in Latin America," in Henry C. Herge, ed., *Disarmament in the Western World*, Conference Proceedings on the Occasion of the 23rd Anniversary of the United Nations, Occasional Publications, no. 1 (New Brunswick, New Jersey: Latin American Institute, Rutgers University, June 1969), p. 37.

[46] The lack of progress in implementing the agreement is very, very briefly discussed by former U.S. ambassador to the Organization of American States, Sol M. Linowitz, in *New Directions for the 1970's: Toward a Strategy of Inter-American Development, Hearings*, Subcommittee on Inter-American Affairs, Committee on Foreign Affairs, House of Representatives, U.S. Congress, 91st Cong. 1st sess., 1969, pp. 342–343.

Carl Solberg
Department of History
University of Washington
Seattle, Washington

RURAL UNREST AND AGRARIAN POLICY IN ARGENTINA, 1912-1930*

From 1912 until the late 1920s Argentina faced an agrarian social and economic crisis of proportions unprecedented in the republic's history. Trapped between unstable prices and the exactions of landlords, thousands of tenant farmers organized, went on strike, and at times sabotaged agricultural production. This unrest swept across the cereal belt, a 160,000,000-acre zone of extremely fertile soil in the provinces of Santa Fe, Entre Ríos, Córdoba, and Buenos Aires, and in the national territory of La Pampa. After 1919, rural unrest acquired new complexity when tens of thousands of landless workers employed by the tenant farmers began strike movements of their own. The purpose of the present article is to analyze the origins and characteristics of this rural upheaval and then to examine the responses to it formulated by the republic's national political leaders.

The disorganization of the international economic system that began with the outbreak of the Balkan War and lasted until the early 1920s largely explains the outburst of agrarian unrest in Argentina during the same period. Exports, primarily to the rapidly industrializing countries of Europe, had absorbed the bulk of national production and had expanded from 150 million gold pesos in value in 1900 to nearly 500 million in 1913. During this same period, the most rapid economic expansion in Argentine history, area under cultivation of cereals and flax increased

* Financial assistance from the National Endowment for the Humanities and from the University of Washington Graduate School Research Fund made possible the research for this article.

from 4.7 million hectares to 14.1 million.[1] Argentina became the world's leading exporter of corn, oats, and flaxseed and the third or fourth major exporter of wheat.[2] Comparisons between the agricultural exports of the United States and those of Argentina demonstrate the heavy reliance of the latter country's agriculture on the world market. (See Table 1.) When the international trading economy failed to function smoothly, Argentina's farmers were bound to suffer.

TABLE 1

PROPORTION OF AGRICULTURAL PRODUCTION EXPORTED
THE UNITED STATES AND ARGENTINA, 1911–1913 AVERAGE

Crop	*U.S. Exported Proportion*	*Argentine Exported Proportion*
Corn	1.7%	77.1%
Wheat	17.5%	60.6%
Oats	1.1%	82.4%
Flaxseed	.04%	81.8%

Source: Laurel Duvall, "The Production and Handling of Grain in Argentina," *Yearbook of the Department of Agriculture* (Washington: U.S. Department of Agriculture, 1915), pp. 285–286.

The economic prosperity of Argentine farmers was particularly vulnerable because they seldom owned the land they worked. A small and exclusive group of upper-class families had held secure ownership over most of the best land in the cereal belt since the mid-nineteenth century. The ownership pattern in the key province of Buenos Aires was typical. In 1928, only 1041 estates occupied one-third the area of the vast province and included much of its best grazing and farm land.[3] After 1880,

[1] The value of the gold peso until 1933 was US $ .9648. An excellent source of agricultural statistics is Juan L. Tenembaum, *Orientación económica de la agricultura argentina* (Buenos Aires: Editorial Losada, 1946). Data on area under cultivation is on pp. 21–22. Another important statistical source is Ernesto Tornquist & Cía. Ltda., *El desarrollo económico de la República Argentina en los últimos cincuenta años* (Buenos Aires: Ernesto Tornquist & Cía. Ltda., 1920). Export statistics are on pp. 133–134.

[2] Vernon L. Phelps, *The International Economic Position of Argentina* (Philadelphia: University of Pennsylvania Press, 1938), p. 141; Laurel Duvall, "The Production and Handling of Grain in Argentina," in *Yearbook of the Department of Agriculture* (Washington: U.S. Department of Agriculture, 1915), pp. 284–285.

[3] Jacinto Oddone, *La burguesía terrateniente argentina*, 3rd ed. (Buenos Aires: Ediciones Populares Argentinas, 1956), pp. 182–185. The standard historical study of Argentina land policy and of the concentration of ownership is Miguel A. Cárcano, *Evolución histórica del régimen de la tierra pública, 1810–1916* (Buenos Aires: Librería Mendesky, 1917). An important recent treatment of the

mushrooming demand for agricultural export crops and for alfalfa to use as cattle feed quickly valorized land in the cereal belt and made owners reluctant to sell their properties. In the rich southern departments of Santa Fe, for example, the price of agricultural land rose from 30.4 gold pesos per hectare in 1887 to 60 in 1905 and to 102.8 in 1912.[4] Landowners in the agricultural regions of neighboring Córdoba enjoyed increases from 36.8 gold pesos per hectare in 1906 to 109 in 1912.[5]

With land values rising so rapidly and in the absence of any workable-land distribution laws, the Italian and Spanish immigrants who flocked to the cereal belt generally could not buy land and instead had to rent it for money payments or for shares of the crop. In 1912 at least two-thirds of the farmers in the cereal belt were renters who operated plots generally between 150 and 200 hectares in size.[6] Prior to 1921 no tenancy laws existed to protect farmers from undue exploitation or to regulate rental contracts. These were short-term, usually for two or three years, which not only permitted owners to renegotiate rents frequently but also enabled them to shift land between agriculture and cattle as market circumstances dictated. Landowners often rented plots to "colonists," as tenant farmers were called, in order to prepare land for alfalfa. When

---

evolution of the land tenure system is James R. Scobie, *Revolution on the Pampas: A Social History of Argentine Wheat, 1860–1910* (Austin: University of Texas Press, 1964).

4 Ezequiel Gallo (h), "Santa Fe en la segunda mitad del siglo XIX. Transformaciones en su estructura regional," in Rosario, Universidad Nacional del Litoral, Facultad de Filosofía y Letras, *Anuario del Instituto de Investigaciones Históricas* 7 (1964): 150.

5 M. E. Greffier, "La propiedad rural en la Provincia de Córdoba," *Revista de Ciencias Económicas* 13 (August 1919): 113. For data on the valorization of rural property in the cereal zone between 1886 and 1929, see José Boglich, *El problema agrario y la crisis actual* (Buenos Aires: Ediciones Aras, 1933), p. 154. Boglich's data are reproduced in the standard economic history of Argentina, Ricardo M. Ortiz, *Historia económica de la Argentina, 1850–1930*, 2 vols. (Buenos Aires: Editorial Raigal, 1964), 2:106.

6 In 1911 68 percent of farmers were tenants in Buenos Aires; 62 percent were tenants in Santa Fe and Entre Ríos, and 72 percent were tenants in Córdoba. See Aaron Pavlovsky, *La cuestión agraria* (Buenos Aires: Talleres de la Casa Jacobo Peuser, 1913), p. 27. This work by a well-known agronomist carefully outlines the land tenure situation in the cereal provinces. In La Pampa, 68 percent of farmers were tenants. For statistics on land tenure in the territories, see Argentine Republic, Ministerio del Interior, Asesoría Letrada de Territorios Nacionales, *Censo general de los territorios nacionales. República Argentina. 1920.* 2 vols. (Buenos Aires: Establecimiento Gráfico A. de Martino, 1923), 2: 22. Ortiz, *Historia económica de la Argentina*, 2: 112–118, presents data on the size of farms in the cereal belt. In 1914, 96.5 percent of farms were less than 500 hectares and, of these, the average size was 176 hectares.

such contracts expired, colonists had to pack up and move elsewhere.[7] The impermanence of tenure that characterized rural Argentina prompted observers to liken the farmer both to the "agricultural Arab" and the "wandering Jew."[8]

Rental contracts imposed a number of heavy burdens on the farmer. Generally he was responsible for transporting the owner's share of the crop to the railroad station in bags which the colonist had to purchase at his own expense, frequently from the owner. Farmers used bags because almost no grain elevators or agricultural cooperatives existed in Argentina to help store and market the harvest.[9] The lack of elevators cost the farmers dearly, for they were unable to provide buyers with a uniform quality of wheat. Furthermore, much grain was exposed to the weather, became damp and deteriorated, and could only be sold at heavy discounts.[10] The intermediaries or "colonization companies" with whom tenant farmers often had to deal constituted perhaps the heaviest burden of all upon the cereal belt's producers. Landowners, wishing to reside in Buenos Aires or Paris, frequently rented huge tracts to these intermediaries, who in turn subrented plots of a few hundred hectares to tenants. Some companies controlled hundreds of thousands of hectares and made profits up to 80 percent a year. Contracts usually required renters to buy hail insurance, to rent threshing machinery, and to purchase bags only from intermediaries, who also operated local stores. To obtain credit, farmers had to guarantee payment with the harvest and had to sell the

---

[7] Mark Jefferson, *Peopling the Argentine Pampa* (New York, 1930), p. 142; Daniel Slutzky, "Aspectos sociales del desarrollo rural en la pampa húmeda argentina," *Desarrollo Económico* 8 (April-June 1968): 97; Curto Érico Hotschewer, *Evolución de la agricultura en la Provincia de Santa Fe* (Santa Fe: Ministerio de Hacienda, Economía e Industrias, 1953), p. 198. Large landowners also hesitated to sell because land ownership conferred social prestige. See Leon M. Estabrook, *Agricultural Survey of South America: Argentina and Paraguay* (Washington: Government Printing Office, 1926), p. 60.

[8] Herbert Gibson, *The Land We Live On* (Buenos Aires: R. Grant & Co., Printers, 1914), p. 17; Emilio A. Coni, "Cuestiones agrarias," *Revista de Ciencias Económicas* 26 (June 1926): 371.

[9] In 1913 there were thirty-four agricultural cooperatives in Argentina with 13,371 members. Almost all were in Entre Ríos Province. Juan B. Tobar, "Las cooperativas agrícolas," *Revista de Ciencias Económicas* 1 (July 1913): 57. The first cooperative grain elevator in Argentina was inaugurated at Leones, Córdoba, in July 1930. See *La Prensa,* 13 July 1930, p. 13. At that time there were only twenty-three grain elevators in the entire republic, with a total capacity of 400,000 tons. For analyses of rental contract provisions, see Pavlovsky, *La cuestión agraria,* p. 27; and the work of another agronomist, Roberto Campolieti, *La chacra argentina* (Buenos Aires: privately printed, 1914), pp. 50–51.

[10] Duvall, "The Production and Handling of Grain in Argentina," p. 296.

entire crop to these storekeepers.[11] The subrenting system, concluded a government inspector after visiting strife-ridden La Pampa in 1912, "constitutes the most odious extreme of absentee ownership." [12]

Since landowners did not pay indemnification for improvements, farmers seldom built decent housing. The colonist's house "is, at best, an enlarged sardine tin," wrote landowner Herbert Gibson in 1914. Many farmers lived in rude mud huts with dirt floors and zinc roofs.[13] Under such conditions, wrote one agronomist, "hygiene is unknown, even by sight." Rural education was deficient, and children of tenant farmers frequently grew up illiterate.[14]

Isolation imposed by bad roads aggravated the harsh life of Argentine farmers. As late as 1925, only 1273 kilometers of all-weather roads existed in the entire republic. In rural areas, as one agronomy professor complained, roads were "a succession of mud-holes," and a constant travail for farmers.[15] Primitive rural transport was an expensive burden;

---

11 For contemporary analyses of the intermediary system, see *La Prensa*, 8 July 1912, p. 13; Hugo Miatello, *Investigación agrícola en la Provincia de Santa Fe* (Buenos Aires: Compañía Sud-Americana de Billetes de Banco, 1904), pp. 279–280; Juan B. Justo, *La cuestión agraria* (Buenos Aires: Tip. "La Vanguardia," 1917), p. 22; and W. P. Rutter, *Wheat-Growing in Canada, the United States and the Argentine* (London: Adam and Charles Black, 1911), pp. 133–134 and passim. A recent evaluation by a distinguished Argentine scholar is Gastón Gori, *El pan nuestro: panorama social de las regiones cerealistas argentinas* (Buenos Aires: Ediciones Galatea-Nueva Visión, 1958), p. 113.

12 Julio B. Lezama, an inspector of the Departamento Nacional del Trabajo, made this report to Minister of the Interior Indalecio Gómez. It was published in Argentine Republic, Ministerio del Interior, *Memoria del Ministerio del Interior presentada al Honorable Congreso Nacional, 1912–1913* (Buenos Aires: Talleres Gráficos de la Penitenciaría Nacional, 1913), p. 519.

13 Gibson, *The Land We Live On*, p. 16. This pamphlet is a fascinating critique of the land tenure system by a wealthy English-born landowner. Also, Scobie, *Revolution on the Pampas*, p. 65.

14 Hugo Miatello, "El hogar agrícola," *Boletín del Museo Social Argentino* 3 (1914): 565. Mariano Vélez, a teacher at Alta Italia in La Pampa, made a local education census in 1931 which revealed that the bulk of rural children were not attending school and that many could not read or write. See his *La situación agrícola de La Pampa* (Buenos Aires: Imprenta "La Vanguardia," 1934), p. 119. As late as 1943, reports Carl C. Taylor in *Rural Life in Argentina* (Baton Rouge: Louisiana State University Press, 1948), p. 316, in Buenos Aires province 15.9 percent of the children between the ages of 6 and 13 never had attached school. Percentages for Santa Fe were 11.8, for La Pampa 12.7, for Córdoba 14.4, and for Entre Ríos 20.7. Taylor's work is a useful study of farm life in the mid-1940s but does not analyze the period under consideration in the present study.

15 Statistics on road mileage are in Alejandro E. Bunge, *La economía argentina*, 4 vols. (Buenos Aires: Agencia General de Librerías y Publicaciones, 1928–1930), 4: 85. See also Guillermo Garbarini Islas, "Consideraciones sobre el estado de nuestro régimen agrario," *Revista de Economía Argentina* 21 (September 1928): 212; and Rutter, *Wheat-Growing in Canada, the United States, and the Argentine*, pp. 133–134 and passim.

in a rainy year, estimated a Rosario businessman, Santa Fe farmers spent 10 percent of their income to transport crops from farms to railway stations.[16]

During the final decades of the nineteenth century and the opening years of the twentieth, farmers were willing to accept their onerous contracts and their often harsh living conditions because they were small-scale entrepreneurs who gambled on the possibility of rapid enrichment through agriculture. If market prices were high, if the weather were favorable, and if the grasshoppers stayed away, a farmer could reap substantial profits. With the hopes of striking it rich, colonists tended to rent as much land as possible and to plant extensively. Agriculture became, as a careful observer pointed out, a "game of chance." [17]

But by 1912 a combination of factors began to frustrate these ambitious small capitalists. Several consecutive years of high prices had encouraged farmers to expand their plantings and to bid up land rents to excessive levels.[18] Rentals in southern Sante Fe had risen from 18 or 20 percent of the crop in 1904 to at least 35 percent by 1912. Then, crop failures and low prices left many farmers unable to meet these rising obligations. In 1911 the corn harvest was ruined by drought and totalled only 713,000 tons—compared with almost 4.5 million the previous year—and the linseed harvest also was poor. The following year the corn harvest was superb and totalled 7.5 million tons, a quantity so great that it sharply depressed the world market price. Unable to obtain credit or pay rents, tenant farmers faced eviction from their lands, while small businessmen in the farming communities went bankrupt.[19]

---

[16] I. Bustos, "Caminos, transportes y elevadores de granos," *Revista de Derecho, Historia y Letras* 43 (October 1912): 223. The Argentine national government did almost nothing to promote road construction. In Congress, organic highway laws were proposed in 1912, 1913, 1915, 1916, 1922, 1923, 1924, and 1925. But no concerted action on highway improvement occurred until the Justo administration of the 1930s. See *The Review of the River Plate* 64 (2 November 1928): 9.

[17] Juan Bialet Massé, *Informe sobre el estado de las clases obreras en el interior de la República,* 3 vols. (Buenos Aires: Imprenta y Casa Editora de Adolfo Grau, 1904), 1: 120.

[18] A number of observers pointed to the speculative character of Argentine agriculture. See, for example, the socialist author Antonio Borras, *Nuestra cuestión agraria: en defensa de la producción y del productor* (Buenos Aires: Editorial "La Vanguardia," 1932), p. 37. Also, *La Prensa,* 21 June 1912, p. 13; and the perceptive French traveller Pierre Denis, *The Argentine Republic: Its Development and Progress,* trans. Joseph McCabe (London: T. Fisher Unwin Ltd., 1922), p. 201.

[19] Corn, quoted in Buenos Aires at 11.35 pesos per 100 quintals in January 1912, fetched 6.65 five months later. For background to the 1912 farmers' strike, see Plácido Grela, *El grito de Alcorta* (Rosario: Tierra Nuestra, 1958), pp. 46–47. Grela's work, the only significant secondary source on tenant farmer discontent, contains useful information despite its disorganization and despite the author's

Faced with expulsion, tenants fought back with the first large-scale rural strike in Argentine history. The strike movement began in the Santa Fe town of Alcorta, center of a rich corn-producing area farmed mostly by Italians. On 25 June 1912 two thousand farmers gathered in Alcorta to demand rent reductions and longer-term contracts and to pledge to strike until these demands were met. Led by Francisco Netri, a Rosario intellectual well acquainted with peasant protest movements in his native Italy, and supported by local small businessmen and rural newspapers, the strike quickly caught on and spread through central and southern Santa Fe, into neighboring Córdoba and Buenos Aires, and finally into La Pampa territory. In some localities, Italian priests sided with their parishioners' cause, declared the strike a "holy crusade," and urged emigration to Tripolitania if satisfactory settlements were not reached.[20] The 1912 strike, although generally nonviolent, effectively halted farm work for two months.[21]

A significant result of the 1912 movement was the formation of Argentina's first and most important farmers' confederation, the *Federación Agraria Argentina* (FAA). Led by Netri, delegates from Santa Fe province met at Rosario on 1 August and within two weeks announced the foundation of the organization, which began to publish a weekly newspaper, *La Tierra*, and to recruit membership throughout the republic. From the beginning until at least 1930, Italian and Spanish tenant farmers formed the bulk of the membership. Landless laborers were not invited to join. After an early power struggle in which a moderate group headed by Netri triumphed over a radical faction favoring violent action, the fundamentally conservative character of the FAA was clearly estab-

---

interpretation of the events of 1912 from the viewpoint of the Argentine Communist party in 1958. Other useful background sources include Lázaro Nemirovsky, *Estructura económica y orientación política de la agricultura en la República Argentina* (Buenos Aires: Librería y Casa Editora de Jesús Menéndez, 1933), pp. 216–218; Damián M. Torino, *El problema del inmigrante y el problema agrario argentino* (Buenos Aires: privately published, 1912), pp. 145, 252; and Jorge Abelardo Ramos, *Revolución y contrarrevolución en la Argentina,* 2 vols. (Buenos Aires: Editorial Plus Ultra, 1957), 2: 155–156.

20 *La Prensa*, 24 March 1913, p. 12; Grela, *El grito de Alcorta*, pp. 18–19.

21 Tomás García Serrano, a Rosario historian who took part in the events of 1912, sets the number of strikers at 100,000. See his *Esteban Piacenza: Apuntes biográficos,* 2nd ed. (Rosario: Librería y Editorial Ruiz, 1967), p. 40. A recent study by Juan Carlos Grosso accepts this figure. See "Los problemas económicos y sociales y la repuesta radical en el gobierno," in Luis Alberto Romero et al., *El radicalismo* (Buenos Aires, 1968), p. 313. Grela, *El grito de Alcorta*, p. 14, estimates that there were 120,000 strikers. A good brief summary of the 1912 agitation is Silvio Spangemberg, "El conflicto agrario del sud de Santa Fe," *Boletín Mensual del Museo Social Argentino* 1 (1912): 522–531.

lished. The organization became primarily a pressure group dedicated to advancing the interests of its petit bourgeois rural members.[22]

Despite the essential moderation of the organized farmers movement, the agrarian conflict of 1912 posed serious political problems, especially in Santa Fe. In that province, the Radical party, a moderate movement emphasizing political reform, led primarily by middle-class urbanites and appealing largely to the native-born masses, had been elected only a few months before and was anxious to end the strike.[23] Continued agitation or a turn towards violence would give the national administration, headed by oligarchic enemies of the Radicals, an excuse to "intervene," as provided by the federal constitution, and to call new elections. Adopting a conciliatory policy, the provincial governor appointed a committee of three Radical leaders to study the agrarian crisis and to make recommendations. Moving with alacrity, the committee travelled widely and interviewed scores of farmers. Its report, issued 21 July 1912, openly favored the tenants and urged reductions in rents, minimum three-year contracts, and restrictions on intermediaries.[24] The provincial government used the publicity generated by this report to pressure landowners to negotiate compromise contracts with their tenants. By mid-August, Santa Fe farmers began returning to work, soon followed by those in neighboring provinces.

In contrast with the position of the Santa Fe Radicals, disdain towards the problems of the tenants characterized the national government of President Roque Sáenz Peña. This government's principal base of support was the landed elite, and a number of powerful landowners held high national office. Vice President Victoriano de la Plaza, who on Sáenz Peña's death in 1914 was to serve as president until 1916, was one

---

[22] *La Tierra,* 1 August 1914, p. 1. The formation of the FAA and the struggle to define its direction are outlined in Grela, *El grito de Alcorta,* pp. 366–376. Also see *La Vanguardia,* 23 August 1912, p. 1.

[23] For analysis of the heterogeneous composition of the Radical party, see Peter H. Smith, *Politics and Beef in Argentina: Patterns of Conflict and Change* (New York: Columbia University Press, 1969), p. 23; Ezequiel Gallo (h) and Silvia Sigal, "La formación de los partidos políticos contemporáneos: La U.C.R. (1890–1916)," in Torcuato S. di Tella et al., *Argentina, sociedad de masas* (Buenos Aires: Editorial Universitaria de Buenos Aires, 1965), pp. 136–137, 152, 163; and Ramos, *Revolución y contrarrevolución en la Argentina,* 2: 59–60.

[24] Members of the committee were Ricardo Caballero, J. Daniel Infante, and Toribio Sánchez. Infante reviewed the committee's work and the provincial government's desire to reach a settlement in a pamphlet, *El problema agrario* (Rosario: Establecimiento B. Tamburini y Cía., 1912), see especially pp. 3, 50, 63, 71. Grela, *El grito de Alcorta,* pp. 132–133, 140–141, quotes important sections of the committee's report. Also see *La Prensa,* 16 July 1912, p. 12; and 23 July 1912, p. 13.

of the largest landowners in Córdoba province. In 1912 he adamantly refused to compromise with his tenants in arrears and instead had the provincial police expel them.[25] Sáenz Peña defended his government's inaction during the agrarian strike by claiming that the state lacked authority to intervene in what legally was a private contractual dispute. The minister of agriculture, who charged in front of the Chamber of Deputies that outside agitators were the main cause of the strike, further reflected the administration's position.[26] The ministry sent investigators to the provinces, but the government did not implement their advice, which urged the formation of special arbitration tribunals to settle contract disputes.[27] Newspapers and intellectuals alike sharply criticized the government's inaction as damaging to agriculture and to national prosperity.[28]

Economic depression, touched off by the Balkan War crisis in Europe and intensified by a marked reduction of European capital flow to Argentina, settled over the republic in 1913 and heightened social tension in the cereal belt.[29] Landowners failed to carry out rent reductions promised the previous year, and tenant farmers again responded with a strike.[30] The movement in Santa Fe, Córdoba, and Buenos Aires was generally peaceful, but serious violence and crop destruction hit La Pampa. In response, the territorial police, directly under command of the national government, intimidated striking colonists while evicting dozens of families whose rent was in arrears.[31] Compromise settlements again

25 *La Prensa,* 16 August 1912, p. 18; interview with Antonio Diecidue, librarian of the Federación Agraria Argentina, Rosario, 2 August 1969.

26 Argentine Republic, Cámara de Diputados, *Diario de sesiones de la Cámara de Diputados*, sesiones ordinarias, I (29 July 1912): 815–832. (Hereafter this source will be referred to as *Diputados*). In his opening message to Congress on 6 May 1913 Sáenz Peña attempted to justify his government's policy by claiming it lacked authority to intervene. See Roque Sáenz Peña, *Escritos y discursos,* 2 vols. (Buenos Aires: Casa Jacobo Peuser Ltda., Editores, 1935), 2: 567.

27 Emilio Lahitte, the Director of Rural Statistics in the Ministry of Agriculture, investigated the conflict and then recommended the formation of arbitration committees. *The Review of the River Plate* 38 (9 August 1912): 335; Emilio Lahitte, *La cuestión agraria* (Buenos Aires: Ministerio de Agricultura, 1912), p. 5; *La Prensa,* 4 July 1912, p. 16.

28 In a series of editorials, *La Prensa* attacked the president's lack of intervention as unjustifiable: 12 July 1912, p. 7; 1 December 1912, p. 11. See also Cárcano, *Evolución histórica del régimen de la tierra pública, 1810–1916,* p. 477.

29 For analysis of the impact of the Balkan War on the Argentine economy, see Phelps, *The International Economic Position of Argentina,* pp. 22–25.

30 Netri emphasized the farmers' bitterness over the rent question in an interview with *La Prensa,* 6 March 1913, p. 16. Also see *The Review of the River Plate* 39 (14 March 1913): 655; and Abel Bengolea, *Conflictos agrarios* (Buenos Aires: Dirección General de Agricultura y Defensa Agrícola, 1913), pp. 2–3.

31 *La Vanguardia,* 15 January 1913, p. 1; *La Prensa,* 7 February 1913, p. 13; 20 February 1913, p. 14; W. Jaime Molins, *La Pampa* (Buenos Aires, 1918), pp. 354–355.

were reached, but the basic structure of the land tenure system remained unchanged.

The contrast between the conciliatory policy the Santa Fe Radicals had adopted during the 1912 strike and the hostile attitudes of conservative politicians raised hopes among farmers that a Radical national government might support agrarian interests. But after the 1916 election it became clear that these hopes were misplaced. The victorious presidential candidate was the long-time Radical leader Hipólito Yrigoyen, a powerful figure who dominated twentieth-century Argentine politics as no other leader before Perón. Once in office, however, Yrigoyen took little interest in the problems of the tenant farmers.

Several factors help explain the Radical administration's indifference to agrarian questions. For one thing, large landed interests held powerful influence in the party and within the Yrigoyen government. The president himself, although urban born, had become a landowner and a stock raiser. Several cabinet ministers, including his first minister of agriculture, were members of the *Sociedad Rural*, the powerful, exclusive, and aristocratic cattleman's association. Yrigoyen's policies, particularly during his first term, favored cattle raising interests.[32]

Yrigoyen's social philosophy, nurtured by his reading of the ethical and spiritualistic writings of the nineteenth-century German philosopher Karl Christian Friedrich Krause, also influenced his government's agrarian policies.[33] The president claimed that he was "predestined by God" to lead a "political apostolate" in which he would govern paternalistically in the interests of all classes and interest groups. Because Yrigoyen was convinced that he alone was equipped to decide policy and to find the right answers in each case, he came down hard on dissidents and viewed those who preached class organization or who led strikes as dangerous agitators out to destroy the alleged unity of Argentine society. The government's social role, according to this viewpoint, was to curb such threats

[32] A vast polemical literature exists on Yrigoyen, but as yet there is no scholarly biography. The most informative study, by Manuel Gálvez, bears the significant title, *Vida de Hipólito Yrigoyen, hombre del misterio* (Buenos Aires: Kraft, 1937). On Yrigoyen's landholdings and his addiction to rural life, see Luis V. Sommi, *Hipólito Yrigoyen: su época y su vida* (Buenos Aires: Editorial Monteagudo, 1947), pp. 292–295; Félix Luna, *Yrigoyen* (Buenos Aires: Editorial Desarrollo, 1964), pp. 57–59. Smith's *Politics and Beef in Argentina* carefully analyzes Yrigoyen's relationships with the *Sociedad Rural* and his policies towards the cattle industry. See especially pp. 48–50, 71–88, 129–136.

[33] For evaluation of the impact of *krausismo* on Yrigoyen, see Sommi, *Hipólito Yrigoyen*, pp. 286–288; and José Landa, *Hipólito Yrigoyen visto por uno de sus médicos* (Buenos Aires: Macland S.R.L., 1958), pp. 254–257.

to the system and to use strong moral suasion to harmonize groups in conflict.[34] "My one dream," wrote the Radical leader, "is to make the Argentine nation a synthesis of the welfare of all classes." [35]

Despite his mystical philosophy, Yrigoyen was a skillful practical politician, and the fact that most farmers lacked the suffrage probably influenced his government's agrarian policies. According to the national census of 1914, 72,995 of the 102,881 farmers in the agricultural provinces were unnaturalized immigrants. (See Table 2.) During the 1930s, Argentine-born sons of immigrant farmers tended to abandon the countryside and move to the cities, and the bulk of the farmers remained citizens of Spain or Italy until their death.[36] In the entire republic, only 33,219 immigrants, or 2.25 percent of the foreign-born male adult population, had become citizens by 1914, and over half of these lived in the national capital.[37] The farmers' miniscule rate of naturalization reflected their lack of identification with Argentine values and institutions, and this lack of identification in turn probably was rooted in Argentina's failure to give them a stake in national life by establishing a workable homestead act or land distribution program.

---

34 Yrigoyen was not a systematic writer and one must glean his social philosophy from his speeches and messages. Particularly revealing is a 1923 manuscript left unpublished until 1957 in which Yrigoyen justifies and rationalizes his "spiritual leadership." See Hipólito Yrigoyen, *Mi vida y mi doctrina* (Buenos Aires: Editorial Raigal, 1957), pp. 46–47, 56–57 and passim. For sympathetic analysis of his social thought, see Gabriel del Mazo, *El radicalismo: ensayo sobre su historia y doctrina*, 3 vols. (Buenos Aires: Ediciones Gure, 1957), 2: 209, 228–229.

35 Quoted in T. R. Ybarra, "Mystery Man of Argentina," *World's Work* 59 (March, 1930): 88.

36 Roberto Campolieti, *La organización de la agricultura argentina (Ensayo de política agraria)* (Buenos Aires: Pedro M. Aquino & Cía., 1929), p. 11; *La Tierra,* 22 September 1930, p. 1. The 1937 agricultural census revealed that 38.1 percent of "agricultural producers" in the four agricultural provinces and La Pampa territory were unnaturalized immigrants. Since "agricultural producers" included landless laborers, most of whom were native-born, and cattle raisers, most of whom also were nationals, the proportion of immigrant farmers was probably considerably higher. See Argentine Republic, Comisión Nacional del Censo Agropecuario, *Censo nacional agropecuario, Año 1937,* 4 vols. (Buenos Aires: Guillermo Kraft, Ltda., 1939–1940), 2: 3.

37 Statistics on naturalization are found in Argentine Republic, *Tercer censo nacional, levantado el 1° de junio de 1914,* 10 vols. (Buenos Aires, 1915–1917), 2: 403–417. Also see Alfredo L. Spinetto, *Ciudadanía conferida a los extranjeros* (Buenos Aires: Tip. "La Vanguardia," 1917), p. 23. The distribution of naturalized immigrants by provinces, based on Ministry of the Interior statistics, is found in *La Vanguardia,* 19 April 1913, p. 1. There were 3981 in Buenos Aires province, 1875 in Santa Fe, 633 in Entre Ríos, 104 in Córdoba, and 27 in La Pampa.

TABLE 2

NATIONALITY OF FARMERS IN THE ARGENTINE CEREAL BELT, 1914

Province	*Argentines*	*Foreigners*	*Total*	*Percentage of Foreigners*
Buenos Aires	13,017	28,841	41,858	69.0
Santa Fe	5,626	22,278	27,904	79.8
Entre Ríos	4,612	6,599	11,211	58.8
Córdoba	6,116	11,794	17,910	65.8
La Pampa	515	3,483	3,998	87.0
Totals	29,886	72,995	102,881	71.0

Source: Sergio Bagú, "Evolución histórica de la estratificación social en la Argentina," mimeographed (Buenos Aires: Departmento de Sociología, Universidad de Buenos Aires, 1961), pp. 108–111. [Bagú's data are drawn from the 1914 national census.]

Virtually excluded from land ownership, many immigrants remained alienated from Argentina and desired to return to their homeland after enriching themselves. As Esteban Piacenza, president of the FAA between 1916 and 1947 put it, the farmers "have migrated to this country . . . to work a few years, as few as possible, to make some money, and then to return. . . . No one has come here from his homeland with the thought of remaining." [38] Actually many farmers did stay in Argentina and eventually did decide to apply for citizenship. But they found that the national government had erected complicated bureaucratic barriers that discouraged citizenship applicants and slowed the rate of naturalization to a trickle.[39]

The Radical party captured the presidency at a time when European conditions again were subjecting Argentine farmers to a cost-price squeeze and bringing on an agrarian crisis. World War I caused a severe shipping shortage, raised the price of essential farm items such as machinery and bags, and ended immigration, thus creating harvest labor shortages. Farm prices, which had risen in 1914 and 1915, fell throughout 1916 because of bumper crops in the United States and Canada. There was almost no

[38] Quoted in García Serrano, *Esteban Piacenza,* p. 51. In the editorial columns of *La Tierra,* Piacenza strongly opposed the tendency of immigrant farmers to remain unnaturalized and repeatedly urged farmers to apply for citizenship. *La Tierra,* 17 May 1918, p. 1; 28 March 1922, p. 1; 17 February 1923, p. 1.

[39] The point is discussed more fully in Carl Solberg, *Immigration and Nationalism: Argentina and Chile, 1890–1914* (Austin: University of Texas Press, 1970), pp. 124–125. Also Adolfo Dickmann, *Los argentinos naturalizados en la política* (Buenos Aires: Talleres Gráficos Juan Perrotti, 1915), p. 23; *La Vanguardia,* 2 August 1920, p. 2; and *La Época,* 8 September 1928, p. 2.

external market for Argentina's 1917 corn crop, which rotted on the ground or was used to fire the republic's power plants, stricken by a shortage of imported coal.[40]

As in 1912, the deteriorating economic situation fostered a strike among tenant farmers which broke out in April 1917 and which spread across Santa Fe, Córdoba, and Buenos Aires. As the strike continued, landlords expelled hundreds of tenants for nonpayment of rents, and Piacenza telegraphed Yrigoyen to ask for a rent moratorium.[41] The administration intervened, not in the manner Piacenza had desired, but with repressive force. Yrigoyen's allies, the Radical governors of Santa Fe and Buenos Aires, ordered the police to arrest striking farmers, to harass the FAA, and to apply the 1910 Social Defense Law, which permitted summary deportation of foreigners suspected of anarchism or labor agitation.[42] Repression on the one hand and rising agricultural prices on the other ended the strike by late June.

While it was acting to put down agrarian unrest, the Yrigoyen government also was formulating policies for the Ministry of Agriculture, the principal administrative link between the national government and individual farmers. The parsimonious budgetary support which the ministry received between 1916 and 1922 hindered its operations and reflected the administration's lack of concern for agrarian problems. As Table 3 demonstrates, during the first Yrigoyen administration budgeting of the agricultural divisions of the Ministry of Agriculture plunged to the lowest amounts, in both absolute and relative terms, of the entire 1912–1930 period. The cuts were partly made in response to a financial crisis brought on by World War I, but when finances eased in 1920 the government did not restore the ministry's budget to its former levels. Although the president's party remained a minority in the Senate throughout his term and

40 The use of corn for fuel for locomotives and power plants is discussed in V. L. Havens, "Fuel in Argentina," *Power* 52 (26 October 1920): 649–650. For background to the 1917 agrarian strike, see *La Prensa,* 12 May 1917, p. 12; and *The Review of the River Plate* 45 (16 June 1916): 1309. Sources for the impact of World War I on farm prices and production in Argentina include Guido di Tella and Manuel Zymelman, *Las etapas del desarrollo económico argentino* (Buenos Aires: Editorial Universitaria de Buenos Aires, 1967), especially pp. 299, 301; Simon G. Hanson, *Argentine Meat and the British Market* (Stanford, 1938), pp. 199, 255; and L. Brewster Smith, Harry T. Collings, and Elizabeth Murphey, *The Economic Position of Argentina During the War* (Washington: Bureau of Foreign and Domestic Commerce, Miscellaneous Series, no. 88, 1920), p. 85 and passim.

41 *La Prensa,* 1 May 1917, p. 14; 8 May 1917, p. 13; 9 May 1917, p. 14; 10 May 1917, p. 13. Also *La Vanguardia,* 8 May 1917, p. 1; 11 May 1917, p. 1.

42 *La Prensa,* 28 May 1917, p. 13; *La Vanguardia,* 25 May 1917, p. 1; *Diputados,* sesiones ordinarias, I (22 May 1917): 159–160.

did not hold a majority in the Chamber until 1920, analysis of the budget debates reveals that the incentive for the reductions came not from the opposition in Congress but from the executive branch. Yrigoyen's minister of agriculture proposed the austere agricultural budgets and Congress approved them, generally with little discussion.[43] This lack of financial support kept total government spending on agriculture, at both national and provincial levels, at only one peso per capita of the Argentine population in 1921, compared with expenditure of 2.55 pesos per capita in the United States and 3.22 in Canada.[44]

TABLE 3

PROPORTION OF THE ARGENTINE GOVERNMENT BUDGET DEVOTED TO AGRICULTURE, 1912–1930

A	B	C	D	E
Year	*President*	*Total Operating Budget (pesos)*	*Amount of Ministry of Agriculture Budget Specifically Related to Agriculture*	*Percentage of Total Operating Budget Spent on Agriculture*
1912	Sáenz Peña	278,674,285	13,087,756	4.7
1913	Sáenz Peña	323,159,964	13,243,857	4.1
1914	Sáenz Peña	346,573,187	13,242,397	3.8
1915	de la Plaza	322,178,805	9,599,576	2.9
1916	de la Plaza	302,767,145	10,009,362	3.3
1917	Yrigoyen	331,238,910	8,151,483	2.4
1918	Yrigoyen	379,896,079	7,311,860	1.9
1919	Yrigoyen	379,896,079	7,311,860	1.9
1920	Yrigoyen	459,171,586	7,562,362	1.6
1921	Yrigoyen	457,477,475	7,562,362	1.6
1922	Yrigoyen	457,477,475	7,562,362	1.6
1923	Alvear	650,033,600	14,708,860	2.3
1924	Alvear	650,033,600	14,708,860	2.3
1925	Alvear	650,033,600	14,708,860	2.3
1926	Alvear	650,033,600	14,708,860	2.3
1927	Alvear	646,795,428	14,351,840	2.2
1928	Alvear	646,795,428	14,351,840	2.2
1929	Yrigoyen	704,724,847	17,707,568	2.5
1930	Yrigoyen	704,724,847	17,707,568	2.5

43 For description of the government's budget procedures during this period, see H. E. Peters, *The Foreign Debt of the Argentine Republic* (Baltimore: The Johns Hopkins Press, 1934), pp. 107–111. Debate on the 1918 agricultural budget is in *Diputados*, sesiones extraordinarias, VIII (24 January 1918): 318–319, 688. Debate on the 1920 budget is in *Diputados*, sesiones extraordinarias, VII (27 January 1920): 441.

44 Ricardo Videla, "La cuestión agraria argentina," *Revista de Economía Argentina* 8 (March 1922): 201.

Note: The Divisions of the Ministry of Agriculture included in Column D as "specifically related to agriculture" are the following: (1) Secretariat, (2) Agricultural Statistics, (3) Agricultural Defense, (4) Agricultural Education, (5) Meterology, (6) General Land Office, (7) Agricultural and Cattle Research Laboratories, (8) Agricultural and Cattle Register.

Other Divisions of the Ministry, not included as "specifically related to agriculture," were (1) Cattle Raising, (2) Mines, Geology, and Hydrology, (3) Commerce and Industry, (4) Patents and Trademarks, (5) Immigration.

Sources: Budgets of 1912–1915, 1917–1918, 1920, 1923, 1927, 1929: Argentine Republic, *Ley de presupuesto general de la República Argentina* (Buenos Aires: Talleres Gráficos del Ministerio de Agricultura, 1912–1915, 1917–1918, 1920, 1923, 1927, 1929). Budget of 1916: Argentine Republic, *Boletín Oficial de la República Argentina* 24 (4 February 1916): 73. Budget of 1919: Law 10,653. See also: Augusto da Rocha, comp., *Colección completa de leyes nacionales sancionadas por el Honorable Congreso durante los años 1852 a 1933*, 27 vols. (Buenos Aires: Librería "La Facultad" de Juan Roldán & Cía., 1918–1933), 20: 10–18. Budget of 1921: Argentine Republic, *Ley No. 11.178 sobre presupuesto general de gastos de la administración y leyes impositivas para el ejercicio de 1921* (Buenos Aires: Talleres Gráficos del Ministerio de Agricultura de la Nación, 1921). Budget of 1922: Law 11,188, in Da Rocha, comp., *Colección completa de leyes nacionales*, 22: 12. Budgets of 1924–1926, Law 11,319 (1924), in ibid., 22: 23–25. Law 11,319 (1925), in ibid., 23: 23–25. Law 11,333 (1926), in ibid., 24: 14. Budget of 1928: in ibid., 24: 164. Budget of 1930: in Argentine Republic, *Boletín Oficial de la República Argentina* 38 (20 February 1930): 705.

Moreover, a number of observers raised doubts that the ministry was devoting its scanty resources to the most pressing needs of agriculture. The FAA in 1921 complained that the ministry had become a "nullity" which "does not even serve as a source of information." [45] In the previous year, the national government had employed thirty-five field agronomists, scattered over all the republic's expanse. Only two served the province of Santa Fe. The ministry's central bureaucracy, added the respected scholar Miguel Ángel Cárcano, was overstaffed and graft-ridden.[46] Corruption became particularly severe in the Division of Agricultural Defense (*Defensa Agrícola*), whose task was to combat rural pests, especially locusts. Although Defensa Agrícola had never been free from corruption, President Yrigoyen greatly increased its budgetary allocations, not to fight insect invasions but to create hundreds of new inspectorships for rural political allies. Between 1917 and 1921, invasions

[45] *La Tierra*, 15 April 1921, p. 1.

[46] Miguel Ángel Cárcano, "Organización de la producción: la pequeña propiedad y el crédito agrícola," *Revista de Economía Argentina* 1 (1918): 524. The number of agronomists employed by the Ministry of Agriculture may be found in Argentine Republic, Ministerio de Agricultura de la Nación, *Memoria presentada al Congreso por el Ministro de Agricultural Ing. Alfredo Demarchi, 1920* (Buenos Aires: Talleres Gráficos del Ministerio de Agricultura de la Nación, 1921), p. 64.

of locusts and other pests fell to the lowest point in over a decade while the budget of Defensa Agrícola rose from 1.87 million pesos in 1917 to 2.95 million in 1920. In 1919 the Division absorbed 39 percent of all the ministry's agricultural funds.[47] Meanwhile, the newly-created inspectorships became the basis of a rural electoral machine, particularly in Buenos Aires and Córdoba provinces.[48]

While lavishly financing Defensa Agrícola, the government slashed the budgets of some of the Ministry of Agriculture's most important activities, particularly agricultural education. In spite of the fact that almost all observers of Argentine rural problems agreed that the low technical and cultural levels of most tenant farmers made agricultural education a pressing necessity, the Yrigoyen administration steadily reduced its financial support.[49] Budget allotments for the republic's twelve agricultural schools, five agronomical institutes, and nine experimental stations fell from a high of 2.9 million pesos in 1912 to 2.2 million in 1916 and to 928,000 in 1920, an amount so low that several institutions closed.[50] The number of students in government agricultural schools declined from a high of 634 in 1914 to 397 in 1920 and to 276 in 1921.[51]

The Ministry of Agriculture came under sharp attack in 1917 and 1918 as a result of its failure to ease the severe shortage of grain bags from which Argentine farmers were suffering. The grain bag was essential

---

[47] The creation and early years of *Defensa Agrícola* are discussed in Scobie, *Revolution on the Pampas*, pp. 145–147. Statistics on invasions of insect pests in Argentina are found in Vicente J. Libonati, *La langosta: su historia en la Argentina (Síntesis)* (Buenos Aires: Editores Casartelli y Fiol, 1927), pp. 37, 78–123 passim.

[48] *La Prensa*, 24 April 1930, p. 15; Guillermo Garbarini Islas, *Derecho rural argentino* (Buenos Aires: Librería de Derecho y Jurisprudencia Restoy & Doeste, 1925), p. 281. The most thorough denunciation of Yrigoyen's use of Defensa Agrícola was made by Conservative Senator Matías Sánchez Sorondo. See his *Historia de seis años* (Buenos Aires: Agencia General de Librería, 1922), pp. 355–359. The farmers themselves were well aware of the corruption. The Second National Agricultural Congress, meeting at Rio IV, Córdoba, in 1919, passed a resolution to the effect that Defensa Agrícola served no useful purpose and ought to be suppressed. See *Diputados*, sesiones ordinarias, I (3 June 1919): 331–332. The president's use of Defensa Agrícola for political purposes also became a theme in Argentine literature. See Arturo Cancela's widely acclaimed short story, "El cocabacilo," in his *Tres relatos porteños*, 2nd ed. (Madrid: Calpe, 1923), pp. 15–115.

[49] A convenient summary of the history and achievements of Argentine agricultural education is Tomás Amadeo, *La enseñanza y la experimentación agrícolas* (Buenos Aires: Talleres Gráficos del Ministerio de Agricultura de la Nación, 1916), especially pp. 53–59.

[50] Budgets for agricultural education between 1898 and 1929 are summarized conveniently in Rodolfo Allen, *Enseñanza agrícola: documentos orgánicos* (Buenos Aires: Talleres Gráficos del Ministerio de Agricultura de la Nación, 1929), p. 30.

[51] Ibid., p. 106.

to the republic's agriculture, and the cost of bags was becoming exorbitant. In Buenos Aires the average unit price rose from 35 centavos during the 1916–1917 harvest to 1.2 pesos the following year.[52] Meanwhile, the press revealed that Argentine bag manufacturers, which simply sewed together hessians imported from India, were making annual profits of 100 percent.[53] When farmers demanded government action to remedy the shortage, the Ministry of Agriculture attempted to solve the bag question quickly by allowing the Royal Commission on Wheat Supplies, housed in the British consulate at Buenos Aires, to import and sell bags directly to farmers at 75 centavos each for the 1918–1919 harvest. However, the government's failure to control distribution undermined the scheme's effectiveness. In practice, to obtain bags colonists had to pay cash in advance.[54] Small farmers who lacked cash had to deal with intermediaries on extortionate terms. Despite assurances that the Royal Commission would supply all the bags Argentina required, German submarines, labor problems in India, and port strikes in Argentina combined to create serious shortages. By late 1918, the Royal Commission filled orders so tardily that some crops rotted on the ground.[55] The farmers furiously denounced the government's inability to supply sacking at reasonable prices.[56]

To attempt to remedy the bag shortage, in 1919 the government severed its agreement with the Royal Commission and entered the bag business itself. Congress passed legislation authorizing the executive branch to spend 25 million pesos to acquire bags and twine, which the Ministry of Agriculture would sell to farmers at cost plus ten percent.[57] But serious

52 Statistics on prices of bags in the provinces are in Argentine Republic, Ministerio de Agricultura, *Memoria del Ministerio de Agricultura. Aplicación de la Ley N° 10.777* (Buenos Aires: Talleres Gráficos del Ministerio de Agricultura de la Nación, 1921), pp. 73, 75.

53 *The Review of the River Plate* 50 (18 October 1918): 977.

54 A report of the terms of the agreement with the Royal Commission and a defense of the latter's policies appears in "Report on the Supply of Bags by the Royal Commission on Wheat Supplies for the Grain Crop of 1918–1919," *The Review of the River Plate* 51 (11 April 1919): 855–861.

55 *La Prensa* gave the bag shortage and the Royal Commission's performance close scrutiny. See 9 January 1919, pp. 11–12; 25 January 1919, p. 9; 29 January 1919, p. 7. Also, *The Review of the River Plate* 50 (18 October 1918): 977; 50 (20 December 1918): 1551. The influential socialist congressman Nicolás Repetto, who was also a Córdoba farmer, describes the difficulties and expense of obtaining bags in *Mi paso por la agricultura* (Buenos Aires: Santiago Rueda Editor, 1959), p. 179.

56 *La Prensa,* 5 January 1919, p. 9.

57 *Diputados,* sesiones ordinarias, III (6 August 1919): 367–368, 401–417; also Argentine Republic, Congreso Nacional, *Diario de sesiones de la Cámara de Senadores,* sesiones ordinarias, I (16 September 1919): 585, 625 (hereafter this source is referred to as *Senadores*).

flaws weakened this scheme. On the one hand, the government did not acquire the bags in time for the 1919–1920 harvest.[58] On the other hand, bags which government agents did purchase were twenty-five percent smaller than ordinary. Since by 1920 the world shortage of sacking was over and prices were falling, farmers turned to the private market rather than to the government's undersized bags, and the ministry found itself with an inventory of 29 million unsold grain bags. To the government's further embarrassment, the press and a congressional investigation uncovered evidence that ministerial corruption had accompanied purchase of the sacking.[59]

Another Yrigoyen policy that alarmed and alienated agricultural producers was the tax on exports that the government, beset by falling receipts from customs duties, levied in 1918. This levy was meant as a temporary emergency measure but was not repealed. The impact of the tax, of course, fell upon rural producers.[60]

While raising the farmers' tax burden, the government gave a low priority to agrarian reform legislation. The opposition parties undoubtedly made the Radical president's legislative task more difficult. At the same time, between 1916 and 1919, Yrigoyen proposed little agrarian legislation and did not encourage Congress to make rural reforms. The one significant piece of agrarian legislation proposed during the first three years of Yrigoyen's term was the "Ley del Hogar" or the "Ley Homestead," as it was frequently called. Sanctioned on 25 September 1917, this law provided for grants of public land to farmers. It was projected as a means of populating the interior, of easing agrarian unrest, and of reliev-

---

[58] In an article entitled "Las bolsas del gobierno nacional," *Cooperación Agrícola*, the newspaper of the Entre Ríos cooperative farmers, complained that the law was useless for the 1919–1920 harvest, 1 (November 1919): 268.

[59] *La Vanguardia*, 12 December 1919, p. 2; *La Prensa*, 27 September 1921, p. 10. The congressional investigating committee's efforts were frustrated by the refusal of the executive branch to cooperate and by the opposition of the Radical majority in the Chamber of Deputies. For information of the committee see *Diputados*, sesiones ordinarias, II (21 July 1921): 216; (3 August 1921): 408; III (1 September 1921): 272. The committee reported to the Chamber on 27 September 1921, sesiones ordinarias, IV: 341–349. Charging lack of cooperation by the president and by his Radical party followers in Congress, Conservative Matías Sánchez Sorondo and Socialist Antonio de Tomaso, the committee's two most prominent members, resigned 21 July 1922. See *Diputados*, sesiones ordinarias, III (21 July 1922): 291. The government attempted to defend its actions in a report, Argentine Republic, Ministerio de Agricultura, *Memoria del Ministerio de Agricultura. Aplicación de la Ley N° 10.777*, especially pp. 3, 8, 9, 12, 16.

[60] For analysis of the 1918 export tax, see Alejandro E. Bunge, *Riqueza y renta de la Argentina* (Buenos Aires: Agencia General de Librería y Publicaciones, 1919), p. 194; and Peters, *The Foreign Debt of the Argentine Republic*, pp. 70–71.

ing urban social tensions. Despite these lofty goals, the legislation was weak and essentially meaningless.

The Ley del Hogar's inspiration was the North American Homestead Act, but Argentine political and economic circumstances differed greatly from the United States. Constitutionally, the federal government could dispose of public land only in the territories, not in the provinces, which contained most of the area suitable for agriculture. The territories, with the exception of part of La Pampa, were located in the far north or the far south and were largely useless for farming. Moreover, as *La Tierra* emphasized, the 200-hectare maximum grants the law provided were much too small to support a family in the territories, and experience had shown that few immigrants were interested in settling in the bleak, isolated southern lands or in the semitropical north. In La Pampa, where a two-hundred-hectare farm was enough for profitable cereal growing, almost no good public land remained, as the territorial governor pointed out.[61] The Ley del Hogar appears to have been primarily a gesture.

Weak as it was, the law had raised hopes for populating the territories, and Yrigoyen's refusal to enforce it brought him scathing criticism. Basing his opposition to the law on what he called "nationalism," the president pointed to provisions which enabled unnaturalized immigrants to apply for land grants. Convinced that the legislation invited virtual foreign takeover of the territories, Yrigoyen ignored congressional pressure and refused to implement it until modified to apply only to Argentine citizens. Since Congress did not make this change, the Ley del Hogar remained a dead letter, a victim of the president's apprehension about the impact of immigration and of his poor working relationship with Congress.[62]

Serious agrarian unrest erupted in 1919 and eventually induced the

---

[61] *La Tierra,* 6 June 1919, p. 1; Molins, *La Pampa,* p. 32. Most of the congressional debate on the legislation emphasized that the farmers and the nation would benefit greatly if the proposal became law. See *Diputados* sesiones extraordinarias, IV (21 December 1916): 2970–2974; sesiones ordinarias, III (20 August 1917): 495–503; and *Senadores,* sesiones ordinarias, II (25 September 1917): 1071–1080. For criticism of the law by a respected intellectual and head of the Progressive Democratic party, see Lisandro de la Torre, *Obras de Lisandro de la Torre,* 6 vols. (Buenos Aires: Editorial Hemisferio, 1954), 6: 30.

[62] The press sharply criticized Yrigoyen's refusal to enforce the law. See, for example, *La Prensa,* 11 March 1919, p. 6; 4 August 1921, p. 10. Deputies attempted a full-scale investigation, but the executive branch refused to cooperate. *Diputados,* sesiones ordinarias, II (21 July 1921): 228–238; (29 July 1921): 341–345; (3 August 1921): 412–413, 437–438. Yrigoyen informed the Chamber of his reasons for opposing the law through a Radical party spokesman, Deputy José A. Amuchástegui of the Federal District. See *Diputados,* sesiones ordinarias, II (9 August 1922): 724–731.

government to propose land tenure reform more meaningful than the Ley del Hogar. The immediate cause of unrest was familiar—world prices for agricultural products again declined, while fixed costs of production remained high. Adding to the distress were heavy rains that damaged the 1918–1919 crop and a prolonged Argentine port strike that curtailed exports.[63] As expulsion of colonists for rent defaults began, the FAA made an urgent appeal to the president for a moratorium on land rent payments, for government loans to finance the corn harvest, and for a decree forbidding creditors to seize farmers' tools and personal property. When the government made no reply, the FAA issued a strike call, and by March (1919) 70,000 farmers responded.[64] In contrast with earlier agrarian movements, in 1919 farmers did not limit themselves to striking for short-term improvements and rent reductions but demanded fundamental changes in the land tenure system to transfer ownership of the land to tenants and renters. Interviewed by the respected socialist newspaper *La Vanguardia,* Piacenza announced that the FAA considered contract renegotiation as only a "transitory and circumstantial remedy" that was no substitute for thoroughgoing land reform.[65] The 1919 movement was not only more militant than previous strikes but also more violent; in a number of locations striking farmers burned crops and destroyed machinery.[66]

Renewal of tenant farmer agitation took place just as anti-Bolshevik paranoia was gripping the upper classes. Between 9 and 13 January 1919 Buenos Aires had witnessed a frightening bloodbath when the police, the army, and groups of upper-class vigilantes forcibly broke up an anarcho-syndicalist general strike. To justify the use of heavy-handed force during the *Semana Trágica,* as the week has been known ever since, the government, along with most of the urban press, magnified out of proportion

---

63 *The Review of the River Plate* 52 (10 October 1919): 929. See also Hanson, *Argentine Meat and the British Market,* p. 255; and Di Tella and Zymelman, *Las etapas del desarrollo,* p. 301; and *La Prensa,* 31 March 1919, p. 5; and 13 April 1919, p. 5.

64 The petition is in *La Tierra,* 7 March 1919, p. 1. Also see ibid., 1–2 May 1919, p. 1; 9 May 1919, p. 1. Piacenza reemphasized the farmers' plight in an interview with *La Prensa* on 10 April 1919, p. 12.

65 *La Vanguardia,* 1 January 1920, p. 1. A University of La Plata Faculty of Agronomy seminar, which surveyed cereal belt farmers on the land tenure question, found that almost without exception farmers aspired to become landowners. The seminar's published report is Emilio A. Coni, *¿Arrendamiento o propiedad?* (La Plata: Universidad Nacional de La Plata, 1920), p. 11. The results of the survey also were summarized in *La Vanguardia,* 19 September 1920, p. 2.

66 *La Tierra,* 11 February 1916, p. 1; *La Prensa,* 24 March 1919, p. 10; 17 April 1919, p. 6; *The Review of the River Plate* 51 (11 April 1919): 855. Also see Grosso, "Los problemas económicos y sociales y la respuesta radical con el gobierno (1916–1930)," p. 143.

the threat of violent social revolution. *La Época,* semiofficial organ of the Yrigoyen government, assured its readers that thousands of Russian "Maximalists," disguised as simple immigrant farmers, were migrating to Argentina to lead a bloody social upheaval.[67]

In this tense atmosphere, the government portrayed the tenants' movement as a revolutionary threat. Yrigoyen made one attempt at peaceful settlement by sending Minister of Agriculture Demarchi on an inspection tour through the cereal belt. Along with assurances that the president was looking after their welfare, Demarchi urged the farmers to return to work and made it clear that the government would not tolerate "vices" like agitation. Colonists, in a sullen and defiant mood, disregarded the minister's pleas and on several occasions shouted him down.[68] When the farmers failed to go back to work, the government turned to police repression. Circulars issued by the Ministry of Agriculture announced that the cause of the strike was agitators "who are conspiring against public tranquility and national order." The provincial police of Buenos Aires received authority to arrest anyone making "seditious" remarks.[69] By May and June of 1919, the repressive campaign was in full swing, and in several areas, police systematically persecuted the strike by breaking up FAA meetings and jailing rural leaders. The reliable British weekly *Review of the River Plate* reported that the government deported over 300 under the Social Defense Law. As in earlier strikes, government repression became particularly severe in La Pampa, where the national police openly threatened to deport farmers who refused to return to work.[70]

---

[67] *La Época,* 15 January 1919, p. 1. For an anarcho-syndicalist viewpoint of the causes and events of the Semana Trágica, see Diego Abad de Santillán, *La F.O.R.A. Ideología y trayectoria del movimiento obrero revolucionario en la Argentina* (Buenos Aires: Ediciones Nervio, 1933), pp. 259–260. An account by a Buenos Aires police officer who served during the Semana Trágica is José Ramón Romariz, *La semana trágica* (Buenos Aires: Hemisferio, 1952). For an apology of Yrigoyen's role in the 1919 events, see Nicolás Babini, *Enero de 1919: los hechos y los hombres de la "semana trágica"* (Buenos Aires: S.E.P.A., 1956).

[68] The Buenos Aires newspapers chronicled the minister's inspection tour with great interest. See *La Época,* 14 April 1919, p. 1; 25 April 1919, p. 4; *La Vanguardia,* 22 April 1919, p. 1; 21 May 1919, p. 1; *La Prensa,* 13 April 1919, p. 5; 18 April 1919, p. 4; 21 April 1919, p. 5; and *The Review of the River Plate* 51 (18 April 1919): 917; 51 (2 May 1919): 1043. The government's principal offer to the farmers was expanded short-term credit for seeds and sowing expenses. See *La Época,* 29 April 1919, p. 1; *The Review of the River Plate* 51 (4 April 1919): 789.

[69] The ministry's circular is reprinted in *La Vanguardia,* 16 April 1919, p. 1. Also see *The Review of the River Plate* 51 (23 May 1919): 1233.

[70] *The Review of the River Plate* 51 (20 June 1919): 1445. Also see *La Vanguardia,* 10 April 1919, p. 2; 15 September 1919, p. 1; *La Prensa,* 11 May 1919, p. 10; 22 May 1919, p. 12; and Repetto, *Mi paso por la agricultura*, pp. 160, 167.

This repression brought forth vigorous protest, especially from the FAA, which complained that "the anarchists, the agitators, and the agrarian propagandists which the government indicts as promoters of the strike exist only in its imagination." [71] After sharp debate, during which Radical deputies again blamed unrest on "professional agitators," the Chamber voted to ask the minister of the interior to explain the persecution of striking farmers. The Yrigoyen government never replied.[72] By mid-June 1919 the strike ended, but the repression increased anger and resentment among tenant farmers.

The well-publicized violence and repression which accompanied the 1919 tenant strike made the land tenure question a major national issue. Since 1912 the small but active Socialist party's congressional delegation had proposed legislation to regulate rental contracts and to force landowners to compensate tenants for physical improvements to rented property. Although reintroduced periodically by the socialists and warmly backed by the FAA, these proposals had been pigeonholed in Congress and ignored by the executive branch.[73] As rural unrest deepened in 1919, a number of dissident congressmen in Yrigoyen's own party joined the Socialists and the Progressive Democrat party, a moderate group based in Santa Fe, to demand not only contract reform but also a stiff land tax which, it was claimed, would force the division and sale of large estates.[74] Spokesmen for the large landowners responded with arguments reflecting the incomprehension of agrarian problems which long had characterized the Argentine elite. According to one socially prominent landowner, the basic cause of agrarian distress was not the land system but the tenant farmer, who "lacks skill, lacks order, lacks economy, and lacks industriousness." Similarly, the official publication

---

[71] *La Tierra,* 16 May 1919, p. 1.

[72] For the Chamber's debates, see *Diputados,* sesiones ordinarias, I (28 May 1919): 146–155.

[73] For an overview of the Socialist party's agrarian program, see Alfredo L. Palacios, *La justicia social* (Buenos Aires: Editorial Claridad, 1954), pp. 178–179, 399–402; Juan B. Justo, *Discursos y escritos políticos* (Buenos Aires: "El Ateneo," 1933), pp. 140–189; and Partido Socialista, *El Partido Socialista y los agricultores. Doce años de acción y de propaganda* (Buenos Aires: Tip. "La Vanguardia," 1913).

[74] Carlos J. Rodríguez, a Radical congressman from Córdoba province, introduced legislation in 1919 calling not only for a national land tax but also for an immediate moratorium on all rural rents. See *Diputados,* sesiones extraordinarias, VI (9 April 1919): 652–653; ibid., sesiones ordinarias, II (16 July 1919): 729–730. The Progressive Democratic party, led by the great intellectual and political reformer Lisandro de la Torre, poposed compensated expropriation of large estates followed by division and sale to small farmers. De la Torre, *Obras,* VI: 17, 23–27.

of the *Sociedad Rural* portrayed farmers as indolent drones who whiled away their time and money playing cards, shooting pool, and drinking.[75]

Taking a middle ground between supporters of land reform on the one hand and the conservative elite on the other, Yrigoyen in July 1919 proposed several moderate agrarian programs. Specifically, the president's proposals would have required owners to make contracts for a minimum of three years and to reimburse tenants for improvements. Yrigoyen also proposed reform of the National Mortgage Bank, creation of an agrarian bank to expand rural credit, and formation of rural arbitration boards to settle contractual disputes.[76] In 1919 the legislators acted on only one of these proposals: the reform of the National Mortgage Bank's charter to permit the institution to make loans to farmers for purchase of rural lots. During debate, legislators predicted the reform would benefit farmers greatly, but in practice the continuing reluctance of large owners to subdivide and sell estates along with the bank's complicated bureaucratic procedures prevented the 1919 law from making a significant impact.[77] The remainder of Yrigoyen's agrarian proposals languished in Congress during 1919 and received no further suuport from the president. As the months passed and the government failed to act, farmers became increasingly resentful.

But the farmers' criticism of the national government subsided temporarily when a major strike of landless rural laborers, or *braceros* as they were often called in Argentina, startled the republic and threatened the interests of the tenant farmers and the landed elite alike. About 200,000 braceros were permanently employed, mostly on the large farms. During most harvest seasons, tens of thousands of additional laborers migrated to the cereal belt. Many of these migrants labored for the small tenant farmers who needed no outside help the rest of the year. Before the war, most migrant workers had come from Italy during the European off-season or from the poverty-stricken northwestern Argen-

[75] M. A. Pueyrredón, "Panaceas," *La Razón,* 5 May 1919; Alberto E. Castex, "El malestar agrícola," *Anales de la Sociedad Rural Argentina* 53 (April 1919): 199–200.

[76] One may read Yrigoyen's proposals in *Diputados*, sesiones ordinarias, II (2 July 1913): 612–615; ibid., sesiones ordinarias (September 29 1919): 717–719.

[77] The reform of the Mortgage Bank also contained provisions to aid cattlemen, which probably explains its rapid passage. Analysis of the impact of the reform, passed as Law 10,676, may be found in Alfredo Bonino and Pedro del Carril, *La subdivisión de nuestras tierras y la evolución agraria del país* (Buenos Aires: Estudio de Agronomía y Colonización, 1926), p. 39; Podestá, *La pequeña propiedad rural en la República Argentina,* pp. 101, 114; and Ortiz, *Historia económica de la Argentina,* 2: 120–121. For the debates, see *Diputados,* sesiones ordinarias, IV (1 September 1919): 28–50.

tine provinces of Santiago del Estero and Tucumán. During World War I, however, Italian migrants were replaced by unemployed Buenos Aires laborers.[78]

Whatever their origin, Argentine rural laborers were generally a repressed and marginal group. During the harvest season braceros labored sixteen or more hours daily, mostly under the searing sun. The wages for this heavy work were low. As late as 1924 unskilled farm labor earned 3 to 3.5 paper pesos daily without board, a substandard wage at the time in Argentina. Farmers retained much of this pay for shelter, fuel, and use of a horse. Some harvest workers, especially machinery operators, earned considerably more, but like other rural laborers isolation often forced them to purchase supplies from employers, who charged "ten for whatever is worth one." When the harvest was finished, thousands of braceros wandered around the countryside looking for work, riding on freight trains and suffering the harassment of provincial police.[79]

Major bracero unrest appeared in Argentina for the first time during World War I, when inflation caused real wages to fall sharply. The weak economic situation created fertile ground for anarcho-syndicalist theories of working-class militancy brought by migrants from the cities in 1918 and 1919. Labor unions, a novelty among Argentine rural workers, formed and began to demand a twelve-hour shift, increased wages, and improvements in working conditions.[80] Farmers, many of whom had suffered severely in 1919, generally rejected such demands, and in December 1919 the workers responded with a mammoth strike. The movement began in southern Santa Fe and in southern Buenos Aires but spread rapidly

[78] Statistics on agricultural workers are found in Ortiz, *Historia económica de la Argentina*, 2: 194. For analysis of the origin of these workers, see Gori, *El pan nuestro*, p. 100; Pedro Pagés, *Defensa de la producción agropecuaria* (La Plata: Universidad Nacional de La Plata, 1928), p. 50; and *La Tierra*, 30 November 1917, p. 1. Unemployment in the Argentine cities increased markedly during World War I, when the government suspended most public works. For analysis of urban working conditions during this period, see José Panettieri, *Los trabajadores* (Buenos Aires: Editorial Jorge Álvarez, S.A., 1967), pp. 169–183.

[79] The value of the paper peso was 44% of the gold peso, or about US $.42. The words quoted come from José Rodríguez Tardati, "Los trabajadores del campo," *Revista de Ciencias Económicas* 26 (June 1926): 386. Other analyses of bracero wages and working conditions are in Estabrook, *Agricultural Survey of South America*, p. 67; Juan Álvarez, "Obrerismo agrario," *La Prensa*, 28 March 1920, p. 6; *La Capital* (Rosario), 18 November 1920, p. 4; and *La Vanguardia*, 31 December 1919, p. 5.

[80] *La Prensa*, 30 November 1919, 7. On an index of 1940=100, real wages of industrial workers in Buenos Aires fell from 68 in 1914 to a low of 42 in 1918. They rose to 57 in 1919. Adolfo Dorfman, *Evolución industrial argentina* (Buenos Aires: Editorial Losada, S.A., 1942), p. 241. Also see Panettieri, *Los trabajadores*, p. 174.

throughout the entire cereal zone and lasted for several weeks. Violence was mostly confined to the destruction of crops.[81]

In a no-nonsense mood, the government quickly moved to crush the bracero strike. In Buenos Aires province, which spent 500,000 pesos in 1919 for police rifles, as well as in Santa Fe, the Radical governors mobilized heavy detachments of gendarmes. Several pitched battles between strikers and police occurred, but more often the government forces met little resistance as they burned literature, jailed leaders, and deported foreigners. *La Época* lauded the Buenos Aires police, who broke the strike after arresting "over 600 professional agitators." In their zeal to crush the movement by eliminating its leadership, provincial police at one point adopted the practice of sniping at labor leaders alighting from rural trains, a practice which killed innocent bystanders.[82]

Now that the tenant farmers were subjected to a bracero strike, their fundamental conservatism became apparent. When their own interests had been at stake, colonists had generated sustained agitation and had indignantly denounced government policy. But the farmers, whose support for agrarian reform hardly envisioned social democracy in the countryside, vigorously applauded the government's use of force to end the bracero strike.[83] In Entre Ríos, meetings of colonists called on the president to send troops to guarantee the "right to work." The FAA viewed the strike with a petit bourgeois spirit of self-righteousness. Farmers, said *La Tierra,* are "true martyrs," who had risen from poverty. "We have frequented neither houses of prostitution, nor gaming establishments, nor horse races," it continued, adding that braceros wasted time drinking, carousing, and gambling. Such shiftless workers, who included a high proportion of "degenerates and vice addicts," certainly had no right to strike for "impossible conditions." The bracero strike, according to the FAA, must be the result of anarchist agitators.[84] The farmers, like the landed elite, the Radical party, and the press, employed

[81] Urban newspapers, alarmed at the extent and intensity of the rural labor strike, gave it close attention. For detailed reports, see *La Vanguardia,* 20 December 1919, p. 2; 29 December 1919, p. 1; 18 January 1920, p. 1; 14 April 1919, p. 1; *La Capital* (Rosario), 1 January 1920, p. 3; 6 January 1920, p. 4; 19 January 1920, p. 4; *La Prensa,* 30 November 1919, pp. 7, 13; 13 December 1919, p. 12; 23 December 1919, p. 12; 18 January 1920, p. 12.

[82] *The Review of the River Plate* 52 (17 October 1919): 995; 53 (2 January 1920): 17; *La Vanguardia,* 26 December 1919, p. 1; *La Prensa,* 20 December 1919, p. 13; *La Época,* 24 January 1919, p. 2.

[83] *La Tierra,* 16 May 1919, p. 1.

[84] *La Tierra,* 26 September 1919, p. 1; 14 November 1919, p. 1; 26 December 1919, p. 1; 5 October 1920, p. 1. For the position of the Entre Ríos colonists, see "Movimiento agrario," *Cooperación agrícola* 1 (March 1920): 486–488.

the conspiracy theory when it served their purposes to shift explanations of social unrest away from economics.[85]

When the Chamber of Deputies convened in May for its 1920 sessions, it contained a Radical majority for the first time, but the legislators responded to the severe unrest among farmers and braceros with the same lack of urgency that previous opposition-dominated chambers had displayed. The deputies showed total disregard for the demands of landless laborers. A proposal to appoint a study commission to investigate the wages, hours, and living conditions of rural workers was promptly and unceremoniously shelved.[86] Although the congressmen took up the rural tenure reform question, they largely emasculated Yrigoyen's 1919 proposals. They did extend the minimum contract period to four years but they also inserted major loopholes into the law. One such clause limited the law's jurisdiction to farms under 300 hectares rented directly from the owner. Landowners could evade the law's intent by renting plots larger than 300 hectares or by employing intermediaries. Another weakness of the legislation was the failure to require written contracts.[87]

Passed by the Chamber on 21 September 1920, the land rental reform encountered studied indifference in the Senate, which refused to consider the question during its regular sessions of 1920 and 1921. The president also passed up an opportunity to force the Senate's consideration when he failed to place tenure reform on the agenda of the special congressional sessions called for January 1921.[88]

Impatient with the Senate's procrastination, the FAA took the step, unprecedented among Argentine farmers, of organizing a demonstration in the capital. After widespread advance publicity and careful organization, about 1400 farmers converged on Buenos Aires on 26 August 1921. At an open-air meeting that night, they loudly cheered speakers who portrayed the farmers' plight and who demanded political action to ease it. The next day, Yrigoyen disappointed the demonstrators when he refused to receive a delegation, but the farmers publicized their cause with

---

85 The *Sociedad Rural* viewed the rural labor strike as an anarchist plot. See Alberto E. Castex, "Propaganda anarquista en la campaña," *Anales de la Sociedad Rural Argentina* 53 (15–30 December 1919): 1017.

86 The proposal to form the study group is in *Diputados*, sesiones ordinarias, I (1 June 1920): 407. The Argentine government enacted no significant legislation to protect rural workers until 1944.

87 *Diputados,* sesiones ordinarias, V (21 September 1920): 341–377. The Radicals held 84 of 152 seats in the chamber during 1920. For information on the composition of the Chamber of Deputies by political party, see Eduardo Zalduendo, *Geografía electoral de la Argentina* (Buenos Aires: Ediciones Ancora, 1958), p. 226.

88 *La Tierra*, 18 January 1921, p. 1; 25 January 1921, p. 1.

a march the length of the Avenida de Mayo through the heart of the business district. Their rude clothing standing out quaintly in a capital which worshipped the latest trends in London and Paris fashions, the rural demonstrators gathered in the plaza in front of Congress, where a number of senators appeared to assure the crowd that the upper house would soon take up the land rental question. After more oratory, the farmers dispersed and began the long trek home.[89]

Within a month, the Senate passed a land rental act identical to the Chamber of Deputies' version. During debate, Radical senators strongly supported the legislation over the protests of their conservative colleagues, most of whom criticized the bill's infringement on property rights.[90] Sanctioned on 24 September 1921, the legislation, known as Law 11,170, guaranteed farmers the right to retain personal property in case of debt foreclosures, prohibited landowners from requiring tenants to sell to, buy from, or insure with any specific parties, and required landowners to compensate tenants for physical improvements to the property at the end of contracts.[91] Without explanation, Yrigoyen refused to sign Law 11,170, but, as the constitution provided, the law took effect without his signature after a delay of ten days. The president then continued to obstruct the law's application. Not until November 18 did he order the Ministry of Agriculture to prepare the decree necessary to administer the legislation, which finally went into effect on 21 February 1922.[92] *La Tierra*, which was aware that the legislation was imperfect but nonetheless considered it an important precedent for future agrarian reforms, condemned Yrigoyen's delay as an insult to the republic's farmers.[93]

As Yrigoyen prepared to leave office in October 1922, the FAA reviewed his term and found much that was unfavorable, particularly the president's failure to formulate a coherent agricultural policy and his stormy relations with the organized farm movement. *La Tierra* expressed

---

89 For reports of the 1921 Farmers' March, see *La Tierra,* 18 August 1921, p. 1; 30 August 1921, p. 1; and 25 March 1925, p. 1; *La Vanguardia,* 27 August 1921, p. 1; 28 August 1921, p. 1; and *La Prensa,* 27 August 1921, p. 11; 28 August 1921, p. 5.

90 *Senadores,* 20 September 1921, pp. 492–496; 24 September 1921, pp. 573–599.

91 The law's complete text is reprinted in Palacios, *La justicia social,* pp. 403–405. It is also found in the standard collection of Argentine legislation for this period, Augusto da Rocha, comp., *Colección completa de leyes nacionales sancionadas por el Honorable Congreso durante los años 1852 a 1933,* 27 vols. (Buenos Aires: Librería "La Facultad" de Juan Roldán & Cia., 1918–1933), 21: 58–62.

92 *La Tierra,* 21 February 1922, p. 1; *La Vanguardia,* 19 November 1921, p. 1.

93 *La Tierra,* 28 October 1921, p. 1.

the alienation between the FAA leaders and Yrigoyen when it editorialized that the president had been a "strong enemy of farmers, as are all Indians . . . when a law was sanctioned, his Indian passions drove him to reject it." [94] Meant as an unkindly slap, the reference to Yrigoyen's mixed racial background reflected Argentina's tragic failure to integrate its rural immigrant population into national political life and to inspire the immigrants' respect for the republic's cultural background.

Largely because world market prices were favorable, the six-year interim between Yrigoyen's first and second presidencies marked a period of respite for Argentina's farmers. Between 1921 and 1925 wheat prices were relatively high and steady, while corn prices rose rapidly. Prices fell in 1926 and 1927 but then recovered, and agricultural prosperity lasted until mid-1929.[95] Farmers were not free from fears of a renewed cost-price squeeze, for land rents and railroad rates mounted steadily until 1927. But as long as farm prices stayed high, no significant rural unrest emerged.[96]

This relatively auspicious economic picture coincided with the presidency of Marcelo T. de Alvear (1922–1928). A member of one of the republic's most distinguished families as well as a long-time Radical, Alvear continued the precedent, set by previous administrations, of granting a low priority to agrarian reform. In fact, Alvear's principal achievement in agrarian matters was to reorganize the Ministry of Agriculture. To accomplish this task, the president appointed as minister Tomás A. Le Bretón, Yrigoyen's widely-respected ambassador to the United States. Working with great energy, Le Bretón suppressed unnecessary positions, fired corrupt bureaucrats, and rooted field employees out of their urban swivel chairs and sent them to the countryside where they belonged. The statistical and experimental bureaus, divisions of the ministry which directly affected farmers, received particularly close attention. Rural statistics, neglected during the Yrigoyen administration, were placed under the direction of Leon Estabrook, a North American expert, and by the mid-1920s the government for the first time published reliable periodical

[94] *La Tierra,* 13 October 1922, p. 1; also see 15 November 1924, p. 2. Yrigoyen's father was a French Basque immigrant; his mother was a native of Buenos Aires and was probably of *mestizo* background. Luna, *Yrigoyen,* pp. 15–16.

[95] For data on farm prices during the 1920s, see Hanson, *Argentine Meat and the British Market,* p. 255; Di Tella and Zymelman, *Las etapas del desarrollo,* pp. 356, 381. Most "farm prices" recorded terminal market data, but for a set of statistics that reported the amounts farmers actually received for their crops, see *Diputados,* sesiones ordinarias, III (5 September 1928): 683–692.

[96] For data on rising land rents in the 1920s, see Nicolás Repetto, "La defensa de la producción agrícola nacional," *Revista de Ciencias Económicas* 33 (September 1929): 731; and Nemirovsky, *Estructura económica y orientación política,* p. 112.

agricultural data.[97] The ministry also began to emphasize scientific seed selection and distribution, which had received less attention in Argentina than in Uruguay or even in poverty-stricken Paraguay. By 1923 European experts arrived to carry out seed experimentation, while the government began an informational campaign to urge farmers to use better seeds.[98]

Improvements in statistics and research were tempered somewhat by the ministry's inadequate attention to agricultural education. Enrollment in the government's agricultural schools rose only slightly—from 331 in 1922 to 443 in 1925—and most of these institutions continued to "function only thanks to the heroism of their directors." [99] The number of field agronomists employed by the ministry rose from 35 in 1921 to only 40 in 1927.[100] Despite these deficiencies, Le Bretón established a good reputation for honesty and efficiency and was the only minister of agriculture whom the FAA publicly praised during the 1912–1920 period.[101]

The Alvear government's record in agrarian legislation was much less favorable than its administrative accomplishments. Like Yrigoyen, Alvear was unable to command a majority in the Senate. Moreover, in the Chamber, the Radical party was seriously divided between "personalists," who desired Yrigoyen's return to power in 1928, and "anti-personalists," who attempted to obstruct that return by sponsoring federal intervention in provincial politics. In both houses of Congress, "political wranglings" over the question of provincial intervention took precedence over constructive legislative work.[102] Between 1922 and 1928 Congress passed only four laws relating specifically to agrarian matters.[103]

---

[97] *The Review of the River Plate* 59 (2 February 1923): 267; Leon M. Estabrook, "Agricultural Statistics in Argentina," ibid. 62 (8 August 1924): 359; Miguel Ángel Cárcano, "Nuestro régimen agrario," *Revista de Ciencias Económicas* 29 (October 1927): 1115. The reorganization of the ministry is outlined in Argentine Republic, Ministerio de Agricultura, *Memoria correspondiente al ejercicio de 1923 presentada al Congreso de la Nación por el Ministro de Agricultura Dr. T. A. Le Bretón* (Buenos Aires: Talleres Gráficos del Ministerio de Agricultura de la Nación, 1924), pp. 5–13.

[98] *The Review of the River Plate* 59 (2 February 1923): 267; 64 (29 October 1926): 7; 66 (30 March 1928): 13. Also Emilio J. Schleh, *Semillas para el agricultor* (Buenos Aires: Imp. Ferrari Hnos., 1924), pp. 13–15.

[99] *La Tierra,* 6 May 1924, p. 1. Enrollment statistics in agricultural schools are from Allen, *Enseñanza agrícola: documentos orgánicos,* p. 106.

[100] Argentine Republic, Ministerio de Agricultura, *Memoria correspondiente al ejercicio de 1927 presentada al Congreso de la Nación por el Ministro de Agricultura Emilio Mihura* (Buenos Aires: Talleres Gráficos del Ministerio de Agricultura de la Nación, 1928), p. 73.

[101] *La Tierra,* 25 August 1925, p. 1.

[102] *The Review of the River Plate* 54 (26 February 1926): 5.

[103] Laws 11,380 of 30 September 1926 and 11,388 of 10 December 1926 dealt with agricultural cooperatives. Law 11,212 of 6 September 1923 appropriated one

The most glaring example of the government's inattention to agrarian needs during the Alvear administration concerned the failure to reform and strengthen Law 11,170. By the mid-1920s the inefficacy of the 1921 land rental act was public knowledge, and tenant farmers were clamoring for reform.[104] The FAA released a survey in 1928 which showed that, despite the law's terms, thirty percent of the tenants in Buenos Aires province held contracts for less than four years. As in the years before 1921, landowners continued to refuse to indemnify tenants for property improvements and frequently continued to require colonists to purchase bags, machinery, and insurance at extortionate rates.[105] On several occasions, congressmen introduced legislation to revise the law, but these proposals all died in committee.[106]

The Alvear government made one basic agrarian legislative proposal. Submitted to Congress in 1924, the legislation would have authorized the executive branch to purchase agricultural land held in large estates, to subdivide it, and to sell it to individual farmers.[107] Minister Le Bretón formulated this proposal, he stated, to combat the trend toward stagnation that was becoming evident in Argentine agriculture by the early 1920s. Area under cereal and flax cultivation had increased only slightly—from 14.1 million hectares in 1913–1914 to 15.1 million in 1924–1925. Production and exports were growing slowly in comparison with other major agricultural countries. Between 1905–1909 and 1920–1924 Argentine wheat exports rose only thirty percent, while Canada's quintupled, Australia's tripled, and those of the United States more than doubled.[108]

Government-sponsored land reform to create a numerous class of property-owning farmers was essential, argued Le Bretón, in order to reverse Argentina's declining importance as an agricultural exporter. The

---

million pesos for emergency seed distribution. Law 11,280 of 20 November 1923, appropriated fifteen million pesos for Defensa Agrícola.

104 For detailed analysis of methods of evading Law 11,170, see Vélez, *La situación agrícola de La Pampa,* pp. 90–96. On the same theme, *La Prensa,* 28 October 1921, p. 9; and Pedro de Paoli, *La reforma agraria* (Buenos Aires: Editorial A. Peña Lillo, 1960), p. 31.

105 The FAA survey was summarized in *Diputados,* sesiones ordinarias, II (1 August 1928): 775. Also see ibid., sesiones ordinarias, V (29 September 1928): 599–600.

106 Reform of Law 11,170 was introduced in the Chamber in 1923, 1925, and 1928, and in the Senate in 1927 and 1928.

107 The proposal is reprinted in *Diputados,* sesiones ordinarias, III (21 August 1924): 480–481.

108 Argentine Republic, Ministerio de Agricultura, *Memoria correspondiente al ejercicio de 1923,* p. 5. For statistics on area cultivated, see Tenembaum, *Orientación económica,* pp. 21–22. For comparative export data, Estabrook, *Agricultural Survey of South America,* pp. 3, 69.

minister's arguments emphasized that the existing tenancy system made farming an unattractive way of life and kept agricultural production low. The difficulty of purchasing land in Argentina discouraged European immigrants from settling in the largely empty cereal provinces and at the same time encouraged farmers already there to abandon agriculture and migrate to the cities. Furthermore, according to Le Bretón, crop yields in Argentina remained lower than in the United States or Canada largely because tenant farmers rented as much land and planted as extensively as possible in hopes of good weather and high prices. Still another unfortunate result of the land system was the reluctance of tenant farmers to engage in diversified agriculture or mixed farming.[109] The government's proposal, finally, was predicated on the fact that many tenants had long been eager to buy land, but large owners, during the 1920s as before, subdivided and sold only a fraction of the land farmers wished to purchase.[110]

Applauded by the FAA, the 1924 land reform proposal attracted widespread support among farmers, and within ten months over 14,000 telegrams arrived in Congress to urge passage.[111] Shortly after the administration presented its proposal, however, rising world cereal prices induced an expansion of planting in Argentina. With agricultural stagnation temporarily ended, Le Bretón's arguments lost some of their force and Congress took no action on the land reform proposal. After Le Bretón resigned in 1925, the administration took little further interest in land reform.[112]

The legislators' inattention to the land question, as well as the government's failure to take action on other fundamental rural problems, did much to discredit Argentine political institutions among the farmers. "The degeneration of Congress is poisoning our faith in democracy," editorialized *La Tierra* in 1925.[113] For over ten years the rural protest movement had publicized the need for basic agrarian reforms, but none of the governments had done much to bring them about. By the mid-1920s farm-

---

109 On low yields in Argentine agriculture, consult Scobie, *Revolution on the Pampas,* p. 87. For analysis of the impact of the land system on agricultural diversification, see Tenembaum, *Orientación económica,* pp. 23–24; Torino, *El problema del inmigrante,* p. 250; and Vélez, *La situación agrícola de La Pampa,* p. 145.

110 *The Review of the River Plate* 63 (12 June 1925): 31.

111 *La Tierra,* 26 August 1924, p. 1; *Diputados,* sesiones ordinarias, III (21 August 1925): 686.

112 *The Review of the River Plate* (24 October 1924), p. 1067; 12 September 1924, p. 679; 65 (25 March 1927): 25. Hectares cultivated with cereal and flax increased from 15.1 million in 1924–1925 to 19.5 million in 1929–1930. Tenembaum, *Orientación económica,* p. 22.

113 *La Tierra,* 25 August 1925, p. 1.

ers were comparing the inactivity of the Argentine government with what they considered the strong and vigorous regime of Fascist Italy. Piacenza journeyed to Rome to meet Mussolini, and *La Tierra* began to print editorials commenting favorably on the Italian political system.[114] While it is a mistake to label Piacenza and the FAA as "Fascist," as some Argentine authors have done,[115] there is no question that tenant farmers were becoming increasingly disillusioned with the accomplishments of parliamentary democracy. Two decades later, Perón's authoritarian political system gathered substantial support among cereal-belt farmers, largely because the dictator enacted many of the reforms for which tenants had been pleading since 1912.[116]

The alienation of the tenant farmers from the prevailing political system accelerated after Hipólito Yrigoyen reassumed the presidency in 1928. The Radical leader, who had maintained his popularity among the native-born masses despite his seventy-six years, swept to power with a large majority of the popular vote. Yrigoyen attracted this support not only by means of his charisma but also by indications that his second administration would assume a more populist stance than had his first. *La Época,* for example, assured its readers that it was the intention of the new administration to "aid the noble producers" by promoting the "development and protection of agriculture." [117]

The government's agricultural policies failed to match these promises. Yrigoyen took office as a rural depression, brought about by a sharp drop in world prices, was emerging. The price of wheat fell from 11.2 pesos per hundred kilograms in March 1928 to 7.35 in September 1930. During the same period, the price of corn fell from 8.8 pesos to 5.15 and the price of flax from 15.25 to 10.6. Drought, which wiped out seventy percent of the wheat and flax crops in 1929, added to the farmers' dis-

---

[114] Ibid., 10 April 1923, p. 1; 10 June 1924, p. 1.

[115] H. García Ledesma, *Lisandro de la Torre y la pampa gringa* (Buenos Aires: Editorial Indoamerica, 1954), p. 55.

[116] In 1945 land rents were frozen; in succeeding years they actually fell because of inflation. In 1948 Perón's Congress passed Law No. 13,246 which extended the minimum rental contract to eight years. Also "provision was made for periodic review and adjustment of rent." Other clauses authorized the Bank of the Nation to loan farmers up to 100 percent of the purchase price to buy the land they were renting. Peronist legislation also established special arbitration tribunals to settle contract disputes, a reform government experts had recommended in 1912. Most of these reforms were rescinded after General Perón's fall in 1955. For additional information on his government's agricultural policies, see Darrell F. Fienup, Russell H. Brannon, and Frank A. Fender, *The Agricultural Development of Argentina* (New York: Frederick A. Praeger, Publishers, 1969), pp. 302–303 and passim; and de Paoli, *La reforma agraria*, pp. 42–54.

[117] *La Época,* 17 August 1928, p. 1.

tress.[118] Land rents and other costs fell only slowly, and by mid-1930 tenant farmers found that sale of the harvest was insufficient to return costs of production.[119] The rapidly deepening crisis created demands for political action, but while the government did initiate some programs to meet the needs of farmers, its attitude towards rural problems recalled the president's first administration. There was a great deal of talk about doing something for the farmers but very little actual accomplishment.

The one occasion during Yrigoyen's second term on which he vigorously exercised his executive powers in a manner that aided the tenant farmers occurred late in 1928, when bitter bracero strikes broke out in Santa Fe for the first time since 1920. As in his first term, Yrigoyen made it clear that he would not tolerate rural labor unrest that might threaten production and exports. The strike, called to press for higher wages and for recognition of rural syndicates, led to considerable violence and threatened to stop agricultural production in southern Santa Fe.[120] After the police failed to enforce the "right to work," the national government took the highly unusual step of sending two army regiments to Santa Fe without the request of the provincial government. Justifying this tough approach by blaming the trouble on "professional agitators," the government swiftly broke the strike. The FAA, which had opposed occasional congressional proposals during the 1920s to improve the rural workers' living and working conditions, applauded Yrigoyen's use of the army.[121]

But the president did not act with similar energy in organizing the Ministry of Agriculture, which after 1928 slid back into incompetence and corruption. Although the ministry's share of the budget rose slightly in 1929 and 1930 (see Table 3), the quality of its services declined. Agricultural statistics, which the *Review of the River Plate* described as in a state of "collapse," exemplified the ministry's sad state. The publication of many important statistics was abandoned, while other data appeared so tardily as to be useless.[122]

---

118 Statistics on agricultural prices between 1927 and 1930 are in Di Tella and Zymelman, *Las etapas del desarrollo,* p. 385. *La Prensa,* in its issue of 10 January 1930, p. 15, recounts the ravages caused by drought.

119 Campolieti, *La organización de la agricultura argentina,* p. 7; Gastón Lestard, "La actualidad agrícola," *La Razón,* 5 November 1930; *La Tierra,* 1 October 1930, p. 4.

120 *La Tierra,* 15 November 1928, p. 1; 24 November 1928, p. 2; *The Review of the River Plate* 66 (30 November 1928): 7; *La Prensa,* 29 November 1928, p. 19.

121 Yrigoyen's use of the army is narrated in detail in *La Tierra,* 8 December 1928, p. 2; *La Época,* 2 December 1928, p. 1; 3 December 1928, p. 1; and 12 December 1928, p. 1. For the farmers' opposition to rural labor legislation, see *La Tierra,* 16 June 1928, p. 1; and 28 July 1928, p. 1.

122 *The Review of the River Plate* 67 (21 June 1929): 15; *La Prensa,* 18 June 1929, p. 17; 2 April 1930, p. 13.

Troubled by the ministry's disorganization, agrarian interests were also perplexed by the executive branch's failure to formulate a national policy to confront the deepening rural depression. The executive proposed no land reform or colonization policies, nor did he suggest controls or reductions of railroad rates, which farmers considered exorbitant. Despite widespread support from farmers, economists, and the press for construction of a network of country grain elevators, Yrigoyen put forward no legislation on the subject. Faced by the diversity of conflicting interests which wished to finance, build, and operate elevators, the government took no action, and Argentina remained virtually without rural grain storage facilities (see footnote 9).

Although the administration showed no concern for agricultural storage and marketing questions, it did propose two reforms farmers long had sought: revision of the 1921 land rental act and creation of a system of rural credit. Despite the opposition of the Sociedad Rural, in September 1929 the Radical-controlled Chamber approved the administration's proposal to strengthen and reform Law 11,170. A few months later, the Senate approved the reform with some modifications.[123] But from that point on, the reform fell victim to the intense political hatreds which polarized Congress into warring factions during 1930. The Chamber, which spent all its sessions between May and August debating the credentials of three anti-Yrigoyen Radicals legally elected from Mendoza and San Juan provinces, was unable to constitute itself and could transact no business. Eventually, the president had his way and the Chamber refused to seat the three deputies-elect, but vital legislation, including consideration of the Senate's modifications of the land rental law, were left waiting.[124] A similar fate befell the administration's proposal to establish a national agrarian bank. Passed by the Chamber in 1929, the proposal was not considered by the Senate that year, and in 1930 the upper house held no sessions, for it could not legally convene until the Chamber had constituted itself.[125]

While the executive and legislative branches continued to devote

[123] For reports of opposition to further land tenure reform, see *La Prensa*, 23 December 1929, p. 10; Genero García, "Leyes agrarias peligrosas," *Revista de Economía Argentina* 24 (May 1930): 340. Only one vote was cast against the reform in the Chamber. See *Diputados*, sesiones ordinarias, III (18 September 1929): 618. For discussion in the Senate, see *Senadores*, sesiones extraordinarias, III (25 January 1930): 311–356.

[124] An excellent analysis of the congressional crisis of 1930 is in Robert Smith, "Radicalism in the Province of San Juan: The Saga of Federico Cantoni (1916–1934)," Unpublished Ph.D. Dissertation, University of California at Los Angeles, 1970.

[125] *Disputados*, sesiones ordinarias, III (25 September 1929): 909–913, 1070.

their energies to political vindictiveness, the economic plight of many farmers became desperate. In Santa Fe, where numerous farmers were evicted in 1930, tenants began to strike for rent reductions. By June 1930 the FAA requested an executive order to place a moratorium on all rural rent payments, but Yrigoyen failed to respond.[126] The plight of thousands of farmers in La Pampa, who requested government grants of seeds to permit planting following the drought of 1929, encountered similar executive inertia, and the government made no seeds available.[127]

By mid-1930 farmers were echoing other segments of Argentine society that the aged president had abrogated leadership in the midst of a national economic crisis, and when a military coup unseated Yrigoyen on 6 September 1930, the FAA shed nary a tear for him or for the parliamentary system. The deposed president, editorialized *La Tierra,* was a man incapable of ruling who had "vegetated . . . surrounded by deceiving and ignorant advisers." Argentine politics, added the agrarian newspaper, had done nothing fundamental to aid or develop agriculture.[128]

This conclusion was accurate. During fourteen years under a form of parliamentary democracy, the national government had passed little legislation of importance to farmers and had enforced little of what was passed. The Radical party in power had failed consistently to support land reform or agrarian development in order to populate the interior, enlarge the national market for industrial goods, and integrate the rural population into national cultural and political life. As a result, Argentine agriculture remained technically backward, the interior remained largely empty, and the bulk of farmers still lived as short-term tenants—isolated, politically weak, and often economically impoverished.[129] The living conditions of landless laborers, moreover, remained dismal. At the national level, Radical party policy had continued a tradition established in earlier administrations of sacrificing the integration and development of Argentina to the interests of the landed elite.

---

126 *La Prensa,* 5 March 1930, p. 17; 20 April 1930, p. 16; *La Época,* 8 June 1930, p. 1; 2 August 1930, p. 1.

127 *La Prensa,* 20 February 1930, p. 13; 10 March 1930, p. 19; 11 April 1930, p. 11; 19 May 1930, p. 8.

128 *La Tierra,* 10 September 1930, p. 4; 12 September 1930, p. 4.

129 The 1937 agricultural census reported that in the provinces of Buenos Aires, Santa Fe, Entre Ríos, and Córdoba and in La Pampa territory, 59 percent of rural producers were renters, 35 percent were owners, and 6 percent held land under other forms of tenure. These percentages included cattle raisers; the proportion of renters among farmers probably was higher. See Argentine Republic, Ministerio de Agricultura, Comisión Nacional del Censo Agropecuario, *Censo nacional agropecuario,* 1: 46.

Ramón Lugo Lovatón
Director of the National Museum
Santo Domingo, Dominican Republic

LA VIRGEN DE LAS MERCEDES EN LA ISLA DE SANTO DOMINGO

En aquella remota época, cuando la mayor parte de España estaba en poder de los árabes, cuando bajo el yugo de los sarracenos innumerables fieles cristianos sufrían en tierras moras amarguísima esclavitud, con grave peligro para la salvación de sus almas y seguridad de sus vidas, la Augusta Reina de los Cielos, atenta a tan graves males, ocurrió en su infinita caridad para redimir a los cautivos.

Como el célebre San Agustín, famoso Obispo de Hipona, autor de las *Confesiones,* en sus fecundos *Soliloquios,* el bienaventurado Pedro Nolasco, cuyo corazón estaba lleno de piedad, meditaba en los medios a escoger para librar a los cristianos cautivos o disminuir las penas de su cautividad. Y se consagró de tal manera, que la Santísima Virgen, apareciéndosele, expresóle que tanto Ella como su unigénito Hijo, aceptaban se fundase una orden de religiosos que se encargara de la liberación de los cautivos cristianos del poder otomano simbolizado por la Media Luna y guiado por los principios de Mahoma.

El Padre Nolasco, varón de Dios, recreado ante esa celestial visión, e impulsado por el ideal que anidaba en su espíritu fecundo, ocurrió aquella misma noche de la aparición a los pies de Raymundo de Peñafort, su confesor, para comunicarle lo sucedido, y cuál no sería su sorpresa al manifestarle su bienaventurado hermano en Cristo, que la Virgen también se le había aparecido con igual propósito. Sorprendidos estaban aquellos santos varones cuando el propio Rey de Aragón llegó hasta ellos para confesarles que la Virgen le había hecho idéntica revelación. En los tres había sido la misma, por lo que ordenó don Jaime se fundase la institución bajo la invocación de Santa María de la Merced. Esta orden ostentaría títulos de Real y Militar, al haberla fundado don Jaime de Aragón en fecha 10 de agosto de 1218.

Ese es el origen de la Orden de la Merced, que la Iglesia acepta en el campo histórico. De los reinos de España y de esa Orden llegaron a la isla de Santo Domingo aquellos religiosos que propagaron en esta tierra la devoción y el culto de la Virgen de las Mercedes.

El culto que siempre se ha tributado en la isla Española, hasta nuestros días, bajo la advocación de Nuestra Señora de las Mercedes, lo debemos a la piedad y al celo de los religiosos de la Orden de la Merced por la redención de los cautivos.

Puede decirse que la antigüedad de su culto concurre con la fundación de sus primeros conventos en la isla. No se conoce la fecha cierta de su comienzo en la ciudad de Santo Domingo. La presencia de Mercedarios en la isla sitúanla algunos historiadores y cronistas con la segunda llegada de Colón a la Española, al encontrar éste destruido el Fuerte de la Navidad. Se ha escrito también que el primer convento de la orden se estableció en la villa de La Isabela, primera ciudad del Nuevo Mundo, construida por disposición del Almirante en la comarca del cacicazgo subalterno de Bohío. Lo cierto es que antes de ser concentrados a la vida monacal a principios del siglo XVI, existían ya en la isla algunos Mercedarios y sin estar sujetos a ningún régimen sin hacer vida en común. Ellos profesaban gran devoción por San Lorenzo, mártir, en cuya festividad, el 10 de agosto, se estableciera la orden de la Merced.

Hacia 1527, en el Capítulo General de la Orden celebrado en Burgos, la reforma de la Orden en la Isla Española fue decretada para establecer la vida regular en común. Y así, con el tiempo, se establecieron los siguientes conventos: el de la ciudad de Santo Domingo, el de Santiago de los Caballeros, el de la villa de Compostela de Azúa, el de la ciudad de Concepción de La Vega, en el Santo Cerro —de que nos ocuparemos de inmediato— y, fuera de la isla, el de la ciudad de León de Caracas, el de la villa de Puerto Príncipe, Camagüey, y el de San Cristóbal de La Habana. La iglesia de Nuestra Señora de las Mercedes fue consagrada por Fray Juan de Galaviz, arzobispo metropolitano, el 5 de septiembre del año 1734, y en su convento, de 1615 a 1618, Fray Gabriel Téllez, Tirso de Molina, clásico español, escribió algunas de sus obras.

Este fecundo escritor dramático, religioso de la Merced, nacido en Madrid en 1571, muerto en Soria en 1648, creador del *Burlador de Sevilla, Don Gil de las Calzas Verdes*, y tantas obras maestras, luego de rememorar en larga crónica los milagros de la Virgen de las Mercedes y la devoción de este pueblo por ella, escribe respecto de su consagración como patrona de la república:

> Intentamos los recién venidos, conociendo el general afecto con que seguían todos esta piadosa verdad y la fé con que abrazaban la inmunidad de su limpia Concepción, que la ciudad admitiese por Patrona a nuestra Imágen milagrosísima con voto expreso de su inmaculada preservación; y aunque el Presidente Gobernador de aquella Real Audiencia e Isla lo contradijo y con él algunos oidores y validos (tan poderosa fué con ellos la familiaridad del superior de los contrarios), pudo más el afecto y devoción de los restantes y así la Real Audiencia y el Cabildo o Regimiento de aquella cristianísima República, con fiestas y demonstraciones regocijadas y otra vez no vistas semejantes, la víspera de su Natividad gozosa y también su día, vinieron en procesión a nuestra Iglesia y celebrando el incruento sacrificio (en que predicó el nuevo Vicario General), la juraron por única Patrona el ya reducido Presidente y sus oidores y oficiales por su Cancillería, y por su Ciudad, los regidores.

II

Pasemos ahora a referir la hermosa leyenda de la primera aparición de Nuestra Señora de las Mercedes en la isla de Santo Domingo.

Empinada sobre enhiesto monte, en una meseta desde donde se domina como una bendición de Dios para los habitantes de esta tierra el amplio y fértil valle de la Vega Real, como si quisiera penetrar la azul inmensidad, se eleva hacia el cielo la iglesia del Santo Cerro, lugar sagrado, venerado e histórico hacia el cual encamina sus pasos el fervoroso y creyente peregrino dominicano. Aquel lugar fue el escenario de una batalla y la pila bautismal de la más hermosa leyenda que conserva nuestro pueblo respecto de la venerada Virgen de las Mercedes.

Corría el año de 1495 y don Cristóbal Colón y su hermano, el Adelantado don Bartolomé, con no crecido número entre hombres de infantería y de caballería, disponíanse a resistir en sus primeros pasos por la conquista de la isla las huestes indígenas que dirigían los caciques Caonabo y Maniocatex, que según noticias, indudablemente exageradas, pasaban de treinta mil.

Colón había plantado en el Cerro su pendón real. Había allí, conforme a la tradición, un árbol muy grande y en toda la isla jamás se halló otro de la misma casta y elevación. El Almirante mandó desgajar sus ramas para que el mástil vertical quedara solo, y cortando otro árbol pequeño que estaba cerca, de diferente clase, lo colocaron atravesado en la parte superior del árbol grande, haciendo así de ambos una cruz que señoreaba, simbólico poder de Cristo, aquella virgen y vasta región.

Alrededor de ella construyeron los españoles un palenque y un fuerte con añosos árboles para defenderse de los indígenas, fieros e intrépidos guerreros. Allí contuvieron muchas veces sus asaltos, con sus armas de fuego, sus lanzas y sus caballos, pero ante la continuidad de las temibles embestidas muchas veces los españoles, mal de su grado, abandonaban el palenque y se retiraban a otros cerros vecinos. Los indígenas, con mucha leña, pegaron fuego a la cruz, y afirman que ésta ardió a la vista de los colonos, peninsulares, y nativos, y aunque ardiera toda ella como un ascua para asombro de Colón y sus hombres, cuando recuperaron el Cerro, allí estaba la Santa Cruz intacta. Tres veces sucedió lo mismo, agrega la leyenda. Los indígenas trataron de quebrar la cruz con hachas y bejucos, pero todo fue inútil.

Un día, víspera de la Cruz de Mayo, ya entrada la noche, gran claridad apareció en lo alto de los cerros, y mucho más intensa en el Cerro de la Cruz. La empeñada lucha era sangrienta; flechas y arcabuces sembraban la muerte y el espanto en ambos bandos, en aquella noche memorable. Dicen que allí estaba Fray Juan Infante, religioso de la Orden de la Merced, quien enardeció las tropas con valerosa arenga. No obstante, todo parecía perdido; se suponía con razón que los indígenas, por su crecido número, vencerían en la contienda, cuando de pronto, como refiere en apasionado relato de aquellos sucesos Fray Gerónimo de Alfaro:

> . . . apareció la Virgen, Nuestra Señora, con su hijo en los brazos y se sentó en el brazo derecho de la Cruz, donde estuvo por más de cuatro horas. Los españoles la saludaron llenos de alborozo. Los indios la arrojaban flechas que con fuerza volvían a los mismos que las arrojaban, que los traspasaron y a otros tres o cuatro que estaban detrás de ellos. Esto puso tanto espanto en los indios que, huyendo del Cerro, no volvieron más a él. Los cristianos prometieron de hacer allí una iglesia del nombre de la Santa Cruz; con ella se fundó después el convento.

Así la batalla fue ganada, como narran los viejos cronistas, por intervención de Nuestra Señora de las Mercedes, que inspirara renovada fe al Descubridor, al Adelantado y a las tropas, infundiéndoles valor. Después, el Emperador Carlos V, al saber del extraordinario milagro, señaló una pensión anual para el monasterio que se edificó en el Santo Cerro y que destruyera el terremoto de 1564. Aquel suceso estableció en la isla de Santo Domingo la devoción de la Santa Reliquia. Los maderos que formaban la cruz en trozos divididos, como reliquias, se repartieron en iglesias de La Española, del Perú y de México, donde aún se conservan como primera floración del milagroso cristianismo en este primer solar americano.

Vamos ahora a referirnos, brevemente, a tres grandes milagros de la Virgen de las Mercedes, que siempre se recuerdan y que contribuyeron a aumentar la veneración que le profesa el pueblo dominicano.

Víspera de su fiesta de la Natividad, en el año 1614, un terrible terremoto sacudió la ciudad de Santo Domingo, y durante cuarenta días sucesivos sacudimientos llenaron de pánico a esta población y a todos los habitantes de La Española.

Cuenta la tradición que al final de aquellos días angustiosos y gravemente amenazada la vida de los habitantes de esta ciudad, en grandes masas se guarecieron bajo las naves de su iglesia y convento, y al no sufrir allí daño alguno y ofrecer por ello penitencia general a la Virgen, el rostro de su inmaculada imagen, que por muchos días había aparecido triste ante el pueblo que la contemplaba, desde la noche del 7 de septiembre, víspera de la Natividad, se mostró radiante y, a partir de esa fecha, la tierra dejó de temblar.

En la tercera parte de este trabajo narramos los otros dos grandes milagros de la Virgen de las Mercedes, que tienen particular significación histórica.

III

Pasan algunas décadas. En 1689, los intrépidos bucaneros de la Isla de La Tortuga, convertidos ya en colonos franceses, en la parte norte de La Española, conducidos por Delisle, caen como bárbaros sobre Santiago, la saquean y la destruyen.

Dos años después, la hidalguía española busca el desquite. Don Ignacio Caro, Gobernador y Capitán General, Almirante Real de la flota de Barlovento, organiza con todas las armas una columna que encomienda a la pericia guerrera del Maestre de Campo, don Francisco Segura Sandoval y Castillo.

Este ejército, y otro francés que le sale al encuentro, el 21 de enero de 1691 hacen contacto en la Sabana Real o de la Limonade. Bajo la invocación de Nuestra Señora de las Mercedes, y portando un lienzo con su sagrada imagen, se inicia el combate que desde sus comienzos se perfila desastroso para los franceses. Carlos de Sigüenza y Góngora, en su relato de aquel suceso épico, manifiesta que el cuerpo derecho se le dió a las compañías de Santiago, el izquierdo a las de Azúa, y en el centro se situaron los lanceros con orden de acometer al enemigo y destruir sus costados.

Mientras aquellas tropas se protegían con el símbolo de las Mercedes, los soldados traídos de la parte oriental de la isla invocaban la protección de Nuestra Señora de la Altagracia, y por ello se dió el extraño caso de que una doble invocación a dos augustas representaciones de la madre de Dios en nuestra isla ayudase a las tropas españolas a obtener el triunfo.

Fortalecida salió de allí la fe en la Virgen de las Mercedes; mayor consagración tributaron desde entonces a la Virgen de la Altagracia, y la fiesta de esta última, que se celebraba el 15 de agosto, a partir de 1692 comenzó a celebrarse el 21 de enero, fecha aniversario de la batalla de la Limonade. Aquel mismo día cerraba los ojos para siempre el héroe de aquella jornada, el Maestre de Campo don Francisco de Segura Sandoval y Castillo.

Transcurren ahora los amargos días de enero del año 1801. El hombre de color más extraordinario y singular nacido en América ha invadido nuestro territorio hasta la ciudad de Santo Domingo con ejércitos que entraron por el norte y el sur de la frontera y, con justificada razón, la sorpresa y el pánico de la familia dominicana no es para contarse. Se acariciaba aún la esperanza de que el Tratado de Basilea de 1795 fuera revisado por España, pero no fue así. Como un ejecutor de aquel doloroso acuerdo en la ciudad suiza de Basilea, alguien contemplaba con ojos de águila la ciudad de los Colones. Se llamaba: Toussaint L'Ouverture.

Comenzó casi inmediatamente el éxodo de numerosas familias dominicanas rumbo a México, Venezuela, Puerto Rico y Cuba. Ilustres apellidos buscaban seguridad y paz en otras playas, mientras cada día se hacía más patente la hostilidad de la población de Santo Domingo, de cepa hispana, con ideales y hábitos completamente distintos al de los invasores.

Toussaint trata de impedir por todos los medios a su alcance la emigración de la isla, y busca rutas para conseguir a su favor la simpatía popular. Sus falsas promesas, sus argumentos, nada logran ante el desprecio y la general indiferencia. En el ánimo de aquel hombre tan temible y temido crece una voz interior que le invita a escarmentar a los españoles. Su rencor crece y su odio se agiganta; con frecuencia sus mismos familiares y edecanes le oyen exclamar estas palabras: *Tous sont des ennemies.*

Una mañana se dirige a la Catedral; solicita al párroco descubrir a Jesús Sacramentado y, colocada la hostia en el viril, dobla las rodillas y salmodia una oración.

Al mediodía varios oficiales le informan que unas "mamiselles" (muchachas) se sonreían sarcásticamente mientras él estaba arrodillado. Toussaint les dice: *Après nous verrons,* y se aleja sombrío como si una idea siniestra cobrara dominio en su mente.

Ni visita a nadie ni recibe visitas. Con su hermano, Paul L'Ouverture, a quien ha designado gobernador del Departamento del Ozama, se ha instalado en el Palacio de los Capitanes Generales de la Colonia. Apenas toca durante las comidas los platos que le sirven. Cierto día, al salir del comedor, en una apartada habitación, comunica a su hermano Paul esta terrible resolución: "Pasar a cuchillo a toda la población". Paul, consternado, porque su alma era distinta, trata de disuadirlo y de calmar el espíritu conturbado de su hermano, pero todo es inútil, y Paul acude a su esposa para informarle la sanguinaria idea de Toussaint, manifestándole que sólo una divina intervención podía detenerlo.

"Mon Dieu! mon Dieu!", exclama la compañera de Paul, que se aleja presurosa hacia un aposento de la casa donde ha visto una imagen de Nuestra Señora de las Mercedes, y pasa la tarde y la noche en orante actitud ante la virgen.

Antes de la oración, ha cundido por el pueblo el grave rumor de que Toussaint ha ordenado un degüello. Los habitantes de la ciudad, por medio de un bando leído en las esquinas, acompañado de tambores, han sido convocados para reunirse a las siete del día siguiente en la Plaza de Armas. Hay un lúgubre presagio en todos los hogares.

A la mañana siguiente un sol magnífico saluda la ciudad. Todos, sin excepción, han ocupado sus puestos en la Plaza de Armas, cuando un agudo toque de corneta anuncia la llegada de Toussaint L'Ouverture. Tambores y pífanos saludan su presencia, mientras sube a una tarima y anuncia a la muchedumbre que ha sido abolida la esclavitud. La muchedumbre calla. Silenciosa espera una hecatombe.

Toussaint baja de la tarima y se dirige al lugar donde están las mujeres agrupadas. Sólo hay españolas. Desea convencerse de que no hay entre ellas fugitivas de la parte occidental de la isla. Con su bastón de mando, símbolo de su jerarquía, las toca una a una, sin respetar el pudor de ellas, y les pregunta: "¿Francesa o española?".

Avanza; toca con su bastón a una dama elegante, de ojos vivos, seno erecto. Ésta, con gesto airado, exclama: "¡Atrevido! ¡Aprenda modales para que sepa tratar a las damas españolas!" Es la señorita Dominga Núñez, sobrina, nada menos, del Dr. don José Núñez de Cáceres. Toussaint ha escuchado sus palabras. Frunce el ceño. Sube de nuevo a la tarima. Jean Philippe, jefe de las tropas, palidece en espera de la señal. Mira a Toussaint pero nada advierte en sus ojos. Sus manos no dejan caer el pañuelo de seda.

De pronto, hacia oriente, el sol oscurece, y un aire fuerte y caliente azota la multitud. De la tierra salen sordos truenos, mientras en el cenit hay un halo radiante de luz solar.

Toussaint L'Ouverture clava sus ojos en el cielo y los fija con detenimiento en el punto luminoso. Repentina ceguera le hace cerrar los párpados. Parece haber visto algo. Ordena a Jean Philippe desalojar la plaza y él mismo con sus edecanes se aleja presuroso. Hay en su voz no contenida agitación. Paul y su mujer se le acercan sigilosamente y Paul, a solas con él en una estancia, escucha el relato de Toussaint, que al sentir la luz que bajaba de lo alto, miró al cielo y pudo advertir la presencia de una dama, con blanco traje talar, que lo contemplaba en arrobadora actitud suplicante.

¡Elle était Notre Dame! ¡Je l'ai vue! (¡Era Nuestra Señora! ¡Yo la he visto! ¡Yo la he visto!)

Al escuchar estas palabras, la esposa de Paul L'Ouverture corrió a la estancia de sus oraciones, y agradecida cayó de rodillas ante la imagen de la Virgen de las Mercedes.

Toda leyenda, señores, constituye un patrimonio común subyacente que enriquece y da belleza a la historia de cada país. La leyenda toca a lo maravilloso y deslumbra; la tradición corresponde a lo histórico y cautiva. ¿En dónde termina la leyenda y comienza la tradición? El primer campo viola con frecuencia los dominios del segundo; a veces, lo que pertenece a la tradición es tan inverosímil, tan raro y maravilloso, que entra franca y caballerescamente en el ámbito de la leyenda. Con la raza humana nació la historia, y con la historia la leyenda. Todo demuestra esa verdad inconclusa.

Las leyendas mayas, aztecas y peruanas constituyen pruebas de que la leyenda es más fuerte en los pueblos que tienen una historia más intensa, porque éstos poseen un grado superior de civilización. Puede afirmarse que toda América es imaginativa en sus concepciones, por ser hija de España. En la conquista del Nuevo Continente, empresa colosal sin paralelo, surgen epopeyas y hombres, milagros y sucesos que apenas caben por su grandeza en el marco de la historia, porque escapan a todo lo que pueda considerarse como verdadero y sucedido para caer en los límites de lo fantástico o de lo inverosímil.

Así, el viaje de Colón y el descubrimiento de las Indias Occidentales, su llegada a Quisqueya, donde deja en el Fuerte de la Navidad un puñado de audaces dignos de la pluma cervantina; la odisea de México, cuyo imperio conquista Hernán Cortés; la hazaña de Pizarro, que traza una raya sobre la arena para que trece descamisados se propongan y realicen la conquista del Perú; Ponce de León buscando en la Florida la Fuente de la Eterna Juventud; Ojeda luchando con los indígenas en La Española; Balboa, que sale de Santo Domingo en un buque, oculto en un túnel, para descubrir el Mar del Sur; el viaje de Magallanes, y los hombres de Hernando de Soto, Pedro Alvarado, Garcilazo de la Vega, Diego Colón, María de Toledo, Las Casas, Anacaona, Enriquillo y un ciento más, tejen en la aurora de la historia de nuestra raza en América una leyenda tras otra, una tradición tras otra tradición, y apenas podemos dar crédito a tanta maravilla en los albores de la civilización y del cristianismo en las tierras vírgenes de América.

¡Virgen de las Mercedes! El recuerdo de tu leyenda, de tus milagros y de tus augustas intervenciones desde el Descubrimiento hasta la creación de la República, y desde 1844 hasta nuestros días, te han hecho nuestra patrona. No olvidamos tu aparición sobre los secos pajonales de Santomé. Continúa alentado y esclareciendo el sagrado destino de este pueblo, fervoroso e inmortal.

Frances M. Foland
Fellow, Institute of Current World Affairs
New York

A PROFILE OF AMAZONIA

Its Possibilities for Development

Amazonia is once again the *nouvelle vague.* Object of intense but ephemeral attention at the turn of the century and intermittently thereafter, the region now confronts a concerted and multi-pronged program for its de facto integration into the nation.

A special issue of *Desenvolvimento & Conjuntura* in March 1967,[1] devoted to Amazonia, editorialized: "O atual interêsse pela Amazônia resulta de duas cadeias causais, de grande profundidade, e que são; primeiro, a consciência nacional da necessidade de acelerar o desenvolvimento de todo o territorio nacional, visando à terminação dos desniveis econômicos; e, segundo a compreensão que temos atualmente de fatôres de âmbito internacional. Estamos cônscios de que chegamos a era do desenvolvimento regional."

In the same publication, a document prepared by the Comissão de Desenvolvimento Econômico do Estado do Amazonas states: "Desenvolver a Amazônia é um dever indeclinável dos brasileiros . . . É uma opção entre o confôrto de ser pequeno e as canseiras de ser grande . . . é uma maneira de permanecer fiel ao destino da nação brasileira, pelo menos para aquêles que acreditam na grandeza dêsse destino."

Two specific motivations for Amazonian development are discussed. Of prime concern is the arrested industrialization blamed on the constricted domestic market: "É uma das maneiras mais eficientes de corrigir tal situação está, exatamente, na política de recuperação das áreas eco-

[1] "Amazônia: Número Especial," *Desenvolvimento & Conjuntura,* Ano XI, No. 3, March 1967, p. 3.

nômicamente atrasadas." Secondly, exogenous factors are cited, primarily the demographic pressure throughout the world. Although this latter parameter is viewed in terms of Brazil's responsibility to maximize its production of foodstuffs, there is a strong underlying concern for "A segurança nacional."

"Amazonia is our new frontier," said former President Costa e Silva, "and we Brazilians intend to make it a part of our nation both in terms of national boundaries—which it already is—and in terms of national integration—which it is not."

Brazilian military leaders' resolve to make theirs a great country will no doubt cause stirrings in Amazonia. But, the vast basin of labyrinthine rivers, vine-matted forests, omnipresent insects, and inundating rainfall dwarfs man and his actions.

THE AMAZONIAN ECOSYSTEM

The Primeval Setting: Hyperbole and Hypocrisy

It has given rise to the most extravagant of claims and epithets. It is Green Hell and El Dorado. By legend it is home to towering, handsome, and pugnacious women, thus its name. Twentieth century science has come up with some other big roles for it: it is the "lungs of the world," and to destroy the forest mantle would doom mankind to death throes, gasping for oxygen. Or, the Hudson Institute's proposal to form a vast inland sea by damming 20 percent of the world's river flow would disturb the earth's balance and affect its rotation.

To say that Amazonia is big is no exaggeration, however. The catchment area of the basin embraces some 23° of latitude and 30° of longitude. Climax forest, dense and evergreen, represents the growth of a millenium over a vast area of 3,620,000 square kilometers. From horizon to horizon this equatorial forest, dubbed "Hylea" by Humboldt, mats the earth with several layers of growth.

It is this luxuriant vegetation which deceives and has mislead many to fanfare the great fertility of the land. But, most Amazonian soils are poor, leached, and acid. Typical of tropical soils throughout the world, the laterite is formed where decomposition of underlying rock exceeds the rate of erosion. The hot, humid climate fosters rapid bacterial action destroying the organic cover and causing a lack of humic acid. Silicate minerals are leached out, particularly calcium, with residual insolubles of iron and aluminum forming rock-like nodules. The red soil resulting from this chemical and mechanical action is of low fertility, short on bases and humus.

Nutrients are concentrated as a thin layer of recently-deposited organic matter, and Amazonian root systems tend to reach out horizontally rather than probing the impoverished strata below. Great trees may then have but a superficial grasp of the earth, and a tropical storm can uproot them with ease, their fall ripping down dozens of smaller trees, vines, and undergrowth. To the native the danger of being crushed by these sudden uprootings far exceeds the threat of reptile and beast.

The Indians long ago perfected the only feasible method of agriculture to cope with the infertile conditions: slash and burn. On the new land the hardy mandioca produces two or three crops, the soil quickly becoming exhausted. Then the Indian moves on, leaving behind a swath victimized by rapid erosion.

After the Amazon forest has been destroyed, the first plants to come back are the sun-loving which could not exist under the previous tree cover. As this first layer grows, another comes on under it, less dependent on the sun. And so the strata accumulate through the centuries, taking 800 to 1000 years to reach the stage of climax forest.

Amazon vegetation subsists on a delicate balance of self-produced organic matter and ample rainfall. Informed scientists agree that the fragile ecosystem of the rainforest is only a few steps removed from a wasteland. If the forest vegetation were to be cleared, says Colombian geologist Carlos Eduardo Acosta, the Amazon basin would become "a desert like the Sahara." [2]

The lowlands along the rivers, about 4 percent of the total area, give some relief to the poverty of the *terra firme*. These alluvial strips, renewed with each year's flooding, are highly productive agriculturally.

Amazonia is not one vast swamp, but rather a low Tertiary plateau of gentle relief, interlaced and inundated by a welter of water formations. Louis Agassiz said of it: "This labyrinth of water is more an ocean of fresh water, cut and divided by the land, than a fluvial network." A Harvard scientist visiting Manáus coined his own epithet: "A liquid desert."

This is a land that wants to be water. Amazonia holds one-fifth of the world's available fresh water, the volume of the Amazon River varying between 60 and 140 thousand cubic meters per second, depending upon the season. At the gorge of Óbidos it reaches a depth of 425 ft. and at its mouth, a width of 125 miles. Seven times the size of France, the basin has over 10,000 navigable miles in its major rivers alone, ten of which are longer than the Mississippi.

To the west the headwaters reach into the ice and snow of the Andes which feed it with their thaws. From the east, more dramatically, come

---

[2] "Brazil: A Prodigy of Growth," *Population Bulletin* 25, no. 4 (September 1969).

the heavy, dark cumuli which, from November to May, swirl over its length propelled by Atlantic winds. Tropical rains drench the land in spasmodic torrents. This is winter in Amazonia—temperature, as ever, averaging in the mid-80s; humidity, as ever, 85 percent or higher; and rains, in this season, heavy and daily.

In a classic treatise based upon a 1912 journey through Amazonia, the Swiss scientist, Dr. Hans Bluntschli, commented:

"The cycle of water, coming from the sea through the air to the ground covered with forest and returning from the forest via the fluvial plain to the eternal sea—this is the great epic that dominates the image of Amazonia, its life and its character. Perhaps in no other part of the world does the powerful force of the cycle of water present itself, within the mental vision of man, with such clarity and evidence." [3]

At floodtide the Amazonas reaches a width of 35 miles. Only prominent features of land protrude—levees, points, and hummocks, called *restingas*—which swirl in roughly parallel contours as if a paisley, brown and green. The variety of water-oriented formations include:*igapó*, an area of dense vegetation continually under water; *caa-igapó*, vegetation associated with moisture-laden soils; *várzea*, floodplain inundated a part of each year; *igarapé*, literally a canoe trail, is a river amid the forest; *paraná*, an arm of the river forming a large island; *furo*, a stream connecting two rivers or other bodies of water; *sacado*, an oxbow lake formed when a river changes course; *rego,* a small channel within a depression; *caa-tinga,* an open forested area (different meaning in northeast Brazil); *terra firme*, high land seldom flooded.

The Traditional Economy

While most agriculture of Amazonia is concentrated on the floodplain and is inexorably governed by the cycle of the waters, even the extractive activities of the terra firme change with the seasons, depending upon the occurrence of rain. A typical *caboclo* of the interior is likely to tend about a hundred rubber trees along a jungle trail during the dry months. But the latex, which drips into small open cups, is spoiled by water, so, with the rains, the caboclo must change his means of livelihood. Often the switch is to Brazil nuts, which are freed from the high branches of the *castanheira* by the storms of the wet season.

Another major extractive industry of the region, lumbering, has its seasonal rhythm. The cutting takes place year round, but the logs must be rolled from the terra firme to the rivers, and if the low-lying várzea be-

[3] Hans Bluntschli, "A Amazônia como Organismo Harmônico," *Cadernos da Amazônia.* Instituto Nacional de Pesquisas da Amazônia, Manaus.

tween is flooded, then transport is impaired. On the other hand, high water is the time for floating the logs down to the sawmill, especially when shoals and rapids must be passed. Also, the logging camps and, for that matter, all population clusters upriver must stock a year's provisions during the months when the boats can reach them.

The very population pattern of Amazonia is determined by the water courses. Myriad metaphors have been coined to describe the hydrographic network of the region. A popular one is that of a tree—the Amazonas as a trunk, the tributaries as branches, and the complex delta areas as the root system. In this case, people are the leaves and lichen which cling to branch and trunk. The rural inhabitants scatter themselves in isolation along the river banks. Then, there are nodules, tucked with epiphytes where trunk and branch join—these are the cities.

This dendritic demographic pattern is explained by one simple fact: *o rio é a rua.* Therefore, as regional say has it: "The boat is the horse; the oar is the bridle."

The boats in Amazonia come in a proliferation of sizes and styles to serve all purposes from hunter to entrepreneur. Indigenous is the *igarité*, a pirogue appropriate for igarapé and igapó. The caboclo enlarged the shell and put in seats to make the *montaria*; generally he propels it sitting at the very prow with a hand-carved paddle the shape of a lollipop. Having no keel, it demands a masterful stroke to keep on course.

Middle Amazonas seems to rely more on motor than on sail for its locomotion. *Gaiolas* abound in all sizes, so called because their superstructure of one or two levels has the appearance of a cage.

From Santarém downstream to Belém, reliance is more upon the sail. As in Manáus, the market of Belém is adjacent to the water. The one-masted sailboats, *vigilengas*, bring in the fruits and fish and vegetables, and crowd against one another in the protected harbor.

The giants of the Amazon are the ocean-going freighters, particularly those of the Booth Line, the one international shipping company that penetrates beyond Belém. Iquitos in Perú is the terminal point. Booth, along with many other English companies, first came to the Amazon because of rubber, in the late nineteenth century. Now the freight is very different. The largest cargoes come in April, May, and June when the harvesting of the Brazil nuts reaches its peak and the waters allow heavy loads.

Pound for pound, the most valuable cargo is the roseoil, base for fragrant soaps and perfumes. One drum is worth $1,000; freight charge to Europe (1967) is $55.

Rubber, Brazil nuts, rosewood oil—produce of the forest, products of an extractive economy dependent upon a highly heterogeneous biochore which consists of over 4000 species. Man sustains himself essentially by handicraft methods; he works alone or nearly so; he depends upon his hands and muscle-power with only the simplest of tools to maximize his body's capabilities; his work is seasonal, juxtaposing excessive work in some months against inactivity in others; his production is low and conducive to wastage of the prime material; his offerings await the pleasures of the market; the extractor is a loner, isolated from colleagues with whom he might organize to improve his situation.

As geography gave rise to the extractive economy, so the latter has sired a sociopolitical relationship among men. The *aviador* is the pivotal institution; a middleman—wholesaler and purveyor—the aviador takes in the gleanings of the harvesters and, in turn, provides them with supplies. Almost invariably the harvester, victim of price-gouging and of his own excesses, becomes indebted to the aviador, and he is likely to continue that way. The human relationship which dominates in this activity is, therefore, that of debtor-creditor. The control and influence of the aviador-patrón, likewise guides political participation in Amazonia.[4]

The common man of the Amazon is seminomadic, moving along the river and streams according to seasons, harvests, and cropping. His home, a *tapirí,* is but a temporary structure of palm fronds. Handicrafts and machetes prevail in the age of the computer; a mandioca culture is coeval with the post-industrial society.

A TALLY SHEET
The Barriers to Development

"Do this sparse population, these wretched health conditions, the deplorably low standard of living, and the lack of industry mean that Amazonian environment is an insurmountable obstacle to development?" [5]

To develop, Amazonia must upgrade its human resources, in both quantity and quality. In terms of number, *Desenvolvimento & Conjuntura* points out: ". . . o rendimento econômico insatisfatório do homen amazônico procede . . . da dispersão de parte dessa população, condicionada pela atividade extrativista, e a falta de um sistema adequado de transporte. A pequena densidade demográfica na área extrativista torna difícil uma divisão e especialização do trabalho." [6]

[4] Amilcar Alves Tupiassu, "Condições Socio-Estruturais e Participação Política na Amazônia." Paper presented at Mesa Redonda a Ciência Política do Rio de Janeiro, International Political Science Assn., October 1969.

[5] Charles Wagley, *Amazon Town: A Study of Man in the Tropics* (New York: Alfred A. Knopf, 1964), p. 5.

[6] "Amazônia: Número Especial," p. 8.

In terms of quality, there is a major problem both in attracting trained personnel and in holding them in the region, even those native-born. Both Manaus and Belém have universities—the former founded in 1913 due to the rubber boom but subsequently closed and reopened in 1964 as a full university including departments of engineering, science, and liberal arts. In Belém the Instituto de Pesquisas e Experimentação Agropecuária do Norte is strengthening its agronomy school. But even those who are born and trained in the region are easily lured by the glamour and higher salaries of the South. And there are negative factors which drive them from Amazonia—climate and disease.

As to the effects of the climate, the director of the Institute Nacional de Pesquisas da Amazônia in Manaus describes it as follows:

"Aceitemos portanto a realidade: o regime térmico da Amazônia é equatorial, e conquanto as afirmações de que o clima da região é 'calunado' . . ., não podemos fugir à verdade de que as temperatures elevadas e constantes, sem as variações tonificadora das estações dos climas temperados, acompanhadas de alta umidade relativa, ensolejamento impiedoso, às vêzes baixa da pressão atmosférica e ventos de pouca velocidade, levam o organismo à fadiga precoce, especialmente ao exercer um trabalho sob o sol, ensejando a perda de litros de suor, com que se eliminam também grandes cotas de cloreto de sódio, que é o estimulador químico das glândulas supre-renais." [7]

In a hot, humid climate a proliferation of men's enemies can be expected—among them, insects. *Fórmigas, vintequatros, sacacaias, piúmes, aranhas, carrapatos*—the Brazilian vocabulary abounds with them. Though the bites of many are poisonous and bring immediate suffering, it is the delayed effect of the anopheles which is the scourge of the country. Malaria is as prevalent as the common cold in a New York winter.

Parasites, virus, fungi, and bacteria also flourish—and the illnesses which result from them. Diseases occurring in Amazonia include typhoid, measles, tuberculosis, yellow fever (once stamped out but now reappearing), malaria (four kinds), filariasis (affects 15–20 percent in Belém), intestinal parasites (amoeba, giardia, hookworm, strongylordes, tricharis, ascaris), leishmaniasis (although the visceral is rare in Amazonia, the cutaneous is common), leprosy, bacterial dysentery, larva migrans, rabies, tetanus, and encephalomyelitis.

To the scientists working at the Instituto Evandro Chagas in Belém, Amazonia is "a wonderfully unhealthy jungle" and a "virologist's happy-hunting ground." In the virus laboratory, research focuses on arthropod-

[7] Djalma Batista, "Da Habitabilidade da Amazônia," *Cadernos da Amazônia.* Instituto Nacional de Pesquisas da Amazônia, Manaus, 1963, p. 25.

borne viruses—therefore on mosquito and tick vectors and the animal reservoirs of viral infection: rodents, marsupials, bats, and cats. Thirty-eight viruses have been isolated at the Belém center of which nine are so far unique in the world.

Brazil's worst health problem, shistosomiasis, has invaded only a small area of the Bragantine in Pará. It is thought that the highly acid waters may discourage the snail vector.

Agriculture, like man, is accosted by disease. Two examples serve to show its effect. One is out of history: the famous case of Fordlândia where, on a concession of one million hectares, 1,600,000 rubber trees were planted with high hopes of supplying the U.S. market. But, the blight struck. The leaves withered and fell, and no remedy could be found. The fungus (*Dothidela Ulei*) raced through the trees and turned the plantation into desolation. Now, the plague is resisted by an elaborate grafting process. But the struggle to control and overcome the leaf fungus forces a constant compromise in the selection of tree stock—not only productivity as criterion but, also, resistance. It is doubtful if Amazonia could ever achieve the high yield common to the rubber trees of the Orient.

A second case in point is the Japanese struggle with the enemy of their major crop, black pepper. They have combatted foot-and-root rot (*Fusarium salani piperi*) for years, grafting and experimenting with different varieties. Although the Amazonian colony of Tome-Açu has slowed it, the fungus inevitably affects the plants, usually after about seven years and especially on soils of high acidity; once it is infected, the land cannot be replanted in pepper again.

Superb agriculturalists, the Japanese farmers face another problem which can be listed as another barrier to Amazonia development: the high cost of imports even though—in fact, especially if—they come from southern Brazil.

The president of the cooperative in Tome-Açu reported that products brought in from the United States and even as far as Japan were cheaper than Brazilian items—and, in addition, they were better. But because of government controls and tariffs, they were forced to "buy Brazilian." In 1967 chemical fertilizers cost Cr.$10,000 in São Paulo, but the same product was Cr.$20,000 in Manaus. The U.S.-European price for black pepper had fallen to $485 per ton which, at that time, was barely enough to cover the cost of the fertilizer. A poorer colony, "Kilómetro 42," near Manaus could not afford chemical fertilizers and, so, relied upon manure. With great quantities needed, the animal population far exceeded the human population. The colony was overrun by chickens with the attendant din and odor.

Cost deterrents affecting the use of fertilizers apply to all other processed goods needed in the area. Local industrialization is limited almost exclusively to the treatment of raw materials of the area: rubber, jute and—at a primitive level—timber and roseoil. An oil refinery in Manaus is a notable exception. Although the development agency, SUDAM (and its predecessor, SPVEA) has tried to instigate industrial growth, Amazonia is still a colonial economy, exporting raw materials and importing almost all of its manufactured goods and much of its foodstuffs. It, therefore, suffers from the inevitable double standard for these products.

Concomitant with this colonial economy is the capital drain. Until the recent *Lei f.174/66*, allowing the diversion of 50 percent of income tax due into Amazon investments, the flow has been almost completely negative.

Detriments suggested explicitly or implicitly in the material to this point include: poor soils, limitations in the transportation system, a heterogeneous forest, an enervating climate, high incidence of disease, a weak economy, scarcity of trained personnel, low population density, minimal industrialization, a primitive agriculture, and a shortage of capital.

Conquests in the Tropics

No deity could shortchange an area so badly. Utilized properly, the resources of Amazonia can be turned to profitable enterprises, and there are concrete examples to prove it.

"The tropical soils have a good physical structure and ample water reserves; large amounts of organic matter accumulate owing to the fast plant growth of the tropical forest. With better knowledge about the physical and chemical properties of the soils, it should be possible to correct the soil's deficiencies with fertilizer and their acidity with lime; and it should also be possible to develop management techniques to increase the productivity considerably. Besides some portions of the tropics have alluvial and volcanic soils of high fertility." [8]

The Japanese have proved that it can be done. Pepper and jute have become, in the last two decades, the two major earners in the export market. The Japanese have achieved their success by dint of very hard work and intensive application of fertilizer. They tried first with low-value crops, such as rice, and with garden produce; the first failed because of the high cost of transport, and the second because of the lack of a local market. Because of the problem with the foot-and-root rot, they are now

---

[8] Kenneth L. Turk and Loy V. Crowder, eds. *Rural Development in Tropical Latin America* (Ithaca, N.Y.: Cornell University Press, 1967), p. 7.

conducting experiments with other high-value crops: cloves, vanilla, and other exotic plants yielding spices and medicinal oils. Always the prime considerations are minimum bulk, maximum price, and an international market.

The publication of the Brazilian Trade Bureau in New York has stated that insecticide and medicinal plants are among Brazil's greatest natural resources—and, also, for the most part, among its least developed ones. Among other exotic sources, it mentions the *timbó* plant, whose root has insect-killing property and which may increase its market now that DDT is losing favor. It grows along the Amazon and its tributaries like the Tapajós, Tocantins, and the Negro. "Where timbó plantations have been established, entrepreneurs have made profits consistently. When they relied on wild harvests, they often went broke." [9]

Other products whose yield could be greatly expanded are tropical fruits and nuts. Beyond bananas, pineapples, and oranges—of which Brazil is one of the world's biggest producers—there are papayas, guavas, conde fruit, *maracujás,* cashew fruit, mangos, *caquis, carambolas, jabuticabas,* and *pitangas.* Until recently many of these were too perishable for shipping, but with new methods of storing and freezing they are accessible to markets in temperate climates. With its navigable waterways and its advantageous location near both the United States and Europe, Brazil could compete effectively if proper organization and marketing methods were adopted.

Amazonia's major export in terms of bulk is Brazil nuts, shipping about a third of its annual production (41,000 to 56,000 tons) to the United States. As a typical extractive practice, the harvesters roam the rainforest during the wet season, gathering the nuts in a haphazard fashion. A recent report estimated that fewer than a million of some eight million trees were visited. Thus the yield could be boosted to 450,000 long tons. Also, its high protein content could be turned to local dietary needs.[10]

Another natural wealth underutilized for commercial purposes in Amazonia is tropical fish. Again they bear exotic names: *piraíba, peixeboi, piracuru, dourado, tambaqui, aruaña, tucunaré, pescada,* and the Amazonian sardine. With some 1,800 species in the area, the fishing industry is still in its infancy.

But these possible exploitations of the flora and fauna are insignificant compared to extant timber operations; Amazonia embraces about 16 per-

[9] "Insecticide and Medicinal Plants Await Investors," *Brazilian Bulletin.* Brazilian Government Trade Bureau, New York. May 1967.

[10] *Brazilian Bulletin.* Brazilian Government Trade Bureau, New York, November 1968.

cent of the world's timberland. In 1967 six major operations had recently acquired land, among them, Georgia-Pacific, Brumasa (the Dutch firm Bruyznell from Surinam), and D. K. Ludwig of New York.

In the mid-1960s Georgia-Pacific purchased 640,000 acres with veneers and plywoods as the objective. The largest producer in Amazonia, Georgia-Pacific produces 234 million square feet per year.

D. K. Ludwig purchased three million acres with a highly diversified development in mind. One of the interesting projects underway in 1967 was the clearing of 100,000 acres of Amazonian forest in order to plant trees: the *gmelina* from West Africa. This fast-growing species would reach a growth in seven years which would serve for pulp for the paper factory yet to be constructed on the Jarí River. Paper and cellulose are seen to be two of the major possibilities as industries for the region.

Since the region will undergo more and more of the clearing process, the method is here described. In the case of the gmelina plantation, it was necessary to sweep the land clean, taking down all but selected quality specimens, and removing the debris. For the Ludwig operation the combination was the D-9 tractor mounted with the Rome KG blade, followed by the chain saws to take down what the blade could not handle. The D–9s are the largest manufactured by Caterpillar, weighing some 35 tons each and standing more than twice the height of a man. The blade—named after the place or original manufacture, Rome, Georgia—is a 2,500-pound angled plow; a heavy spike called a stinger, on one end, is used to split larger trees before they are felled. The blade cuts even secondary growth close to the ground and windrows it to the side. One plow pushed by a tractor can clear about 2,700 yards an hour. At the Ludwig camp, it was estimated that the cost would be about $80 per acre—i.e., $800,000 to clear the 100,000 acres in order to plant trees.

A cruder, faster, cheaper way is sufficient where cattle-grazing is to follow and, thus, the secondary growth and debris can be left. Again, the motive force is the big tractor, this time two in parallel with a heavy anchor chain stretched between them. A huge hollow steel ball, eight feet in diameter and weighing nearly three tons, acts as rolling support for the chain. As the huge tractors cleat into the forest the chain pulls the trees over. The huge matted root system is torn from its bed, leaving a large hole; this method is not advisable where top soil is thin and should be preserved.

This latter onslaught is underway in the 180,000 acre holding of the King Ranch, some 300 miles south of Belém. There it is planned that "300–h.p. fifty-ton tractors, supported by auxiliary earthmoving gear, will clear 100,000 acres of the forest, and have grass on the land, in 12 years. Clearing, seeding, and fencing will cost $30 an acre... Including the purchase price of land and the cost of a starting herd, the capital investment will approach $5 million.... The region lies five days closer by ship to the European market than do the Argentine slaughter-houses." [11]

Though unusual in its high level of capitalization, the King Ranch's venture is but one of many cattle-raising undertakings recently initiated in Amazonia. According to Isaac Sabbá—native of the region, self-made millionaire, so-called "King of the Amazon"—development of the region should emphasize cattle:

"The first step should be to clear the forest in order to make pasture land for cattle—clearing the forest will yield lumber and cellulose. With the astounding population increase, land is becoming more and more valuable—there are fewer spaces with open pasture necessary for cattle-grazing. The valorization of land will work to the advantage of Amazonia. In addition, cattle are a good first step for Amazonia because the activity requires little population—let's say, about 10 *vaqueiros* per 1,000 hectares." [12]

Whereas cattle-raising is yet an infant activity, mineral exploitation is at least an adolescent. Foreign and Brazilian firms are active from one end of Amazonia to the other:

Amapá. The ICOMI manganese deposit is 51 percent Brazilian-owned, 49 percent Bethlehem Steel. This huge operation consisting of railroad, city, port, and loading facilities is currently producing about 1,500,000 tons of ore per year—all that can be sold.

In this new state there is also some *garimpeiro* production of cassiterite, gold, and semi-precious stones; these are found in eluvial-alluvial deposits derived from the weathering of pegmatites. Minor amounts of diamonds are also produced which are presumably derived from the weathering of diamond-bearing conglomerates in northern Amapá.

Pará. U.S. Steel (Cia. Meridional de Mineração) has announced the discovery of large reserves of iron ore in the vicinity of the Itacaiunas River (between the Xingu and Tocantins). These may rival the Minas Gerais deposits, but development will doubtlessly depend on a long-term agreement with the Brazilian government.

A considerable quantity of gold and lesser amounts of cassiterite and Wolfram (tungsten) have been produced in the vicinity of Jacaré-Acanga on the Rio Tapajós for the past six years. Recorded gold production which passed through Santarém in 1967 was 178,490 grams (US$ 1.00/Gm.). This probably represents only 10–20 percent of the actual

[11] "The King Ranch South of the Border," *Fortune*, July 1969, p. 144.
[12] Personal interview, Manaus, 1967.

production because the gold is generally bought illegally and flown out from bush strips, thus bypassing the tax people in Santarem. The Tapajós deposits are alluvial-eluvial and are generally small, though rich. No serious exploration or development has been undertaken due to the complete lack of law enforcement, disputed titles, garimpeiro control, etc.

A vast area north of the Amazon remains to be explored. A small quantity of cassiterite and gold has been extracted by hand washing alluvial gravels 150 miles north of Santarém. No roads and few airstrips exist in the area, and most rivers are not navigable. However, the potential is very good.

Roraima. There is minor diamond production by garimpeiros but practically no serious exploration. The potential is good.

Rondônia and adjacent parts of Mato Grosso and Amazonas. Cassiterite has been and probably will continue to be the principal mineral produced from this area. One foreign company, Billiton, has purchased several mining concessions and is now in production. These properties are all accessible to the Pôrto Velho-Cuiabá highway. Mining of the cassiterite alluvial-eluvial deposits is by conventional placer methods: gravel pumps and earth-moving equipment are employed to feed washing plants incorporating mineral jigs and sluices.

Other foreign interests have been watching the Amazônia tin situation closely but are hesitant to invest until the government can control the garimpeiros who physically hold many of the better deposits. In many instances, Brazilians who have been granted exploration concessions cannot safely enter their lands to perform exploration work as required by law.

General. Additional investigation will, no doubt, reveal other areas in Amazonia with the proper geologic environment for mineral deposits. The principal minerals to be expected are those which have already been discovered and which are often associated with highly acid granites; these are cassiterite and gold. Wolfram (tungsten) is also common but currently not marketable. Diamond production is expected to increase but will not contribute significantly to the economy.

Amazonia, and Rondônia in particular, promises to be a major competitor with such major tin producing countries as Bolivia, Congo, Indonesia, Malaysia, Nigeria, and Thailand. The alluvial deposits are rich and might well be competitive in the world market, providing (1) the garimpeiro problem is resolved, solution depending on action by the government; and (2) the government encourages foreign investment and guarantees against nationalization.

While private enterprise tackles other facets of development, the

Brazilian government is trying to attract increased investment into Amazonia and to encourage industrialization. The Constitution of 1946 decreed that 3 percent of the federal budget must be invested in the area; the current charter contains no such clause, but a 1966 law allows 50 percent of income tax due to be diverted into the Banco da Amazônia for investment purposes. By mid-1968, the Superintendency for Amazon Development (SUDAM) said a total of 135 projects had been approved; few individual projects are large, but they represent a total investment of about $196 million.[13]

Another stimulant applied by the government is the creation of a Free Zone in Manaus which, according to a leading business man in that city, immediately brought on "a mercantile revolution." In 1967 Sr. Samuel Benchimol said that his prices dropped 35–40 percent as a result of the zone and that now the cost of living was comparable to that in other parts of the country: "This is essential to attract people to live here as the climatic conditions are such as to necessitate other attractions to overcome its disadvantage." [14] Marshall Whitlock, the U.S. consular agent in Manaus, observed: "It's been a scramble . . . but the so-called Free Zone could be abandoned overnight." He explained that heavy industry is not joining the boom to create the kind of industrial base envisaged by the plan. U.S. businesses have been particularly reluctant, a major drawback being inadequate electric power.[15] (An English company put in the thermo-electric plant at the time of the rubber boom, but, because the government did not allow rate increases, the plant deteriorated and was finally abandoned. Manaus was without electricity for 15 years, 1946–1962, depending on candles and kerosene lamps. In that year Westinghouse generators were installed.)

Isaac Sabbá insists that "the first phase in the development of Amazonia is not industrialization—there is not a consumer market." [16]

EVALUATION

In Rondônia monitors ejecting jets of water at high pressure are cutting liquid swaths through the forest, washing tin-bearing sands and gravels into sumps where they begin the processes of concentration culminating in a smelter in Volta Redonda. In Pará, south of the Amazon, tractor-drawn balls and chains drag down the forest cover. In Pará, north of the Amazon, Rome blades and Caterpillars carefully dismantle the ancient vegetation.

13 *The Wall Street Journal*, 3 December 1968.
14 Personal interview, Manaus, 1967.
15 *The Wall Street Journal*, 3 December 1968.
16 Personal interview, Manaus, 1967.

The will and the wealth to tackle one of the world's largest "last frontiers" seems at hand. Both will and wealth are needed in abundance. Amazonia is big on all counts, and any attempt to subdue it must likewise be on a grand scale. Bushmasters must be routed to clear ground for camps deep in the forest. Workers must be primed with malaria pills, yellow fever inoculations, and nutritious foods to keep them going. Spare parts and fuel must creep up river on barges to maintain an operation. Technicians must commute in small planes. Roads must be bludgeoned through the mantle, harbors built, dams constructed, and the product transported out thousands of miles to the point of processing and consumption.

Big, very big, money is involved, and, therefore, foreign interests risk capital. Attendant upon this type of investment are xenophobic resentments, dependence of local population upon an impersonal employer, a tendency toward paternalism, decision-making by exogenous leadership—the syndrome born of the mega-enterprise in a frontier setting. It does not promise a balanced economy and healthy sociopolitical structure.

Success in the short run does not assure success in the long run. Will the exotic gmelina of Nigeria better resist the Amazonian ravages than did the native *hevea*? Will any area cleared better survive than did the one major focus of colonization to this time—a Região Bragantina?

The Bragantine is a zone between Belém and the city of Bragantine in western Pará. In 1883 construction of a railroad was begun, eventually spanning the 228 kilometers between the two cities. Spontaneous colonization flooded the area, especially with small farmers from northeast Brazil, Spain, and Portugal. As a result:

"A região, outrora coberta de densa mata virgem, da verdadeira Hiléia Amazônica, hoje em dia se apresenta ao viajante como uma imensa capoeira, testemunho da ação do homen, sob o pretexto de colonização.

". . . uma vez interrompido o ciclo vegetativo com a destruição das matas, as terras em pouco tempo esgotaramse das reservas nutritivas . . . Com as derrubadas e queimadas sucessivas, tornaram-se as terras exaustivas, até chegar ao ponto atual onde a região está se transformando passo a passo, num semideserto, formando-se carrascos como no nordeste . . . Depois disso . . . houve naturalmente uma evaporação excessiva das águas, resultando daí um sensível rebaixamento no volume dos rios e igarapés." [17]

Today the poverty-stricken inhabitants rely for their livelihood largely on *uma praga*, a weed, *malva* or mallow which renders a fiber of commercial value. Where the wiry shrub is allowed to flourish, it chokes out all other crops.

[17] Fritz Louis Ackermann, "Geologia e Fisografia da Região Bragantina," *Cadernos da Amazônia.* Instituto Nacional de Pesquisas da Amazônia, pp. 11–19.

Scientific observers closely studying the Amazon rainforest suggest that the key to life is a symbiotic association of a soil fungus with the roots of certain plants. This closely woven mass, enveloping the rootlets or penetrating the root cells, is called mycorrhiza and enables vegetation to survive on poor soils. When the roots go, so goes the fungus.

There is a Brazilian law that for every tree destroyed, two must be planted. But in Amazonia, with no forestry service, "se obedece pero no se cumple." In fact, the law being unheralded, it is doubtful if even the conscience "se obedece."

It can be argued that foreign companies will exercise greater care in reforestation and that increased wealth and attention will assure better law enforcement and conservation. Advocates of development can also emphasize advances in science and technology as assurance that, in the last half of the twentieth century, man knows how to transform hostile areas and make them produce. But nature has a way of disrupting the manmade balance. Recent irrigation systems in India and Pakistan have raised the water level and contaminated the top soil with salt which rose from the earth with the water. Control of Nile flooding by the Aswan Dam has deprived the alluvial plains of their annual rejuvenation. Throughout the tropics, ambitious irrigation projects are breeding more schistosomes than food crops.

In the past, Amazonia has enervated the invaders, turning them away or subduing them before they made an impact of any significance. However, larger forces are now mounting which are coming to bear upon the region: the need for nonreoccurring resources; population pressure, both internal and external: a soaring world demand for food; the development dynamic of Brazil; the advance in science and technology.

It seems likely that, quite independent of conscious development efforts by the government, there will be ambitious incursions into the area. Armed with methods and mechanisms recently acquired, man's ability to dominate the tropics may begin to match nature's power to repel him. The next decades will add to the human equipment: nuclear power could compensate for the low hydroelectric potential, solar agriculture may end dependence on the soil, ecology research may ameliorate living conditions, husbandry may perfect breeds fit for the tropics, innovations in transport may erase problems of distance and inaccessibility, and The Big Dam might transform the whole physical setting of Amazonia. The list is as long and varied as the possibilities of what the future may bring. The major issue, hovering as incubus above all, is the consequence upon the total environment.

JOHN H. PETERSEN
Department of Government
Western Kentucky University
Bowling Green, Kentucky

STUDENT POLITICAL ACTIVISM IN GUATEMALA

A Research Note

Scholarly interest in student political behavior has grown markedly in recent years.[1] Among those who have done research and written on Latin American students a good deal of effort has gone into attempts to develop some generalizations about bases of student activism. A major objective of these efforts has been to try and explain why students become politically active and what differentiates the politically active from the inactive students. Several hypotheses have been advanced in this research attempting to explain high degrees of student political involvement by relating it to factors in the students' backgrounds or environment. Some of the hypotheses which stand out in the literature have been selected for analysis here. They will be examined in relation to data gathered during recent research on university students in Guatemala.

The data base for this study comes primarily from two 1967 surveys. In one the University of San Carlos of Guatemala requested students to complete a questionnaire aimed, in part, at gaining socioeconomic information. This survey was selective and reported 4,540 respondents out of a total enrollment of 9,388. The other data source is statistics gathered from all of the 9,388 students as part of their enrollment requirements for the 1967 school year. Responses to the surveys were broken down by fac-

[1] Much of this research has been summarized in Seymour Lipset, ed., *Student Politics* (New York: Basic Books, 1967), pp. 1–53. For a discussion of the literature on Latin American students see John H. Petersen, "Recent Research on Latin American University Students," *Latin American Research Review* 5, no. 1 (Spring 1970): 37–58.

ulty. In addition, some data from a 1963 student census were utilized. For the purposes of the present study, questions from these surveys that provided information relevant to hypotheses on student activism were selected out. This provides the data base for the analysis that follows.

STUDENT POLITICS IN GUATEMALA

Students at the national university of Guatemala, the University of San Carlos, as their counterparts in most Latin American countries, have been deeply involved in national politics for many years. In 1944 they played an important role in organizing and leading the movement that overthrew the long-entrenched dictator Jorge Ubico and ushered in a period of reform government in the country. During the moderate-to-leftist regimes of Juan José Arévalo and Jacobo Arbenz (1945–1954), students played important roles in supporting as well as opposing governmental policies. In the period of conservative reaction that followed the Carlos Castillo Armas seizure of power in 1954, students led the resistance to the repressive policies of the government. In 1962 they were one of the leading elements in an anti-government movement that nearly succeeded in overturning the government of Miguel Ydígoras Fuentes. In sum, university students in Guatemala constitute one of the significant groups in the national political system.

Studies of students and politics show that not all students are politically active to the same degree. Some spend most of their time on politics, others occasionally participate, while others rarely, if ever, do. At the national university of Guatemala the faculties of law, economics, and humanities have long been the centers of political activism. Detailed studies of student politics in the country show that these faculties have consistently been the most politically active over the past twenty-five years.[2] Less active have been the faculties of medicine and engineering, while the least active faculties have been agronomy, architecture, dentistry, pharmacy, and veterinary science. Students enrolled in the faculty of general studies are excluded from this classification inasmuch as the faculty had been established only a short time and had no political reputation. (In addition,

[2] See, for example, Miguel Ángel Reyes, *El Poder Político de los estudiantes universitarios* (Guatemala: Facultad de Ciencias Jurídicas y Sociales, Universidad de San Carlos de Guatemala, 1967), p. 5; John H. Petersen, "The Political Role of University Students in Guatemala, 1944–1968" (unpublished Ph.D. dissertation, University of Pittsburgh, 1969); and Mario Monteforte Toledo, *Guatemala: Monografía Sociológica* (Mexico, D.F.: U.N.A.M., 1965), p. 334. All agree that the faculties of law, humanities, and economics stand out as the most politically active at the university. The same general breakdown of faculty activism is found at other Latin American universities according to the summary presented in Lipset, *Student Politics*, p. 45.

as a result of student pressure, the faculty of general studies was disbanded in late 1968.) For this analysis, the three most active faculties are grouped and compared with the seven less active faculties.[3]

TABLE 1

CLASSIFICATION OF FACULTIES, BASED ON STUDENT POLITICAL ACTIVISM

Most Active	*Least Active*	
Law	Medicine	Agronomy
Economics	Engineering	Architecture
Humanities	Pharmacy	Veterinary medicine

This division is made for the purpose of the analysis that follows. The categories are general ones that hide individual differences and will be used only to make general statements about the correlates of political activism. There is no claim, for example, that all law students are more activist than all agronomy students, only that as a group law students have been more active than agronomy students. It is group differences that will be compared in this study.[4] We will be interested in what characteristics, if any, differentiate the active group of faculties from the less active group. Since the university faculties in Guatemala are quite independent of one another, it is reasonable to speak of them as separate entities.

CORRELATES OF POLITICAL ACTIVISM

The "Professional" Student Syndrome

Many writers have asserted a relationship between longevity at the university and political activism, suggesting that the activists are more likely to be those with longer experience as students.[5] They point to the so-called "professional" students as political leaders on campus. Alistair Hennessy says that "professional students, often but not necessarily

[3] In this study, activism is defined as participation in student political meetings, support for petitions and position papers, and participation in demonstrations and strikes. It does not refer to ideological division among students, i.e., radicalism, liberalism, conservatism, which represents a separate dimension.

[4] For a strong endorsement of the use of aggregate statistics in Latin American political research see Philippe C. Schmitter, "New Strategies for the Comparative Analysis of Latin American Politics," *Latin American Research Review* 4, no. 2 (Summer 1969): 83–110.

[5] For example, Lipset, *Student Politics*, p. 24. Also see E. Wright Bakke, "Students on the March: The Cases of Mexico and Colombia," *Sociology of Education* 37 (Spring 1964): 204; and S. Walter Washington, "Student Political Activity in Latin America," in *Latin American Politics*, Robert Tomasek, ed. (New York: Doubleday and Co., 1966), p. 118.

Leftists, and whose careers may span several student generations, come to play a vital role in student politics." [6] Francis Donahue also maintains that older, "professional" students are likely to be the instigators of intervention into national politics.[7] This suggests that the university experience socializes students into politically active roles, and the more activist students are likely to have been at the university the longest. Contrary conclusions, however, have emerged from studies by Richard Walter in Argentina and Frank Bonilla in Chile. These two studies indicate that there is no relationship between the "professional" students and political activism at the universities they studied.[8] The role of such students, therefore, remains a matter of controversy in the literature.

In order to test this relationship, one could hypothesize that there is a positive correlation between political activism and longevity at the university and/or between political activism and greater ages of students. To examine this hypothesis in Guatemala two sets of statistics from the 1967 surveys at the University of San Carlos have been employed. One deals with the average age of students in each faculty and the other with the average time taken to gain a degree in each faculty.

The following statistics are based on the entire enrollment for the 1967 academic year at the University of San Carlos and show the average age of students enrolled in each faculty.[9] By dividing the faculties into most and least politically active according to the categories established, the following averages emerge:

TABLE 2

AVERAGE AGE OF STUDENT BY FACULTY,
GROUPED MOST AND LEAST ACTIVE

Faculties	*Average Age*	*N*
Most Active	30.99	2623
Least Active	25.50	1992
		4615

[6] Alistair Hennessy, "University Students in National Politics," in *The Politics of Conformity in Latin America*, Claudio Veliz, ed. (London: Oxford University Press, 1967), p. 132.

[7] Francis Donahue, "Students in Latin American Politics," *Antioch Review* 24 (Spring 1966): 94.

[8] Richard Walter, *Student Politics in Argentina* (New York: Basic Books, 1968), p. 193; Frank Bonilla, "The Chilean Student Federation," *Journal of Inter-American Studies* 2 (July 1960): 329.

[9] "Edad media de los estudiantes inscritos por facultad, ciclo académico 1967," *Boletín Estadístico Universitario,* Año VI, no. 6 (Guatemala, C. A.: Oficina de Registro, Universidad de San Carlos, 1967): 23.

Students in the most politically active faculties were, on the average, more than five years older than students in the less active faculties. Another way of looking at this is in terms of the percentage of students in each of the faculties who are over thirty-five years of age. The age distribution of students in each of the groups of faculties is presented in the following table:[10]

TABLE 3

AGE DISTRIBUTION OF STUDENTS IN EACH GROUP OF FACULTIES

Faculties	*Under 35*	*Over 35*	*Totals*
Most Active	74.8% (1944)	25.2% (679)	100% (2623)
Least Active	94.9% (1889)	5.1% (103)	100% (1992)
			4615

One of every four students in the most active group of faculties was over thirty-five years of age, while only one in twenty was over thirty-five in the less active faculties. The results show clearly that the students in the group of faculties which have been most active politically are, on the average, older than students in the less active faculties. Thus, although the evidence is circumstantial, these data tend to support the hypothesis that age and activism are related.

Other data bearing on this hypothesis deal with the average time spent in each faculty to obtain a degree.[11] They provide information on the length of student careers among those who succeed in completing their work. This gives an indication of how long individuals in each of these faculties remain students. Again by dividing the faculties into most and least active groups, the following averages emerge:

TABLE 4

AVERAGE YEARS TAKEN TO GAIN DEGREE, FACULTIES GROUPED MOST AND LEAST ACTIVE

Faculties	*Average Years Taken To Gain Degree*	*N*
Most Active	14.21	2256
Least Active	11.56	2472
		4728

[10] Ibid., p. 22.

[11] "Resumen de los requisitos académicos y del progreso académico estudiantil en cada carrera, facultad y ciudad universitaria," *Progreso académico de los estudiantes de la Universidad de San Carlos de Guatemala* (Guatemala: Instituto de Investigaciones y Mejoramiento Educativo, Universidad de San Carlos de Guatemala, 1964), pp. 15–17.

As these data reveal, students in both groups take a substantial number of years to complete their degree work. However, students in the most active faculties spend more than two and one-half years longer in pursuit of degrees than do students in the less active faculties, even though the requirements are about the same. This would suggest a positive relationship between the amount of time spent at the university and the likelihood of political activism.

In short, the data here presented show a positive relationship between both age and time spent at the university to gain a degree and political activism. The most politically active faculties are those with older students and longer average student careers in comparison with students in the less active group of faculties. This would support the assertion that "professional" long-time students play an important political role in Guatemala and confirm the findings of Hennessy, Donahue, and Seymour Lipset.

Student Living Patterns

Several analysts of student political behavior have suggested that political activity is related to the student's residence and relationship with parents.[12] It is argued that students living at home and economically dependent on their parents are less likely to be political activists than those who are economically independent and live away from home. Living at home under the influence of parents is said to have a restraining and conservative effect on student political behavior. Students living away from home and on their own resources are conversely thought to be more free to participate politically.

This leads to the testable hypothesis that the most politically active students are those who live away from home and are relatively independent economically, while the least active are those who live with their parents and are economically dependent on them. The following data have been recombined from the 1967 socioeconomic survey of students at San Carlos.[13]

---

[12] For example, Frank Bonilla, "Students in Politics: Three Generations of Political Action in a Latin American University" (Unpublished Ph.D. dissertation, Harvard University, 1959), pp. 250–255; and Lipset, *Student Politics*, p. 25.

[13] "Estudiantes enquestados por facultad y personas con quienes viven," *Estudio de las condiciones socio-económicas de los estudiantes* (Guatemala: Oficina de Registro, Universidad de San Carlos, 1967), p. 9.

TABLE 5

STUDENT LIVING ARRANGEMENTS

Faculties	*Living with Parents/Family*	*Living Away From Parents*	*Totals*
Most Active	40.4% (209)	59.6% (308)	100% (517)
Least Active	67.3% (693)	32.7% (337)	100% (1030)
			1547

$\chi^2 = 102.1$, $p < .001$[a] $Q = -.504$[b]

[a] chi-squares will be indicated to show the level of significance of the distribution in each table.

[b] Q is a measure of association to determine how closely two variables are related to one another. Q can range from complete positive or negative relationship at +1 or −1 to no relationship at 0. In this study, a Q of .01 to .33 is considered a weak relationship, .34 to .66 a moderate relationship, and .67 to 1 a strong relationship.

The table reveals a pattern which lends support to the above hypothesis. A majority of students in the most active faculties live away from home while the reverse is true for those from the least active faculties. These differences are significant at the .001 level, based on *chi square.* In other words, these observed differences could be attributed to chance less than one time in a thousand. The Q measure of association at a −.504 level indicates a moderate relationship between the two variables.

Another index bearing on this hypothesis is the source of economic support for the students. According to the hypothesis, those who are economically dependent on their parents will be less likely to engage in political activity than those who are relatively independent of parental support. Available statistics on students' primary sources of economic support in 1967 were divided into those who depend on their own work and hence are independent economically, and those who are primarily dependent on their family for support. A third category covers those supported by scholarships, fellowships or unclassified sources of income.[14]

TABLE 6

PRIMARY SOURCE OF STUDENT ECONOMIC SUPPORT

Faculties	*Work*	*Support by Family*	*Other*	*Totals*
Most Active	85.8% (462)	12.1% (65)	2.0% (11)	100% (538)
Least Active	49.5% (529)	47.3% (505)	3.1% (33)	100% (1067)
				1605

$\chi^2 = 200.7$, $p < .001$ $Q = +.74$ (eliminating "other" category)

[14] "Fuente principal de ingresos del estudiante," ibid., p. 15.

The evidence clearly indicates that students in the more activist faculties are more likely to be living away from their parents and to be financially independent of them when compared with the less active group of faculties. Based on the *chi square* test, the difference indicated is significant at the .001 level.

The Q measure of association at a +.74 level indicates that there is strong relationship between the two variables. In sum, one thing that clearly differentiates the activist group of students from the less active is economic independence from parents. Taken together, the data on student living arrangements and economic support confirm the hypothesis relating activism to independence from parental control.

Socioeconomic Background

Several writers have suggested a link between students' political activism and their class and economic background.[15] It has been argued that students from relatively more privileged class backgrounds are more likely to be satisfied with the status quo and hence less likely to be politically active. Relatively lower class students, on the other hand, are likely to seek change of the existing arrangements and hence become more politically active. For example, studies conducted by Myron Glazer in Chile and S. Walter Washington in Venezuela show greater political activism among lower-class students.[16] However, Orlando Albórnoz, after analyzing studies from a variety of Latin American countries, concludes that no correlation between political involvement and social class exists.[17] Thus, no consensus has been reached in the literature on this point.

In order to examine the relationship with data from Guatemala the following proposition will be tested: that students from the more active faculties will be from relatively lower class backgrounds than students from the less active faculties.

Available statistics provide the following types of social class indicators for students at the University of San Carlos: (1) whether the student graduated from a public or private secondary school, (2) the average monthly income of the student's family, and (3) the education of the student's father.

The first indicator of social class, whether the student attended a

15 A summary of these studies is presented in Lipset, *Student Politics*, p. 29.

16 Myron Glazer, "Student Politics in a Chilean University," *Daedalus* 97 (Winter 1968):104; S. Walter Washington, "The Political Activity of Latin American Students," in *Latin American Politics*, by Robert Tomasek, ed., p. 125.

17 Orlando Albórnoz, "Student Opposition in Latin America," *Government and Opposition* 2 (Oct. 1966–Jan. 1967): 108–109.

public or private secondary school, gives a good indication of class and economic background. In Guatemala almost everyone who can afford it sends his children to private schools. Virtually the only students who attend public schools are those too poor to do otherwise. The 1967 student census provide the following data on educational background. The faculties have again been grouped according to their political activism.[18]

TABLE 7

STUDENTS' SECONDARY EDUCATION

Faculties	*Public School Grads.*	*Private School Grads.*	*Totals*
Most Active	59.1% (1505)	40.9% (1045)	100% (2550)
Least Active	34.8% (674)	65.2% (1261)	100% (1935)
			4485

$\chi^2 = 257.6, p < .001$ $Q = +.46$

This evidence clearly shows that students from the most active faculties are more likely to have graduated from public schools than those from less active faculties. The differences shown are significant at the .001 level on the *chi square* test. The Q level of association at +.46 indicates a moderate degree of association between these variables. From this we can logically assume that there is a substantially higher proportion of lower class students in the activist faculties and hence an apparent connection between lower class background and disposition toward political activism. (One could also argue, of course, that the public schools socialize students differently than do private schools, which causes the variety in behavior. The question remains open for future research.)

The second indicator of class is the average income of the student's family. Based on the 1967 student body, the average family income for each of the groups of faculties is as follows:[19]

TABLE 8

STUDENTS' FAMILY INCOME

Faculties	*Family Income Per Month*	*N*
Most Active	$251.15	2623
Least Active	$294.53	1992
		4615

[18] "Estudiantes inscritos por tipo de establecimiento donde obtuvieron el título o diploma que les sirvió para ingresar a la universidad," *Boletín Estádistico Universitario*, p. 32.

[19] "Valor mediano de los ingresos familiares y percápita," *Condiciones socio-económicas de los estudiantes*, p. 21.

The pattern of lower income, hence lower class background, for the more active faculties continues to hold true, although the differences are less than might be expected in light of the public school—private school division shown above. The relatively high level of both these averages is significant. All fall into the upper-to-lower middle-class range on a national scale which indicates that we are dealing only with the relatively privileged sector of society.

The third available measure of class background is the level of education attained by the student's father. These statistics are grouped according to whether the students' fathers' highest educational level was primary school, secondary school, or the university.[20]

TABLE 9

STUDENTS' FATHERS' EDUCATION

Faculties	*Primary (Partial or Comp.)*	*Secondary (Partial or Comp.)*	*University (Partial or Comp.)*	*Totals*
Most Active	48.2% (228)	36.2% (171)	15.6% (74)	100% (473)
Least Active	28.2% (276)	43.4% (424)	28.4% (278)	100% (978)
				1451

$\chi^2 = 62.2$, $p < .001$ $G = +.35$*

* G or gamma is a measure of association similar to Q, except that it can be used on 2x3 tables while Q cannot.

These figures indicate that the students from the more active faculties are more likely to have fathers of relatively low educational attainment in comparison to the students from the less active faculties. Conversely, students from the less active faculties are more likely to have better educated fathers than those in the more active group. The differences indicated are significant at the .001 level, based on the *chi square* test. The degree of association, +.35, indicates a low-moderate relationship between the two variables. If we make the reasonable assumption that there is a close relationship between educational attainment and class level, then it follows that the most politically active faculties are more likely to be made up of students from relatively lower class backgrounds and the least active faculties of students from relatively higher class backgrounds.

In sum, the three indicators agree with, and the data from Guate-

[20] "Estudiantes enquestados por facultad y nivel educational del padre," ibid., p. 13.

mala lend support to the hypothesis that political activism at the university tends to be associated with students from relatively lower class backgrounds. It must be kept in mind, however, that lower class here applies only in a relative sense, that is, in relation to the student body. It does not mean that these students come from or represent the lower classes of the society as a whole. The lowest classes in Guatemala, which means primarily the Indians, are essentially unrepresented at the university. Even among the "ladinized" [21] elements of the population, the rural and urban proletariat classes send very few to the university. It is in this context that the findings set forth above must be understood.

CONCLUSIONS

The composite picture that emerges shows the most politically active faculties to be those which are made up of students who are older, have a longer university career, live independently from their parents, and are of lower social class origins in relation to those students in less active faculties. There is a close relationship between activism and independence from parental control, and a moderate to low relationship between activism and both relatively lower class background and "professional" student status. This combination of factors by no means fully accounts for political activism among Guatemalan students. They have, however, been shown to be related to activism to a greater or lesser degree, and they in combination with other, as yet unidentified, variables account for the variation among students on the dimension of political activism.

These data, of course, cannot be used for any final conclusions on the questions raised. At most, they can be only one more piece of evidence to add to the ongoing discussion on the nature of student political behavior. The indicators available here are very gross, and the results must be taken with a note of caution. Much further research, particularly of a comprehensive comparative nature, is needed before the bases of political activism among students will be fully identified.

---

21 Guatemalan society is divided between Indians, who retain their traditional dress, language, religion and customs, and *ladinos*, who are "westernized" in dress, language, and culture. The distinction is primarily cultural, not racial.

Frederic Hicks
Department of Anthropology
University of Louisville
Louisville, Kentucky

INTERPERSONAL RELATIONSHIPS AND *CAUDILLISMO* IN PARAGUAY*

Paraguay has a relatively open (for Latin America) class structure, a strong national consciousness, a two-party political system, and mass involvement in national politics, all of which are features that some writers[1] believe should be associated with representative democracy of the North American type. In Paraguay, however, these features are associated with, and in fact reinforce, a political system which for most of the past century has consisted of a series of conservative and unstable dictatorships.

It will be suggested in this paper that this association is made possible by the development of certain kinds of interpersonal relationships which have been called "dyadic contracts" [2] since they bind two individuals in either patron-client relationships or colleague relationships. They take various institutionalized forms in many peasant societies that lack

---

* Material for this paper was gathered, at first casually and only later systematically, between March 1963 and September 1965 while I was a visiting professor of anthropology at the Universidad Nacional de Asunción under the Fulbright-Hays program. I have not been able to keep in touch with developments in Paraguay since leaving that country, however, so except where otherwise noted, the political system is here described as it was in 1965.

1 E.g., Theodore Wyckoff, "The Role of the Military in Latin American Politics," *Western Political Quarterly* 13 (September 1960): 745–763.

2 George M. Foster, "The Dyadic Contract: A Model for the Social Structure of a Mexican Peasant Village," *American Anthropologist* 63 (December 1961): 1173–1192; idem. "The Dyadic Contract in Tzintzuntzan, II: Patron-Client Relationships," ibid. 65 (December 1963): 1280–1294.

corporate descent groups, having been described for Italy,[3] Spain,[4] and the Philippines,[5] as well as Latin America. Among their effects is to link the peasantry and other lower class sectors to the elite, including the political elite. This effect has been noted in many countries. What seems distinctive about Paraguay is the way the dyadic contract complex is linked to the national political party system. This has the effect of politicizing the peasantry (and the urban lower classes), yet directing their political energies to the support of conservative groups which do not usually act in their interest. It is also related to the preservation (in modified form) of *caudillismo*, a political system involving a succession of leaders who achieve power chiefly through violence with the support of a personal following which expects a share of the spoils that accrue to the powerholder.[6]

DEVELOPMENT OF THE PARAGUAYAN POLITICAL SYSTEM

The present Paraguayan political system began to take shape in the decades following the War of the Triple Alliance (1865–1870), in which Paraguay fought the combined forces of Brazil, Argentina, and Uruguay. The war, which Paraguay lost, devastated the country, wiped out an estimated one-half of its population, and brought widespread political, economic, and social disruption.

Politically, the relative isolation of the country under its three great dictators, Gaspar Rodríguez de Francia (1814–1840), Carlos Antonio López (1844–1862), and Francisco Solano López (1862–1870), ended with the death in the war of the younger López. Under the eyes of the Brazilian occupation forces, a new constitution was drawn up by a number of educated liberal Paraguayans who had fled their country before the war and in many cases fought on the side of the Allies for the purpose, as they saw it, of liberating their country from the tyranny of López. The new constitution, which remained in effect until 1940, provided for a liberal, democratic government, with an elected president and a bicameral

---

3 Jeremy Boissevain, "Patronage in Sicily," *Man*, new ser., 1, no. 1 (March 1966): 18–33; Sydel F. Silverman, "Patronage and Community-Nation Relationships in Central Italy," *Ethnology* 4, no. 2 (April 1965): 172–189.

4 Michael Kenny, "Patterns of Patronage in Spain," *Anthropological Quarterly* 33 (January 1960): 14–23.

5 Mary R. Hollensteiner, "Social Structure and Power in a Philippine Municipality," in Jack M. Potter et al, eds., *Peasant Society: A Reader* (Boston: Little-Brown, 1967), pp. 200–212.

6 Merle Kling, "Toward a Theory of Power and Political Instability in Latin America," *Western Political Quarterly* 9 (March 1956): 21–35; Eric R. Wolf and Edward C. Hansen, "Caudillo Politics: A Structural Analysis," *Comparative Studies in Society and History* 9, no. 2 (January 1967): 168–179.

legislature, freedom of the press, universal suffrage, and the inviolability of private property. Although an enlightened document for its time, it was the product of a foreign culture, imposed upon Paraguay and quite alien to the Paraguayan tradition.

Many landowners had abandoned their properties in their flight to escape the war's devastation. After the war, the country was opened up to hordes of adventurers and speculators, of diverse nationalities, who poured in to take advantage, for personal gain, of the disorganized conditions and the corruption which soon prevailed. A series of questionable financial machinations plunged the country ever deeper into debt.

A way out of the financial problems was eventually found in the sale of public lands. Between 1883 and 1887, a series of laws were passed to permit the sale of vast quantities of state-owned lands, inherited from the López era or acquired after their owners had abandoned them during the war, and which meanwhile had been occupied by peasants or small farmers. The lands were sold exclusively in large parcels, at prices that were extremely low but too high for the penniless Paraguayan peasants, and the conditions of sale were such that few but foreigners could meet them. Within ten years, virtually all of the productive, accessible public lands were owned by foreigners, for the most part land speculators who lived outside Paraguay. As a result of the land sales, thousands of peasants were driven from lands which, in some cases, they had occupied for generations. With no place to go, many suffered extreme privation. Working conditions, for those few able to find work, got steadily worse. For the first time, Paraguayans in appreciable numbers began to emigrate from their country.[7]

It was under these conditions of defeat, foreign economic domination, and economic insecurity that the modern Paraguayan political system began. The system as it developed was adapted to these conditions, which recall those prevalent earlier in many other parts of Latin America when caudillismo as a political system developed,[8] and under which, in Kling's analysis,[9] chronic political instability should prevail. They also recall those of Sicily, for which Boissevain[10] has described a system of patronage similar to that of Paraguay. While today it is doubtful that foreign economic domination and economic insecurity are appreciably greater in Paraguay than in most Latin American countries, their forms

---

[7] Alcides Codas Papalucá, *Cuestiones rurales del Paraguay* (Buenos Aires: Editorial Tupã, 1949); Carlos Pastore, *La lucha por la tierra en el Paraguay: proceso histórico y legislativo* (Montevideo: Editorial Antequera, 1949).

[8] Wolf and Hansen, "Caudillo Politics."

[9] Kling, "Theory of Power."

[10] Boissevain, "Patronage in Sicily."

have undergone little change since the late nineteenth century. The political system, with its pattern of patronage and instability,[11] still bears the marks of the conditions under which it arose, and to some extent it functions to maintain those conditions.

The two political parties which still today dominate the political life of Paraguay trace their origins back to two rival clubs, of limited membership and influence, that were formed shortly after the war. They did not begin to organize on a national scale, however, until 1887. In June of that year, a group of businessmen, professionals, and intellectuals formed the *Centro Democrático*, later called the *Partido Liberal*, to defend their interests against a clique which, with the support of the government, threatened to monopolize economic opportunities. In response, members of the government under the leadership of the president, General Bernardino Caballero, formed in September of that year the *Asociación Nacional Republicana*, also called the *Partido Colorado* after the red banner it adopted as its emblem (the Liberals adopted the color blue).[12]

Through a network of friendships, patron-client relationships, and group interests, membership in one or the other of the two parties spread throughout the country, involving people of all social classes, so that today the membership of the two parties is assumed to be about equal. To the extent that ideologies were involved, both parties adopted the liberal principles that were the order of the day, but party affiliation reflected primarily personal loyalties, not political principles.

Historians write that the Colorado party ruled until 1904, when the Liberal era began, lasting until 1941 except for a brief interlude in 1936–1937. Then came the dictatorship of Morínigo, a nonparty man, which lasted until the revolution of 1947, when the Colorados regained power, which they hold to this day. In reality, however, there has rarely been much party cohesion. Factional splits have occurred repeatedly. At risk of

---

11 At this writing, President Alfredo Stroessner has succeeded in holding office for more than fifteen years, longer than any president since Carlos Antonio López, and many Paraguayans understandably regard this as "political stability." However, he has retained office simply by being able to triumph over all attempts to oust him so far, or, as Kling (see footnote 6) would put it, by "a series of successful anticipatory revolts."

12 Policarpo Artaza, *Qué hizo el Partido Liberal en la oposición y en el gobierno* (Buenos Aires: Talleres Gráficos Lucania, 1961), pp. 15–19; Justo Pastor Benítez, *Formación social del pueblo paraguayo* (Asunción & Buenos Aires: Editorial América-Sapucai, 1955), pp. 152–153, 165; Carlos P. Centurión, *Historia de la cultura paraguaya* I (Asunción: Biblioteca "Ortiz Guerrero", 1961), pp. 408–413; Justo Prieto, *Paraguay, la provincia gigante de las Indias* (Buenos Aires: Librería-Editorial "El Ateneo", 1951), pp. 132, 195; Paul H. Lewis, *The Politics of Exile: Paraguay's Febrerista Party* (Chapel Hill: University of North Carolina Press, 1968), pp. 17–25.

gross oversimplification, one can perhaps say that it is common for factions to develop within the party in power over the division of the spoils, and in the party out of power over the best way to get in. The violence which has so often characterized Paraguayan political life is due as much to these factional splits as to the rivalry between the two parties.[13]

Efforts to establish third parties or new political movements have been made from time to time, but they have not had lasting success. During the resurgence of nationalism in the 1920s and 1930s, there was much talk of building a "New Paraguay." [14] A Communist party was formed, and it made some headway among the country's few urban workers. More important was the Febrerista party, originally composed of the followers of Chaco War hero Colonel Rafael Franco, who held the presidency briefly following a coup in February, 1936. More recently, a Christian Democratic movement was established in 1960, and it became a political party in 1965. Today, the Febrerista and Christian Democratic parties both have legal status, but they have few adherents outside the urban bourgeoisie.[15] The vast majority of Paraguayans continue their allegiance to one or the other of the two "traditional" parties, Colorado and Liberal. This is despite the fact that these parties are both avowedly "rightist," while the smaller parties espouse programs which might be expected to have wide mass appeal.

Both of the traditional parties are, however, affected by factionalism. Shortly after the revolution of 1947, the Colorado party split into factions known as "Guión Rojo" and "Democrático," and while these factions have not yet been completely amalgamated, they work together now on a national level and have become largely overshadowed by a new generation of Colorados owing allegiance only to President Stroessner, who, as head of the armed forces, seized the presidency in 1954 and has held it since that time. A dissident Colorado faction known as the *Movi-*

---

[13] Artaza, *Partido Liberal*, pp. 33–38; Manuel J. Cibils, *Anarquía y revolución en el Paraguay* (Buenos Aires: Editorial Américalee, 1957), pp. 29–31; Lewis, *Politics of Exile*, pp. 25–37; Pastore, *Tierra en Paraguay*, pp. 144ff; Rodolfo Rivarola, "El Paraguay Político", *Revista Argentina de Ciencias Políticas*, Año 1, 2 (1911): 5–23; Harris G. Warren, *Paraguay, an Informal History* (Norman: University of Oklahoma Press, 1949), pp. 265–268.

[14] Harris G. Warren, "Political Aspects of the Paraguayan Revolution, 1936–1940," *Hispanic American Historical Review* 30 (February 1950): 2–25.

[15] The Febrerista party has repeatedly split into factions, usually identifiable as "left" or "right", over ideological and tactical issues (see Lewis [footnote 12] for a summary and analysis of these schisms). Generally the more conservative factions have remained active in Paraguay, while the more radical ones have continued their separate organizations in exile. The latter sometimes make news with declarations issued in exile, but their impact on affairs inside Paraguay is negligible.

miento Popular Colorado (MOPOCO), formed between 1955 and 1958, operates clandestinely both inside and outside of Paraguay. The Liberal party split into factions in 1963 over the issue of participation in the fixed presidential elections of that year (they were offered one-third of the seats in congress and one ambassadorship or two, regardless of vote count, if they would participate in the elections). The government recognized the small dissident faction that favored participation as the only legal Liberal party. The majority of the Liberals remained aloof until 1966, when they accepted legal recognition under the name *Partido Liberal Radical,* but they are still understood to be the majority faction of the Liberal party.

National elections are customarily held at periodic intervals (every five years, normally), but rarely if ever have these been credible tests of popular political preferences. Elections in which the dominant party's candidate runs unopposed, or with only token opposition, have been the rule. Political power has never passed from one party to another as the result of an election, and knowledgeable Paraguayans doubt that it ever will under the present political system.

CLASS AND POLITICIZATION

Paraguay is a relatively homogeneous nation culturally, and its social class system is not marked by the rigid barriers to mobility that are so characteristic of the Andean countries and Central America.[16] In particular, the great social gulf that separates the laboring *peón* class from the non-*peón* classes in those countries is virtually absent. Indeed, many Paraguayans hold almost as a dogma that social class differences do not exist in their country, only wealth differences. The difference is a real one, although it can be overstated. Wealth of course brings advantages, but it is primarily wealth, not ascribed status or cultural background, that brings them.[17] Political activity and the fruits of such activity are not expected to be withheld from any sector of society because of its wealth, education, background, or occupation.

The social distinction which perhaps best correlates with a difference in political behavior is that between people with a cosmopolitan, somewhat intellectual, urban cultural orientation, on the one hand, and people of a more provincial orientation, less intellectually inclined, on the other.

---

16 Ralph L. Beals, "Social Stratification in Latin America," *American Journal of Sociology* 58 (January 1953): 327–339.

17 The distinction between the *baile oficial* and the *baile popular,* which the Services found so useful as an indicator of class differences in Tobatí (see Elman R. Service and Helen S. Service, *Tobatí: Paraguayan Town* [Chicago: University of Chicago Press, 1954], pp. 136–137) is either absent or much less formalized in many Paraguayan communities, and is definitely on the decline.

This is not entirely a wealth difference, for the social system provides opportunities for members of the latter group to become wealthy (usually through the armed services, politics, or commercial agriculture and stock-raising) without acquiring an urban, cosmopolitan orientation. It is only a somewhat more rural-urban difference, because even Asunción, the capital and largest city, is sufficiently provincial, so that the contrast between it and many rural towns is not extreme. A moderately urban environment and a certain minimum of economic resources are necessary for the acquisition of a cosmopolitan outlook and the values that go with it but do not assure their acquisition.

The associated difference in political behavior is this: the cosmopolitan, urban-oriented intellectual tends to be concerned with political principles and ideologies and may regard politics as a potential instrument for bringing about social or economic change. He knows from his formal education that this is what politics is supposed to be about. The less cosmopolitan, more provincially-oriented persons—and such are of course the vast majority—see politics primarily or exclusively as a means of manipulating people so as to achieve advancement and power for themselves or their clique. To them, politics is "politicking"—*politiquería.*

Most of what is written about politics in Paraguay is written by members of the intellectual, cosmopolitan group. It is primarily members of this group also that are attracted to the newer, smaller, ideologically-oriented parties. The larger, traditional parties, however, provide more opportunities for advancement through political activity, especially in the rural areas. So these parties have greater appeal for people of a more provincial, less intellectual orientation.

Regardless of social class, Paraguayans have a highly developed national consciousness. There are no *patrias chicas* in Paraguay; there is a good deal of geographical mobility and very little regional variation.[18] Almost without exception, sentiments and loyalties are directed toward the nation, not toward any particular locality within it. This, plus the relatively open class structure, means that Paraguayans of all classes and regions can have the satisfaction of being involved in a form of political activity which, as will be seen, brings rewards and is significant on a national scale; but their involvement does not lead to politically-initiated changes favoring the lower classes, and this is largely the result of the way the dyadic contract works in a political context.

---

[18] Domingo M. Rivarola, "Bases preliminares para el estudio de la movilidad social en el Paraguay," *Revista Paraguaya de Sociología*, Año 1, no. 1 (September–December 1964), pp. 9–29.

THE DYADIC CONTRACT AND CAUDILLISMO IN PARAGUAY

Like many Latin American countries—and underdeveloped countries throughout the world—Paraguay has few impersonal means of providing economic and legal security for its inhabitants. It had virtually none in the decades following the War of the Triple Alliance, when the present Paraguayan political system was taking form. For people of the lower classes, the social welfare programs are inadequate to meet the need; there are few opportunities for secure employment, and court or bureaucratic procedures are invariably beyond their level of sophistication. On the upper social levels, there has in the past been relatively little dependable government protection of business interests; government favoritism and arbitrariness, as well as economic fluctuations, have added to investment risks, particularly for Paraguayan nationals.

These conditions have led to the development of other means of providing the individual with the security he needs. These means are based on the establishment of ties of mutual loyalty and obligation on a person-to-person basis. They take various forms, depending on the context and the status of the person involved, but for the most part are of the type that Foster has called "dyadic contracts," [19] since basically they are ties binding two individuals. Foster distinguishes two types of dyadic contract operating in Tzintzuntzan, Mexico. Colleague relationships "tie people of equal or approximately equal socioeconomic status, who exchange the same kinds of goods and services," while patron-client relationships "tie people . . . of significantly different socioeconomic status (or order of power), who exchange different kinds of goods and services." [20] The proliferation of such relationships may create a network permeating virtually the entire society, but it will be a network based on individual relationships, rather than on class unity and opposition.

One form of patron-client relationship is the well-known institution of *compadrazgo*—ritual co-parenthood—which is widespread throughout the Latin world. This institution serves to provide the individual with a number of pseudo-kin with whom he is linked by obligations and responsibilities which include mutual aid.[21] In Paraguay it is important primarily in the rural areas, and, as in many other countries, *compadres* (coparents) are often chosen not merely out of friendship but with a view toward cementing relationships of certain useful kinds. A conscious

19 Foster, "Dyadic Contract."

20 Foster, "Dyadic Contract in Tzintzuntzan," p. 1281.

21 Sidney W. Mintz and Eric R. Wolf, "An Analysis of Ritual Co-Parenthood (Compadrazgo)," *Southwestern Journal of Anthropology* 6 (Winter 1950): 341–368; Service and Service, *Tobatí*, pp. 126–127.

effort is often made to obtain compadres for oneself, and *padrinos* (godfathers) for one's offspring, who would be able to provide economic assistance or influence should circumstances make this necessary. The man who is potentially in a position to give aid (the patron) receives from the relationship the loyalty of his client compadre and feels free to call on him for such assistance as he can provide, including assistance which can only be effective if it is voluntary, such as votes or their functional equivalent and talk which will promote a favorable image for the patron among his client's associates.[22]

A less institutionalized form of patron-client relationship is exemplified by a behavior pattern generally called "paternalism" which, primarily in employer-employee relationships, is characteristic of much of Latin America.[23] Typically, and especially in small concerns which are not unionized, the employer is expected to display a certain sense of noblesse oblige which may require him to provide for his workers more than their usually meager wage. He may be expected to pay a worker's medical expenses or the school expenses of his children, to pay a large share of the funeral expenses of a former worker, and to advance loans.[24] The worker, for his part, may often be called upon to provide personal services for his employer beyond what would usually be expected of him in highly industrialized countries. Elman and Helen Service's description of peasant behavior in a wage working context in Tobatí, in this case involving very small rural concerns, applies to most smaller Paraguayan communities and to a large extent to smaller concerns in Asunción as well. The attitude is somewhat as if the employer (patrón) were doing the employee a favor by hiring him and, to at least an equal degree, the employee is doing the patrón a favor by working for him. The exchange of money is played down as if it were only a minor part of the arrangement.

It is not unusual for the employer to become the padrino of one of the employee's children, so that the two men become compadres, but this is not a necessary part of the pattern. The breaking of the employer-employee relationship becomes a delicate matter, as both parties are considered to be bound by ties that go beyond the purely economic, even if the compadre relationship is not present.[25] This does not mean that wage work is in itself undesirable. On the contrary, a steady job,

---

[22] Service and Service, *Tobatí*, chap. 12; cf. for Mexico, Foster, "The Dyadic Contract in Tzintzuntzan," pp. 1283–1284.

[23] Robert J. Alexander, *Today's Latin America* (Garden City: Doubleday Anchor Books, 1962), pp. 88–90.

[24] Frederic Hicks and Egidio Picchioni, "Algunos aspectos de la industrialización en una comunidad paraguaya," *Suplemento Antropológico de la Revista del Ateneo Paraguayo* 2, no. 1 (Diciembre 1966): 31–54.

[25] Service and Service, *Tobatí*, pp. 126–127.

with a regular salary, is a very attractive alternative to the subsistence farmer whose sole monetary income, if any, comes from the small surplus his wife may be able to sell. However, if the peasant must abandon farming to take up employment, he is likely to suffer extraordinary hardship if he is suddenly dismissed; hence the effort to create personal bonds of a more permanent nature.

Colleague relationships,[26] in which the participants are of approximately equal status, are important in Paraguay mainly in the upper socioeconomic strata. It is considered a friendly gesture, if not actually an obligation of friendship, to grant to friends, and of course to relatives also,[27] what favors one can by virtue of one's position, knowledge, or skills. It is assumed that the favor will be returned should an appropriate occasion present itself. A friend in customs gets one's package out quickly and with little formality; a friend in the railway administration gets one a sleeper reservation on short notice; a member of the opposition Liberal party retains his government job, a youth of Liberal parents gains easy admittance to the national *colegio*, or a left-wing Febrerista remains unmolested because they have Colorado friends or relatives in high government positions. One is not expected to wait his turn and comply with all the formal details of a bureaucratic procedure if he has a friend through whom he can by-pass them, and the friend would be hurt if the favor were not asked of him.

Most Paraguayans would be shocked if this were called "corruption." To those who can participate in it, it is seen simply as a manifestation of a characteristic trait of friendliness and hospitality of which Paraguayans are justifiably very proud. They emphasize that no money ever changes hands; to offer an outright bribe would be extremely improper. The point is that by doing a favor, one creates an obligation on the part of the person favored to return it, while bribery creates no such tie. It is rumored that some bribery does occur in Paraguay, but it is said to be confined to the highest levels of the political or military bureaucracy, and I suspect that, if so, it involves mainly foreigners or others with whom enduring reciprocal obligations cannot be established.

The emphasis on reciprocal loyalities and obligations, as manifested in the system of dyadic relationships, is a theme of Paraguayan culture that finds its natural expression in the realm of politics. It can function to provide certain individuals with large personal followings which they can

---

26 Foster, "Dyadic Contract in Tzintzuntzan," p. 1281.

27 For the purposes of this paper I believe that kinship ties may be treated as dyadic relationships; they are often very strong but still dyadic.

use to political advantage.[28] It forms the basis for caudillismo, a political system which, I would maintain, is still very much alive in Paraguay, not only on a local level in rural areas but on a national level as well, involving the highest offices in the government.

Wolf and Hansen[29] have argued that as a political system, caudillismo (or as these authors term it, *caudillaje*) began to give way in the 1870s, when the particular balance between landowning *criollo*, lower class *mestizo*, and foreign interests, on which the system depended, was upset by a shift in the nature of foreign investment. I would suggest, however, that while Paraguayan caudillismo is somewhat modified, and necessarily more discreet than the form which was so prevalent throughout Latin America a century ago, its essential features are still present today. These features include personal rule (rather than rule through the authority vested in a political office) maintained by building up a loyal personal following, a following which is retained by rewards of wealth or the power to bestow patronage through control of access to the sources of wealth.[30]

The core of this following is said to consist of a group of military officers who are President Stroessner's closest associates.[31] Although often of intermediate rank (majors or colonels, usually), and holding titles which in some cases sound inconsequential (e.g., chief of the military cabinet of the presidency, commander of the presidential escort batallion), they are in fact among the most powerful men in the country. They include those in actual command of troops, and their loyalty is retained by granting them unusual opportunities for self-enrichment. Many of the more lucrative business enterprises in the country (and a few in neighboring Brazil) belong to military men. The various expanding state enterprises—the alcohol monopoly, meat packing and export, shipping, the railway, an airline, electric power—provide sources of wealth and patronage easily disposable as rewards. Rumors circulating in 1964 were that one of the most powerful military units received a regular sum siphoned

---

[28] Ramiro Domínguez, "El valle y la loma: comunicación en comunidades rurales," *Suplemento Antropológico de la Revista del Ateneo Paraguayo* 1, no. 2 (February 1966): 127–242.

[29] Wolf and Hansen, "Caudillo Politics," pp. 177–178.

[30] Domingo M. Rivarola, "Universidad y estudiantes en una sociedad tradicional," *Aportes* 12 (Abril 1969): 63–64.

[31] The statements in the remainder of this paragraph cannot, of course, be documented, and I must present them simply as rumors. These and others like them, however, come with great consistency from a diversity of sources, and I have no doubt that they are true in essence, if not always accurate in detail. I present them despite the lack of substantiation because the Paraguayan political system cannot be understood without taking this kind of information into account.

off from the state alcohol monopoly to retain its loyalty. The large-scale traffic in contraband items of all kinds, which is carried on quite openly throughout the country, is generally understood to be run by military men. They are also said to direct much of the cattle-stealing that prevails in the more remote parts of the country. Men in these positions can in turn control the access of others to economic opportunities and can grant such access as favors.

It must all be done discreetly, however, lest Paraguay's international relations be jeopardized. The picture conveyed by Wolf and Hansen[32] of predatory armed bands more or less openly engaging in "the systematic pillage of 'free' resources" is too gross to apply generally to present-day Paraguay. While no one doubts President Stroessner's *machismo*, he is certainly not a flamboyant public personality. His very obscurity however, helps preserve the system by not calling international attention to it. Visiting journalists are viewed with great apprehension by officials, and much of the press censorship, which is particularly effective because it relies on informal pressures and understandings rather than on official decrees, seems designed simply to prevent Paraguay from becoming an international news center.

Possibly the caudillo system persists in Paraguay today because the balance of interests referred to above has not yet been sufficiently altered, but it may also be that the relationship between the dyadic contract complex and the traditional political party system has enabled it to survive some degree of economic alteration. In any case, its existence as a system is recognized by most Paraguayans, and many consider it a praiseworthy system—despite its more predatory aspects, which they shrug off as something one must put up with for the sake of peace.

It is by its nature a conservative system, however, because it functions by utilizing existing power relationships which the people involved, whether as patrons or as clients, are obliged to maintain. Lacking the experience for bettering one's condition through hard work or business acumen, one seeks advancement by allying himself with someone already in a position to bestow favors. As the Services noted, "the most usual response from a peasant who is queried about his economic or technical difficulties is not that he needs a good steel plow, better seed, or a yoke of oxen, but that he needs a good patrón who will help him." [33] An individual who is sufficiently adept may be able to work his way up the political ladder through the system, so there is a turnover of personnel, but neither the system nor the existing power relationships are thereby

---

32 Wolf and Hansen, "Caudillo Politics."

33 Service and Service, *Tobatí*, p. 125.

changed. In fact, the system provides a certain amount of opportunity for people of relatively humble origin to achieve a moderately high political position, and many who consider themselves aristocrats are annoyed that they must deal with such "simple brutes" as often occupy positions of authority.

THE POLITICAL PARTIES

The most striking feature of Paraguayan politics is the near-universal adhesion to one or the other of the two traditional political parties, Colorado and Liberal. The vast majority of Paraguayans, rural and urban, of all social classes and in all but the most remote parts of the country, see themselves as belonging to one or the other of these parties, whether or not they are formally inscribed in the party rolls.[34] One is expected to remain always loyal to his party; to change one's party affiliation is considered little short of treasonous. Except for members of the cosmopolitan, intellectual class concerned with such matters, this loyalty does not involve the ideology or program of the party, of which most people are only vaguely aware, but the symbols and slogans of the party. The party leaders are not above criticism, but however bitterly an individual member may criticize them, he always affirms his unwavering loyalty to the party.

Once one does become allied with a particular political leader, however, he is expected to remain loyal to him. This means that in a political contest, for example, one should vote with the man to whom one owes loyalty and should remain loyal to the candidate this man supports, whether he wins or loses. Consequently, voting (for example, in an election of local party officials) frequently results in the formation of factions, as the followers of the losing candidate quite commonly (normally, according to many Paraguayans) refuse to reunite and cooperate with the winner.[35]

Thus factions readily form, and the existence of factional splits within a political party, on either a national or a local level, is perhaps the second most striking feature of Paraguayan politics. The factions formed after one election tend to endure for long periods of time, the same ones appearing in election after election. This is understandable considering that elections seldom involve ideological issues but rather are contests

[34] At present the Liberal party is split into what are officially two parties (see below). Similar situations have existed in the past and have so far always proved ephemeral.

[35] This pattern is apparently not limited to political elections among the rural or provincially-oriented sector. I know of at least one such case involving an election among the highly-educated membership of a professional society in Asunción.

for positions from which to form a power base through opportunity to bestow patronage. The candidate's supporters are those who hope for suitable rewards if he wins. If he loses, they can expect no consideration from the man they opposed, who is obliged to reward only his supporters. Indeed, he rarely has the means to tempt his former opponents after rewarding his supporters, who would in any case resent further division of their share of the spoils. Theoretically, a particularly successful factional leader might become so successful as to acquire a larger following than he could reward, but the two-party system precludes such an eventuality by placing a limit on the number of followers that even the most successful leader can acquire, since they can be drawn only from his own party. Thus the best course of action for followers of a losing candidate is to stick with the man they supported and hope for better luck next time. One who switches allegiances is clearly not to be trusted; since it is unlikely that he would do so out of a change in his convictions, his motivation could only be personal gain.

It follows from this that, aside from the urban, intellectual, cosmopolitan class, everyone must have an "opinión"—a commitment to one or another party or faction. One does not know how to deal with a person without knowing what his political affiliation is. One does not know how to interpret his statements, nor how one's own will be interpreted. Since Paraguayans are fully aware of the functional relationships between politics and so many other aspects of their culture, few topics of conversation can long remain wholly free of political implications; so one quite commonly feels uneasy talking with someone whose political affiliation is unknown. If a person attempts to maintain a position of aloofness or neutrality, he is likely to be regarded with suspicion and mistrusted by nearly everyone. People often express their dissatisfaction with such persons by calling them "Communists," which is understood to mean someone who works undercover toward subversive and vaguely evil ends. The truth is probably that lack of a party or factional commitment is an indication not of one's political beliefs but of his attitude toward society. He declines to be either client or patron; he presumes neither to need the support of his fellows nor to offer his own. A sincerely neutral person could only be antisocial, or if not that, then a spy or otherwise somehow subversive.[36]

The foregoing description applies to the vast majority of Paraguayans but not to all. A great many of the cosmopolitan, urban intellectuals have either become disillusioned altogether with the two traditional par-

[36] Frederic Hicks, "Politics, Power, and the Role of the Village Priest in Paraguay," *Journal of Inter-American Studies* 9 (April 1967): 273–282.

ties or cynically seek to take advantage of the prevailing pattern of party membership to suit their own purposes. From the former group arise the leaders of the newer and smaller parties, such as the Febrerista and Christian Democratic, plus the occasional true Communist and those who are simply apolitical. From the latter group are drawn many of the holders of civilian political posts, plus the inevitable bureaucrat who has learned to adjust to the situation as it is and to *añembotavy*, that is, to appear to accept everything in innocent good faith and retain a satisfactory middle-class job. But there are also many members of this class, including some of the country's foremost intellectuals, who are just as firmly loyal to the symbols and traditions of their party as is any peasant and whose view of politics is much the same.

LOCAL ORGANIZATION AND THE ROLE OF POLITICAL PARTIES

On the local level party members are organized into territorially based wards, called *seccionales* in case of the Colorados, and *comités* in the case of the Liberals. In theory and to a large extent in practice, the entire country is divided into wards whose boundaries generally coincide with other administrative boundaries, such as *distritos* (units comparable to New England townships or small Southern counties), *barrios* (wards) of cities, etc.[37] It is on this level that voting behavior and other forms of political activity can be most easily observed in Paraguay.

The party members of each ward elect a *comisión*, or governing body, which is charged with the task of mobilizing the party members and, particularly in the case of the Colorado seccionales, exercising vigilance over the opposition. Since the Colorado party is in power, the leaders of its seccionales often play important roles in local political affairs, and, especially in small communities, the presidency of the seccional is generally considered one of the three most important political positions, the others being that of *intendente*, or mayor (in those towns large enough to have this office), and that of police *comisario*. The activities of the seccionales and comités will presently be examined in more detail, but it will be worthwhile to examine first the electoral procedure. Unfortunately, I have sufficient data only for the Colorado party.

Each seccional is governed by a comisión of from twelve to thirty members, consisting of a president, one to three vice-presidents, one or two secretaries, a treasurer, and members-at-large (*vocales*). This leadership is elected by the vote of all Colorado party members in the ward and

---

[37] In Asunción, for example, there are (as of 1965) twenty-five Colorado *seccionales*, which are divided into *subseccionales*, and a reported forty-six orthodox Liberal (now Radical Liberal) *comités*.

holds office for three years. The election is supervised by the *Junta de Gobierno* (governing board) of the party, which has headquarters in Asunción, through an agency called the *Comisión de Reorganización Partidaria.* When the officials of a given seccional are about to complete their term of office, this agency appoints a delegation (*delegación*) to supervise the election of a new comisión. The delegation is normally headed by a prominent, well-known figure in the national government, assisted by one or two lesser party functionaries. Their duty is to go to the community in question, talk to the more influential party members, and try to get them to nominate and elect a comisión acceptable to the Junta de Gobierno.

The delegation generally tries to get all of the party members to agree on a single slate of candidates which can be elected without opposition, because this promotes party unity more effectively and avoids the formation of irreconcilable factions. This effort often requires repeated visits by the delegation to the community, in the course of which they make suggestions and then give the people time to consider them informally. Thus the precise date of the election is not set far in advance but merely for the winter of a given year; the actual election takes place when all preparations are complete. If a single slate of candidates cannot be agreed upon, a system of proportional representation assures the losing slate of at least some positions on the governing comisión, provided its margin of loss is slim.

Since the power of the seccional president depends heavily on his acceptance by the Junta de Gobierno, from which he derives his ability to bestow patronage, the delegation can pressure the electorate to vote for the slate it favors.[38] If not done adroitly, however, this can cause bitterness and may even intensify factional differences, leading many Colorados to be critical of what they regard as undue interference by the Junta delegation.

The seccional election takes place during the course of an *asamblea partidaria,* and is a major political and social event. The delegates come[39] and make speeches to the assembled party members in which they extoll

---

[38] Reasons for favoritism are various. For example, in Capiatá, in 1965, the party was divided into two factions, and the leader of the faction favored by the Junta de Gobierno impressed me as much less capable than his opponent, until it was pointed out to me by a Junta official that the latter man commuted to work in Asunción (20 km away) and often spent weeks away from Capiatá, hence could not keep closely in touch with local affairs.

[39] The description which follows is based on an asamblea which I witnessed, as a guest of the delegation, in a community not far from Villa Hayes in August 1964. Supplemental information was provided by informants who had witnessed or participated in other asambleas.

the party and its past and present leaders, particularly President Stroessner, and urge party unity, vigilance over the opposition, etc. Then the voting takes place, by acclamation if possible. This is followed by a feast, as lavish as local resources will permit, attended by the delegates and, ideally, most of the party members who were present at the voting. Drinking begins before the meal, and beer or wine is served with it. Toasts are offered with some regularity, and a dance is held in the afternoon.

The delegates from the Junta de Gobierno are expected to participate in all this. The chief of the delegation is usually a nationally prominent politician whose name has appeared frequently in the newspapers and is familiar to the people; except for this occasion they would probably never be privileged to actually meet him. But as the alcohol and the general festive mood breaks down reserve, ordinary peasants engage him in conversation and present to him their problems; he dances with the local girls, and the feeling is fostered that the leaders of the Colorado government, however exalted, maintain a close personal interest in the well-being of their fellow party members, however poor, in all parts of the country.

The occasion also provides an opportunity for young men seeking political advancement to bring themselves to the attention of the delegates (offering toasts and making impromptu speeches is one way of doing this) and to make contacts which may later be useful. At the same time, the delegates, representing the national party leadership, come to know and evaluate the principal party leaders in the community. I have had occasion to be impressed with the extent to which party officials in Asunción, through the obligation to serve on such delegations, have come to know and understand local problems and personalities in many parts of the country. From what little information I have been able to gather, the same appears to be true of their Liberal counterparts.

It is primarily through the local seccional organization that party cohesion is maintained, and this in turn is an important factor strengthening government control over the country, lightening the task of the police and military forces in keeping such control.

One of the stated functions of the seccional organization is to attend to the welfare of fellow party members. Sometimes this is done in a very direct way, by paying funeral expenses, providing legal aid, distributing necessary school supplies to children of poor Colorado families, and the like. If necessary, collections are taken up locally, but the party headquarters also provides funds for this purpose (all government employees are required to donate 5 percent of their salary to the party).[40]

---

[40] The published expenses of the party for the period September 1963-September 1964, which total Gs. 7,481,906, include as the largest single item Gs.

In other cases such welfare is attended to by means of recommendations. A letter of recommendation from the president of a seccional is important and sometimes essential in order to obtain government employment of any kind, and such a recommendation may carry more weight than one from a teacher in gaining admission to one of the country's few public (virtually free) secondary schools. The seccional leadership may attempt to exert pressure on private employers to give preferences in hiring to persons recommended by them or to make contributions to the welfare of the seccional, but their power to do this varies; they are likely to be more successful where the community is heavily Colorado and where the enterprise concerned is Paraguayan-owned and dependent on government contracts or patronage. The government, however, is the country's largest employer, and as in most underdeveloped countries, jobs are scarce and much in demand. A steady job makes an excellent reward for political services rendered.

Another acknowledged function of the seccional and one of the most important from the point of view of the national government is political vigilance. Party members are supposed to keep watch over all public institutions, to see that they are operated properly. But more important, they are urged to watch all opposition political activity and report whatever they observe to the seccional leaders or, if appropriate, to the police. They are warned to be on guard against "Communists" (a term applied to all people who agitate for change without government approval), mysterious strangers, and the like. Especially in the more remote areas of the country, any stranger is regarded with suspicion, and if the suspicion is great enough, force may be used to drive him from the community.

The seccional leaders and their followers are expected to watch for any gathering of people known to be affiliated with opposition parties and to be sure the local police detachment is informed (during much of its recent history, Paraguay has been under a state of siege, and any meeting has required a police permit). This emphasis on vigilance has given rise to the individual called a *pyragüé,* originally a furtive character out of Guaraní folklore, whose body is all covered with hair, even the soles of his feet so he can walk very silently. The term now refers to

2,000,000 for 20,000 *guardapolvos*—the white smocks that form the principal part of the obligatory school uniform. Other items include Gs. 440,000 for 40,000 "President Stroessner" school notebooks, Gs. 100,000 for 40,000 pencils, Gs. 66,500 for 700 first and second grade readers, and Gs. 154,000 for 15,400 boxes of colored pencils. Also in the list of expenses were Gs. 312,000 for the distribution of 1,200 blankets, Gs. 496,350 for medicines and hospital bills, and Gs. 381,000 for the distribution of toys on epiphany (*Patria* [Asunción], 27 September 1964).

a person who seeks to listen in and inform the authorities of opposition political activity.

The Liberal party's directorate corresponds to the Colorado party's Junta de Gobierno. However, since this party is out of power, its members are only part-time political workers. They seek to maintain contact with Liberal leaders in all parts of the country, train future political leaders, and take care of the material needs of the local comité members as best they can. Providing legal aid for its members is a particularly important function of this party. Liberals are encouraged to contribute financially to their party, and because of their numbers they are able to obtain enough to keep the party organization functioning, although they are unable to require such contributions. The party directorate works on a national level to reduce discrimination against Liberals with regard to economic opportunities. On a local level, the Liberals frequently take sides as a bloc in Colorado factional disputes. Lacking voting power, they cannot influence directly the outcome of seccional elections, but by their numbers and what economic resources they command they can give their favorite some additional power or influence in the community. Since the party, except for a small splinter group, was technically illegal prior to its reorganization in 1966 as the Radical Liberal party, the activities of the Liberal comités, including their elections, had to be carried on quietly and unobtrusively.

The Colorado and Liberal parties are the only ones that have this extensive local organization. In small communities, members of other parties are rarely encountered. One may find an occasional Febrerista, usually a Chaco War veteran who became a follower of Franco during the war and who, now middle-aged or older, has retained this loyalty. An occasional thoughtful, dissatisfied, and religious man may declare himself a Christian Democrat. But the two traditional parties retain their hold over the mass of the people, despite the fact that the leadership of these two parties has usually been in the hands of men whose understanding of and responsiveness to the needs of the lower classes has generally been limited to the minimum necessary to retain an adequate degree of party cohesion.

This hold is maintained, however, not because of the ideologies of the parties—indeed, they are rarely thought of as having ideologies—but because of their function as mutual aid societies and channels of social mobility. They function this way because they are among the most important channels through which patronage is dispensed. The two traditional parties (and only these two) provide the means whereby a man can achieve the power to become a patron and thereby acquire a clientele which may bring him still greater power. Opportunities to achieve power outside the political party structure are few, and even these generally require the power-holder to maintain a balance between power blocs which are based on the party structure.[41]

A side effect of this role of the political parties is that when non-intellectually-inclined, provincially-oriented Paraguayans become concerned over matters of civic improvement, or social or economic conditions, they are not likely to think of these as problems to be tackled in the political arena. They are not likely to support candidates for political office who would promise to improve conditions. To them, politics means patronage. Civil or social improvements have nothing to do with politics, and must be brought about in other ways.

THE TWO-PARTY SYSTEM AND THE STABILITY OF CAUDILLISMO

The maintenance of the Paraguayan political system depends, I suggest, on the assumption that each of the two traditional parties has approximately the same number of members, each drawing its membership from all socioeconomic levels, and between them commanding the loyalty of the vast majority of the people. No figures are available on the precise numerical strength of either party, and it would be imprudent to try to gather such information. It seems to be generally understood that whichever party is in power tends to gain membership at the expense of the other because of its greater access to sources of patronage; but it has been assumed that such gains are relatively small and that the numerical strength of the two big parties is more or less equal.[42]

Such equality, or the assumption of such equality, seems essential for two reasons. The first is that it keeps attention focused on the mutual-aid role of the political parties and the second that it diverts attention from the fact that basic social and economic problems are not being met. The Colorado party is able to retain the allegiance of its people largely by its ability to maintain a spirit of rivalry against a powerful opposing party and by giving its followers certain advantages in the competition for jobs, political favors, and protection. Advantages, that is, over the Liberals;

---

[41] See Hicks, "Politics Power," for an illustration.

[42] A survey conducted among Asunción university students in 1965 revealed that, of those willing to respond to a question concerning political affiliation, 36 percent claimed Colorado affiliation, 32 percent Liberal, 20 percent Christian Democratic, and 12 percent Febrerista (university students presumably represent largely the urban, cosmopolitan sector, hence the high proportion of nontraditional affiliations). However, 62 percent declined to give their political affiliation. See Domingo M. Rivarola, "Universidad y estudiantes," pp. 62–63.

and it is because there are so many Liberals to oppose and to compare themselves with that the Colorados can see this relative advantage. If this comparison were not kept constantly before them, they might make other comparisons, which could lead to increasing discontent with the system.

The Liberals are in a similar position. Because their party is out of power, they must stick together for mutual protection against the Colorados. Because of its large following, the Liberal party is able to provide a measure of security for its people by giving them some legal and financial aid when needed. By being well organized and led by sophisticated and influential men (whose influence is often derived from colleague relationships with their Colorado counterparts), it can also prevent excessive oppression by the dominant Colorados. Again, rivalry with the Colorados, and the need for protection, leads rank and file Liberals to concentrate on the distinction between Liberal and Colorado rather than on social and economic distinctions.

The second reason for the maintenance of the two-party system is that it limits the clientele among whom patronage need be distributed. As the nature of foreign investment in the Paraguayan economy changes and the proportion of economic resources available for disposal through the patronage system diminishes, the system of caudillismo is able to survive because the proportion of the population that need be benefited is limited to the membership of one political party and, on a local level, often to only one faction within it. Because of the prevailing view of the role of political parties, this forms a socially acceptable way of depriving half or more of the population of a share of the scarce benefits. The rank and file Liberals complain of specific instances of this deprivation, but they accept the system, for they know that when the day comes that their party can seize power the tables will be turned.

Significantly, the Colorado party does not maintain a policy of encouraging wholesale and indiscriminate recruitment of Liberals to the Colorado banner. Apparently, neither party has ever maintained such a policy when it was in power. Joining a political party is a formal matter. As he nears voting age, a youth of Liberal parents may sometimes be approached to become a Colorado, or he may solicit membership in the party, but he must have the acceptance of the seccional leadership and will be provided with a political "tutor"; he is not admitted to formal party membership until his continuing loyalty seems certain. The prevailing pattern is to respect the Liberal who stays with his party even when it is at a disadvantage. Despite the flamboyant and militant rhetoric heard at political rallies, the frequent harassment of Liberal political leaders, and even the occasional periods of anti-Liberal terrorism, the ruling Colorados have consciously refrained from taking any measures that would seriously diminish Liberal party membership.

It also appears that local Colorado factional leaders do not seek to gain more adherents than are necessary for them to control access to patronage. However, the national party leadership does strive to prevent local factions from forming, since in the past dissident factions of the party in power have sometimes helped the rival party to overthrow the government.

This is a system in which national elections, with the presidency at stake, would appear to be dysfunctional. Yet, due to a combination of historical circumstances and the nature of Paraguay's international relations (which require that a somewhat democratic image be projected), periodic elections must be held. Prior to 1968, such elections were usually single-candidate affairs, or otherwise conducted in such a way as to make one think they were deliberately designed not to be taken seriously. The assumption that the two parties were numerically equal was never put to the test. However, as the world-wide spirit of reform and revolution began to be felt in Paraguay, it must have become evident that the system would be endangered by keeping the Liberals underground and thus receptive to ideas which, in Paraguay, are best diffused underground. The Febreristas and Christian Democrats had been granted recognition as political parties, eligible to participate in elections, in 1964 and 1966 respectively. Lacking a ready-made clientele, they could hardly do otherwise than campaign on issues of policy and ideology.

In 1965 many Liberals supported Febrerista candidates in the nationwide municipal elections. A survey of political preferences of Asunción university students in that year showed rather striking gains for the Christian Democrats.[43] By 1968 there was little choice but to allow the Liberals (now called Radical Liberals) full participation in the national elections. The alternative would have been the growth of the ideologically-based parties at the expense of the patronage-based Liberals, and a change in the whole nature of politics.

The published figures gave the Liberals only about one quarter as many votes as the Colorados.[44] Paraguayans have been conditioned not to expect their elections to be honest and so may not accept these figures. They are at least plausible, however, and if people accept them as true, they must also acknowledge that the two parties are in fact quite unequal in numbers. The Liberals will thus have to gain adherents from the

[43] Ibid.
[44] *Louisville Times,* 12 February 1968.

Colorado ranks, which they may find they can most easily do by introducing real issues and advocating meaningful and significant reforms. In any case, electoral competition between the two major parties, which circumstances have apparently forced the government to accept, may well prove incompatible with the continuation of caudillo politics.

Emily M. Nett
Department of Sociology
University of Evansville
Evansville, Indiana

THE FUNCTIONAL ELITES OF QUITO*

When the educated natives of the capital city of Ecuador are questioned about social class and the power structure of their country, the answer comes unhesitatingly and with little variation. Everyone, and of course the educated are as yet few in number, knows who is who and what is what. The sampler of random opinion concludes that the real power is no longer in Quito but in the port of Guayaquil. This has been documented by Díaz,[1] who claims that the traditional aristocracy today owns only about 50 percent of sierran acreage, most of it impoverished and ruined, and that this class is declining steadily with the growth of various coastal "bourgeoisie" classes which stem from the commercial and banking interests of the coast. Politically, too, according to Lang,[2] the coastal influence is undermining that of the sierra, the deposition of the military junta in 1966 being attributable to pressures from the Guayaquil commercial oligarchy.

Furthermore, it is generally believed that the eligible members of the old upper class, formerly the source of political and intellectual leaders, are not acting in these capacities relative to prior modernization trends set in motion since World War II. Members of the Quito upper class

* Partial funds for the research reported in this paper were provided by a Faculty Research Grant, Texas Southern University, Houston, Texas, 1967–1968.

1 A. Díaz, "Cambios sociales de las clases dominantes del Ecuador," *Revista mexicana de sociología* 25 (1963): 721–736.

2 Norris G. Lang, "Plutocrats, Managers, and Workers: An Analysis of the Social Organization of a Coastal Ecuadorian Plantation." (Doctoral dissertation, Department of Anthropology, University of Illinois, Urbana, Illinois, 1969).

may still exercise some authority behind the scene, mostly blocking and preventing programs originating elsewhere, but their leadership contributions to the affairs of the country are negligible, according to popular belief.

The purpose of this paper is to focus on questions stemming from the second of these widely held opinions, that is: the Quito upper class influence on the elites is declining. It must be presumed that the consensus of educated quiteños regarding the power structure of the nation is at least an approximation of the situation. The coastal-sierra split is a political reality, although undoubtedly a gross oversimplification as an explanatory concept. The division is certainly more than a matter of conservative versus liberal politics today, as Blanksten[3] points out. Perhaps the international economic interest theory of Lang[4] combined with the legitimacy vacuum theory of Needler[5] contributes to a better understanding of the power situation. At any rate, these data on functional elites in Quito are presented with the knowledge that their ultimate interpretation requires a framework which is known mostly by conjecture.

Ecuador is a country which should by no means be considered "typical" of Latin America, if indeed any such country exists. Perhaps it is typical of the "witness people" as described by Ribeiro,[6] but if so, it is distinguishable by at least the following three characteristics: its geographic isolation, its size, and its primarily agricultural economic base, which has taken the form of monoculture. These variables are all reflected in the appearance and structure of the capital. Quito today is considered one of the most beautiful and conservative capital cities of Latin America, though not the most traditional city in Ecuador. It is relatively quiet, colonial in style of architecture, and its streets are crowded with barefoot Indians in native dress. The factors mentioned for the country as a whole have special significance for Quito when combined with some others also in evidence in most Latin American cities. The political instability of the national government it houses, the influx of illiterate rural migrants without corresponding employment opportunities, and the remarkably persistent remnants of feudalism would all seemingly have

---

[3] George I. Blanksten, "Ecuador: The Politics of Instability," in *Political Systems of Latin America,* Martin C. Needler, ed. (Princeton, New Jersey: D. Van Nostrand Company, Inc., 1964).

[4] Lang, "Political Instability: The Industrial Elite of Coastal Ecuador" (presented to the Third Annual Conference on Latin America, University of Houston, 1968).

[5] Martin Needler, *Anatomy of a Coup d'Etat: Ecuador 1963* (Washington: Institute for the Comparative Study of Political Systems, 1964).

[6] Darey Ribeiro, "Universities and Social Development," in *Elites in Latin America,* Seymour Lipset and Aldo Solari, eds. (New York: Oxford Press, 1967).

given special advantages to the members of the traditional upper class in maintaining what Lenski[7] originally termed "status crystallization" and what Whiteford[8] identified in his study of the traditional unchanging Colombian city, Popayán, as a lack of "incongruities in the possession of the symbols of social status" among the upper class.

On the other hand, modernization, to be understood in Eisenstadt's[9] meaning of increasing separation of roles held by individuals, a high level of technology and specialization and intensification of power in central agencies which is accompanied by rationality and populism, is occurring even in the sierra of Ecuador. Silvert[10] has characterized the rate of economic development of the country as "average" for Latin American countries.

To the extent that both forces toward traditionality and modernity are operating, the following hypotheses are suggested for Quito:

1. Members of the upper class participate in the sociocultural life of the city as elites to a lesser extent than formerly but to a greater extent than they are required to do where modernization is taking place rapidly or has already been accomplished.

2. The elite turnover rate in the last ten or fifteen years has not been as great in Quito as that for more modernized cities, the same people who are active today having been in important positions a decade ago. Younger persons are more specialized and less extensively engaged.

Distinguishing the elite from the upper class, Baltzell[11] concluded,

> The *elite* concept refers to those individuals who are the most successful and stand at the top of the functional (objective) class hierarchy. These individuals are leaders in their chosen occupations or professions; they are the final decision-makers in in the political, economic, or military spheres as well as leaders in such professions as law, engineering, medicine, education, religion, and the arts. On the other hand, in any comparatively stable social structure, over the years, certain elite members and their families will tend to associate with one another in var-

---

[7] Gerhart Lenski, "Status Crystallization: A Non-Vertical Dimension of Social Status," *The American Sociological Review* 19 (1954): 405–413.

[8] Andrew H. Whiteford, *Two Cities of Latin America: A Comparative Description,* (Beloit, Wisconsin: The Legan Museum of Anthropology, 1960).

[9] S. N. Eisenstadt, *Modernization: Protest and Change* (Englewood, New Jersey: Prentice-Hall, Inc., 1966).

[10] Kalman Silvert, "Nationalism in Latin America," in *The Dynamics of Change in Latin American Politics,* John D. Martz, ed. (Englewood, New Jersey: Prentice-Hall, Inc., 1965).

[11] Edward D. Baltzell, " 'Who's Who in America' and 'The Social Register': Elite in Upperclass Indexes in Metropolitan America" in *Class, Status, and Power,* 3rd ed., R. Bendix and S. M. Lipset, eds. (New York: Free Press, 1966), pp. 266–276.

> ious primary group situations and gradually develop a consciousness of kind and distinctive style of life. The *upper class* concept, then refers to a group of families, descendents of successful individuals (elite members) one, two, or three generations ago, who are at the top of the social (subjective) class hierarchy.

In a later formulation of the elite concept, Aron[12] has distinguished between what he calls the elite as the broadest category, which includes all those in diverse activities who are high in important or privileged positions either in terms of wealth or prestige, and two other narrower categories, the political class and the ruling class. The political class is comprised of those who actually exercise the political function of government. The ruling class includes those privileged people who, without exercising actual political functions, influence those who govern and those who obey. The influence of the ruling class derives from the moral authority which they hold, or from the economic or financial power they possess. In this paper "elite" is used in Aron's broadest sense; the prerogative to make final decisions which Baltzell extends to all elites is viewed as being only that of the ruling class. Keller's[13] term "strategic elites" seems to include the same categories of influential persons that Baltzell's more operationally derived "functional elites" covers.

The method of the study is similar to that of Baltzell, who used the *Who's Who* as an indicator of elite status and the *Social Register* as an index of upper-class groupings. Lacking both sources for Quito in recent years, I obtained lists of traditional upper-class families and new upper-class persons from informants and of elite persons from newspapers and organizational directories. Information for 1951 was obtained from a *Who's Who in Quito* (1954). Returns from an autobiographical questionnaire mailed to the 532 elite persons active in 1964 constitute about 14 percent of the mailing, a total of 76 questionnaires being the basis for the following discussion. In terms of the two major classes to which individuals had been assigned, the returns were representative of the mailing, approximately 78 percent having been middle-class and 22 percent upper-class. Within the upper class, there was a slight overrepresentation of the traditional upper class and an underrepresentation of the new upper class.

The traditional upper class are well-established Quito families (same

---

[12] Raymond Aron, "Social Class, Political Class, Ruling Class," *European Journal of Sociology* 1 (1960): 260–281, translated in Bendix and Lipset, eds., *Class, Status, and Power*.

[13] Suzanne Keller, *Beyond the Ruling Class* (New York: Random House, 1963).

maternal and paternal name) of good reputation (ideally descended or with the myth of descent from Spanish royalty or conquistadors) who view intermarriage as the ideal and tend to exclude as marriage mates for their children persons of other classes. Included are three foreigners (United States, Spain, Colombia) who had married into good Quito families and several other upper-class families from other Ecuadorian cities who as a result of long-time residence and interests were thought to belong. The new upper class are socially acceptable but not yet married into the traditional upper class.

Figures comparing the elite sample with the questionnaires mailed, by social class, are shown in Table 1.

TABLE 1

THE SAMPLE OF ELITES COMPARED WITH THE QUESTIONNAIRES MAILED, BY SOCIAL CLASS

Social Class	*Questionnaires Mailed*	*Questionnaires Returned*
Traditional Upper	7%	13%
New Upper	16	9
Middle	77	78
Total	100	100
N	532	76

The first hypothesis of this investigation related to differential participation in the sociocultural life of the city by the upper class. Taking a hypothetical model of absolute monopoly of the elite positions by the upper class of 100 percent and complete abandonment of these positions to the middle class as zero percent—both of which conditions never exist in actuality—Quito with the upper class contributing 20 percent of the elites appears far from a situation of perfect status consistency. This distance from the model of absolute monopoly appears to be the result of the emergence and subsequent growth of the "middle sector," as Gillin[14] has termed this category. The expansion of this class of persons in turn reflects changes in the occupational structure. The proportion of upper-class to middle-class employed adults for the entire country has been estimated by Torres[15] as six persons in occupations called upper-class for each 94 persons in middle-class occupations. I believe the uni-

[14] John P. Gillin, "Some Sign Posts for Policy," in *Social Change in Latin America Today,* Richard N. Adams et al, eds. (New York: Harper and Brothers, 1960).

[15] Reinaldo Torres Caicedo, *Los estratos socioeconómicos del Ecuador* (Quito, Ecuador: La Junta de Planificación y Coordinación Económica, 1960).

versity attendance reflects more accurately the occupational distribution of employable adults for the city than the census data for the country as a whole. The 1965 data of Blaise and Rodríquez[16] show that for each 20 upper-class students there are 80 middle-class students in the two universities in Quito. The replication of the elite proportions in the student population does not appear to me as coincidental; both phenomena stem from the occupational structure or the sometimes-called "objective" stratification system.

The 20 percent of the elites deriving from the upper class in Quito can be compared with the average upper-class participation of 23 percent in the twelve oldest metropolitan areas in the United States in 1940 reported by Baltzell. Upper-class contributions to the elites in those cities ranged from a high of 29 percent for Philadelphia, an old conservative eastern seaboard city, to 11 percent for Chicago, one of the younger, more rapidly changing social structures.

In the above analysis participation has been viewed from the point of view of upper-class contributions to the elites. The question under consideration was, "What percentage of the elites are upper-class?" Focusing on the social class instead of the functional position, the question can be rephrased, "What percentage of the upper class are elites?" In Quito in 1964 fifteen percent of the traditional upper-class active adults were elites. This compares with only four percent for Philadelphia in 1940. From this perspective the Quito upper class appears to be highly involved in the community. This involvement can only be interpreted, however, in terms of the type of participation.

By occupation as well as by degree of participation, Quito upper-class elites differ from their counterparts in North American cities. If occupations are combined into five categories of functional elites, in both Quito and Philadelphia the upper class as a proportion of all in the category is highest for the business elite, "business" including industrialists, businessmen, lawyers, engineers, and bankers. Table 2 shows the percentage distributions. The Quito upper-class occupations in this category are lawyers and industrialists; the Philadelphia elite is in medicine and architecture. The Quito upper class is not represented among either the artists and authors elite or the church and educators elite; in Philadelphia there were upper-class persons in both these elite categories. The Quito middle-class elites are similar to the Philadelphia ones except that the Quito middle class contributes to a slightly greater extent to the busi-

[16] Hans Blaise and Luis Rodríguez, "Students and the Social Order," manuscript, 1967 (study of institution building by the University of Pittsburg; an AID Project).

ness elite and to the church and educators elite than the Philadelphia middle class does.

TABLE 2

FUNCTIONAL ELITES FOR QUITO 1964 AND PHILADELPHIA 1940

Elite Category	*Philadelphia* Social Register	Who's Who	SR as Pct of Total	*Quito* Upper Class	Middle Class	UC as Pct of Total
Business*	47%	20%	49%	58%	32%	34%
Opinion & Political	6	13	16	18	15	25
Medicine & Architecture	12	8	39	6	8	17
Church & Education	17	40	15		15	
Artists & Authors	11	14	24		12	
Others	7	5	38	12	15	17
Total	100	100	29%	100	100	22%
N	226	554		16	56	

* Includes Businessmen, Lawyers, Engineers, and Bankers.

The second hypothesis of this study is that elite turnover in Quito has not been great, although younger elites of today are more specialized occupationally than those who were also elites thirteen years prior to the investigation. About half of the persons participating in the affairs of the community in 1964 had also been active in 1951; upper-class persons, more than middle-class persons, tend to be active in both periods as can be seen in Table 3. Persistence in personnel at this rate is found despite two new constitutionally elected governments, both coalition types, and two coup d'etats, one of which installed the military junta which was in power at the time of this study. In connection with this low turnover rate, Needler[17] has described the men involved in the military overthrow as almost all having been active in previous governments. The same is the case with the candidates for the recent elections of June 1968. All three of the prospective candidates for the past coalition of radical liberals and socialist parties, called the Ecuadorian Left Wing Front, were elites, two of whom are listed in the 1951 Quito *Who's Who*, the other one being a Guayaquileño. (The candidates for the nomination were Dr. Raúl Clemente Huerta [Guayaquil], Dr. Andrés Córdova, and Dr. Julio Moreno Espinosa. Dr. Córdova received it.) Both the populist and right wing candidates were former presidents of the nation and of course both were

[17] Needler, *Anatomy of a coup d'Etat.*

listed in the same publication. (Dr. José María Velasco Ibarra was the candidate of the Velasquista party and Dr. Camilio Ponce Enriques of the Christian Social Democrats.) The winner of the election, Dr. Velasco Ibarra, has three times before filled the office.

TABLE 3

QUITO ELITES IN *Who's Who* FOR 1951 AND 1964, BY CLASS

Class	*Both 1964 and 1951*	*Only 1964*	*Both as a Pct of Total*
Traditional Upper	19%	7%	70%
New Upper	11	7	57
Middle	70	85	43
Total	100	99	48%
N	37	39	

With regard to specialization, younger men were more likely to hold a university degree and to have training beyond that degree, as indicated in Table 4. Except for the fact that age differentials do not exist for participation as government officials, younger men differ by type of occupation. Many more persons under fifty-three years of age were engaged in business, industry, and banking. (The average age for all elites was forty-eight years. The standard deviation was not computed, but five years were arbitrarily added to ensure the older group did include mostly those of another generation.) Furthermore, they held corresponding degrees in business administration, economics, engineering, and public administration. These persons fifty-three years and over were more likely to be practicing the traditional professions of law, medicine, and university teaching, to be artists, musicians, and writers, or to be career military men or religious functionaries. These percentages appear in Table 5.

TABLE 4

EDUCATION OF ELITES BORN BEFORE 1912
COMPARED WITH THOSE BORN IN 1912 AND AFTER

Education	*Date of Birth* *Before*	*After*	*1912 & After as a Pct of Total*
Primary	5%	0%	0%
Secondary	10	4	50
Special Training	16	7	57
University Attendance	16	9	62
Graduated University	37	54	81
Postgraduate	16	26	82
Total	100	100	73%
N	19	54	

TABLE 5

PRESENT POSITION OF ELITES BORN BEFORE 1912 AND BORN IN 1912 AND AFTER

Position	Date of Birth: Before	Date of Birth: After	1912 & After as a Pct of Total
Government Official	35%	38%	75%
Business & Industry	10	22	85
Practicing Profession	10	16	82
Banking		7	100
Officers in Professional & Scientific Organizations	20	5	43
Officials in University or Other Cultural Organizations	5	4	67
Fine Arts & Literature	10	4	50
Politics & Opinion		2	100
Military		2	100
Religious Functionary	5		0
Retired	5		0
Total	100	100	73%
N	20	55	

In general, these scant data lend support to the expectations of the investigation: that, even though modernization is occurring in sierran Ecuador, the upper class continues to influence the life of the community visibly. The elites as a whole, though the upper class to a lesser extent than the new middle class, reflect structural changes in the social system. Younger elites function in more specialized and technologically based roles. Thus the evidence is also in accord with the popular notion that the upper class today is not participating in the community in the same manner it previously did; and the difference is not so much in terms of the quantitative differences.

Members of the elite are involved in a more limited range of occupations and positions than formerly, having been displaced almost altogether in art and literature, but they are still dominant in the area of politics and opinion-making. Unless, or until, the educational base in Ecuador is considerably broadened, the upper class will continue to be the source of recruitment for the functional elites in greater degree than it is in more modern nations. However, the characterization of the functional elites is obviously becoming more middle-class. That is, increasingly the elites include people who are neither of the governing class nor of the ruling class. The evidence seems to lend support to Keller's[18] thesis that modern societies have specialized but functionally interdependent elites in place of a traditional ruling class. Perhaps Ecuador has gone "beyond the ruling class."

[18] Keller, *Beyond the Ruling Class* (New York: Random House, 1963).

Edward J. Mullen
Department of Modern Languages
Purdue University
Lafayette, Indiana

CONTEMPORÁNEOS IN MEXICAN INTELLECTUAL HISTORY, 1928-1931

The controversial Mexican literary periodical *Contemporáneos* (1928–1931) has recently received considerable attention from literary critics who view it as a significant document in the history of twentieth-century Mexican *belles lettres*.[1] The journal was not, however, exclusively a literary review but, as the subtitle (*Revista de Cultura Mexicana*) clearly indicates, a magazine of varied cultural pursuits as well. It contained a number of important essays in which the members of Mexico's post-revolutionary intelligentsia attempted to define and interpret national problems. It will be the purpose of this essay to discuss the role played by the journal in Mexican intellectual history.

In June 1928 the first issue of *Contemporáneos* appeared in the bookshops of Mexico City. The events leading up to its publication and the reasons for its sudden cessation in December 1931 can be traced to the activities of a group of young Mexican intellectuals later to be classified by the title of this their most significant literary review. The writers who have been grouped within this literary generation are: Jorge Cuesta (1903–1942), Enrique González Rojo (1889–1939), José Gorostiza (1901–), Salvador Novo (1904–), Bernardo Ortiz de Mon-

[1] For the most complete study of the literary aspects of the journal and the group of writers who edited it see Merlin Forster, *Los Contemporáneos 1920–32, perfil de un experimento vanguardista mexicano* (México: Ediciones de Andrea, 1964). Professor Forster's work contains copious bibliographic data on all of the editors of the journal (see pp. 127–145). No attempt has been made to reproduce these citations in the present study which focuses primarily on nonliterary aspects of the review.

tellano (1889–1949), Gilberto Owen (1905–1952), Jaime Torres Bodet (1902–), and Xavier Villaurrutia (1903–1950).

The formation of the "Contemporáneos," this famed "grupo de amigos," [2] began with the association of the aforementioned writers in the Escuela Nacional Preparatoria during the chaotic period of post-revolutionary adjustment. Of particular importance in the intellectual formation of the Contemporáneos was the influence of the members of the renowned Ateneo de México: Antonio Caso, Enrique González Martínez, Alfonso Reyes, and José Vasconcelos.[3] Torres Bodet wrote: "Más que su influencia directa, lo que recibimos a través de ellos fue el mensaje del mundo literario y filosófico, en que iban plasmando sus propias conquistas" (*C*, II, 4, 26).[4] In 1918 the bonds of group solidarity among the Contemporáneos were further strengthened by the organization of the Ateneo de la Juventud. More literary than philosophic in orientation, the Ateneo brought together a number of Mexico's young thinkers.

Characteristic of Spanish American letters, political phenomena strongly influenced the activities of the Contemporáneos. With the fall of the government of Venustiano Carranza in 1920 and the inauguration of sweeping changes by Álvaro Obregón, many of the Contemporáneos secured positions in the new bureaucracy. Torres Bodet, for example, was appointed secretary of the Escuela Nacional Preparatoria in 1921 and in 1922 became head of the Department of Libraries. Fortified with the financial backing and prestige of their government positions, many of the writers collaborated on a series of literary reviews from 1920 to 1928. The fruition of their experiences on these journals was the publication of *Contemporáneos.*

The first eight numbers, published with the support of Dr. Bernardo Gastélum under the auspices of the Department of Health, established the format of the review and subtly stated its basic credos. Internal political changes in the Mexican government, caused by the assassination of President Obregón in July 1928 and the election of Emilio Portes Gil as chief of state, were to affect the publication of the last thirty-five issues of *Contemporáneos.* As a result of the political upheaval, Gastélum lost the directorship of the Department of Health and, accompanied by

[2] Alfredo Cardona Peña, *Semblanzas mexicanas* (México: Ediciones de Libro-Mex., 1955), p. 126.

[3] For a discussion of the influence of this group on Mexican thought, see María Rosa Santos, "El Ateneo de la Juventud: su influencia en la vida intelectual de México" (unpubl. diss., University of Florida, 1965).

[4] All references to the journal *Contemporáneos* will follow this form in my text.

González Rojo, went on a diplomatic mission to Italy. Another central figure in the group's activities, Torres Bodet, accepted a diplomatic position in Paris. After this sudden loss of patronage in the Department of Health and the absence of several of the editors, the directorship of *Contemporáneos* was delegated to Ortiz de Montellano. The financial backing of the journal was assumed by Genaro Estrada,[5] assistant secretary in the Ministry of Foreign Relations.[6]

Ortiz de Montellano edited the journal until its sudden cessation in December 1931. A careful examination of the last numbers gives no reason to suspect economic or editorial difficulties.[7] The sudden termination of the review has been variously explained. Alfredo Cardona Peña attributed it to the simultaneous illness of Ortiz de Montellano and the loss of Genaro Estrada's patronage in the Department of Foreign Relations.[8] Jefferson Rea Spell did not refer to the sickness of the director but alluded to a general decline in the solidarity of the editors caused by the absence of Estrada: "Its demise is traceable to the departure for Madrid of Genaro Estrada, the inspiration of the younger poets." [9] Salvador Novo explained that the journal's cessation was due to the entrance of a number of the editors into the diplomatic service: "Su repentina suspensión se debió a que simultáneamente ingresaron en el servicio diplomático los principales autores de la publicación, y se alejaron de México." [10] Abreu Gómez spoke of political factors: "Los cambios políticos dieron al traste con la revista. Ya no hubo dinero para sostenerla." [11]

While explaining the immediate circumstances which forced the journal to cease publication, the aforementioned factors fail to account

---

5 Alfonso Reyes (*Obras Completas*, 18 vols. (Mexico: Fondo de Cultura Económica, 1958, XII, 175) spoke of him in the following manner: "Era Genaro Estrada una de esas instituciones de la ciudad, uno de esos hombres centrales que hacen posible la organización de las pléyades literarias (El Pen Club de México sólo vivió mientras estuvo a su sombra, y lo mismo la revista *Contemporáneos*). Era un padrino natural de los libros. Y era la suya una de esas bondades sin aureola y sin exceso de santidad, tan lejana de la falsa austeridad y de los morbosos lujos de aislamiento y tebaidas [sic]."

6 Cardona Peña, *Semblanzas,* p. 21.

7 For example, only two issues before the cessation of *Contemporáneos* the editors welcomed the collaboration of Antonio Castro Leal: "*Contemporáneos* cuenta a partir de este número, con la inteligente colaboración que desde Europa le ofrece Antonio Castro Leal, ensayista muy estimado por sus estudios de la literatura inglesa" (*C,* XI, 38–39, 112).

8 Cardona Peña, *Semblanzas,* p. 121.

9 Jefferson Rea Spell, "Mexican Literary Periodicals of the Twentieth Century," *PMLA* 54 (September 1939): 840.

10 Personal letter from Salvador Novo, 30 June 1967.

11 Abreu Gómez, *Las revistas literarias de México* (México: Instituto Nacional de Bellas Artes, 1963), p. 183.

for the feelings of hostility towards the journal's editors harbored by prominent members of Mexican literary circles. This hostility may explain, in part, why Ortiz de Montellano was not able to find financial backing for the review after the departure of Genaro Estrada in 1931.[12]

The arguments of the critics of *Contemporáneos* who claimed that the journal was a "capilla hermética y europeizante" [13] lose all validity when an inventory of the essays treating Mexican themes is undertaken. The entire spectrum of Mexican culture is treated in the journal. Although the majority of the writers treated specialized aspects such as art, literature, or history, Bernardo J. Gastélum, Alfonso Reyes, and Samuel Ramos wrote a series of broadly philosophic interpretations of Mexican life.

Gastélum, the founder of *Contemporáneos,* contributed six important essays which treated diverse aspects of Mexican culture, history, and politics. One of the basic concerns of Gastélum's writing is the theme of cultural regeneration. In his essay, "Espíritu del héroe" (*C*, I, 1, 1–14), which served somewhat as a manifesto for the journal, he called for a reevaluation of contemporary beliefs. The Renaissance, Gastélum affirmed, was the last period of intellectual growth. Modern man, stifled by tradition, has entered into a period of cultural stagnation. "Espíritu del héroe" is a plea for the creation of a new set of esthetic values: "Edifiquemos con estos valores—en el presente—el estilo de una nueva sensibilidad ética y abandonemos el absurdo de descubrir en las ruinas de una realidad que fue" (p. 4).

The same plan for intellectual revitalization was sounded in "Pensar en vez de recordar" (*C*, VI, 20, 8–20). Since the days of the Roman Empire, Gastélum notes, man has done nothing but "recurrir a lo tradicional para plasmar el presente" (p. 15). This recourse to memory rather than thought has fatal implications for modern society. A failure to keep abreast of technical advancement and social change through creative thinking points the way to cultural retardation. Gastélum draws his argument from the plane of the abstract to the concrete in his closing remarks: "Hay que preguntarse si a la revolución mexicana no la distingue este carácter, si lleva dentro de sí algún propósito y si se ha preocupado por la

[12] With reference to the problem of financial backing Abreu Gómez (*Las revistas,* p. 183) wrote: "Bernardo, entusiasta y crédulo, pensó que era posible que cada número lo pagara una secretaría. Hizo gestiones . . . hablamos con señores y señorones y hasta con señoras de copete. . . . Al fin nos dimos cuenta que hacía falta otro Genaro Estrada. . . . La revista había muerto."

[13] Ermilo Abreu Gómez, *Sala de retratos* (México: Ediciones Botas, 1946), p. 47.

dirección educativa de la raza en la diversa serie de perspectivas que comprende un Estado" (p. 19).

In a singular essay, "Democracia asimétrica" (*C*, II, 6, 244–256), Gastélum proposed a concrete plan for the intellectual regeneration of his nation based on a theory of biological determinism. To save Mexico from mediocrity and cultural stagnation, he advanced a theory of miscegenation: "Importar buena simiente equivale a nulificar ciertos aspectos peligrosos de nuestro medio y que tienen su raigambre en una oscura y feroz ascendencia" (p. 250). Gastélum's essays, while broadly philosophic in their scope, always make direct allusion to Mexico's political realities. Nowhere is this tendency more clearly evidenced than in his interpretations of the Mexican Revolution, "La revolución mexicana (I Canción de la libertad)" (*C*, IX, 33, 140–151), and "La teoría del sufragio" (*C*, VII, 23, 34–46).[14]

In "La revolución mexicana" Gastélum examines the underlying cause of the conflagration of 1910—political conservatism. The wars for independence and the formation of a Federal Republic in 1821, he asserts, succeeded only in changing exterior structural aspects of government. The malignancy of political and intellectual conservatism continued to prevent the formation of an enlightened, imaginative political organization. The apogee of conservative power was reached during the dictatorship of Porfirio Díaz, the prelude to castastrophic social change. Throughout the essay Gastélum develops with great explicitness his thesis that social melioration can be achieved only in a climate of intellectual creativity.[15] The causes and effects of post-revolutionary political chaos are examined in Gastélum's "Teoría del sufragio." The Revolution of 1910, the author affirms, was not totally successful, because it failed to obtain the basic prerequisite for the advancement of culture—free public franchise. Responsible for this betrayal were the intelligentsia, who, bowing to conservative forces, failed to guide the masses to political liberty.

"Un Hombre" (*C*, I, 3, 221–228), one of the journal's rare commentaries on the contemporary scene, is a eulogy written after the assassination of President Álvaro Obregón. This essay is particularly signif-

[14] A footnote to the essay reads: "Segundo capítulo del libro en prensa, *Cinco ensayos de la revolución mexicana*" (p. 34). It has been difficult to verify the publication of this book.

[15] E. Martínez Ulloa in his essay "Cultura y política" (*C*, VI, 20, 57–80) also asserted that the amelioration of Mexico's political organization was dependent upon the creation of a spirit of concern among the general populace: "Adoptemos una actitud severa y en lugar de lamentarnos de nuestros males, procuremos corregirlos, indagando sus causas y viendo la manera de no reincidir en ellos" (p. 76).

icant because it synthesizes the attitude of the journal towards political phenomena and expresses the essentially universalist outlook of the editors. For Gastélum, Obregón was more than a political figure; he represented a cultural ideal, an opportunity for Mexico to reap the best of modern ideology: "En estos días de apasionado trabajo reconstructivo, *Contemporáneos* deplora la ausencia definitiva de este gran espíritu que ajeno a toda tendencia dogmática, permanecía continuadamente abierto a las más ondulantes inquietudes. Fue una de las más amplias ventanas por donde la revolución inquiría las curiosidades filosóficas y sociales que la ampliación de todo método inteligente de gobierno supone" (pp. 227–228).

Alfonso Reyes (1889–1959), one of Mexico's most distinguished scholars, also attempted to examine the nature of Mexican character and predict his nation's cultural destiny in his rambling essay "Discurso por Virgilio" (*C*, IX, 33, 97–131). Similar to the theory of biological determinism advanced by Gastélum, Reyes affirmed that the essence of Mexican character emanates from its Latin heritage: "El expíritu mexicano está en el color que el agua latina, tal como ella llegó ya hasta nosotros, adquirió aquí, en nuestra casa, al correr durante tres siglos lamiendo las arcillas rojas de nuestro suelo" (p. 105). Similarly, he asserted that the future hope of Mexico rests with miscegenation: "Lo que ha de salir no será oriental ni occidental, sino amplio y totalmente humano" (p. 124). The author also echoed Gastélum's affirmation that a revitalization of Mexican culture can only be effected through the reclamation of the nation's uneducated masses and the expression of national consciousness within a framework of universality.

Samuel Ramos (1897–1959) presented the most penetrating analysis of the national character in his essay "La cultura criolla" (*C*, XI, 38–39, 61–82).[16] His essay was unique in several ways. It was not only the first attempt to define the psychology of the Mexican but it synthesized as well the edict of his contemporaries that Mexican thought should be incorporated within the broad framework of Western culture. Ramos began his study by affirming, as Reyes had done, that Mexican character is essentially a product of European culture: "Debemos aceptar que nuestras perspectivas de cultura están cerradas dentro del marco europeo" (p. 60). Consequently, the most important force operative in the formation of creole culture has been an element of Western European tradition —Catholicism. From the earliest examples of colonial architecture to

[16] Ramos' essay was included in the anthology *El ensayo mexicano moderno*, 2 vols., José Luis Martínez, ed. (México: Fondo de Cultura Económica, 1958), 2: 455–469.

José Enrique Rodó's philosophy of idealism, Latin American culture has been molded by a spirit of religious fervor.

The most significant phase of the development of creole thought, Ramos continues, was marked by the activities of the Ateneo de la Juventud, which, in an attempt to broaden Mexico's cultural horizons, introduced currents of contemporary European thought. The Mexican, Ramos argues, should not reject the avenue to intellectual creativity introduced by the Ateneo but use it as a vehicle for the interpretation of autochthonous themes. His closing remarks are an apology for *Contemporáneos'* essentially apolitical, literary orientation:

> No es desprecio a su país, ni la incomprensión de sus problemas la causa de que el intelectual mexicano no haga citas de la realidad circundante; es que cuando el espíritu quiere expresarse tiene que hacerlo en un lenguaje propio que no ha creado todavía el suelo americano y que sólo puede dárselo la cultura europea. No es siempre nuestro "europeísmo" un frívolo estar a la moda, o un mimetismo servil; es también estimación de los valores efectivos de la vida humana y deseo de entrar al mundo que los contiene (p. 81).

Apart from these broad interpretive essays, a number of more specialized works treating various aspects of Mexican culture appeared in *Contemporáneos.* Typical of the works treating Mexican politico-historical phenomena are the studies of Luis Chávez Orozco, "Orígenes de la autocracia de Porfirio Díaz" (*C*, VI, 21, 153–182) and "El mecanismo de la autocracia de Porfirio Díaz" (*C*, X, 36, 144–164).[17] The fundamental thesis of Chávez Orozco is that the violence of the Mexican Revolution was a direct result of Díaz' political regime: "Todo lo que tuvo de sangrienta y vengativa la Revolución de 1910 se debió a los procedimientos del gobierno de estos tiranuelos ínfimos que con saña inaudita pisotearon la dignidad del campesino y del artesano" (p. 159).

The theme of the Mexican Indian, his historical evolution, philosophy, folklore,[18] and political destiny also formed the topic of a number of specialized studies. Ortiz de Montellano, in "Indios,' a prologue to a chapter of Guillermo Prieto's *Viajes de orden suprema* (1857) (*C*, XI, 42–43, 234), noted the importance of indigenous themes. Typical of the journal's apolitical policies, the discussion of autochthonous themes is

---

[17] Jose G. Heredia's monograph "En busca de las siete ciudades" (*C*, II, 5, 160–193; IV, 14, 314–340) also falls within this grouping. The study is a defense and justification of Coronado's activities in Mexico.

[18] Two translations of indigenous literary works appeared in the journal: Ortiz de Montellano, "Antiguos cantares mexicanos" (*C*, IV, 12, 100–119), and A Mediz Bolio, "El Chilam Balam de Chumayel" (*C*, IV, 13, 240–256).

restricted to a historical-philosophic framework. Outwardly pro-Indian propagandistic literature never appeared in *Contemporáneos.* The most important examples of studies of this nature are: Miguel O. de Mendizábal, "La conquista y la independencia religiosa de los indígenas" (*C*, I, 2, 149–199); "Evolución religiosa de los pueblos indígenas de México" (*C*, III, 8, 32–73); and Salvador Domínguez Assiayn, "Filosofía de los antiguos mexicanos" (*C*, XI, 42–43, 209, 225).

The examination of Mexico's role in music and the plastic arts formed a popular essay theme.[19] Two extensive studies of Diego Rivera appeared: Samuel Ramos, "El sueño de Diego" (*C*, VI, 21, 113–126; VII, 24, 103–118) and Gabriel García Maroto, "La obra de Diego Rivera" (*C*, I, 1, 43–75). Ramos' study is particularly important because more than a technical evaluation of the painter's work, it represents an effort to place Rivera in his proper historical perspective. Rivera's paintings, according to Ramos, mark a definite phase in the evolution of Mexican culture. They represent the crystallization of the spirit of the Mexican Revolution and the adaptation of modern artistic techniques to express national themes.

While the writers associated with *Contemporáneos* were perennially concerned with explaining problems related to Mexico's historic destiny, it should be noted that they reflected in their essays emerging trends in European philosophic thought. The essays of Bernardo Gastélum, Samuel Ramos, José Romano Muñoz, and Enrique Munguía, Jr. evince a desire to apply new philosophic concepts to the realities of the Mexican social milieu.

Among the most important of these trends was the influence of José Ortega y Gasset.[20] Speaking of the latter, Samuel Ramos wrote in *Historia de la filosofía en México:* "Una generación intelectual que comenzó a actuar públicamente entre 1925 y 1930 se sentía inconforme con el romanticismo filosófico de Caso y Vasconcelos. . . . En esta perplejidad, empiezan a llegar a México los libros de José Ortega y Gasset,

---

19 Briefer articles on this theme are: Aaron Copland, "Carlos Chávez, compositor" (*C*, II, 7, 407–412), and Xavier Villaurrutia, "Fichas sin sobre para Lazo" (*C*, I, 2, 117–122).

20 For commentary on the influence of Ortega y Gasset in Mexico see Arthur Berndtson, "Latin American Philosophy," in *The Encyclopedia of Philosophy,* 8 vols., Paul Edwards, ed. (New York: The MacMillan Co., 1967), 4: 397; Samuel Ramos, *Historia de la filosofía en México* (Mexico: Imprenta Universitaria, 1943), pp. 149–158; Patrick Romanell, *Making of the Mexican Mind* (Lincoln: University of Nebraska Press, 1952), pp. 141–185; Aníbal Sánchez Reulet, *La filosofía latinoamericana contemporánea* (Mexico: Unión Panamericana, 1949), pp. 14–15; and Jaime Torres Bodet, *Contemporáneos, notas de crítica* (México: Ediciones Contemporáneos, 1928), p. 124.

y en el primero de ellos, las *Meditaciones del Quijote,* encuentra la solución al conflicto en la doctrina de *razón vital."* [21] Thus, as Ramos admits, the Contemporáneos found in the pivotal dictum of Ortega y Gasset, "Yo soy yo y mi circunstancia," a challenge to effect a revitalization of Mexican philosophic thought.

The most effective synthesis of the latter's doctrine of a fusion of the self and environmental reality was presented in Ramos' essay "La cultura criolla." The first attempt to present a psychoanalysis of creole culture, it reflected postulates developed in *Meditaciones del Quijote.* Man's prime intellectual task was to bring national aspirations in harmony with currents of contemporary world thought by freeing himself from the limitations of Cartesian rationalism.

The essays of Gastélum, "Espíritu del héroe," "Pensar en vez de recordar," and "Democracia asimétrica" are also concerned with the theme of intellectual regeneration. Gastélum repeatedly asserts that a dependence on past ideology can no longer suffice. The individual in interaction with his historic and biological circumstances must create a new set of values. Likewise, E. Martínez Ulloa synthesized the essentially dynamic, activist orientation of the philosophy of Ortega y Gasset in "Cultura y política" (*C*, VI, 20, 57–80). Mexico's future is dependent, he asserted, on the creation of a proper intellectual climate—a *cultura política* from which a new political structure can arise. In the past the nation has had only inept, uninspired leaders: "Nunca un destello de genio, una inteligente vislumbre de orientación decidida" (p. 74).

Another basic theme in the writings of Ortega y Gasset, his aristocratic distrust of democracy and contemporary mass society, was developed with great explicitness in *Contemporáneos.* This doctrine was best reflected in "La doble solución al problema del valor de la vida" (*C*, III, 10, 206–213) by José Romano Muñoz. Romano Muñoz asserted that through the cultivation of the creative faculties, man could combat the intellectual analgesia engendered by a materialist society: "Hay que cultivar el genio . . . es el único que nos diferencia de las bestias y nos hace semejante a Dios" (p. 210).

Ortega's highly controversial thesis that the decadence of modern society is due to the absence of rule by the intellectual elite was expressed in a number of essays. Although tacitly implied by Romano Muñoz and Samuel Ramos, Gastélum advanced the theory most clearly in "Espíritu del héroe" and "Ciencia del caballero." In the former he declared: "El héroe y el santo edifican. Los demás forman la multitud, la masa que trasmite a la posteridad su historia" (p. 5).

---

[21] Ramos, *Filosofía en México,* p. 149.

A number of conclusions, essential to an appreciation of *Contemporáneos,* can be drawn from an examination of the expository prose in the journal. A survey of the nonfictional prose contents proves conclusively that the journal was not solely an organ of European thought. In fact a major portion of the articles, essays, and monographs are dedicated to national themes. While Bernardo Gastélum, Samuel Ramos, and Alfonso Reyes wrote broad interpretive essays, numerous specialized studies dedicated to all aspects of Mexican culture appeared in the review. Proof of the journal's interest in the social destiny of Mexico is evidenced in the concern expressed for the uneducated masses. Gastélum, Reyes, and Chávez Orozco all voiced their belief that the spiritual and political destiny of Mexico rested with the redemption of the Indian.

The interest expressed in Mexico in *Contemporáneos* is neither nationalistic nor propagandistic but an attempt to interpret the role of the nation within a framework of world culture. In a series of subtle journal manifestoes, Gastélum, Ortiz de Montellano, and Torres Bodet explained and defended the journal's apolitical position against those who wished to see *Contemporáneos* become an organ of political propaganda. It was the opinion of the editors that literature itself was revolutionary; to make it a vehicle for dogma was to debase its inherent value. Repeating the postulates of the Ateneo de la Juventud, *Contemporáneos* sought continuously to express the finest of Mexico's cultural heritage within a framework of intellectual universality.[22]

In their totality the selections of nonfictional prose represent not only works of literary value but an invaluable source for the study of postwar intellectual development in Mexico. Henrique González Casanova, speaking of the Contemporáneos has written with insight: "No es en balde una generación de ensayistas a la par que de poetas." [23]

---

[22] Henrique González Casanova has commented on the universalist orientation of the Contemporáneos in his essay, "Reseña de la poesía mexicana siglo XX," *México en el Arte,* nos. 10–11 (1950), p. 18: "Otro elemento que los caracteriza es su mexicanismo, nacionalista, pero no por los temas y los giros como lo hubieran querido muchos de sus contemporáneos de miradas más limitadas, sino por el afán de situar a México dentro de lo universal en términos de igualdad, y sin temor al qué dirán de las naciones extranjeras" (p. 18).

[23] Ibid., p. 19.

Ursula Lamb
Department of History
Yale University
New Haven, Connecticut

UNITS OF ONE AND THE VISIBLE EVENT

*Reflections Based Upon the Historiography of New Spain**

On the occasion of a meeting of Mexican and United States historians a discussion was scheduled to deal with the historiography of the sixteenth and seventeenth centuries of New Spain. For the purposes of this paper, the period will be extended to the 1760s or about the time when the Bourbon reforms became effective. Although the following reflections were prompted by this topic and the illustrations are drawn from that period and place, the frame of reference is largely incidental to the discussion of a problem which is typical of all narrative history. New Spain serves here only as a convenient base to supply a structure to the inquiry and to give a convenient support of detail.

One problem of the history of conquest and colonization in New Spain is that of the uneven visibility of men and developments at the beginning and toward the end of the period, 1500–1760. The bunching of events which leads to the dramatic contrast in density is in part responsible for the distinct styles of treatment used by historians. Action and extravagant effect are most frequently presented in detail for the conquest, and construct and trend are the preferred methods for writing about the later period. To deal with this problem, the historian who writes narrative history might profit from looking at the significance of the human unit chosen by historians to carry their meaning, whether it be the unit of one or of many.

Few events and subsequent epochs show the importance of this choice to such critical advantage as does the conquest of America. In very simple

* This article is based on a paper read at one of the sessions of the Third Conference of Mexican and U.S. historians at Oaxtepec, Mexico, in November, 1969.

terms, the problem first appears when the conqueror is seen in the singular and the conquered in the plural. The conqueror is one, the hero, while the conquered appear in the plural as "Indians." For even when Cortés is joined by his band of companions, they do not make a very satisfactory collective. A company of heroes weakens the idea of the heroic and soon becomes a surfeit of heroes. Whenever Indian heroes such as Moctezuma or Cuauhtémoc appear and are joined by other princes, as in fact they were—in most accounts save native ones—all of them promptly turn into the collective "Indians" when the action starts. This results in an uneven match of the *visión de los vencidos* with the *hechos de los castellanos.*

Another way to show the problem is that in conquest narrative the goals of the individual Spaniards are realistically plural. Spaniards wanted to be rich, to be ennobled, to talk with kings and ride with grandees, to marry well and establish or maintain a legitimate line, and to live in comfort without toil. All of these aims are present to various degrees and in varied combinations among the conquerors.

The Indians, on the contrary, are reduced to unsuccessful resistance and to sorrowful lament of a common fate, even in most of the Indian literature. No enumeration of troubles, no counting of Indian dead can in the end evoke in the reader more understanding of the abject tragedy of the fate of their race. It is the magnitude of this single grief which fuses the many into one powerful entity without differentiation, while the conqueror and his companions are as distinguishable for their content as they look separately.

One answer to this imbalance of the individual who represents the event has been for the parties of the conquest to penetrate the other's domain. So Cuauhtémoc, the Indian leader, was made a Renaissance hero to match Cortés, and the Marqués del Valle was made *un comunero*[1] blending into the *grupos de conquistadores.*[2]

A really new level of understanding of the Indian, however, was reached only by a look at the many, or at how the natives lived, as in the *Daily Life of the Aztecs* (Soustelle), *The Aztecs Under Spanish Rule* (Gibson), and the "Civil Congregation," studied by Cline.[3] In such dis-

[1] Manuel Jiménez Fernández, *Hernán Cortes y su revolución comunera en la Nueva España* (Madrid: CSIC, 1948); Eulalia Guzmán, *Relaciones de Hernán Cortés* (Mexico, 1958).

[2] Mario Góngora, *Los grupos de conquistadores en Tierra Firme, 1509–1530* (Santiago de Chile, 1962). This book treats of Central America but concerns typical bands of conquistadores.

[3] Jacques Soustelle, *La Vie Quotidienne des Aztèques a la veille de la conquête Espagnole* (Paris, 1955); Charles Gibson, *The Aztecs Under Spanish Rule* (Stanford, 1964); Howard F. Cline, "Civil Congregations of the Indians in New Spain, 1598–1666," *Hispanic American Historical Review* 29, (1942): 349–369.

cussions the concreteness of deed in daily life gives reality to an Indian who is no longer reduced solely to bearing the burden of sentiment (which has been the lot of crowds ever since Gustave Le Bon). Accounts of daily life of the natives have led to a better understanding of where the Indian was vulnerable and how he endured. The problem of the individualism of the many conquering heroes on the other hand, yielded to studies of concepts which they shared. The world of Western ideas united the Spaniards behind cohesive programs such as those discussed by Silvio Zavala in his works on Utopias and by John L. Phelan in his *Millennial Kingdom of the Franciscans.*[4] These books and others of their kind show how the *Hechos de los castellanos* (Herrera)[5] gave way to the *Obra de España en América* (Carlos Pereyra).[6]

A tendency can thus be discerned in recent writings which breaks down the traditional conventions regarding the visibility of Indians and Spaniards in the history of the conquest. Our seeing the sixteenth-century conquest has been as learned as our seeing the picture of a crucifixion, where the body of a Christ on the cross signifies life and the portraits of living donors to either side imply mortality. The explanation of such a point of view needed as much translation as does our picture of the conquest.

If the sixteenth century has for too long been the history of the conquerors, the succeeding period, prior to independence, suffered from a lack of visible events. Caught as it is between cataclysmic military conflicts, it is the epoch in which the ordinary prevails over the extraordinary so that one gets an impression of quiescence. The true problem is that the period lacks great names attached to spectacular changes. As people are visible in events, a history without heroes is anonymous history, and a history without names becomes the inevitable history of trends. In the case of New Spain, this is determined by its origin in conquest and its outcome in independence. The middle epoch must therefore be restored to autonomy as a distinct period in which the viceregal system fully matures and the colony presents, as Morales Padrón puts it, *Un mundo que se expresa.*[7]

This expression is made visible by the common fate of groups of

---

4 Silvio Zavala, *La Utopía de Tomás Moro en la Nueva España* (México, 1937); *Ideario de Vasco de Quiroga* (México, 1941); John L. Phelan, *The Millennial Kingdom of the Franciscans in the New World* (Berkeley, Cal., 1956).

5 Antonio de Herrera, *Historia general de los hechos de los castellanos en las islas y tierra firme del mar Océano* (Madrid, 1601–1615).

6 Carlos Pereyra, *La obra de España en América* (Madrid, 1920).

7 Francisco Morales Padrón, *Historia de América,* vol. V of *Manual de Historia Universal* (Madrid, 1958), part III.

people, by their concerted action and the cumulative effects of it and by the persistence of social roles which are characteristic of the epoch. In such groups the individual appears submerged, but still it is he who carries the meaning of "many conquests," as used by Professor Phelan.[8] Such a meaning of conquest for the later colonial period could be derived from the etymological antecedent of our use of the word, when *conquirere-conquisitium* meant to seek to live together. Most naturally the product of this search in Mexico was the mestizo, and mestizaje in the widest sense—from Magnus Mörner to Brigitte Leander[9]—has been identified as the single most important phenomenon of change during this epoch. In other words, the unit of one which characterizes visible change in this epoch is an entire population, the product of two inheritances.

A collective of individuals identifiable only as members of a social group such as *Los vagabundos de Nueva España* studied by N. F. Martin, or the widows and orphans who so consistently appear in colonial legislation, might serve as units to draw our attention to otherwise unnoticeable social phenomena. Another visible unit could be made by a collection of mini-biographies or of multiple short lives. The technique of short lives can be used with precision to investigate historical problems which are otherwise inaccessible. This method, in fact, diminishes the merely evocative and sentimental elements in lives which characterize the *Grandes Biografías*. Moreover, short lives might check the tendencies of using mere compilations of figures in narrative history, where numbers sometimes lead to "misplaced concreteness" (in Whitehead's phrase used in another connection), as when, on occasion, sex, age, and station, in lists, do not answer more than they stand for but rather less.

Then there is the composite unit of one. Informed by all the accessible data a new kind of *vida ejemplar* can be envisioned. This matches a man to a job, the job to a task, and the task to the society and environment. Julio Caro Baroja introduced this genre in his *El Señor Inquisidor y Otras Vidas por Oficio*,[10] where he shows the fit of a man to his office—if indeed he was not a mere pensioner[11]—and, in that case, the fit of the office to the problems under its purview over a sufficient length of time

---

[8] John L. Phelan, "Many Conquests." Title of one of two papers given at session II in Oaxtepec, November 1969, Third meeting U.S.-Mexican Historians.

[9] Magnus Mörner, "La política de segregación y el mestizaje en la Audiencia de Guatemala," pp. 137–153, and B. Leander, "Mestizaje ecológico en México," pp. 87–153, and the rest of the number, *Revista de Indias*, Números 95–96, 1964.

[10] Julio Caro Baroja, *El Señor Inquisidor y Otras Vidas por Oficio* (Madrid, 1968).

[11] John H. Parry, *The Sale of Public Office in the Spanish Indies Under the Hapsburgs* (Berkeley, Cal., 1953).

to tell the story, regardless of the number of individuals holding it. Such a *vida por oficio* is not a collection of *vidas*, nor does it bring portraits in the sense of depiction. All one must know is which of two models is discussed, male or female, and which color, red, white, black, yellow, or mixed. Beyond that it needs not be stated that there are two eyes and that these are on either side of the nose. The *vida por oficio* is a portrait in vivid fragment which catches men and events over a span of time in essence and not in a single likeness. So one may avoid writing on the one hand about offices without people, a useful and well established branch of history though this is, and on the other, about office-holders whose lives fall largely outside their assigned tasks.

Historians who do not tool up for a "systems" approach to research, nor stay immersed in one locality for a long stretch of time, have ample scope for new ways in traditional history by the varied use of its basic ingredient, namely the number of men whom they choose to carry visible events. In sixteenth-century historiography it was seen that the traditional preference for singular over plural lives restricted the meaning of the conquest for Indians as well as for Spaniards. The early conquest was better understood when Indian societies were seen to be the unit which rendered observable the profound changes in the nature and role of the individual. The Spanish opponent was made more comprehensible when a common pool of ideas was seen to motivate him, and the hitherto unwieldy numbers of heroes were shown to be carriers of a shared heritage made visible in the New World.

For the period of the later Habsburgs and up to the time that the Bourbon reforms affected New Spain it has been shown that new human units can be put together by historians which demonstrate change independent of the tyranny of chronology and in the absence of visible or apparent change. With the help of such units one might explore the human condition over a longer time span and the alternatives, chosen or ignored, which were characteristic of that epoch.

It has been the purpose of this paper to show the usefulness of looking at the numbers of people who are made to carry historical narrative, first as an analytical method for event-dominated epochs, and second as imaginative constructions for periods of apparent or traditional quiescence.

Robert E. McNicoll

NUEVAS CORRIENTES*

Regarding Allende

Oiga of Lima, Peru, 6 November 1970.

"Con una carga tan pesada sobre sus hombros, no era de extrañar que Allende desinflara los deseos de algunos exaltados que querían ver ya a Fidel Castro entre los primeros invitados al Palacio de la Moneda y soñaban con que la primera medida del nuevo gobierno fuese la ruptura con Estados Unidos . . . (p. 20).

"Sin embargo, en la conducción de su política todo indica que Allende parece estar dispuesto a andar con prudencia. Y es posible que él intente un modus vivendi razonable con los capitales norteamericanos a fin de mantener la comercialización del cobre en el área del dólar . . . Finalmente, completando su táctica de prudencia, el nuevo presidente chileno intentará, no muy revolucionariamente, mantener buenas relaciones con los militares. En esta política de apaciguamiento parecen haber influido los consejos dados a Allende por Fidel Castro . . ." (p. 21).

Caretas of Lima, Peru, November 1970, p. 15.

"El compañero presidente"

"La 'revolución con sabor a empanadas y vino tinto' como llama Allende a lo que se viene, se inició el martes 3 con festejos en la Alameda, con mucha cueca y 'tallas' al por mayor, y con una juerga que siguió el

---

* *Editorial Note:* This section is reincorporated into the *Journal* after a lapse of seven years. The purpose is to bring to the attention of readers current matters of interest and, hopefully, to provide a channel for dialogue among Latin Americanists on topics of future research. There is probably no recent event of greater implications than the victory of Salvador Allende in Chile. The comments of Latin American publications, although tentative and greatly influenced by their origins, should be provocative of thought and discussion by scholars of the various disciplines.

4 y culminó el 5 en la tarde, con un festival popular en el Estadio Nacional. Allí Allende dio su primer discurso formal.

"Sin embargo, no dejan de haber diferencias y, a veces, suspicacias entre socialistas y comunistas. Comúnmente se considera que los socialistas son los mas 'revolucionarios'. De hecho, el partido incluye una mescolanza de tendencias que parecen abarcar desde social demócratas hasta maoístas y trotskistas. Los comunistas, por su lado, son sindicados como más 'conservadores' y, sin duda, son infinitamente más disciplinados. Por lo pronto controlan la Central Única de Trabajadores.

"La edicion original que [Allende] tiene en su biblioteca de 'La Guerra de Guerrillas' del Che Guevara tiene la siguiente inscripción: 'A mi amigo Allende que está tratando de lograr lo mismo por otros medios' ".

Andrés Cisneros in *Confirmado* of Buenos Aires, September 1970, p. 27.

"La unción de un presidente marxista resulta una completa contradicción. Si cumple su programa a la letra, provocará la intervención de las fuerzas armadas. Si no lo cumple, defraudará el electorado, desviándolo hacia el escepticismo o la democracia cristiana, con lo que el juego recomenzaría ... Es predicible que el nuevo presidente agite banderas socialistas, pero aplique, en la práctica, el programa de Tomic ... Hoy ya nadie duda ... que lo que América latina necesita son cambios revolucionarios. Esto es, profundos e inmediatos. Y no se sabe de ninguna revolución donde los ejércitos se hayan mantenido prescindentes. A favor o en contra, siempre son protagonistas. Cuando no participan es, sencillamente, porque no hay revolución".

Technology and Science

"The extent to which anti-*yanqui* sentiment in Spanish America continues to influence decisions affecting efforts to incorporate technology and science, as they are creatively used in contemporary society, will work toward keeping the area dependent or 'colonial' in relation to the rest of the world. This is so no matter what validity the sentiment may have or what political purpose it may serve."

John P. Harrison in "The University versus National Development in Spanish America," 1968 Hackett Memorial Lecture, University of Texas.

German Publication

Der Institut fur Internationales Recht of Kiel University has announced the publication of *Die Organisation der Amerikanischen Staaten* (OAS) by Gerhard Kutzner. The work of 40 pages describes the history of the inter-American system from the "beginning of last century to the 13th Meeting of Consultation of Ministers of Foreign Affairs (1969/70)." It also "deals with the juridical and political aspects of the OAS. It includes such controversial issues as the exclusion of the present government of Cuba, the relation between UNO and OAS, the plan to establish a permanent inter-American force and Canada's attitude towards the hemisphere organization." A third part describes the functions of the different organizations under both the old and the modified OAS charters.

The publication is distributed by Hansischer Gildenverlag Joachim Heitmann Co., Hamburg, Germany.

A Letter

Gentlemen:

We have forwarded to you the first issue of our *Boletín Documental Sobre la Mujer* and hope you have received it and given it due attention.

. . . .

Knowing that your interest in the human development of Latin America is sincere, we take the liberty to ask you if on occasion your documentation services would be generous enough to keep us informed regarding any articles or books of real value about women in general, and about women in Latin America, in particular.

Thanking you in advance
Sincerely Yours
E. M. Hollants
Coordinación de Iniciativas para el Desarrollo de América Latina.
Calle Rió Fuerte No. 3
Cuernavaca, Mor., México.

We are happy to bring this to the attention of our readers.

Center for Advanced International Studies
University of Miami

CENTER NOTES

NEW DIRECTOR FOR INSTITUTE OF INTER-AMERICAN STUDIES

The University of Miami's long-established program of Latin American Studies is being strengthened with the appointment of Dr. John P. Harrison as the new Director of the Institute of Inter-American Studies in the Center for Advanced International Studies. Dr. Harrison, who will assume his position in January 1971, brings to his new assignment a wealth of experience gained as Latin American specialist with the Rockefeller Foundation and as Director of the Institute of Latin American Studies at the University of Texas from 1962 to 1967, as well as a national and international reputation among Latin Americanists.

THE JOSÉ A. BALSEIRO INTERNATIONAL AWARD

The José A. Balseiro International Prize Committee and the Institute of Inter-American Studies of the Center for Advanced International Studies, University of Miami, are pleased to announce the opening of competition for the Balseiro International Award. This award was instituted in 1968 for the best essay written by a graduate student in the fields of Hispanic Literature or Philosophy. All graduate students in these fields are invited to participate, and faculty members are asked to aid in making known to students the possibility of participation and the availability of this prize. In 1969 the prize was awarded to Miss LaVonne C. McGee of Bryn Mawr College for her essay, "Un estudio crítico de *Los crepúsculos del jardín* de Leopoldo Lugones."

AWARD:	$200.00 and consideration for publication in the *Journal of Inter-American Studies and World Affairs.*
ELIGIBILITY:	Open to graduate students in the fields of Hispanic Literature or Philosophy at U.S. or Latin American universities.
REQUIREMENTS:	Essays on Hispanic Literature or Philosophy, in Spanish or English, 25-50 typewritten

pages in length, double-spaced on 8½ x 11″ paper. Three copies should be submitted.

Deadline for submission: 1 March 1971.

Date of Award: June 1971.

Entries should be submitted to:

Associate Director
Institute of Inter-American Studies
CAIS
University of Miami
Coral Gables, Florida 33124

A Review Article by
MANUEL ORTEGA*

BOOKS

DICTATORSHIP AND TRANSITION IN THE DOMINICAN REPUBLIC

Wiarda, Howard J. *Dictatorship and Development: The Methods of Control in Trujillo's Dominican Republic.* Latin American Monographs, Second Series, Number 5. Gainesville: University of Florida Press, 1968. Preface bibliography, index. 225 pp. $3.75.

Wiarda, Howard J. *The Dominican Republic: Nation in Transition.* New York, Washington and London: Frederick A. Praeger, 1969. Preface, photographs, suggestions for further reading, index. viii, 249 pp. $7.00.

Entre los académicos norteamericanos interesados en la investigación de la realidad socio-política de la República Dominicana es sin duda el profesor Howard J. Wiarda, del departamento de ciencias políticas de la Universidad de Massachusetts, quien hasta el presente ha producido un mayor número de estudios sobre tema dominicano. Además de dedicar a este tema tanto su tesis de licenciatura como su disertación para el doctorado, el profesor Wiarda ha publicado, a partir de 1963, más de media docena de artículos en revistas especializadas y ha presentado igualmente algunas ponencias en congresos de ciencias sociales analizando distintos aspectos del sistema político dominicano. También han aparecido, en revistas de divulgación, comentarios suyos a la cambiante situación socio-económica y política de la República Dominicana contemporánea. Finalmente, el profesor Wiarda tiene editadas una guía a las elecciones generales dominicanas de 1966 y una bibliografía anotada sobre política y gobierno en la República Dominicana entre 1930 y 1966.

El carácter académico de todo este cuerpo de publicaciones está respaldado por los ocho años que aproximadamente lleva el autor profundizando en el tema del cambio social y el desarrollo político en la República Dominicana, por una abundante colección personal de publicaciones y documentos dominicanos y extranjeros, así como por no menos de seis viajes de estudio a ese país.

Con las dos obras objeto de la presente reseña, el profesor Wiarda da comienzo a una etapa nueva en la publicación de sus investigaciones dominicanas. Por primera vez, lo que él nos ofrece no son ya trabajos más o menos

* Research Assistant, Center for Advanced International Studies, University of Miami.

breves, sino libros en los que un tema determinado ha sido desarrollado extensamente.

El primero de estos libros, *Dictatorship and Development: The Methods of Control in Trujillo's Dominican Republic,* viene a llenar un vacío en la literatura de habla inglesa acerca de la Era de Trujillo. Aunque existía la excelente biografía del "Generalísimo" escrita por Robert D. Crassweller, *Trujillo: The Life and Times of a Caribbean Dictator*, faltaba sin embargo un estudio analítico de su dictadura en el que se considerasen los mechanismos de control que permitieron a Trujillo permanecer en el poder por más de treinta años. Es cierto que el profesor Jesús de Galíndez había realizado una brillante aportación inicial a dicho estudio. Pero su obra, *La Era de Trujillo: Un Estudio Casuístico de Dictadura Hispanoamericana,* además de no haber sido publicada en inglés en forma de libro, sólo cubre la dictadura hasta 1955. La trágica desaparición de su autor, ocurrida en 1956, impidió todo análisis del importantísimo quinquenio final de la Era.

La obra *Dictatorship and Development* no debe ser mirada como una biografía de Trujillo ni tampoco como una historia completa de su larga dictadura. El libro se orienta claramente a un doble fin. En primer lugar, presentar en su perspectiva histórica el sistema político implantado por Trujillo, mediante un análisis detallado de aquellos pilares sobre los que el "Generalísimo" basó su casi absoluto control político y económico sobre la República Dominicana desde 1930 a 1961. En segundo lugar, ofrecer una doble aportación al estudio comparado de los sistemas políticos, tratando de ubicar al régimen de Trujillo dentro de la variada gama de sistemas dictatoriales, así como de determinar las implicaciones que la Era tuvo para el desarrollo y modernización de la República Dominicana.

Ahora bien, mientras que al primero de los dos fines señalados se consagran los siete capítulos centrales del libro; al segundo se dedican tan sólo una parte del capítulo introductorio—en el que se ofrece un marco teórico de análisis— y dos secciones del capítulo final —en donde brevemente el autor ubica al régimen trujillista y apunta sus implicaciones para el desarrollo y modernización del país. Esta aparente desproporción parece deberse al hecho de que el núcleo principal del presente libro, o sea sus siete capítulos centrales, es en realidad una versión ampliada y perfeccionada de la tesis de licenciatura defendida por el autor en 1962. Dicha tesis carecía casi en absoluto de marco analítico, reduciéndose a describir los principales métodos de control de la dictadura de Trujillo. Teniendo esto en consideración, las secciones en los capítulos primero y último de *Dictatorship and Development* —en donde su autor intenta hacer la doble aportación arriba señalada— nos dan la impresión de ser un esfuerzo posterior por enriquecer el estudio con un marco teórico que permita colocarlo dentro de una perspectiva tan de actualidad hoy día en el campo de las ciencias políticas como es el análisis comparado de los sistemas políticos. Dicho en otras palabras, nos parece tratarse de un esfuerzo por dar valor generalizable a otros países en vías de desarrollo a algo que originalmente no pasaba de ser un estudio casuístico individual.

A nuestro juicio, sin embargo, este esfuerzo no está plenamente logrado. Creemos, en efecto, que ni el marco teórico inicial, ni las que su autor llama "implicaciones para una teoría de las dictaduras y para el desarrollo y modernización de la República Dominicana", están suficientemente desarrollados ni totalmente integrados al núcleo principal del libro. Por otra parte, opinamos que es precisamente en los siete capítulos centrales —de carácter preponderantemente informativo-descriptivo— donde se encuentra el mérito principal de la obra. En ellos se da a conocer lo que fué el sistema socio-político y económico creado por Trujillo, su estructura y su funcionamiento. El autor nos describe, en este orden, los orígenes del régimen y la personalidad del dictador; su dominio sobre las fuerzas armadas, la estructura formal del gobierno, y la economía nacional; la ideología oficial del régimen; las técnicas para controlar la vida cultural y religiosa de la nacion; y por ultimo el trágico fin de la Era.

Pasando ya a hacer algunos comentarios más de detalle, se deben en primer lugar alabar la abundancia y calidad de las fuentes que el autor emplea a lo largo de su obra. Con todo, es de lamentar a este respecto el que en ocasiones el sentido de algunos pasajes de fuentes en castellano no haya sido correctamente interpretado. Sin embargo, en absolutamente ninguno de los casos notados se trata de errores que hayan influido en las conclusiones a que llega el estudio. Carece igualmente de trascendencia algún que otro lapso histórico que se le escapa al autor; tal como el confundir (p. 142) al historiador eclesiástico Carlos Nouel con su hijo el arzobispo Adolfo A. Nouel, o el dar (p. 165) como fecha de la división de la arquidiócesis de Santo Domingo el año 1958 cuando en realidad ésta ocurrió el 25 de septiembre de 1953.

En relación al capítulo quinto —"The National Economy and Socio-economic Groups"— es de lamentar que la fecha en que este libro fue dado a la imprenta impidiera a su autor incorporar los aportes de la reciente controversia que sobre el papel desempeñado por Trujillo en el desarrollo socio-económico de la República Dominicana han sostenido autores dominicanos tales como Juan Bosch, Juan Isidro Jimenes Grullón, Franklin Franco y otros. La misma razón del tiempo de publicación impidió, de seguro, incorporar lo que más o menos esos mismos autores han polemizado en los últimos meses acerca de las clases sociales en el pasado y el presente dominicano.

El capítulo sexto —"Trujillo's Political Ideology"— es a nuestro juicio una del las más interesantes contribuciones que la obra del profesor Wiarda hace al estudio de la Era. Sin compartir necesariamente todas y cada una de sus afirmaciones al respecto, creemos que el autor obró acertadamente dedicando un capítulo entero a compensar la casi total falta de atención que otros autores habían prestado a este tema. El resumen que de la "filosofía política" de Trujillo hace el profesor Wiarda nos parece una de las aportaciones más originales de todo el libro.

Finalmente es de alabar el estilo a la vez académico y claro empleado por el autor. Esta cualidad, no siempre presente en las obras especializadas de ciencias sociales, hace sumamente interesante la lectura de todos y cada uno de los capítulos de este libro.

Para juzgar con objetividad la segunda obra del profesor Wiarda, *The Dominican Republic: Nation in Transition,* se debe tener muy presente el fin específico que su autor se propuso al componerla. Este fin ha sido ofrecer al lector norteamericano no especializado una introducción tanto a la geografía e historia como a la realidad cultural, socio-política y económica de la República Dominicana. Una obra así era echada de menos por cuantos en los Estados Unidos se interesan por conocer mejor aquel pequeño pero interesante país del Caribe. No existía en inglés obra alguna escrita para el público general por un solo autor en un volumen y en la que, para hacer más asequible la lectura, se hubiese renunciado al uso de notas al calce así como a los tecnicismos propios de las ciencias políticas, la sociología o la economía. Ahora bien, es esto precisamente lo que en su libro *The Dominican Republic* nos ofrece el profesor Wiarda. En sucesivos capítulos quedan descritos: el marco geográfico; el proceso histórico desde el descubrimiento de la Hispaniola hasta nuestros días; la composición racial, lenguaje, religión y mundo de valores del pueblo dominicano y su estratificación social contemporánea; las estructuras gubernamentales; la vida política nacional; la economía; y finalmente los programas de desarrollo, así como la política exterior de la República Dominicana principalmente en relación a los Estados Unidos de América.

Abundan todo a lo largo de la obra observaciones sumamente atinadas acerca de las instituciones y pueblo dominicanos. Esto supone de parte del autor, además de una seria y prolija labor de investigación, una apreciable dosis de empatía con la sociedad objeto de su estudio. He aquí algunos de esos aciertos de interpretación:

En el capítulo tercero —"The Pattern of Historical Development"— el autor nos recuerda como a consecuencia de no haber recibido la Hispaniola la influencia de ninguno de los movimientos innovadores de la edad moderna —Reforma, revolución científica, revolución industrial, desarrollo de la democracia representativa— sus tradiciones intelectuales, religiosas, ecónomicas y políticas permanecieron medievales. De este modo, como muy bien nota el autor, "la época colonial dejó tras de sí una herencia que la República Dominicana no ha podido aún superar".

En el capítulo sexto —"The People"— el profesor Wiarda resalta justamente el hecho de que, sin existir en la República Dominicana la pluralidad étnica o cultural que tan negativas consecuencias ha tenido para otros países en vías de desarrollo, sus habitantes, sin embargo, distan mucho de constituir una nación bien integrada. La sección final de este capítulo, dedicada al tema de los valores y conducta del pueblo dominicano, nos describe, con simpatía, sí, pero al mismo tiempo con todo realismo, los rasgos más sobresalientes de ese pueblo. La conclusión a que el autor llega —a saber, la gran dificultad de construir sobre esa base una sociedad democrática de acuerdo al modelo anglosajón— no parece ser fácilmente impugnable. Figuras dominicanas de prestigio como el ex presidente Juan Bosch van más allá hoy día negando la conveniencia misma para su país de la democracia representativa.

Es de alabar por su exactitud y valentía la descripción que en la capítulo séptimo —"The Social Structure"— se hace de las clases populares dominicanas especialmente los campesinos. Estimamos igualmente acertado el modo como el autor presenta a los sectores medios: su heterogeneidad y falta de conciencia de clase, así como la acentuada tendencia de su parte a imitar el tren de vida de la clase más pudiente. También coincidimos con el profesor Wiarda cuando describe a la dominicana como una sociedad en donde las barreras de clase no acaban todavía de caer, pero en la que comienzan a darse cambios profundos al igual que una embrionaria mobilidad social.

En el capítulo octavo —"Education and Culture"— es de especial interés la sección dedicada a la "nueva ola" cultural dominicana.

El capítulo décimo —"Governmental Structures"— no se limita a describir con exactitud la ineficiencia de la administración pública, sino que ofrece una muy acertada explicación de la situación existente. Otro tanto se puede decir de la presentación que, al final del mismo capítulo, el autor hace del sistema legal dominicano.

El capítulo doce —"Public Policy and Foreign Affairs"— es quizás uno de los más logrados de todo el libro. En primer lugar, por ofrecernos un análisis detallado de los intentos, reales o ficticios según los casos, que sucesivos gobiernos dominicanos han hecho por realizar un programa nacional de reforma agraria. El profesor Wiarda sabe destacar los diversos factores que en cada uno de los casos han conducido al fracaso de dichos programas. De esta forma, la suerte corrida por la reforma agraria sirve para ilustrar los problemas y dificultades casi insuperables que confronta llevar a término una política gubernamental de desarrollo en la República Dominicana hoy día. En segundo lugar, este capítulo, al describir el tipo de influjo que los Estados Unidos ejercen sobre los asuntos dominicanos, destaca la aparente paradoja de que dicho influjo, a pesar de lo enorme de sus proporciones, resulta en ocasiones sumamente limitado en sus logros.

Fijando la atención ahora en sus limitaciones, *The Dominican Republic* contiene algunas incorrecciones de detalle que por carecer de trascendencia omitimos mencionar aquí. Igualmente se ofrecen en él ciertas interpretaciones y juicios a nuestro entender debatibles. Sirva de ejemplo, entre otros varios, la valorización totalmente negativa que el profesor Wiarda hace de la ocupación haitiana de 1822 a 1844 (pp. 27–28). Aunque ésta haya sido por mucho tiempo en la República Dominicana la interpretación tradicional, hoy día es puesta en tela de juicio por la más reciente historiografía dominicana. Véanse, por ejemplo, *La República Dominicana: Una Ficción*, publicada en 1965 por Juan Isidro Jimenes Grullón, y *La Revolución Haitiana y Santo Domingo*, 1968, del profesor Emilio Cordero Michel.

Pero sobre todo queremos criticar una cierta tendencia —manifestada no sólo en este libro sino en otras publicaciones anteriores del autor— a considerar a la clase alta dominicana y a la militar como si cada una de ellas fuera más homogénea y actuara con una mayor cohesión interna de lo que nos parece ser la realidad, comprobada una y muchas veces así en el pasado como el momento actual dominicano. Reconociendo la existencia de poderosos intereses institucionales tanto en la llamada "oligarquía" como en las fuerzas armadas, hubiéramos deseado, sin embargo, que especialmente en los capítulos séptimo —"The Social Structure"— y undécimo —"Political Processes"— se hubiese hecho mayor hincapié en la heterogeneidad existente en la seno así de los cuerpos castrenses como de las "élites" dominicanas.

Antes de terminar, permítasenos dejar de nuevo constancia de que, en nuestra opinión, así como *Dictatorship and Development* constituye un valioso aporte a la investigación de uno de los casos más interesantes de dictadura "de transicíon" en la América Latina contemporánea, *The Dominican Republic* es, por su parte, la mejor introducción general que sobre la República Dominicana haya sido escrita recientemente en lengua inglesa. Sin lugar a dudas, las dos obras contribuyen a hacer del profesor Wiarda uno de los autores a consultar con fruto por cuantos deseen conocer más profundamente la realidad socio-política dominicana.

BOOK REVIEWS

Moreno, Francisco José. *Legitimacy and Stability in Latin America: A Study of Chilean Political Culture*. New York: New York University Press, 1969. Acknowledgments, introduction, appendixes I, II, and III. xviii, 197 pp.

Why does a democratic political process exist in some Latin American countries but not in others? Why does political reality in most of the Latin American countries diverge from the prescriptions contained in their constitutions? Why have most of the efforts to institute democracy proved unsuccessful? Why has political stability eluded most of the Latin American countries? What accounts for the stability that a few countries do enjoy?

It is to questions such as these that Moreno directs attention in his analysis of the Chilean political system. As is stated on the dust-jacket, *Legitimacy and Stability in Latin America: A Study of Chilean Political Culture* offers "an original evaluation of Chilean politics, . . . [which] challenges the prevailing view that Chile's stability is the result of pluralistic democratization. Instead, it asserts that the Chilean political system has been legitimized on the basis of its appeal to traditional tendencies. . . ."

Moreno's analysis of Chilean politics centers around the concept of *authoritism* and the contention that "authoristic government is in conformity with cultural and psychological forces deeply felt in the Chilean community . . ." (p. 173). Authoritism, as the term is used by Moreno, refers to the ". . . existence of a single center of legitimate political power, the legal supremacy of which is sanctioned in the name of justice and whose actions are, therefore, not to be bound by written regulations . . ." (p. 24). Both stability and legitimacy characterize authoristic government. Authoritism, Moreno argues, existed in Spain and was instituted in its colonies. Authoristic government is not necessarily personalistic, although it may be. In Spain and in the colonies it was institutionalized. The stability of Spanish and colonial authoritism and the legitimacy accorded it are accounted for by the social, psychological, and cultural factors of the populous. As the author puts it: "The stability of Spanish institutional authoritism should not be attributed as much to any intrinsic quality of the system as to the fact that this form of political organization must have coincided with the inclinations and expectancies of those who were ruled by it" (p. 29). Spanish and colonial authoritism is treated in chapters 1 and 2.

Collapse of the colonial system and Chilean independence are treated in chapter 3. The author attributes these events to Napoleon's overthrow of the authoristic system in Spain. "Removal of the king from his throne altered the colonial arrangement. The traditionally accepted mechanism for resolving disputes and preserving order no longer operated . . ." (p. 72). The result was a political vacuum in Chile. The vacuum "incited the different parts of the [Chilean] colonial apparatus to struggles for total power" (p. 84). From those struggles—intracolonial struggles—came the independence movement—and independence.

Independence did not work a total transformation of Chilean society. The political culture—attitudes and orientations toward politics and the political system—that existed before independence remained. Or, as Moreno describes it, "the new country had to be built with the same people who were there before independence, and their political attitudes could not be changed by the stroke of the pen or the desire of the intellect" (p. 82). The preindependence political culture of Chile was one that accepted and accorded ligitimacy to absolutistic, monistic, authoristic rule—a type of rule that had provided stable government and socioecomonic progress during the colonial years—and not one conducive to pluralistic democracy.

Chile's postindependence political development is surveyed in chapters 4–7. Among the events reviewed are: the chaos that marked the country's first two decades of independence, the Portales period which established stability and presidential dominance, efforts to institute pluralistic democracy, the Balmaceda administration and the insurrection against it, parliamentary government, the 1925 Constitution, the Arturo Alessandri presidency and the reestablishment of presidential dominance, and the Frei Administration. The review is descriptive and explanatory. Moreno's analysis leads him to the conclusion that "Political pluralism has traditionally failed in Chile. The relative high degree of stability the country has enjoyed has been the product of its adherence to a monistic system capable of eliciting the allegiance of the politically important sectors" (p. 176).

On the basis of his analysis of Chile's political past, Moreno offers a projection about the country's political future:

> Leadership, to be successful, will have to remain caudillistic, or it will have to be firmly institutionalized. In either case, the president will be looked upon by most Chileans as the undisputed ruler of the nation, the leader who is to lead in the name of an abstract concept of justice that takes precedence over written laws. Sharing of power will be seen as a sign of weakness, and it will lead to lack of confidence and support (p. 176).

Moreno argues that the only alternatives to an authoristic system are dictatorship and anarchy because "Chile, as a society, lacks sufficient social cohesiveness to permit the government to cease acting as a powerful collective unifying factor" (p. 176).

While the authoristic system may be undemocratic, it need not be so. Authoritism and democracy are not inherently contradictory or incompatible. Moreno holds that "a political system culturally accepted and understood, provides . . . more opportunities for participation than one that is not. In the former the people understand the mechanisms through which their opinions can be expressed and their interests defended" (p. 177). Clearly, of course, the democracy that exists in an authoristic context is not and cannot be the pluralistic variety of democracy.

The book focuses on Chile's political development. However, the analysis and explanation presented are relevant to Latin America as a whole. The psychological and cultural factors shaping Chilean political development and the functioning of the country's political system exist elsewhere in Spanish Latin America.

In sum, Moreno's study is refreshing, insightful, and thought-provoking. It deserves to be read by the student who seeks to understand the Chilean political system and Latin American political systems generally; and it deserves to be read by the reformer who seeks to change Latin American political institutions and processes.

JAMES D. COCHRANE
Associate Professor of
Political Science
Tulane University

Corten, André and Corten, Andrée. *Cambio Social en Santo Domingo.* Instituto de Estudios del Caribe, Estudio Especial No. 5. Puerto Rico: Instituto de Estudios del Caribe, 1968. Prefacio, anexo: cuestionarios. x, 180 pp. $4.00.

There is a paucity of published sociological accounts on the Dominican Republic. This study provides much-needed hard data on the way of life of the poor marginal sectors of the population of Santo Domingo, the main city and capital of that country. The sample consisted of 421 families (households) with whom interviews were conducted in September 1964. The sampling appears to have been accomplished efficiently and according to standard practices. Their model required 475 units, but they candidly admit that some interviews could not be obtained and others were eliminated because they were incomplete. Data were collected on family structure, *compadrazgo,* neighborhood *barrio* organization, education, religion, employment patterns, the usage of medical services, participation in the lottery, consumption of alcohol, and the attitudes towards violence. At the time of the study the authors were teaching sociology at the Universidad Autónoma de Santo Domingo. Selected students were used as interviewers, which was undoubtedly a valuable experience for them in their development as sociologists. Thus, in a rather unusual sense, this might be called "action research."

The theoretical concept of the dual society underlies the whole analysis. Frequently, this concept refers to the fact that modern complex societies are made up of "haves" and "have-nots." The Cortens pose the dichotomy in terms of "traditional" and "modern." Their criteria for classifying families and individuals rest on the kind and duration of employment, and on the level of income for those in business or otherwise self-employed. In addition, two transitional stages were recognized. The first such category included those who had been regularly employed for less than two years, or those who had had such employment within the past five years, even though they had since lost their jobs. The second transitional class comprised those who had been steadily employed less than five years, but more than two. The "moderns" were those steadily employed more than five years. It was suggested by the authors that the type of employment was crucial in determining income, and at the same time reflected nontraditional skills, both of which they feel are crucial as indicators of "modernity." This would seem to be a kind of "culture of poverty" argument in reverse. There is also the assumption that "modern" is an urban phenomenon, while the traditional is primarily rural. Data are then presented in contrasting sets of modern vs. traditional.

To my mind, this is putting the cart before the horse. I do not believe that they have achieved meaningful definitions of traditional and modern. These classifications are neither emic nor etic, and their justification or rationale for the selection of employment as a basic criterion of modernity is not convincing. It would be interesting to take some other criterion—such as participation in voluntary associations—and try correlating differences in this with the other characteristics. It could be that componential analysis or Guttman scaling might be revealing of some undiscovered relationships and/ or processes involved in modernization.

Quite apart from the above criticisms, I very much enjoyed reading the book. It was most informative regarding "how the other half lives in Santo Domingo." The latter was the title of a journal article published by the same authors as a preliminary report. The book is a highly elaborated extension of that article.

It is to be hoped that the facts and perspectives reported here will serve as a basis for future studies, and that the conceptual apparatus may at least be useful as a heuristic device for future sociological studies in that country. Perhaps some of the students trained by the Cortens will do follow-up research on the same or related topics.

NANCIE SOLIEN GONZALEZ
Professor of Anthropology
University of Iowa

Grieb, Kenneth J. *The United States and Huerta.* Lincoln: The University of Nebraska Press, 1969. List of abbreviations, introduction, acknowledgments, note on the sources, index, maps and illustrations, xiv, 233 pp. $7.95.

Woodrow Wilson's policy toward the government of Victoriano Huerta in Mexico has been the subject of much criticism by historians. This book does not contest the conventional treatment of Wilson's first major effort at missionary diplomacy, but it does explore the episode in considerable detail and provides additional evidence for an excoriation of the president's behavior.

Beginning with an account of the circumstances under which Huerta came to power, the author reveals the involvement of U.S. Ambassador Henry Lane Wilson and the favorable reaction in Washington to the new government. The promise of stability appeared to determine the American attitude, although this stability was threatened by the prospect of a pro-Madero uprising and the uncertain position of Venustiano Carranza, governor of Coahuila. Ambassador Wilson recommended recognition of the new administration and Secretary of State Philander Knox indicated it would be extended provided outstanding issues between the two countries could be settled by formal agreement. Such was the situation when a new chief executive took office in Washington.

The president first applied pressure on the new government by denying recognition, and the author carefully recounts the steps by which Wilson escalated his coercive methods in an effort to remove Huerta. Detailed accounts of the Lind mission, the domestic upheaval in Mexico, the role of other nations, military incursions, and the Niagara Falls Conference reveal the complex maneuvers that contributed to Huerta's expulsion.

The author assesses Wilson as "an ardent moralist" who rejected compromise and was intolerant of opposition. Motivated by abstract ideas rather than the national interest, Wilson was inclined to impose his own beliefs on others, often to the detriment of the United States and the nations with which he was dealing. This reviewer does take exception to the seemingly over-simplistic view of Wilson's motives (which were multiple, as the author indicates in portions of the narrative) and his inflexibility, although the author mentions that the president in his subsequent diplomacy may have profited from this unpleasant involvement in Mexican affairs. In regard to nonrecognition, the author states: "By adopting this stance, Wilson reversed traditional American policy. Historically, the United States had always recognized *de facto* regimes, and such statesmen as John Quincy Adams and James Buchanan had affirmed this doctrine." Actually, Adams added a new criterion to American recognition policy, namely, that a government must observe accepted standards of international behavior. Recognition was denied the government of Buenos Aires until it cancelled letters of marque issued to privateers, recognition of the Díaz government in Mexico was withheld for nearly a year, and numerous other pre-Wilsonian examples exist. The "constitutional legitimacy" principle emerged when the Southern states seceded, and it was applied to the Maximilian regime when the United States continued to recognize the government of Benito Juárez.

But essentially this work is a well-balanced, generally objective explanation of this long and painful episode. The major figures, sharply drawn, emerge in full dimension as their characteristics and personalities are related to their actions under the circumstances. The author has utilized archival resources and personal papers in Mexico, Great Britain, and the United States to provide a valuable contribution to an understanding of these events.

RAYMOND G. O'CONNOR
Professor of History
University of Miami

Petras, James *Politics and Social Forces in Chilean Development.* Berkeley and Los Angeles: University of California Press, 1969. 377 pp. $8.50.

This book has been promised by the University of California Press for several years. Now that it has appeared one can perhaps understand the delay in publishing it, for despite its length and scholarly apparatus it is a work of propaganda rather than of scholarship. The reference on page 125 to the period "after Germany invaded the Soviet Union and World War II broke out" is a clue to the political sympathies of the author, which are further revealed in his caricature of the Christian Democratic party as dominated by "corporatists" who are concerned with "maintaining the status quo" (p. 199) through a paternalistic, hierarchical organization of society, as well as in his prediction of the imminent triumph of the Communist-Socialist FRAP coalition through an alliance of peasants and workers.

Not all the Christian Democrats are tarred with the corporatist brush. Some trade union members (not identified) and the leader of the Christian Democratic peasant union (Hector Alarcón of the *Unión de Campesinos Cristianos*) are identified as "populists," but President Frei is accused of repression, bloodshed, and selling out to foreign investors (p. 199). The Christian Democratic party is described as attempting to establish a "quasi-one-party system such as Mexico's where the opposition is ineffective and where the major social sectors are integrated into corporate bodies" (p. 250), and the government-sponsored Popular Promotion program is said to be concerned with "inhibiting the populace from influencing basic decisions which will continue to be made by the economic and political elites" (p. 236).

The evidence for these assertions is scattered, unconvincing, and surprisingly dated for a book with a 1969 publication date. As proof that "very little land reform has been accomplished and little seems likely in the future," Petras cites the 1962 Alessandri agrarian reform law (p. 165), a speech by Frei in 1965 (p. 226), and a 1966 report by the Agrarian Reform Agency (p. 349). There is no mention of the extensive expropriations since the passage of the Christian Democratic agrarian reform law in 1967. (At last count 18,000 families have received land.) To prove the stagnation of the Chilean economy, Petras uses figures from the 1950s (pp. 26 and 149), and to demonstrate that the American copper companies exploit the Chilean economy he refers (p. 47) to a thesis written in 1962, well before the "Chileanization" program was implemented in 1967.

The basic problem, however, is the corporatist-populist analytic framework. There are, of course, good reasons to stress the importance of corporatist thinking in Latin America, both because of the existence of social groupings and loyalties which make it particularly appropriate and the influence of this type of Catholic thought in Latin American history.

Yet there is an important difference between the static hierarchical outlook of corporatism and the democratic pluralism of Christian Democracy. It is because Christian Democratic parties in Latin America have been deeply committed to incorporating the "marginal" socioeconomic groups into effective decision-making and democratizing the economic system that they have been able to appeal to students, intellectuals, and radical reformers. Aside from a brief and obviously interpolated reference to President Frei's difficulties with the "rebel" sector of his party (never analyzed or related to the corporatist-populist dichotomy), there is no analysis of the internal dynamics and the important ideological and practical differences among the Chilean Christian Democrats, and not a single reference to its longtime second-in-command and now presidential candidate, Radomiro Tomic, who stands considerably to the left of Frei on many issues.

There is also no mention of the fact that the real income of the lower classes in Chile has increased by 54 percent since Frei's accession to office. Petras admits in a footnote (p. 106) that "under the Frei government an income tax has been more or less effectively applied, and apparently has cut into the income of the salaried middle class, if not that of the upper-income groups." But he sees the Christian Democrats, like the Radicals before them, as instruments of a Latin American middle class which is concerned with "stability" rather than "political insurgency," shows "an increasing tendency to identify with the established order," and supports military coups to protect its social and economic position (p. 26).

There is some justification for the recent reaction by writers on Latin America against the earlier naive belief that the middle class would automatically support constitutional democracy, but it is equally simplistic to assume that "the Latin American pattern of political development" (whatever that is) is always one of "assimilation" rather than "reformism" on the part of the middle classes (p. 34). The leadership of the Christian Democrats is largely middle-class, but it is also deeply committed to reform. The Chilean municipal elections of 1967 and the congressional elections of March 1969 showed a considerable drop in middle- (and lower-) class support of the Christian Democrats, and a striking revival of the voting strength of the right-wing National party (a fusion of the former Liberals and Conservatives). If the Christian Democrats are indeed the instruments of an authoritarian and assimilationist middle class, it is difficult to explain this. However, anyone who has lived in either the United States or Chile in recent years can explain it easily. Reform costs money, raises taxes, and increases inflationary pressures. The middle-class backlash is a response derived from the pocketbook rather than from devotion to the established hierarchical order in society.

In another interpolation at the end of chapter 3, Petras alludes to the recent resurgence of the National party and the strong possibility of the election of former president Jorge Alessandri in 1970. This contradicts his other assertions about the "plummeting popular support for the Right" as well as his description of the Christian Democrats as "the last political institution capable of preventing the Socialist-Communist rise to power" (p. 251). The author's own evidence indicates why the right wing is doing so well. In addition to the rising tax load on the middle and upper classes (in the latter case the heavy patrimonial tax), the 53 percent of the peasantry who own land, and the large group of traditionalist voters who supported Frei in 1964 out of fear of a victory by the Left have contributed to the new strength of the National party. Above all, there is the personalist factor which does not figure in the author's Marxist categories. Jorge Alessandri is so beloved by Chileans that the members of his family who ran for office in the 1969 elections ran up two of the largest majorities of any congressional candidates. One of them, running in a working-class area where Alessandri is director of a paper factory, received nearly twice as many votes as any other candidate in the country.

The book is no more satisfactory when it treats the Left. In the chapter on the FRAP (the electoral alliance of the Communists and Socialists), the Socialists are described as "neutralist" in foreign policy. They may be neutral between Peking and Moscow but certainly not between East and West—the usual meaning of the term. The 1967 split into two Socialist parties gets one sentence in a footnote but is not analyzed, and there is little attention given to the Socialists' idealogical and electoral differences from the Communists. The debate on the relation of revolution to electoral politics is not discussed, and there is no mention of the differing policies of the Communist and Socialist parties to the Castroite MIR (*Movimiento de la Izquierda Revolucionaria*). The Radicals are dismissed as a right-wing party, although they have been moving left for the past several years and are now attempting to enter an electoral alliance with the FRAP. (Recently they expelled the former right-wing leaders from the party—including their 1964 presidential candidate!)

Inevitably in a work of this length, there are factual errors. The Chilean epithet for the right wing ("mummies") is *momios*, not *momias* (p. 112); the latest figures indicate that 16 percent, not 12 percent of the Chilean labor force is unionized (p. 237); the agrarian reform cooperative settlements run for 3–5 years, not 2 years (p. 258); and there is little reason for pro-Catholic bias in the civil service (p. 306), since it is dominated by adherents of the anticlerical Radical party.

On the positive side, this study emphasizes a number of important aspects of Chilean politics and society which earlier works have ignored. The considerable role of the state in the Chilean economy is noted, and Petras' description of the system as "state-subsidized capitalism" seems accurate. The collectivist orientation of the bureaucracy and its importance in mediating and resolving conflict is discussed, and some interesting survey data presented. The limited participation in Chilean elections until the last decade and the corruption produced by the voting system in use until 1958 are properly underscored. The importance of education (especially but not exclusively private school education) for social mobility is discussed also, although it is not related, as it should be, to the rise of power of the middle-class reformist parties (Radicals and Christian Democrats).

There is another way in which this book is important. It gives the American reader an insight into the way that many Chilean-Left intellectuals see their own society. For basically what Petras has done is to take the assertions of the Chilean Left as working hypotheses and attempt to back them up with a mixture of historical evidence and survey data. If this method does not do justice to the complexities of Chilean politics and social life, it is because the Marxist orientation that provides the author with some interesting hypotheses and questions about Chile also prevents him from giving a balanced assessment of the evidence for and against his initial assumptions.

PAUL E. SIGMUND
Associate Professor of Politics
Princeton University

BOOKS RECEIVED

General and Regional Latin America

Aguayo, Leopoldo González. *La Nacionalización de Bienes Extranjeros en América Latina* (Partes I y II). Ciudad Universitaria, México: Universidad Nacional Autónoma de México, Facultad de Ciencias Políticas y Sociales, Serie Estudios, 7 y 18, 1969. Parte I: Bibliografía. vi, 412 pp. Parte II: Indice. 294 pp.

Foster, David W. and Foster, Virginia Ramos, compilers. *Manual of Hispanic Bibliography*. Seattle and London: University of Washington Press, 1970. Introduction, index. x, 206 pp. $11.00.

Hildebrand, John Raymond. *Economic Development: A Latin Emphasis.* Austin, Texas: The Pemberton Press, 1969. Preface, appendixes A-C, index. x, 155 pp.

Krause, Walter and Mathis, John F. *Latin America and Economic Integrational Planning for Development.* Iowa City: University of Iowa Press, 1970. Foreword, preface, statistical appendix, bibliography. xii, 105 pp. $4.00.

Pearson, Lester B. *The Crisis of Development.* (The Russell C. Leffingwell Lectures Published for the Council on Foreign Relations by Praeger Publishers.) New York: Praeger Publishers, 1970. Foreword by John J. McCloy, index. viii, 117 pp. $4.95.

Sigmund, Paul E., ed. *Models of Political Change in Latin America.* New Work, Washington and London: Praeger Publishers, 1970. Introduction. xiv, 338 pp. $9.00.

Stavenhagen, Rodolfo, ed. *Agrarian Problems and Peasant Movement in Latin America.* Garden City, New York: Doubleday & Co., Inc., 1970. Preface, introduction. xi, 583 pp. $2.45.

Tomasek, Robert D., ed. *Latin American Politics: Studies of the Contemporary Scene.* Garden City, New York: Doubleday & Co., Inc., 1970. Preface to the first edition, preface to the second edition. xiv, 584 pp.

Véliz, Claudio, ed. *The Politics of Conformity in Latin America.* London, Oxford and New York: Oxford University Press, 1970. Foreword, abbreviations, note on contributors, index. x, 291 pp. $2.25.

Countries of Latin America

Bolivia

Malloy, James M. *Bolivia: The Uncompleted Revolution.* Pennsylvania: University of Pittsburgh Press, 1970. Preface, introduction, notes, glossary, index. x, 396 pp. $11.95.

Brazil

Ianni, Octavio. *Crisis in Brazil.* Phyllis B. Eveleth, New York and London: Columbia University Press, 1970. Preface, notes, glossary, abbreviations, bibliography, index. 244 pp. $8.50.

Levine, Robert M. *The Vargas Regime: The Critical Years, 1934–1938.* New York and London: Columbia University Press, 1970. Acknowledgments, abbreviations, notes, bibliography, index. xvi, 270 pp. $9.00.

Caribbean Region

Huberman, Leo and Sweezy, Paul M. *Socialism in Cuba.* New York: Monthly Review Press, 1969. Preface. 221 pp. $2.95.

Liebman, Arthur. *The Politics of Puerto Rican University Students.* (Latin American Monographs, No. 20.) Austin: The University of Texas Press, 1970. Acknowledgments, introduction, bibliography, index. x, 205 pp. $6.00.

Colombia

Richardson, Miles. *San Pedro, Colombia, Small Town in a Developing Society.* (Case Studies in Cultural Anthropology.) New York: Holt, Rinehart and Winston, 1970. Foreword, preface, introduction, bibliography. xiv, 98 pp. $1.95.

Guatemala

Adams, Richard Newbold. *Crucifixion by Power, Essays on Guatemalan National Social Structure, 1944–1966.* Austin and London: University of Texas Press, 1970. Acknowledgments, introduction, works cited, index. xiv, 553 pp. $10.00.

Mexico

Albers, Anni. *Pre-Columbian Mexican Miniatures.* New York: Praeger Publishers, 1970. Foreword by Ignacio Bernal, introductory text by Michael D. Coe, photographs by John T. Hill. xx, 92 pp. $15.00.

Casanova, Pablo Gonzales. *Democracy in Mexico.* Danielle Salti, trans. New York: Oxford University Press, 1970. Foreword by Irving Louis Horowitz, introduction, tables, name and subject indexes. xvii, 245 pp. $7.95.

Craine, Eugene R. and Reindorp, Reginald C., trans. and eds. *The Chronicles of Michoacán.* Norman: University of Oklahoma Press, 1970. Foreword, appendixes, suggested readings, index. xxii, 259 pp. $7.95.

Flores, Edmundo. *Vieja Revolución, Nuevos Problemas.* Guaymas, México: Editorial Joaquín Mortiz, S. A., 1970. Prólogo, índice. 125 pp.

Vázquez, de Knauth, Josefina. *Nacionalismo y Educación en México.* Guanajuato: El Colegio de México, 1970. Prólogo, introdución, bibliografía, índice onomástico, vii, 291 pp.

Wilkie, James W. *The Mexican Revolution: Federal Expenditure and Social Change Since 1910.* Berkeley and Los Angeles: University of California Press, 1970. Foreword by Howard F. Cline, introduction, list of symbols, tables, maps, graphs. xxxii, 337 pp. $9.00.

Peru

Schwartz, Robert N. *Peru: Country in Search of a Nation.* Los Angeles, California: Inter-American Publishing Co., 1970. Preface, introduction, notes, bibliography, appendix, index. xiii, 178 pp.

Austin, Allan G. and Lewis, Sherman. *Urban Development for Metropolitan Lima.* (Praeger Special Studies in International Politics and Public Affairs.) New York: Praeger Publishers, 1970. Foreword by Lyle C. Fitch, list of maps, charts and tables, glossary, selected bibliography, about the authors. xv, 187 pp. $12.50.

INTER-AMERICAN RELATIONS

Rout, Leslie B., Jr. *Politics of the Chaco Peace Conference, 1935–1939.* (Latin American Monographs, No. 19.) Austin: University of Texas Press, 1970. Preface, acknowledgments, bibliography, index. xviii, 268 pp. $7.50.

Slater, Jerome. *Intervention and Negotiation: The United States and the Dominican Republic.* New York, Evanston and London: Harper and Row, Publishers, 1970. Foreword by Hans J. Morgenthau, preface, notes, bibliography, index, illustrations. xviii, 254 pp. $7.95.

Wagner, R. Harrison. *United States Policy Toward Latin America, a Study in Domestic and International Politics.* Stanford, California: Stanford University Press, 1970. Introduction, notes, index. 246 pp. $7.95.

MISCELLANEOUS

Briones, Angel Valbuena. *Literatura Hispanoamericana.* (Tomo IV de la *Historia de la Literatura Española.*) Barcelona, España: Editorial Gustavo Gili, S. A. Índice, índice de obras, índice onomástico. 556 pp.

César Vallejo: An Anthology of his Poetry. Oxford, New York and Toronto: Pergamon Press, 1970. Introduction and notes by James Higgins. ix, 183 pp. $4.00.

Clissold, Stephen, ed. *Soviet Relations with Latin America 1918–68, a Documentary Survey.* London, New York and Toronto: Oxford University Press, 1970. Preface and acknowledgments, abbreviations, list of documents and extracts, introduction, notes, index. xx, 313 pp. $12.00.

Gillett, Theresa and McIntyre, Helen, compilers. *Catalog of Luso-Brazilian Material in the University of New Mexico Libraries.* Metuchen, New Jersey: The Scarecrow Press, Inc., 1970. Introduction, abbreviations, index. xiii, 961 pp. $20.00.

Gutiérrez, Fermín Estrella. *Estudios Literarios.* (Estudios Académicos IX.) Buenos Aires: Academia Argentina de Letras, 1969. Prólogo, índice. 363 pp.

Magis, Carlos H. *La Lírica Popular Contemporánea: España, México, Argentina.* (Centro de Estudios Lingüísticos y Literarios, Nueva Serie 1.) Guanajuato, México: Colegio de México, 1969. Introducción, bibliografía, glosario, índices. 724 pp.

Phelan, John Leddy. *The Millenial Kingdom of the Franciscans in the New World.* Berkeley and Los Angeles: University of California Press, 1970. Prologue, notes, bibliography, index. 179 pp. $6.75.

Reindorp, Reginald C. *Spanish American Customs, Culture and Personality.*

Available through the College Bookstore, Wesleyan College, Macon, Georgia. Copyright 1968. Preface, introduction. xvi, 344 pp.

Rohde, Jorge Max. *Humanidad y Humanidades, Estudios Literarios.* (Estudios Académicos X.) Buenos Aires: Academia Argentina de Letras, 1969. Índice. 361 pp.

GREAT SEAL UNIVERSITY OF MIAMI
CORAL GABLES FLORIDA 1925

APRIL 1971
VOLUME XIII—NO. 2

JOURNAL OF INTER-AMERICAN STUDIES and WORLD AFFAIRS

JOURNAL OF INTER-AMERICAN STUDIES and WORLD AFFAIRS

Vol. XIII, No. 2 APRIL 1971

La Ganadería americana: una propuesta para la historia comparativa	MANUEL A. MACHADO, JR.	159
Bolivian Oil and Brazilian Economic Nationalism	PETER SEABORN SMITH	166
Interim Adjustment Policy in the CACM	JOSEPH PINCUS	182
Situación demográfica de Guatemala y sus efectos socio-económicos	JOSÉ A. VILLAMIL	197
Juan M. Thome, Argentine Astronomer from the Quaker State	JOHN E. HODGE	215
Provincial Participation in Canadian Foreign Relations	GÉRARD F. RUTAN	230
The Image of Christ in Spanish America As a Model for Suffering	MILES RICHARDSON MARTA EUGENIA PARDO AND BARBARA BODE	246
The Contribution of Capistrano de Abreu to Brazilian Historiography	KATHERINE FRINGER	258
The Catholic Church in Brazil	PHILIP RAINE	279
Nuevas Corrientes	ROBERT E. MCNICOLL	296
Books		300

Published Quarterly for the

CENTER FOR ADVANCED INTERNATIONAL STUDIES

by the

UNIVERSITY OF MIAMI PRESS

Coral Gables, Florida

CONTRIBUTORS

MANUEL A. MACHADO, JR., is a Ph.D. graduate from the University of California, Santa Barbara. In addition to recent research on Aftosa and the Mexican cattle industry, he will soon be publishing a book on United States-Mexican relations 1919–1924 * * * PETER SEABORN SMITH completed research for his article under a Doherty Fellowship in 1966–1967 and two Canada Council grants in 1967–1968 and in 1970. He received his Ph.D. from the University of New Mexico * * * JOSEPH PINCUS served in the U.S. Department of State and the Agency for International Development in Costa Rica, Paraguay, and El Salvador. He is a Ph.D. graduate from the American University, Washington, D.C., and the author of a number of books and articles on economic problems in Latin America * * * JOSÉ A. VILLAMIL is a Guatemalan economist trained at Louisiana State University, whose particular field of interest is the role of demography in economic development * * * JOHN E. HODGE received his Ph.D. from the University of Illinois and is the author of a number of articles on nineteenth-century Argentina * * * GERARD F. RUTAN, whose primary research interest is Canadian politics, holds a Ph.D. degree in political science from the University of North Carolina and is a member of the executive committee of the Association for Canadian Studies in the United States * * * MILES RICHARDSON, Ph.D. graduate of Tulane University, has done field work in Colombia and Costa Rica; BARBARA BODE is a doctoral candidate in anthropology at Tulane University who had done field work in Guatemala and Costa Rica; MARTA EUGENIA PARDO, a graduate of the University of Costa Rica, is now a Master's degree candidate in anthropology at Louisiana State University in Baton Rouge * * * KATHERINE FRINGER, a doctoral candidate at Columbia University, has been a Herbert Lehman Fellow for the past three years and is currently preparing her dissertation in Bahia, Brazil, where her husband is serving as Peace Corps physician * * * PHILIP RAINE whose last post, before retirement, was minister-counselor of the U.S. embassy in Rio de Janeiro was also Visiting Lecturer at Temple University in 1968. He is presently in Costa Rica where he has acquired a coffee farm and is writing a book on Brazilian politics.

All correspondence concerning manuscripts or exchange information should be directed to the Editor, *Journal of Inter-American Studies and World Affairs*, Box 8134, University of Miami, Coral Gables, Florida 33124. Correspondence regarding book reviews should be sent to the Book Review Editor, *Journal of Inter-American Studies and World Affairs*, Box 8123, University of Miami, Coral Gables, Florida 33124. Subscriptions and business correspondence should be addressed to *Journal of Inter-American Studies and World Affairs*, University of Miami Press, Drawer 9088, Coral Gables, Florida 33124. Annual subscription, $8.00; students, $6.50. Single issues available; please inquire concerning prices.

The *Journal of Inter-American Studies and World Affairs* is indexed in *Public Affairs Information Service, Historical Abstracts, Social Sciences and Humanities Index, Indice Bibliográfico, Current Contents: Behavioral, Social, and Management*, and others.

PRINTED IN THE UNITED STATES OF AMERICA

Manuel A. Machado, Jr.
Department of History
University of Montana
Missoula, Montana

LA GANADERÍA AMERICANA: UNA PROPUESTA PARA LA HISTORIA COMPARATIVA*

Cuando Herbert Eugene Bolton, en 1932, enunció su tesis sobre la integración histórica de los países americanos despertó gran conmoción entre los historiadores sobre la validez de su tesis. Lo que propuso, simplemente, era que existían raíces comunes en todos los países americanos y que éstos necesitaban un estudio integrado para comprender los puntos complejos de dicha historia y darle una perspectiva continental. No cabe duda que a partir de 1932 varios historiadores han corregido ciertos aspectos de su tesis, pero a la vez, sigue íntegra como base para empezar un estudio económico y social de la ganadería americana. El problema con la tesis de Bolton aparece durante el período después de la independencia de los varios países y a la vez con la unión continua del Canadá con el Imperio Británico. He aquí donde muchos historiadores lo critican sin considerar que casi todos los países tomaron sus inspiraciones intelectuales de Europa y también de los Estados Unidos. A la vez, no se puede rechazar una tesis tan importante sin estudiar los aspectos no políticos e internacionales. Por esta razón, es de mayor importancia darle consideración a la ganadería como fuerza social, política y económica.

En todo el Hemisferio occidental la ganadería tuvo importancia en la vida cotidiana y en el desarrollo de la historia de todos los países. En los Estados Unidos durante su época colonial fue necesario empezar la cría de ganado para la producción de leche, carne y cuero. Aunque la cría no era

* Este trabajo fue presentado en una de las sesiones del Pacific Coast Council of Latin American Studies reunido en la Universidad de California, Santa Barbara, los días 5–7 de noviembre de 1970.

considerable, sirvió como base para darle a los coloniales experiencia en el manejo del ganado. Con la independencia en 1783 y la siguiente expansión de los Estados Unidos hasta el Mar Pacífico empezó un gran movimiento demográfico en ese país. Creció una sociedad fronteriza, creándose instituciones relativamente indígenas que resultaron de la necesidad de la gente para adaptarse al nuevo ambiente. En esto también se puede ver la importancia de la ganadería en la historia. El ganado, por un tiempo durante los años 1865 a 1895, reinó como la industria suprema de las regiones occidentales de los Estados Unidos. Crecieron en esa región grandes latifundios no muy diferentes en función y extensión de las haciendas mexicanas o las estancias argentinas. Era cría de ganado extensiva y no intensiva. Alrededor de 1870–1875, empezó la importación de razas finas de ganado europeo, principalmente de Inglaterra. Con el aumento de ganado fino que por fin reemplazó al ganado criollo un cambio sutil apareció. La ganadería perdió muchos de sus aspectos fronterizos. Ahora se trató como inversión de capital. Banqueros, inversionistas, especuladores y los mismos ganaderos empezaron a pensar de una manera completamente comercial. Se hablaba de ganancia o pérdida, de la necesidad de cercar el ganado para que los toros sementales no perdieran su esperma en vacas criollas, de sueldos, de los gastos de mandar el ganado a Chicago o Nueva York por los nuevos ferrocarriles. A la vez empezó el conflicto con el agricultor. La dotación de tierras a los labradores precipitó a veces guerras sangrientas entre ganaderos y agricultores. Surgió también conflicto entre ganadero y ferrocarrilero sobre los elevados gastos de mandar el ganado a los centros metropolitanos. Esta relación compleja entre ganadero, agricultor, ferrocarrilero y comprador de la metrópoli indica la importancia del ganado. Había demanda de carne en la costa del Atlántico pero el ganado estaba en el oeste. Al mismo tiempo, la evolución del ferrocarril mejoró la situación en el este pero los gastos de mandar el ganado no dejaron que el ganadero aumentara su ganancia. El conflicto entre las regiones ganaderas-agricultoras y las ciudades grandes del este aumentó y sigue teniendo impacto hasta la época actual.

También hay que tomar en consideración a la ganadería norteamericana en el siglo XX. La época romántica del siglo XIX con sus grandes extensiones pastoriles, la figura del *cowboy* y la libertad fronteriza pasó a la historia y al olvido cuando los centros metropolitanos tomaron el control del gobierno. Hay que analizar entonces la manera en que los ganaderos norteamericanos adoptaron nuevas normas durante el siglo actual. ¿Cómo, por ejemplo, se organizaron para mantener íntegra la industria ganadera? A la vez, ¿cuáles cambios fueron introducidos a la cría ganadera en los Estados Unidos para que esa industria pudiera competir con otras entidades económicas? ¿En qué manera se organizaron los ganaderos norteamericanos? Hay necesidad de examinar cuidadosamente la historia de las organizaciones ganaderas norteamericanas.

En la América Latina, especialmente en las regiones ganaderas de México, Argentina, Venezuela, Uruguay, Brasil y partes de Chile y el Perú durante la época colonial crecieron grandes latifundios dedicados a la cría del ganado. A la vez, se nota un fenómeno particular: en casi todos los casos la cría de ganado empezó donde había necesidad de suministrar las minas de una región con carne y cuero. En México, por ejemplo, con el descubrimiento de las minas de Zacatecas en 1546 y con la siguiente guerra contra los chichimecas, los mineros, sin contacto comercial directo con la ciudad de México-Tenochtitlán, tuvieron que establecer haciendas para la cría del ganado. En la Argentina, cuya historia colonial varía bastante de la de México o del Perú, empezó también la ganadería mas con el propósito de exportación de cueros en vez de la carne del animal. En Brasil, con el descubrimiento de ricas minas de diamantes y de oro a fines del siglo XVII y a principios del siglo XVIII empezó en Rio Grande do Sul y la región del Matto Grosso, la cual es extensión de la Pampa rioplatense, una extensa cría de ganado para suplir a los mineros. Esto fue propagación de la cría ganadera que se había establecido en la región del Rio São Francisco.

Durante esta importante época colonial, se ve el establecimiento de instituciones españolas, portuguesas y criollas. Estas instituciones —la hacienda, el peonaje— tuvieron gran impacto en la historia de la América Latina después de la independencia. En México, la Mesta, gran organización trasladada de España, sirvió como manera de controlar la ganadería mexicana durante el virreinato. Era como la rama ganadera del imperio español. A la vez, en el virreinato del Perú no se estableció la Mesta porque en esa entidad no hubo el extenso desarrollo ganadero que existía en México.

Se ve también un desenvolvimiento social que tendrá su mayor influencia en los años después de la independencia: es decir, el mestizaje. La mezcla de sangre española o portuguesa con la indígena creó al mestizo (o mameluco en Brasil) que forma la gran parte de los que manejaron el ganado. Rechazado por los blancos y por los indios, el mestizo se escapó a la frontera donde se metió en el trabajo más importante de esas regiones: la ganadería. En México los mestizos sirvieron como los vaqueros de las haciendas norteñas. En la Argentina, el Uruguay, el Paraguay y en el suroeste del Brasil el gaucho, y en el noreste brasileño el *vaqueiro,* derivado de sangre mezclada, formaron la mayoría de los hombres que manejaban los grandes rebaños de ganado bovino y ovino. La frontera latinoamericana sirvió como escape para el mestizo cuya vida hubiera sido limitada por la organización formal y casi rígida de las ciudades y de la metrópoli.

Durante la época de la independencia fue el mestizo el que formó gran parte de los ejércitos libertadores. En Venezuela el llanero José Antonio Páez, gran ganadero y soldado, pudo cambiar el balance a favor de los ejércitos de Simón Bolívar. En México, hombres como José María Morelos, Vicente Guerrero, Guadalupe Victoria y hasta Agustín de Iturbide dependieron de la masa mestiza para formar sus ejércitos. Esto no fue pura casualidad porque los mestizos eran diestros en el manejo de caballos y ganado que se necesitaban en un ejército compuesto principalmente de cuerpos de caballería e infantería.

Después de la independencia, casi todos los países latinoamericanos sufrieron gran caída económica. Años de guerra debilitaron a la industria ganadera y les tomó casi medio siglo para reestablecerla. Al mismo tiempo, los líos políticos que padecían los países latinoamericanos no dejaban que se desarrollara la ganadería. Cuartelazos y caudillos contínuamente causaban gran desequilibrio a la ganadería y a la economía en general. Abigeato por los varios ejércitos de gauchos, llaneros o vaqueros no dejaba que la ganadería se estableciera como entidad íntegra.

Alrededor de 1870, en muchos países latinoamericanos la estabilidad empezó a formarse en el cuerpo político. A la vez, inversionistas extranjeros aumentaron sus inversiones en empresas ferrocarrileras, la ganadería, la minería y el comercio de la América Latina. Desde la independencia, intereses extranjeros se habían metido en la América Latina, pero al lograrse cierta estabilidad en países como Argentina, Brasil y México aumentó en gran proporción la inversión de los Estados Unidos y de Inglaterra. En la Argentina, la construcción de ferrocarriles dejó que el ganado de Córdoba o La Rioja llegara a Buenos Aires. En esa ciudad se construyeron mataderos y frigoríficos para la matanza de las reses y el empacamiento de la carne. A la vez, con el descubrimiento de la refrigeración, se pudo exportar carne a Europa y así aumentar la importancia económica de la ganadería. Como en los Estados Unidos, el desarrollo ganadero argentino hizo que se importara ganado de pura raza para mejorar el criollo existente. Al mismo tiempo, el conflicto entre las regiones ganaderas y las ciudades que se vió en los Estados Unidos se manifestó también en la América Latina. Conflictos entre Buenos Aires y la provincias, desacuerdo entre los hacendados norteños y los consejeros positivistas de Porfirio Díaz, conflicto entre los llaneros venezolanos y los habitantes de Caracas—todo fue manifestación de los líos políticos, económicos y sociales entre lo rural y lo metropolitano.

El siglo XX dio a luz un gran movimiento revolucionario en la

América Latina que se manifestó claramente en México. Las clases bajas y medias salieron triunfantes durante una guerra civil sangrienta que duró más que catorce años. Derrotaron a la clase criolla y a la vez casi destruyeron la ganadería. Pasaron muchos años antes que la ganadería mexicana se restableciese como aspecto importante de la economía nacional. En el resto de la América Latina la ganadería sufrió como resultado de las vicisitudes políticas y sociales. En la Argentina, el gaucho como tipo social ya sólo vivía en el poema épico *Martín Fierro* de José Hernández y en las novelas gauchescas. Los labradores que se dedicaban al trigo convirtieron a la Pampa de una región donde antes vagaban grandes rebaños de ganado y borregos en un lugar con cercas y de vida más organizada. Pero esto no quiere decir que la ganadería perdiera su importancia. La industrialización forzó a la ganadería a una posición secundaria con el impulso moderno para la industria y la exportación comercial. La ganadería, considerando las tendencias positivistas de los gobiernos modernos latinoamericanos, tuvo que competir con otros aspectos de las economías nacionales.

En la América latina también fueron organizados grupos ganaderos a fines del siglo XIX. En la Argentina, por ejemplo, la Sociedad Rural Argentina ejerció gran poder sobre el destino político y económico del país rioplatense. En el siglo presente dicha sociedad perdió un poco de su poder, especialmente con el énfasis industrial que la economía recibió por medio de Juan Domingo Perón. México tuvo experiencia también en la organización ganadera especialmente después de 1930. Estos grupos —las uniones regionales ganaderas— formaron un balance contra la influencia agraria que se avanzó con los grupos campesinos. En los otros países de la América Latina han crecido grupos ganaderos que tratan de ejercer su influencia sobre el cuerpo político y económico de sus distintos países. El problema para el historiador viene en que tendrá que empezar de nuevo. Hay muy poca literatura histórica sobre la ganadería latinoamericana en este siglo.

La ganadería del hemisferio presenta ciertos problemas históricos. Siguiendo la tesis de Bolton, hay que analizar los varios aspectos de la ganadería americana y comparar el desarrollo ganadero en los varios países del hemisferio. Esto se puede hacer formulando varias preguntas. ¿Cuál, por ejemplo, fue el impacto político de la ganadería en los países del continente? ¿De qué manera se manifestó la fuerza política de la ganadería? A la vez, ¿cuáles procesos de modernización afectaron la influencia política de los ganaderos? En su aspecto fronterizo, ¿cuáles factores comunes contribuyeron al desarrollo en los Estados Unidos, Argentina, México, Brasil y los otros países del continente? ¿Cuáles herencias coloniales contribuyeron al desarrollo ganadero en la época moderna?

Más importante es el impacto social de la ganadería en la historia. Como se puede ver, la frontera sirvió como escape para el mestizo en la América Latina. En los Estados Unidos, los que querían escaparse de las presiones metropolitanas también se fueron a las regiones fronterizas. Con esto se crearon tipos sociales distintos: el vaquero en México, el gaucho o vaqueiro en las regiones rioplatenses y brasileñas, el llanero venezolano, el cowboy norteamericano. Usando la historia comparativa como método de estudio, ¿cuáles factores tenían en común todos estos tipos sociales que resultaron del desarrollo ganadero en la Américas? Al mismo tiempo, ¿cuáles factores contribuyeron a la caída de estos tipos sociales? ¿Cuáles fueron los procesos en que la ganadería tuvo que adaptarse a la vida moderna para sobrevivir como aspecto íntegro de la economía y de la sociedad?

En su aspecto económico, ¿qué efecto tuvo la ganadería en la vida material de países como los Estados Unidos, México, Argentina, Brasil y Venezuela? ¿Cómo se adaptó la ganadería a la totalidad de la economía de estos varios países? ¿De qué manera se forzó la modernización de la ganadería? ¿Cuáles factores de competencia militaron contra la expansión de la ganadería para que pudiera tener importancia en la época actual? A la vez, ¿cuáles factores biológicos han tenido impacto en la ganadería de este hemisferio?

Una cosa que se debe considerar es la importancia de las enfermedades del ganado como aspecto de la ganadería del hemisferio. En esto, hay que hacer estudios del desarrollo veterinario y zootécnico en los países ganaderos del hemisferio. Tomando como ejemplo la fiebre aftosa, se puede ver que dicho mal por los menos destruye un 25 porciento del ganado de toda la América del Sur. Hay que tomar en cuenta que en países como Venezuela, Ecuador, Perú, Chile y Argentina la fiebre aftosa no deja que se desarrolle la ganadería como industria de gran exportación. En los Estados Unidos y en la Argentina la aftosa apareció alrededor de 1870. Después de varios brotes, los Estados Unidos pudieron controlar y erradicar el mal. En la Argentina, dicho mal sigue siendo una gran amenaza a la industria ganadera. Se prohibe la importación de ganado argentino a los Estados Unidos, México y los países centroamericanos, todos libres del mal. Por razones económicas y sanitarias los Estados Unidos ha prohibido la importación de ganado o carne de la América del Sur. Esto inhibe producción total de ganado. A la vez, con una pérdida anual de un 25 porciento de la producción total, hasta los mercados domésticos sufren escasez de carne. También la industria lechera sufre porque las vacas infectadas con la fiebre aftosa no pueden producir leche para consumo humano.

¿Cuál ha sido el efecto de las enfermedades del ganado en la América latina? ¿De qué manera se relacionan las enfermedades ganaderas con el desarrollo económico de esa industria? ¿Cuál ha sido el impacto internacional de estas enfermedades, como la fiebre aftosa, en la política de los varios países del hemisferio? Es decir, ¿cuál es la relación entre estas enfermedades y la historia general de la ganadería americana?

Lo que se propone en este ensayo esquemático es otra manera de estudiar la historia de los países americanos. La historia comparativa puede servir como vehículo para enriquecer el entendimiento entre los varios países del hemisferio. Hay que empezar con estudios muy específicos que consideren una región o un tema con mucha profundidad. Las monografías que dan luz a esta clase de estudios deben ser muy detalladas para que se pueda hacer síntesis de las tendencias comunes en la ganadería del hemisferio. A la vez, usando la ganadería como punto de partida, se pueden ver las fuerzas comunes que han determinado el desarrollo histórico del hemisferio. Esta clase de estudio, también, requiere adiestramiento especial.

El historiador de esta época necesita saber más que el análisis de documentos. Tiene que apreciar los procesos económicos, sociológicos y biológicos que se mezclan en la evolución de un pueblo. Para esto, hay que adiestrar a los jovenes historiadores en el manejo de datos derivados de la psicología, la sociología, la economía y las ciencias naturales. Hay que cambiar la orientación provinciana y rígida de algunos historiadores para que puedan ver las fuerzas generales que contribuyeron a la evolución histórica del hemisferio. De esta manera, posiblemente la historia del hemisferio se pueda librar de los prejuicios políticos que tiñen a la literatura histórica. El estudio de aspectos históricos no políticos puede llevar a cabo un entendimiento de las culturas diversas del Nuevo Mundo. Con tal comprensión, posiblemente se puedan mejorar las relaciones entre los países del hemisferio y quitar como obstáculo los prejuicios que existen en los varios países. Al mismo tiempo, una comprensión comparativa de las varias culturas del continente, por medio de un estudio minucioso, ayudará a encontrar maneras de elevar el modo de vida de muchos de los habitantes sin imponer ideas extrañas que no tienen relación a la realidad particular de estos países.

Peter Seaborn Smith
History Department
St. Jerome's College
Waterloo, Ontario

BOLIVIAN OIL AND BRAZILIAN ECONOMIC NATIONALISM

Early in 1938, Brazil signed a treaty with Bolivia that would open part of the apparently oil-rich Chaco region to Brazilian exploitation. Up to that time, Brazil's growing but still negligible national effort to find oil within her own territory had proved fruitless; the treaty, however, seemed to guarantee it a supply of oil not controlled by the great international petroleum companies, an important proviso during the nationalistic Vargas administration. Yet Brazil failed to pursue the prospect opened by the treaty until the 1950s, and then its attempts to implement it were defeated by internal economic nationalism. This essay deals with Brazil's abortive efforts in the 1950s to frame and implement a policy for developing its oil concessions in Bolivia. The incident is an isolated example of the difficult international relations which prevail in Latin America.

The sequence of events begins on 17 November 1903 in the signing of the Treaty of Petrópolis ending the "War of Acre" and several years of tension between Brazil and Bolivia.[1] Both nations secured highly desired

[1] The problem had concerned the present Brazilian state of Acre, which the Brazilian imperial government had recognized as Bolivian territory by the Treaty of Ayacucho (27 March 1867), signed during the Paraguayan War when Brazil had been courting traditionally unfavorable Bolivian public opinion. Alvaro Lins called the treaty "perhaps the most generous . . . which Brazil, during the Empire, signed with its neighbors." Further, since the area was then unexplored, its limits were left vague, to be ratified later in accordance with "limits more natural and convenient to each nation." Acre, however, was "entirely inhabited by Brazilians," who by 1880 had established a thriving rubber production. In 1899 Bolivia decided

concessions from the treaty. Brazil acquired the extensive and rich natural-rubber-growing territories in the Amazon Valley, an area roughly corresponding to the present state of Acre. Bolivia gained egress to the outside world: both to the Paraguay River by the cession of some territory near the Brazilian city of Corumbá and to the Amazon River when Brazil would construct a railway from Madeira to Mamoré, bypassing rapids and with a bridge across the Mamoré River linking the railway to Villa Bella, Bolivia. In addition, Brazil agreed to pay Bolivia two million pounds sterling.[2]

A quarter of a century later the bridge to Villa Bella had not been built. Negotiations concluded by the "Christmas Treaty," 25 December 1928, stipulated that Brazil should expend the approximately million-pound cost of the Mamoré River bridge in building instead a railway from Santa Cruz de la Sierra to Cochabamba, Bolivia. This agreement in its turn was not implemented by Brazil in the course of the following decade.[3]

The question of Brazilian concessions to Bolivian oil resources entered the picture when a further round of negotiations betwen the two nations was concluded on 26 February 1938. Under the new arrangements a more ambitious 743-kilometer-long railway, including the bridging of the Paraguay River, was to be built from Santa Cruz to Porto Esperança, Brazil.

Clearly this railway would cost more than the million pounds at issue between the nations, and in return for the extra Brazilian aid, Bolivia set aside part of its "Subandean" oil zone under a Treaty for the Extraction and Development of Bolivian Petroleum. The zone, from the Parapetí River north to the Ichilo River, was to be surveyed jointly, after which Brazilian-Bolivian companies would be formed for exploitation. After ful-

---

to turn over the exploitation and administration of Acre to the Bolivian Syndicate, a company backed by United States and British capital. The inhabitants of Acre stubbornly resisted Bolivian attempts to enter the region. Brazil, in order to compel Bolivia to protect Brazilian citizens in Acre, soon suspended Bolivia's shipping rights on Brazilian rivers. Negotiations, led by the Baron of Rio-Branco, culminated in the 1903 treaty (Alvaro Lins, *Rio-Branco* [Rio de Janeiro: José Olympo, 1945]), 1: 366–74; 2: 401–34.

[2] Ibid., 2: 434–35; Gordon Ireland, *Boundaries, Possessions, and Conflicts in South America* (Cambridge, Ma.: Harvard University Press, 1938), pp. 48–49; José Maria Bello, *História da República,* 5th ed. (São Paulo: Companhia Editora Nacional, 1964), p. 230; [Refinaria e Exploração de Petróleo União S.A.], *Petróleo Boliviano e Mercado Brasileiro* (São Paulo, 1956), p. 13. Brazil, in the 1867 Treaty of Ayacucho, had already promised to build the Madeira-Mamoré railroad: Lins, *Rio-Branco,* 2: 435.

[3] Ireland, *Boundaries,* pp. 52–53; *Petróleo Boliviano e Mercado Brasileiro,* p. 13; Ambassador Raul Fernandes to Chamber of Deputies, 16 May 1955, *Diário do Congresso,* 31 May 1955, cited in ibid., pp. 35–36.

filling Bolivian consumption requirements the surplus oil would be offered to Brazil, and whatever balance remained would be exported. The agreement further stipulated that Brazil would provide Bolivia with rail facilities and allow it the right to construct pipelines (if needed). Both countries would erect refineries to process the oil produced under the treaty.[4]

For Bolivia, the fundamental impulse behind the several treaties was its persistent drive to the sea. Ever since the War of the Pacific, by which it had lost its last fragment of coastline, Bolivia had been expending every possible effort to win from its rather uncooperative neighbors some guaranteed means of access to the sea. Its relations with Chile, despite "free port" privileges in Antofagasta and Arica and Chile's construction of a railway linking La Paz with Arica, have been troubled by a legacy of bitterness over the 1883 settlement. Bolivia was wise to seek an alternate port.[5]

For Brazil the Chaco region of Bolivia exercised a fascination, particularly since Paraguay and Bolivia had fought a war over it and Standard Oil had invested a lot of money in its exploration.[6] Bolivia was willing to share the petroleum which apparently was there in return for a means of access to the Atlantic. Brazil was looking outside its territory for a supply of oil, and eager to take advantage of the unique opportunity to meet its need.

Bolivia's nationalization in 1936 of Standard Oil of New Jersey's holdings added a new dimension to its negotiations with Brazil. Anxious that the Standard should not be able to maneuver through Brazil to regain control of Bolivian oil, the directors of Yacimientos Petrolíferos Fis-

---

[4] The *New York Times*, 27 February, 17 March 1938; *Petróleo Boliviano e Mercado Brasileiro*, pp. 13–14; Ambassador Fernandes, *Petróleo*, pp. 36–37. The treaty stipulated that each country would allot $1,500,000 to the survey; Ambassador Fernandes said that Brazil did so but that Bolivia offered maps of the region confiscated from Standard Oil, for which Bolivia had paid $950,000 (Standard Oil had apparently spent $17,000,000 in compiling them). The text of the Treaty for the Extraction and Development of Bolivian Petroleum may be found in *Petróleo*, pp. 27–28. The sides of the treaty zone (on the east and west) were not delineated.

[5] Preston James, *Latin America*, 3rd ed. (New York: The Odyssey Press, 1959), pp. 226–27; Harold Osborne, *Bolivia; A Land Divided*, 3rd ed. (London: Oxford University Press, 1964), p. 60.

[6] The Standard Oil Company of New Jersey obtained a concession in the Camiri region, in the vicinity of the Parapetí River (it would later become one of Bolivia's major producing zones) in 1922. Until 1937, when the operation was expropriated, the highest crude production was approximately 450 barrels per day. Jersey Standard also built two small topping plants, which had a combined capacity of 450 b.p.d. in 1935. See Robert J. Alexander, *The Bolivian National Revolution* (New Brunswick, N.J.: Rutgers University Press, 1958), p. 160; Cornelius H. Zondag, *The Bolivian Economy, 1952–65; The Revolution and Its Aftermath* (New York: Frederick A. Praeger, 1966), p. 112.

cales Bolivianos (YPFB), the state oil company, put pressure on Brazil to form a state agency to handle oil exported under the 1938 treaty. The result was Brazil's creation, in May of the same year, of the National Petroleum Council (Conselho Nacional de Petróleo—CNP), a state entity with full control over all phases of the Brazilian oil industry. Further, the CNP immediately announced plans to erect oil refineries, a move calculated to emphasize Brazil's interest in the treaty.[7]

Brazil, however, discovered oil within its own territory less than a year after signing the treaty with Bolivia and immediately turned its attention to development of the field under CNP supervision. Further, after World War II a wave of economic nationalism, based on the slogan, "*O petróleo é nosso*" (The oil is ours), inflamed the debate over a national oil policy; its culmination was a state-monopoly company, Petróleo Brasileiro S.A. (Petrobrás), formed late in 1953 for development of national oil reserves. With massive infusions of public capital, Petrobrás began to improve substantially the still negligible Brazilian production figure.

The Bolivian oil zone seemed unimportant to Brazilians by comparison. Although construction of the railway had begun, it proceeded so slowly that after more than a decade work in the Subandean zone had not progressed beyond the surveying stage.[8]

Meanwhile, in Bolivia YPFB had kept crude-oil production at a modest 1000 barrels per day—from the former Standard Oil field at Camiri—for about a decade. However, the 1952 revolution swept the MNR under Víctor Paz Estenssoro into power, and one of the new govern-

---

7 General Júlio C. Horta Barbosa, opening address to CNP, 12 September 1938, "Sessões Realizadas," in CNP *Relatório, 1º triênio, 1938–41* (Rio de Janeiro, 1941), p. 4; John D. Wirth, *The Politics of Brazilian Development* (Stanford: Stanford University Press, 1970), 149–50. Wirth notes that the two chief executives of YPFB were "disgruntled former officials of Standard of Bolivia . . . [who] wanted old scores with Standard to stay settled."

8 In 1941 Brazil discovered that Argentina had a similar railway concession (to be paid off over a period of time by Bolivia) which passed through the Brazilian treaty zone to Santa Cruz. In answer to a Brazilian protest, Bolivia replied that Argentina had no rights to oil within Brazil's concession, since the latter had legal control by virtue of its prior claim. By 1952 some delineation had been made of the zone's east and west sides, but it was not precise; a "Reversal Note" (meaning an exchange of diplomatic notes between two countries dealing with a single topic) to this effect was exchanged in 1952: Ambassador Fernandes in *Petróleo Boliviano e Mercado Brasileiro,* pp. 37–38; Brasil, Câmara dos Deputados, *Anais da Câmara dos Deputados*, 1960, 9: 608–9. In 1951 and 1952 President Getúlio Vargas reported that exploratory drilling was about to begin, and diplomatic notes were exchanged to that effect in 1952 and 1953. See Getúlio Vargas, *O Govêrno Trabalhista do Brasil* (Rio de Janeiro: José Olympo, 1952), 1: 93; Vargas, *O Govêrno Trabalhista do Brasil: Os Problemas de Base da Economia Nacional* (Rio de Janeiro: José Olympo, 1954), 2; 133–34; the *New York Times,* 7 January, 13 August 1953. By January 1953, only fifty miles of track remained to be laid, the *New York Times,* 7 January 1953.

ment's first economic objectives was to increase the output of YPFB. Exploration activity increased substantially, and a new field, near Camiri, was discovered almost immediately.[9] From this it appeared highly probable that the zone reserved under the 1938 treaty for joint Brazilian-Bolivian exploration and exploitation, lying as it did immediately north of Camiri, would yield oil.

Late in 1954, Paz Estenssoro sent a sharp complaint to his Brazilian counterpart, João Café Filho, about Brazil's lack of interest in exploring the treaty zone. A ceremony on 5 January 1955, inaugurating the finally completed Porto Esperança-Santa Cruz de la Sierra railway brought the two presidents together.[10] Paz Estenssoro called upon Brazil to relinquish its rights to all Bolivian territory reserved to it under the treaty of 1938. The area would be explored and controlled by YPFB, and a refinery built in Santa Cruz to serve the local Bolivian market and neighboring Mato Grosso state. Exploitation would be open to anyone, including Brazilian companies, by means of concessions.[11]

In his memoirs, Café Filho described his shock when, upon arriving in Santa Cruz, he was met by demonstrators shouting "O petróleo é nosso," not against the United States but against Brazil. He said Paz Estenssoro "complained long and bitterly" over Brazil's inactivity in connection with the 1938 treaty, which he said he had opposed as a deputy. Paz Estenssoro emphasized the "psychological effect" upon his countrymen of this unhappy state of affairs: in comparison with Bolivia, Brazil was "rich and growing," and yet it had neglected Bolivia and had even held back its overall growth by retaining sovereignty over part of the nation. Finally, he pointed out that he had come to power at the head of a revolutionary movement which had expelled the foreign owners of tin mines. The implication of his remarks was not lost upon the Brazilian president.[12]

Café Filho did succeed in having further action on the treaty postponed until after the forthcoming Brazilian presidential election. Upon returning to Rio de Janeiro he asked his cabinet for their opinions on the question; he also asked Minister of Finance Eugênio Gudin if Brazil could find enough foreign exchange ($4,000,000) to comply with the treaty. The

---

[9] Alexander, *Bolivian Revolution*, pp. 160–62; Zondag, *Bolivian Economy*, pp. 112–13.

[10] The *New York Times*, 8 January 1955; Mário Leão Ludolf, *Da Conveniência da Exploração do Petróleo Boliviano* (Rio de Janeiro: Confederação Nacional Da Industria, Conselho Econômico, 1959), p. 11; *Petróleo Boliviano e Mercado Brasileiro*, p. 34.

[11] *Petróleo Boliviano*, p. 34.

[12] João Café Filho, *Do Sindicato ao Catete: Memórias Políticas e Confissões Humanas* (Rio de Janeiro: José Olympo, 1966), pp. 445, 447–48.

reply was that it would be "difficult, if not impossible" to find the funds.[13]

Late in 1955 Paz Estenssoro decreed a Petroleum Code which abandoned the nationalistic policy established in 1937. Clearly short of capital and foreign exchange, and anxious to explore substantially Bolivia's oil potential, the government made available all but 7 percent of national territory to exploration by concession. Within a year, a number of foreign oil companies had entered the country attracted by the possibilities of the Subandean zone, in which Argentina as well as Bolivia had discovered petroleum.[14]

Because of its own shortage of foreign exchange as well as pressure from Bolivia, Brazil might well have agreed to let its rights to Bolivian oil lapse at this time had not an element among its defense experts opposed such a move. General Canrobert Pereira da Costa, chief of staff of the armed forces, and the chiefs of staff of the army and navy all advised retaining the treaty unaltered. They envisaged a continental supply of petroleum for Brazil, and thus wanted to preserve the treaty for reasons of national security. In time of war, they argued, Brazil would be more secure if it did not have to rely on maritime transport for oil imports. The National Security Council, largely composed of men of like mind, also called for retention of the Bolivian treaty land but said the 1938 agreement should be "reexamined." President Café Filho accordingly directed Itamarati (the Foreign Office) to begin conversations with Bolivia "to discuss the hypothesis of the suggested revision." [15]

By December 1956, talks between the two nations had proceeded well, to the point that Itamarati began to seek and interview Brazilian groups which might be authorized to develop oil on her behalf in the treaty zone. Those mentioned at the time were connected with two consortia: Refinaria de Petróleo do Distrito Federal S.A., which owned and operated

---

13 Lúcio Glauco Torres, "Petróleo da Bolívia," *O Observador Econômico e Financeiro* 279 (May 1959): 52; Café Filho, *Do Sindicato*, 452; Juarez Távora, "Quem Matou Vargas; Notas à Margem do Tema," *Manchete* 822 (20 January 1968): 127.

14 Zondag, *Bolivian Economy*, pp. 113–14; Alexander, *Bolivian Revolution*, pp. 164–66. Gulf Oil Company, through a wholly-owned subsidiary, Bolivian Gulf Oil Company (BOGOC), acquired the largest number of concessions (by 1967 more than 4,000,000 acres) and had the greatest success of any of the firms in discovering oil. Under terms of its contract (drawn up late in 1956), the company paid Bolivia 11 percent royalty in oil from production plus 19 percent development tax. See "Gulf Bolivian Subsidiary Will Conduct Exploration," *World Oil* 143, no. 6 (1956): 227; "Gulf Seeking New Fields in Bolivia as Oil is Exported," ibid. 164, no. 2 (1967): 95; Enrique T. Mauri, "Bolivian Oil Interest Warming Up," ibid. 145, no. 1 (1957): 183–84.

15 Café Filho, *Do Sindicato*, pp. 450–52; Torres, *O Observador Econômico e Financeiro* (May 1959), p. 52; *Petróleo Boliviano e Mercado Brasileiro*, pp. 34–35.

a refinery at Manguinhos, on the outskirts of Rio de Janeiro, and Refinaria e Exploração de Petróleo União S.A., whose refinery was at Capuava, between Santos and São Paulo.[16]

At this early date Petrobrás was not under consideration as a possible Brazilian agency in the Bolivian oilfields. One Brazilian newspaper, discussing the state company in this context, remarked on the obvious hypocrisy of such participation: Petrobrás had been founded upon anti-imperialism and radical nationalism and it was an embodiment of the state; for it to operate in Bolivia would be nothing short of an invasion of a sovereign nation.[17]

Discussions between the two countries continued through 1957. As many as seven private Brazilian firms indicated interest in developing the Bolivian treaty area; at least two of them were rumored to have foreign (U.S. or British) backing. Bolivia made it clear that Petrobrás would not be allowed to participate in the exploitation of the area in question. However, Colonel Janari Nunes, president of Petrobrás, insisted in 1957 that his company be included in discussions with Bolivia and, further, that it be the sole company exploiting the Bolivian concession.[18]

In May 1957 a Brazilian mission went to La Paz to discuss the 1938 treaty. Nunes represented Petrobrás, but his presence proved a stumbling-block to negotiations. Bolivia remained firmly opposed to Petrobrás' participation in the exploitation of the treaty area. Nunes' return to Brazil in July led observers to believe that Petrobrás had been defeated in its effort to dominate, or even participate in, Brazil's exploitation of Bolivian oil.

Apparently Bolivia was still putting pressure on Brazil to relinquish its claim to Bolivian territory under the 1938 treaty. The Andean country

[16] *O Jornal* 8 December 1956; *Última Hora*, 12 January 1957.

[17] *O Jornal*, 11 December 1956. This newspaper, which had commented on Petrobrás, espoused "orthodox" economics and private enterprise. The Bolivian Petroleum Code (decreed on 26 October 1955) stipulated, by Article 16, that "no foreign state, ostensibly or discreetly, may obtain a petroleum concession in Bolivia." See *Petróleo Boliviano e Mercado Brasileiro*, 29; the *New York Times*, 19 January 1957. General Henrique Teixeira Lott, then minister of war, pointed out that "it would seem absurd . . . that we should have a foreign orientation on different bases than those which we have adopted for our internal orbit." See Café Filho, *Do Sindicato*, p. 451.

[18] The *New York Times*, 19 January, 24 February 1957; "Brasileiros no Petróleo da Bolívia," *O Observador Econômico e Financeiro* 252 (February 1957): 83–84; "A Setback for Petrobrás?," *Petroleum Week*, 19 July 1957, in Anderson O. Mascarenhas, *Roboré, um Torpedo contra a Petrobrás* (São Paulo: Editora Fulgor, 1959), pp. 157–61. Foreign capital—in this case Gulf Oil Corporation—was interested in building a pipeline from the treaty zone to Santos, but existing Brazilian legislation would not permit such activity by a foreign company; the *New York Times*, 14 August 1956.

needed foreign exchange. Brazilian companies were under no obligation to pay exploration taxes to Bolivia while working in the treaty zone. On the other hand, the Bolivian Gulf Company (BOGOC) had expressed interest in the southern half of the treaty area; not only would it pay exploration taxes but it would pay them in dollars, thus contributing to Bolivia's meager foreign-exchange reserves.[19]

Negotiations reached a stalemate toward the end of 1957. Brazil was eager and determined that Petrobrás be allowed to exploit the treaty zone, and Bolivia adamantly opposed such a move. Bolivia, moreover, wanted at least part of the zone opened to foreign-capital development and Brazil feared that under such conditions Bolivia would become a "back door" by which the great international petroleum companies (the "trusts" to Brazilian nationalists) could enter Brazil and undermine Petrobrás.

The press of both countries then took up the controversy. Nationalistic Brazilian newspapers charged that Bolivia was "under the control of the trusts," and their Bolivian counterparts charged Brazil with "imperialism." Indeed, Bolivia even went so far as to accuse Brazil of evoking separatism in Santa Cruz de la Sierra Province to annex it and its oil to Brazil.[20]

Early in November 1957 Brazil agreed to a Bolivian proposal that the foreign ministers of each country meet to attempt a resolution of the stalemate.[21] During January 1958 negotiating teams met in the Bolivian town of Roboré, on the railroad Brazil had built under one of the 1938 treaties. Clearly, Brazil could hope to stay in Bolivia only if it reduced its claims; on the other hand, Bolivia wanted an outlet for her oil and other

---

19 "A Setback for Petrobrás?," in Mascarenhas, *Roboré*, pp. 157–61; the *New York Times*, 22 July 1957. The newspaper also noted that "Bolivia had become the hottest oil area in South America after Venezuela and that foreign companies were actively competing for concessions" since liberalizing her oil policy in November 1956 (when Congress implemented the 1955 code).

20 *Última Hora*, 16–22 July, p. 31; 4–6 September, 30 October, 1, 5 November 1957; *O Estado de São Paulo*, 4 October 1957; the *New York Times*, 6 October, 2 November 1957; *O Semanário* 21–28 February 1957. Senator Lourival Fontes (PTB), former press secretary to Vargas and a strong nationalist, accused Henry F. Holland, former United States Assistant Secretary of State for Inter-American Affairs and subsequently an attorney for several United States groups with interests in Latin America, of interference in the Brazilian-Bolivian negotiations: *New York Times*, 6 October 1957. *Última Hora*, 4–6 September 1957, charged that Holland and the "trusts" had written Bolivia's 1956 petroleum law. Zondag (p. 113) says, "The United States Operations Mission to Bolivia made available to the Bolivian Government the services of a United States consulting firm for the purpose of drawing up a new petroleum code." Alexander (pp. 168–169) notes that Holland held his State Department post while the code was being drawn up; within a few months he appeared in Bolivia as a lawyer for oil interests seeking concessions there. It would be easy to conclude that the United States had pressured Bolivia into an oil policy favorable to the "trusts" and U.S. interests.

21 The *New York Times*, 2 November 1957.

exports through Brazil. On January 27 the parties reached an agreement, details of which were soon released to both countries.[22]

The settlement, known as the "Roboré Agreement" (*Acôrdo de Roboré*), was in the form of thirty-one separate clauses.[23] It dealt with a variety of topics, among which was the implementation of the 1938 Treaty for the Extraction and Development of Bolivian Petroleum. Clause Six reduced the area open to Brazilian exploitation from 34,000 to 13,500 square kilometers, and limited its development to "private companies of Brazilian capital," subject to the Bolivian Petroleum Code. Under the terms of the other clauses referring to petroleum, Brazil agreed to purchase in "convertible currencies" (dollars or sterling) 100,000 barrels per day of crude oil produced in Bolivia (by any company), 5000 of which were to be supplied by YPFB. The oil was to be purchased "in the conditions and prices of the international market." Private Brazilian firms were to exploit the Bolivian field solely for Brazilian consumption; if such production exceeded 100,000 barrels per day, the companies were free to dispose of the surplus as they saw fit. The oil produced was to be given free passage throughout Brazil and be subject only to normal tariffs.[24]

Brazil's nationalistic press was initially enthusiastic about the Roboré Agreement. Rio de Janeiro's *Última Hora* hailed the pact as "one of the greatest negotiations in our history" and said that Brazil had been lucky to get so much, since it had been dealing with the "trusts" rather than with Bolivia. The newspaper saw the agreement as a "victory for the realistic nationalism" of President Juscelino Kubitschek and heaped praise upon Foreign Minister Macedo Soares, who had headed the mission to Bolivia (he had also participated in the negotiations over the 1938 treaty).[25]

The National Bank of Economic Development (BNDE) accepted proposals until 12 September 1958 from groups interested in exploiting the treaty zone. By the deadline, six had applied. According to the *New*

---

22 *Última Hora*, January 1959 (the newspaper ran a series of articles throughout the month on the negotiations, expressing the hope that the 1938 treaty would be implemented); Torres, *O Observador Econômico e Financeiro* (May 1959), p. 52; Cafe Filho, *Do Sindicato*, pp. 452–53.

23 The clauses were known as "Reversal Notes."

24 "Bolivia," *World Oil* 149, no. 3 (1959): 131–32; Café Filho, *Do Sindicato*, pp. 452–453; Ludolf, *Da Conveniência*, pp. 13–14; *O Jornal*, 1 April 1958; *Folha da Manhã*, 10 July 1958; Torres, *O Observador Econômico e Financeiro* (May 1959), p. 52. The question of how the anticipated oil was to be transported to Brazil was not resolved: a pipeline seemed the least expensive means, but Brazil probably could not have expended the necessary capital on such an ambitious project and she could not allow any foreign concern to build one; Brazil favored using the railway.

25 *Última Hora*, 30–31 January, 7 February, 2 April 1958; Torres, *O Observador Econômico e Financeiro*, p. 52.

York Times, most of them were negotiating with U.S. and West European interests for the financing of their operations.[26] The BNDE, while considering the applications, indicated that it would favor those from groups which had their own sources of funds. The BNDE did not have the dollars to finance such a venture.

For *Última Hora* such a preference on the part of the BNDE represented a "tacit acceptance" that the "trusts' would have a hand in financing the Brazilian companies in Bolivia. The newspaper charged that there were indeed some "figurehead" organizations among the six applicants.[27] The CNP pointed out to President Kubitschek that foreign oil capital might enter Brazil through the private companies working in Bolivia. The BNDE delayed for several months its decision on which companies should go to Bolivia, and the controversy over how Brazil should develop its treaty zone continued unabated.[28]

Unfortunately for the scheme, negotiations for financing coincided with a very unpopular anti-inflation drive by the Brazilian government. In response to rapidly growing inflation and foreign debt, as well as strong pressure from the International Monetary Fund to apply a "shock treatment" approach to stabilization, President Kubitschek attempted in 1958–1959 to introduce a measure of austerity into parts of the national economy. The move stirred widespread resentment, particularly from nationalists, against "foreign pressures." [29] In such a climate, foreign financing for companies proposing to exploit Brazil's "concession" in Bolivia would be bound to arouse strong reaction from nationalists as another example of foreign pressure.

Early in January 1959 the BNDE chose three companies for developing the Bolivian zone. A representative of each was called before a Chamber of Deputies investigating committee; their subsequent testimony revealed that each firm had made arrangements for some foreign backing.[30]

---

[26] *Última Hora*, 13 September 1958; the *New York Times*, 13 September 1958. *Última Hora*, 25 April 1958, had warned about national companies acting as fronts for the "trusts" in Bolivia. The companies that submitted proposals were: *União Brasil-Bolívia de Petróleo S.A.* (a subsidiary of *Refinaria e Exploração de Petróleo União S.A.*); an unnamed consortium headed by Oscar Hermínio Filho; *Petróleo Andino S.A.*, ("*Petrolansa*"); *Petróleo da Bolívia S.A.* ("*Petrobol*"); and two others still in the process of organization.

[27] *Última Hora*, 23 September 1958. The president of the BNDE was Robert de Oliveira Campos, an "orthodox" economist who already had been a target for the nationalistic press as an "*entreguista*," selling out Brazil to foreign interests.

[28] *Última Hora*, 22 October, 6 November 1958.

[29] Thomas Skidmore, *Politics in Brazil, 1930–1964; An Experiment in Democracy* (New York: Oxford University Press, 1967), pp. 174–80.

[30] *Última Hora*, 12–14 January 1959; Torres, *O Observador Econômico e Financeiro* (May 1959), p. 52. The three companies were *União Brasil-Bolívia de*

Macedo Soares and Colonel Alexínio Bittencourt, a former president of the CNP and a member of the mission to Roboré, appeared before the same committee and attacked the BNDE for breaking with the nationalistic precedent set by Brazil in its negotiations with Bolivia.[31] Roberto Campos, president of the BNDE, also testified before the committee and stressed the risks involved in the undertaking. It was better, he said, that foreign rather than national capital be gambled in such an uncertain venture.[32]

Opposition among nationalists to the Roboré Agreement grew rapidly and was widespread by the end of January 1959. On 28 January Rio de Janeiro police broke up a student demonstration in front of the BNDE. *Última Hora*, which had earlier praised the accord, now spoke strongly against it on the grounds that it had brought the "trusts" close to, if not into, Brazil. Public figures in increasing numbers denounced the agreement as not in Brazil's best interest.[33] Senator Lourival Fontes, for example, asserted that Bolivia had betrayed the "patriots of yesterday" and had broken the 1938 treaty. It had done so in obedience to the "American monopoly," led by Gulf Oil Corporation, which hoped to retard Brazilian development.[34] Deputy Sérgio Magalhães saw no reason for interest in Bolivia "when we have so much to do, right here, in terms of petroleum." The Roboré Agreement, he said, "should be abandoned." [35]

The Clube Militar took an interest in the Bolivian question at this time,

Petróleo S.A., *Brabol*, and *Petrolansa*. The first company had arranged with the Anderson Clayton group to "swap" dollars for *cruzeiros* (a fortuitous meeting of two complementary needs); the second had a connection with DeGolyer & MacNaughton Co., Pan American Land and Royalty Co., and Intercontinental Financial Co.; and the third had arranged a loan of $9,000,000 from a syndicate of four U.S. companies (Tennessee Gas, Union Oil and Gas, Lion Oil, and Murphy Corp.), repayable in dollars after production had been initiated.

31 *Última Hora*, 15, 17 January 1959.

32 *Jornal do Comércio* 21 January 1959. Celso Furtado, later to become a controversial figure in Brazil and to lose his political rights after the 1964 revolution, was at the time a director of the BNDE and supported Campos' policy.

33 *Última Hora*, 22, 27–31 January 1959; the *New York Times*, 29 January 1959; "Petróleo Boliviano," *O Observador Econômico e Financeiro* 275 (January 1959): 3, 13–14. At this time a columnist in *Última Hora* (22 January 1959) raised the problem of a pipeline from Bolivia. After noting the legal difficulties involved in building the pipeline and the financial restraints facing Petrobrás, the columnist said that if oil should be found and a pipeline built by Petrobrás, it would be carrying oil belonging to a private company, probably under the control of the "trusts."

34 Lourival Fontes, *Política, Petróleo e População* (Rio de Janeiro: José Olympio, 1958), pp. 55–56. On this theme see also Joel Silveira and Lourival Coutinho, *História de uma Conspiração (Bolívia, Brasil e Petróleo)* (Rio de Janeiro: Editôra Coelho Branco, 1959), passim.

35 *Última Hora*, 24 January 1959. Magalhães, like Fontes, was a member of the PTB, which tended to have more nationalists within its ranks than the other major parties.

reflecting both the continuing interest of the military in a ready supply of oil as an aspect of national security and the nationalism of the club executive elected in June 1958.[36] Late in January 1959, Army Colonel Albino Silva addressed the club, calling for a return to the terms of the 1938 treaty and pledging support for Petrobrás.[37] Air Force Colonel Anderson O. Mascarenhas, in the *Revista do Clube Militar*, the club's official organ, took Albino Silva's points to their logical conclusion. He charged that the Roboré Agreement could make Brazil "a colony of the international petroleum cartels" and that it signified "the definitive and inescapable abdication of our economic emancipation in the face of the international petroleum groups." [38]

Mascarenhas also published a book in which he set out the main arguments of the nationalists against the Roboré Agreement. The bone of contention was that the "trusts" would get into Brazil and break the state petroleum monopoly, as embodied in Petrobrás, through the "back door." Each of the companies approved by the BNDE to exploit the zone had connections with foreign oil concerns; these companies would ship oil to Brazil, and this would represent the first step in an "inevitable takeover" of the country by the "trusts." Further, even if the companies approved by the BNDE were financed solely by Brazilian capital, Bolivia was in the hands of the "trusts," which was enough to threaten Petrobrás.[39]

Nationalistic deputies, led by Gabriel de Rezende Passos, charged that the Roboré Agreement was not just "enabling legislation" but a new treaty because it changed the 1938 treaty. It would then have to be submitted to Congress, where nationalists believed they could bring about its defeat. Itamarati, however, contended that the Roboré Agreement

---

[36] General Justino Alves Bastos became president of the club in June 1958 as a result of a growing wave of nationalism within the organization. See *Última Hora,* 27 June 1958. The Clube Naval, in a rare demonstration of independence from the Clube Militar, held a series of lectures in *support* of the Roboré Agreement; ibid., 14 February 1959.

[37] *Última Hora*, 29 January 1959. From about 1957 until the 1964 revolution, to pledge support for Petrobrás seems to have served as a loyalty oath for radical nationalists. Albino Silva became president of Petrobrás in 1963, serving for several months.

[38] Colonel Anderson Oscar Mascarenhas, "O Acôrdo de Roboré," *Revista do Clube Militar* 152 (January 1959): 33–34.

[39] Mascarenhas, *Roboré, um Torpedo contra a Petrobrás.* The book included contributions from other radical nationalists, such as Gondin da Fonseca, Teixeira Lott, Osny Duarte Peireira and Gabriel de Rezende Passos. Mascarenhas exposed a "plot," engineered by the "trusts" to destroy Petrobrás and all it represented for the independence of Brazil. The details are unimportant, but it is worth noting that the military had been, for Mascarenhas, the single entity which had been able to thwart the plot since its inception in 1950.

merely implemented the old treaty, which action did not require congressional approval.[40]

The CNP recommended to President Kubitschek, on 6 March 1959, that the three companies selected by the BNDE be authorized to work in Bolivia as long as they could prove financial capacity to both governments.[41]

The issue, however, was reopened on 25 January 1960. Gabriel Passos recommended in the Chamber of Deputies that those clauses in the Roboré Agreement dealing with petroleum be submitted to Congress and that Congress reject them as contrary to the interests of Brazil.[42] In October 1960 the Chamber demanded that the relevant clauses be submitted to it for examination.[43]

Less than a year later the administration of Jânio Quadros accepted the proposition that the Roboré Agreement was in fact a new treaty and submitted the entire accord to Congress.[44] Bolivia, however, refused to discuss any change in the agreement, maintaining that it was satisfied with the "Reversal Notes" which both sides had accepted in 1958. There the matter rested, as far as the Brazilian Congress was concerned, which took no further action.[45] Yet, since an agreement already existed (the 1938 treaty), in 1961 four Brazilian companies were allowed to venture into Bolivia to develop the "concession."

Two of the companies did not reach the drilling stage. Petróleo da Bolívia S.A. was dissolved for financial reasons before it could begin operations, and Petróleo Andino S.A. (*Petrolansa*) made geologic surveys only and failed to drill (apparently also for financial reasons).

---

[40] Mascarenhas, *Roboré*, pp. 230–33; Gabriel de Rezende Passos, *Estudo sôbre o Acôrdo de Roboré* (São Paulo: Editôra Fulgor, 1960), p. 7. Passos was minister of mines under João Goulart until his death in 1962.

[41] *Última Hora*, 7 March 1959. The CNP recommended that companies arrange for their foreign exchange either by the "swap" method, used by *União Brasil-Bolívia de Petróleo S.A.* and the Anderson Clayton group, or by recourse to the open market.

[42] *Anais da Câmara dos Deputados*, 1960, 345–53; Olympio Guilherme, *A Verdade sôbre Roboré* (Rio de Janeiro: Livraria Freitas Bastos, 1960), p. 81. Guilherme wrote his pamphlet, calling for retention of the agreement, in answer to Passos' work *Estudo sôbre o Acôrdo de Roboré.*

[43] *Última Hora*, 27 October 1960; *Anais da Câmara dos Deputados*, 1960, 19: 99–100. Passos had presented the bill on 15 June 1960: *Anais*, 1960, 9: 526–628.

[44] Minister of Foreign Relations Afonso Arinos, in *Diário do Congresso Nacional* (Seção II), 8 June 1961, p. 946; Café Filho, *Do Sindicato*, pp. 452–53. The reason for the long delay in securing congressional consideration was probably the dramatic success Petrobrás was enjoying in production, apparently reducing the significance of a possible Bolivian oil source.

[45] Personal interview, Dr. Lauriston Pessôa Monteiro, Rio de Janeiro, 15 July 1970. Dr. Monteiro is a superintendent of *União Brasil-Bolívia de Petróleo S.A.*

A third company, Companhia Petrolífera Brasileira S.A., struck oil in the one well it drilled. In common, however, with the two firms already mentioned, it could not raise the capital necessary to exploit its concession. Further, the Bolivian government charged the company with smuggling in connection with imports of equipment, expropriated its holding, and turned it over to YPFB.

The fourth company União Brasil-Bolívia de Petróleo S.A., drilled four wells in two of which (in the foothills of the Andes) "shows" of gas and oil were found. Encouraged, the company decided to seek more funds from its shareholders; but at the time (1962–1963) the Brazilian government, under João Goulart, was debating the expropriation of the few private refineries within the national territory, one of which (at Capuava, São Paulo) was owned by the company's parent, Refinaria e Exploração de Petróleo União S.A. The threatened move was part of a radicalization of Brazilian nationalism over which Goulart had no control, and which took for one of its chief symbols Petrobrás and the "economic emancipation," for which it purportedly stood. In such an uncertain climate for private enterprise in petroleum, União Brasil-Bolívia de Petróleo S.A. felt it could not approach its shareholders. Late in 1963 the company sought permission from the Bolivian government to build a refinery at Santa Cruz de la Sierra, but the persistent threat to the parent company's refinery in Brazil (principal source of capital for the entire União organization) prompted Bolivia to refuse the offer. União Brasil-Bolívia de Petróleo S.A. then released over half its concession to Bolivia. It still holds the remainder, against the day when an effective oil treaty is signed between Brazil and Bolivia.[46]

Bolivia recently nationalized the holdings of BOGOC and, as a result, no longer has a market for its surplus oil. Brazil, on the other hand, continues to produce less than half the oil it consumes. Accordingly, Brazil's interest in Bolivian oil and gas and Bolivia's interest in the Brazilian market have apparently been reawakened. At first glance, Brazilian imports of Bolivian petroleum would seem both compelling and easy to arrange: (1) a railroad already exists from the Bolivian oilfields to Brazil's industrial heartland, São Paulo, and a multi-products pipeline could be constructed along its right of way; (2) since Chile is reluctant to allow substantial exports from Bolivia through its ports and, moreover, significant

[46] Café Filho, *Do Sindicato*, pp. 452–53; personal interview, Dr. Lauriston Pessôa Monteiro, Rio de Janeiro, 6 November 1967. Dr. Monteiro said he was optimistic about the gas possibilities of his company's concession. He also pointed out that all machinery needed in the Bolivian operation had been shipped from Santos by rail to the drilling site south of Santa Cruz; Brazilian industrial products could thus be carried to Bolivia in exchange for oil.

consumption on the Bolivian Altiplano does not yet exist, it would seem more feasible to ship to the Atlantic; and (3) Bolivian gas could serve the projected Brazilian petrochemical complex in the interior of São Paulo.[47]

The cost of such a pipeline, however, would be enormous (perhaps half a billion dollars) and, even if production and reserves were sufficient to justify such an expense, the political climate would seem to mitigate against the undertaking. Relations between the two countries have been troubled for decades, and it is doubtful that a nationalistic Bolivian government would tolerate being tied to Brazil. The possibility that Petrobrás might be given concessions and allowed to export oil to Brazil would, for the same reasons, seem highly unlikely. Finally, it is also equally doubtful that Brazilian companies, possibly foreign-financed (however indirectly), would be allowed to exploit concessions in Bolivia and export oil and gas directly to Brazil, considering the strong official support still given Petrobrás' monopoly on oil importing. Thus it would appear that the treaty (1938 or 1958) will remain a dead issue.

Economic nationalism clearly was instrumental in the collapse of the Brazilian effort to develop conjectured oilfields in Bolivia. On the one hand, it seems safe to say that Brazil would have done little about the 1938 treaty had not Bolivia's economic nationalism and thirst for dollars threatened Brazil with the loss of its Bolivian "concession." Yet when Brazil tried to implement the 1938 treaty—finally negotiating the Roboré Agreement—it ran afoul of its own economic nationalism. First, negotiations nearly broke down because Petrobrás tried not only to enter but to monopolize them (it is ironic that Petrobrás, a state-monopoly company and the creature of economic nationalism, should have been cast as an "agent of economic imperialism"). But perhaps the most important reason for the collapse of the effort was that Brazilian economic nationalism channeled massive amounts of capital (and significantly, of foreign exchange) into Petrobrás and even threatened the capital formation of private oil companies. It thus proved impossible to find sufficient funds to finance the Bolivian venture. In the end, the campaign of economic nationalism did not stop companies going to Bolivia (although, nationalistic

[47] Michael Sieniawski, "Brazil again Eyes Oil from Bolivian Sources," *Christian Science Monitor*, 11 February 1970; "Óleo Boliviano," *O Globo*, 11 June 1970. Bolivia is reported interested in supplying Brazil's west, through a refinery in Corumbá, Mato Grosso. Personal interview, Dr. Lauriston P. Monteiro, Rio de Janeiro, 15, 19 June 1970; Monteiro, "Relatório Sucinto da Viagem de Observação à Bolívia, Realizada entre os Dias 8 e 22 de Novembro de 1969," unpublished report to *União Brasil-Bolívia de Petróleo S.A.* (Rio de Janeiro, 1969), passim. Petrobrás remains unwilling to consider Bolivian oil and gas imports, citing reasons of "national security" and "political-economic problems."

opposition to the Roboré Agreement did delay the start of operations), but the uncertain climate it produced in Brazil in the early 1960s restricted work to very limited exploration. Bolivian economic nationalism in the late 1950s had stirred Brazil to action, only to be confounded by the rise of Brazilian economic nationalism in the succeeding decade.

This episode presents a microcosm of the difficulties besetting Latin American cooperation, as the region appears to be trying to move toward economic integration. Economic nationalism currently holds sway—just as it defeated a Brazilian-Bolivian attempt at cooperation in one commodity only, so it is delaying implementation of a hemispheric common market.

Joseph Pincus
Department of Economics and Finance
Louisiana Tech University
Ruston, Louisiana

INTERIM ADJUSTMENT POLICY IN THE CACM

The long-term revenue and balance of payments policies of the Central American Common Market (CACM) countries are (1) to achieve harmonization of their tax structures and improve tax administration; and (2) to establish a Central American Monetary Union capable of (a) assisting member countries suffering from temporary balance of payments disequilibria; (b) operating as a Federal Reserve Bank-type system; and (c) serving as a clearinghouse for intra-CACM as well as external payments. These policies have been receiving considerable study. On 25 February 1964 the central banks of the five CACM countries signed in San Salvador an Agreement for the Establishment of a Central American Monetary Union. The foregoing policies were enunciated at a meeting of the Central American presidents in San José, Costa Rica, on 19 March 1963, when they agreed "to establish a monetary union and a common policy in fiscal, economic and social matters, within the framework of the Economic Integration Program." A Central American Monetary Council was created by the Agreement. The Council comprises the presidents of the five central banks of the CACM countries.

At a meeting of the Central American Monetary Council in San Salvador in January 1968,[1] it was decided to create a Central American Monetary Stabilization Fund to coordinate CACM monetary policies, facilitate financial assistance to countries having temporary balance of

[1] Twenty-fourth Extraordinary Meeting.

payments difficulties, and assure the maintenance of monetary stability and convertibility of the respective national currencies. This fund was to serve as an intermediate step toward the long-range objective of achieving a monetary union. Through U.S. government auspices, the services of two well-known monetary experts (Robert Triffin and Richard M. Cooper) were obtained to study and recommend the form and functions of the Central American Monetary Stabilization Fund. Their recommendations were presented to a Tripartite Meeting (Monetary Council, Economic Council, Executive Council) that took place in San Salvador in mid-1968, and the Fund came into being on 1 December 1969. It was to work closely with the International Monetary Fund (IMF) in providing emergency assistance, including Special Drawing Rights (SDR), to individual CACM members. Over a period of years, the Stabilization Fund was to acquire increasing holdings of member central bank foreign exchange reserves; it could invest these reserves in the region and abroad; it was to incorporate the functions of the existing Central American Clearing House;[2] and it was to coordinate monetary policies in the CACM. Eventually, the creation of a Central American currency was contemplated.

While negotiations leading to the adoption of partial long-term policies for curing Central America's balance of payments problems were in progress, tumbling world prices for coffee and bananas and a drop in Nicaraguan exports of cotton resulted in considerable strain on the balance of payments of the Central American countries, especially Nicaragua and Costa Rica. (Costa Rica introduced a dual exchange system in January 1967, which prohibited the banking system from selling foreign exchange at the official rate for imports from outside the CACM.) Inasmuch as there are also serious revenue repercussion effects in these countries associated with a drop in export earnings, fears became widespread in the CACM that further unilateral actions might be taken by members and that the integration mechanism would be imperiled. Thus a partial interim regional solution to these problems was sought through the negotiation of the San José Protocol at about the same time that the longer-range policies were under consideration.

This paper discusses the interim adjustment policies adopted in the San José Protocol and attempts to estimate the possible effects of these policies. Their implementation was still awaiting the adoption of appropriate regulations as 1971 began.

---

[2] Established by an agreement signed by the Central American central banks on 28 July 1961.

BALANCE OF PAYMENTS POSITION

International Liquidity on the Eve of the Protocol

The International Monetary Fund defines Central Bank international reserve liquidity as the sum of its holdings of gold and foreign exchange plus its IMF gold tranche position.[3] From the data according with this definition (see Table 1) it appears that the international liquidity position

TABLE 1

CACM COUNTRIES: INTERNATIONAL LIQUIDITY OF THE CENTRAL BANKS, 1960–1969*
(In millions of U.S. dollar equivalents)

End of Year	*Costa Rica*	*El Salvador*	*Guatemala*	*Honduras*	*Nicaragua*	*CACM*
1960	13.44	33.00	54.00	13.31	11.73	125.48
1961	6.28	24.50	54.80	12.33	13.53	111.44
1962	12.62	26.30	45.80	13.30	15.23	115.25
1963	15.64	44.40	56.70	12.45	31.82	161.01
1964	18.62	53.40	59.50	19.69	38.94	190.15
1965	19.84	56.30	67.80	23.39	57.32	224.65
1966	17.11	56.90	60.70	27.38	58.12	220.21
1967	18.18	54.80	65.10	25.08	32.09	195.25
1968	20.55	62.00	65.50	31.54	48.47	228.06
1969	29.17	63.80	71.60	30.92	44.22	239.71

Source: International Monetary Fund, *International Financial Statistics*, May 1968; December 1967; and September 1970.

* Data include gold, foreign exchange, and IMF gold tranche; but exclude Central Bank gold and foreign currency subscriptions to other international institutions. Reported in U.S. dollar equivalents.

of the CACM central banks declined from US$125.5 million in 1960 to $111.4 million in 1961 and rose in subsequent years, reaching a peak of $224.7 million in 1965; their liquidity position deteriorated during the subsequent two years, so that gross international reserves of the CACM central banks stood at $195.3 million at the end of 1967, a decline of 13% from the 1965 level. As shown in Table 2, the net foreign asset position of the CACM banking systems during 1960–67 was far worse than the liquidity position of the central banks.

Foreign Assets

The net foreign asset position of the CACM central banks followed the same pattern as their liquidity position during 1960–67. However, while four of the five central banks consistently had foreign assets in excess

[3] Central Banks' gold and foreign currency subscription to other international institutions are excluded by this definition, but are included in the concept of "foreign assets."

TABLE 2

CACM COUNTRIES: NET FOREIGN ASSETS, 1960–1969
(In Millions of U.S. dollar equivalents)

End of Year	*Costa Rica*	*El Salvador*	*Guatemala*	*Honduras*	*Nicaragua*	*CACM*
1960	1.98	15.48	48.50	6.68	7.56	80.20
1961	– 7.32	10.92	44.50	6.68	5.53	60.31
1962	– 1.04	16.64	31.50	6.94	11.06	65.10
1963	– 2.72	29.04	42.40	6.80	18.26	93.78
1964	–11.47	30.24	39.00	10.41	21.19	89.37
1965	–23.08	38.36	34.00	15.49	19.10	83.87
1966	–31.32	25.16	23.90	16.68	3.46	37.88
1967	– 8.44	23.72	16.90	13.33	–23.41	22.10
1968	– 5.03	25.92	15.70	22.34	–34.23	24.70
1969	10.84	20.92	24.20	17.80	–41.56	32.20

Source: International Monetary Fund, *International Financial Statistics,* December 1967; May 1968; and September 1970.

Data correspond to line 31 in the country reports.

Conversion Rates:

Costa Rica : US$1 = 5.615 colones (1960); and US$1 = 6.625 colones (1961–67)
El Salvador : US$1 = 2.50 colones
Guatemala : US$1 = 1 quetzal
Honduras : US$1 = 2 lempiras
Nicaragua : US$1 = 7 córdobas

of their foreign liabilities during these eight years, the Central Bank of Costa Rica had the obverse experience, i.e., its foreign liabilities consistently exceeded its foreign assets, and by substantial amounts. Costa Rica's situation showed a doubling in foreign assets from 1960 to 1965, some deterioration in 1966, and a modest recovery in 1967. On the liability side, however, the Central Bank of Costa Rica increased its obligations about 3.5 times from 1960 to 1966, and dramatically reduced them 33% in 1967, although they still remained in excess of its foreign assets in that year.

The major factor affecting the net foreign asset position of the CACM countries was the steep rise in foreign liabilities of the deposit money banks. This growth was most marked in Nicaragua (3,800%), Honduras (800%), Guatemala (500%), and Costa Rica (417%), between 1960 and 1967; El Salvador's commercial bank liabilities increased only 139% during this period. From 1962, the net foreign position of the CACM commercial banks worsened annually, reaching a net deficit of $81.4 million (equivalent) by the end of 1967.

In consequence of the foregoing, by 1967 the net foreign assets of the CACM banking systems aggregated only $22.2 million, or less than one-fourth on the peak achieved in 1963 (see Table 2). The extremely dangerous level of net foreign assets in relation to import levels (see Tables 3 and 4)—let alone total foreign exchange requirements for

TABLE 3

CACM COUNTRIES: VALUE OF IMPORTS (C.I.F.), 1960–1969
(In millions of U.S. dollar equivalents)

Country	*1960*	*1961*	*1962*	*1963*	*1964*	*1965*	*1966*	*1967*	*1968*	*1969*
Costa Rica	110	107	113	124	139	178	178	191	214	245
El Salvador	122	109	125	152	191	201	220	224	214	214
Guatemala	138	134	136	171	202	229	207	247	247	279
Honduras	72	72	80	95	102	122	149	165	186	184
Nicaragua	72	74	94	111	137	160	182	202	185	177
TOTAL	514	496	551	653	771	890	931	1,029	1,046	1,099

Source: International Monetary Fund, *International Financial Statistics.*

TABLE 4

CACM: RATIO OF NET FOREIGN ASSETS TO IMPORTS, 1960–1969
(In millions of U.S. dollar equivalents)

Year	*Net Foreign Assets*	*Value of Imports (CIF)*	*Ratio of Assets to Imports (In percent)*
1960	80.20	514	15.6%
1961	60.31	496	12.2%
1962	65.10	551	11.8%
1963	93.78	653	14.4%
1964	89.37	771	11.6%
1965	83.87	890	9.4%
1966	37.88	936	4.0%
1967	22.10	1,029	2.1%
1968	24.70	1,046	2.4%
1969	32.20	1,104	3.4%

balance of payments transactions—caused justifiable concern in the Central American countries and their regional institutions.

Conclusions and Policy Decisions

From the data cited in the foregoing tables we may deduce that (1) the international asset-earning capacity of the Central American countries has been most inadequate to meet their development needs; (2) the sharply rising net liability position of the commercial banks, if left unchecked, would impair seriously the credit position of Central American importers vis-à-vis their foreign suppliers; (3) imports must continue to rise to sustain a minimum satisfactory rate of economic growth;[4] and (4) while Nicaragua's foreign asset condition has been the most difficult in Central America, none of the five countries may be characterized as being in a satisfactory net reserve position. At the end of 1967 the gross reserve (international liquidity) position of the CACM as a whole represented only about 2.3 months of regional imports, improving slightly to 2.6 months by the end of 1969.

The Central American area's chronic deficit in international goods and services transactions during the decade of the 1960s is shown in Table 5. Prior to the signing of the San José Protocol, the CACM deficit in these items had reached a peak (in 1967) of US$267 million (equivalent).

TABLE 5

CACM: BALANCE ON GOODS AND SERVICES TRANSACTIONS, 1960–1969
(In millions of U.S. dollar equivalents)

Year	*Costa Rica*	*El Salvador*	*Guatemala*	*Honduras*	*Nicaragua*	*CACM*
1960	−19.7	−28.7	−25.6	3.1	−11.3	− 82.2
1961	−21.8	− 2.7	−24.2	0.5	− 7.2	− 55.4
1962	−32.8	− 1.7	−23.0	− 2.8	−13.3	− 73.6
1963	−34.1	−17.3	−20.8	−16.8	− 9.0	− 98.0
1964	−32.6	−32.0	−45.7	−17.4	−14.6	−142.3
1965	−76.2	−26.0	−41.8	−10.7	−29.7	−184.4
1966	−52.5	−50.8	−23.3	−23.5	−56.8	−206.9
1967	−59.0	−35.2	−69.4	−33.3	−70.0	−266.9
1968	−51.5	−23.2	−57.1	−30.9	−46.1	−208.8
1969	−63.1	−31.2	−37.4	−37.3	−42.2	−211.2

Source: International Monetary Fund, *International Financial Statistics,* individual country data.

FISCAL SITUATION

The five Central American countries, in the aggregate, produced chronic fiscal deficits in every year of the past decade (see Table 6). During the years 1960–1969, CACM revenues rose at a compound annual rate of 5.9%, while expenditures increased at a yearly rate of 7.4%. As a result, the respective countries experienced increasing difficulty in providing sufficient local currencies to match external resources available for public sector investment programs. The need for increasing revenues as well as for controlling expenditures had become apparent to the CACM

[4] This statement allows for a shift in the composition of imports toward more capital goods imports and an equivalent reduction in the value of "nonessential" consumer goods imports. However, imports of nonessential goods must take place to provide rewards for entrepreneurial effort. The question is to what extent can these imports be reduced without an adverse effect on local investment?

governments during 1966 and 1967, and positive action was urged by the CIAP [5] and international lending agencies. While improvements in tax administration were producing limited revenue increases in some of the Central American countries, the increments were not nearly sufficient to meet growing investment needs.

TABLE 6

CACM COUNTRIES: CENTRAL GOVERNMENT FINANCES, 1960–1969
(In millions of U.S. dollar equivalents)

	Costa Rica	*El Salvador*	*Guatemala*	*Honduras*	*Nicaragua*	*CACM*
A. Revenues/						
1960	62.2	76.2	94.9	36.8	33.3	303.4
1961	48.0	81.3	98.4	37.6	36.0	301.3
1962	58.3	74.2	93.6	37.8	41.2	305.1
1963	58.4	76.8	95.3	39.8	49.3	319.6
1964	65.8	89.2	106.1	46.5	53.2	360.8
1965	71.8	110.5	122.6	54.4	63.9	423.2
1966	78.7	100.4	122.5	60.2	65.6	427.4
1967	81.6	103.2	126.5	64.7	68.6	444.6
1968	96.0	90.5	138.5	73.4	66.7	465.1
1969	108.6	102.8	152.0	76.8[a]	69.7	509.9
B. Expenditures/						
1960	63.0	73.8	93.3	40.8	37.5	308.4
1961	50.8	88.5	98.0	39.9	35.8	313.0
1962	61.5	80.6	89.7	41.8	42.3	315.9
1963	70.3	78.3	104.3	42.6	46.1	341.6
1964	73.0	81.2	116.0	49.8	52.3	372.4
1965	78.6	100.3	128.5	54.3	61.5	423.2
1966	90.4	112.1	138.8	59.6	71.5	472.4
1967	98.4	103.9	150.0	68.2	80.8	501.3
1968	102.6	95.8	146.4	75.1	72.7	492.6
1969	127.8	114.8	165.5	97.8	81.3	587.2
C. Balances/						
1960	− 0.8	+ 2.4	+ 1.6	− 4.0	− 4.2	− 5.0
1961	− 2.8	− 7.2	+ 0.4	− 2.3	+ 0.2	−11.7
1962	− 3.2	− 6.4	+ 3.9	− 4.0	− 1.1	−10.8
1963	−11.9	− 1.5	− 9.0	− 2.8	+ 3.2	−22.0
1964	− 7.2	+ 7.9	− 9.9	− 3.4	+ 0.9	−11.6
1965	− 6.8	+10.2	− 5.9	+ 0.3	+ 2.4	0.0
1966	−11.7	−11.7	−16.3	+ 0.6	− 5.9	−45.0
1967	−16.8	− 0.7	−23.5	− 3.5	−12.2	−56.7
1968	− 6.6	− 5.3	− 7.9	− 1.7	− 6.0	−27.5
1969	−19.2	−12.0	−13.5	−21.0	−11.6	−77.3

[a] Preliminary.

Source: Consejo Monetario Centroamericano, *Boletín Estadístico*, Vol. VI, No. 6, 1969, pp. 149–153; No. 1, September 1965, pp. 98–102.

[5] Inter-American Committee of the Alliance for Progress (*Comité Inter-Americano Pro Alianza para el Progreso—CIAP*).

Attempts at structural tax reform had had rather limited success in Central America during the decade of the 1960s. The active opposition of vested interests, the absence of governmental public relations activities in educating the public to tax reform, and the lack of success in at least one country (Guatemala) in imposing a hurriedly conceived consumption tax appeared to make any further efforts in this direction impossible to achieve on a unilateral basis. The combination of balance of payments and fiscal disequilibria in the CACM countries led to the negotiation and signing of the so-called "San José Protocol," in June 1968, as an interim measure for dealing with these problems. This Protocol is discussed below.

THE SAN JOSÉ PROTOCOL

Article X of the General Treaty For Central American Economic Integration (signed 13 December 1960 and effective from 4 June 1961) provides, in part:

> In the event of serious balance-of-payments difficulties which affect or are apt to affect monetary relations of payments among the signatory states, the Executive Council, at its own initiative or at the request of one of the parties, shall immediately study the problem in collaboration with the Central Banks in order to recommend to the signatory governments a satisfactory solution compatible with the maintenance of the multilateral free-trade system.

In keeping with this provision, and after consultation with the Central American Economic Council, the Monetary Council, and the Ministers of Finance of the respective countries, the five Central American governments signed the "San José Protocol" to the General Treaty of Economic Integration on 1 June 1968. It contains "emergency measures in defense of the balance of payments" and was to remain in force for five years from its initial effective date. Its provisions call for the levying of certain tax measures as a short-run solution ("medidas de corto plazo") to the balance of payments problem. It was generally understood that these taxes would, if adopted, constitute the maximum structural tax reform package politically acceptable at this time. (Previous attempts at instituting a sales tax in certain CACM countries failed because of strong opposition of special-interest groups.)

The key provisions of the San José Protocol are: (1) a 30% surcharge on the amount of import tariffs paid is to be imposed for a period of five years, dating from the effective date of this Protocol, on all but a specified list of imports from outside the Central American Common

Market area.[6] This surcharge is to be called an Economic Stabilization Tax. (2) In addition, the signatory states shall be able to levy on specified commodities, divided into two lists, a one-stage consumption tax of 20% and 10%, respectively, regardless of the origin of these commodities. These lists may be expanded with the consent of the Economic Council, following upon prior approval by the Executive Council.

The Economic Stabilization Tax was to apply to the imports even of those enterprises that have obtained duty-free concessions under various incentive laws.[7] In such cases, however, the tax is not to become effective until all five CACM countries have deposited their instruments of ratification with the Organization of Central American States (ODECA).

In spite of the foregoing provision, the Protocol permits the executive power of any signatory state to exonerate totally or partially from the payment of the Economic Stabilization Tax imports of capital goods, raw materials, semiprocessed and packaging products, and fuels and lubricants for industrial use (except gasoline) when these are to be utilized by enterprises pertaining to new industries of special interest to the economic development of Central America. When the aforementioned items are produced in Central America in satisfactory amounts, quality, and prices, then such tax exonerations or reductions are not to be permitted.

Items of prime necessity, agricultural machinery, seeds, fertilizers, gasoline, vehicles for commercial uses, etc. would not be subject either to the Economic Stabilization Tax or to the internal consumption taxes permitted (but not made mandatory) under this Protocol. A mechanism was provided for granting exemptions from the Economic Stabilization Tax to the imports of agricultural and industrial enterprises that could prove injury under this Protocol. A decision of the Executive Council of the General Treaty is required after prior approval of the Permanent Secretariat of the General Treaty of Central American Economic Integration (SIECA).

The effective date of the Protocol was to be eight days after the deposit of the third instrument of ratification, for the initial three countries, and for each of the remaining two countries upon the date of deposit of their respective instruments of ratification. It became operative on 9 No-

[6] For imported items that have not had uniform Central American tariff rates established, the surcharge also was to be 30%. However, the contracting parties could impose higher surcharges on such items in accordance with their respective laws, or lower surcharges to equalize the total levy with that of any CACM country having a lower tariff duty on such an item.

[7] The surcharge was to be levied on the duties that such enterprises would have to pay if they did *not* have concessionary privileges.

vember 1968 with respect to Nicaragua, El Salvador, and Guatemala; in March 1969 for Honduras; and in August 1970 for Costa Rica. However, implementing regulations had not yet been adopted by the end of 1970. The "Migration War" of July 1969 between El Salvador and Honduras aggravated a long-felt dissatisfaction on the part of Honduras with its share of any benefits occurring from the regional integration scheme. Current indications (January 1971) of the possible withdrawal of Honduras from the CACM may serve to delay adoption of these Regulations and hence to limit further any benefits that might emerge from implementation of this Protocol.

The proponents of the San José Protocol believed that it would accomplish two vital objectives: (1) a reduction in nonessential imports, thereby relieving the pressure on the balance of payments of the CACM countries, and (2) an increase in fiscal revenues resulting from the Economic Stabilization Tax and, if levied, the consumption taxes. It was argued that these additional revenues would assist the CACM governments materially in making their local currency contributions to capital projects receiving partial external financing.

Comments on the San José Protocol

a) The Economic Stabilization Tax would appear to penalize mildly present and new entrants into existing production fields; duties on capital goods imports and raw materials in general are low in Central America. On the other hand, it encourages entry into new industrial fields of interest in the economic development of Central America, provided that the psychological reactions to the ex post facto nature of this tax were not overriding. Some authorities in Central America believe that a number of enterprises have been established in the CACM solely to take advantage of the national incentive laws and have taken their profits and folded when their benefit periods have expired. If such were the case, the Economic Stabilization Tax would serve as an interim measure for obtaining revenue from such enterprises until the incentive laws themselves were amended to correct the situation. But the Protocol is contradictory on this point, as it permits the exemption from the surcharge to firms establishing in new (basic) industries.

New priority industries appear to be encouraged by the provisions of this Protocol. Such industries are defined in the text as those that will (a) produce raw materials or capital goods; (b) produce containers or semimanufactured articles, always provided that at least 50% of the total value of raw materials, containers, and semimanufactures utilized in the production process are of Central American origin; or (c) generate important net benefits to the balance of payments and have a high-value added characteristic in their output. Once such basic industries have been established in the CACM, the importation of similar items from outside the region would be subject to the Economic Stabilization Tax (provided that it were still in effect).

b) The San José Protocol is, in part, an emergency measure to relieve the CACM balance of payments pressures by reducing imports (through raising their cost) and stimulating exports. The lists of items that may be subject to internal consumption taxes include many products having possibilities for export to non-CACM markets. The internal price elasticities of demand for the items included in the tax lists are not known, but certainly some reduction in the consumption of the affected products must be expected. Unless definite increases in exports to third countries were achieved, processing industries would be discouraged and important domestic resources (e.g., fish, nuts, chicle, chocolate and its components and preparations, meat products) might remain underutilized. Hence it would appear logical to dedicate a portion of the revenue from such consumption taxes to export promotion programs aimed at non-CACM markets.

c) The Protocol would favor imports from non-CACM countries and equipment for the agricultural sector by excluding such products from the 30% import tax surcharge, while leaving such inputs for much of the industrial sector subject to the Economic Stabilization Tax.[8] The exception to the latter would be those plants established in desired new industries whose capital goods requirements could not be met (in price, quantity, and quality) from CACM sources of supply, and therefore could be permitted to import these needs from third countries without the payment, in whole or in part, of the 30% tax surcharge liability. The agricultural sector would thus receive preferential treatment, permitting the mechanization and modernization of agricultural production without the burden of the 30% import duty surcharge.

While encouragement of the agricultural sector certainly is a desirable project, it is not stated in the document why the Protocol discriminates (albeit mildly) against a major portion of the industrial sector. However, given the Protocol's permissive special treatment of new industries, we might deduce that many existing industries already have adequate—indeed, surplus—productive capacity and that fiscal incentives no longer are required in these lines. Presumably, revisions in the incentive laws will

[8] However, the duties on all types of machinery are relatively low, so that the degree of discrimination would be slight.

be made during the five-year life of the Protocol and will take the capacity factor into account.

d) The dual objectives of the Economic Stabilization Tax—reduction of imports and increase in revenues—appear to be feasible, provided that the administration of collections is adequate and that the additional revenues will be applied to meeting local costs of capital projects. It is highly unlikely that the price elasticity of imports would be greater than unity, so that the expected reduction in imports from third countries at best would not exceed the value of 30% import duty surcharge;[9] the permitted total or partial exemptions noted above would further constrain the import-reduction effect. Thus an increase in fiscal revenues as a result of this tax is consistent with some reduction in imports. An estimate of the probable effects of the 30% Economic Stabilization Tax, based on the participation of all five countries in its application, is given below:

CALCULATED EFFECTS OF 30% IMPORT DUTY SURCHARGE ON CACM IMPORTS AND TARIFF REVENUES, 1967 DATA

	Before Surcharge	*After Surcharge*	*Change*
	(In millions of U.S. dollar equivalent)		
Total imports (CIF)	1,029	977	
Less Imports from CACM	214	214	
Imports from Third Countries	815	763	
Less Duty-Free Imports[10]	126	126	
Dutiable Imports from Third Countries	689	637	−52
Assume Average Duty of 25%; Yield	172	159	(− 7.5%)
Add 30% Surcharge	....	48	
Estimated Revenue	172	207	+35 (+20.3%)

The estimated results of the San José Protocol would appear to be in the neighborhood of a 7.5% decline in dutiable imports from third countries and a 20.3% increase in imports tax collections. While these results undoubtedly are desirable, they nevertheless are inadequate by themselves to overcome the sizable annual balance of payments and fiscal deficits discussed earlier in this paper. For example, the increased revenue ($35 million, equivalent) estimated on the basis of 1967 data would amount to 61.7% of the CACM fiscal deficit in that year. If Honduras

[9] The effects of possible consumption taxes are not included in this calculation, as these taxes would apply to a limited number of items, not important in relation to total imports.

[10] Government imports and private imports entering duty-free under exonerations permitted by the Protocol. Estimated at 15% of imports from third countries.

were excluded from all the calculations, the increased revenue (of only \$30 million, equivalent) would amount to only 56.4% of the fiscal deficit of the remaining four countries.

In the foregoing analysis it was assumed that the incremental revenue obtained from the import duty surcharge would be used entirely for domestic financing and would not enter the import stream. An assumption also was made regarding the price elasticity of the demand for imports. While the income effect on the propensity to import was not discussed, obviously the effect of the 30% surcharge on the balance of payments also would depend upon the rate of growth of disposable income in Central America in relation to the rate of price inflation in third country sources of supply. The inflationary trends in the United States and Europe in recent years would tend to strengthen the corrective measures adopted in the CACM.

Any success of the foregoing program, assuming that the CACM continues intact, will rest primarily on its administration—assuring that the incremental revenues are used internally, that contraband does not become a serious problem, and that the customs authorities do a proper job of classifying and valuing imports. It probably would be much easier, from an administrative viewpoint, to levy a consumption tax on nonbasic consumer goods and to devalue the Central American currencies on a uniform basis to avoid internal disruption within the CACM. However, these measures appear to be unacceptable politically in spite of their potentially greater effect in restoring fiscal and monetary balance.

ALTERNATIVES TO THE EMERGENCY MEASURES

As previously discussed, the chronic balance of payments disequilibria of the CACM members have resulted from a faster growth of imports as compared with the growth of exports. Attempts at developing markets for new (nontraditional) export products thus far have had very limited success. In general, it has been found that production costs in Central America's leading industries are equal to or higher than retail prices for similar products produced on a mass basis in the United States. Also, the quality of many CACM products does not meet U.S. market requirements; and supplies from Central American plants are inadequate and/or uncertain. Some prospects have been identified in lower unit volume, higher priced, hand crafted Central American products (e.g., hand-sewn shoes), but these would not provide substantial increments of exports from the region.[11] It was felt by some of the investigators that

[11] Investigations undertaken in 1968 on behalf of the Central American Bank

opportunities for exporting Central American manufactures might be greater in markets outside the United States, especially in the Caribbean area. Nevertheless, it appears that the five CACM countries will have to rely largely on their traditional exports for their foreign exchange earnings for some time to come. Consequently, continued sizable inflows of external financing will be required to finance economic growth in the CACM.

The CACM fiscal deficits have arisen from numerous causes: growing social requirements of an exploding population; inability to effect needed changes in tax structures and in rates of government-operated utilities; inefficient revenue administration; limited markets for government debt obligations; IMF-imposed restrictions on central bank lending to the central governments, as part of stabilization programs aimed at maintaining fixed exchange rates; and a rather low productivity in the government service. As indicated earlier in this paper, the Central American governments have been constrained to adopt second or third best corrective measures because of the inability to enact and implement basic reforms. There is small doubt that improved tax collections at the national level and preparation of import taxes on imports from third countries (as contemplated in the agreements creating the CACM) would eliminate all or at least a major part of the fiscal deficits in these countries. Also, simplification of the tax systems and a modification of the fiscal incentives for establishing or enlarging manufacturing enterprises might yield meaningful additional revenues without harming the investment climate. One important investigation of such incentives concludes that, without detailed investigation, we should not assume that special stimulation for investment in fixed capital is a necessary component of a development program; and that it is extremely doubtful that such incentives will ever be sufficient in themselves to launch a wave of development spending.[12] When such fiscal incentives are employed, they should be integrated closely with other phases of the development effort, such as tax reform, financial and other controls, expenditure programs, and generally the body of law and practice that influences the investment climate.[13]

We conclude that the fiscal and foreign exchange gaps in the Central American economies can be overcome, in time, only if basic steps are taken to improve revenues, control expenditures, expand domestic markets for locally produced goods, and adopt combinations of productive factors

for Economic Integration, and in early 1969 on behalf of the U.S.A.I.D. Regional Office for Central America and Panama (ROCAP).

[12] Jack Heller and Kenneth M. Kauffman, *Tax Incentives for Industry in Less Developed Countries* (Cambridge, Ma.: The Law School of Harvard University, 1963), p. 194.

[13] Ibid.

appropriate to enhancing the competitive position of selected commodities in third country markets. Although these conclusions are well-known and tend to be widely accepted, accomplishments in the directions indicated have been limited to date. The region-wide adoption of poor policy compromises is not the solution to the problems considered here. Perhaps greater individual efforts to strengthen national economies—a direction in which Honduras appears to be heading—may prove more salutary in the long run. If this is true a temporary slowdown in the economic integration timetable may permit a consolidation of existing gains, a rethinking of the basic premises of the CACM, and a subsequent revitalization of the program through "integration from strength." This would enhance the possibilities for a more equitable sharing in the benefits of regional integration on the part of the five member countries that constituted the Central American Common Market.

Selected Sources of Information

Consejo Monetario Centroamericano, *Boletín Estadístico,* No. 1 (1965) and No. 6 (1969).

Jack Heller and Kenneth M. Kauffman, *Tax Incentives For Industry In Less Developed Countries* (Cambridge, Ma.: The Law School of Harvard University, 1963).

Inter-American Development Bank, Social Progress Trust Fund, annual reports on *Socio-Economic Progress In Latin America* (Washington: Inter-American Development Bank).

International Monetary Fund, *International Financial Statistics* (monthly).

Secretaría Permanente del Tratado General de Integración Económica Centroamericana, *Carta Informativa* (Guatemala: SIECA, monthly).

José A. Villamil
Facultad de Ciencias Sociales
Universidad del Valle de Guatemala
Guatemala, Guatemala, C.A.

SITUACIÓN DEMOGRÁFICA DE GUATEMALA Y SUS EFECTOS SOCIO-ECONÓMICOS*

El 24 de octubre de 1970 el doctor Norman E. BarLang, quien recibió el premio Nobel de la Paz por su labor para mejorar las cosechas de trigo, advirtió en una conferencia de prensa en la ciudad de México que "la actitud irreal del mundo hacia el desmedido crecimiento de la población mundial es el mayor problema que encaramos en la actualidad" [1].

Esa actitud irreal que señala el Dr. BarLang es la que prevalece en nuestra América, especialmente en Guatemala y el resto de Centroamérica. Aparentemente existen tres grandes posturas ideológicas en lo que se relaciona a la situación demográfica en Centroamérica:

A. Los grupos de extrema izquierda minimizan el problema con posturas simplistas e irracionales. Para ellos no hay ningún problema poblacional real ya que éste ha sido creado artificialmente por el "imperialismo norteamericano" para producir un pánico general que nos lleve a implementar métodos de control de natalidad y, siguiendo la lógica de estos grupos, a la subsiguiente despoblación de Centroamérica. Detrás de este argumento que apela al nacionalismo y a la emocionalidad del centroamericano hay un verdadero motivo por el cual es necesario para estos grupos impedir un análisis lógico y empírico de la situación demográfica. Todos, obviamente, están comprometidos a la creación de una revolución violenta en Centroamérica y tienen la esperanza que en un futuro no muy lejano las

* Este trabajo fue presentado ante el International Seminar on Human Development celebrado el 3 de noviembre de 1970 en la Universidad del Valle de Guatemala.

1 Diario *La Nación*, Ciudad de Guatemala, 24 de octubre de 1970.

masas empobrecidas que se multiplican rápidamente (multiplicando por ello su pobreza) los llevarán al poder por medio de la "revolución del proletariado".

B. Las oligarquías nacionales que ostentan el poder real en muchas de nuestras naciones muestran cierta pasividad en relación al problema del rápido crecimiento de la población. Para estos grupos tal parece que el problema se solucionará por sí solo y que un análisis racional de la situación es innecesario. Cabe preguntarse sin embargo si detrás de esta racionalización no está un motivo predominantemente económico. Es decir, al reproducirse la población a pasos vertiginosos la oferta de trabajo aumenta en una tasa geométrica cada año y, por consiguiente, los salarios tienden a disminuir o, en el mejor de los casos, a permanecer en los mismos bajos niveles de siempre.

C. La postura de la iglesia católica, que, aunque ha cambiado mucho en los últimos años, sigue siendo uno de los obstáculos mayores para un análisis científico del crecimiento de la población y de programas de planificación familiar.

Aunque simplificadas, éstas son las corrientes ideológicas que tristemente encontramos en Centroamérica. El problema de la población se esgrime con fines políticos, económicos o religiosos; se utiliza para satisfacer las necesidades y creencias de cada grupo obstaculizando un análisis racional de la presente situación demográfica en Centroamérica.

El presente estudio intenta analizar teórica y cuantitativamente la situación demográfica en Guatemala con atención a sus efectos socioeconómicos. Más que un análisis profundo y extensivo se espera que sirva de marco analítico para otros estudios más completos y para llevar al frente de la polémica el rápido crecimiento de la población como una de las tantas variables del desarrollo económico.

El acelerado crecimiento demográfico en Guatemala, y en el resto de los países en vías de desarrollo, no es un fenómeno fortuito sino que tiene sus raíces en lo histórico. Por consiguiente para tener una perspectiva del problema en el siguiente capítulo presentaremos una breve reseña del crecimiento de la población en el mundo y especialmente en Guatemala.

EL CRECIMIENTO DE LA POBLACIÓN MUNDIAL[2]

Antes del siglo XVIII, las naciones del orbe sufrían un alto grado de mortalidad. En todas partes del mundo un gran número de cada generación moría en la infancia, de suerte que la población aumentaba lenta-

[2] Descripción histórica tomada de "The Determinants and Consequences of Pop. Trends" (New York: U.N., 1953). Traducción libre del autor.

mente a pesar de que los tipos de natalidad eran universalmente altos. Este difícil y delicado equilibrio de alta fertilidad y gran mortalidad fue destruido en Europa al comienzo de la Era Moderna por la mejora de las condiciones de vida de las masas debida a los efectos económicos de las revoluciones agrícola e industrial que concluyeron en una importante reducción del tipo de mortalidad. El resultado fue que la población europea creció realmente como los hongos. Se ha calculado que entre 1750 y 1900 la población de Europa aumentó casi cuatro veces, aun incluyendo las personas que emigraron. Sin embargo la explosión demográfica de esos países, llamados hoy en día económicamente desarrollados, ha sido contenida por una baja en el tipo de natalidad. Las causas de este decrecimiento de la natalidad estaban ligadas a cambios profundos en las condiciones de vida introducidos por la evolución de la sociedad urbano-industrial:

A. Los hombres dieron menos valor a la satisfacción de una numerosa descendencia y un mayor valor a las comodidades materiales y a la independencia personal que pudieran lograrse con la limitación en el número de hijos. Es decir, al abrirse las estructuras sociales que antes permanecían rígidas, los hombres buscaron el ascenso *vertical* en la sociedad por medio del mejoramiento de la familia. Un gran número de hijos entorpecía este ascenso social y el hombre reaccionó limitando su familia.

B. Los grandes adelantos en el descubrimiento y aplicación de métodos anticonceptivos junto con la expansión de la educación sexual en las escuelas y universidades permitieron a un gran número de personas planificar sus familias.

El resultado ha sido que en aquellas naciones que experimentaron las revoluciones agrícola e industrial la población ha crecido en los últimos veinte años a un ritmo que les permite ofrecer un aumento constante en el nivel de vida a sus habitantes. Junto con una tasa baja de mortalidad debida a los adelantos en las ciencias médicas y a la universalización de los sistemas de sanidad pública encontramos una tasa baja de natalidad causada por las variables endógenas que intervinieron para crear una sociedad urbano-industrial.

En la mayoría de los países subdesarrollados, entre ellos la República de Guatemala, la historia del crecimiento de la población ha adquirido otras características que es necesario describir y analizar para poder apreciar el fenómeno que hoy llamamos “explosión demográfica”.

En nuestras regiones el precario balance entre una tasa alta de mortalidad y una tasa alta de natalidad fue deshecho por la importación de técnicas médicas y sanitarias que permitieron disminuir drásticamente la tasa de mortalidad de la población. A partir de la Segunda Guerra Mundial se han señalado notables avances en la lucha contra la mortalidad prematura en regiones en vías de desarrollo. En Guatemala, como en la mayoría de los países iberoamericanos, la mortalidad actualmente supone sólo una fracción de lo que era antes de la mencionada guerra. En la República, la tasa de mortalidad general ha descendido de 21,8 por millar en 1950 a 17,2 por millar en 1963[3]. Si analizamos solamente la tasa de mortalidad infantil podemos comprobar que también ha bajado en forma muy significativa en el indicado período pasando de 106,8 a 92,4 por millar de niños nacidos. En 1971 se espera que esta cifra alcance solamente el 44,6 por millar de niños nacidos[4].

La tasa de natalidad en Guatemala, al igual que en toda Centroamérica, ha permanecido relativamente constante en las últimas dos décadas ya que las condiciones sociales y económicas que causaron una disminución en esa tasa en los países ahora desarrollados no se han dado en Guatemala. El país continúa siendo predominantemente agrícola, utilizando métodos primitivos de producción con baja productividad por trabajador y un alto grado de rigidez en sus estructuras sociales. El campesino guatemalteco busca su ascenso en la sociedad por medio de la movilidad horizontal hacia los centros urbanos, ya que su ascenso vertical está impedido por la rigidez de las estructuras sociales.

En Guatemala las revoluciones agrícola e industrial no han ocurrido y, por lo tanto, los valores de la sociedad no han experimentado cambios radicales. Esta situación da lugar a que la tasa de natalidad no haya sufrido cambios drásticos. Sin embargo, la tasa de mortalidad, como hemos podido observar, sí ha evidenciado un notable descenso ocasionando un desequilibrio entre muertes y nacimientos que causa la llamada explosión demográfica. El famoso demógrafo Kingsley Davis sintetiza la situación poblacional de las áreas subdesarrolladas de la manera siguiente:

> Las enfermedades infecciosas han sido controladas en las regiones económicamente atrasadas . . . por medio de la transferencia de conocimientos científicos, personal calificado y ayuda financiera de las regiones industrializadas hacia esas áreas poco privilegiadas . . . La dramática baja de la mortalidad en los países subdesarrollados ha sido entonces llevada a cabo por la ayuda internacional en el control de enfermedades no por los cambios resultantes del crecimiento económico de dichas regiones. No ha requerido cambios radicales en las costumbres e instituciones de los habitantes de esas regiones[5].

---

[3] Tasas tomadas de la Dirección General de Estadística.

[4] Ibid.

[5] Traducción libre del autor de Kingsley Davis, "The unpredicted Pattern of

En los países ahora desarrollados, para extender el análisis de Davis, las bajas en la mortalidad general y la natalidad se debieron a adelantos en la ciencia y en las economías de esas naciones. La modernización de la vida fue la causa principal de las espectaculares disminuciones en las tasas de mortalidad y natalidad. En Guatemala y otras naciones "económicamente atrasadas" las bajas en la mortalidad general han sido causadas, en su gran mayoría, por variables exógenas y no por cambios endógenos. La tasa de natalidad alta sigue igual debido a que no ha habido cambios en las estructuras socio-económicas de la nación y seguirá siendo alta mientras Guatemala no tecnifique y desarrolle su economía. El problema estriba en que el rápido crecimiento de la población obstaculiza en grado sumo la tecnificación y el desarrollo de la economía. En Guatemala nos encontramos en un "círculo vicioso de crecimiento poblacional".

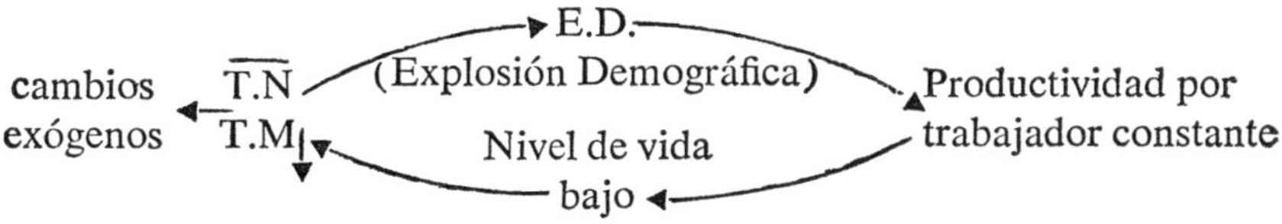

Tampoco debemos caer en el error de pensar que en un futuro próximo el problema desaparecerá por sí solo. Sociólogos y demógrafos afirman que en la república, debido a sus fuertes núcleos de indígenas semi-aislados, existen grandes reservas de poblacion[6]. Esto indica que cuando los adelantos médicos lleguen a todas las regiones del país, la tasa de mortalidad general bajará aún más dramáticamente aumentando la tasa de crecimiento demográfico a niveles todavía más elevados con el consiguiente deterioro en el nivel de vida del guatemalteco.

Nos queda entonces analizar, en el siguiente capítulo, los efectos socio-económicos de la presente situación demográfica de Guatemala.

LA VARIABLE DEMOGRÁFICA EN GUATEMALA: SUS EFECTOS SOCIO-ECONÓMICOS

América Latina es en la actualidad la región de más rápido crecimiento demográfico en el mundo[7]. El área de esta región que presenta los más altos índices de crecimiento poblacional es Centroamérica (creciendo con una tasa vegetativa del 3.1% anual). Costa Rica y Guatemala representan el primero y segundo lugar en todo el continente.

Population Change", *Annals of the American Academy of Political and Social Science* (mayo de 1956), pp. 56–57.

[6] Desarrollo Económico y Crecimiento Demográfico en Centro América (Guatemala: ICAPF, 1968).

[7] África 2.5%, Asia 2.5%, Latinoamérica 2.9% (1963–1967).

En Guatemala, los censos de población han sido muy escasos y la mayoría de las cifras se basan en proyecciones de los censos de 1950 y 1964. Vale la pena indicar que en toda la América Latina éstos y otros censos estadísticos son escasos y tienen un bajo grado de confianza. Se hace necesario, para una mejor planificación económica de nuestros países, mejorar y acelerar la recolección y el procesamiento de datos.

A continuación presentamos en términos absolutos el vertiginoso crecimiento de la población guatemalteca.

TABLA 1

Población de la República de Guatemala, años 1950–1964 y su proyección para 1970

Año	*Población (número de personas)*
1950	2.790.868
1964	4.284.473
1970	5.141.367

Fuente: censos de población de 1950 y 1964. La proyección fue basada en datos de 1964, utilizando la ecuación $A = P(1 + i)^n$ y con un parámetro poblacional del 3.1% anual.

Comparando los resultados de los censos de 1950 y 1964 vemos que se registró un crecimiento de población de 1.493.605 personas, lo que arroja una tasa geométrica promedio de incremento anual del 3.1%. Utilizando esta tasa constante de crecimiento vegetativo y por ende subestimando la población actual, la proyección para 1970 indica que existen 5.141.367 guatemaltecos, o sea, que la población práticamente se ha duplicado en el corto período de veinte años con la subsiguiente presión que este incremento ocasiona en los limitados recursos de la nación. Es decir, solamente para mantener el mismo bajo nivel de vida de 1950, la república tiene que haber duplicado su producción anual de bienes y servicios.

Encontramos, a la vez, ciertas características geográficas y estructurales de la población guatemalteca que concretan un análisis más detallado que el análisis global de la población. La Tabla II presenta la división de la población guatemalteca por edades en los años 1950 y 1970.

TABLA 2

Composición (%) por edades de la población guatemalteca, 1950 y 1970:

	0–14	15–64	65 y más
1950	42,5%	55,0	2,5
1970	45,7%	51,3	3,0

Fuente: Sieca

La composición por edades de la población refleja el efecto histórico acumulativo de los patrones de fecundidad y mortalidad que afectan a dicha población. Podemos notar por el análisis de la tabla anterior que "la pirámide de la población guatemalteca" tiene una base ancha y un cono estrecho, lo que indica una población típicamente "joven". Sin embargo, esta composición de la población por edades, que es un resultado directo de una alta tasa de crecimiento demográfico, tiene un efecto adverso en el desarrollo económico del país al causar un aumento gradual de la población económicamente dependiente (en el caso de Guatemala podemos llamarla de 0–14 años). Para 1980 se estima que el 46.5% de la población estará comprendida entre 0 y 14 años, lo que creará una mayor presión en la población económicamente activa para proveer de bienes y servicios a un núcleo cada vez mayor de niños.

La república no solamente sufre de un rápido crecimiento de población sino también de una mala distribución geográfica de la misma y de una corriente migratoria interna hacia los ya sobrecargados centros urbanos, especialmente hacia la ciudad capital, que está experimentando un crecimiento demográfico de un 5 % anual.

Guerra Borges, geógrafo guatemalteco, describe y analiza los efectos de la concentración humana en ciertas regiones del país en su libro, *Geografía Económica de Guatemala:*

> Geográficamente la población guatemalteca se encuentra más concentrada en una faja de tierra templada o fría que corre paralela a la costa del Pacífico. La faja comprende los departamentos de San Marcos, Quetzaltenango, Totonicapán, Sololá, Chimaltenango, Sacatepéquez y Guatemala . . . se trata de un territorio que no dispone de grandes riquezas, ni tampoco cuenta con una agricultura más desarrollada. Por el contrario, en esta faja densamente poblada, encontramos a una población que a duras penas sobrevive[8].

Se hace urgente entonces un programa efectivo de redistribución de la población. El problema se complica cuando observamos que en Guatemala la mayoría de las tierras fértiles ya tienen propietarios y que la región de El Petén contiene suelos muy pobres para la agricultura. Además, tenemos que pensar en el gasto real que significa el establecer colonias en tierras vírgenes y la resistencia tradicional del campesino indígena de emigrar de su región de origen. La situación actual es bien clara, una población que crece vertiginosamente en una cantidad fija de tierra por ende poco fértil y cansada con el consiguiente estímulo al minifundio y en detrimento de la productividad agrícola del país.

Esta situación fue dramáticamente expuesta por el Padre Breene,

---

[8] A. Guerra Borges, *Geografía Económica de Guatemala* (Guatemala: Universidad de San Carlos, 1968), pp. 193–96.

director de la orden Mary Knoll en Centroamérica: "Hay hambre en el Altiplano de Guatemala. El indígena se está muriendo de hambre y miseria, está dispuesto a emigrar a otras regiones simplemente para poder sobre-existir" [9].

La fuerte corriente migratoria, mayormente compuesta por ladinos hacia la ciudad capital y otros centros urbanos se puede apreciar en la siguiente tabla:

TABLA 3

Distribución de la población entre urbana y rural en %, años 1950, 1960*, 1970*

Año	*% de la población urbana*	*% de la población rural*
1950	24,1	75,9
1960	27,3	72,7
1970	31,9	68,1

*—Proyección

Fuente: Datos elaborados por la División de desarrollo de S.I.E.CA. con base en información elaborada por C.E.L.A.D.E.

La teoría del desarrollo y la experiencia de las naciones desarrolladas indican que estas corrientes migratorias deben esperarse en una nación que se encuentra experimentando cambios estructurales causados por la tecnificación de la economía. En Guatemala, sin embargo, esta corriente migratoria *no se debe* a la tecnificación del agro y del sector urbano sino que es engendrada por la atracción que ejercen los centros urbanos (como polos magnéticos) en los campesinos empobrecidos que buscan su ascenso vertical en la sociedad por medio del movimiento hacia las ciudades.

La rigidez de las estructuras agrarias en Guatemala junto con el abandono a que ha estado sujeto el sector primario han causado esta corriente migratoria, la cual no ha sido el resultado de los cambios estructurales implícitos en el desarrollo económico. Podemos observar a la capital y a otros centros urbanos de Guatemala inflados artificialmente por esta inmigración que crece a ritmo acelerado creando el desempleo, el subempleo, las áreas marginales, el vicio y la criminalidad en estos centros.

Hemos visto, entonces, como el rápido crecimiento de la población de la república acentúa los problemas económicos y sociales presentes. No habría motivo de alarma si los problemas de población disminuyeran al seguir adelante el desarrollo. Nos falta analizar sin embargo, si este acelerado crecimiento demográfico previene que esos cambios necesarios se lleven a cabo y que, por consiguiente, atrape a la nación en un cuasi-

[9] Conferencia en el Colegio Americano de Guatemala a los quintos años de bachillerato, mayo de 1970.

equilibrio de alto crecimiento de población y baja productividad per cápita.

Para el economista, el desarrollo significa algo más que un incremento en la renta real per cápita de una nación. Verdadero desarrollo implica cambios en las estructuras y en los métodos de producción de la economía que lleven a un alza continua en la productividad del trabajador y a un mejoramiento en el nivel de vida de la mayoría de los habitantes de un país. La renta real per cápita, aunque se considera una medida bastante cruda del nivel de desarrollo de una región, es una de las más usadas. En la siguiente tabla estadística presentamos el P.N.B. per cápita de Guatemala.

TABLA 4

Producto Nacional Bruto total y per cápita de Guatemala
(P.N.B. en millones de quetzales, per cápita en quetzales)
(A Precios constantes de 1967)

AÑO	*P.N.B.*	△ *PNB %*	*Población (en miles)*	*PNB pob*	△ *RPC %*
1960	1.013	—	3.911	259	—
1961	1.056	4,2	4.044	261	,8
1962	1.094	3,6	4.181	262	,2
1963	1.197	9,4	4.323	277	5,8
1964	1.251	4,5	4.470	280	1,1
1965	1.306	4,4	4.613	283	1,1
1966	1.367	4,7	4.761	287	1,4
1967	1.416	3,6	4.913	288	,4
1968	1.487	5,0	5.070	293	1,8

Fuente: Indicadores Económicos y Sociales A.I.D., 1969.

La baja renta real per cápita de la república la sitúa como una de las naciones menos desarrolladas de América Latina. Podemos notar que el P.N.B. per cápita ha permanecido casi estático desde 1960 al 1968, pues de Q.259 que alcanzó en 1960 se incrementó sólo en Q.34 en los siguientes ocho años. Es decir, en este período el P.N.B. per cápita creció a un ritmo promedio anual de 1.7%, lo cual es muy bajo para mejorar significativamente el bienestar del guatemalteco. Para poder doblar la renta real per cápita en viente años, ésta debería crecer a un ritmo del 5% anual y el producto nacional bruto, asumiendo una población que crece al 3.1% anual, a un ritmo del 8.1%. Por lo tanto se necesita una tasa de incremento muy por encima de la presente.

Podemos afirmar, sin embargo, que será casi imposible para la república realizar y sostener de una manera constante el ritmo de crecimiento necesario para obtener una renta real per cápita el doble de la presente en veinte años. Una población creciendo a un ritmo tan acelerado como el de Guatemala ejerce una presión tan grande en los recursos productivos que previene un desarrollo rápido y autosostenido. Guatemala se debe contentar con mantenerse solamente medio paso adelante del crecimiento de la población.

Una de las críticas más fuertes de la renta per cápita real como medida del bienestar económico de la nación es que ésta no da una indicación de la distribución del ingreso total entre los distintos sectores de la población. En nuestros países una élite económica acapara los recursos productivos y recibe un porciento elevado y desproporcionado de la renta en relación con su número relativo en la población total. En la república, como en el resto de Centroamérica, la desigualdad de la distribución de la renta nacional es muy pronunciada y da lugar a que un grupo muy reducido de personas reciba una proporción muy alta del ingreso total de la nación, mientras que el gran núcleo de la población recibe una proporción muy pequeña de la renta total. Si asumimos (un caso bastante real) que esta población mayoritaria y sumergida en la miseria recibe una proporción constante del ingreso total cada año y que es en este sector de la población donde la explosión demográfica se hace sentir con todo su peso, podemos vislumbrar la caótica situación. El rápido crecimiento de ese sector acentúa la ya alta desigualdad que existe en la distribución de la renta y causa, dada la baja tasa de crecimiento del PNB en Guatemala, un empobrecimiento ascendente entre la clase más populosa del país.

La renta real per cápita, aunque una medida útil y fácil de computar, es un indicador muy limitado del nivel de desarrollo económico de una región. Una renta per cápita baja es más bien uno de los efectos y no la causa principal del subdesarrollo económico de un área. El bajo cociente resultante de la relación producción-fuerza laboral, o sea, una baja productividad por trabajador, es considerada por muchos economistas como la causa primordial del subdesarrollo. Podemos sintetizar esta capacidad productiva per cápita de una economía por medio de una función matemática de producción; esto es, una descripción de la relación que existe entre la cantidad de producción y las magnitudes de los insumos que afectan la mencionada cantidad de producción. En este caso en que describimos una función de producción en términos generales, ésta no indica la naturaleza de la relación cuantitativa entre cada insumo y producción, solamente indica que hay una relación. Así en estos términos generales podemos exponer que:

$$Y/N = F(r/n, k/n, e/n, t)$$

Y/N = producción por trabajador (o por hombre-hora)

R/N = recursos naturales por trabajador

K/N = capital por trabajador

E/N = administradores por trabajador
T = progreso tecnológico

Para simplificar nuestra función y con fines analíticos podemos asumir que todos los recursos naturales son creados por la inversión y considerarlos entonces bajo la variable capital (K). También podemos suponer que los administradores necesarios para organizar cualquier innovación de manera efectiva aparecerán automáticamente cuando la mencionada innovación sea desarrollada. Por consiguiente, podemos asumir la variable E bajo la variable T (progreso tecnológico): $Y/N = F\ (K/N, t)$, o dicho más ampliamente, que la productividad por trabajador depende de la relación capital-trabajo y de las técnicas de producción en la economía.

En Guatemala, como en el resto de los países subdesarrollados, la productividad por trabajador es baja debido a la poca tecnología de la economía (un pequeño stock de capital en relación con la fuerza de trabajo) y a métodos primitivos de producción en la mayoría de los casos. Para poder incrementar la productividad de la economía es necesario, entonces, "intensificar" el capital en relación a la fuerza laboral (aumentar K en una proporción mayor que el incremento de N) y mejorar las técnicas de producción. (Para fines analíticos mantendremos constante nuestras técnicas de producción [t].)

Al tratar de incrementar el stock de capital en relación con la fuerza de trabajo encontramos que la explosión demográfica impide la tecnificación de la economía de dos maneras:

1) obstaculiza un aumento constante y autosostenido en la variable K al actuar de manera adversa en la tasa de ahorro y por consiguiente en la tasa de inversión neta de la nación.

2) la fuerza de trabajo (n) aumenta cada año en una tasa geométrica neutralizando o, en el mejor de los casos retardando los esfuerzos que hace la república para "profundizar" su stock de capital en relación a la fuerza de trabajo (k/n).

El punto No. 1 requiere un análisis más profundo para entenderlo con claridad y precisión y notar su importante significado. Al principio de este capítulo nos encontramos que la población de Guatemala es predominantemente joven (0–25 años) y que debido al rápido crecimiento demográfico este grupo tiende a crecer en términos absolutos y relativos a la población total. Este fenómeno ocasiona que cada año haya una mayor carga sobre la población económicamente activa que tendrá que enfrentar una crecida masa de población que aún no está en capacidad de trabajar.

TABLA 5

Clasificación de la Población

	Población dependiente	*Población económicamente activa*
1950	1.828	977
1965	3.110	1.387

Fuente: División de desarrollo de S.I.E.C.A.

Debido al alto número de la población dependiente, una gran proporción del Producto Interno Bruto de la nación tiene que ser canalizado para vestir, alimentar, enseñar y cuidar a este grupo no productivo y poco queda para el ahorro y la inversión en capital:

> En Guatemala, la propensión media a consumir (PMC) es muy alta, casi todo el ingreso se dedica al consumo quedando un remanente muy reducido para el ahorro lo cual ocasiona que exista en Guatemala, una tasa de inversión sumamente baja[10].

Las estadísticas corroboran nuestro análisis. Entre 1960 y 1967, Guatemala tenía una propensión media a consumir de ,90 como promedio (es decir el 90% del PNB lo genera el sector consumo), una proporción muy baja del ahorro nacional bruto en relación al PNB (9% como promedio anual entre 1958 y 1966) y una tasa de inversión geográfica bruta que crecía a un ritmo del 4.6% anual en los últimos veinte años[11]. En la inversión geográfica bruta se toman en cuenta los gastos de depreciación de capital (reparación y sustitución de capital existente). Podemos inferir entonces que el ritmo de crecimiento de la inversión geográfica neta (creación de nuevo capital) fue mucho más lento que el de la inversión bruta. Comparando esta tasa lenta de crecimiento del stock de capital con la tasa acelerada de crecimiento de la fuerza de trabajo (entre 1960 y 1970 la fuerza de trabajo creció a un ritmo de 3,3% anual) llegamos a la conclusión de que la necesaria "intensificación" de capital no se está llevando a cabo y que a duras penas se logra la "expansión" de capital (K/N se mantiene *relativamente* constante). Esta situación perpetúa la baja productividad del trabajador guatemalteco y mantiene a la república en un cuasiequilibrio que solamente genera pobreza y subdesarrollo. Claro que hay sectores de la economía que han "intensificado" el capital en relación a la fuerza de trabajo (el sector secundario por ejemplo). Sin

---

10 Leonel González "Descripción y diagnóstico de la Economía Guatemalteca Actual" en el *Reto del desarrollo en Guatemala* (Guatemala: IDESAC, julio 1970), p. 93.

11 Computaciones hechas por el autor basadas en datos obtenidos del Banco de Guatemala.

embargo es el sector primario en el que depende la gran mayoría de los guatemaltecos para su subsistencia, donde los resultados indican que ha habido una verdadera descapitalización.

Un tratado teórico-analítico de los efectos del rápido crecimiento demográfico en la economía guatemalteca no es el propósito final de esta limitada investigación. A continuación se cuantiarán y analizarán en síntesis los efectos que ocasiona la variable de la población al obstaculizar y prevenir la acelerada tecnificación de la economía:

1. Una renta real per cápita que apenas se incrementa cada año y que está muy por debajo de la mayoría de las naciones latinoamericanas.

2. Un sector primario (agricultura, caza y pesca) estancado y en decadencia como resultado directo de la baja productividad del agricultor guatemalteco. Con 6 de cada 10 guatemaltecos trabajando en la agricultura, la república no es autosuficiente en la producción de productos básicos para el consumo interno y cada año tiene que *importar* (con la consiguiente erogación de escasas divisas) una cantidad mayor de esos productos. Vemos que durante los últimos tres años (1966–1968) la oferta interna de productos básicos creció a un ritmo de 3% anual mientras que la demanda efectiva creció en una tasa promedio anual del 4.12% [12]. Estos datos tienen serias implicaciones:

a) Un deterioro constante en el nivel nutricional del guatemalteco que ya es uno de los más bajos de América Latina según la encuesta nutricional de Centroamérica y Panamá llevada a cabo por el INCAP en 1965. A continuación se reproducen algunos de los datos proporcionados por dicha investigación:

TABLA 6

Disponibilidad de alimentos en Guatemala
1965 y 1970*

Aumento	*Ingesta recomendada por adulto, g/día*	*Disponibilidad 1965*	*1970* *
huevos	24	40%	40%
carnes	90	42%	40%
frijoles	75	36%	35%
trigo	114	16%	15%
maiz	228	180%	173%
arroz	45	29%	29%

* Proyección

Fuente: Datos obtenidos de la *Encuesta Nutricional de Centroamérica y Panamá*

[12] Datos para la oferta obtenidos del *Socio-Economic Progress and Trust Fund* (Washington: BID, 1968). La reciente publicación del Banco de Guatemala (Estudio económico y memoria de labores) indica que en 1969 la situación empeoró más al

Como se puede apreciar en 1965 la disponibilidad de alimentos estaba muy por debajo de aquella recomendada por el INCAP ya que en la mayoría de los casos la disponibilidad era menor del 50%. Basados en las proyecciones para 1970 advertimos que ha habido un detrimento en la disponsibilidad de las carnes, de los frijoles, del trigo y del maíz. Solamente los huevos y el arroz permanecieron en la misma baja proporción. Aunque para 1970 solamente son proyecciones y a pesar de que las bajas acusadas son muy insignificantes para indicar un deterioro en las proporciones sí podemos inferir que la baja disponibilidad de alimentos ha permanecido estática. No ha habido el incremento necesario en la producción total como para siquiera aliviar la caótica situación alimenticia en Guatemala. También tenemos que tomar en cuenta la desigualdad en la distribución de la renta. La baja disponibilidad de alimentos es acaparada por el reducido número de personas de las clases alta y media, dejando a la clase de menor poder adquisitivo con apenas una dieta de subsistencia, no digamos adecuada.

Si entendemos por desarrollo económico un aumento constante en el nivel de vida de la mayoría de los guatemaltecos, podemos llegar a la conclusión de que éste no existe en el país, que es solamente una utopía en vez de la realidad. Lo que existe es un lento pero constante deterioro de la situación alimenticia causado por la baja producción por trabajador en el lado de la oferta y, por el lado de la demanda, por una creciente población que exige cantidades mayores de artículos cada año.

b) Otro efecto de la baja productividad agrícola es que el naciente y pujante sector secundario demanda una cantidad cada vez mayor de materias primas que el sector primario no puede abastecer.[13] Esta situación causa "cuellos de botella" en las industrias aumentando el costo del producto final y obstaculizando la implantación de industrias en gran escala. También incrementa nuestro ya alto grado de dependencia en el sector internacional al tener que importar materias primas para las industrias nacionales y agudiza el problema del déficit crónico en la balanza de pagos de Guatemala.

c) Estimulado por la baja producción del sector primario de Guatemala el célebre "dualismo" económico se acentúa cada vez más como se puede observar en la siguiente tabla estadística:

---

haberse incrementado la producción en sólo un 2.7%. Para estimar la demanda de estos productos se utilizó la ecuación $D = np + g$.
b

[13] Programa de Desarrollo Industrial para la República de Guatemala (1965–69) Secretaría Nacional del Consejo de Planificatión Económica y Social, Guatemala.

TABLA 7

Distribución del PGB per cápita por regiones y % de la población económicamente activa en el sector primario — 1966

Región	*PGB per cápita*	*% de la población económicamente activa en el sector primario*
Central	Q. 1.111,21	14,6%
Sur	Q. 240,24	73,6%
Petén	Q. 107,93	66,7%
Oriental	Q. 65,37	82,1%
Norte	Q. 41,20	84,2%

Fuente: Censos de 1964 y Banco de Guatemala

Como se puede observar existe una correlación muy alta entre un bajo PGB per cápita y el % de la población económicamente activa en el sector primario. Si observamos que las regiones central y sur son las más industrializadas, podemos darnos cuenta de la baja productividad del campesino guatemalteco. Dos implicaciones importantes se pueden hacer de los datos presentados en el cuadro: (1) En Guatemala existe un alto grado de "dualidad" económica. Esto implica la monopolización de los recursos de producción en una región que por ende tiene una población relativamente menor que el resto de las regiones del país. Este dualismo, entonces, condena a la mayoría de los guatemaltecos a una vida de pobreza. (2) La baja productividad del campesino del país lo coloca con un poder adquisitivo tan bajo que se imposibilita la introducción en Guatemala de las industrias a gran escala debido a las limitaciones del mercado.

d) El encarecimiento de la vida que afecta a todos los guatemaltecos, especialmente a aquellos que viven en áreas urbanas, es el efecto de una demanda ascendente que se encuentra con una oferta de productos insuficiente. En la capital ha habido en los pasados meses grandes carestías de productos básicos con la subsiguiente presión en los precios de los mismos.

e) La creciente tasa de desempleo está directamente relacionada con la evolución lenta de la economía y con una oferta de trabajo que se incrementa en una tasa geométrica:

Tasa de Desocupación en Guatemala
1950–1970

	Tasa de desocupación abierta
1950	5,4
1970	8,5

Fuente: S.I.E.C.A.

La tasa de desocupación real, sin embargo, debe ser mucho más alta ya que gran parte de la población que en las estadísticas figura como ocupada está en realidad desempeñando cargos que tienen una productividad marginal de cero, constituyendo por lo tanto un "desempleo disfrazado" [14]. En resumen, el crecimiento de la economía guatemalteca no puede ofrecer empleo a una proporción mayor cada año de guatemaltecos. La situación es todavía más crítica en el sector capitalino debido a la fuerte corriente migratoria proveniente del campo. En 1969, por ejemplo, 81.500 nuevos trabajadores disponibles se lanzaron hacia las 1.500 nuevas plazas industriales[15]. El sector industrial de la capital que utiliza una alta proporción de capital en relación a la mano de obra, simplemente no puede absorber la corriente humana que pide trabajo cada año. La alta tasa de desempleo y subempleo tiene serias implicaciones tanto económicas como sociales. Económicas porque el número de desempleados implica una pérdida real de un recurso de producción que pudiera ser productivo y que es, debido a las circunstancias, una carga económica para la sociedad. Sociales porque negarle el trabajo a un ser humano que lo necesita desesperadamente lleva a este sujeto a la negación de su propio ser y del sistema que lo denigra. La tasa alta de criminalidad y violencia de la nación está en relación directa con el alto número de desempleados.

ALGUNAS OBSERVACIONES FINALES

A través de esta limitada investigación el énfasis ha sido en el análisis más bien económico de los efectos de una alta tasa de crecimiento demográfico; los efectos sociales, obviamente, están implícitos en muchos de los resultados económicos. Es imposible, en la vida real, desligar las variables sociales y económicas ya que las mismas están íntimamente relacionadas. Así vemos que un alto porcentaje de desempleados tiene efectos tanto económicos como sociales y que la fuerte migración hacia los centros urbanos se debe tanto a una razón económica, el estancamiento del sector primario, como a una social, buscar el ascenso en la sociedad por medio de la movilidad horizontal hacia la ciudad.

El desarrollo del sector social, sin embargo, necesita de una sólida base económica para mantener intactos sus logros y avanzar hacia un bienestar social y una salud pública cada vez mejores. Aunque no es el propósito de esta investigación entrar en un análisis detallado del sector socio-educativo, las siguientes observaciones merecen mención para que sirvan de marco analítico a futuros estudios:

---

[14] Comité ad hoc del Comité de los Nueve de la Alianza para el progreso. *Evaluación del Plan de desarrollo económico y social de Guatemala* (1965–69).

[15] Programa de Desarrollo Industrial para la República de Guatemala (1965–69).

1. Una proporción cada vez mayor de personas en edad escolar (0–25) demanda una cantidad ascendente de aulas, maestros y material didáctico que los limitados recursos de la nación están imposibilitados de ofrecer.

2. A pesar de los encomiosos esfuerzos del Ministerio de Educación al aumentar cada año el número de maestros y aulas, la población escolar que no podrá ser atendida en 1972 será de 585.299 individuos, que comparada con la de 1966 que fue de 573.404 acusa un aumento total de 65.031 niños.

3. En 1968 la cifra existente de 4.197 aulas constituía en el sector rural apenas un 29% de las necesarias. Para 1972 este porciento habrá disminuido al 25,5%.

4. En 1968 laboraron 12.917 maestros, lo que constituía el 48,1% del número necesario (26.882 maestros). Para 1972 la cifra de maestros laborantes habrá alcanzado los 14.493, lo que significa un 47,8% para 1972 [16].

Como se puede observar, aun este breve análisis indica que la república no puede incrementar sus recursos educativos en relación con el rápido crecimiento de la población escolar. Cada año se condena a los futuros ciudadanos del país a recibir una educación cada vez más deficiente, lo cual repercute adversamente en la productividad y en el bienestar social de la nación.

CONCLUSIONES

En Guatemala existe una actitud irreal y despreocupada en relación con el grave problema de la explosión demográfica. El crecimiento de la población se utiliza para satisfacer fines políticos, económicos y religiosos minimizando sus verdaderos efectos.

El comportamiento demográfico de Guatemala tiene sus raíces en lo histórico. La importación de técnicas para el control de enfermedades después de la Segunda Guerra Mundial ha dado lugar a la llamada "explosión demográfica", sin que haya habido cambios básicos en las estructuras socio-económicas.

La variable demográfica obstaculiza en grado sumo que se realicen los cambios estructurales necesarios para que la tasa de natalidad disminuya. Esto ocasiona que exista en Guatemala un alto grado de desequilibrio entre las tasas de mortalidad y natalidad.

Dados los escasos recursos materiales del país y la baja calidad de

[16] Los cómputos educacionales a continuación fueron elaborados con datos obtenidos del *Plan Nacional de Educación para la República de Guatemala.* Cuadrienio 1969–1972 del Ministerio de Educación (OPIE).

sus recursos humanos, el rápido aumento demográfico mantiene a la economía en un cuasiequilibrio de subdesarrollo constante.

El sector educativo también sufre las consecuencias del rápido crecimiento de la población escolar. Cada año habrá un número mayor de niños que no podrán ser atendidos y un déficit cada vez mayor de maestros necesarios. El problema adquiere proporciones dramáticas en el sector rural.

Urge la creación de un centro demográfico con carácter oficial bajo el Consejo de Planificación Económica y Social de la República. Este centro se encargaría de la rápida recolección, procesamiento y análisis de datos demográficos y de diseñar, basado en los datos obtenidos, los programas de población necesarios. El rápido crecimiento de la población debe ser considerado como una variable importante y no como un parámetro más del desarrollo económico.

(Las ideas presentadas en esta investigación representan únicamente las del autor y no necesariamente las de la institución donde labora.)

John E. Hodge
Department of History
Greensboro College
Greensboro, North Carolina

JUAN M. THOME, ARGENTINE ASTRONOMER FROM THE QUAKER STATE

The founding of the Argentine National Observatory and much of its later development were the results of unusual inter-American cooperation. In 1870 the noted American astronomer Benjamin Apthorp Gould had realized his dream of inaugurating a major observatory in Argentina in order to extend to the Southern Hemisphere the kind of detailed examination of the stars already undertaken by the great observatories of the Northern Hemisphere.[1] After a few false starts Gould was able to begin work in Córdoba thanks to the enthusiasm of President Domingo F. Sarmiento and the wholehearted support of his minister of public instruction, Nicolás Avellaneda. The Argentine government appropriated funds for the construction of an observatory and the purchase of a modest but adequate inventory of instruments.

The project was furthered by the benevolent patronage of the government of the province of Córdoba and the friendly reception by the people of the city of Córdoba, combined with donations of equipment and publications from individuals, government agencies, and learned societies in the United States and Europe. The first three directors of the observatory —Gould (1870–1885), John M. Thome (1885–1908), and Charles D. Perrine (1909–1936)—were all from the United States. The second of these spent his entire adult life in Argentina in the service of the republic

[1] Details on the establishment of the observatory can be found in the author's "Benjamin Apthorp Gould and the Founding of the Argentine National Observatory," in the forthcoming July 1971 issue of *The Americas* (Academy of American Franciscan History).

and the advancement of astronomy. From the day in 1870 when he arrived fresh from college with no experience in astronomy until his death in 1908, Thome labored with unceasing devotion and industry, first as an assistant and then as director.

John Macon Thome was born in Palmyra, Pennsylvania, 22 August 1843. He eventually entered Lehigh University as a second classman in September 1866. After four years he was awarded the degree of C.E. (Civil Engineer) in June 1870. During his last two years Thome was cited as "Distinguished Student" based on annual examinations and during his senior year served as secretary to the president, Dr. Henry Coppée.[2]

When Benjamin Gould was unable to persuade any former students or colleagues from Harvard to make the long trek to remote Córdoba, Thome was one of the four young men contacted through Gould's academic connections who was willing to give it a try. The other three assistants, equally young and inexperienced, were William M. Davis, later head of the Argentine Meteorological Office, Clarence Hathaway, and Miles Rock, also a C.E. from Lehigh and an instructor there in minerology and geology.

From the very beginning Thome stood out over his fellows by his keen interest, precision in detail, and his incredible industry, which allowed him throughout his life to turn out more work than seemed humanly possible in a given period of time with the equipment at hand. It was this last quality which most impressed his close friends and fellow astronomers in many parts of the world. As an assistant, as director with assistants under him, and as an astronomer working virtually alone during the depression of the 1890s, he continued to supervise the publication of the results of the observatory's work during the Gould era (1870–1885) and to contribute the great bulk of the observations and reductions for the *Córdoba Durchmusterung* (hereafter Córdoba DM) which was his own life's work. These achievements, when set alongside innumerable observations and publications regarding planets, comets, asteroids, and other heavenly phenomena, must come close to a record for sheer perseverance and endurance. Benjamin Gould had set a high mark, but Thome more than matched it. It should be noted that in the period 1885–1908 over 1,800,000 observations for the Córdoba DM alone were made and

2 *Lehigh University Register (1870)*; Mary E. Riley (Lehigh University Library) to the author, 30 March 1970. Thome did not receive the degree of D.Sc. as is often stated in obituary notices and elsewhere. He was, however, awarded a Ph.D. by Lehigh in recognition of his services in Córdoba, probably in June 1888. After that date the degree appears with his name in the *Lehigh University Registers*. The statement found in all Argentine biographical sketches that he was a graduate of "Flower University" is based on an error in the long obituary article published in *La Nación*, 29 March 1908, by his friend Julio Lederer. The mistake probably arises from confusion with the Flower Observatory of the University of Pennsylvania.

recorded in spite of overwhelming financial difficulties and steadily deteriorating weather conditions.

When Thome and the other three assistants arrived in Córdoba, 17 October 1870, Gould was waiting for them; but no work on the construction of the observatory had yet begun. By October of the following year enough of the building had been erected to permit a formal inauguration. In the meantime, Gould had put the staff to work compiling observations with the naked eye for what ultimately became the *Uranometría Argentina*. Due to the unusual transparency of the Córdoba skies, in the early days of the observatory's history every star in the southern heavens down to the seventh magnitude was observed and recorded in the catalogue and charted in the accompanying *Atlas*.[3]

Without meaning to belittle the work of the other three assistants, one must note the preponderant contributions of Thome to both publications. Since Gould's nearsightedness precluded his participation in the work of the *Uranometría*, all observations were made by the four tyros who learned their trade on the job under the director's demanding supervision. Total observations made by Thome amounted to 15,815—as compared to 11,123 (Rock), 10,779 (Davis), and 6,793 (Hathaway). By far the largest number of sightings of stars dimmer than the seventh magnitude were also recorded by Thome.[4]

Similarly, in the preparation of the *Atlas* Thome led his colleagues. In the original plan the entire field of vision from the pole to 10 degrees north was to be contained in seventeen maps. Five of these were the responsibility of Thome, while his fellows were assigned four each. This project was later expanded to provide for forty-one more detailed maps, covering the same area as the original seventeen with six additional maps of the Magellanic Cloud and certain portions of the Milky Way. Of these, thirteen each were the work of Thome and of Davis, while Hathaway and Rock turned out eleven and ten respectively.[5]

Although the *Uranometría*, which earned for Gould the Gold Medal of the Royal Astronomical Society, did not appear until 1879 due to maddening delays at the printers hundreds of miles away in Buenos Aires, the observations were completed by the end of 1871. The work was

---

[3] Published as *Resultados del Observatorio Nacional en Córdoba* (Buenos Aires: Coni, 1879), vol. I. Hereinafter cited as *Resultados*. The *Atlas* was published two years earlier but was withheld until 1879 in order to be a companion volume.

[4] *Resultados*, I, pp. 100–102.

[5] Ibid., pp. 7–8. This work was revised and reprinted much later under Thome's supervision as *Atlas de la Uranometría Argentina que contiene las estrellas del hemisferio sud por el Observatorio Nacional de Córdoba* (Buenos Aires: J. Peuser, 1905).

constantly being revised and, when Gould returned briefly to the United States in April of 1874, Thome alone of the original American contingent remained at his post to undertake a new and complete revision of the entire *Uranometría.* When it finally saw the light of day, Gould went to great lengths to acknowledge his debt to Thome, pointing out that there was

> no portion of the work to which he [had] not contributed important aid whether in the estimates of magnitude, determination of position, the delineation and scrutiny of charts, the detection of misidentifications, the comparison of the finished Atlas with the heavens, or the revision of the proof sheets.[6]

The next fourteen volumes of the *Resultados del Observatorio* contain the results of observations made while Gould was director. Only volumes II through IV, and VII and VIII appeared while Gould was still in Argentina.[7] It was Thome who supervised the publication of all the others, which included many new observations, revisions of manuscripts, and corrigenda of work already printed. The Zone Catalogues (vols. VII and VIII), dedicated to Mary Gould, had been printed abroad and came out much earlier than volumes V and VI, which were published, as most of the *Resultados* were, by the well-known Buenos Aires firm of Paul Coni. Thus, from 1885 onwards, in addition to the new work being undertaken by the observatory, Thome had the full responsibility for seeing to it that much of Gould's work was checked and rechecked and seen safely through the press.

Even before the end of Gould's tenure Thome had exercised the nominal directorship of the institution for extended periods of time during Gould's visits to the United States or Europe in 1874, 1880, and 1883. During the Gould era assistants came and went; generally a year or two was all they could stand of the monotony of the work and the isolation of Córdoba. Only Thome and Davis were on hand in 1885 when Gould took his leave. Davis became much more interested in the weather business than in astronomy after Gould organized the Argentine Meterological Office in 1872. He eventually became its director when in 1885 it was separated from the observatory and moved to its own building in Córdoba.[8] Thome visited the United States in 1877 but was soon back at the

---

6 *Resultados*, I, p. viii.

7 Vol. II (1881); vols. III, IV, VII, and VIII (all 1884); vols. V (1886) and VI (1887). Vols. IX–XV appeared at intervals from 1887 to 1896.

8 Prior to Gould's arrival Argentina had no means of forecasting the weather. The Meteorological Office operated out of the Observatory from 1872 to 1885 through a nationwide telegraphic system linking it with various *colegios nacionales* used as weather stations.

observatory where he had found his métier in stellar astronomy of precision. Like Gould before him, he remained a steadfast practitioner of classical astronomy and appeared to take no interest in the newer and potentially more rewarding field of astrophysics.

Although his contributions as first assistant and sometime director from 1870 to 1885 were noteworthy, it was with Gould's departure in March of 1885 that Thome's career of service to Argentina, the observatory, and the astronomical world really began. His principal achievement was the Córdoba DM which is made up of volumes XVI, XVII, XVIII, and XXI (in two parts) of the *Resultados del Observatorio.*

Thome's proposed project was to extend the *Bonner Durchmusterung* from –22 degrees to the pole, following as exactly as possible the techniques, estimates, and scope of that great work begun by Friederich Argelander and continued by Eduard Schönfeld in the Northern Hemisphere and in the upper part of the Southern Hemisphere.[9] Observations for the strip from –22 degrees to –42 degrees were commenced in September 1885 and completed February 1891.[10] The work was continually and systematically revised by the director and his assistants during a period in which, at least till 1889, the government could allow the observatory sufficient funds to pay trained staff members. In this belt over 1,100,000 observations were made, determining the location of 340,380 stars within 6075 square degrees of a great circle with an average of 56.2 stars per square degree and as many as 160 per square degree in the region of the Milky Way.

The technique used illustrates the makeshift quality of much of the observatory's equipment and the need for Yankee ingenuity. The Córdoba optics consisted of a Repsold meridian circle, used by Gould for the Zone Catalogues which were continued by Thome; a "large" equatorial with photographic and viewing objectives of eleven-inch aperture; and a small equatorial with a fine five-inch Clark lens (12.5 cm.) which had hardly been used at all.[11] It was this last instrument which Thome used exclusively to compile the Córdoba DM. By itself it did not have the power to reach stars of the ninth magnitude (Argelander) much less 9.4 (Schönfeld), but when adapted with the eye piece of the large equatorial it served ad-

[9] The *Bonner Durchmusterung,* published by Argelander from 1852 to 1862 and continued by Schönfeld from 1875 to 1885, formed a catalogue of over 300,000 stars of the Northern Hemisphere with accompanying Atlas, and over 130,000 stars of the northern portion of the Southern Hemisphere. It forms the basis of catalogues still in use by modern astronomers.

[10] *Resultados,* XVI (1892), p. vi.

[11] The equipment of the observatory is described in detail in the author's article already cited. For the small telescope see also Deborah Jean Warner, *Alvan Clark & Sons Artists in Optics* (Washington: Smithsonian, 1968), p. 48.

mirably to show stars of the tenth magnitude with high resolution. Its objective was equipped with a reticule and, though offering only a small field of view, was perfectly suitable for separating stars and determining position in the many extremely dense portions of the Milky Way. The telescope was clamped and used as a transit instrument in conjunction with a chronograph and was so serviceable that Thome decided to extend the limits of his *Durchmusterung* to the tenth magnitude.[12] The end result was the recording of many more stars than had been noted by Argelander and Schönfeld, who had averaged 15.2 and 18.5 stars per square degree respectively in their northern belts.[13]

Observations for the belt of the next ten degrees down to –52 degrees were made from January 1894 to December 1897 and were the last whose results Thome was to live to see safely through the press.[14] From 1894 onwards he had the use of a polarizing photometer for the determination of magnitudes lent by Professor Edward Pickering of Harvard from the Harvard Observatory's southern station at Arequipa, Peru.[15] It was at this time that the observatory in Córdoba began to face obstacles which only the zeal of a fanatic could have overcome.

The first of these was the collapse of the Argentine economy with the subsequent bankruptcy of the national government. The immediate result of these disasters was that, after 1890, the appropriation for the observatory was paid in the greatly depreciated paper currency of Argentina. Formerly the observatory had been able to count on its 44,000 in *pesos fuertes*. This new development made the hiring and retention of trained astronomers as well as the acquisition of new equipment virtually impossible. Although the official appropriation remained constant at 44,000 pesos, the actual purchasing power of that money throughout the 1890s averaged about one third that amount. Throughout the decade Thome worked alone, observing, reducing, and recording; on occasion he was aided in a secretarial capacity by Mrs. Thome and a Mr. Gustavus Schuldt.

The general financial situation and the constant threat of war with Chile over the boundary made it impossible for Thome to get his paper allocation increased for several years, even after the country went back

---

[12] *Resultados*, XVI, pp. vii–x. The equipment and technique are described in detail.

[13] Ibid., p. xvii. Vol. XVI contained –22 degrees to –32 degrees; vol. XVII (1894) from –32 to –42.

[14] *Resultados*, XVIII (1900).

[15] This photometer was still in the possession of the observatory when the work was completed in 1932. Thome had met Pickering in Chicago in 1893 and had been particularly grateful for his interest in the work at Córdoba.

to a policy of convertible currency in 1899 at the rate of forty-four centavos gold to one peso paper fixed by law. Indeed, in 1898, 12,000 paper pesos were cut from the observatory's budget of 44,000 pesos "by a stroke of the pen," to use Thome's phrase.[16] The cause of astronomy in Argentina suffered from the wave of anti-United States sentiment that swept across the country in the wake of the Spanish-American war. Thome attributed the loss of the 12,000 pesos to this hostility as in the "scuffle [for money] the observatory, being officered by 'Yankees,' was completely helpless and unprotected." That the armaments race with Chile was not the sole reason for the government's action was made clear by the transfer of 10,000 pesos of the observatory's lost 12,000 to a fund for the establishment of a kindergarten. Thome applied to various European astronomers for expressions of support and "received a few notable and most convincing replies, especially from Paris and Berlin," with which he went to Buenos Aires and "begged for reconsideration." With the advent of what Thome termed "another and better President and Minister" he hoped for restitution. He had pointed out to the retiring administration of José E. Uriburu that he had "no doubt that if *they* would not publish the results which he had so painfully and laboriously accumulated during many long and thankless years, that he was sure the '*Yankees*' would do so!" At any rate, Thome was able to get the more enlightened government of General Julio Roca to reestablish the original appropriation without such threats.[17] Although the money continued to be in the paper currency of Argentina, by the time of his death in 1908 his salary had been doubled and the observatory's share of the national budget greatly increased.[18]

At the very time the financial support of the observatory was swept away, the weather in and around Córdoba began to change. A network of irrigation canals and an artificial lake created just to the west of the city greatly increased the humidity of the atmosphere, causing mists and clouds where the skies had once been unusually transparent. Perhaps a broad change in weather patterns was also a factor, as the number of good observing nights began to decline steadily. Hardly a dispatch from Thome to the astronomical journals of Europe and the United States failed to men-

---

[16] This information and all the quoted material are from a private letter which clears up the confusion caused by discrepancies in the official budget and some of Thome's published statements, which are guarded and appear contradictory. Thome to Edward Pickering, 10 January 1899. Harvard College Observatory Archives, courtesy of Mrs. Lyle G. Boyd.

[17] *Resultados*, XVIII, p. vii. For a thorough analysis of the financial picture in Argentina at this time see A.G. Ford, *The Gold Standard 1880–1914 Britain and Argentina* (Oxford: Clarendon Press, 1962), pp. 90–109.

[18] República Argentina, *Congreso Nacional Diario de sesiones de la cámara de senadores* (1908), p. 437.

tion the poor weather, as time and again comets were not seen until days after they should have been sighted and lost sooner than had been the case in the 1870s and 1880s. By 1896 Thome could report: "There seems to be no doubt that our clear skies have vanished—the percentage of working nights during the year has been below 50. Attempts at observing the planets were alike futile." [19] Similarly, he reported to the Royal Astronomical Society in 1903 that the average number of suitable nights per year since 1890 had been reduced from 270 during the first fifteen years of the observatory's operation to 189.[20] These are just two examples selected at random from a score of similar comments over the years.

By the time of his death Thome had compiled about ninety percent of the observations for the field of –52 degrees to –62 degrees.[21] When Charles Dillon Perrine, formerly of the Lick Observatory, assumed the directorship in June 1909, he found that the Clark object glass of the small equatorial had been broken. After considerable delay it was replaced with a similar lens[22] and the project was carried forward, interrupted by various changes of personnel and the demands of Perrine's own work. Under the new director's supervision the small portion of the ten-degree belt down to –62 degrees was completed and the results published in 1914. The work on the DM was then suspended for some time in favor of other matters until 1923 when Perrine instructed Mr. E. Chaudet of the staff to work on it. Chaudet extended the cataloguing from –62 degrees to –64 degrees and completed the polar region from –82 degrees to –90 degrees by the end of 1926. In that year José Tretter joined the observatory and was put in charge of the completion of Thome's work, an undertaking to which he devoted himself exclusively from August 1926 to December 1928. Tretter then spent the next two years in making revisions, and the final portion of the *Córdoba Durchmusterung* saw the light of day twenty-four years after its planner's death and forty-seven years after its inception.[23]

Although the *Córdoba DM* is a justly famous work and one which is inseparably linked with Thome's name, it would be a serious mistake to assume that it was the only significant enterprise he undertook during his long directorship. From 1885 onwards he maintained a steady stream of reports, usually to the *Astronomical Journal*, the *Astronomische Nachrichten*, or the Royal Astronomical Society. For his work on the DM and other contributions the last named society elected him Foreign Associate 10

19 *Astronomische Nachrichten*, CXXXXII (1897), cols. 355–356.

20 *Monthly Notices of the R.A.S.* 64 (June 1904): 812.

21 *Resultados*, XXI, pt. 1 (Córdoba: n. pub., 1914), preface.

22 Perrine did not give details on the manufacturer.

23 *Resultados*, XXV, pt. 2 (Córdoba: n. pub., 1932).

November 1899. Shortly thereafter he undertook another highly specialized task.

In April 1887 the International Congress of Astronomers, composed of French astronomers and thirty-six others, met in Paris, to discuss the organization of a worldwide network for the great *Carte du Ciel*, or photographic chart of the entire heavens.[24] The instrument chosen by the assembly was a thirteen-inch photographic refractor, the mechanism and telescope to be constructed by the firm of Paul Gauthier and the lens by that of the Henry Brothers, Paul and Prosper. Both these Paris companies were internationally known as the makers of the finest astronomical pieces, and it was the intention of the Congress that each participating observatory have this equipment in order to insure uniformity of results. Of the three stations selected in Latin America one was in Argentina. It was not, however, the National Observatory but the newly founded observatory of the province of Buenos Aires in the city of La Plata which was assigned the photographs of the belt –23 degrees to –31 degrees. By 1900 it had become apparent that the La Plata Observatory would not be able to fulfill its commitment.[25]

In one of the great experiences of his life Thome was present at the International Astronomical Conference in Paris in 1900 as the delegate from Argentina. For a man used to the isolation and anonymity of life in a remote observation point, Paris and the convocation of so many celebrated astronomers proved to be overwhelming. Not the least memorable aspect of his visit was the recognition he met on all sides for the work he had been turning out and meeting those people whom, except for a brief period in Chicago in 1893, he had never dealt with on a personal basis. "I felt deep emotion," he wrote the minister of public instruction,

> to see and speak to such notable astronomers some of whom I recognized from having seen them [in Chicago]. Later, when at the invitation of the President, I presented my own paper, describing the work performed in the Cordoba Observatory, I was warmly congratulated by all with friendly salutation. . . .[26]

[24] For a complete record of the conference, including minutes of all general sessions and committee meetings, a copy of the invitation sent, a list of all French and foreign delegates by their observatories or titles, notes or letters sent to the conference by astronomers, and all resolutions adopted see Academie des Sciences, *Congrès Astrophotographique International* (Paris: Gauthier Villars, 1887). Much more accessible is a capsuled version published in *L'Astronomie Revue d'Astronomie Populaire* 6 (1887): 161–69.

[25] For aid in obtaining materials, many of which were hard to find, regarding the original conference and the subsequent sessions, particularly that of 1900, the author would like to thank the Yale University Library.

[26] Thome to Oswaldo Magnasco, 22 February 1901, printed in *Memoria presentada al congreso nacional de 1901 por el Ministro de Justicia, Culto e Instrucción*

Thome was convinced not only of the great importance of the *Carte du Ciel* (eventually abandoned because of the very immensity of the task) but also, more significantly, that South America and particularly Argentina should play a part in its creation. The project involved more than zeal on his part, however, since Argentina would be expected to purchase all the necessary specialized equipment in Paris at a cost of 30,000 pesos. Fortunately for Thome, Julio Roca was president for the second time (1898–1904) and still vitally interested in the position of Argentina as a civilized nation in the eyes of Europeans.[27]

Before Thome left for the Paris conference of 1900 he had decided to offer the services of the Córdoba Observatory in place of those of the La Plata station. Roca's government sent a recommendation to the Senate in May that funds for the project be approved. After a brief study by the Finance Committee it passed, vigorously supported by Senator Carlos Pellegrini of Buenos Aires, an ex-president and like Roca a strong advocate of economic development and "Europeanization." In the Chamber of Deputies the measure was taken up a few days later and sent to the auxiliary committee of the budget which reported it out in two days, recommending swift action. The actual bill called for the appropriation of 24,000 pesos, since the Roca administration had already set aside 6,000 pesos for new equipment for the observatory. With the outspoken support of Deputies Eleazar Garzón (Córdoba) on the floor and Leonidas Zavalla (Entre Ríos) in his presentation from the special budget committee the measure passed easily. Thome left Argentina for Paris armed not only with credentials from the government proclaiming him the official Argentine delegate but also with authority to spend 30,000 pesos.[28]

Pública (Buenos Aires: República Argentina, 1901), 2: 364–73. These annual reports will be cited hereinafter as *Memoria*, followed by the year it was submitted to Congress.

[27] Julio Roca, the strongman of the dominant oligarchy, had been president earlier (1880–1886) during Gould's tenure and was reelected in 1898. In his messages to Congress he often mentioned the observatory in favorable terms, calling attention to the role it was playing in enhancing the reputation of Argentina as a civilized country. A longtime supporter of foreign investment and technology, Roca regarded the observatory as a badge of achievement rather than a costly luxury. For characteristic statements readily accessible see Heraclio Mabragana, ed., *Los mensajes: Historia del desenvolvimiento de la nación, redactada cronológicamente por sus göbernantes, 1810–1910*, 6 vols. (Buenos Aires: Compañía gral. de fósforos, 1910), 4: 171; 6: 36.

[28] The burden of the arguments in the Senate and the Chamber of Deputies was that this expense represented an opportunity for the Argentine to amount to something in the eyes of Europeans and to make a significant contribution to the march of science. *Congreso Nacional, Diario de sesiones de la cámara de senadores, 1900,* May 10 and 12. *Diario de sesiones de la cámara de diputados, 1900,* I, May 16 and 18. The bill became Law N. 3924.

The astronomer was still at some pains to convince the government a year later that the money had been well spent, as he referred to the "great delight" of the International Congress upon learning that the Córdoba Observatory would enter the league. "This step," he went on, "is a great leap forward, because by it, not only does Argentina find herself in the ranks of the most progressive and illustrious nations, but also because it has put her at the head of all the South American nations in the view of all concerned." [29]

Thome returned to his adopted land in January of 1901 after an extended tour of European observatories which included a two-week stay at Greenwich and almost two months at the Paris Observatory where he studied carefully all its instruments and especially the latest techniques of celestial photography.[30] Shortly after his Paris visit he was awarded the LaLande Prize for astronomy by the *Académie des Sciences*, one of the profession's most prestigious medals.[31]

Much of 1901 was spent in preparing the observatory for the equipment which began to arrive in Buenos Aires in January of 1902. The telescope was erected, but the Lumière plates, which were essential to the work, did not arrive until April. Another maddening delay was endured when it was found that the plates were 161 mm. instead of 160, and Thome had to wait till the end of summer before a new gross arrived. Then the weather turned bad, and during the remainder of 1902 only the nights of 1 September, 3 October, 2 November, and 2 December were good enough for photography. By the summer of 1903, however, Thome had produced 208 plates which in his words "seem[ed] to meet the requirements." [32]

Aside from his brief trip to the United States in 1877 and his participation in the International Conference of 1900, Thome left Argentina only twice. In 1893 he abruptly suspended work and hurried to his dying mother's bedside in Pennsylvania and was able to see her for the last time.[33] The sadness of the occasion was somewhat alleviated by the recognition accorded him in the press and at the Chicago Columbian Exposition, where a large group of astronomers were gathered to assess the progress of their discipline, particularly in regard to techniques and equip-

---

[29] Thome to Oswaldo Magnasco, loc. cit.

[30] Ibid.

[31] For the citation see Académie des Sciences, *Comptes Rendus* 133 (1901): 1059–61.

[32] Thome to Joaquín Gonzales, 20 March 1902, printed in *Memoria* (1902), pp. 631–40; Thome to Juan R. Fernández, 31 March 1903, printed in *Memoria* (1903), pp. 346–53; *Monthly Notices of the R.A.S.* 63 (June 1903): 549–52.

[33] National Archives. Thome to Josiah Quincy, 27 June 1893; Thome to Edward H. Strobel, 3 July 1893, in *Despatches from the United States Consuls in Córdoba Argentina*, I.

ment. From June to November Thome had nothing to do but talk shop and inspect new astronomical devices of every type. He reported later that, after years of hard work and grinding routine, it was wonderful for once in his life "to enjoy the attitude of *dolce far niente* with no obligation except that of admiring the activity of others." [34] He noted with intense satisfaction the "lively interest" manifested in the Córdoba Observatory and reported that it would have been hard to imagine more sincere concern and sympathy for the development of all science in Argentina than he encountered at the World's Fair. He could not forbear, on this occasion, pointing out to the minister of public instruction that, although the equipment of the Córdoba station was primitive compared to what he saw all about him in North America, when it came to work turned out, Argentina was "in the first rank." [35]

It would seem that the Argentine government in 1893 had some doubts about that and was wondering whether or not the observatory justified its meager appropriation in the depths of the terrible depression of the 1890s. The Argentine commissioner to the exposition sent letters to various leading observatories in the United States, asking for an evaluation of the Córdoba Observatory. The replies, which were later printed in 1905,[36] were all glowing testimonials to the quality, quantity, and significance of Thome's work. Thome's satisfaction can best be understood in the light of sentiments expressed several years earlier that "the approval of these [distinguished and noble astronomers] in regard to the steps taken by this observatory have been the great inspiration to me during the long and solitary hours of work." [37] While in Chicago Thome took every occasion to express publicly his gratitude to the Argentine Republic. One of such instances was during an address in which he told his audience that his long residence in that country had been "invariably agreeable and pleasant, and his intercourse with the citizens of all classes in different parts of the Republic, enabl[ed] [him] to testify to their many noble, generous and brilliant qualities." [38]

For all his affection for the country and the length of his sojourn there, Thome never became a naturalized Argentine citizen. Not only did

[34] Thome to José V. Zapata, 12 April 1894, printed in *Memoria* (1894), 2: 126–40.

[35] Ibid.

[36] *Memoria* (1905), 2: 259–62. These included letters from Lewis Boss, Simon Newcomb, Edward S. Holden, John Hagen and C.A. Young.

[37] Thome to Amancio Alcorta, 20 April 1893, printed in *Memoria* (1893) 3: 171–84.

[38] From his paper, "The National Argentine Observatory," read in August of 1893 at the Congress of Astronomy and Astro-physics in Chicago, printed in *Astronomy and Astro-Physics* 13 (January 1894): 8–14.

he and the small colony of Americans in Córdoba celebrate the Fourth of July and keep their native land uppermost in their hearts, but Thome served as U.S. vice-consul in Córdoba from 1877 until the closing of the consulate in 1906. He served first under an ex-Confederate physician, Dr. B. W. Green, until 1881, after which he was the sole consular official, operating from his office in the observatory. The entire inventory of the consulate never amounted to more than a few papers, a seal, and a flag which had to be replaced from time to time. His functions consisted in turning in an annual report—usually "no business"—and answering a few requests for information from American businessmen.[39]

Thome sometimes took himself a bit too seriously. When the consulate was closed in 1906 for lack of business and the State Department proposed to designate Thome consular agent, the astronomer submitted his resignation on the grounds that "as the dean of consular officials in Córdoba" such a demotion would put him to considerable embarrassment.[40] Though his friends and acquaintances agreed that he was jovial and enthusiastic in the face of impediments and real hardship, he did not like the Córdoba Observatory to be taken at anything less than his own estimate of it. When a report on Southern Hemisphere observatories was published in Washington in 1903 apparently indicating that the National Observatory of Argentina had gone to seed after the departure of Benjamin Gould, Thome came up swinging.[41] In a rather petulant communiqué to the R.A.S. he sought to set the record straight, pointing out that in spite of overwhelming financial problems, poor weather, and various other disasters, an immense number of observations had been made for the Córdoba DM, while work continued with the meridian circle and

---

[39] The entire consular correspondence is contained in one volume of the *Despatches from the United States Consuls in Córdoba,* already cited. During the period 1871–1906 hardly a hundred dollars' worth of business was transacted. On a few occasions Thome sent in reports on the local scene; some light is shed on the American community in Córdoba, and Thome's trips abroad (up to 1900) can be pinpointed through these records.

[40] Thome to Robert Bacon, 24 June 1906, ibid. A pencilled note from "H.W." to W. Carr enclosed in the file reads: "Mr. Thome seems an intelligent man, and I fear his feelings are hurt. Let us say the nicest possible things in accepting his resignation in order to earn his good will, —if he is as 'all right' as he seems."

[41] The passage to which Thome took such exception was really quite mild. "A strong national observatory was organized at Córdoba, in the Argentine Republic, in 1870, under the direction of Dr. B. A. Gould. This ranked among the leading observatories of the world for many years; but the financial disasters of Argentina have had a depressing effect upon that observatory, which, though it still continues its valuable work with perseverance and effect, is certainly in no position to undertake any additional obligations beyond that of a share in the photographic chart and other works there in progress." *Report of the Committee on Southern and Solar Observatories* (Washington: Carnegie Institution, December 1903), p. 26.

random observations were made with the large equatorial. On top of this he had accepted the responsibility for the work originally delegated to the La Plata Observatory in the *Carte du Ciel* project.

Calculating the declining number of working nights with nice precision, Thome decided that 69,192 observations more *could have been made* with the meridian circle if the weather had been the same since 1885 as it was from 1870 to 1885. When this number was added to those actually made with that instrument during his tenure as director the total would have been 272,582 for him and 265,758 for Gould.[42] In his sensitivity Thome had taken an isolated and rather friendly statement in a long report devoted to solar astronomy as a direct affront when he felt that encouragement, not criticism, was in order. That Thome took the reputation of the Córdoba Observatory as a personal matter is clear from his reports and communications, whether in the form of grateful acknowledgement of any foreign recognition or in his warnings to the government to keep visitors away from the observatory for fear of the poor impression it might make.

Thome was forever trying to make clear to the Department of Public Instruction that what passed for up-to-date and expensive equipment in Argentina would be laughed at by anyone familiar with the observatories of many of the universities of the United States and the great national observatories of Europe. He never tired of the theme that the reputation of Argentina in astronomy would have to rest on the publications of the Córdoba station and not on its physical plant. He was distressed before foreign astronomers at his standard of living and that of his assistants (when he had any) which was, he thought, "humiliating." He was fond of citing the example of the director of the Uppsala Observatory, who had been dumfounded by the primitive installation that had turned out the great Córdoba DM volumes as well as Gould's work, all of which, in this distinguished visitor's estimate, would have honored the oldest and best equipped observatories in the world.[43]

In the light of these expressions it is not difficult to imagine the depths of his emotions when he was so resoundingly welcomed in Chicago in 1893 and Paris in 1900. Although Thome wished the Córdoba Observatory to receive its due, he did not exaggerate his own contribution to astronomy, which was, he noted in Chicago, more the result of diligence than brilliance.[44] He had poured his life into his work, and the value of his

---

42 *Monthly Notices of the R.A.S.* 64 (June 1904): 810–12.

43 Thome to Antonio Bermejo, 15 April 1895, printed in *Memoria* (1895), 2: 243–62.

44 *Astronomy and Astro-Physics,* loc. cit.

life and the worth placed on the Córdoba station by the world's great astronomers were as one to him. His somewhat embarrassing displays of pique do not alter the fact that he was a man of enormous character and goodwill.

In 1907 Thome made his last trip abroad when he went in search of a new meridian circle to replace the old one brought to Argentina by Gould in 1869.[45] It was the same celebrated firm of Repsold which undertook to construct the new one, though Thome would not live to see it. When he died quite unexpectedly in March of 1908, he was planning new projects while still working on the Córdoba DM. His passing was mourned by astronomers in many parts of the world, by the people of Córdoba, and by many friends throughout Argentina. Friendly Argentines, knowing nothing of astronomy, looked upon him with awe as something of a combination of wizard and long distance runner. The measured evaluation of E. B. Knobel, former President of the R.A.S. and member of its council at the time of Thome's death was typical of the assessment of his peers:

> It is impossible not to speak in the highest terms of the ability and untiring devotion of Thome in prosecuting and accomplishing the important and valuable contribution to astronomy. He will always occupy an honourable place in the roll of the great workers of science.[46]

For a young man from Lehigh with no experience in astronomy who had made the long journey to Córdoba, Argentina, the same year the first railway line was opened from Rosario to Córdoba, it had indeed been a long and distinguished career in a new field and a new country. The life and work of John M. Thome remain an exhilarating example of the spirit of adventure, a job well done, the love of science for its own sake, and, last but not least, inter-American cooperation. Perhaps the most rewarding aspect of the study of his career has been the unearthing by the author of so many testimonials of sincere friendship between Thome and countless natives of the Río de la Plata.[47]

---

[45] *Astronomische Gesellschaft, Vierteljahrschrift* 44 (1909): 99–100. For interesting comments on the new instrument see the papers by M.L. Zimmer and A. Estelle Glancy in *Proceedings of the Second Pan American Scientific Congress,* 10 vols. (Washington: Government Printing Office, 1917), 2: 102–9.

[46] *Monthly Notices of the R.A.S.* 69 (February 1909): 255–57.

[47] Two in particular are worth noting: Julio Lederer, "Juan M. Thome. Director del Observatorio de Córdoba," *La Nación*, 29 March 1908 (University of Pennsylvania Library); and a pamphlet, Enrique Legrand, *Breves apuntes sobre los trabajos de Juan M. Thome* (Montevideo: A Barreiro y Ramos, 1909)—Library of Congress.

Gerard F. Rutan
Department of Political Science
Western Washington State College
Bellingham, Washington

PROVINCIAL PARTICIPATION IN CANADIAN FOREIGN RELATIONS

I

We do not feel that it is dangerous or harmful to the federation if provinces enter into relationships with other nations to develop for example educational or similar programs.

Hon. Harry E. Strom, Premier of Alberta, in a letter to the author

Within the past decade a perennial and intriguing problem concerning Canadian foreign relations has gained new prominence. Can the government of Canada as empowered under Heading VI (Section 91) of the *British North America Act* (1867) conclude contractual relations with foreign states when the terms of such contractual relations can be given legal implementation only by legislation of the provinces in areas reserved to them under heading VI (sections 92 and 93)? Or more precisely, since certain classes of legislative subjects are specifically reserved to the provinces, can the individual province then engage in "foreign relations" vis-à-vis those reserved subjects?

With the signing of the *Franco-Quebec Agreements* of 15 September 1967, which provided for increased cultural, scientific, and technological cooperation between France and Quebec,[1] and the developments leading up to and flowing from this *Accord*, the problem of the role and extent of provincial powers in regard to foreign relationships again came to the fore. Many Canadian scholars, politicians, and diplomats have taken an active interest in this problem and the Canadian news media have also

[1] From 11 to 15 September 1967 M. Alain Peyrefitte, minister of national education of France, and M. Jean-Jacques Bertrand, then Quebec minister of education, negotiated and concluded a seventeen-point *Accord* which provided *inter alia* for a ten-fold increase in cultural, scientific, and technical exchanges between France and Quebec. The *Accord* represented an expansion of the *entente culturelle* concluded between France and Quebec in 1965. These arrangements between the governments of France and Quebec were finalized without reference to the Canadian federal government.

offered some examination of it although often of a rather simplistic nature and too often with the focus upon Quebec alone.

Of more importance, some provincial governments, supported by politicians and scholars, and some eminent scholars on their own, have advanced arguments buttressing the claim of provincial powers to one degree or another in the area of foreign relations within the last several years. These claims are put forward with a *logica interna* that makes them difficult to ignore. Some of these advocates of provincial powers in foreign relations center their arguments upon Quebec since this province is most observably "different" from the rest of Canada (or so the argument runs). For example, the *Working Paper* of the Quebec Delegation to the Constitutional Conference of February 1969[2] states that the heightened activities of the federal government on the inter-national level since World War II, and the Dominion's increased participation in the work and activities of international organizations, coincides with "Quebec's need to assume its powers to the full." Thus Quebec, over the past two decades but with emphasis within the past five or six years, has taken the lead among the provinces in instituting what Quebec officialdom likes to call "parallel activity" in foreign relations. Understandably, such parallel activity in an area claimed exclusively by the federal government in Ottawa can cause a good deal of political heartburn and runs the risk of serious tensions within Canada as well as confusion and possible ill-feeling abroad.

I think it is important that we remember, however, that Quebec is certainly not the first or the only Canadian province to see itself possessed of some type of power in the field of foreign relations.[3] In 1937, in its arguments before the Judicial Committee of the Privy Council, the government of the province of Ontario in the now famous *Labor Conventions Case* sought to convince Their Lordships [lords Atkin, Thankerton, Macmillan, Wright, and Sir Sidney Rowlatt] of provincial hegemony of at least a partial nature:

> There are no grounds whatever for saying that the parties to advise His Majesty in matters relating to the jurisdiction of the

[2] Gouvernement du Quebec, Ministère des Affaires Intergouvernementales, *Document de Travail Concernant les Relations avec l'Etranger,* Quebec, 5 February 1969. Hereinafter called the Quebec Working Paper.

[3] In 1970 I wrote to the premiers of the ten provinces, asking them their attitudes and observations. All of the premiers except those of Ontario and British Columbia responded to my little "survey" but since the *n* here was so small, no attempt at analysis will be made. Rather it will suffice here to say that the responses can be roughly divided into two approximately equal groups: 1) those that generally recognize some kind of federal supremacy and 2) those who generally recognize—with or without qualifications—what Premier Strom of Alberta calls "a delicate equilibrium which characterizes division of powers." [Author's note]

> Provinces have in some way come to be the Dominion Ministers. The Province has the right to advise the Crown in matters where its legislative powers apply. Ontario has a right to enter into an agreement with another part of the British Empire or with a foreign State.[4]

Professor J.-Y. Morin, of the University of Montreal, has striven to give scholarly backing to the Quebec claim of provincial external abilities,[5] while Professor F. G. Stanley of the Royal Military College of Canada, a self-proclaimed "Compact Theory" scholar, has advanced the argument that in matters concerning education, research, cultural affairs, labor, and technology the federal government cannot claim centralist powers.[6] Other students of the problem, such as J. G. Castel and Ivan Head,[7] while steering a more compromising path aimed at cooperation between federal and provincial governments, nevertheless advance compelling arguments for a "new federalism" wherein are recognized the rights and the prerogatives of the provinces as guaranteed by Sections 92–93 of the *British North America Act.*

II

> *. . .Quebec has been led to organize with certain countries—particularly those whose language and culture are French—exchanges it considers indispensable in order to exercise its powers under the constitution.*
>
> From the Quebec *Working Paper*
> of February 1969, pp. 3–4.

The most recent statement of the arguments for provincial participation in foreign relations is to be found in the Quebec *Working Paper.*[8] This

---

4 Quebec *Working Paper*, p. 4. See also *Attorney-General for Canada (Appellant); and Attorney-General for Ontario and others (Respondents) On Appeal From the Supreme Court of Canada, January 28, 1937*, A.C. 326 and following. The *Law Reports*, House of Lords, Judicial Committee of the Privy Council, 1937.

5 Jean-Yves Morin, "La conclusion d'accords internationaux par les provinces canadiennes à la lumière du droit comparé," *Canadian Yearbook of International Law* III (1965): 126.

6 George F. G. Stanley, *A Short History of the Canadian Constitution* (Toronto: The Ryerson Press, 1969), pp. 208–9. See also discussion of Compact Theory, vii-viii.

7 See J. G. Castel, "Canada and the Hague Conference on Private International Law: 1893–1967," *Canadian Bar Review* 45 (1967): 1. See also I. L. Head, "The 'New Federalism' in Canada," *Alberta Law Review* 4 (1966): 389.

8 I find the rank of the signer of the letter of transmittal interesting. The Quebec *Working Paper* is issued over the signature of M. Claude Morin, under-minister of the Ministry of Intergovernmental Affairs. Ten months after the issue of this statement the federal government's "reply" (if indeed it is such) appeared in the Department of External Affairs' publication *External Affairs* (November 1969) in an article by one Jean-Pierre Goyer, parliamentary secretary of the secretary of state for External Affairs. Perhaps I read too much into this.

document argues that Quebec "has always felt free to enter into agreements with foreign governments in matters within its jurisdiction." As examples, the *Working Paper* offers the agreements concluded between Quebec and some ten American states on trucking and the reciprocal arrangements concerning probate and estate taxes concluded between Quebec and the United Kingdom, Quebec and Trinidad and Tobago, and Quebec and Northern Ireland.

As mentioned above, however, the real growth of Quebecois foreign relations began roughly five years ago, in 1965, with the Franco-Quebec *Accord* on education and culture. The 1967 *Agreements*, vastly extending the range of cooperation between the two governments, added icing to the cake. One could go back to 1964 and mention the agreement setting up cooperation between the Quebec Education Department and the semi-public French agency ASTEF (*Association pour l'organization de stages en France*). All of these different and related relationships between Quebec and France and implemented by a singular body known as the Permanent Commission for Franco-Quebec cooperation (*Commission permanente de co-opération franco-quebecoise*).[9]

The government of Quebec argues that it will be "obvious" to anyone who reflects upon these many and varied exchanges, whose numbers grow with each passing year, that such relations both benefit the province of Quebec and (more importantly) substantiate its claim to at least partial sovereignty in the area of external relations. They represent, or so it is maintained, "a concrete effort to break the cultural isolation in which events have contrived to keep Quebec for two hundred years"—which is a nice way of saying that the *Hégémonie à l'anglaise* in existence since the battle on the Plains of Abraham is now to be shrugged off. Quebec's cultural and educational relations of a foreign (external) nature are now to return to that authority to which they legitimately and constitutionally always belonged. The final argument in this regard is as follows:

> In their fashion, tailored to the French way of thinking, they provide Quebec with the same kind of cross-fertilization from Europe as the other Canadian provinces have always received from the British Isles.[10]

Finally, the Quebec *Working Paper* argues that the very nature of these agreements, whose exact substance and implementation is determined yearly by the Franco-Quebec Permanent Commission, makes clear

---

[9] For a detailed examination of the exchanges and missions carried out under this Commission see Quebec *Working Paper*, p. 7.

[10] Quebec *Working Paper*, p. 9.

why the government of Quebec and not the government of Canada must be one of the two high contracting parties:

> All these exchanges require an intimate knowledge of governmental machinery and educational institutions. Before anything can be done, needs have to be determined and priorities set, which entails carrying on discussions with departments and teaching establishments; then the entire programme has to be negotiated each year with the French authorities; this done, funds have to be appropriated and results assessed. Now, in accordance with the constitution and the nature of things, only the Quebec Government is competent to perform this task.[11]

This argument is of a double nature, i.e., both constitutional and practical. The reasoning appears to be that the federal government would not be able to weigh accurately the need for various kinds of teachers, or to assess practically the professional competence of educators from France, without ultimately having to ask for the expertise of the Quebec government anyway . . . or overstep the bounds of the federal constitutional mandate if it tried to implement terms without so consulting the Quebec authorities. In any case, it is argued that these decisions and scores of others like them are *ultra vires* sections 91 and 132 and thus beyond the constitutional capacity of the federal authority as well as beyond its more practical abilities.[12]

III

> *The question involved is one of principle: who is responsible for Canadian representation abroad, whether in matters of education or any other matters within provincial jurisdiction?*
>
> Hon. Mitchell Sharp, *Federalism and International Conferences on Education* (1968)

The lines and varieties of argumentation in support of provincial foreign relations powers seem almost endless and quite complex to the investigator who makes the mistake of stumbling into this area of research. Morris[13] manages to isolate at least four different themes or main lines of

---

[11] Ibid., p. 10.

[12] As explained by Ontario Supreme Court Justice Bora Laskin: "It is too much to expect the Canadian courts to torture the words of the section [Section 132] sufficiently to give it modern relevance even with respect to the question of implementation to which it was directly related. Accordingly, section 132 must be deemed obsolete in all practical respects." Hon. Justice Bora Laskin, Canadian Constitutional Law (Toronto: Carswell Publishers, Ltd., 1966), 3rd ed., p. 290. In March 1970, Mr. Justice Laskin was appointed to the Supreme Court of Canada.

[13] Gerald L. Morris, "The Treaty Making Power: A Canadian Dilemma," *Canadian Bar Review* 45 (September 1967): 481.

argumentation utilized by those supporting an enhanced provincial power in this regard. These are:

1. *the domestic constitutional argument* based upon the fact that an exclusive federal power is not detailed in the Canadian constitutional documents, and what is more, the power of the province to handle its own foreign relations in certain specified areas is implied without being explicitly denied. As Morris states it:

   > An integral part of this argument is the claim that the exclusive right currently conceded to the provinces to implement certain treaties must logically and necessarily carry with it the right to negotiate and sign those treaties, since the process of negotiation cannot realistically be separated from internal implementation.

2. *the comparative constitutional argument* which attempts to show that in other federal states constituent members are constitutionally empowered and/or functionally capable of entering into treaties and handling their own foreign relations. Morris maintains that these precedents are submitted as "evidence" of the commonality and feasibility of provincial claims within the Canadian context.

3. *the international practice argument* which especially relates to international bodies of a service nature such as some of the bodies and bureaus of the United Nations. This line of argumentation is somewhat weaker, in my opinion, than the first two, hinging as it does on the definition given the term "international agency." Such agencies, it is argued, regularly engage in relationships of an external nature even while their membership is often made up in part of participants who are not fully independent and sovereign states. In a vicarious or secondhand manner these nonindependent states are indeed engaging in international relations.

4. *the "What must be done to meet the needs of Canadian federalism?" argument* which Morris properly labels more political then constitutional/legal. This argument is the one that this author concludes to be the focus of explanation for the development within the past year of functional arrangements ameliorating for the present the problem of provincial participation in Canadian foreign relations. But to develop the thesis at this point would be to steal my own thunder. Suffice to say now that constitutional and legal strictures are often at variance with the realities of political life. The major element of success in the Canadian experiment over the past century and more, I submit, has been a high tolerance for paradox and an ability on the part of the

> Canadian societies—and the various governmental structures—to live with a good deal of "slack" in the system.

The arguments against the provincial role in Canadian foreign relations have in the main centered around two themes: 1) the constitutional mandate giving the federal authority complete and ultimate control over external relations, and 2) the impracticality of a divided mandate in foreign relations, i.e., the real world foolishness of multiple foreign relations all carried on in the name of, or by member states of, a single federal authority. I do not want to bore you trying to attempt to develop here the long and at times complicated legal argumentation underlying the federal government's case. Such is well presented already in *Federalism and International Relations.*[14] It is sufficient to note that, through fifty years and more of development, both in terms of practice and in terms of legal decisions by the Privy Council and the Supreme Court of Canada, the federal authority in Ottawa (specifically the Department of External Affairs) has claimed "exclusive competence" [15] in the field of foreign relations. The most recent and succinct presentation of the federal government's point of view is to be found in the article "Foreign Policy and the Provinces" by M. Jean-Pierre Goyer, parliamentary assistant to the secretary of state for External Affairs and Liberal MP from Dollard (Quebec). We can be certain, I am sure, that M. Goyer's article—appearing as it did in *External Affairs*—expresses the point of view of the present government at the federal capital.

M. Goyer rehashes, but most articulately, the arguments already put forth in 1968 by the then almost out-of-office Pearson government in its lengthy document *Federalism and International Relations.* The points are driven home by M. Goyer, however, with a cleanness and precision that merit respect: 1) "In constitutional and international law, only the Federal Government has competence in the field of foreign relations." [16] Great stress is laid upon the majesty of sovereignty, and thus upon the unique and sovereign nature of Canada as it is found in its natural repository . . . the federal government. 2) "The international community would not accept the theory of a so-called external sovereignty for the provinces." [17] M. Goyer declares that, constitutional arguments aside, the theory of provincial "sovereignty" runs headlong into a major defect, namely, "it is completely incompatible with the facts of international life." The international

[14] Hon. Paul Martin, secretary of state for External Affairs, *Federalism and International Relations* (Ottawa: Queen's Printers, 1968).

[15] Jean-Pierre Goyer, "Foreign Policy and the Provinces," *External Affairs* 21 (November 1969): 387.

[16] Ibid., p. 387.

[17] Ibid., p. 389.

community will never accept provincial foreign relations powers, we are told, for it would fragment the world community into hundreds—even thousands—of participating agents. While this argument is, perhaps, logical it lacks conviction as far as I am concerned for reasons I will enumerate below.

IV

> *Their Lordships are satisfied that neither case affords a warrant for holding that legislation to perform a Canadian treaty is exclusively within the Dominion legislative power. For the purposes of ss. 91 and 92, i.e., the distribution of legislative powers between the Dominion and the Provinces, there is no such thing as treaty legislation as such. The distribution is based on classes of subjects; and as a treaty deals with a particular class of subjects, so will the legislative power of performing it be ascertained.*
>
> From the decision of the Judicial Committee of the privy Council in the *Labor Conventions Case* (1937). A. C. 351.

In regard to Goyer's first argument, the constitutional or legal, it must be admitted that the 1937 *Labor Conventions Case* is a determining precedent. Yet Goyer does a masterful job of handling what is for him a knotty problem:

> It is often claimed that the argument concerning the Letters Patent is nullified by the judgement of the Privy Council in 1937. *Labor Conventions Case* has the effect of permitting the provinces to establish direct, separate relations with foreign countries and even to sign international agreements in the fields of their jurisdiction. I seriously question the level of legal knowledge of people who can come to such conclusions. Thirty-two years after the judgement was handed down, people should really know what it is about.[18]

In fact, says Goyer, all the Judicial Committee of the Privy Council said back in 1937 was that in those matters which are under the exclusive jurisdiction of the provinces, as delineated in the *BNA Act*, the federal parliament cannot assume for itself the right to legislate for implementation of treaty terms. Neither can the federal government claim that such legislative power should be assumed by it in order to carry out a treaty it negotiated. Yet from this state of affairs Goyer draws the following conclusion:

> . . . The Privy Council did not cast doubt in any way on the exclusive right of the Federal Government to conclude treaties,

[18] Ibid., pp. 387–88.

> and as a consequence, to conduct Canada's international relations. I agree that there can be no interference in the international legislative competence of the provinces in Canada, but there can also be no provincial interference in the ultimate competence of the Federal Government abroad.[19]

At the risk of appearing to "lack legal knowledge," I myself question Goyer's rather brisk dismissal of the *Labor Conventions Case.* While it is true that the Privy Council did not cast explicit doubt upon the sovereign power of the federal government to conclude treaties, yet it in no way reserved foreign relations "exclusively" to the federal authority nor did it proclaim any "ultimate competence" of the federal government abroad. And that is the thrust of the case . . . that is why it has been discussed and examined lo these many years since 1937! And that is what Goyer misses or overlooks.

If one agrees that there can be no interference in the *international* competence of the provinces of Canada (as Goyer does) then one must follow out his own logic: the provinces possess the "ultimate competence" over certain aspects—certain classes of subjects—of their own lives, and even the federal government cannot carry on international relations without depending upon provincial implementation in law of terms in those areas exclusively reserved to the provinces. Thus, logically, the provinces possess an *international* character in that they can refuse to implement in law terms of an international agreement they themselves find not to their liking. To have this kind of power, even in a negative sense, is for a provincial government an affirmation that it is in a position quite different from that of being without any abilities in the field of international relations. The provinces in Canada are not American states; they are not subsumed under any "exclusive competence of the Federal Government" no matter what M. Goyer may say.

Further, it can be argued that the *Labor Conventions Case* not only recognizes the international character of the Canadian province, but actually reserves certain areas of international relations to the provinces themselves.[20] Yet this is beyond the concern of my paper. All I wish to do

---

19 Ibid., p. 388.

20 See the decision of the Judicial Committee of the Privy Council in this case A.C. 352: "In other words, the Dominion cannot merely by making promises to foreign countries, clothe itself with legislative authority inconsistent with the constitution which gave it birth." See also A.C. 353–54: "It must not be thought that the result of this decision is that Canada is incompetent to legislate in performance of treaty obligations. In totality of legislative powers, Dominion and Provincial together, she is fully equipped. But the legislative powers remain distributed, and if in the exercise of her new functions derived from her new international status

here is to show that M. Goyer has been somewhat less than exacting in his handling of the *Labor Conventions Case*, or else has a very different interpretation of it than I do.[21]

More interesting, in my opinion, than the subtleties of constitutional law and legal development are the actual practices of the federal and provincial governments in this problem area. As was stated briefly above, political realities are often at variance with formal structures. Goyer's second argument (which is a distillation of most such similar arguments) is that "the international community would not accept the theory of a so-called external sovereignty for the provinces," that "it is completely incompatible with the facts of international life." In other words, Goyer advances an argument of political impracticability.

Now the problem with arguments of impracticability is that they have a strange way of turning on their user. It is my experience that one often ends up arguing what *ought* not to be practicable rather than what *is* not practicable. The functional aspects of life in general, and certainly of political life in particular, are most often rather confusing and hard to articulate since they possess a goodly capacity for paradox and a nice ability to digest contradictions. In a society which depends rather more upon compromise and unstructured consensus than most, Canadian political realities are very often confusing and contradictory. That is why, I am certain, so many problems are left to solve themselves in Canadian political life. There is a general if necessarily unspoken realization that a lot of problems will simply "go away" (i.e., seek and find their own answers) if one leaves them in the in-basket long enough . . . if you do not "fiddle" with them. In what would once again appear to be in opposition to the conclusions of M. Goyer, I submit that the federal and provincial governments have arrived at just such a practicable understanding, and

---

Canada incurs obligations they must, so far as legislation be concerned, when they deal with Provincial classes of subjects, be dealt with by the totality of powers, in other words by co-operation between the Dominion and the Provinces."

[21] For example, Goyer makes the statement that "the authority to enter into international agreements resides exclusively with the federal auhority." To support this thesis he quotes from *Federalism and International Relations* (1968) cited above, in which is found yet another quotation: "The Canadian Executive, again, constitutionally acts under responsibility to the Parliament of Canada, and it is Parliament alone which can constitutionally control its conduct of international affairs. The above is a statement by Chief Justice Duff of the Supreme Court of Canada, and is part of that court's decision on the *Labor Conventions Case*. The statement is quoted at greater length in *Federalism and International Relations* (1968) and is a key stone in Goyer's argumentation. But what must be understood, and what is never mentioned by Goyer, is that this statement was made *before* the Privy Council reversal of the Supreme Court of Canada decision! If one reads only Goyer, one gets the faulty impression that Duff's dictum stands unimpaired, or so it seems to me.

that while it may not be perfect in its constitutional "fit," it is both fuctional within Canada and generally acceptable abroad.

V

> *Thus the Quebec Delegation would like to propose that each State [Province] commit itself to communicate to the central government the terms of any agreements it wishes to make with foreign countries in due time before they are signed. Whenever the object of an agreement lies wholly within State jurisdiction, the federal government should examine the proposed text for the sole purpose of determining whether it is compatible with Canadian foreign policy and, in case it withholds its approval, state its reason for doing so. Whenever agreements relate to matters of joint jurisdiction, in which the federal Parliament has primacy under the BNA Act, the federal government could refuse its assent for reasons of internal or foreign policy. Such a procedure would avoid all later complications in implementing an agreement.*
>
> From the Quebec *Working Paper* (1969)

An international conference, the first of its kind, was held on 17–20 February 1969 at Niamey, capital of the Republic of Niger. This conference was attended by thirty countries, scattered over four continents, in which French is either the official language or is widely spoken (*les pays francophones*). Both the Canadian federal government and the government of Quebec were separately invited to attend the Niamey Conference. A series of "informal" discussions between Ottawa and Quebec City resulted in a practicable *modus vivendi* that had been several months in the making: it was agreed that Quebec would send its own delegation, which, however, upon arrival at Niamey would "unite" with the Canadian federal delegation. When Premier Bertrand announced this compromise on 11 February, he went to some effort to point out that in this manner the Quebec delegation at Niamey sitting behind its own flag and nameplate would be separately identified, while the fact that it would sit "with" other Canadians would assure "Canadian representivity." [22]

This kind of practicable arrangement, I conclude, grew out of the debacle high-lighted by two earlier *francophone* conferences. The government of Quebec independently participated in a conference of education ministers from France and eighteen other French-speaking lands twice the year before the Niamey Conference, i.e., in 1968. The first of these was in Liberville, Gabon, on 5–10 February 1968, and a second con-

[22] The Canadian delegation was led by M. Gerard Pelletier, secretary of state of Canada, and the Quebec delegation was led by M. Jean-Guy Cardinal, the provincial minister of education.

ference met in Paris during 22–27 April. Quebec participated independently and as a full and equal member, and this led to serious protest action by the Canadian federal government.

Mr. Lester Pearson, then prime minister of Canada, announced on 4 March 1968 that his government had sent a note to the Gabonese government accusing it of having acted in a manner not in keeping with the demands of international law. Mr. Pearson also told the Gabonese that they were responsible for endangering "the close and friendly relations between Canada and Gabon."

But of more importance, at least as far as I am concerned, the note recalled that during discussions with both the government of Quebec and the government of Gabon, the Canadian federal government had proposed that M. Cardinal should lead a *Canadian* delegation, *thus reconciling the provincial responsibility for education with that of the federal government for external affairs.* Unfortunately, both Quebec and Gabon ignored, at that time, the Pearson proposal for what Stanley calls "ad hoc" cooperative federalism,[23] and Canada temporarily suspended diplomatic relations with the Liberville administration. The April 1968 conference in Paris led to the same kind of tensions, although the French administration was careful to be much more discreet than the Gabonese. Relations between Ottawa and Paris were already strained, and it is doubtful that either side wanted to exacerbate an already delicate situation.[24]

It was out of this Liberville-Paris episode, and similar events during that time, that the compromise of Niamey arose . . . or so I submit here. Mr. Trudeau, who had succeeded Mr. Pearson as federal prime minister, announced only eighteen days after taking office that he had sent to the provincial premiers another federal position paper entitled *Federalism and International Conferences on Education* (8 May 1968).[25] This supplement to the earlier *Federalism and International Relations* (7 February 1968) stated that the conduct of Canadian foreign relations could not be divided into watertight compartments, some of which were within the

[23] Stanley, *A Short History*, p. 209.

[24] M. Johnson, then premier of Quebec, described the federal government's note to Gabon as "premature," especially at a time when both levels of government in Canada were seeking to delimit spheres of international jurisdiction following the previous month's Federal-Provincial Conference. In Paris M. Yvon Bourges, French secretary of state for foreign affairs (Co-operation), said on 26 April that the Quebec delegation had attended as "observers." On 30 April M. Georges Gorse, French minister of information, stated that M. Cardinal had been present at the Conference "not in the quality of an observer but as a full participant." The Canadian federal government's note to France was announced by Ottawa to be "part of a dialogue," and neither the Canadian nor French governments published its contents.

[25] Hon. Mitchell Sharp, *Federalism and International Conferences on Education* (Ottawa: Queen's Printers, 1968).

competence of the federal government and others of provincial or local concern. Further, the federal position paper held that to question the integrity of Canada's external personality inevitably involved a challenge to national unity.

Yet, the Trudeau government in this 8 May document went to great lengths, or so it seems to me, to say that within this basic framework there is a wide, almost permissive, latitude for cooperation. Federal and provincial governments can work together regarding intergovernmental conferences and other areas of international collaboration, and the inference, if not the explicit wording, is that they will work together as equals. This kind of cooperation, we are told, should give full scope to provincial interests as well as protect the prerogatives of the federal government.

The federal position paper maintains that the policy in Ottawa always has been to work closely with the provincial governments to establish balanced delegations for international conferences and negotiations! This quest for "balance"" will in the future be expanded to take into account both the federal claims regarding foreign relations and increased provincial responsibilities in fields such as education, cultural advancement, technology, and so forth. The reasoning seems to be that where the provinces are recognized as having responsibilities they must be recognized as having some powers.

Further, the new federal government announced that it had also made a number of suggestions about intergovernmental meetings on education within the framework of *francophonie*, which, while safeguarding national unity, gave full recognition both to provincial jurisdiction over education and to the special interest in *francophonie* of Quebec and other provinces with large French-speaking minorities. These suggestions are now hanging fire, waiting for fuller discussion by the permanent committee on the constitution.[26] Nevertheless, there was established in May 1968 what I call an atmosphere, or an attitude, of permissive adaptability . . . a willingness to accept *ad hoc* arrangements between federal and provincial levels

[26] Perhaps one reason for the announced suggestions was the fact that on 3 May (five days before the release of the position paper) the French Ministry of Education released a communique announcing that M. Peyrefitte and M. Cardinal had examined the state of advancement in the different questions concerning Franco-Quebec cooperation in educational affairs," and had agreed in principle on a common program and on measures aimed at "guaranteeing the volume of credits affected by such co-operation." The two ministers discussed mutual exchanges of civil servants and students, the admission of Quebec students to French schools, the distribution of French-language text books, and the mutual recognition of educational diplomas. In addition, M. Cardinal raised the question of reciprocity in social benefits for French and Quebec students, facilities in France for Quebec archaeologists, and the participation of French television experts in Quebec programs of adult education. For a fuller discussion see *Montreal Star*, 4 May 1968.

regarding foreign relations. While this phenomenon had been many months in the making, it bloomed under Mr. Trudeau's careful preelection handling.

VI

> *And those who are bored or offended by the platitudes and irrelevancies that often seem to pervade debates in the House of Commons would do well to remember that beneath them is usually to be detected by an attentive ear a whole network of conversations—conversations between the past and the present, between one part of the country and another, between the provinces and the federal government, between French and English.*
>
> From Douglas LePan, "The Canadian Dialectic" in *Notes for a Native Land* (Oberon Press, 1969).

In February 1969, nine months after the release of *Federalism and International Conferences on Education*, the government of Quebec issued its own *Working Paper* to which I have referred above. What should be noted is that while maintaining in print (and with verve) the right of the government of Quebec or of any other province to sign agreements [note that the term "treaty" is not used] and pursue relations with foreign governments on matters wholly subject to provincial jurisdiction, this Quebec *Working Paper* declares that the texts of any such agreements should be submitted in advance to the federal government to avoid any conflict with overall Canadian foreign policy.[27] This is a significant announcement, for it marks a change in emphasis, a moderation in the position formerly taken by the Quebec government. Just twelve months before, in a brief submitted to the Dominion-Provincial Conference in February 1968, the Quebec prime minister stated with emphasis that education, research, cultural affairs, labor, and technology in its broadest sense were all provincial responsibilities, and that Quebec

> cannot allow them to be dealt with internationally by the Federal Government alone. The content of agreements in these fields has such a close bearing on the day-to-day implementation of policies that, if the Federal government were to have a monopoly on international affairs, it would gradually take over *de facto*—if not *de jure*—international jurisdiction over matters which, constitutionally, do not fall within its competence.[28]

The 1969 position is softer than the 1968 one and tends to allow much greater room for maneuver and ultimate compromise. With this softened

---

[27] Quebec *Working Paper*, pp. 22 infra.

[28] Government of Quebec, *Brief on the Constitution: A Document Submitted to the Canadian Intergovernmental Conference, Ottawa, 1968* (Quebec City, 1968), pp. 13–14.

attitude of both Quebec and Ottawa a functional *modus vivendi* has been reached . . . at least for the moment. As Stanley put it:

> Having gained its point that it had a special interest in the French-speaking world—*la francophonie*—Quebec joined Federal representatives and those of New Brunswick and Ontario in accepting invitations to international conferences at Paris, France, and Niamey, Niger.[29]

M. Goyer not withstanding, what ought not to have been practicable was.

In mid-March of 1970 a second *francophone* conference was held in Niamey, Niger. The problem of Quebec representation was solved (after some pressure from other national delegations) along the lines already developed above. M. Gerard Pelletier, secretary of state for Canada and head of the Canadian delegation, announced in concert with M. Jean-Guy Cardinal, head of the Quebec delegation and minister of education of Quebec at that time, that the Quebec delegation would be viewed by all others concerned as "a participating government in terms of provincial jurisdiction." Quebec would sit "with" the Canadian delegation to assure Canadian representivity but would retain is own prerogatives over matters of purely provincial concern. Just what this means today in exact detail is not known . . . only the evolution of the federal-provincial relationship throughout the 1970s can allow us to see the significance for the rest of Canada beyond Quebec.

Yet the implications are somewhat more clear. The Canadian provincial governments will continue to press for and to exercise foreign powers unthinkable in the American, Mexican, or Brazilian state contexts. These powers will sooner or later become articulated and entrenched in the proposed Canadian constitution (discussed in Ottawa in February 1971 by the provincial premiers and the prime minister, and to be further detailed in Victoria in June). Just as Quebec has laid the foundations for provincial participation in foreign relations, so the other provinces will now begin to build upon them.

Certainly the Canadian experiment must be watched with great interest. In a time when decentralization is seen as one method of offsetting or correcting centralist excesses there is an importance beyond the Canadian scene attached to the Ottawa-Quebec confrontations of the 1960s; and now that western Canadians are demanding special recognition,[30] the

---

29 Stanley, *A Short History*, pp. 208–9.

30 In Edmonton, in December 1970, the Western Canada Party (WCP) came into existence. Aims of the new party are: to hold a majority of western Canada's seventy seats in the House of Commons and to initiate "western teamwork" in Parliament; to give western Canada, through the WCP a strong influence on national

actions of Quebec portend a significance for all provinces of the Dominion. The problems associated with provincial participation in foreign relations during the 1960s essentially involved Quebec. But during the 1970s the Quebec precedent will have ever greater influence in the other provinces of Canada, and one can look forward to heightened provincial activity in the foreign relations of Canada.

policies; to look after the "interests" of western Canada, both national and "international". At the same time British Columbia has adopted a position contrary to that of the Canadian federal government regarding the proposed raising of the level of Ross Lake. This issue involves serious relationships with the United States and has a twenty-year history of provincial prerogatives exercised in the area of foreign affairs.

Miles Richardson and Marta Eugenia Pardo
Department of Geography and Anthropology
Louisiana State University, Baton Rouge

Barbara Bode
Department of Anthropology
Tulane University, New Orleans

THE IMAGE OF CHRIST IN SPANISH AMERICA AS A MODEL FOR SUFFERING

*An Exploratory Note**

Holy Week in San Pedro, Colombia, a small town near the bustling city of Cali, begins with a procession that commemorates Jesus' triumphal march into Jerusalem. The week climaxes on Holy Friday with processions and rites which act out Christ's crucifixion and death. The remaining days of Saturday and Sunday, days that ostensibly glorify Christ's victory over death, evoke little enthusiasm; only the priest and a few hard-core faithful trudge through the rites necessary to terminate the week.

The events which lead to the agony of Christ (his march into Jerusalem and the Last Supper), most of all the agony itself (the struggle up Calvary), are the events that the townspeople celebrate. A *sanpedrano* explains:

> No, this is not fatalism. It is the lesson of Christ's life. Christ

*Field work (1962–1963) in San Pedro, Colombia by Miles Richardson was financed by the International Center for Medical Research and Training, Tulane University and Universidad del Valle. The field work (June-August 1967) in Puntarenas, Costa Rica, by Richardson and Bode with assistance from Pardo was supported, in part, by Public Health Service Training Grant T01–AT–00007 and Public Health Service Research Grant TW00148, National Institutes of Allergy and Infectious Diseases, and by the Louisiana State University Medical School.

We also thank George Tracy, Department of Sociology, Louisiana State University, for his helpful advice about chi square; and Valerie Richardson for her several, most helpful comments. The responsibility for what we did with their suggestions is ours. We continue to be in debt to the people of San Pedro and Puntarenas. A version of this paper was read at the Association of Social and Behavioral Sciences, Nashville, Tennessee, 24 April 1969.

> lived so that we may die. Christ taught us how to die. He set an example, an example of how to suffer patiently. Today, humans do not suffer correctly. They fight against death. This is bad. We must try to suffer and to die in the manner of Christ, who was God.[1]

The image of Christ which emerges from the events of Holy Week and from the explanations of the *sanpedranos* differs strikingly from that of Anglo-Protestantism in the United States. In Anglo-Protestantism the major ritual event is on Resurrection Sunday. With special sunrise services many Protestant groups greet the Sunday morning sun with the resounding phrases of "Hallelujah! Christ Arose!" Suffering is important to Anglo-Protestants, both their own personal suffering and that of Christ. Christ, however, suffered in order to redeem men from their sins so that they may gain eternal life, as exemplified in this stanza:

> Blessed Redeemer! Precious Redeemer!
> Seems now I see Him on Calvary's tree
> Wounded and bleeding, for sinners pleading,
> Blind and unheeding, dying for me.[2]

In a single religion appear two distinct, almost contradictory images of the same god: the Anglo-Protestant conqueror of death and the Spanish American sufferer on the cross.

In this exploratory note we want to consider the cultural imagery of Christ in Spanish America. On the basis of data gathered principally from Colombia and Costa Rica, we suggest that the Spanish American Christ is a model, a set of instructions, on how to face suffering. Furthermore, the data indicate that this model cuts across many socioeconomic barriers and has a universal distribution in Spanish America.

CHRIST AS AN INSTRUCTIONAL MODEL

Perhaps like all religious figures, Christ in Spanish America is a model for guiding human thought and action. As a model he provides a source of perfect information that men can draw upon as they wrestle with the problems of suffering and death.[3] In his capacity as instructor, Christ takes on the qualities of a role model similar to the way in which parents are role models for their children. However, behind every parental role model there

---

[1] Miles Richardson, *San Pedro, Colombia: Small Town in a Developing Society* (New York: Holt, Rinehart and Winston, 1970), p. 78.

[2] Walter H. Sims, *Baptist Hymnal* (Nashville, Tn.: Convention Press, 1956), pp. 106, 113.

[3] Clifford Geertz, "Religion as a Cultural System," in Michael Banton, ed. *Anthropological Approaches to the Study of Religion* (London: Tavistock Publication, 1966), pp. 1–46.

is an empirical being, an "individual," [4] who engages in dynamic interplay with his child. Sooner or later the parent's behavioral miscues leak through the screen of images, and the child learns with sadness that he is dealing with an imperfect creature. Behind the image of Christ stands no empirical referent. Because Christ does not empirically interact with people, they receive no behavioral information that the image of Christ is less than perfect. The only variations are in the ways different people depart from the model. The model itself is constant, absolute, and with a hard perfection that glitters against the murky inadequacies of the empirical world.

More concretely, the Spanish American Christ provides specific information on how people should suffer. The specific information is conveyed through the physical representations of a thorn-crowned Christ struggling to carry his cross up to Calvary. The way Christ suffered on this occasion is the way that people should suffer. The way Christ suffered was not through loud, heroic combat with his enemies, but it was with quietness and above all *con paciencia.*

Paciencia (patience) belongs to that group of basic Spanish American concepts expressed through such key words as *respeto* (respect), *fe* (faith), *formalidad* (formality), *conformidad* (conformity), and *resignación* (resignation). So rich are these words that their analysis can carry us deep into the basic postulates of Spanish American social existence. Without any pretension to complete understanding, we are able to suggest the manner in which these words and their concepts form a construct. The details of this construct come from one of our Costa Rican informants, Mario Ortiz. After long conversations with Mario, a man of conviction and insight, Miss Bode saw three major components in his view of God and man. The components are conformity, commitment, and resignation.[5]

Conformity connotes limiting desire to an appropriate level, to act con formalidad (formally) and con respeto (respectfully). To be in a state of conformity before God is to limit one's passions and not to engage in an endless pleading with God. God is an absolute, an immovable being, and to exceed the occasional appropriate prayer will gain nothing. Commitment, expressed in the phrase *yo tengo fe* (*I* have faith), is a deeply personal act through which man established a relationship with God. Commitment to God comes from the individual man, from you. You, as a distinct

---

4 Fred Gearing, "Social Structure: Societies as Arrangements of Personnel," in James A. Clifton, ed. *Introduction to Cultural Anthropology* (New York: Houghton Mifflin Company, 1968), pp. 160–81.

5 Barbara Bode and Miles Richardson, "A Case Study in the Nature of Faith," *Human Mosaic* 3 (1968): 13–40.

being, initiate and maintain the connection with God. God cannot be coerced, but it is through *your* faith that he moves. The third component is resignation. Resignation to Mario does *not* mean "Let God's will be done." Mario does *not* resign himself, as American Protestants may, to an uncontrollable universe. He resigns himself to his own inadequate acts of commitment. If man does not resign himself to his own fallibility, he will break out of the balanced state of conformity and endlessly knock himself against life, over which he now has no control. He will have lost his paciencia.

With his paciencia lost man exposes himself to the contradictory demands of life. He opens the door to endless ambition and engages in a fruitless struggle to achieve nothing. He will have no guard against people with *interés* who lie in wait, ready in an instant to exploit him for their own selfish ends.

A sick person without paciencia will fight sickness and will become more ill; a man without paciencia fights suffering, and so he suffers more.

The ideal man is the one who always acts with conformity, commitment, resignation, and patience. Such a man was Christ. As the perfect man, Christ conformed himself to his Father's wishes, he committed himself to man, and he resigned himself to the cross. On the cross he suffered with patience. If Christ, who was God, suffered patiently, then surely man must do likewise.

Both Costa Rican and Colombian informants insist that when man follows the image of Christ hanging in agony on the cross, he is not following a fatalistic philosophy. The lesson that Christ teaches is not that man should suffer but *how* to suffer. Man should not seek suffering; he should strive to exercise control over it.

For the sake of man Christ voluntarily placed himself in a position of intense suffering. He allowed himself to be tortured and nailed alive to a cross. (The intensity of Christ's pain is developed through the use of grotesque statuary. The Holy Friday procession in San Pedro is headed by a Christ bleeding from his crown of thorns, bent almost double under the weight of the cross, and flayed by the whip of a Roman soldier.) Despite the intensity of his suffering, Christ did not permit the external pain to penetrate into his inner self. Because he was God, Christ was able to maintain his own personal faith, his own personal worth as a human being.

Christ's refusal to allow suffering to destroy his inner self is the lesson of his crucifixion. Man should approach suffering in such a way that it does not destroy the balanced composure that he has erected to separate himself from the sensory world of pain. Like Christ, man controls suffering through suffering con paciencia. Through suffering patiently, man is able to maintain the most precious quality of his existence, his own personal sense of worth, his sacred humanity.

The dynamic, positive quality of the lesson on how to suffer is amplified when we see how the image of Christ fits into the binary contrast between *cultura* and *monte*. In Colombia, cultura closely resembles the humanist notion of culture. Cultura includes the "manifestations of human creativity: art, science, knowledge, refinement—*those things that freed man from nature*." [6] In contrast monte is the state of untamed, dangerous nature; it is the absence of civilization. In the view of the people of San Pedro, only Indians, people without cultura, and bandits, people who have lost cultura and who have consequently reverted back to being animals, live in the *monte*.

Man, say the *sanpedranos*, must gain cultura. He cannot be fully human until he has separated himself from the monte. Consequently, occupations which directly expose man to nature, such as work in the sun, carry less prestige in San Pedro than do occupations, such as office work, which shield man from nature.[7] The town's dirt streets are periodically cleaned of grass, because a street is a part of man's cultura, and grass is monte, insidiously invading man's domain. Wattle and daub houses with thatched roofs and dirt floors are despised because their construction materials are too close to the monte and do not adequately testify to the occupants' departure from nature.

The people of San Pedro equate cultura and Christianity. To be a Christian is to have cultura. The priest, disgruntled with attendance at church, charges that the townspeople lack cultura and therefore do not come to mass. The size of a *cristiano*, a human, is indicated with the hand outstretched and turned on edge; the size of a *bestia*, an animal, is measured with the palm turned downward. Indians are savages without cultura *and* without Christianity; and bandits, because they have killed, have forsaken Christ and so likewise live without cultura in the wilds of the monte.

Thus, to have cultura is to be able to separate oneself from raw nature and thereby to conquer it. To be a Christian is to be like Christ, who refused to be destroyed by the raw experience of the crucifixion. So to seek cultura and to follow Christ are identical ways that man uses to exercise control over his surroundings. To learn how to suffer like Christ is to learn how to maintain cultura, or human qualities, in face of the monte,

---

6 George W. Stocking, Jr., "Franz Boas and the Culture Concept in Historical Perspective," *American Anthropologist* 68 (1966): 867–82. Emphasis added.

7 Miles Richardson, "The Significance of the 'Hole' Community in Anthropological Studies," *American Anthropologist* 69 (1967): 41–54.

or dehumanizing experiences. To learn how to suffer con paciencia is to learn how to be fully human.

To summarize: the figure of Christ in Spanish America is a set of instructions on how to suffer. The key concept in the message is expressed in the word paciencia. The concept is part of a construct composed of the components of conformity, commitment, and resignation. The construct calls for a balanced relationship between man and his world. When man is properly composed, he has paciencia. When he loses his paciencia, he departs from the balanced relationship and destroys himself in fruitless, *un-Christ-like* struggles.

Christ in Spanish America is not a fatalistic figure. While hanging in agony on his cross, he is nonetheless teaching man how to exercise control over experience. By not allowing the inhuman torture of the cross to destroy his inner self, he epitomizes the ideal man of cultura. By suffering con paciencia, he demonstrates how man should maintain his sacred humanity in the face of an inhuman world.

Parenthetically, it would appear that the image of Christ as a set of instructions on how to control suffering conflicts with what Gillin describes as the Spanish American's search for an extraordinary experience.[8] On the one hand, the effort is toward controlling experience; on the other, it is toward savoring experience. However, the two drives are necessary complements. As the perfect man, Christ was able to control the experience of the crucifixion. Man tries to be like Christ, but he fails because he is not perfect and lacks commitment. When he fails to achieve the perfect state of composure, man returns to the world of raw experience and explodes in a fireworks display of emotion. His failure and subsequent search for the extraordinary enhances the perfect quality of Christ's suffering; the perfection of Christ depends on man's imperfections. Thus, the two cultural drives are necessary complements. Only in a culture that is preoccupied with the magic of emotions can the image of Christ as the conqueror of emotions have meaning.

THE DISTRIBUTION OF THE MODEL IN SPANISH AMERICA

The question that arises next is the distribution of the model of Christ in Spanish America. Is the model tightly bounded by a number of geographical, social, or cultural barriers, or does it cut across these barriers and teach the same lesson to many different types of people? Is the model a particularistic one or is it universalistic? A conclusive an-

[8] John Gillin, "Ethos Components in Modern Latin American Culture," *American Anthropologist* 57 (1955): 488–500.

swer to this question requires much more data than we have at our command. However, we do have information that bears on this important point, and we will present it, fully aware of its limitations.

One component of the model of Christ is the concept that God may act to reinforce the message of Christ, that is, God may send illnesses to teach man how to suffer.[9] Included in our survey of one section of Puntarenas was a question asking if the respondent agreed or disagreed with this concept. If we compare the responses to strategic variables which frequently segregate populations, the results will indicate either that this component of the model is associated with certain variables and thus is particularistic or that the component cuts across the categories and is universalistic.

The survey population of 200 people is not a random sample of Puntarenas, and some of the wealthiest and most powerful people in the city are not included. Yet the survey population is economically mixed with monthly income ranging from approximately 15 to 165 dollars. The population also varies in birthplace, education, sex, occupation, and a number of other factors. Thus, the survey group approximates a representative slice of Puntarenas. Puntarenas itself is a city of some 20,000. It is Costa Rica's main Pacific port and enjoys a mildly licentious reputation.

Eighty-five percent of the 200 Puntarenians agreed that God may send illnesses to teach the way of suffering. Clearly the concept is not restricted to rural, peasant life.

Many people who presently live in Puntarenas have moved there from other parts of the country. Perhaps those who were born in nonurban places have brought the concept to the city. Table 1 compares the responses of those born in an urban place with those born in a nonurban one (i.e. small town or rural). The chi square of 0.186 (calculated, as are the others, with the Yates correction formula) indicates no significant relation between birthplace and concept. The sickness as a lesson concept is not limited to those who presently live in a city but were born in a nonurban place, that is, the concept tends to be universalistic.[10]

---

[9] It is extremely important to note that this concept does *not* prevent people from assigning a naturalistic cause to a particular disease. Nor does it prevent them from seeking out modern, professionally trained physicians. As is the case with the general model, this particular component is not fatalistic. For other details on Costa Rican popular medicine see Miles Richardson and Barbara Bode, "Urban and Societal Features of Popular Medicine in Puntarenas, Costa Rica," *Publications of the Middle American Research Institute* (Tulane University, in press at this writing).

[10] Our data force us to define urban as the national and provincial capitals, Puntarenas being a provincial capital. This is not a satisfactory definition of urban and nonurban. However, since the vast majority of people born in an urban place were born in the city of Puntarenas, and since the majority of those born outside the

TABLE 1

COMPARISON OF BIRTHPLACE WITH THE CONCEPT THAT GOD MAY TEACH SUFFERING BY SENDING AN ILLNESS

Agreement	Birthplace		
	Urban Place	*Nonurban Place*	
Yes	101	65	166
No	15	7	22
Totals	116	72	188

$X^2 = 0.186$

People in the survey were asked to place themselves on an economic scale composed of low, middle, and high categories. Only two people considered that they belonged to the high position, and for the purposes of calculating Table 2, these two were put in the middle group. The self-placement should indicate a degree of perceived economic success. People who placed their economic position in the middle category considered themselves economically better off than at least some other people. Perhaps such people find the concept that God teaches man through sending an illness incompatible with their relatively higher economic position. However, Table 2 reveals no significant relation between economic placement and agreement with the concept. Economic placement and the concept appear to vary independently; the concept tends to be universalistic.

TABLE 2

COMPARISON OF ECONOMIC PLACEMENT WITH THE CONCEPT THAT GOD MAY TEACH SUFFERING BY SENDING AN ILLNESS

Agreement	*Economic Placement*		
	Low	*Middle*	
Yes	85	81	166
No	11	11	22
Totals	96	92	188

$X^2 = 0.0145$

Perhaps the better educated people reject the concept of illness as a God-sent lesson? Because the survey included only two people who had some measure of university training, the comparison of educational levels is essentially limited to those who did not or did attend high school.

city were from a clearly rural area, an urban nonurban dichotomy, if it is in the data, should appear. Dirección General de Estadística y Censo, *Censo de Población; 1963* (San José: Ministerio de Industria y Comercio, 1966).

TABLE 3

COMPARISON OF EDUCATIONAL LEVELS WITH THE CONCEPT THAT GOD MAY TEACH SUFFERING BY SENDING AN ILLNESS

Agreement	*Educational Levels*		
	Low (0–6 Years)	*High* (7 & Above)	
Yes	144	22	166
No	17	5	22
Totals	161	27	188

$X^2 = 0.752$

Table 3 suggests that no significant relationship occurs between educational levels and agreement with the concept. Both a high school graduate and a person with no formal education will accept God's role as a teacher on how to suffer.

For a number of reasons we may expect that the Spanish American woman finds in the image of the suffering Christ a mirror portrait of herself. Traditionally, she sits at home (or in church) and endures the *machismo* antics of her action-oriented husband. Yet both in San Pedro, Colombia, and in Puntarenas, Costa Rica, the individuals who gave the fullest account of the suffering message of Christ were men. Table 4 shows that the connection between sex and the concept is significant only at the unacceptable level of .10. At the rigorous level of .05, sex and agreement that God may send an illness to teach suffering vary independently. Once again the data strongly hint that the concept tends to be universalistic.

TABLE 4

COMPARISON OF SEX OF RESPONDENT WITH THE CONCEPT THAT GOD MAY TEACH SUFFERING BY SENDING AN ILLNESS

Agreement	*Sex of Respondent*		
	Female	*Male*	
Yes	152	20	172
No	18	6	24
Totals	170	26	196

$X^2 = 2.173$

Thus, in Puntarenas the concept that God may send illnesses to reinforce the message of Christ seems to cut across urban and nonurban birth places, perceived economic position, educational attainment (at least up to the university level), and sex. As the concept is a component of the larger image of Christ as a model for suffering, the data indicate that the model is not bounded by particularistic features but that its appeal *tends* to be universalistic. This is not to say that it is universal but only that we do not know the parameters that bound the model. Without a review of what is an extensive literature, we can only offer the following possible parameters. We will be most appreciative of any suggestions from the readers of this article.

Within Spanish America, one possible parameter which the model of a suffering Christ may not cross is to be found in ethnic subcultures, such as the "Modern Indian." Modern Indians are contemporary groups whose culture is a European-aboriginal synthesis effected in colonial times.[11] The aboriginal facet of the synthesis has long drawn the attention of anthropologists, yet among Middle American Indians the "pervasive character of Roman Catholicism in the structure of fiestas . . . is clearly recognized." [12] The point of contact between Catholicism and the Indians, at least the Nahuatl in Mexico, seem to be the Virgin. Of "the many 'santos' and 'Cristos' worshipped in Mexico, the Virgin of Guadalupe is the most benevolent and the most representative of Christian ethical values," [13] In contrast, the people of Saucío, the descendants of the Chibcha Indians and the conquistadores of Colombia, depict Christ as "the long-suffering, thorn-crowned Son of God, nailed to a cross and resigned to his death. . . ." [14] These cases appear to indicate that the question of whether or not the Modern Indian type is a parameter that bounds the model of the suffering Christ dissolves into another question: around which Christian image, that of the Virgin or that of Christ, does the Modern Indian gather?

The other large ethnic group in Spanish America, the Afro-American, may be a more effective boundary. Certainly the image of a God who suffered in order to teach the control of suffering does not appear in the works of Herskovits.[15] However, most of Herskovits' data came from Negro groups who do not live in a Spanish American country.

Social parameters may be as important as, or even more so, than ethnic ones. The lack of difference in our data between people born in a

---

[11] Charles Wagley and Marvin Harris, "A Typology of Latin American Subcultures," *American Anthropologist* 57 (1955): 428–51.

[12] Ruben E. Reina, "Annual Cycle and Fiesta Cycle," in Manning Nash, ed., *Social Anthropology*. Vol. 6 of *Handbook of Middle American Indians,* ed. Robert Wauchope (Austin: University of Texas Press, 1967), p. 330.

[13] William Madsen, "Religious Syncretism," in Manning Nash, ed., *Social Anthropology,* vol. 6 of *Handbook of Middle American Indians,* ed. Robert Wauchope (Austin: University of Texas Press, 1967), p. 378.

[14] Orlando Fals-Borda, *Peasant Society in the Colombian Andes* (Gainesville: University of Florida Press, 1955), p. 228.

[15] Melville J. Herskovits, *The Myth of the Negro Past* (Boston: Beacon Press, 1958).

nonurban place and those born in an urban one may indicate a widespread sharing of traits that stops at the point where people's position in society allows them to exercise power.[16] More and more in contemporary Spanish America people who occupy such a position have university training. Their education in the sciences may make it difficult for them to accept the concept of God sending an illness. It is more likely that to the extent that they depart from accepting the traditional model of Christ, their departure is based on the intoxicating, godlike experience of exercising power over the social environments and the emotions of others.

It must be emphasized that the conscious model of Christ is acted out in the major ritual of the year, Holy Week. The model is not only in the mind; it is also in ritual behavior. In considering both ethnic and social parameters, we have to examine not only the mental departures, which are expressed verbally, but also the ritual ones, which are expressed behaviorally. For example, people in power may verbally disagree with the model, but for one or another reason they may participate in the ritual which supports the model.

Another possible parameter is the religious one. The model of Christ as an example of how to suffer seems closely tied to Catholicism. The Protestant model, at least in the United States, appears to differ sharply. Protestant suffering is instrumental and gains an individual peace, in the after life. The difference between Catholicism and Protestantism may well reflect still another parameter, the difference between the cultural heritage of the New World colonies. The divergence in cultural heritage may go back to the Reformation or even beyond, to a division between Northern, Germanic culture and Mediterranean, Roman culture.

"TO CHRIST CRUCIFIED"

As perhaps is true of all religious personages, the figure of Christ is a model that supplies perfect information on how man should face suffering and death. Unlike the Anglo-Protestant conqueror of death, the Spanish American figure conveys the specific information that man maintains his humanity by suffering in the manner of Christ on the cross. The manner in which Christ suffered was *con paciencia*. Through suffering with patience, Christ exhibits to the perfect degree the values of conformity, commitment, and resignation. The lesson of Christ is not fatalistic; instead it teaches how man should exercise control over the raw experiences of the untamed world. Christ is the ideal man of *cultura* who refuses to allow the crude pain of the cross to destroy his own personal faith and his sense

[16] Richards N. Adams, *The Second Sowing: Power and Secondary Development in Latin America* (San Francisco: Chandler Publishing Company, 1967).

of inner worth. By suffering patiently, Christ demonstrates how man should hold fast to his sacred humanity in face of an inhuman world.

A component of the Spanish American model of Christ is the concept that God may send illnesses to reinforce the message of suffering. The concept seems to vary independently of birthplace, perceived economic position, educational attainment, and sex. The data from Costa Rica suggest that the component concept and the larger model are universalistic and appeal to many different types of Spanish Americans. However, possible parameters that may bound the model in Spanish America are ethnic subcultures, particularly the Afro-American; social parameters, especially positions of power; and Catholicism. The Protestant-Catholic dichotomy may express a more ancient cultural dichotomy between Northern-Germanic and Mediterranean-Roman heritages.

The image of Christ in Spanish America as a model for suffering stretches back at least to Miguel de Guevara, a Mexican *criollo* friar. In 1634 he wrote "*A Cristo Crucificado*" to describe how he felt when facing the image of Christ on the cross. Today Costa Rican children, under the nun's approving eye, continue to repeat his words.

I am not moved, God, to love you
By the Heaven you have promised;
Nor does the Hell so feared move me
To stop offending you.

You move me, Lord; it moves me to see you
Nailed to a cross and scorned;
Seeing your body so wounded moves me;
Insults to you, and your death, they move me.

Your love moves me in such a way
That were there no Heaven, I would love you,
And were there no Hell, I would fear you.

You do not have to give me so that I'll love you,
For though I were not to hope for that which I hope,
I would still love you as I love you.[17]

---

[17] Miguel de Guevara, "A Cristo Crucificado," *An Anthology of Spanish Poetry from Garcilaso to García Lorca* (Garden City: Doubleday & Company, 1961), p. 340. Above translation by Barbara Bode.

Katherine Fringer
Ph.D. Candidate in History
Columbia University
New York

THE CONTRIBUTION OF CAPISTRANO DE ABREU TO BRAZILIAN HISTORIOGRAPHY

João Capistrano de Abreu changed the course of Brazilian historiography. Unlike previous historians who had oriented their studies toward colonial history as an expression of Brazil's connections with European culture, he pointed to the socioeconomic and psychological aspects of the evolution of the Brazilian interior as the most significant part of Brazilian history. By reinterpreting familiar sources and uncovering new material, he reconstructed the Brazilian colonial experience from a totally original point of view. Dating from the publication of his two major works, *Os Caminhos Antigos e o Povoamento do Brasil* (1889)[1] and *Capítulos de História Colonial* (1907),[2] the perspectives of historiography in Brazil have altered, and historians have reoriented their studies to emphasize the development of Brazil as an independent nation rather than as an appendage of Portugal.[3]

This article will attempt to trace Capistrano's central thesis as it appears in his works: the great social and economic mobility in the

---

[1] *Os Caminhos Antigos e o Povoamento do Brasil* was first published in 1889 in three articles in the *Jornal do Comércio*, Rio de Janeiro, and reappeared in 1930 as the title of a collection of essays by Capistrano de Abreu. See *Os Caminhos Antigos e o Povoamento do Brasil* (Rio de Janeiro: Briguiet, 1930).

[2] Capistrano de Abreu, *Capítulos de História Colonial* (1500–1800), 4th. ed. revised and annotated by José Honório Rodriques (Rio de Janeiro: Briguiet, 1954).

[3] José Honório Rodrigues, "Capistrano and Brazilian Historiography," in E. Bradford Burns, ed., *Perspectives on Brazilian Historiography* (New York: Columbia University Press, 1967), p. 176. For an essay on colonial Brazilian historiography in English, see the introduction by E. Bradford Burns in his *Perspectives.*

sertão, which allowed the settlers to live relatively free from Portuguese administrative rule in the urban centers along the littoral, brought about the development of an independent and separatist attitude which eventually turned into Brazilian nationalism.

Until the appearance of Capistrano de Abreu's works, the administrative acts of the principal authorities in the colony and the struggles against foreign invaders, better classified as battle history, formed the subject matter for history textbooks and historical writings. Afonso de Taunay, the paulista historian and disciple of Capistrano, wrote of this state of affairs:

> The *bandeirantes*' campaign which resulted in the territorial expansion of Brazil was not considered as important as their aid in the extinction of the *quilombo* at Palmares. . . . Fleeting references were made to the sorties into the interior without any commentary on the obstacles opposing such a difficult conquest. The chapter on gold mining was always the least significant. The era of the dawn of Brazilian cultural development was reduced to the citation of a few titles from eighteenth-century literary academies.[4]

With its emphasis on memorization of names, dates, and battles, it is no wonder that history was considered one of the most boring subjects in nineteenth-century Brazilian schools.[5] Dom Pedro II showed his innocence of the truth of Brazilian history with his phrase "The history of Brazil is modest but honest." [6]

Capistrano aimed at changing this attitude. In 1883, he wrote:

> I am dealing with the foundation of an historical association less pompous and less protected than the Instituto Histórico which, however, I hope, will be more effective. It will be called Clube Taques Paes Leme and will occupy itself almost exclusively with *bandeiras* and *bandeirantes*, old trails, methods of transportation, and the economic history of Brazil.[7]

He planned to begin with the sixteenth century and to give each member a printed manuscript to examine, edit, and discuss. Finally, all of the contributions would be collected and published with a general introduction

---

[4] Afonso de E. Taunay, "Capistrano de Abreu," Curso Capistrano de Abreu, *Revista do Instituto Histórico e Geográfico Brasileiro* 221 (October/December 1953): 200.

[5] Ibid.

[6] Ibid—in Portuguese the expression is "modesta mas honesta."

[7] Letter to Antônio Joaquim Macedo Soares, 1883, in Capistrano de Abreu, *Correspondência*, 3: 2. The correspondence was published in three volumes, organized and prefaced by José Honório Rodrigues (Rio de Janeiro: Ministério de Educação e Cultura, Instituto Nacional de Livro, 1954).

tying up all the data obtained. In this way, Capistrano envisioned the entire colonial past being synthesized into collections of pertinent documents, a revolutionary idea for Brazilian historiography.

José Honório Rodrigues commented upon the role of Capistrano in the revision of Brazilian history:

> It is especially with Capistrano de Abreu that the new historiography is initiated as an expression of the new Brazil. Upon writing *Os Caminhos Antigos e o Povoamento do Brasil* (1889), although still a colonial theme, he rejects the emphasis formerly put upon European origins and relations with Europe. His theme is entirely national, since he invited Brazilian historians not to centralize their interests on the coastal settlements, but rather on the interior, on archaic Brazil, it is true, but on the origins of an autonomous Brazil: the mines, the *bandeiras,* the trails. The rejection of colonialism is contained within his colonial theme.[8]

In order to understand the development of Capistrano de Abreu into Brazil's foremost historian, one has only to look at his correspondence. Although he never left any explanatory introductions to his books, his letters reveal his methodological formation and the development of each of his works.

His basic orientation was toward the Rankian school of German realism; his goal was to narrate what actually happened on the basis of thorough documentation. He did not merely read the documents but he interpreted their meaning. Writing to his friend Guilherme Studart, the Cearense historian, Capistrano reprimanded him for failing to interpret documents and to use the Rankian method of citing sources.[9] This rigorous demand for exact citations was new to Brazilian historians; many still ignore the criteria established by the German methodologists for scholarly works.

Perhaps the most profound and lasting influence on Capistrano was the idea of the English Positivist historian Thomas Henry Buckle to study the masses, instead of great men, to find out what really shaped history. Capistrano wrote to the Portuguese historian João Lúcio de Azevedo in 1917:

> I remember the first time I thought of writing the history of Brazil. I was in Ceará . . . with a few books, far from all intellectual

[8] José Honório Rodrigues, *Teoria da História do Brasil* (São Paulo: Companhia Editora Nacional, 1957), 2: 12.

[9] Capistrano de Abreu, *Correspondência.* Letter to Guilherme Studart, April 1904, 2: 165–66.

> companionship. I had just read Buckle in the original, I read Taine once more, and I had finished the voyage of Agassiz.[10]

With his strong feeling that the history of Brazil did not begin and end in lists of Portuguese administrators and battle accounts, Capistrano was immediately attracted to Buckle's coherent presentation of a history depending not only upon kings, statesmen, and generals but upon the totality of human activity. Capistrano wrote:

> . . . in history we only point to the dominant figures, those who destroyed or built up, leaving behind a trail of blood, or a ray of light. We do not remember the shoulders which bore them, or the courage of the masses which gave them their strength, the collective mind which exalted their minds, the unknown hands which pointed out to them the ideal which only the most fortunate attained. And often the unknown man is the one whose cooperation was most vital in bringing about the great event.[11]

Capistrano's concept of anti-heroic history went to such extremes that he gave no importance to Tiradentes. He jokingly said about his *Capítulos de História Colonial*: "The only thing I kept in mind was the following: to show that the entire history of Brazil can be written without even mentioning the name of Tiradentes." [12]

In his tireless research to uncover new sources of information, Capistrano unfortunately lost the time needed to write a complete history of Brazil. Consequently, his books number far fewer than would be expected from a historian of his stature. In fact, a major criticism of Capistrano is that he did not produce even one long work. He believed instead that the greatest contribution he could make to Brazilian historiography was to uncover new sources. He formulated concepts for the use of ethnography, geography, anthropology, economics, statistics, psychology, the natural and physical sciences, and social history and customs in the study of Brazilian history. It was Capistrano who, in 1907, first saw the importance of the *Casa Grande* and *Senzala* in the Northeast.

Before going into a detailed discussion of Capistrano's major works, it is important to consider the works that he edited, or commented upon, which became sources for his synthesization of Brazilian history.

Between 1881 and 1887 he identified Fernão Cardim, José de Anchieta, Padre Manoel da Nóbrega, and Frei Vicente do Salvador with their works. In 1886 he published the fundamental texts of Nóbrega,

10 Ibid., 19 March 1917, 2: 37–38.

11 Capistrano de Abreu, *Ensaios e Estudos*, 3 vols. (Rio de Janeiro: Briguiet, 1931), 1: iii

12 Quoted by Tristão de Athayde in "Capistrano de Abreu," *Revista do Instituto de Ceará* 43 (1928): 134.

Anchieta, and the other Jesuits' letters and also identified André João Antonil as the pseudonym for João Antônio Andreoni.

By 1889 he had published his first edition of the annotated *História do Brasil* by Frei Vicente do Salvador and had translated the geographies of J. E. Wappaeus and A. W. Sellin and the travel account by Herbert Smith. These translations were of primary importance to Capistrano since he believed it was necessary to understand Brazilian geography in order to know how to write the history of the exploration of the interior, which depended vitally upon the location of rivers and the natural features of each area.[13]

In his 1901 introduction to Ambrósio Fernandes Brandão's *Diálogos das Grandezas do Brasil*, written in 1617, Capistrano noted its important interpretive contribution to Brazilian historiography in sensing the changes taking place in Brazil. Brandão wrote of Brazil's future: "... then nothing will be lacking and the land will abound with all necessities. Her great fertility and abundance will be discernible to everyone, and no longer will she need to import anything from Portugal." [14] When he first began work on the *Diálogos*, Capistrano felt an immediate affinity with its author, who praised the riches and beauty of Brazil and proclaimed in a primitive way its future independence from Portugal. This affinity expanded into Capistrano's whole concept of the "Brazilianization" of Brazil:

> From the third and fourth decades of the seventeenth century, Portuguese, *mazombos, moleques, caboclos, mulatos, mamelucos,* all denominations felt the differences which separated them. But they felt closer to one another than to the Dutch, and therefore they fought from 1624 to 1654 until the invader left Brazil. The same feeling of solidarity grew to a point where in the first and second decades of the eighteenth century, the Portuguese changed to the category of enemy, and the wars of the *mascates* between Pernambucans and of the *emboabas* among the paulistas broke out.[15]

In 1918 Capistrano published the final critical edition of Frei Vicente do Salvador's *História do Brasil*, receiving high acclaim for his work.[16] Based on interviews, the history covers the period between the discovery of Brazil and the Dutch Wars. Capistrano wrote: "Frei Vicente

[13] Capistrano de Abreu, "A Geografia do Brasil," *Ensaios e Estudos*, vol. 2. His translations are: J. E. Wappaeus, *A Geografia Física do Brasil,* 1884; A. W. Sellin, *Geografia Geral do Brasil,* 1889; Herbert Smith, *Viagem pelo Brasil,* 1886.

[14] Ambrósio Fernandes Brandão, *Diálogos das Grandezas do Brasil,* introduction by Capistrano de Abreu (Salvador, Bahia: Livraria Progresso, 1956), p. 21.

[15] Ibid.

[16] Frei Vicente do Salvador, *História do Brasil,* introduction by Capistrano de Abreu (Sao Paulo: Weiszflog Irmãos, 1918), p. xx.

is truly the basis of our history from 1580 to [1]627." [17] In the introduction, he mused on what might have happened had the work been published and read when it was first written. More would have been known about the sertão, more anecdotes would have been collected, "breaking the solemn and pedestrian monotony with which the historians like Rocha Pitta dared to publish." [18] Considering this a vital work for a history of the sertão, Capistrano concluded his introduction: "Frei Vicente finished the *História do Brasil* in 1627; only one century later Sebastião da Rocha Pitta came out with his *História . . . da América Portuguêsa*." [19] Thus, by his title, Rocha Pitta identified Brazil as a Portuguese colony, whereas Frei Vicente had referred to his land more nationalistically as "Brasil," omitting all reference to its status as a Portuguese colony.

An important essay written early in Capistrano's career was his 1882 critique of Francisco Adolfo de Varnhagen, Brazil's leading historian during the Second Empire and author of *História Geral do Brasil*, long considered a standard survey of Brazilian history.[20] In this essay, composed eight years before *Os Caminhos Antigos e o Povoamento do Brasil*, Capistrano clearly outlined his formula for writing Brazilian history. He stated that Varnhagen's major shortcoming lay in his failure to develop any theory of Brazilian history or to formulate general laws based on his research, but Capistrano also acknowledged the indebtedness of future historians to Varnhagen for the immense amount of primary material that he discovered and compiled. His findings were invaluable, but unfortunately he had turned them into an amorphous mass of uninterpreted material that had to be sorted out and annotated in order to make his work usable. Capistrano wrote:

> In Varnhagen's hands the history of Brazil was standardized, its distinct features blurred, its characteristics mixed together, and its colors faded. It appeared to be a flat and level surface which was reminiscent of the pages of a book that a heedless binder had carelessly repeated. Even people who knew infinitely less about Brazilian history than Varnhagen could see that his periods followed one another without reference to what pre-

---

[17] Capistrano de Abreu, letter to Studart, 19 October 1892. *Correspondência,* 1: 140.

[18] Capistrano de Abreu, introduction to Frei Vicente do Salvador, *História do Brasil*, p. xx.

[19] Ibid.

[20] See Capistrano de Abreu, "*A Critique of Francisco Adolfo de Varnhagen*," first published *História Geral do Brasil* in Madrid in 1854. For the third edition, revised by Capistrano de Abreu, see Varnhagen, *História Geral do Brasil* (Rio de Janeiro: Laemmert, 1907).

> ceded each one and often without continuity. This monotony need not exist. I suggest the following periodization.[21]

In this unsurpassed periodization of Brazilian history, Capistrano separated the years between 1500 and 1850 into eras differentiated by certain basic economic and social motivations but unified by the general process of development from colony to nation. Capistrano characterized the first century, from 1500 to 1614, as transoceanic, an era of dependence on Portugal when privations and danger of Indian attacks gave the colony an aura of melancholy. The Portuguese consistently discriminated against anyone born in Brazil, even if his ancestry were completely European.

The years between 1614 and 1700 formed the second period, a time of internal migration and movement:

> On the São Francisco River Paulistas descend and meet Bahians and Sergipans who travel upriver. The banks are rapidly settled and cattle raising assumes enormous proportions. One of the breeders, in pursuit of Indians who raid his property, accidentally discovers the Piauxí River. Almost at the same time, Gomes Freire de Andrada sends an expedition to explore the trail between Maranhão and Bahia.[22]

Capistrano discerned that in the years between 1600 and 1750 important psychological changes took place. The Dutch were defeated, the Paulistas and cattle breeders explored and settled the hinterlands, and hostilities between Portuguese and natives of the colony, between aristocrats and the common people, gave rise to the wars of the Mascates and of the Emboabas. The Brazilian feeling of inferiority to Portugal, which characterized the early days of colonial settlement, gradually changed to a feeling of superiority, which "grew and gave us the 7th of September." [23]

From 1700 to 1750 the mines dominated the movement towards the Brazilian sertão:

> Minas Gerais, Cuiabá, Goiás, Mato Grosso, which had already been traveled by the *bandeirantes* in their hunt for Indian slaves, are penetrated by gold hunters. All of the interior is explored and settled. Agriculture is abandoned. Slaves are imported in large numbers. Anarchy takes unprecedented proportions. Racial rivalries open up, never again to be settled.[24]

---

[21] Capistrano de Abreu, "Critique of Varnhagen," in Burns, *Perspectives*, p. 149.

[22] Capistrano de Abreu, *Ensaios e Estudos*, 1: 207–8. See also Burns pp. 149–50.

[23] Capistrano de Abreu, *Ensaios e Estudos*, 1: 75–76.

[24] Ibid., pp. 207–8.

When the Portuguese crown realized the enormous wealth coming from the mines, administrative reforms were undertaken in order to centralize power in Portugal, first to avoid the rising anarchy, and later to collect revenues more efficiently.

Within the period between 1750 and 1808, Capistrano delineated the consolidation of the colonial system. The municipalities were annulled, the Jesuits expelled, the hereditary captaincies abolished, the capital transferred from Salvador to Rio de Janeiro, and the mining output declined. The rivalries between the colonists and the Portuguese came to a boiling point: the idea of independence was the result. From 1808 to 1850 the colonial system disintegrated and Brazil became a nation.[25]

The major themes set forth in this periodization became the basis for his lifelong work: the exploration and settlement of the interior in connection with cattle breeding and the gold rush, the discovery of overland trails linking the fluvial transportation network, and the important psychological changes brought on by these events.

Capistrano's first original historical essay, *O Descobrimento do Brasil e Seu Desenvolvimento no Século XVI*, was the winning thesis presented in 1883 in the competition for the highly coveted chair of History at the Imperial Colégio de D. Pedro II.[26] It was praised for its original conclusions, its synthesis of Brazilian history, and a bibliography that included the use of linguistics, folklore, and indigenous studies, a novelty in Brazilian historiography. In this study, Brazilian history became a "lively, documented analysis of the activities of the discoverer and colonizer and of their reactions to Brazil." [27] Capistrano presented here his objectives as a historian: to give more importance to the *sertão* as a factor in shaping national life and to study the ethnic and cultural mixtures in the colonization of Brazil. Although this thesis presented a completely new interpretation of Brazil's past, Capistrano managed to write it in only forty days. He later said: "I left the essay almost intact: in the last chapter I was forced to reduce to propositions what on a primitive level should give rise to many other chapters. In short, I hope to be able to finish this and other works." [28]

All of these propositions were astonishingly original and provocative, for example:

---

[25] Ibid.

[26] Capistrano de Abreu, *O Descobrimento do Brasil* (Rio de Janeiro: Briguiet, 1929).

[27] Gustavo Barroso, "Capistrano de Abreu e a interpretação do Brasil," *Revista do Inst. Hist. e Geog. Bras.* 221:96.

[28] Capistrano de Abreu, letter to Studart, 23 February 1887. *Correspondência,* 1: 138.

> In the eighteenth century the Brazilian people were generally conscious of their superiority over the Portuguese people. *Indianismo* is the literary form of this feeling. . . .
> The Dutch had considerable influence on the exploration of the *sertões* of the North.
> In the spirit of resistance aroused by the Dutch lies one of the causes of the later revolutions in Pernambuco.[29]

In a letter written to the Baron of Rio Branco in 1887, Capistrano outlined the work that was to earn him the respect and admiration of future historians:

> When I began my studies of national history, the sixteenth century called my special attention. Even today I enjoy studying this period, but now what attracts me most is the seventeenth century, especially after the Dutch War. I see in it so many questions and, above all, so much obscurity. In Varnhagen there is almost nothing to represent this century. To fill these lacunae is, therefore, my major interest. For the State of Maranhão the problem is not difficult, but for the rest, without chroniclers and almost without official documents, the task will be arduous.[30]

In 1889, Capistrano published *Os Caminhos Antigos e o Povoamento do Brasil.* José Honório Rodrigues wrote of this essay:

> *Os Caminhos Antigos e o Povoamento do Brasil* is for Brazilian historiography what Turner's 1893 essay, *The Frontier in American History*, was for historiography in the United States. With one essay, the entire spirit of Brazilian historiography was renovated and the investigation and clarification of an entirely new area hitherto either unknown, abandoned, or neglected, was stimulated. The investigation of the *bandeiras* received from that moment a new, decisive impulse, and our historical knowledge was profoundly amplified.[31]

Just as Turner had shown the development of "Americanism" from barbarism to civilization on the frontier in the United States, Capistrano pointed out the conditions of anarchy and savagery on the Brazilian frontier where the settlers first came in contact with the indigenous Brazilians. The bandeirantes of the São Paulo region were mostly half-Indian. They lived in the interior and felt no connection with the mother

---

[29] Capistrano de Abreu, *O Descobrimento do Brasil*, pp. 135–36.

[30] Capistrano de Abreu, letter to Rio Branco, 9 April, 1887. *Correspondência*, 1: 112–13.

[31] José Honório Rodrigues, *Teoria da História do Brasil*, p. 266. See also Rodrigues, "Capistrano and Brazilian Historiography," in Burns, *Perspectives*, pp. 156–80.

country. Brazil was the only land they knew. How could these isolated people feel themselves to be anything other than Brazilian? The only strong ties with Portugal were in the major administrative centers along the coast, not in the sertão.

Capistrano formulated *Os Caminhos Antigos* as the reply to a question he posed in the introduction: "Can the settlement of Brazil be reduced to a few principal centers comparable to the way in which all the waters of some nations gather into a few large basins?" [32] For an affirmative answer to this question, Capistrano studied the settlement of four areas: Pernambuco, São Vicente, Bahia, and Maranhão, which he successfully showed to be the focal points for the colonization of Brazil. For each of these areas he traced the results of the people's perception of the geographical deterrents to settlement and how, once they were able to overcome these obstacles, they proceeded to colonize these four regions.[33]

Pernambuco was where the first colonization took place. Under Duarte Coelho and his heirs, Pernambuco expanded both to the north and to the south until the Dutch invasion held up this advance. By the 1750s Recife had only penetrated fifteen leagues into the sertão, and the rest of the Pernambucan interior had become an extension of Bahia. The real impulse to settlement came from the appearance of numerous cattle *fazendas* after the pacification of the hostile Cariri Indians.

The second and greatest center for colonization of the interior was São Vicente. Traveling over the coastal range which blocked the coast from the interior, the settlers founded São Paulo, with its network of rivers linking the highlands with northern and northeastern Brazil. The discovery of the gold mines in 1695 robbed this area of its original vitality, and São Paulo was not to regain vigor until the nineteenth century with the rise of coffee, when its geographical factors were reevaluated and used in terms beneficial to the development of the area.

The major vehicle for the successful settlement of the Bahian interior was cattle raising. Capistrano wrote:

> It was urgent to give the *caatingas* a destiny because of their enormous area. To ignore them amounted to a failure to profit from the major part of the country.[34]

---

[32] Capistrano de Abreu, *Os Caminhos Antigos e o Provoamento do Brasil*, p. 48.

[33] In order to avoid needless repetition, I shall merely outline the principal conclusions Capistrano reached for each of the four areas and include a more detailed look at these themes in the discussion of *Capítulos de História Colonial*. See infra, pp. 269.

[34] Capistrano de Abreu, *Os Caminhos Antigos*, p. 78.

Up and down the São Francisco River and its affluents, an extensive area of cattle fazendas appeared. The settlement of this cattle zone was for Capistrano one of the most important factors in Brazilian colonial history. One of his sources for this area, the *Roteiro do Maranhão a Goiás pela capitania do Piauxi,* contained a description of the formation of cattle settlement areas that so impressed Capistrano that he summarized a long passage from it which is worth repeating in the context of this paper:

> In the areas of breeding, open and full of plains, little is moved on the surface of the land. Once a house is raised, covered mostly with straw, some corrals are built, and cattle introduced, three leagues of land are settled. The mulattoes, the mestizos, and the freed blacks enter this area with pleasure, in the hope that some day they will be *fazendeiros,* and such a dream can easily come true, because the *vaqueiros* are paid in kind, so that in a few years they have the basis with which they can fight life from a more advantageous position.
>
> But what most clearly manifests the power of cattle raising and its advantage over agriculture as an export in a country as sparsely populated as it is vast, is the capacity to conquer distances. The cattle do not need to be carried; they bear their own weight on the long treks with hardly any need even to be guided.
>
> In these marches, some cattle would get tired or go astray, or almost die for lack of water. Experience taught certain settlers to establish themselves along the trails, to make dams, to plant food which did not need to be exported because it was sold to travelers at the gates, to buy stray or weak cattle, which, treated carefully, were either eaten or resold at a profit. . . . Thus the trails were slowly settled, and Bahia became more thickly populated than any other area, except a few cattle raising areas of Pernambuco.[35]

The fourth and last center of expansion was Maranhão. Because the tradewinds off the coast made voyages from Maranhão to any other point in Brazil impossible during half the year, this region became isolated from the rest of Brazil. Therefore, overland trails were sought, and, in the process, much of the territory was explored. The discovery of the trail linking Maranhão with Bahia was, in Capistrano's estimation:

> . . . one of the most important events of the history of Brazil: it signified the victory over the tradewinds which during half the year blow in only one direction, thereby hindering any continuity in reciprocal maritime communications.[36]

After outlining the colonization efforts in Pernambuco, São Vicente, Bahia, and Maranhão, Capistrano concluded his study:

---

[35] Ibid., pp. 100–101.

[36] Capistrano de Abreu, "A Geografia do Brasil," *Ensaios e Estudos,* 2: 40.

> Thus, at the beginning of the last century, the whole country was linked, although imperfectly, by means of overland routes and rivers. Would it form a conjunct, a nationality? The colonial system meant divergency and particularism: the center remained in Portugal.
>
> Under well-known circumstances the Portuguese court moved to Brazil, and the center, which had been abroad, now remained within the country. D. João VI reigned for thirteen years, D. Pedro I for ten, and the convergence of the parts began so harmoniously, the process of Brazilian unification ran so smoothly, that, in spite of the profound revolutions that occurred during these two reigns, a gradual and genuine evolutionary process underlined the events. The achievement of nationality was so well consolidated that it defied the crises accompanying the Regency and the beginning of the Second Empire.[37]

Capistrano's other major work and only book length study was *Capítulos de História Colonial*, published in 1907. As early as 1890, in a letter to Rio Branco, Capistrano outlined this work:

> I give you great news (at least for me): I have decided to write a history of Brazil, not the one of which I dreamed so many years ago in Ceará, after having read Buckle and in the enthusiasm of that reading which formed an era of my life, but a modest history, in broad strokes, until 1807. I am writing it because I can thus unite many scattered matters, and I hope to link better certain facts, to call attention to cerain new things, and at least to break the iron fetters of Varnhagen's method which, introduced by Macedo in the Colégio de Pedro II, are still today the basis of our teaching. The *bandeiras,* the mines, the trails, the cattle, are all as yet unknown, as is almost the entire seventeenth century, aside from the Spanish and Dutch Wars.[38]

From the first chapter, "Indigenous Beginnings," Capistrano did indeed break away from the Varnhagen tradition. Whereas Varnhagen began his *História Geral do Brasil* with Portuguese antecedents, Capistrano began with an anthropological and geographical description of Brazil, emphasizing the fact that the Indians were the first Brazilians. He outlined Brazil's discovery by the Portuguese, its occupation and settlement, colonization, penetration, and definition of the borders. Throughout this outline was interwoven the formation of the development of Brazilian national consciousness. Capistrano devoted only thirty pages to the Dutch Wars

---

[37] Capistrano de Abreu, *Os Caminhos Antigos*, p. 117.

[38] Capistrano de Abreu, letter to Rio Branco, 17 April 1890. *Correspondência,* 1: 124

and more than one hundred to the chapter on the sertão, almost in inverse proportion to these themes as they appeared in Varnhagen's history.

After chapters on indigenous Brazil, the Portuguese discovery, and first attempts at settlement, Capistrano delineated the first hereditary captaincies and explained their feudal character. Then he proceeded to his true interest: the description and interpretation of colonization and expansion into the sertão and the geographical determinants involved.

> Then there were attempts at settlement: even today towns exist which were founded in the 1640s; but the colonists were confronted with virgin forests, rivers filled with cataracts, and pathless mountain ridges which, at first, they did not know how to overcome. They only gave impetus to the history of Brazil after these obstacles were conquered.[39]

In the chapter titled "Frenchmen and Spaniards," Capistrano showed that the Spanish domination over Portugal from 1580 to 1640 presented certain advantages to Brazil: the French were eliminated from the area and the colonists were freer to expand westward, especially in the Amazon. As both the east and west coasts of South America were under the Spanish Crown, inward expansion became a more cohesive venture in seeking a tie between Brazil and the western coast via the Amazon. But the great disadvantage that arose as a result of Spanish rule was the onset of the Dutch Wars. During this sixty-year period, Capistrano saw certain social forces at work:

> Forces of dissolution dominated the social organism. . . . There was no conscience of unity, but rather of multiplicity. Only very slowly did this movement of general dispersion cease, around the middle of the seventeenth century. . . . In spite of their many differences, all groups felt a common bond against the Dutch invader: from this feeling resulted the war begun in 1624 and brought to its conclusion . . . after thirty years.[40]

Capistrano devoted the next chapter to the Dutch Wars, and once again he delineated the changes moving Brazil toward a national spirit and final independence in 1822:

> Holland and Olinda represented mercantilism and nationalism. The national spirit prevailed. Portuguese like Francisco Barreto, Azoreans like Vieira, Brazilians like André Vidal, Indians like Camarão, Negroes like Henrique Dias, *mamelucos, mulatos, caribocas, mestiços* of all shades, felt unified by the cause of liberty.

---

[39] Capistrano de Abreu, *Capítulos de História Colonial*, p. 98.

[40] Ibid., p. 140.

> Under external pressure, solidarity grew—superficial, imperfect, but at least a beginning of solidarity, developed among the diverse ethnic groups.
>
> The warriors of Pernambuco, who had defeated the Dutch, who had, in turn, defeated the Spanish, who were once lords over Portugal, felt a community spirit, that of a community of heroes.
>
> . . . After the first moments of enthusiasm, the native Portuguese wished to reassume their protective attitude of superiority. From this moment dates the irreparable and uncontrollable separation between Pernambuco and Portugal.[41]

The following chapter, on the sertão, constitutes more than one-third of the entire work. Capistrano explained the reason for its importance in Brazilian colonial history:

> The Flemish invasion constituted a mere episode in the occupation of the coast. The settlement of the sertão, begun in diverse stages, from separate points, until it formed an interior current more voluminous and more fertile than the tenuous thread of settlement along the coast, surpasses it in all respects.[42]

In a concise and lucid presentation, Capistrano divided the material on the sertão into five main topics similar to those featured in *Os Caminhos Antigos*: São Vicente and the Paulistas, Maranhão, the expansion of cattle, the mines, and the changing psychology of the colonists, especially as manifested in the wars of the Mascates and of the Emboabas.

Dealing with São Vicente, Capistrano began with the same geographical description of the isolation of the inhabitants on the Piratininga highland as he had used in *Os Caminhos Antigos*. The bandeirantes were natural offspring of their wild environment: their formation was initially into *bandeiras* to enslave other human beings in a primitive manner. In their hunts, they followed trails previously forged by the indigenous population and, in time, linked the Paraíba River to the São Francisco, and the Paranaíba, Goiás, and Mato Grosso regions to the Amazon through the Madeira, Tocantins, and Tapajós Rivers. The early bandeirantes centered on the Tietê and Paraíba Rivers, where the Jesuits from Asunción had established their reductions:

> A more tempting prey for slave hunters cannot be imagined. Why venture to unknown lands, among strange, untamed people, speaking incomprehensible and confusing languages, if nearby were inhabitants of numerous villages initiated in the art of peace, accustomed to the yoke of authority . . .? [43]

---

[41] Ibid., pp. 175–76.
[42] Ibid., p. 177.
[43] Ibid., p. 182.

Capistrano described the horrible treatment inflicted by the bandeirantes on the Indians, and wondered, "Are such horrors compensated by the consideration that the lands devastated by the bandeirantes, because of them, now pertain to Brazil?" [44]

Another, more heroic, feat of the bandeirantes was their assistance in the pacification of warring Indians in the north. Many Paulistas remained in the north, and Capistrano noted the change which accompanied their decision to stay: "From bandeirantes, that is, depopulators, they became conquistadores, forming fixed residences." [45] Even before the great exodus from São Paulo during the mining period, there were more than one hundred Paulista families on the banks of the Velhas and São Francisco Rivers, "dedicated to cattle raising." [46] Thus the formerly nomadic and barbarous bandeirantes settled down as cattle raisers and characterized, for Capistrano, the process of development from primitive to civilized colonizers of Brazil.

To summarize the section on the Paulistas achievements, Capistrano quoted at length an anonymous letter written to the Portuguese king after 1690 to recommend them, because of their past feats of territorial expansion, for a future role in the conquest of lands for Portugal:

> They are men capable of penetrating all the *sertões*, where they continually go with no more food than the animals they hunt . . . wild fruits and roots from various trees, unworried about spending year after year in the *sertões*, being accustomed to that life. And even if these paulistas are, in some instances, insolent, no one can deny that the entire settled portion of the *sertão* was conquered by them from the savage natives. . . .[47]

The second section, on the sertão of Maranhão, begins with the first major figure in the expansion into the hinterland, Bento Maciel Parente, a native of Portugal raised in Pernambuco, who, from 1616 to 1626, made sorties into the sertão, following the example of the bandeirantes. Another explorer, Pedro Teixeira, made a trip to Quito in 1638 via the Amazon to open relations with the Spanish colonies. When the Dutch heard of his voyage, their intentions to take possession of Maranhão strengthened, since Pedro Teixeira had pointed out vividly the contiguity of that area with Spanish America.

The most notable fact in the years following the final expulsion of the Dutch from northeastern Brazil was the introduction of the Jesuits.

---

[44] Ibid., p. 184.
[45] Ibid., p. 187.
[46] Ibid., p. 188.
[47] Ibid., pp. 191–92. Quoted from "Informação do Estado do Brasil e de suas necessidades," *Revista do Inst. Hist. e Geog. Bras.* 25 (1862): 473.

In 1652 nine Jesuits went to Pará and, a year later, Antônio Vieira, the historian of the first missions, arrived with three other priests. Capistrano added, "Finally, people arrived to defend the Indians." [48] After innumerable trips and sermons made to promulgate their cause, in 1693 the Jesuits were given mission rights on the south banks of the Amazon.

Capistrano finally got to his favorite subject: the opening of the land trail between Maranhão and Bahia. In the 1680s João Velho do Vale was charged with finding a means of communication between Maranhão and the rest of Brazil. He did, and the fact that his narrative of the discovery was lost remained one of Capistrano's great regrets:

> In my opinion there is no question more important than the break in the great curve of the São Francisco, the *entrada* into the Parnaíba, the land trail from Maranhão to Bahia. I think I would faint if I found the logbook of João Valho do Vale, done by order of Gomes Freire. The ideal history of Brazil would be one in which the place occupied by the Dutch and Spanish Wars went to these other events.[49]

The third section of the chapter on the sertão traces the connection between the first moves into the interior and the phenomenal rise in economic importance of the area through the development of the cattle industry. Capistrano wrote that the sugar plantations of the Northeast all remained within the area close to the coast and the navigable rivers, since it was unprofitable to transport the cane from any great distance to the coastal markets. The first chroniclers complained that their contemporaries "clutched at the coastal sands like crabs, instead of moving into the interior." [50] The westward movement was easy in São Paulo because of the Indian hunts being a general activity for the settlers, and in the Amazon, with its natural abundance; but in the middle zone, another solution was needed. The solution was cattle. Here Capistrano repeated the theme of the destiny of the *caatinga*, which had first appeared in *Os Caminhos Antigos*:

> Cattle dispensed with the need for a nearby coastal outlet, since, like victims of the bandeirantes, they transported themselves for long distances, and even more easily. They were successfully raised in regions unfit for sugar . . . ; they needed few people . . . , important in a sparsely populated country; they almost abolished the need for capital, since they were fixed and cir-

[48] Capistrano de Abreu, *Capítulos de História Colonial*, p. 202.

[49] Capistrano de Abreu, letter to João Lúzio de Azevedo, 14 September 1916. *Correspondência*, 2: 16.

[50] Capistrano de Abreu, *Capítulos de História Colonial*, p. 213.

> culating capital in one, multiplying without intervention; they furnished constant food, superior to shellfish. . . .[51]

Cattle raising first developed near the city of Salvador. The conquest of Sergipe extended cattle along the right bank of the São Francisco, while, on the Pernambucan side, the movement was weaker. However, by the outbreak of the Dutch War in 1624, both banks of the São Francisco supported cattle. Capistrano added, ". . . for no other reason, Mauritz of Nassau incorporated them into the territory of the West India Company, and the patriots defended them with such tenacity." [52]

Cattle development along the course of the São Francisco necessitated trails to connect the river with the coast. The people who lived in the sertão, along the trails and on the fazendas, were completely dominated by cattle raising. In a famous passage, Capistrano described the era as the "age of leather." Everything they did involved either cattle or cattle hides:

> The entrances to their huts were leather, as was the crude bed set out upon the hard ground, which was also used as the bed of childbirth; all the ropes were leather, the water carrier, the saddle-bags used to carry provisions, the hammock to store clothes in, the saddle-cloth to mount the horse, the shackles to hold in the horse on a journey, the knife sheathes, the small bags, the clothes worn to enter the brushlands . . . the snuff was even crushed in leather.[53]

Capistrano repeated Antonil's description from *Cultura e Opulência do Brasil* of the cattle drives and an account of the settlement of the area by people who remained along the routes of the drives. The population density of the Bahian-Pernambucan region of cattle was equalled only when Rio de Janeiro grew after the discovery of the mines. Because of the relatively dense settlement, by 1690 no fear was involved in travel to the sertão, and many men brought their wives and families to the cattle fazendas. Antonil's data on the extension of the lands occupied by cattle raisers and on the number of cattle revealed the following:

> The heads of cattle of Bahia certainly pass the half million mark, and there must be more than 800,000 in Pernambuco, although the Bahians use the cattle more than the Pernambucans, and many more drives are to Bahia.[54]

Capistrano brought up an important point in connection with the cattle and their relationship to the mines, first noted in *Diálogos das Grandezas do Brasil*, in 1618:

---

[51] Ibid., pp. 213–14.
[52] Ibid., p. 214.
[53] Ibid., p. 217.
[54] Ibid., p. 222.

> Beside the feeling of pride inspired by the wealth, by the removal of effective powers, by their impunity, cattle raising also had an effect which had important repercussions: due to the cattle it was possible to discover the mines. From 1618 the author of *Diálogos das Grandezas do Brasil* said that the problem of mining was not in finding the ore—this existed without any doubt; the problem really consisted in the difficulty of feeding the miners.[55]

After linking the cattle and mining industries, Capistrano continued to the section on the mines, beginning with the origin, in Gabriel Soares de Sousa's *Tratado Descritivo do Brasil em 1587*, of the belief that Brazil was full of hidden riches. This sixteenth-century chronicle encouraged the great voyages into the interior in search of allegedly inexhaustible silver mines.[56]

Soon after 1690 an unknown explorer discovered gold in Minas Gerais. In 1719, miners moved to Cuiabá; in 1734 new mines found in Mato Grosso opened up that area; in 1736 a land route was forged from Cuiabá to the Paraguay River. Through the Jesuits, the miners moving northwards discovered that they were in the Madeira basin, thus establishing a link between the mines and the Amazon.

Goiás became a center whose late appearance in the history of the mines and relative proximity to populated centers saved the miners from the privations suffered in Minas Gerais and Mato Grosso. The trail from São Paulo was the only official one, but many others were opened, and adventurers and cattle came from Minas Gerais, Bahia, Pernambuco, Piauí, and Maranhão. By way of the Amazon, Parnaíba, Paraná, and São Francisco Rivers, Goiás had connections with all parts of Brazil.

After discussing Portuguese attempts to centralize the administration of the mines, Capistrano cited the causes given by Teixeira Coelho for the eventual decline of the mines: the poverty of the miners, the lack of Negro slave labor, the abuses in the concessions made by customs officers, the demands made on the privileges of the miners, poor methods of mining, a scarcity of mining lands and water, and the division of the mines through inheritance.[57] Capistrano observed that the first signs of decadence in mining were explained by the continuous upsurge in losses caused by the

---

[55] Ibid., p. 225.

[56] Ibid., pp. 228–29. See Gabriel Soares de Sousa, *Tratado Descritivo do Brasil em 1587* (Rio de Janeiro: Laemmert, 1851) and *Revista do Inst. Hist. e Geog. Bras.* 14 (1851).

[57] Capistrano de Abreu, *Capítulos de História Colonial*, p. 246. See J. J Teixeira Coelho, "Instrução para o Governo da Capitania de Minas Gerais," *Rev. do Inst. Hist. e Geog. Bras.* 15 (1852): 257ff.

multiplicity of the routes of communication.[58] He also mentioned the two principal causes for the decline cited by Guilherme de Eschwege: the people had at their disposal the limitless mines, without inspection over their work, and also lacked restrictive laws adequate for the situation in Brazil. The miners, due to their ignorance, probably lost about half of the valuable ore. The people turned, therefore, to cattle, sugar, tobacco, cereals, and cotton.[59]

In the final part of the chapter on the sertão, Capistrano explained the changing psychology of the colonists:

> The triumphs in wars against foreigners, the feats of the bandeirantes, . . . the abundance of cattle animating the immense sertões, the large sums remitted to the Portuguese government, the numerous fortunes made, the increase in population, influenced considerably the psychology of the colonists. . . . The humble and ashamed mazombos of the beginning of the seventeenth century no longer were able or wished to call themselves inferior to those born in Portugal. For their services to Portugal, for their wealth, for the magnificence of their native land, they counted themselves among the most well-deserving under the Portuguese Crown.[60]

Portugal soon realized this feeling of at least equality, if not superiority, on the part of the colony, and the first manifestation was the War of the Emboabas in 1708 and 1709. The War of the Mascates, in 1711, was basically a war between, on the one hand, the planters, the Portuguese-oriented government, and the ecclesiastical hierarchy of Olinda, and, on the other, the mercantilists of Recife.

Capistrano cited as another example of the new psychological development of the Brazilian colonists the important work of the Jesuit Andreoni, *Cultura e Opulência do Brasil por suas drogas e minas,* written in 1711, which he used as a source for the feeling of Brazilian superiority over Portugal and the subsequent reactions in Portugal. Andreoni took over the Jesuit rectory in Bahia in 1697 and, in his book, he described what he saw on the sugar plantations, in the mines and cattle fazendas, and in the tobacco culture. This firsthand statistical documentation of Brazil's opulence was confiscated immediately by the Portuguese government under the pretext that it gave away secrets of Brazil to foreigners. In truth, Portugal feared the reaction in Brazil to a narrative that "showed the secret of

---

58 Ibid.

59 Ibid., pp. 246–47. See Guilherme B. de Eschwege, "Extrato de uma memória sôbre a decadência das minas de ouro da capitania de Minas Gerais e sôbre vários outros objetos Montanísticos," *História e Memórias da Academia Real das Ciências de Lisboa* (Lisbon, 1868), vol. 4, part 2, pp. 222–23.

60 Capistrano de Abreu, *Capítulos de História Colonial*, p. 248.

Brazil to the Brazilians, showing all of its power, justifying all of its claims, clarifying all of its greatness."[61]

Continuing his study of the last period of Portuguese rule in Brazil, Capistrano cited Pombal's expulsion of the Jesuits in 1759 as a grave error since he believed that the Order had played an invaluable role in the settlement and formation of Brazil. He wrote: "Colonial history is mostly a history of the priests."[62] One of Capistrano's most valuable suggestions for Brazilian historiography was a history of the Jesuits in Brazil: "A history of the Jesuits is an urgently needed work. While we do not possess this it is presumptuous to want to write a history of Brazil."[63]

He concluded his chapter on the sertão by writing, ". . . the attacks against the Jesuits reveal very little intelligence. Instinctively one's sympathy turns to the disciples and companions of Nóbrega, Anchieta, Cardim, Vieira, Andreoni, the teachers of youth, the founders of American linguistics."[64]

After a chapter on the formation of Brazil's territorial limits, Capistrano ended *Capítulos de História Colonial* with a section foreshadowing Gilberto Freyre's *Casa Grande e Senzala* in its description of the geographical distribution of population, crops, cattle raising, foods, the way of life in the casa grande, education, the Masons, the church, and the habits and customs surrounding daily life of the men and women of Brazil at the end of the colonial period. Cited as sources were Henry Koster, G. von Eschwege, August Saint-Hilaire, Spix-Martius, J. E. Pohl, John Luccock, and Thomas Lindley, all of whom, as foreign observers, had written down the scenes of Brazilian life which most impressed them. Capistrano thus demonstrated through his original use of travel accounts the different sources that could be used successfully to write Brazilian history.

He summed up the colonial experience in the last sentence of the book, in which he showed the evolution of a distinctly Brazilian personality as he had documented it throughout his narrative:

> Five ethnographic groups, linked by the active community of language, the passive community of religion, formed by the environmental conditions of five diverse regions, having for the natural resources of their land an abounding enthusiasm, feeling aversion or scorn for the Portuguese, but not esteeming one

---

[61] Ibid., p. 267.

[62] Capistrano de Abreu, "Notícias Atrasadas," *Ensaios e Estudos*, 3: 183.

[63] Capistrano de Abreu, *Capítulos de História Colonial.* A history of the Jesuits was finally written in 1938 by Serafim Leite. See *História da Companhia de Jesús no Brasil*, 11 vols. (Rio de Janeiro, 1938–1949).

[64] Capistrano de Abreu, *Capítulos de História Colonial*, p. 278.

> another in any particular way—here is, in short, the work of three centuries.[65]

In conclusion, the contribution made by Capistrano de Abreu to an understanding of the relative values in Brazilian history can never be overestimated. Twentieth-century historians all look back to his writings as a watershed in Brazilian historiography. Sérgio Buarque de Hollanda wrote in an essay titled "Historical Thought in Twentieth-Century Brazil": "The state of historical thought in Brazil during the last half-century is not easy to understand unless we recognize the prominent role of Capistrano de Abreu, the man who took the first step toward expanding its perspectives." [66]

This new school of historians is today following the advice of Capistrano to research developments of the colonial period which turned what was to become modern Brazil toward the West and the New World, away from the coastal settlements dominated by European traditions and customs, imitating foreign manners and political doctrines, remaining forever colonials at heart because they refused to learn what differentiated their new land from Portugal. Capistrano's studies all pointed to the uniqueness of Brazil through the use of geography, ethnography, linguistics, and folklore. He showed that the valuable essence of Brazilian history was a knowledge of how the people had adapted to conditions peculiar to Brazil through trailblazing, cattle raising, mining, and missionary work, all of which led to the formation of Brazil as an independent nation.

---

[65] Ibid., pp. 337–38.

[66] Sérgio Buarque de Holanda, "Historical Thought in Twentieth-Century Brazil," in Burns, *Perspectives*, p. 181.

Philip Raine
U.S. Foreign Service Officer
(Retired)

THE CATHOLIC CHURCH IN BRAZIL

The church in Brazil suffers many but by no means all of the ills usually ascribed to Catholicism in Spanish American countries. Concern over these problems has grown throughout the Catholic world, as well it might. One-third of the world's Roman Catholics live in the southern part of the Western Hemisphere. According to many churchmen a state of spiritual bankruptcy confronts the church in most of these countries.[1] Basically it is a matter of the irrelevance of a system still rooted in hierarchic and paternalistic spiritual guardianship among people in transitional societies whose goals are modern, affluent egalitarianism. In simpler terms, more and more people in Latin America learn about widespread wealth among others, and fewer and fewer believe that their own disadvantages are preordained and can be changed for the better only in the next world—as the church has long taught. The result is that many have lost interest in the church altogether; others find comfort in Protestant sects, and still others have found a substitute for spiritual religion in materialistic political movements, usually extremist in nature. The mother church has recognized the problem and beginning with John XXIII has taken revolutionary steps to meet it by seeking to identify closer with the poverty stricken masses and to change their condition. This is the reason for the papal encyclicals *Mater et Magister* (1961) and *Populorum Progressio* (1967).

Despite widespread awareness of the need for change in the church in

[1] Ivan Vallier, "Religious Elites," in Seymour M. Lipset and Aldo Solari, *Elites in Latin America* (New York: Oxford University Press, 1967).

Brazil, the Roman Catholic hierarchy and the priests differ among themselves as to what changes are to be encouraged and how they are to be brought about. The problems are of critical importance not only in spiritual matters but in the modernization process in developing nations where Roman Catholicism is the principal cultural element in society. The church in Brazil must therefore be considered in the context of its relationship to the universal Church, how secular modernization has affected it, and its influence on the changing nation.

THE BRAZILIAN CHURCH

The Brazilian church, founded on the Portuguese, was more liberal than those of Spanish origin.[2] In colonial days and during the empire from 1822 to 1889, it was often accused of being too worldly, too closely tied to Brazilian society and the mundane problems of the people, with too little attention given to spiritual matters which most concerned Rome. Brazil's second and last monarchical ruler, Emperor Pedro II, kept a firm hand over the national church. He sometimes quarreled with Rome and presumably had no objections to conditions described by Father Julio María in 1900, eleven years after the empire fell, as "ceremonies that do not edify, devotions that do not refine spirituality; books of novenas that do not reveal fervor; processions that only divert; feasts, finally, that do not profit souls nor give glory to God—behold to what the great and majestic Catholic cult is generally reduced in Brazilian parishes." [3]

But what the church lacked in spirituality, it gained in closeness to its flock. This became evident when the Papacy established firmer control over the Brazilian hierarchy. The spiritual level of the church's pastoral work was elevated but it lost the interest of many Brazilians and found it increasingly difficult to recruit priests. By the church's own estimate, only about 15 percent of nearly 100 million Brazilians today are practicing Catholics, although 90 percent claim Catholicism as their religion. In 1960, forty percent of Brazil's 10,000 priests were foreign-born.[4] As in other Latin American countries, the situation of the Brazilian church was reaching crisis proportions.

[2] See the summary study of Brazilian Catholicism by the French sociologist Roger Bastide, "Religion and the Church in Brazil," in T. Lynn Smith and Alexander Marchant, *Brazil, Portrait of Half a Continent* (New York, 1951).

[3] From "A Religião," in *Livro do Centenario*, Rio de Janeiro, 1900, quoted in João Cruz Costa, *Panorama of the History of Philosophy in Brazil* (Washington: Pan American Union, 1962).

[4] Data on the church hierarchy can be found in Winfredo Plagge, A. A., *A Igreja no Brasil* (Rio de Janeiro: CERIS, 1965). Current data is from *Jornal do Brasil*, 21 July 1968.

To better understand recent developments in Brazil, it is necessary to review developments among the elites in the universal Church. These elites, as identified by Ivan Vallier, consist of 1) the traditional, politically-oriented hierarchy, 2) the papists, 3) the pastors, and 4) the pluralists.

In simplest terms: members of the traditional hierarchy seek to preserve the church's position based on alliances with the power structure of secular society while the papists believe in strong leadership from Rome. They seek to establish a militant, modern Catholicism which will contribute to religious renewal through a church that builds on its own resources and is less beholden to either government or elite groups than it has been in the past. It seeks to penetrate the social milieu and to establish closer ties with rising status groups, particularly the urban proletariat. Direct political involvement with political parties is usually forbidden, although individuals may be politically active under the laws of the country.

The pastors represent a growing group of bishops and priests who seek to create a spiritual body of priests, people, and the sacraments. Less importance is attached to personal piety than to a more active role for laymen within homogeneous communities. Although this view of Catholicism has been common during the past decade or more in the United States and other parts of the world, in Latin America it has been exceptional until very recently.

The pluralists form the third important new group. They are the most revolutionary in outlook and activity. They believe, contrary to conventional wisdom, that Catholicism is a minority faith in Latin America and that, in collaboration with other groups of similar mind, the church's principal objective should be to develop activity which will help to institutionalize social justice. Attention tends to concentrate on basic ethical action rather than traditional religious concerns. Whatever furthers economic development and social integration is considered essentially religious in nature. Ecumenical ties and cooperation are encouraged.[5]

This classification holds generally for divisions among the Brazilian hierarchy. Mutchler in 1965 divided it into ultraconservatives, conservatives, moderates, and progressives. It is a reflection of the changing positions within the church that Mutchler's typology would better fit the situation in 1970 by removing the ultraconservative classification and adding one somewhat more to the left of the progressive. Ultraconservatives no longer exist in sufficient number or have sufficient power to warrant a separate classification. Father Godofredo Deelen, a sociologist in the church-sponsored social research organization called CERIS (Cen-

[5] Vallier, *Religious Elites*, pp. 204–6.

tro de Estadística Religiosa e de Investigação Social), classifies the priests as conservatives (the politicians), moderates (the papists), pastoral (the pastors), and progressive (the pluralists). Mutchler correctly adds a leftist group of priests who believe that violence is necessary to achieve church goals. Their number is small but they were an important factor in the confrontation between the church and the government from 1965 to 1970. Their part in moving the hierarchy toward a more progressive stand was important.[6]

Until little more than a decade ago, the church hierarchy in Brazil was under the control of the politicians. Cardinal Sebastião Leme and Cardinal Jaime Camara, who succeeded him and remains a fortress of conservatism, were probably the most effective of these leaders. Others among the conservative bishops who have taken an active part in condemning the work of the progressives and supporting the military-controlled governments since 1964 are Dom Geraldo de Proença Siguad, archbishop of Diamantina, and Dom Antonio de Castro Mayer, bishop of Campos. There is a community of interest between them and the *latifundistas*, the less progressive-minded industrialists, and commercial leaders who believe that communism is at the root of all problems in Brazil.

To judge by the character of pronouncements by the *Conferencia Nacional dos Bispos do Brasil* (CNBB—National Conference of Brazilian Bishops), the weight of opinion in the Brazilian hierarchy rests somewhere between the moderates and the progressives, that is, the papists and pluralists as described by Villier. Because of conditions among the flock in the endemically poverty-stricken Northeast, bishops from that part of Brazil exercise an influence in the CNBB beyond their weight in numbers. Leaders among the moderates are Cardinal Rossi until recently of São Paulo and the newly-named Cardinal Sherer of Porto Alegre. Cardinal Eugenio Sales of Bahia, formerly a very active progressive bishop of Natal, commands an important following in this group as does Cardinal Sherer in the south. Cardinal Sales, who gained considerable fame for his work in Natal where he was chief coordinator of the "Natal Movement," which fostered radio schools, labor unions, cooperatives, health clinics, agricultural clubs and other community efforts, is another leader of the pastors.

Dom Helder Pessoa Camara, archbishop of Recife and Olinda, has long been recognized as the leader of the progressives or the pluralists.

[6] See David Mutchler, S. J., "Roman Catholicism in Brazil," *Studies in Comparative International Development* (St. Louis, Mo.: Washington University, 1965), vol. I, no. 8, for a study made shortly after the 1964 revolution when the conflict between church and state first became apparent for all to see. Father Deelen's typology was printed in *Jornal do Brasil*, 21 July 1968.

Internationally he is perhaps the best known of Brazilian churchmen as a result of his work as auxiliary bishop of Rio de Janeiro and his outspoken criticism of the existing order. His extreme political and social position—he is a strong critic of capitalism and refuses to blame communism for all Brazil's problems—has made him a principal target of the latifundistas of the Northeast and of the military. His unrelenting fight for radical social change has generated so much animosity that his life has been threatened and one of his aides was murdered in 1969.

Dom Helder Camara does not preach violence; in fact, he has specifically forsworn violence as a means for achieving church goals. He has labeled his methods as "Liberating Moral Pressure" designed to force the government to make social reforms. Indeed, his pronouncements leave no doubt that his goals will be hard to achieve without resort to extreme pressure. Writing in the July-August 1969 *Catholic Worker* of Milwaukee, after observing that superficial revisions of the underdeveloped world are inadequate, he noted that "it will take a structural revolution" to break away from "a sort of internal colonialism, in which the wealth of a small number of privileged people is bought with the misery of millions of their fellow citizens." Dom Helder Camara would doubtless have been silenced a long time ago were he not a personal friend of Pope Paul VI as he was of John XXIII. He took a leading role among the progressives at Vatican II.

Less adept than Dom Helder at gaining public attention—or less interested in working in the glare of publicity—is Dom Avelar Brandão Vilela, archbishop of Teresina, who has been secretary general of the CNBB and president of the Latin American Episcopal Conference. Dom Avelar is a convinced pluralist, with a firm belief in the need to give national churches more autonomy than Rome seems prepared to grant.

It would be well here to review briefly the succession of events that have signaled the changing temper of the Brazilian church, irrespective of the divergent views held by individual bishops and priests. Discontent in and out of the church with its sternly conservative role during the 1940s, when it was largely concerned with a decline in morality and the threat of communism, coincided with a growing concern in the Vatican over its declining position. Changes were made among the hierarchy and liberal papal nuncios were assigned. In the 1950s, Pope Paul VI, then Cardinal Giovanni Montini, took a leading part in bringing these changes about. Bishop Helder Camara was made secretary-general of the newly formed National Conference of Bishops. In 1962, "at the request of Pope John XXIII, and conscious of the very special position in which the Church in Brazil finds itself, [the CNBB] undertook . . . an intensive effort at pastoral renewal based on the Emergency Plan." The Emergency Plan was replaced several years later with the Joint Pastoral Plan (1966–1970).[7]

How far the church had moved by early 1963 can be seen in the statement of bishops made 30 April of that year, reluctantly approved even by the conservative Cardinal Camara, who apparently signed only after certain expressions were changed and an injunction against birth control added.[8] Of particular importance in this document, entitled *Pacem in Terris and the Brazilian Reality*, is a section devoted to the expropriation of land, a subject on which conservative churchmen had long been adamant in support of the latifundistas. Noting that the social system is "still debased by the heavy weight of the capitalist tradition . . ." it states that

> the majority . . . is deprived of the exercise of many of the fundamental and natural rights which are mentioned in the encyclical *Pacem in Terris*: the right of existence and to a decent standard of living, the right of human liberty and dignity, the right to participate in the benefits of culture; in other words the right to live as a man in society. . . . No one can ignore the situation of millions of our brothers living in the rural areas who cannot share in the development of our nation, who live in conditions of misery which are an affront to human dignity. . . . [Let it be known] that the expropriation of land in such situations is in no way contrary to the social doctrine of the Church.

The liberal press published the document under headlines; some conservative papers refused to print it or strongly condemned it. However, conservative reaction then, and subsequent even sharper reaction, failed to sidetrack the new programs first stirred to life at Vatican II. The Joint Pastoral Plan institutionalized and activated changes hitherto limited often to statements of aspirations. The plan envisions the creation of "means and conditions for the church in Brazil to adjust, as rapidly as possible, to the spirit of Vatican II." It calls for the church to assume "a fully civilizing role" in areas of the country where partriarchal structures and subsistence economies persist. Its role is established as "animating the people to a leavening role for the construction of a better world." In other words, it will urge upon communicants an active role in seeking a better life—itself a revolutionary concept. This has been called *consciêncialização*, or transformation of passive lower classes to individuals aware both of their condition and that they can have a role in determining their

---

[7] Conferencia Nacional dos Bispos do Brasil, *Plano de Pastoral de Conjunto, 1966–1970* (Rio de Janeiro: Livraria Dom Bosco, Edit., 1967), p. 13.

[8] Mutchler, "Roman Catholicism", p. 109.

destiny. This concept, endorsed by the Latin American Episcopal Conference in August 1968, has been explained as education that liberates as opposed to education that "domesticates"—or teaches a man to accept his lot without complaint. In the words of the Brazilian educator Dr. Paulo Freire, "The result of a liberating education is that it moves the student to act on or transform his world." [9]

Consciêncialização in the sense used by Paulo Freire has been employed by a relatively small number of priests and bishops. These are the pluralists, the strong progressives and far Leftists among the priests. Their orientation has been revealed at such meetings as the VII General Assembly of the Conference of Religious Orders of Brazil held in Rio de Janeiro in July 1968. The basic document of that Conference was approved by a vote of 387 to 6. It reveals political, social, and economic sophistication that differs sharply from traditional ecclesiastical thought: "Vast rural estates little cultivated or not cultivated at all, deterioration of the terms of international trade; lack of savings and capital; inequality of opportunity and income as between regions and classes; economic and political colonialism masking pressures and domination under the appearance of independence and autonomy; obsolete educational systems and methods," are held to be responsible for retarding economic growth and social progress. "The unity of a whole, fraternal and dynamic people is destroyed," the document goes on to say, "by the interests of minorities, by the wealth of a small number contrasted to the marginalization of the majority of the population."

The document takes to task those who "seek a solution [to out-dated capitalism] through the simple installation of a communism equally contrary to Christianity," but ends with the charge that anti-communism often blinds people to the need for "indispensable and radical reforms of structures and mentalities." [10]

The temper of many even more radical priests is evident from one of several statements issued by 102 priests of Rio de Janeiro during the assembly, which denounced the capitalist system and the profit motive, holding them and private property to be responsible for Brazil's "hunger, misery, sickness, promiscuity . . . exploitation and hemorrhage of our resources." This statement was repudiated by twelve bishops, led by the bishop of Diamantina, in a letter to President Costa e Silva contending that the progressives in the church, although a noisy group, were a minority.

The conservatives and the moderates probably outnumber the pro-

---

[9] *The Washington Post*, 14 February 1970.
[10] *Jornal do Brasil*, 28 July 1968.

gressives by a wide margin, particularly among the diocesan bishops, but it should also be observed that the ideas accepted by the conservatives today would have made them the radicals or progressives of yesterday.

THE LAITY

Paralleling developments within the church hierarchy, a new militant and socially conscious movement grew in lay organizations. This movement had its base among the middle and upper classes and exerted a profound influence on the church itself, forcing it to change more quickly than had it been subjected to pressures only from the lower classes. This Catholic Left was, however, a minority, and one of the principal objectives of the Pastoral Plan continued to be to influence the mentality of the upper classes to the need for social reform.

Unlike the experience of several other Latin American countries where strong Christian Democratic political parties have been a channel for Catholic lay political activities, the Brazilian Christian Democratic party was slow to develop and never became popular. This may be due to the success of the Family Electoral Alliances and Catholic Electoral Leagues founded during the Vargas dictatorship. These church-guided groups were successful in electing candidates who met their criteria and in defeating leftist candidates.[11]

It had also suited Vargas' interests to incorporate their demands, based on papal encyclicals *Rerum Novarum* (1891) and *Quadregesimo Anno* (1931), into the 1934 constitution. These successes seemed to make a strong Christian Democratic party unnecessary and, in any event, Cardinal Leme discouraged Catholic lay political activities. That this judgment was wrong can be deduced from the fact that in countries where a CD party has prospered, social reform has moved far more rapidly and politics have been more stable. A Christian Democratic political party provided an effective channel for Catholic lay leaders to work within the system. There are exceptions, but in countries like Brazil, Ecuador, Peru, Argentina, Paraguay, and Guatemala, where no or only weak CD parties exist and the governments have often been repressive, reformers and reform movements have moved into illegal channels to carry on what they would call effective activities.

The period of great economic development in Brazil, beginning in the 1930s and reaching peaks in the late 1940s and late 1950s, led many

---

[11] Thomas G. Sanders, "Catholicism and Development: The Catholic Left in Brazil," in Kalman M. Silvert, ed., *Churches and States: The Religious Institution and Modernization* (New York: American Universities Field Staff, Inc., 1967). Sanders gives sympathetic treatment to the Catholic Left, including the far-Left.

Brazilians to the conclusion that the conservative churchmen were derelict in their responsibility to adjust to the spiritual and material needs of hundreds of thousands moving from semi-feudal rural Brazil to urban centers unprepared to receive them. A Catholic Left, including professional politicians, scholars, students, journalists, and clergy strongly motivated by concepts of nationalism and development, as well as social justice, began to take shape.

Some of the newly arrived foreign priests named to strategic posts, such as the young Dominicans placed in charge of Catholic Action, a lay socially-oriented group, brought radical ideas from other countries. The relative conservatism of Jacques Maritain, who had inspired the youth of midcentury and earlier, was replaced by the ideas of the existentialist Emmanuel Mounier, who saw capitalistic institutions as the "principal agents of oppression of the human person." The French Dominican Father Lebret, an economist, developed a concept of a world made up of the northern hemisphere of developed nations which were indifferent to the southern hemisphere of undeveloped nations. This concept had a profound influence not only on the Catholic Left but on national policy in all Latin America. Herbert Marcuse has also influenced Latin American youth, as he has influenced youth in the United States and elsewhere.

The most extreme group in the Catholic Left arose from the old *Juventude Católica Universitaria* (JUC—Catholic University Youth) organization, the university branch of Catholic Action. The JUC developed close ties with the *União Nacional de Estudantes* (UNE—National Student Union), the major university student organization in the country. Believing that their objectives could be reached more quickly and effectively by alliances with the Left than the Right, some of the JUC leaders gained control of the UNE with open young-Communist support. Another, even more radical group formed *Açao Popular* (AP—Popular Action) in 1962 as a nonconfessional political-ideological organization. By 1964 it had a largely university student membership of about 3,000. One of its basic precepts was that the tide of history gives the underdeveloped world the role of a revolutionary to further international socialism seeking human betterment. Many in AP sought to work with independent labor groups or worked with the Communists, convinced at that time (1963–64) that President Goulart, who claimed to be fighting for "basic reforms," was no more than an opportunist seeking to perpetuate himself in office.[12] The church hastened to disassociate itself when AP took a strongly leftist tack.

---

[12] Many Brazilians and foreign observers believed Goulart was either a crypto-Communist or was under Communist control, a judgment which known facts did not support.

How representative it is or was of the Catholic Left is not clear, but most of the evidence indicated that the AP and UNE are a small minority. Nevertheless, their capacity for creating large problems cannot be ignored, particularly when, as often happened, excessive repression brings them sympathy and support from moderate groups.

More moderate members of the laity have been active politically as well as in community or educational work that has led them to see the need for social change if Brazil is to become a modern nation. These included men and women in all branches of society, particularly professors in the social sciences, journalists, writers, and even high ranking military officers.

The extreme Catholic Left was instrumental in polarizing the opposing views of the church and the government. The AP and other Catholic youth were the leaders of student demonstrations which began by promoting student grievances and ended by calling for the overthrow of the military dictatorship. Some of the more progressive churchmen were swept up in the reaction against police and military authorities and directly defied state authority, as when they allowed the outlawed UNE to hold clandestine meetings in seminaries. The government, moreover, claimed to have uncovered direct links between members of religious orders and terrorist or guerrilla groups.

CHURCH VS. STATE

The AP was outlawed early in the Castello Branco government (1964–1967) and the UNE was shorn of its semiofficial status as university student representative. In their zeal to uncover Communists, some regional military commanders questioned or jailed priests. A number were forced by the government to leave the country. Many radical Christian Democrats fled the country when Goulart was overthrown by the military. Political calm was the general rule in a period characterized in the beginning by Castello Branco's efforts to get back to democratic procedures and to promote economic stabilization and a number of important economic and social reforms. Later, in 1966, after the government reinstituted "revolutionary" (read "dictatorial") rule in consequence of pressure from hard-line colonels and lower-ranking officers, terrorist activity began. Increasingly repressive measures to meet rising terrorist and nascent guerrilla activity, coupled with the government's failure to move on the educational front, soon brought mounting protests from the students.

There is no need to go into detail of a situation where protest gives rise to defensive repressive measures which often get out of hand and bring ordinarily passive middle-class citizens, priests, and others to the side of the protesters. The phenomenon has a dynamic of its own. Urban terrorism on the part of students and dedicated revolutionaries often leads to mindless police action that turns thousands against the government at home and abroad. An extreme but accurate example is that noted in a laconic Reuters dispatch from Rio de Janeiro dated 14 November 1969 which reported that the archbishop of Riberão Preto, São Paulo, had excommunicated the chief of police for "using electric shock tortures on an imprisoned convent mother superior" because she allegedly "allowed her convent to be used as a cell for a leftist guerrilla movement."

How far such incidents can lead is illustrated by the analysis of one senior churchman who told a Los Angeles Times reporter (*Washington Post*, 21 January 1970) that "for several years, there has been a very small, but growing number who feel social conditions are so desperate and the likelihood of change so small that the only way social justice will come is by armed revolution." After commenting that many priests want to keep out of the controversy, the clergyman added: "But the atmosphere has changed in the past year. Men I once knew as conservatives are moving towards the center. More join the radicals calling for action."

The government continues to uncover subversive activities in which it alleges the involvement (and is almost certainly right in many instances) of priests and nuns who see violence as the only means to achieve social justice in a society where semifeudalism exists in many parts of the country side by side with great urban centers.

Relations between church and state promised to improve after President Emílio Garrastazu Médici, a devout Catholic who is trying to base his government at least partly on popular support, assumed office late in 1969. Subsequent events, however, have shown how difficult it is to regain control of powerful forces, like militant priests and over-zealous police and military officers, once they have escaped the restraining hand of central authority.

On the one hand, churchmen state their subversive position very clearly. An important example was that of the seven Dominican priests who, under arrest on charges of aiding terrorists, smuggled a document out of a São Paulo prison giving their controversial views. In direct opposition to the more moderate policies of the Brazilian hierarchy and the even more accommodating policies of the Holy See, they speak of the church's responsibility as a Christian body. As quoted by Father McCabe, a British Dominican, editor of the Blackfriars magazine, the imprisoned priests had reached the conclusion that "Christian love must have a political dimension or be nothing." The Christian response to the Brazilian situation, the priests wrote, must be revolution: "The only way a violent dictatorship has left to us is the way of revolution. This is the rightful self-defense of a people desperate under oppression—the right to fight for its life." [13]

On the other hand, the proliferation of security agencies, which sprouted when it became apparent that the regular police were fighting a losing battle against the urban terrorists, had made it all but impossible for the government to control them. Not only do police and military security officers often act virtually autonomously—particularly in areas far from the capital or the large urban areas—but they work under varying criteria depending on the local military commander. Some police and military see all opposition, whether politically or religiously inspired, as Communist.

Even President Médici's resolutions and promises often proved ineffective. In early 1970 the president said there would be no mistreatment and certainly no torture of prisoners. Shortly thereafter, a prominent democratic labor leader of São Paulo died after detention and "questioning" by the police. The government also promised not to arrest priests without prior notice to the church hierarchy. Nevertheless, arrests continued. Father José Antonio de Magalhaes Monteiro was arrested 3 August in Maranhão by local authorities and, according to a carefully documented report prepared by churchmen, tortured.[14] Father José Antonio and a French priest, arrested at the same time, were cleared of charges of subversion by a military court early in October, but local authorities, as they always do, denied charges of torture.[15]

In all these cases the president seemed reluctant to take any action against comrades-in-arms except in absolutely clear cases of defiance of authority, which are rare. Exceeding authority is far from rare.

An uneasy truce between the government and the hierarchy had been reached when the National Conference of Bishops early in 1970 adopted a resolution deploring violence of any kind, meant to apply to both church and state. The government for its part promised to speed up trials of all political prisoners (the government denied any were political prisoners, insisting all were arrested on charges related to subversive terrorism) and to move more cautiously when churchmen were involved. Nevertheless, the situation soon deteriorated, as has been noted, to the point that the Brazilian government was being charged with persecuting the church. A study of torture and repression made by churchmen in Brazil was publicly noted by Pope Paul and the Vatican organ *L'Osservatore Romano*, in late October 1970, denounced "arbitrary repression" and "interference

[13] *Miami Herald*, 22 November 1970.
[14] *La Prensa Libre* (San José, Costa Rica), 2 October 1970.
[15] *Miami Herald*, 11 October 1970.

by the State in Church affairs in Brazil." [16] This latter charge was based in part on continued harassment of Archbishop Helder Camara. These and other charges were detailed in a letter from Cardinal Sales of Bahia to President Médici which was delivered personally to the president by the conservative Cardinal Jaime Camara with other complaints drawn up by the CNBB against repression of churchmen. Many church authorities had come to the conclusion that the government was using the archbishop of Recife to justify anti-clerical policies.

In an effort to heal the widening breach between church and state, Pope Paul instructed Cardinal Rossi of São Paulo to issue a statement to the press denying a campaign against the church in Brazil. The note, dated 20 October, appeared in the Latin American press on 1 November. After noting some "Christian efforts" on the part of President Médici, and acknowledging that difficulties had arisen by reason of arbitrariness and injustice on the part of some authorities, the statement said that "the Pope knows that these problems do not constitute religious persecution as has been held, with evident exaggeration, in the press and on radio and television in Europe, the United States, and Canada." The note concluded with the somewhat opaque observation that the pope "is not unaware that darnel and wheat are to be found together wherever there are men, in whatever position they may hold." [17] This statement seemed to be trying to say that good men and evil men can be found on both sides of the dispute in Brazil.

That the Brazilian hierarchy and the Vatican at this time were working at cross purposes was apparent from the action of the Central Committee of the CNBB at an emergency meeting four days before issuance of Cardinal Rossi's note. The committee condemned the abuse of human rights in Brazil and called on the authorities "to take the most effective and earliest measures to assure a climate of solidarity, justice, and liberty, indispensable for the realization of the great destiny of the nation and for the projection of its true image in the community of peoples." [18]

Beclouding the issue even more, Cardinal Rossi, who had been chairman of the Central Committee of the CNBB, shortly after these events transpired was transferred to the Vatican as prefect of the congregation for propagation of the faith. The transfer raised many questions and brought many allegations on the one hand that the cardinal had been removed from the political scene to appease the Brazilian government and, on the other, by some who were less aware of the cardinal's leader-

[16] *La Nación* (San José, Costa Rica), 20 October 1970.
[17] *La Nación* (San José, Costa Rica), 1 November 1970.
[18] *La Nación* (San José, Costa Rica), 18 October 1970.

ship of the moderate-progressives, because he had been too accommodating with the government. Protests were so insistent that the pope took the unprecedented (in modern times) step of publicly denying that the transfer had any other motive than to put an able churchman at the head of an activity held by the pope to be of the highest importance. He specifically stated that any suggestions that the cardinal's removal had some relationship "with certain aspects of the political situation in Brazil" are entirely without foundation.[19]

NATIONAL V. UNIVERSAL CHURCH

Inextricably linked to the matter of church vs. state is that of national vs. universal church. How far can the Vatican tolerate or—perhaps more pertinent—control activity within national churches which may damage the mother church? And how far can the national church let itself be restricted in fighting for principles and social justice involving its suffering and wavering flock.

It is apparent that the church is gaining new strength and prestige through closer identification with the Brazilian masses. The percentage of foreign clergy had dropped from 40 percent in 1960 to 35 percent by 1968.[20] The change has probably brought the church closer to its early colonial position of independence, when it was concerned more with the realities of life than with purely spiritual values of the then universal Church. At the same time, an increasing number of commissions, national and regional secretariats, and Vatican councils bring the word and policies of Rome and other national episcopates. Foreign priests and bishops, many of papist persuasion, do the same. The establishment of the National Conference of Bishops of Brazil as well as its social program resulted from papal initiative.

The pluralist-progressives and some others believe nevertheless that too close control from Rome will inhibit the effectiveness of national churches. The decision of Rome in 1969 to accede to pressure from the Brazilian government (1) by transferring a liberal papal nuncio alleged to be encouraging revolutionary attitudes among the hierarchy and (2) restricting pronouncements by Archbishop Helder Camara to his own diocese, are illustrative of such inhibitory actions.[21] The papacy must also deal with reality and the pope is advised, among others, by sage, politically-minded but very old cardinals who probably find it hard to overlook some

---

19 *La Nación* (San José, Costa Rica), 5 November 1970.

20 As in other parts of the world, recruiting of priests in Brazil is still a serious problem, but the causes are related more to the universal than the Brazilian church.

21 *Jornal do Brasil*, 21 October 1969.

of the aberrations of emerging societies. Viewing it differently are many pluralist and even moderate Brazilian churchmen who are more concerned with solving the people's problems than with accepting the slow pace of reform decreed by the military leaders, or being counseled by the curia at Rome.

These problems are directly related to issues debated at the Extraordinary Synod of Bishops held in the fall of 1969 in Rome. They concern the degree of local autonomy to be exercised by national churches, and the degree of ultramontane influence to be allowed in decisions made at the Vatican. During the Extraordinary Synod, Dom Avelar Brandão Vilela, archbishop of Teresinha, criticized "the rigid control exercised by the Roman Curia over the Church," suggesting that it should take into account "the native culture of each region," adopting pluralism as the way most "capable of concretely expressing the dynamic and local contribution of the local Churches within the universal Church." [22] But the Vatican can well ask itself, if the national churches are given too great latitude, will some become so radical as to destroy themselves—and, in the process, the universal Church? Such questions must be raised when the Brazilian hierarchy and the Vatican apparently are at odds on how far the government is to be accommodated in its fight against subversion when not only the people but churchmen themselves are unjustly dealt with.

THE CHURCH AND MODERNIZATION

A thesis has been developed that the pace and ultimate success of programs of modernization and development in underdeveloped Latin America will rest on the ability of the church to adapt to the changing order in the world and to exert its cultural and religious influence to hasten social change.[23] This thesis accepts the premise, which most developmental economists and political scientists are not yet prepared to agree to, that the church in Latin America is probably the only agency with sufficient moral authority to bring about the kind of social change necessary for modernization without using revolutionary means.

It is apparent that the church in Brazil has embarked on a course aimed at achieving social justice and integrating the poverty-stricken part of the population into the developmental process. It is not yet clear that it set out to do this. Rather, the liberal Pope John XXIII saw that the Brazilian church, like many others, faced the fate of the church in Cuba and other Communist countries if it did not exert itself to become more relevant to the masses in their problems of day-to-day living. The church

[22] Ibid.
[23] See Vallier, *Religious Elites.*

is now consciously an agent of change, seeking to bring about further changes which were first sought by no more than a handful of priests and a few bishops who had been born in poverty.

Another spur to renewal, along with the Communist inroads among the masses, is the effective work of evangelical sects who do outstanding social work among the newly arrived urban poor,[24] work which many Catholic churchmen believed could not be done. Not only has the church been moved by an increasingly popular existential theology that insists it must adapt to the changing order in the world if it is to survive in its diminishingly dominant role, but Catholic lay leaders have also joined with activist church leaders to fortify the pastoral and pluralistic role of the church. It is also clear that the moderate and progressive elements within the church in Brazil, influenced by the more extreme progressives, effectively make the principal decisions.

The question then remains how effective will the church be in forcing change in a society still dominated by entrenched elites buttressed by the conservatives in the armed forces? Following a succession of confrontations which began in 1964 and threatened an open break between church and state, by 1970 efforts were being made on both sides to bring about an acceptable *modus vivendi*. However, the priests and nuns who march with and protect students and workers and the bishops who have accepted Archbishop Helder Camara's "Liberating Moral Pressure" methods will

---

[24] For some considerations on the size and importance of non-Catholic religious movements in Brazil, see Emilio Willems, "Religious Mass Movements and Social Changes in Brazil", in Eric Baklanoff, ed., *New Perspectives in Brazil* (Nashville: Vanderbilt University Press, 1966). Reliable statistics on the size of non-Catholic movements are not available. The count of Protestants in *Anuário Estatístico* was 2,484,968 at the end of 1965. However, Pentecosts estimated their numbers alone to be 2 million in 1961, of a total of more than 4 million Protestants in the country. It is possibly more difficult to estimate the number of Spiritualists, the other important religious movement. The "scientific spiritualists," followers of Kardec, by official count numbered 732,784 at the end of 1965. *Umbandista* Spiritualists, who are an offshoot of the African Macumba (disowned by the Kardecists), were numbered at a little more than 100,000. Catholic sociologists, on the other hand, believe the number of *Umbandistas* to be much higher, since many of them (to the despair of the hierarchy) consider themselves to be Catholics practicing a variation on folk Catholicism, and they classify themselves accordingly to census takers.

The church has noted the rapid growth of Spiritualism in the backward Northeast states, where Catholic proselytising is least effective. (The *Boletim Informativo* of CERIS [July/September 1966, pp. 77–79] estimated that Spiritualists in Brazil had increased by 78 percent from 1940 to 1950, and Protestants by 62 percent. The total population increased only 26 percent, while Catholics increased by 24 percent.) However, Pentecostalism and Spiritualism are largely urban phenomena, explained principally by the failure of the Catholic church to fill the need of recent arrivals from the rural areas for a substitute family, community, and *patrão* for those that they left behind.

bring on more confrontations unless the government adopts measures to further social justice. These differences will be difficult to deal with even under military-controlled government because of the clergy's high prestige in Brazilian society. After a series of critical confrontations with students, in which the administration appeared more reactionary than it liked to, the Costa e Silva government found it wise to take important steps toward educational reform and moved with spectacular success in the area of housing.

But the church will have to change the mentality not only of the industrial and rural elites but also that of many military leaders in order to ease the way to reform. The military as a group may or may not favor social change but many high-ranking generals and active "hardline" colonels do not understand social ferment except as a present danger to national security.

More important than the serious and not so serious confrontations are the basic documents issued by the Brazilian church which, for the first time, put a stamp of legitimacy on radical social reform. The long-run effects of these documents are almost certain to force on conservative elites a clearer understanding of the need for social change and require the government to hasten the present slow pace of improving living standards for millions of poverty-stricken Brazilians.

ROBERT E. MCNICOLL

NUEVAS CORRIENTES

A major purpose of this column is to bring to the attention of readers items in the Latin American journals, or elsewhere, that indicate currents that should be taken into account by Latin Americanists in the United States. While the selection is made by the writer, based solely on his own opinion, it is also hoped that the subjects may be of enough interest to readers to elicit a response of some sort.

North American writers have spoken of the "responsibilities of the foreign scholar to the local scholarly community." Undoubtedly these responsibilities include that of knowing what the scholars of the "host country" want and particularly what they don't want and what they fear. There are many indications that what they fear is the subject of the following item.

Cultural Imperialism

The concept that foreign, and particularly American, ideas either backed by selective grants of money or the powerful inducement of successful example, is a greater threat to Latin American independence than past interventions or colonial bonds has been widely expressed recently. Probably no one has stated it more clearly than Rector Carlos Monje Alfaro of the University of Costa Rica who made it the lead article in *Jornada* (October 1970, pp. 1 and 16) the official publication of the *Consejo Superior Universitario Centroamericano* of which he is president:

Imperialismo Cultural

> Hasta el presente la mayor parte de las instituciones universitarias han efectuado una labor significativa en el campo de la enseñanza, que ha incidido en el desenvolvimiento cultural, institucional y mental de las sociedades. Pero lo han hecho sin percatarse de los radicales cambios operados en el seno de éstas y del extraordinario desarrollo económico ocurrido en las zonas de mayor influencia del mundo, lo cual ha traído consigo un aumento de la dependencia de los países pobres, subdesarrolla-

> dos con respecto a los ricos. O sea, al imperialismo político y económico se ha agregado un peligroso imperialismo cultural-científico y tecnológico. Cualquier iniciativa o fórmula que surja de las naciones latinoamericanas, por ejemplo, crear bloques de integración, sufre la influencia de los modelos e intereses de los llamados países desarrollados. Horacio Flores de la Peña, ilustre economista mexicano, coordinador del Comité de Planificación de la Universidad Autónoma de México, dice en un interesante ensayo intitulado: "La educación universitaria y el desarrollo": Dominación "bastante común es señalar que los países subdesarrollados son altamente dependientes de las grandes potencias que ejercen sobre ellos diversas formas de dominación, desde la económica hasta un claro dominio tecnológico y cultural".
>
> ¿Conviene a los países de América cerrar los ojos ante esa dependencia —una forma disimulada de esclavitud— sin perjudicar programas que apunten a darle fisonomía auténtica a nuestros pueblos, a ponerlos en posesión de sí mismos, y aprovechar al máximo sus recursos humanos y naturales? ¿Por qué Latinoamérica, que tiene 274 millones de habitantes —tantos como la U.R.S.S., y más que los Estados Unidos de América— y riquezas naturales —subsuelo, suelo, aguas etc—, ha de seguir sojuzgada política, económica y culturalmente a las poderosas naciones del orbe, sea de esta o de aquella filiación ideológica? Ya los grandes maestros y pensadores americanos de fines de siglo y principios de éste hablaron de la auténtica respuesta de América Latina a la historia universal; de alcanzar independencia en todas sus formas. El desarrollo de la ciencia y de la tecnología en lugar de traer bienestar cierto y cabal a nuestros pueblos, en lugar de estimular la búsqueda de la felicidad y la afirmación de la libertad, más bien se ha convertido en un instrumento fuerte de dependencia, más que las amarras coloniales de los siglos XVI, XVII y XVIII. . . .

In the last issue we quoted Dr. John P. Harrison to the effect that nationalism would sometimes forego the benefits of modern techniques if they had to come through the agencies of the United States. In February of 1971 a similar fear was expressed regarding education by television even though the project was sponsored by the UNESCO. The Peruvian magazine OIGA (5 February 1971, p. 10) says of a Lima conference of the ministers of education from the Andean group:

> La UNESCO presentó un proyecto para desarrollar un programa educativo, elaborado en Estados Unidos y difundido por vía satélite. A primera vista, el proyecto es sumamente atractivo. Se trata de utilizar el máximo aporte de la tecnología en las telecomunicaciones. Pero . . .
>
> El Perú ha expresado sus reparos sobre los peligros de un sistema de educación masiva efectuada a distancia y cocinada

> en calderas ajenas a la región andina, elaborado por técnicos no solamente ajenos al proceso de trasformación e independencia cultural y económica que fluye en los países del área andina, en especial del Perú, Chile, Ecuador y Bolivia, sino que podría considerarse contrarios al mismo. En vez de ser un instrumento de afirmación de la conciencia nacional y regional sería, por el contrario, un instrumento de dominación cultural.
>
> Sobre este tema, el ministro chileno Mario Astorga, dijo a OIGA en tono enérgico: "Nosotros tenemos también los mismos temores respecto de ese proyecto. Nos preocupa seriamente. No podemos aceptarlo sin más, por el riesgo que él implica. Las ideologías extrañas ya han causado mucho daño a nuestros pueblos. Y, aunque se nos ha prometido y asegurado que al estar a cargo de la UNESCO es toda una garantía, y que no habría peligro de influencias extrañas ni de intereses culturales de dominio, sin embargo, digo, en Chile hemos llegado a la conclusión de que es mucho mejor diferir este proyecto de tele-educación para toda el área. Diferirlo durante un tiempo prudencial. Así, cada uno de los países incluidos en el mismo, podrá estudiarlo con calma y decidir por su cuenta, para luego tomar una decisión común y coherente".

United States scholars, with apparently a new-found concern for the opinions of Latin colleagues, must take the lead in removing the reasons for this fear which may seem excessive. Certainly, there should be avoided the enforced exportation of American standards sometimes shown by both our government and the great foundations. The attitude referred to was clearly expressed by a foundation official when he said: "We shall make a survey of the universities of country X and determine which are worthwhile. These we shall aid by grants of money, of scholarships, and encouragement, leaving the others to die on the vine." How can an American determine what schools are useful in the context of another culture and another society? Must they all conform to the ideas of Middle American Tech? Would this be helpful or ruinous to Country X if it were possible? This is part of the complex of "Cultural Imperialism" and if I were a Latin American I would oppose it also.

A Third Nobel Prize for Argentina

The announcement by the Swedish Academy of Sciences in October 1970 that the prize for chemistry has been given to Dr. Luis F. Leloir of Argentina made the third Nobel Prize won by Argentines. The two earlier ones were awarded to Carlos Saavedra Lamas, Peace Prize, 1936, and to Dr. Bernardo Houssay, physiology, 1947. Despite the fact that Dr. Leloir had won five international prizes previously and that he headed the prestigious *Instituto de Investigaciones Bioquímicas* in Buenos Aires the announcement took most Argentines—including the recipient—by surprise.

The Nobel committee stated that "few discoveries have had as much impact on investigation as those of Leloir. . . . His work and that which he inspired in others have given us real knowledge in a field where we previously had to be satisfied with vague hypotheses." His field is the study of the chemical bases for the transformation of carbohydrates into sugars within the human body. In 1948 he discovered that a special carbohydrate, *galactoquinasa,* became toxic in a baby's body in the absence of a special protein necessary for its conversion to sugar. The toxic condition could easily lead to death but Leloir's discovery made correction easy by changing the diet. This is merely one of the practical results of his inquiries into the inner mechanism of the digestive factors that led to the identification of nearly sixty sub-types of sugar nucleii.

In the Argentine magazine *Análysis* (3 November 1970, pp. 36–38) an attractive view is given of the prizewinner who has donated all his previous prize monies to the work of his Institute. When asked what he would do with the $73,000 (U.S.) Dr. Leloir said that he had not thought about it yet but that surely it also would go to his Institute.

In the same interview Dr. Leloir was asked about the "brain drain" to other countries from Argentina. He said:

"After all, in Argentina we work at less than the optimum level and I believe the exodus of scientists will continue as long as there are more highly developed countries." He referred to the fact that the top pay for scientists in Argentina reached a level only half as high as that in the United States. "But," he said, "Argentina is my country and here I stay."

BOOKS

BOOK REVIEWS

Dean, Warren. *The Industrialization of São Paulo, 1880–1945.* Institute of Latin American Studies Monograph No. 17. Austin and London: The University of Texas Press, 1969. Tables, bibliography, 263 pp., $7.50.

São Paulo, as the dust jacket of Warren Dean's *The Industrialization of São Paulo, 1880–1945* states, "is one of the few places in the underdeveloped world where an advanced industrial system has grown out of a tropical raw-material-exporting economy." "By 1960," it continues, "there were 830,000 industrial workers in the state, producing $3.3 billion worth of goods. It had become Latin America's largest industrial center."

For those interested in how this impressive feat was accomplished, I am afraid that Dean's book will be a disappointment. This is not to discredit the author, or the quality of his work. The fault, I believe, is to be found either in the specific facts of history, or in the nature of the craft Professor Dean practices. But more of this later.

Manufacturing and industry begin in earnest in São Paulo in the late nineteenth century as a response to the increased demand for industrial goods created by the rapid expansion of coffee exports. The type of goods whose importation becomes prohibitive due to their size and bulk—i.e., bricks, cement, etc.—first were produced locally. Later, in spite of consumer preferences for foreign commodities, some capital went into the production of a limited number of items domestically—which usually were packaged and labeled as imports.

Little encouragement was given São Paulo industry during the empire. The republic (established in 1889), however, figured prominently in industrial expansion. During the republican period Brazil was a federation of semi-independent states. Authority and responsibility in economic matters was in the hands of the state governments. São Paulo, in contrast with other Brazilian states at the time, was able to obtain the revenues it needed from the coffee trade; there was no need to tax, and therefore inhibit, incipient industry. More important, however, the planters were able to control the new state government—and use it in the advancement of their own interests, some of which were commercial and industrial. Not only was the control of the government necessary to legitimize their claims to land, given the confusion of the Brazilian landholding system, but it also enabled those in control to take advantage of "undertakings the state government could concede as monopolies, such as railroads, utilities, and emission banks or projects that could be strongly assisted through government favoritism" (p. 44).

Examination of the origins of the early entrepreneurs in part I of the book reveals that they came, for the most part—and no statistical breakdowns are presented—from two distinct social groups. The first was the planter class—hopefully setting straight, at least for Brazil, the mistaken Marxist derived interpretation that planters and industrialists represent two competing groups; the second group was composed of immigrants of a *petit bourgeoise* background in Europe. The capital used by both groups came from overseas, either through the market for the financing of coffee, or directly through the contacts the immigrants had in their country of origin. By the early decades of the twentieth century, however, the immigrants had been absorbed into the planter class—through marriage, merger, etc.

Part II focuses on the period 1914–1930. Chapter 6 is a refutation of the long accepted theory that World War I contributed to the expansion of industry in São Paulo. Dean instead argues convincingly that the productive plant was not enlarged and that the fortunes made "grew out of new lines of exports, twenty-four-hour-a-day production, or out of mergers and reorganizations" (p. 104).

No rapid accumulation of industrial capital occurred in the interwar period. Following the lead of the group of sociologists formerly at the University of São Paulo, Dean demonstrates how little the industrialists did to advance their own industries, or the cause of manufacturing.

In part III, the author shows how the descendents of the entrepreneurs who established the industrial base in São Paulo gradually became overly conservative, only to loose out in the long run.

Chapter 9, for example, examines the relationship between the industrialists and their labor force. Various forms of paternalism were tried in an effort to keep costs down (and profits up). The attempts were frustrated primarily because a number of the laborers who came to work in São Paulo brought with them from the Old Country "the European tradition of labor militance . . ." (p. 156). They exposed and challanged the attempt and were supported by many of their fellow laborers. This precipitated a period of open conflict between management and labor. The industrialists, instead of looking beyond the immediate situation to expanding production, to opening new markets, and to exploring new avenues for profit making, chose to concentrate on fighting labor and unionism. In addition, during the 1920s and 1930s there developed a strong interest among the industrialists in varieties of European facism (p. 171). These authoritarian attitudes are related by Dean to the lack of effort and interest in developing a technically trained manpower pool (p. 176).

Getúlio Vargas came to power in Brazil in 1930. In the early years he had little, if any, interest in industry. He was interested in the State of São Paulo, and acted rapidly to both defuse and control the rich and populated state, which was a potential threat to his tenure of office and to his efforts to reestablish Brazil as a unified political entity. São Paulo had prospered during the Old Republic. The planter-industrialists who had controlled the state feared loosing their privileged position. In addition, Vargas at first favored the policy of free trade and the end of state support for industry. All told, the São Paulo industrialists were in the position of being odd-man-out during the early Vargas years. And when as dictator, after the establishment of the Estado Nôvo in 1937, Vargas came to the realization that industrial development was essential for the future of the nation, they shunned his invitation to partnership by refusing to invest their capital.

The result was that the Vargas government, after it decided on industrialization as its top priority, proceeded almost independent of the São Paulo industrialists. The federal government then, and not private initiative, spearheaded the later industrial development of the nation. Agencies of government were created to perform the tasks handled by private firms elsewhere in the capitalist world. In spite of this, however, Vargas, in his typical manner of absorbing potential enemies, brought the industrialists back into the picture in his plans for the post war period.

With the end of the war, however, came the end of the dictatorship; and with the liberal politics of the post war period came a brief return to liberal economics and free trade. By the time the Brazilian political order came to realize the futility of free trade and other positions it had taken, the economy was so far out of hand that the door had been opened wide to a completely new situation.

And this is where the book, at least to this reviewer, becomes a frustration and a disappointment. After 233 pages about the history of industry in São Paulo, the author tells us in a brief five page concluding chapter that as the result of miscalculations in the post war period—and perhaps some earlier ones by the industrialists themselves—foreign capital came in and did the job Brazilians were unable to do themselves. "By the early 1960s," Dean tells us, "perhaps half of the industrial capital in São Paulo's private sector . . . was foreign owned and controlled" (p. 237). Foreign corporations transformed their sales agencies into branch manufacturing operations. The larger Paulista firms, we are told, did not go under. Instead, whole new lines, like automobiles, pharmaceuticals, tobacco, construction equipment, tires and electronics, had been developed by foreigners.

The impressive modern industrialization of São Paulo, the feat that resulted in the largest industrial center in Latin America, was not the product of the efforts and activities about which Professor Dean had been writing; instead it was essentially a repeat of the general story of the expansion of European- and North-American-based world corporations.

History may be thought of most generally as the chronological reconstruction of events to tell the story of (explain) how certain things have come to pass. At times the relevant antecedent events are to be found in the same place as the end product; as often, however, they are to be found elsewhere. In the latter case the historian must relate events in time and space, selecting what is relevant for each specific story. The activities of peoples in distant places must be brought in when it is relevant to the understanding of the end product. At times, however, specific events of the past, as well as persons and groups, may be singled out for intensive examination. Such studies are for the specialist and not for the general reader. Warren Dean's *The Industrialization of São Paulo, 1880–1945* is such a study.

What Professor Dean has done is to explain why the São Paulo industrialists did *not* develop an advanced industrial system. For the story of how this did come about the reader must look elsewhere—to the activities not of the São Paulo industrialists but to those of the politicians, diplomats, capitalists, investors, and entrepreneurs in Rio de Janeiro, Brazília, Washington, New York, London, and other commercial, financial, and political centers.

If the goal of the reader is to learn something about the social and other characteristics of the first people to establish industries in São Paulo, Dean's book does this, and does it well. However, if the objective of the reader is to find the explanation for what is so impressive to the economist, the sociologist, the student of development, and the general observer, he had best look elsewhere.

SIDNEY M. GREENFIELD
Professor of Sociology
The University of Wisconsin-Milwaukee

Stein, Stanley J. and Barbara H. *The Colonial Heritage of Latin America. Essays on Economic Dependence in Perspective.* New York: Oxford University Press, 1970. Introduction, bibliography and sources, index. viii, 222 pp. $5.00.

Why Latin America, after three centuries of Iberian rule and 150 years of independence, remains largely underdeveloped rather than part of the Atlantic industrial world, is the basic question the authors set out to answer. Spain and Portgual, they point out, entered their imperial careers "imperfectly organized, export-oriented, and lacking a national bourgeoisie or merchant capitalist group capable of stimulating indigenous growth" (p. 19). Spain might have developed industries to supply her expanding empire, as England did later, but no such development occurred.

There was, however, a vast difference between Spain of 1500 and England of 1700. In 1500 the medieval heritage was still powerful and the centuries of intermittent warfare against the Moslems had emphasized the militant roles of aristocracy and church. When the reconquest was completed, the mercantile class might have been able to gain the ascendancy and set the tone for future development but for the discovery and conquest of the New World, which gave the warriors renewed opportunities. While other nations of western Europe were abandoning ancient attitudes toward privilege, church, government, and economy, Spain was reproducing her medieval institutions and values in the New World.

The Latin American economy was export-oriented from the outset. On the ruins of Indian agriculture the Spaniards created the hacienda, a descendant of the medieval manor, and the plantation. The former raised livestock for local consumption, and the latter raised crops for the European markets. Indians and Negro slaves provided the labor for both.

The characteristic features of colonial administration were well established by 1700. "Public office at all levels was seen as a legitimate instrument to further private interest over public weal. A monarchy extorting a share of a viceroy's spoils of office symbolized, indeed legitimized, venality, encouraged corruption and showed itself demonstrably incapable of controlling malfeasance in office. . . . To the elite, law became a norm honored in the breach. To the unprivileged, law was arbitrary and alien, therefore without moral force" (pp. 80, 81). Much of the social unrest of Spanish America in the past century, the authors conclude, was simply an extension of the struggle for access to property and occupational opportunities that the lower classes began in the eighteenth century and which was suppressed in the nineteenth. "It is in the twentieth century that the long struggle for social vindication, rooted in the colonial past, is again re-emerging" (p. 119).

In considering the economic basis of neocolonialism the authors ask why two former colonial areas, the United States and Latin America, developed such different patterns of economic growth after independence. The trade with Britain and British investments helped greatly to stimulate American economic development, while the Spanish American republics had neither trade with nor financial aid from Spain. And unlike most of the Latin American wars, the American Civil War had a major impact on industrial production. In Spanish America, furthermore, elite groups remained entrenched after independence, and their influence on economic affairs was decisive. Owing to regional and other conflicts, national economic policies similar to that created by the United States at an early date were unattainable in Latin America. Yet another factor was the persistence of the hacienda and the emphasis on land as the most desirable form of wealth.

In considering the relative lack of industrial development in Spanish America in the nineteenth century, a comparison of Spain's industrial progress with that of other European nations might be instructive in the search for cultural causes of economic stagnation. Spanish Americans inherited not only Spain's cultural values that contributed to Spanish economic backwardness but the legacies of the conquest and the colonial era. Former colonial areas, as the authors emphasize, do not easily escape the heritage of dependence.

In an "Epilogue" the authors look briefly at the present. After World War

II many Latin Americans hoped, through evolutionary changes, to attain economic autonomy by creating new industries and stimulating production generally. The disappointing results have convinced others that only by revolutionary changes in economic policies, governmental systems, and social organization can progress be achieved. The establishment of basic industries requires both a capital outlay and a domestic market, but a rapidly growing population, regressive tax systems, and the concentration of wealth have prevented the spread of purchasing power and the accumulation of savings for investment. The prospects for Latin America's economic future are generally not promising, although Mexico has become a model for underdeveloped nations to consider. As the authors of this thoughtful study conclude, "the area as a bloc does not constitute a structure of society, economy, and politics perceptibly transformed beyond what was present at the end of the nineteenth century" (p. 198). The search for an escape from neocolonialism has been largely unsuccessful, and pessimism over the failure of evolutionary methods has already produced numerous guerrilla movements dedicated to remaking Latin American societies by more drastic and effective methods.

DONALD E. WORCESTER, Chairman
Department of History
Texas Christian University

Pineda, Virginia Gutiérrez de. *Familia y Cultura en Colombia.* Coediciones Tercer Mundo y Departamento de Sociología Universidad Nacional de Colombia. Colombia: Tercer Mundo, 1968. Presentación, introducción, índice, citas bibliograficas, bibliografía. 415 pp.

This book presents a scholarly description of the structure and dynamics of the Colombian family. The author recognized at the outset that it was impossible to deal with the Colombian family as an entity, in much the same way that one cannot speak of "Latin America" as though it represented a single entity. As a social institution the Colombian family is structurally integrated with varying economic and religious institutions, which in turn evolved from different historical processes; variations within the country's family institution thus make this unitary approach impossible.

Consequently, Dr. Pineda created a typology of the various family forms and placed them into four major categories. Each of these categories represents a subculture or complex with differing values and norms; the basic differentiating indices for these four major categories are their ethnic and geographic dissimilarities. The four complexes or subcultures are the Andean or American, the Santanderean or Neo-Hispanic, the Mountain or Antioquenian, and the Coast-River-Mining or Negroid complex.

Within each culture complex the author includes a detailed description of geographic conditions, the economy and its concomitant land tenure system, religiosity and church ties, and the ethnic modality. These factors are then related to the various marriage and family types. Besides the aboriginal Indian communities which have preserved their basic character, the major distinction is between legal family versus *de facto* family, with the presence or absence of the marriage ceremony differentiating the two forms. The legal form is preferred everywhere, but de facto monogamy is very frequent, especially in the Coast-River-Mining complex.

The forms of de facto monogamy are *amano* (trial living together without a ceremony) which Dr. Pineda claims has pre-Colombian Indian origins, *madre-solterismo* (single mothers) where both mates live with their own families of orientation and each mate, living his separate life, may or may not have a succession of mates. Whereas these two monogamous forms are transitional, the *union libre* (which is the most frequent for Colombians) may have a more stable character; the couple actually forms a monogamous family unit and may live together the rest of their lives. The concubinate is a non-monogamous de facto family pattern where the male, already legally married, lives with another mate.

The author then correlates the legal conjugal and extended family forms with attitudes toward legitimacy, socialization, inheritance customs, masculinity patterns, status, and historical antecedents; these she in turn contrasts with the de facto family forms in each culture complex. The frequency of occurrence of each of these family patterns within each culture complex is also described.

It is evident that a great deal of careful work went into this study. Field techniques such as depth interviews, questionnaires, and participant observation have been supplemented by biographical, economic, geographic, and historical background data. The results have eminently justified the effort; this book makes a highly significant contribution to the entire study of family organization everywhere and is undoubtedly one of the major sources of scholarly material on Colombian family patterns.

AARON LIPMAN
Professor of Sociology
University of Miami

Sierra, Justo. *The Political Evolution of the Mexican People.* Translated by Charles Ramsdell. Austin, Texas: The University of Texas Press, 1969. Publisher's note, introduction and foreword by Edmundo O'Gorman, prologue by Alfonso Reyes, index. xviii, 406 pp. $8.50.

Justo Sierra stands in the select band of historians who, in the classical pattern, played in the life of their country a role equal to their place in its letters. As a teacher he created the history he taught, and as a historian he framed the instruments for teaching. The student of Mexican history has long needed *The Political Evolution of the Mexican People* in English. The introduction by Edmundo O'Gorman and a prologue by Alfonso Reyes make this as obvious as does the experience of one who has attempted to teach Mexican history in English-speaking countries. That translator Charles Ramsdell has effaced himself to allow these three distinct voices to be heard, each in his own tone, is the highest praise which can be given him, and the only reward he needs for his difficult task.

While a Spanish-language encyclopedia notes Sierra's title "Teacher of the Americas," leading English-language encyclopedias do not even list the Latin American writer whose writings are most just to British and Anglo-American actions. Such is the fate of the man of whose masterpiece Reyes wrote: "Whosoever does not know this history does not know us, and whosoever does know it will hardly deny us his sympathy." The views of three generations of Mexican students have been molded by the master, and now the foreign reader can appreciate with them Reyes' encomium: "Justo Sierra's political evolution marches on, and so does the inspiration of his work. . . . The gratitude of his people is his companion."

The brevity of this book precludes its being an adequate history of Mexico. In "what happened" it cannot be compared with the vast accumulation of material in *Méjico a través de los siglos*, upon which it draws heavily, or Hubert Howe Bancroft's *History of Mexico*, both of which are contemporary and coextensive in scope. But Sierra's work looms above them, as it does above the later and similar works by Henry Banford Parkes and Leslie Byrd Simpson, for reasons made clear by O'Gorman and Reyes.

The value of this volume is not limited to a more true picture of Mexican history. The incisive introduction by O'Gorman places Sierra's book at the crossroads of Mexican historiography. After earlier historians had failed "to explain what indeed seemed to be the tremendous historic failure of independence," casting blame on extra-historical forces of God or Nature, or outside influences of the Enlightment and the United States, Spain and the Roman Catholic church, Sierra pointed the way toward explanations, not yet fully explored, within an historical process of the development of people and nation as realistic as it is sympathetic. The effect of positivism, more difficult to trace in the historiography of the United States, is clear in Sierra's writing. In contrast to the bitter, even ridiculous, cast given by positivism to the work of Francisco Bulnes, whose career and historical writings so closely parallel that of Sierra, in the latter positivism and the liberalism of the French Revolution are seen at their best. Despite the conservative drift of the Porfirean regime within which Sierra flourished, the ideals of the Maestro were undimmed in his last years when his world was crushed by the Revolution. José Vasconcelos, the heir of both Bulnes and Sierra, gained fame and recognition of the world for Mexican letters. Yet Sierra could leave his newly-founded National University for honorable exile and death in a diplomatic post in Madrid without the bitter, self-pitying disillusionment which marred the career and writings of Vasconcelos. The *mestizo* nature of Mexico and the Mexicans was a matter of shame to Bulnes, to be apologized for in the writings of Vasconcelos, but both explanation and hope for Sierra.

The preeminent position of Alfonso Reyes in letters lends authority to his appraisal of Sierra the man of humane letters, and he is no less enthusiastic than O'Gorman. The demise of the "art" of writing history is lamented by those who praise the "science" of modern writing of history. Reyes says of Sierra:

> Thus his narrative was enriched with the evocative and interpretive gifts of a stupendous poet who, the better to express himself, had abandoned rhyme and meter. . . . He resolves in an instant, with almost dizzying clarity, some points in Mexican history which, before him and since, have given rise to long-drawn-out arguments and disquisitions. . . . Sierra's eminent success with synthesis would have been impossible without his well-muscled esthetic faculties, for historical synthesis is the greatest challenge to literary technique. . . . Devoid of malice or of any appeal to base prejudice, frank to tell the truth when necessary, it is a long essay in understanding, with the accompaniment of a chorus of facts.

The universality of the appeal of Sierra's pen rises above method and style to respond to his ideals. Sierra closed his book: "Thus our duty is plain: to educate, which means to make strong. Liberty, the marrow of lions, has always been, among nations as among individuals, the patrimony of the strong; the weak have never been free. Mexican social evolution will have been wholly abortive and futile unless it attains the final goal: liberty." Time-entrapped positivism is lost in contemporaneity. The University of Texas Press has lowered the barriers of language and obscurity to give student and scholar this essential volume.

ROBERT L. BIDWELL
Professor of History
East Texas State University.

Gonzalez, Nancie L. *The Spanish-Americans of New Mexico: A Heritage of Pride.* Albuquerque: University of New Mexico Press, 1969. Introduction, illustrations, bibliography, tables, index. xv, 246 pp. $7.95.

This revised and enlarged version of the work that originally appeared as a report for the Mexican American Study Project of the University of California, Los Angeles, is a welcome addition to the literature on the Mexican American minority in general and that of New Mexico in particular. Although the published literature on Mexican Americans in the Southwest has been growing in the last few years, the one on New Mexico is still very limited. However, a vast number of unpublished theses and dissertations is available on this large ethnic group of New Mexico (every fourth inhabitant of the state pertains to it). The author, who is an anthropologist, has systematically surveyed that unpublished literature, extracted the essential contributions from it, reassembled them in line with her own objective, enriched them by her own observations and researches, and put them within the larger context of the well-known studies on Mexican Americans in other parts of the Southwest. She makes it explicit that the primary purpose of her book was "to present an up-to-date, synthetic account of the socio-cultural system of the Spanish Americans in the state of New Mexico." This purpose she has ably fulfilled.

Her work represents a serious, balanced, and honest account. In contrast to some recent newcomers into the field of Mexican American studies, who attempt to inflate the importance of their own work by dismissing in cavalier fashion the writings of those who preceded them, Professor Gonzalez treats these contributions accurately, even when her findings and interpretations differ. Alas, also noteworthy at this time is the fact she did not succumb to the malaise—which has inflicted some social scientists, particularly those writing on minority problems—of abstaining from the use of terminology, observations, and explanations that might offend the ideologists. Even when one disagrees with her, one cannot help but respect her integrity.

Take the use of "Spanish-American" in the title and throughout the book. I felt discomforted by it when I took the book in my hand, and I wondered why and how she decided to employ this term, in face of the other alternatives, such as Mexican Americans or *Chicanos*. I also regretted that she did not specify in the introduction the reason for her decision (after all, the issue of what is its proper name is a lively issue within the minority group which is the object of her study). However, by the end of the book, if one reads it carefully, one comes to appreciate that in making any choice among the existing terms one was apt to offend some members of his minority community. Although the former consensus about the propriety of the term "Spanish-American" or "Hispano"—which has prevailed in this ethnic group of New Mexico since World War I—has been disturbed in recent years, many of its members still insist on these terms. They, and especially those among them who belong or aspire to the middle and upper classes, would have deeply resented being referred to as Mexican Americans, let alone *Chicanos*, terms that smack to them of lower-class status. Still, were I the writer, I would have settled on Mexican Americans, because it is used more and more by the young. But my choice is not more valid than hers. If anything, it reflects a difference in values. Of course, another possibility also exists, that of confining oneself to the term *La Raza*—to which there is little objection anywhere—and thus avoiding the consequences of either of the above choices. Dr. Gonzalez does discuss and occasionally use this term which is widely used by members of this minority to refer to themselves as a collective entity. She makes clear that, although its literal translation is "the race," its meaning does not denote physical characteristics. In her words, "the translation 'the people', meaning 'my people', seems appropriate."

Were one bent on finding a weakness in this book, one might point to the theme running through it that the "Spanish-American" group in New Mexico is quite "different from other areas in the United States with large-sized

Spanish surname populations." One somehow wonders whether inadvertently the author has not been influenced by the "New Mexico legend," which she discusses so perceptively in her book. She begins her book with emphasis on their uniqueness and continues with it almost until the end, page 200, where she suddenly seems to vacillate on this question. Here she says that after reviewing the available evidence, she feels "that the answer cannot be given in an unequivocal Yes or No," whether they are so different or not.

Soon, however, the author reverts to the original theme and finishes on this note: "To the extent that the Spanish-American heritage has become the New Mexican heritage, it will be preserved by Hispanos and Anglos alike. It may fairly be said that, in this sense, the New Mexican situation is different from that in other areas, but the primary differences seem to be in the social behavior relating the various classes and ethnic groups to each other and to the whole." In the peculiar way that the first part of this statement is true, I can safely say that it is also true of California, where I concentrated my studies. Now, as far as the "Spanish heritage" is concerned, one could also claim that it has become the Californian heritage. Here, too, certain aspects have become "preserved by Hispanos and Anglos alike," as reflected in the names of towns and streets. And California also has its "Hispano myth." As a matter of fact, I would venture to say on the basis of my observations and research that hardly any of the important phenomena to which Dr. Gonzalez points to as distinctive of New Mexico is completely lacking in California. They may, however, vary in degree and intensity.

I think that the book could have profited from a theoretical discussion of the concept of "differences" in cultural and social phenomena. For example, the question of quantitative versus qualitative differences is very pertinent and so is that of the net balance of similarities and differences between the Mexican American community in New Mexico and those in other parts of the Southwest. It is unquestionably more traditional, and yet we find in it a rapid growth of political activism, even if it arrived a bit later. The author does, however, discuss this activism, although she did not place it in such a theoretical frame.

A new chapter on "Activism in New Mexico, 1966–69," which did not appear in her original report, has been added and it deserves special attention. The analysis of the Alianza movement, led by Tijerina, as a naturalistic, revivalistic cult, is thought-challenging. Taking into account the work of Frances Swadesh and Joseph Love, who argue that the Alianza has to an increasing extent taken on the characteristics of civil rights movements, Dr. Gonzalez nevertheless maintains that it is better understood if one approaches it as a nativistic cult than as a civil rights movement. She also discusses the other activist organizations in New Mexico, such as the Brown Berets, the United Mexican-American Students (UMAS), *Los Caballeros de Nueva España,* and *Los Comancheros.* While pointing to their growth and articulating their aims, she also balances her discussion by describing who within the community oppose them and why. She tells us that those who oppose them tend to be successful "Hispanos" who have achieved positions which "they appreciate and value. . . . Called *vendidos* themselves [by the militants], many of them feel that it is the militants who are 'selling out' *la raza* by bringing the issue of ethnicity into what would be a war on poverty."

Because of this attempt at balance, I shall be curious to see how this book—dedicated by the author to her two sons "of Spanish, Anglo, and Indian descent"—will be received by the intellectual mouthpiece of Mexican American militancy, the journal *El Grito*, which has branded the "Anthropology and Sociology of the Mexican Americans" in general as "the distortion of Mexican American history."

CELIA S. HELLER
Professor of Anthropology
Hunter College

Alisky, Marvin. *Uruguay: A Contemporary Survey*. New York, Washington and London: Frederick A. Praeger, 1969. Preface, bibliography, index, photographs. vii, 174 pp. $6.50.

Marvin Alisky is professor of Political Science and director of the Center for Latin American Studies at Arizona State University, and editor of *Latin American Digest*. These academic credentials plus the fact of field work undertaken in 1967, insure that we may trust the accuracy of data and sophistication of analysis in this smallish book.

Most of the book is devoted to modern Uruguay, with descriptions arranged under such familiar topical heads as government, finances, education, foreign relations, and culture. The first fifty pages succinctly describe the natural setting, colonial history, and the founding of the modern governmental institutions.

Uruguay is an unusual Latin American country in several respects. It seems tiny as we view it wedged between huge Brazil and Argentina (it is actually about the size of New England). It is composed of a nearly homogeneous population of European origin. Above all, it is famous for an unusually long modern history of a stable, democratic, representative government and the perpetuation of Latin America's first welfare state.

Inflation has become a terrible problem, as has unemployment. In 1967 the cost of living rose by 136 percent, and in 1968 unemployment totaled 12 percent of the potential adult work force. Since then wage-price regulations have slowed inflation dramatically, but a 20–30 percent rise is still expected in 1970. The overwhelming problem for the future is whether civil liberties, increased welfare benefits, and political stability can be maintained in the face of the considerable abilities of the unions and radical parties to sabotage economic growth.

Uruguayan democracy has weathered such other storms as the depression of the 1930s and World War II, and today "stands as a reminder to all Latin America that traditional representative government can speak for all the citizens of a nation." Professor Alisky sounds hopeful when he subheads his *Summary* chapter: "Somehow it All Works." But, as he says, the 1970s will test Uruguay as never before.

ELMAN R. SERVICE
Professor of Anthropology
University of California at
Santa Barbara

BOOKS RECEIVED

General and Regional Latin America

Carr, Raymond, ed. *Latin American Affairs.* (St. Anthony's Papers, no. 22.) New York and London: Oxford University Press, 1970. Notes on contributors. 157 pp. $5.75.

Duncan, W. Raymond and Goodsell, James Nelson, eds. *The Quest for Change in Latin America, Sources for a Twentieth Century Analysis.* New York: Oxford University Press, 1970. Preface, xiv, 563 pp. $12.50.

Geyer, Georgie Anne. *The New Latins; Fateful Change in South and Central America.* New York: Doubleday & Co., Inc., 1970. Introduction, Bibliography, index, xix, 340 pp. $7.95.

Jorrín, Miguel and Martz, John D. *Latin-American Political Thought and Ideology.* Chapel Hill: The University of North Carolina Press, 1970. Preface, introduction, index. xiii, 453 pp. $12.50.

Maritano, Nino. *A Latin American Economic Community.* Indiana: University of Notre Dame Press, 1970. Preface, introduction, abbreviations, selective bibliography, index. xvi, 265 pp. $9.95.

Parker, Franklin. *Travels in Central America; 1821–1840.* Gainesville: University of Florida Press, 1970. Prologue, topical index, bibliography, index. xiv, 340 pp. $12.50.

Petras, James. *Politics and Social Structure in Latin America.* New York: Monthly Review Press, 1970. 382 pp. $9.50.

Ramos, Joseph R. *Labor and Development in Latin America.* New York and London: Columbia University Press, 1970. Foreword, introduction, selected bibliography, index. xvi, 281 pp. $12.50.

Ross, Stanley R., ed. *Latin America in Transition.* Albany: State University of New York Press, 1970. Acknowledgments, introduction, notes on contributors. xxxi, 150 pp. $7.50.

Countries of Latin America

Argentina

Alejandro, Carlos F. Díaz. *Essays on the Economic History of the Argentine Republic.* New Haven, Connecticut: Yale University Press, 1970. Foreword, preface, statistical appendix, index. xvi, 549 pp. $18.50.

Bolivia

Klein, Herbert S. *Parties and Political Change in Bolivia, 1880–1952.* (Cambridge Latin American Studies 5.) New York and London: Cambridge

University Press, 1970. Preface, list of abbreviations, glossary, bibliography, index, xvi, 451 pp. $14.50.

Caribbean Region

Emmanuel, Issac S. and Emmanuel, Suzanne A. *History of the Jews in the Netherlands Antilles*, vol. 1. Netherlands: Royal Vangorcum Ltd., 1970. Preface, list of illustrations, picture credits, abbreviations, glossary, bibliography, index. 533 pp.

Emmanuel, Issac S. and Emmanuel, Suzanne A. *History of the Jews in the Netherlands Antilles*, vol. 2. Netherlands: Royal Vangorum Ltd., 1970. Abbreviations of names. pp. 539–1165.

Wagenheim, Kal. *Puerto Rico: A Profile*. New York, Washington and London: Praeger Publishers, 1970. Foreword by Piri Thomas, preface, introduction, annotated bibliography, index. xv, 286 pp. $8.50.

Chile

Burnett, Ben G. *Political Groups in Chile, The Dialogue Between Order and Change*. (Latin American Monographs, no. 21, Institute of Latin American Studies, The University of Texas at Austin.) Austin: The University of Texas Press, 1970. Preface, bibliography, index, xiv, 319 pp. $8.50.

Colombia

Towards Full Employment. A Programme for Colombia Prepared by an inter-agency team organised by the International Labour Office. Geneva: International Labour Office, 1970. Preface, list of diagrams. viii, 471 pp. $4.00.

Riley, Harold; Harrison, Kelly; Suarez, Nelson; Shaffer, James; Henley, Donald; Larson, Donald; Guthrie, Colin; Lloyd-Clare, David. *Market Coordination in the Development of the Cauca Valley Region—Colombia*. (Research Report No. 5.) East Lansing: Michigan State University, 1970. Foreword, table of contents, bibliography, appendixes A-D. xii, 386 pp.

Mexico

Barkin, David and King, Timothy. *Regional Economic Development, The River Basin Approach in Mexico*. (Cambridge Latin American Studies, no. 7.) New York: Cambridge University Press, 1970. List of figures, list of tables, preface, appendixes, index, x, 262 pp. $10.50.

González Navarro, Moisés. *Raza y Tierra: La Guerra de Castas y el Henequén*. Guanajuato, México: El Colegio de México, 1970. Apéndices, fuentes, bibliografia, índice onomástico, índice analítico. x, 393 pp.

Iduarte, Andrés. *Niño: Child of the Mexican Revolution*. Translated by James F. Shearer. New York, Washington and London: Praeger Publishers, 1971. Translator's preface, glossary. xii, 156 pp. $5.95.

Bazant, Jan. *Alienation of Church Wealth in Mexico, Social and Economic Aspects of the Liberal Revolution, 1856–1875*. Edited and translated by Michael P. Costeloe. (Cambridge Latin American Studies 11.) Cambridge University Press, 1971. List of tables, preface, acknowledgments, list of abbreviations, list of sources and works cited, index, maps. xvi, 333 pp. $17.50.

MISCELLANEOUS

Cartey, Wilfred. *Black Images.* New York: Teachers College Press, 1970. xiv, 186 pp. $7.95.

El Kodsy, Ahmad, and Lobel, Eli. *The Arab World and Israel.* Translated by Brian Pearce and Alfred Ehrenfeld. New York and London: Monthly Review Press, 1970. 137 pp. $6.00.

Elliott, J. H. *The Old World and the New, 1492–1650.* (Cambridge Studies in Early Modern History.) New York and London: Cambridge University Press, 1970. Preface, select bibliography, index. x, 118 pp. $5.95.

Franco, Jean. *The Modern Culture of Latin America: Society and the Artist.* Baltimore, Maryland: Penguin Books Inc., 1970. List of illustrations, acknowledgments, references, bibliography, index of names, index of subjects and titles of works. 381 pp. $2.95.

Güiraldes. Ricardo. *Don Segundo Sombra.* Edited by Angela B. Dellepiane. New Jersey: Prentice-Hall, Inc., 1971. Introducción, índice de palabras y expresiones anotadas. v, 255 pp. $4.95.

Johnson, Cecil. *Communist China and Latin America, 1959–1967.* New York and London: Columbia University Press, 1970. Introduction, bibliography, index. viii, 324 pp. $9.95.

Mandel, Ernest. *Europe vs. America: Contradictions of Imperialism.* New York: Monthly Review Press, 1970. Introduction, bibliography. 160 pp. $5.50.

McNerney, Robert F., Jr., trans. and ed. *Bolivar and the War of Independence.* (Memorias del General Daniel Florencio O'Leary. Narración. Abridged Version.) Austin and London: University of Texas Press, 1970. Translator's foreword, preface, index, list of illustrations and maps. xvi, 386 pp. $9.50.

Oswald, J. Gregory, comp. and trans. *Soviet Image of Contemporary Latin America, A Documentary History, 1960–1968.* Austin and London: University of Texas Press, 1970. Introduction by Herbert S. Dinerstein, foreword, bibliographical index of items. xvi, 365 pp. $15.00

Rockland, Michael Aaron, trans. *Sarmiento's Travels in the United States in 1847.* New Jersey: Princeton University Press, 1970. List of illustrations, introduction, index. xiii, 330 pp. $9.50.

Samuels, Michael Anthony. *Education in Angola, 1878–1914: A History of Culture Transfer and Administration.* New York: Teachers College Press, 1970. Acknowledgments, introduction, maps, index. xiii, 185 pp. $7.95.

Swinfen, D. B. *Imperial Control of Colonial Legislation, 1813–1865.* New York: Oxford University Press, 1971. Abbreviations, introduction, bibliography, index. 202 pp. $8.00.

Vives, Jaime Vicens. *Approaches to the History of Spain.* Translated by Joan Connelly Ullman. Berkeley: University of California Press, 1970. Foreword. by way of prologue, commentary on bibliography, index. xxx, 189 pp. $2.45.

GREAT SEAL UNIVERSITY OF MIAMI
CORAL GABLES FLORIDA 1925

JULY–OCTOBER 1971
VOLUME XIII—NOS. 3 & 4

JOURNAL OF INTER-AMERICAN STUDIES and WORLD AFFAIRS

JOURNAL OF INTER-AMERICAN STUDIES and WORLD AFFAIRS

Vol. XIII, Nos. 3–4 JULY–OCTOBER 1971

International Air Transport Association: Some Historical Notes	JOHN C. LESLIE	319
Jobs and Housing: Alternative Developments in the Venezuelan Guayana	JOHN S. MACDONALD AND LEATRICE D. MACDONALD	342
Post-Emancipation Race Relations: Some Caribbean and American Perspectives	DAVID LOWENTHAL	367
Cuban Refugee Children	BRYAN O. WALSH	378
Policy-Making for the Brazilian Amazon	H. JON ROSENBAUM AND WILLIAM G. TYLER	416
Argentine Letters and the Peronato: An Overview	MARTIN S. STABB	434
Impressions of the Peruvian Agrarian Reform	JOHN S. GITLITZ	456
Presidential Succession in Ecuador: 1860–1968	GEORG MAIER	475
Nuevas Corrientes	ROBERT E. MCNICOLL	510
Books		517
Indexes to Volume XIII		543

Published Quarterly for the

CENTER FOR ADVANCED INTERNATIONAL STUDIES

by the

UNIVERSITY OF MIAMI PRESS

Coral Gables, Florida

CONTRIBUTORS

JOHN C. LESLIE retired as the Senior Vice President-International Affairs of Pan American World Airways 1970 and is now Director of the PAN AM HISTORY PROJECT * * * JOHN S. MACDONALD heads the Department of Sociology and Psychology, Chelsea College, University of London, and LEATRICE D. MACDONALD (Mrs. John S. MacDonald) is a fellow of the Institute of Latin American Studies, University of London * * * DAVID LOWENTHAL, noted for his work in the field of Caribbean studies, studied at Harvard, the University of California at Berkeley, and is a Ph.D. graduate of the University of Wisconsin. He further taught at Vassar College and was a Fulbright research fellow at the University of West Indies (Jamaica) * * * MONSIGNOR BRYAN O. WALSH, Irish-born, is a graduate of Mungret College, Ireland, and St. Mary's University, Baltimore, Maryland, and is now doing graduate work in Inter-American Studies at the University of Miami * * * H. JON ROSENBAUM currently is a Research Asssociate, Center for International Affairs, Harvard University, and a member of the political science faculty at Wellesley College * * * WILLIAM G. TYLER, now teaching Economics at the University of Florida, served in Brazil as a Latin American Teaching Fellow and a consultant for the Agency for International Development * * * MARTIN S. STABB, author of *In Quest of Identity* and a book on Jorge Luis Borges, heads the Department of Spanish, Italian, and Portuguese at the Pennsylvania State University * * * JOHN S. GITLITZ (a Ph.D. candidate at the University of North Carolina, Chapel Hill) spent over a year in Peru (1967-68) with a Fulbright scholarship and returned the summer of 1970 with a NSF grant * * * GEORG MAIER, a frequent visitor to Ecuador, has written a number of articles and has co-authored a book on the history of that country.

All correspondence concerning manuscripts or exchange information should be directed to the Editor, *Journal of Inter-American Studies and World Affairs*, Box 8134, University of Miami, Coral Gables, Florida 33124. Correspondence regarding book reviews should be sent to the Book Review Editor, *Journal of Inter-American Studies and World Affairs*, Box 8123, University of Miami, Coral Gables, Florida 33124. Subscriptions and business correspondence should be addressed to *Journal of Inter-American Studies and World Affairs*, University of Miami Press, Drawer 9088, Coral Gables, Florida 33124. Annual subscription, $12.00; students, $6.50. Single issues available; please inquire concerning prices.

The *Journal of Inter-American Studies and World Affairs* is indexed in *Public Affairs Information Service, Historical Abstracts, Social Sciences and Humanities Index, Indice Bibliográfico, Current Contents: Behavioral, Social, and Management*, and others.

PRINTED IN THE UNITED STATES OF AMERICA

EDITORIAL NOTE

In this enlarged, combined July-October issue of the *Journal of Inter-American Studies and World Affairs* we add a somewhat new dimension to the role or function of a scholarly journal, in that three of our eight articles were written by men (with proper scholarly credentials) reporting on history-making actions in which they had personally participated in some respect. One might regard them (in kind, if not in degree) as late twentieth-century counterparts of Hernán Cortés, Bernal Díaz del Castillo, or Pedro Cieza de León four and a half centuries ago. Like the conquistadores, these authors—a man of business, a member of the ecclesiastical hierarchy, and a budding political scientist—have felt the compulsion to tell the story as it happened before—as it inevitably does—it vanishes into folklore, mythology, or oblivion: to make these primary source materials available immediately and permanently to interested scholars. Already scholarly studies are appearing on two of these subjects, some of them unsatisfying because they are based on inadequate materials. (Bernal Díaz' plaint against Father López de Gómara's book comes to mind!)

Mr. John C. Leslie, whose historical notes on the International Air Transport Association are to be found in the first article of this issue, holds a B.S. degree from Princeton University, and a B.S. in Aeronautical Engineering and an M.S. in Business and Engineering Administration from Massachusetts Institute of Technology. His forty-one year career with Pan American World Airways, from which he retired in 1970 as Senior Vice President-International Affairs and a member of the Board of Directors, brought Mr. Leslie into the arena of world affairs and made him a major participant in the development and activities of IATA about which he writes. He represented Pan American at the Havana Organization meeting of IATA in April 1945, at Montreal in October of the same year, and at many General Meetings thereafter. He also served on the Executive Committee of IATA from 1947 to 1950 and again from 1952 to 1970.

More than a major participant, when Monsignor Walsh writes the story of the Cuban Refugee Children, he does so as the prime (if not the sole) creator and director of a program designed to meet a sharp, immediate, incredibly complicated situation of human need and distress in our time. Quite properly, therefore, he writes directly in the first person, from his own knowledge and records, supplemented by those of his colleagues in this venture. Both personally and professionally, Father Walsh (currently also a graduate student in Inter-American Studies at the University of Miami) shares the concern of historians and social scientists to get this story clear in the record and, at the cost of great personal effort, taken from his busy life, presents it here on pages 378-415.

The Gitlitz article (see pp. 456-474), in contrast to the two mentioned above, shows a scholar-author as neither director nor participant but rather as a young political scientist using his newly-learned methodologies and skills to report on and give a preliminary analysis of the Peruvian reform as he saw it in its first year. Something more than a traveler's account or journalist's report, certainly less definitive than a field research project, we feel that John S. Gitlitz' comments will be useful to *Journal* readers both now and later.

Definitions and descriptions of the role of a scholarly journal vary widely and will continue to do so. Within their own tightly held limits, scholars cherish their individuality and freedom and one could probably get as many different definitions as there are scholars offering them. The *Journal of Inter-American Studies and World Affairs* has always been oriented toward purposeful innovations and its total independence (subject only to its own Board of Editors) gives it an enviable freedom of action in this respect along with a greater challenge and responsibility for exploring new areas of interest or creative action than other journals with different priorities. Your comments are invited about this—our latest venture.

IONE S. WRIGHT
Editor

JOHN C. LESLIE
Fellow of the American Institute of Aeronautics and Astronautics; also of the Royal Aeronautical Society (London)

INTERNATIONAL AIR TRANSPORT ASSOCIATION: SOME HISTORICAL NOTES

A worldwide scheduled air transportation system for passengers, cargo, and mail has been created since World War II. In its global scope it is almost unique; the International Air Transport Association's only prototype is the Universal Postal Union, which for over a century has been the intergovernment vehicle for arranging the expeditious, reliable interchange of foreign mails between nations. Somewhat comparable to IATA in purpose but much more limited geographically, are such arrangements as those which provide for the transfer of electric power across the border between the United States and Canada, the coordination of highway, waterway, and railway traffic respectively in Europe, and the international telephone, cable, and radio services. The general public does not know—and has little need to know—what has gone on behind the scenes to create these facilities which in essence are large international public utility systems. A typical person's impressions would probably reflect his nationality. An American would probably assume that the individual components of such a utility system were privately owned and operated for commercial profit (except for the Postal Service). A European would tend to assume that electric power companies, railroads, airlines, telecommunications companies, and the Postal Service would all be owned by some government. Each would be substantially correct in his own context.

In fact, every variety of airline ownership can be seen in the world airline community, from subsidized government departments to sizable airlines owned entirely by individuals—and in between, for example, the national air corporations of Great Britain and the private-capital airlines of the United States.

The cosmopolitan nature of this community is suggested by the fact that the International Air Transport Association (IATA) today has 92 Active and 16 Associate Members from 86 countries; they speak three official IATA languages (English, French, and Spanish) plus a large number of other mother tongues; all continents are represented and every form of government from monarchy to communism. A majority based on the principle of "one member-one vote" prevails (except in specific constitutional matters). In the Traffic Conferences, unanimity is required; here a single veto can be effective whether cast by a very small or a very large member.

The only obstacle to referring to this worldwide airline network as an "industry" is that this may conjure up the impression of "private" industry and the further assumption that only private capital seeks to earn a return on its investment. The fact is that capital is needed to create and expand any airline and it makes little difference for the purpose of this article whether this capital is invested by private citizens or by governments. Furthermore, the enterprise to which capital has been dedicated is expected by the owner, whether private or governmental, to earn a return. In Britain, for example, the national corporations are given specific targets in terms of return on capital. In the Soviet Union this practice is said to be growing. Regardless of the nature of international airline ownership, moreover, there is general agreement on the goal of "economical" operation, which in broad terms means the avoidance of losses and the earning of some reasonable return on invested capital.

In this context, it may seem difficult to establish a line of demarcation between the "commercial" and "governmental" sectors. Most international scheduled airlines are owned by, regulated by, or are responsive to the civil aviation departments and the foreign offices of their respective governments. Even in the case of the privately-owned U.S.-flag airlines, many of the agreements into which they may enter in IATA are subject to approval by the Civil Aeronautics Board. With few exceptions, however, trial and error has demonstrated the wisdom of airlines, even when government owned, being set up as autonomous, "commercial" entities. The word "businessman" certainly includes the senior traffic official, for example, of British Overseas Airways Corporation or the Soviet Union's Aeroflot as of TWA or Pan Am. As we trace the history of IATA we will be looking at an organization which is much more than a domestic trade association but is still classified as non-governmental and commercial.

There must, of course, be an immense amount of liaison and cooperation between the airline side and the government side. As described later, the primary working relationship is between IATA, representing the scheduled international airlines, and the International Civil Aviation Organization (ICAO), representing the many governments which have adhered to the Chicago Convention.

ICAO is a "specialized agency" of the United Nations, a term which presumably requires no elaboration here. ICAO and IATA customarily exchange Observer status and IATA is invited to present proposals and recommendations to ICAO at all working levels. In almost the same category of importance to civil aviation are three other specialized agencies of the United Nations: the International Telecommunications Union, the World Meteorological Organization, and the World Health Organization. With all of these, as with the Universal Postal Union, IATA represents the non-governmental side. To use another accepted word, IATA represents the "operator" of the aircraft used in scheduled international air service.

The "systems" concept of the world airline network has many facets, only some of which will be touched upon in this paper. The one that first concerns the reader is how he himself arranges to go by air from one country to another. Here his personal experience is likely to color his thinking. One reader will visualize a simple journey like New York-Montreal or London-Paris. Another will think of complicated itineraries involving, for example, a half dozen countries in Europe, or a dozen countries on a world tour embracing the six continents. One time in four, the average passenger books a journey on two or more airlines. In some six cases out of ten he buys his tickets through an IATA authorized travel agent, of whom there are some 16,000 around the world. He expects firm reservations, no matter how many different airlines may be involved on a single itinerary; he expects to pay in one currency at one location; he knows he can check his several pieces of baggage through to different destinations on different airlines, but under a standard form of baggage check; when he changes his itinerary, as he almost certainly will, he looks to a rapid rearrangement and confirmation of the new reservations.

The passenger also takes for granted the system of air navigation and air traffic control built up over the years by the many governments concerned. Obviously, the amount of traffic in the air today has to be controlled in order that all may use the airspace safely and economically. Consider the chaos if each individual country in Europe started to control the traffic over its own territory, disregarding the actions of air traffic controllers in the other countries all around its borders! Or think of the consequences if each country along an air route chose to adopt a different instrument landing system; each airliner would have to carry a half dozen or a dozen different radio receivers on board and the captain would have to accomplish the impossible task of learning a half dozen or a dozen different systems. That the government and the airlines must collaborate is self-evident, and they do. This is part of what IATA, and ICAO, are all about.

The Paris Convention of 1919 established the International Commission for Air Navigation (ICAN), a farsighted effort in Europe to establish some international rules to facilitate civil aviation. Veterans of World War I had access to surplus aircraft and were positive they could induce people to fly commercially. To do this, they soon found that they needed lots of little aids like place-names on roofs along the embryonic airway from London's Croydon Airport to Paris' Le Bourget Airport, and special markers on the beaches on both sides of the English Channel to help the pilots depart over the right point. Another simple need not then easy to achieve in practice was the creation of a weather reporting network and some codes for transmitting local weather reports to aircraft before take-off. (At first, there was no radio to transmit the information to the pilots aloft.)

These simple needs, and others which could even then be foreseen, led to the creation of the first IATA—the International Air Traffic Association—at The Hague on 25 August 1919. The original incorporators were one British, one Dutch, one German, and three Scandinavian airlines.

This is the place perhaps to try to make clear a bit of philosophy, without which it might be difficult to accept some later statements in this article. It will be mentioned that senior airline officials made available for service on the Executive Committee and the Standing Committees of IATA serve under a mandate to regard themselves as individuals working for the best interests of the industry, not as partisan representatives of their individual companies. Is this idealistic or a mere pretense? No, because it was always evident, as it is today, that no international airline system could exist—and therefore no individual international airline could realistically hope to prosper—without cooperative effort on a hundred different problems. This cooperation had to take place between airlines, and between airlines and governments. It has never been difficult to see that the successful solution of the myriad problems on IATA's agenda would, on balance, also mean a greater degree of success for the individual airlines.

It was also plain to the founders of international civil aviation that the opportunities for legal chaos were about as great as in the technical field. This also would have to be averted by the cooperative action of governments and airlines.

For example, it seemed necessary to provide by treaty for the respective rights and responsibilities of passengers, shippers, and airline operators in the event of loss, injury, or death. This resulted in an international treaty called the Warsaw Convention of 1929 (later amended by the Hague Protocol). This established a relatively absolute but financially limited liability on the part of the airlines, while it placed considerable burdens on them for documentation, etc. Likewise liabilities between airlines for damage to aircraft on the ground or in the air, and damage to third parties on the ground, had to be fixed by treaty—the 1933 Rome Convention.

Title to aircraft, and questions of authority, jurisdiction, and liability in the event of crime aboard aircraft, all became subjects of treaties. Currently pending is an international convention on hijacking. IATA was involved in the drafting and negotiation of these treaties affecting, as they did, the rights and responsibilities of the international airline operators.

There is another aspect of the international airline environment which must be understood in order to understand later paragraphs. The reader may be accustomed to thinking of the phrase "freedom of the seas" and he may assume there is also "freedom of the air." Without going into excessive detail, the seventeenth century saw a general acceptance of the doctrine of "freedom of the seas" by which was meant the High Seas beyond territorial limits. It became recognized, after much debate and some armed conflict, that no nation had a right to claim dominion over the High Seas. However, it was not until the nineteenth century that it became common practice to grant foreign vessels the right to trade within the territory of sovereign nations—what may be called "freedom of the ports." These two doctrines make it possible, for example, for a Belgian vessel to solicit a cargo in Baltimore, carry it across the High Seas, and discharge it in Beirut.

The opposite case prevails with respect to international air commerce. The late 19th and early 20th centuries found governments beginning to worry, mostly from the defense point of view, about foreign balloons and aeroplanes moving indiscriminately through the air over their own territories; the use of balloons in the Franco-Prussian war of 1870 and Louis Blériot's cross-Channel flight in 1909 are good examples. By the time the Allies met at Versailles to write the Paris Convention in 1919, they had mostly decided to claim sovereign jurisdiction over the airspace above their respective territories, i.e., no one could enter that airspace without express permission. This was first enshrined in the Paris Convention. It appeared in later treaties, such as Havana 1928, until it was again set forth in the Chicago Convention of 1944. Meanwhile, it had been proclaimed in various national legislation, including in the U.S. the Air Commerce Act of 1926 and the Civil Aeronautics Act of 1938.

The doctrine of air sovereignty obviously meant that there could be no international air transportation except by agreement between at least two nations concerned. That is, no one could start an airline between London and Paris unless the British and French governments agreed on the terms and conditions. These terms and conditions included three major subjects: routes to be flown, the amount of capacity to be offered, and fares and rates to be charged. Routes and capacity were preempted for discussion between governments; these topics are not discussed within IATA.

As will be shown later, IATA has a limited responsibility for providing the machinery within which fares and rates can be discussed by the airlines and appropriate recommendations made to all governments concerned for their approval.

THE OLD IATA

When the International Air Traffic Association was formed in 1919, the first sessions were dedicated to discussions concerning traffic of the member companies. The measure of traffic in 1919 was not great. A total of 3,500 passengers was carried approximately 700,000 passenger-kilometers, averaging one passenger per aircraft. Only 50 years later, in 1969, air transport carried more than 300 million passengers some 350 billion passenger-kilometers, with the average number of passengers per aircraft exceeding 50. At the Annual Meeting in 1925 there was considerable discussion about the price to be charged for the carriage of children; also work was started at this time on a standard airline ticket and international consignment note (cargo airwaybill), as well as agents' commissions. These three subjects appeared time and again on the agenda of subsequent meetings.

Starting also in 1925 was discussion of the carriage of mail, and in September 1927 there was a full-scale conference attended by the airlines and representatives of postal authorities throughout Europe. In the same year, the standard ticket and cargo airwaybill were adopted. It was not until the end of 1933 that a standard code for seat reservations had been accepted.

On the technical and operating side, the civil aviation industry in 1919 was tiny and primitive. As previously mentioned, one of the first requirements was to paint some place names on roofs and put up some guideposts on the beaches of the English Channel. While much of the technical work in the 1920s was accomplished by the chief executives of the airlines working through IATA, it ultimately became expedient to establish an IATA Technical Committee of expert airline officials. This was done on 15 March 1930. Between 1930 and 1932 some decisions were reached by this committee which are so taken for granted today that it seems incredible there was ever any question—but there was. For example: should the throttles move forward or backward to reduce power?—which way should the needles on the various dials in the cockpit move?—even, in which direction should the primary aircraft controls move in order to produce the desired change in aircraft attitude (whether one should press on the right end of the rudder bar to turn right, or on the left end as in the case of a sled turning right)? During this period, spark plugs, propeller hubs, and fuel tank filler caps were standardized. Pipes and wires were assigned standard color-coded markings. Much attention was given to radio communication and the allocation of suitable wavelengths, including provisions for radio navigation. In 1937 the first international teletype reservations system was set up.

By the time the old IATA was holding its Annual Meeting at Budapest in 1938, much progress had been made on the European airline network, but politically "the lights were going out" in Europe. At that meeting, Pan American Airways had joined IATA, the first airline outside the continent of Europe to do so. The 1939 meeting was to be held in New York, and Mr. Juan T. Trippe, president of Pan Am, was to be elected as the next president of the old IATA. The outbreak of war in Europe in August 1939, of course, required the cancellation of this meeting. Everything would have to wait for the end of the war when international air transport was to be reborn—in 1945, as it transpired.

THE NEW IATA: ORGANIZATION

As World War II progressed, it became possible and appropriate to plan for the postwar expansion of international air transport which was certainly going to take place. Aircraft and aircraft power plants had vastly improved, as had radio and radar technology. Airports had been built almost all over the globe. Hitherto land-bound (mentally as well as physically) U.S. domestic airlines had been drafted to serve abroad as contractors to the U.S. Air Transport Command. For the first time, the U.S.-flag air routes which Pan Am had pioneered began to seem attractive to others. At the same time, the pre-war group of experienced, imaginative, and strong-minded international airline executives clearly foresaw a demand for international air transportation which would greatly expand the lines which they had already extended from Europe to the Far East, from the United States to Latin America, and across the Pacific to the Orient, in the decade before World War II. (The transatlantic civilian air service had commenced in the summer of 1939, but was soon overtaken by the outbreak of war in Europe in August of the same year: it continued to operate throughout the war to the neutral countries of Ireland and Portugal. Whether old-timers or newcomers in international civil aviation, the leaders of the industry perceived that much of the prospective expansion could only be achieved by the joint efforts of the airlines and through co-operation between IATA and ICAO. They did not have to wait long to take practical steps in this direction.

In 1944 the United States government invited the Allied nations to a civil aviation conference in Chicago; the war was still going on but its end could be foreseen. Some of the governments, including the United States, aspired to put across their own ideas of the commercial organization of the industry after the war. Specifically, they wanted very much to do something about routes and capacity. The United States at that time was espousing "freedom of the air," a policy later and fortunately abandoned. Other nations were advocating rigid control of routes and capacity, including the possibility of an all-powerful International Civil Aeronautics Board—a concept also happily abandoned.

Very little progress was made at Chicago to resolve differing government views about the future regulation of the industry. Optimists had hoped for a multilateral commercial treaty of some kind but were disappointed, as they were again when the same effort was made in 1947. They did, however, accomplish something very useful; they formed the Provisional International Civil Aviation Organization (PICAO), and made provision in its statutes for an ultimate successor to be known as the International Civil Aviation Organization (ICAO). As described in testimony to the United States Senate when the treaty was presented for ratification, ICAO was to be largely a technical organization, and certainly not an international regulator of commercial matters. As such, it has served well for the past 25 years. Its headquarters were placed in Montreal, Canada, a neat compromise between the conflicting desires of the Europeans and the Americans.

The Chicago Conference, of course, was at the government level and the senior delegates were government officials. However, many delegations included airline advisers. This meant that a number of pre-war foreign airline executives, familiar with the old IATA, were in Chicago attached to national delegations. With the consent of their respective delegations, they formed a Drafting Committee[1] to draw up the Articles of Association of a new IATA to succeed the old IATA. The old IATA had its headquarters in Europe and had confined its activities to Europe; the only outside member was Pan American Airways. Now it was necessary promptly to form a new association with a global outlook and worldwide membership. A fresh start was psychologically and practically necessary.

In April 1945, just a few months after the completion of the Chicago Conference, the new IATA had its organization meeting in Havana, Cuba. Sixty-one airlines met at the Hotel Nacional to consider and adopt, as amended, the Articles of Association proposed by the Chicago Drafting Committee. With that, the new IATA was launched on 19 April 1945. (Legally, the Association was unincorporated until its Canadian charter was issued on 18 December 1945.)

As to the old IATA, the atmosphere was nostalgic at the windup meeting held in London on 17 September 1945 in a handsome, wood-paneled London hotel dining-room. The then Chairman of British Overseas Airways Corporation, Lord Knollys, presided. He said he understood that there was a good tradition to be bequeathed to the new IATA, namely, that the presence of the delegates' wives did much "to soothe the savage beast" and contribute to mutual understanding and harmony. (The new IATA accepted the tradition and has indeed benefited greatly from it.)

In October 1945 the first Annual General Meeting was held in Montreal, Canada. The 41 airline companies represented authorized an invitation to Sir William P. Hildred (then Director General of Civil Aviation of the United Kingdom)[2] to become the first Director General of the Association. They also elected an Executive Committee (equivalent to a Board of

---

[1] The drafting committee consisted of John C. Cooper, Jr., as Chairman (Pan American World Airways), Major J. Ronald McCrindle (British Overseas Airways Corporation), Per Norlin (Scandinavian Airlines System), John Slater (American Export Airlines), Henry Gorecki (LOT of Poland), Pedro Chapa (Cía. Mexicana de Aviación), Luis Machado (Companía Cubana de Aviación), and F. Flocon (France).

[2] A veteran of World War I, William P. Hildred entered the Treasury from the University of Sheffield in 1919. He was Deputy Director General of Civil Aviation 1938–1939. During World War II he served in the Air Ministry and the Ministry of Aircraft Production until he became Director General of the Ministry of Civil Aviation 1941–1946. A man of abundant energy, eloquent in both spoken and written English, studious in his approach to problems, an experienced diplomat, he was uniquely qualified to direct the new IATA during its formative years. He was aptly described in the 5 June 1971 issue of the *Economist* (London) in the following terms: "The first boss of IATA, Sir William Hildred, a former British civil servant, treated the airlines as any competent permanent civil servant would treat his minister; that is, he steered, cajoled, advised, warned, bullied and occasionally rebuked in tones reminiscent of an English nanny—and to some effect."

The retirement of Sir William Hildred, C.B., O.B.E., M.A., LL.D., to take

Directors) consisting of twelve members from airlines of the following countries: Australia, Brazil, China, Egypt, France, India, Netherlands, Sweden, United Kingdom, and United States.[3] The thirteenth seat authorized by the Articles was tacitly held open—optimistically, as it turned out—for the Soviet airline; it has not yet joined.

One of the provisions in the Articles adopted at Havana was that the principal office of the new IATA should be in the same city as the headquarters of the International Civil Aviation Organization (ICAO),[4] and so it was decided to request the government of Canada to allow IATA to incorporate in that country. An act to incorporate the International Air Transport Association was assented to by His Majesty on 18 December 1945 by and with the advice and consent of the Senate and the House of Commons of Canada. The purposes, objects, and aims of the Association are contained in this Charter. They read as follows:

(a) to promote safe, regular and economical air transport for the benefit of the peoples of the world, to foster air commerce and to study the problems connected therewith;
(b) to provide means for collaboration among the air transport enterprises engaged directly or indirectly in international air transport service;
(c) to co-operate with the International Civil Aviation Organization and other international organizations.

Even today, LATA could not officially amend its purposes except with the approval of the Canadian Parliament and it has a self-evident duty to carry out these purposes to the best of its ability.

---

effect in April 1966, was announced at the 21st Annual Meeting held in Vienna in October 1965.

He was succeeded as Director General by Mr. Knut Hammarskjøld of Sweden. Educated at Stockholm University, he is the son of a former member of the Court of International Justice at the Hague and nephew of the late Secretary General of the United Nations. A member of the Swedish Foreign Service in the grade of Minister, Mr. Hammarskjøld had also been attached to the Swedish Board of Civil Aviation, dealing with international air transport agreements. His embassy posts had included Moscow and other Eastern European countries. At the time of his appointment by IATA he had been serving since 1960 as Deputy Secretary-General of the European Free Trade Association. Fluent in a number of languages, Mr. Hammarskjøld is serving IATA with distinction.

[3] W. Hudson Fysh (Australia); J. Bento Ribeiro Dantas (Brazil); T. H. Shen (China); Hassan Sadek Pasha (Egypt); Rene Briend (France); A. F. T. Cambridge (India); Albert Plesman (Netherlands); Per A. Norlin (Sweden); J. Ronald McCrindle (United Kingdom); John C. Cooper (U.S.A.); John E. Slater (U.S.A.) and T. B. Wilson (U.S.A.).

[4] See Articles of Association, Article II.

In recent years IATA has established another principal office, in Geneva, Switzerland. The large and important IATA technical organization remains in Montreal to assure maximum liaison with its counterparts in ICAO. The Traffic and certain other departments are headquartered at Geneva. The Director General divides his time between the two locations.

The active membership of IATA was to be comprised exclusively of air transport enterprises engaged in scheduled international air service. Further, membership was to be open to any air transport enterprise engaging in duly authorized scheduled air service under the flag of a state eligible to membership in ICAO. This included the flag-airlines of states that were or were to become Communist, such as Poland, Czechoslovakia, and Yugoslavia. The question of neutral states and former enemy states was a delicate one at the ICAO level, but Germany, Italy, and Japan were ultimately admitted to ICAO and their airlines to IATA. The USSR, which has always been eligible, has recently joined ICAO; however, the Russian-flag airline, Aeroflot, has not yet applied for membership in IATA. It will be interesting to see what course is followed by the Peoples Republic of China and its airline.

Fundamentally, power in IATA rests in the Annual General Meeting, where the principle of "one man-one vote" prevails—the largest and the smallest member each has identical voting power. On the other hand, the necessity for maintaining momentum and decisiveness between Annual Meetings was foreseen. This resulted in a strong Executive Committee and broad delegation of authority to the Director General.[5]

The Executive Committee exercises the executive functions of the Association plus any additional powers delegated to it by resolution of the General Meeting. Specifically, the Executive Committee has the power and duty for the general management and control of the affairs, funds, and property of the Association; to represent the Association and determine its policy; and to control and supervise activities of local or regional IATA organizations; to establish committees and appoint members; to fix the rules and regulations for the conduct of Traffic Conferences.

The Executive Committee, having elected a Director General subject to confirmation by the General Meeting, determines his term of office, duties, and remuneration. The Director General is responsible to the Executive Committee and appoints his staff, except that the Executive Committee elects the Secretary and the Treasurer, both of whom are subject to the supervision and authority of the Director General. In short, the Director General is the chief executive and administrative officer of the Association and is wholly responsible to the Executive Committee.[6]

As regards the U.S. members who were founding members of IATA (11 Active and 6 Associate),[7] they submitted the Articles of Association

---

[5] Articles of Association VII and IX.

[6] Articles of Association IX and Rules and Regulations of the Executive Committee II (2).

[7] *Active Members*: American Airlines, American Overseas Airlines, Braniff Airways, Colonial Airlines, Northeast Air Lines, Northwest Airlines, Pan American

adopted at Havana in April 1945 to the U.S. Civil Aeronautics Board for approval since, under the Civil Aeronautics Act of 1938, they could not enter into such commitments without Board approval. Approval was granted by Order No. 3728, dated 5 June 1945 (happily, well before the first Annual Meeting in October). This approval was probably facilitated by the fact that Article VIII (6) contains an escape clause in the event that a resolution passed by a general meeting would require the member to contravene an applicable law or regulation, or the official policy, of the state of which that member is a national. This clause has rarely been used, but is no doubt a source of comfort both to governments and airline members. It has sometimes been cited as an argument against the adoption of resolutions which a member thought would be distasteful to his government.

Under the supervision of the Director General, four secretariat units were promptly organized to serve the corresponding Standing Committees comprised of senior officials of member airlines. These committees provide guidance for the respective functions of IATA and also serve as their spokesmen before the Executive Committee and the General Meeting. (A Medical Committee was added in 1950, making the present total of five Standing Committees.) It should be repeated that the members of these committees have been generally successful in following their mandate to serve the overall interests of the industry in their personal capacities and specifically not to regard themselves as partisan representatives of their own companies. This has been effective not only because of the personal integrity of the members but also because it represented the conviction of company managements that only by such cooperative effort could the tremendous joint problems of the industry be solved.

Typical functions of the Standing Committees, vital components of the IATA structure, are outlined in the paragraphs that follow.

Technical Committee

The area of concern of the Technical Committee is all technical matters connected with international air transport, particularly the following:

(i) Operations, including promotion of safety and efficiency of flight;
(ii) Standardization of equipment;
(iii) Communications and radio aids for navigation;
(iv) Meteorology;

World Airways, Pan American-Grace Airways, Transcontinental & Western Air, United Air lines and Western Air Lines. *Associate Members*: Alaska Air Lines, All American Aviation, Delta Air Lines, Eastern Air Lines, National Airlines and Pennsylvania-Central Airlines.

(v) Airworthiness and maintenance matters;
(vi) Aerodromes, air routes and ground aids.

Following the precedent of the old IATA, the new Technical Committee has elected from the beginning to place reliance on Technical Conferences, where representatives of airlines, governments, research and development organizations, the military, and manufacturers could engage in free and frank discussions without being forced to agree upon final resolutions. The Fourth Technical Conference in 1950, for example, had only one theme: Turbine Powered Aircraft. At another, in 1961, more than 600 delegates discussed the Supersonic Transport. In the intervening years, conferences were held on instrument approach and landing systems—pilot training—future requirements for meteorology, air traffic control, navigation, and communications. In recent years, renewed emphasis has been given to airport and terminal building design especially as to functional requirements.

Another Technical Department function is "Facilitation," which means the easing or elimination of any red tape at national frontiers that is burdensome to travelers and shippers. Following a preliminary document issued by PICAO early in 1946, ICAO, advised and assisted by IATA, issued the first edition of so-called Annex 9 (Facilitation) in 1949. Both these documents set forth standards and recommended practices for the simplification of frontier formalities by governments. Committee members and Facilitation staff of IATA have since journeyed throughout the world cajoling governments into eliminating or simplifying documents demanded for the clearance of passengers, cargo, and aircraft. Enough progress has been made to be pointed to with pride, but not nearly enough to satisfy all the requirements of high speed modern air transportation.

Legal Committee

The area of concern of the Legal Committee is all legal matters having a bearing on international air transport, particularly the following:

(i) International conventions on public and private law;
(ii) Current and proposed national laws, orders, and regulations affecting international air transport;
(iii) Legal aspects of agreements relating to Agency and Traffic documents, procedures, and practices, including conditions of carriage;
(iv) Legal aspects of agreements relating to Technical documents, procedures, and practices;
(v) Potential legal problems arising out of technological and other developments in air transport;
(vi) Legal aspects of such other matters, including matters

> proposed for consideration by other Committees and by Traffic Conferences, as may be referred to it by the Executive Committee or the Director General.

Some of international air transport's most complex problems have been and are of a legal nature. At the last General Meeting of the old IATA in 1938, views were already being expressed on such matters as amendment of the 1929 Warsaw and the 1933 Rome Conventions—also how to achieve uniform traffic documentation—how to provide simple documentation for transportation of passengers and goods by air and surface modes combined.

The various international conventions dealing with air law are, as mentioned earlier, of particular importance to IATA. Some of these multilateral treaties are primarily concerned with the rights and duties of sovereign states in relation to international civil aviation. Foremost among such "public law" conventions is the 1944 Chicago Convention, which created the International Civil Aviation Organization (ICAO), the intergovernmental body which provides the forum and the staff for intergovernmental action in the field of civil aviation.

Of even greater concern to the air transport industry are the "private law" conventions which directly affect the legal position of air carriers vis-à-vis passengers and consignors of goods. In this category the 1929 Warsaw Convention (to which 103 states are parties) is the earliest and most widely accepted, as previously mentioned.

Revision of the Warsaw Convention has been a constant theme in the IATA Legal Committee's work since 1946. In 1954 and 1955 IATA took an active part in the discussion which led to the signature of the Hague Protocol amending the Warsaw Convention. As IATA had feared, the Hague provision was considered inadequate by some states as a result of which, in 1966, international airlines operating to the United States entered into the so-called Montreal Agreement which increased passenger limits of liability to, from or via the United States. Recognizing that this Montreal Agreement is not a treaty and is therefore only an interim solution, IATA has supplied ICAO with detailed proposals for a revision of the Warsaw/Hague system.

The Legal Committee has also given continuing attention to the Rome Convention which deals with air carriers' liability for damage caused by aircraft in flight or by objects falling from such aircraft. Some of IATA's recommendations were taken into account when the Rome Convention of 1933 was revised in 1952. Another treaty which has had the continuing attention of the Legal Committee of IATA is the 1963 Tokyo Convention concerning offenses committed aboard aircraft.

The old IATA reached agreement on standard conditions of carriage —something which has so far eluded the new IATA. On the other hand, the Legal Committee of the new IATA was successful in developing uniform conditions of contract for incorporation in the passenger ticket and airwaybill. These were approved by all governments concerned, as were amendments in 1967–1968.

Some long-standing legal problems will assume new importance in the 1970s. Some of these relate to agreements between airlines for the joint use or interchange of aircraft, spare parts, and maintenance services. Such arrangements are becoming more common and it will be desirable to standardize as far as possible those terms which deal with respective liability of the airlines involved with the traveling public or shippers. Such problems as aircraft noise and sonic boom will become more acute and undoubtedly bring lawsuits and new legal principles in train.

The work of the Legal Committee is accomplished by airline lawyers trained in one or the other of two fundamentally different legal systems (Anglo Saxon and Civil Code), speaking three IATA official languages and any number of mother tongues. The practical incentives toward compromise and agreement are fortunately real and influential. Moreover, the intellectual atmosphere is congenial; airline lawyers, like their other IATA colleagues, have happily not been immune to the spirit of adventure, to the frame of mind which seeks to accomplish something which has never been done before.

Financial Committee

The area of concern of the Financial Committee is financial matters connected with international air transport, particularly the following:

- (i) Standardization of methods of rendering, verifying and settling accounts for revenue transactions as between Members;
- (ii) Clearing House;
- (iii) Insurance questions;
- (iv) Taxation, Audit Procedures, and Data Processing;
- (v) Statistical matters;
- (vi) Currency and Exchange Rate Matters;
- (vii) Potential financial and economic problems arising out of technological and other developments in air transport;
- (viii) Financial aspects of such other matters including matters proposed for consideration by other Committees and by Traffic Conferences as may be referred to it by the Executive Committee or the Director General.

Over the years, the airlines through the Financial Committee of IATA have been able to reconcile the financial and accounting systems developed independently in many parts of the world before carriers were extensively linked by the intercontinental routes. Standard Manuals of Revenue Accounting Practices have been agreed and published. Standard electronic data processing techniques have been adopted where appropriate.

One outstanding example of the airlines' cooperative work in the financial field is the IATA Clearing House, through which the airlines settle monthly accounts for interline revenue transactions. It enables them to collect and pay their worldwide inter-airline debts simultaneously by a single cash settlement and to do so either in dollars or convertible sterling regardless of the number of national currencies involved.

By offsetting accounts, the Clearing House eliminates the necessity for cash payment of all but a small amount (about 10%) of the total value of all monthly claims. It assures regular and punctual settlements of interline debts, eliminates much correspondence and other paper work, saves substantial foreign exchange expense, and, moreover, affords protection in the event of currency devaluations.

A good measure of the Clearing House's usefulness is provided by the two-way annual clearance totals, which have risen from an initial $10 million in 1947 to over $5.5 billion in 1970. The offset ratio consistently runs over 90%, which means that only 10% has to be settled in cash.

Medical Committee

The area of concern of the Medical Committee is the physiological, psychological, hygienic, and general medical aspects of all matters affecting the safety and efficiency of aircrew and passengers, in flight and at airports, and of all ground personnel, particularly the following:

- (i) Aircraft;
- (ii) Aircraft equipment;
- (iii) Accommodation;
- (iv) Water and food supplies;
- (v) Sewage disposal;
- (vi) Disinsectization;
- (vii) Quarantine;
- (viii) Immunization;
- (ix) And such other matters as may be referred to it by the Executive Committee.

Close liaison is maintained with the World Health Organization, with joint concern for such matters as sanitary water and food supplies for aircraft and preventing the spread of communicable diseases. Particular regard is paid by the committee to the transportation of infants, severely ill patients, and elderly persons; as a general rule it has been found that such persons may travel safely long distances by air, even at the speeds and altitudes of modern airline operation.

Traffic Advisory Committee

The Traffic Advisory Committee concerns itself, in a policy advisory capacity and subject to and consistent with the Provisions for the Regulation and Conduct of the Traffic Conferences, with all Traffic and Sales matters connected with international air transport, particularly the following:

(a) The matters set forth in Section IV of the Provisions for the Regulation and Conduct of the Traffic Conferences;
(b) Standardization of Traffic practices in the interests of promoting efficient, regular, and economical air transport service for the public;
(c) Creating and appointing such working groups, sub-committees, and rapporteurs as it may deem necessary as to Conference and other Traffic matters (not including postal, facilitation, or compliance machinery matters); deciding their terms of reference and to whom they shall report, and examining and evaluating the results of their activities;
(d) Appointing acting Traffic Conference Officers (except the Secretary, Traffic Conferences) to fill vacancies occurring between regular Fall meetings of the Traffic Conferences; and making interim appointments to fill vacancies and providing for substitutions of membership, between Traffic Conference meetings, on Sub-Committees and working groups created by the Traffic Conferences;
(e) Acting as a steering committee to the Conference(s) when in session; and
(f) Such other matters as may be referred to it by the Executive Committee or the Director General.

The preparation by the Traffic Department of uniform passenger tickets, baggage checks, and cargo airwaybills has previously been mentioned. Following such standard travel documents, came a multilateral form of interline traffic agreement which had the effect of bringing into one unit the services of member and even nonmember airlines throughout the world. Each of these steps has meant months, probably years, of work by IATA staff and expert sub-committees, including many meetings of legal and accounting experts, and final review by the Standing Committees concerned.

Likewise with respect to the approximately 16,000 IATA passenger agents previously mentioned, procedures have been developed over the years for the qualification and servicing of these many agents around the world, such as recording and reporting sales, remitting proceeds, and safeguarding ticket stocks.

IATA members saw the requirement for mechanization and computerization in the early 1950s. The first computer reservation system was placed in service in 1956. Such systems are now constantly being developed in the direction of automatic passenger and cargo handling.

As other examples of airline cooperation for the benefit of the traveling and shipping public, regulations for the carriage of restricted articles by air were approved worldwide some years ago, as was a standard container program.

Last, and certainly not least, the membership decided to organize "Traffic Conferences" somewhat on the old maritime pattern so that members could discuss fares and rates in their respective areas of interest, reach common positions if possible, and recommend any such positions to all governments concerned for their review and approval. The first Traffic Conferences were held in Rio de Janeiro in October 1947; at this time there were nine conferences—a number subsequently reduced to three. The U.S.-flag members of IATA were allowed to join these Traffic Conferences as a result of a proceeding and conditionally favorable decision by the Civil Aeronautics Board, Order No. 4525 dated 19 February 1946. (Matters pertaining to the carriage of air mail by U.S.-flag carriers were excluded from the approved jurisdiction of the Traffic Conferences.)

Traffic Conferences

Because the Traffic Conferences have been the most publicized and least understood feature of IATA's activity, the following clarification is offered.

The Conferences are autonomous bodies in which each participating member has a equal vote. A single negative vote can defeat any proposal. The delegates to the Traffic Conferences negotiate only for their own company and do not represent the industry in general.[8] IATA headquarters provides administrative and clerical support, both at meetings of the conferences and throughout the year. The Executive Committee, subject to government approvals, promulgates the rules and regulations for the conduct of Traffic Conferences.

It is sometimes asserted that IATA is a "cartel." In the accepted definition of a cartel, its members agree to limit production, allocate markets, and fix prices. Neither IATA nor the Traffic Conferences do any of these things. There are no discussions or agreements that would tend to limit production (capacity) or allocation of markets (routes) because these matters are arranged between governments, usually through bilateral

[8] It is often said in the press that "IATA does . . ." or "IATA decides . . .". IATA decides nothing at Traffic Conferences. The conferences themselves decide, subject to approval of all governments concerned.

agreements. There is no fixing of prices, because airline recommendations on fares and rates are subject to approval by all governments concerned.

Why do there have to be any agreements on fares and rates at all? Fundamentally, scheduled air transportation is a business affected with the public interest and inherently subject to regulation. Transportation economics are such that limited entry and price stabilization are unavoidable. But specifically, international law as far back as 1919 (in the Paris Convention) has specified that each nation has complete control over its own airspace; it can admit or exclude anybody it wants. It can fix the terms and conditions under which airlines will be allowed to enter and leave its territory, and this includes control of fares and rates.

In theory, this would require complicated negotiations between governments so that, for example, fares across the Atlantic to Ireland, London, Paris, Brussels, Amsterdam, Frankfurt, Vienna, and Rome would bear a reasonable relationship to each other, would be economic, and would not be discriminatory as between one destination or class of traffic and another. Having neither the specialized staff nor the financial responsibility for negotiating fares and rates in such detail, most governments over the years have officially delegated this chore, in the first instance, to the Traffic Conferences, retaining for themselves the right to approve or disapprove Conference recommendations.

At present, there are three IATA Traffic Conference Areas. One comprises the Western Hemisphere; the second, Europe and Africa; the third, the Orient and Australasia. Composite Conferences deal with fares and rates across the borders between two areas, and with worldwide agreements. The difficulty of reaching a consensus between scores of airlines—some large, some small—some directly concerned and some only indirectly—each with the same single vote and the right to veto—cannot be exaggerated. The fact that agreements have been reached and government approvals granted in so many cases over a period of 25 years shows what can be accomplished on an international scale, given goodwill and the commercial incentive. At this writing, when the North Atlantic fares are under discussion, the conference machinery is subject to unusual stress. A recession in international travel has created economic difficulties for the airlines. The cut-rate nonscheduled charter operators have cut deeply into scheduled airline traffic. There may be an interval on the North Atlantic of severe rate-cutting, but to suggest, as some have, that tariff problems of this type could spell the "demise of IATA" has no basis. As should be evident, the many other functions of the Association would be as essential as ever and would continue regardless of any open rate situation in the Conference areas.

Before leaving the Traffic Conference machinery, mention must be made of the Enforcement (now called Compliance) section which is administered by IATA headquarters. The airlines are under an obligation to the governments with which they have filed tariffs to see that such tariffs are in fact those charged the traveling public, without discrimination. Likewise, they have a duty to each other to apply the approved tariffs because they are at the very heart of the economic forecasts and financial results of each member. From the earlier days of the Traffic Conferences, there has been a group of IATA enforcement officers under the direction of a Chief Enforcement Officer. Their function has been to detect evidence of malpractice on the part of members. Cases of malpractice are brought to a Breaches Commission which, after hearing the evidence and argument, issues a judgment. The early commissions were made up of three members, one man of legal training as chairman, and two experts from traffic departments. In later years, the duty of Commissioner devolved upon one man only, of legal training, and he has had the full power to exonerate the accused or to assess various penalties up to $25,000 for each single offense.

The enforcement machinery has faced perennial major challenges, particularly those occasioned by differences in regional commercial practices, financial circumstances, and degree of management sophistication. It will continue to be needed as long as the airlines and the governments concerned are able to agree on binding tariff regimes.

REFLECTIONS

What was it like at the Stevens Hotel, when the historic Chicago Conference convened there in November 1944?

The war was still on. The representatives from such countries as France, the Netherlands, Belgium, and Poland came from governments-in-exile, mostly based in London. In Britain as on the Continent everyone was suffering from shortages of housing, fuel, food, and clothing. It is almost a miracle that some of the delegations were able to be there at all, much less holding firm government instructions. In fact, a delegation was apparently enroute to Chicago from the Soviet Union when its orders were cancelled and it had to return to Moscow.

There seem to have been virtually non-stop meetings in the vast Stevens Hotel, so many and so protracted that some of the delegates are reputed never to have left the hotel during the month-long Conference. If they did get outside they long talked about Chicago's cold, bitter winter winds.

A few of the nations came prepared with strong and well-publicized positions on civil air policy. Prominent among these were the United States, the United Kingdom, Canada, New Zealand, and Australia. Britain, a great pioneer in civil aviation, was fearful that its future opportunities would be handicapped because it had built fighter aircraft during the war while the United States had concentrated on building transport aircraft for itself and the Allies. France, the Netherlands, and Belgium reflected on their distinguished aviation traditions and worried about how to "get back on the line" when the war was ended.

Even the then civil aviation policy of the United States Government, loosely "freedom of the air," did not enjoy the unanimous support of the U.S.-flag airline community. Pan American World Airways, which had pioneered the United States' international routes from 1927 to 1941, feared that such a policy of non-regulation would be detrimental to the United States, if implemented. Most of the U.S. domestic airlines proceeded on the basis that such a policy would aid them in their newly-discovered aspirations to fly abroad.

To all, it was evident that the American and European international airlines would at last confront and parallel each other, which had not been the case in the prewar years. Only in 1937 had Pan American and Imperial Airways commenced infrequent flights between New York and Bermuda—and only briefly in 1939 had they done so across the Atlantic.

Given these conditions, it is remarkable that the government delegates were able to agree upon the Chicago Convention, and their airline advisers to agree upon the draft Articles of Association for the new IATA.

En route to Havana for the IATA Organization Meeting in April 1945, the IATA delegates received the word of President Franklin Roosevelt's death and Mr. Truman's accession as President. The dropping of the atomic bomb was still to come. And yet, as the delegates sat debating and finally signing the Articles of the new IATA in front of the open windows of the Hotel Nacional, with the gentle Caribbean breezes stirring in the palms, this writer sensed a degree of harmony and optimism which promised well for the new days just ahead.

Those present at Havana, and at the first General Meeting the same year in Montreal, were largely professional men—executives, pilots, engineers, lawyers, marketers, and financial experts. Most of them felt strongly that their embryonic airlines existed to serve the public and make money, not to be pawns in political games. From their pre-War operations across Europe and India to the Far East, across the Pacific to the Orient, from the United States to South America and Africa, they had already glimpsed the vision of a self-supporting, coordinated, worldwide scheduled air transport system. Whether from the technical or the marketing point of view, they already saw that any attempt by a single airline to "go it alone" would be impractical.

Given the composition of IATA, the origins and ownerships of the members, and the political systems at home, it was crystal clear that discussions of politics, national rivalries, and systems of government should be taboo in IATA. They have largely been so. Both Arab and Israeli airlines are Active Members of IATA, yet Middle East differences have usually been expressed in IATA in diplomatic and nondisruptive ways, such as abstention from voting or temporary absence from the room. A deviation from the no-politics rule was attempted at the Annual General Meeting in Rome in October 1963 when some of the IATA members from Africa proposed sanctions against the IATA member airlines from South Africa and Portugal. Some lively debate ensued on the floor of the Assembly, in the course of which it was observed that if IATA had not long since taken a firm policy stand against the discussion of political matters, there would have been no IATA still in existence where the current members could be making their speeches. The crisis was surmounted as a result of private conversations and an agreement to defer certain issues to the next Annual Meeting. Basically, however, the point was successfully made that IATA was not the place in which to contest international rivalries or conflicts and that IATA could not long survive any effort to do so.

These founders of the new IATA, what kind of men were they? They were talented, joyful in their work. Veterans of World War I or World War II, they were wedded to the concept of using aircraft in peaceful commerce. Having struggled successfully against balky engines, dangerous weather, and leaky finances for so many years, they rarely lost their optimism. Accustomed to fighting for business in the marketplace, they nevertheless knew from experience that any public transportation enterprise must somehow be regulated in the public interest. Still more, they shared the soaring spirit of the pioneer flying man himself—his taste for adventure—his striving to see the earth as a whole (the way the astronauts later saw it)—his determination to surmount disappointments, obstacles, and perils.

That was the spirit of 1945. Did it change very much up to 1970? Very little, particularly considering the enormous growth of the industry. The scale of annual revenues went for some companies from 1 million in the 1930s to 100 million to 1,000 million dollars in what seemed an amazingly brief period to those who lived it. Flight speeds went from 100 miles per hour to 150, to 300, and then to 550 (the jets). Passenger capacities per aircraft grew from 12 to 44 to 89 to 160 to almost 400. Most of the men managed to grow too. Because they did, IATA did.

REFERENCES

(1) "The Right to Fly" by John C. Cooper (New York: Henry Holt & Company, 1947).
(2) "Aeronautical Statutes and Related Material" published by U.S. Civil Aeronautics Board June 1970. Superintendent of Documents, U.S. Government Printing Office, Washington, D.C. 20402.
(3) "IATA News Review" 1969. These and other IATA documents can be obtained from the Public Relations Department, International Air Transport Association, 1155 Mansfield Street, Montreal 113, P.Q., Canada, and P.O. Box 315, 1215 Geneva 15 Airport, Switzerland.

John Stuart MacDonald
Department of Sociology and Psychology
Chelsea College, University of London

Leatrice D. MacDonald
Institute of Latin American Studies
University of London

JOBS AND HOUSING: ALTERNATIVE DEVELOPMENTS IN THE VENEZUELAN GUAYANA*

The appraisal of development projects is often complicated by the fact that they rarely occur in isolation. In Latin America, the effectiveness of public housing programs and the reactions of the people involved are, as a rule, bound up with the whole complex of heterogeneous developments we call "urbanization." And when public housing reaches the villages, it typically goes hand in hand with agrarian reform. This is generally the case in Venezuela, where large public housing schemes have been in operation since 1958.

Consequently it is difficult to disentangle and then evaluate the impact of industrialization per se from social infrastructure development in the towns, or agrarian reform per se from social infrastructure development in the villages. The Guayana region of Venezuela is one of the few areas where a production-oriented project and a social welfare project have operated discretely, but within a uniform socioeconomic context.

The Guayana is in the southeastern part of Venezuela beyond Ciudad Bolívar. It remained outside the modern sector until after World War II.[1] The large iron mines and loading facilities at the confluence of

* Fieldwork and data processing for this paper were supported by the Corporación Venezolana de Guayana, the Housing and Productivity Program (UCLA), the Institute of Social and Economic Studies (UWI), and the Joint Center for Urban Studies (Harvard/MIT).

[1] The eastern Venezuelan oilfields, started in the mid-1930s, were all above the Orinoco; and most, if not all, of the pipelines and transshipment facilities led away from the Venezuelan Guayana. Iron mining was started in a small way by Bethlehem Steel in the Orinoco Delta on the eve of World War II, when it was

the Caroní and Orinoco rivers were not started until 1952, when the old market town on the site held 5,000 inhabitants.[2] The wedge of economic development driving south from the Caroní-Orinoco junction was strengthened by the national steel mill, started in 1956 and put into production in 1961, when the population reached 42,000. In the same year, the settlements formed around the plants were named Ciudad Guayana and came under a presidential regional development authority, the CVG,[3] which started urban public works and public housing. Until 1966, when the population exceeded 70,000,[4] all the public housing and most of the social infrastructure in Ciudad Guayana went to the minority of executives, professionals, and technicians whom the development and private corporations brought in from Venezuela's modern sector and from abroad.

By contrast, in the adjoining counties of Piar and Roscio, the only notable change until 1960 was the improvement of the highway which led to the outside world, past Ciudad Guayana. This did little more for

suspended. Small-scale gold and nickel mining in the countries of Piar and Roscio continued at a slow pace after the gold rush to the southeast in the last century.

2 Bethlehem Steel resumed iron mining in 1948, when it moved operations up the Orinoco to what became Ciudad Guayana. However, iron mining only assumed massive proportions when U.S. Steel built its main camp there in 1952, dwarfing the pre-existing village of San Félix.

3 Corporación Venezolana de Guayana. For its program, see: CVG, *Informes Anuales* (Caracas: occasional); *Guayana* (Caracas: 1963); *The Guayana Economic Program* (Caracas: 1966); *The Guayana Region* (Caracas: 1963); *Plan de desarrollo urbano* (Caracas: 1966).

J. Friedman, *Regional Development Policy* (Cambridge: MIT, 1969).

N. McGinn and R. Davis, *Build A Mill, Build A City, Build A School* (Cambridge: MIT, 1969).

L. Rodwin and Associates, *Planning Urban Growth and Regional Development* (Cambridge: MIT, 1969).

4 For demographic perspectives, see: Banco Central de Venezuela, *Encuesta sobre ocupacion y desempleo en Santo Tome de Guayana* (Caracas: mimeo., 1962). 5 vols.

Banco Central de Venezuela, *Encuesta Sobre características demográficas, etc.* (Caracas: mimeo., 1965). 2 Vols.

C. Chen, *Movimientos migratorios en Venezuela* (Caracas: Universidad Católica Andrés Bello, 1968).

Dirección General de Estadística, *Encuesta regional de hogares por muestra Ciudad Guayana* (Caracas: Ministerio de Fomento, 1968).

J.S. MacDonald, "Anticipating City Growth," *World Population Conference 1965 Belgrade* (New York: United Nations, 1967). Vol. III, section B.5.

J.S. MacDonald, "Componentes de la urbanización en una nueva ciudad," *Conferencia Regional Latinoamericana De Población 1970 Mexico* (Liège/Santiago: IUSSP/ECLA, in press).

J.S. MacDonald, "The Social Demography of A New City," *International Union for the Scientific Study of Population 1967 Sydney* (Bangkok/Liege: ECAFE/IUSSP, 1968).

L.D. MacDonald, "Motives And Objectives Of Migration," *Social and Economic Studies,* 17(4), Dec. 1968.

the inhabitants than facilitate their migration to the steel town and beyond. The economic base remained shifting cultivation, extensive cattle ranching and diamond prospecting, supplemented by fishing, riverboat work, and smuggling.[5] These had also been the customary occupations in the area of Ciudad Guayana.

The big change for Piar and Roscio came in 1960 when the government's Vivienda Rural program[6] rapidly introduced public housing for peasants—in greater density, relative to a population of 65,000, than in other parts of Venezuela. During the period from 1960 to 1965, 10,000 people were accommodated in 2,000 Vivienda Rural houses in Piar and Roscio. The program there was distinctive in not being accompanied by the social benefits or land reform which usually went with it in other parts of Venezuela. So these two counties present an extraordinary opportunity for isolating the effects of improved housing on rural development, since, in other cases, improved housing is typically accompanied by a set of other developments, often the whole urbanization complex.

The effect of heavy industrial development from the contiguous area of Ciudad Guayana is also clear. The main effect was to pull migrants from Piar and Roscio. There was a net migration balance of 7,000 from 1960 to 1965.[7] The steel town, being very recent and highly concentrated in large enterprises, had very slight multiplier or secondary effects on its neighbors, other than pushing up consumer prices, including the prices of the large component of consumption brought to the villages from the modern sector in the north of Venezuela. Commuting from the villages,

---

[5] For socioeconomic background on the hinterland, see: CVG, *Reconocimiento agropecuario forestal del Oriente de La Guayana Venezuela.* (Caracas: Ministerio de Agricultura y Cría, 1961). Vol. VI.

D. Fairchild, "Report On El Palmar 1962" (Cambridge/Caracas: CVG/Joint Center for Urban Studies, mimeo).

K. Schwerin, *Oil and Steel* (Los Angeles: UCLA, 1966).

J.S. MacDonald, "Identifying Types Of Rural SocioEconomic Structure," *Community Development And Local Government 1968 Port-of-Spain* (Santiago: ECLA, 1969).

Mission IRFED, "Région De Guayana," Rapport Annexe *Pour Un Développement Equilibré et Harmonisé Du Venezuela.* (Caracas: CORDIPLAIN, Mimeo., 1965?).

[6] See Appendix I. Also:

Banco Obrero, *1965 Politica De Vivienda B.O.* (Caracas B.O., 1965)

Dirección de Malariología, *Programa Nacional de Vivienda Rural* (Caracas: Ministerio de la Sanidad, 1966).

División de Vivienda Rural, Dirección de Malariología, "Campaña del Programa de Vivienda Rural," *Congreso Católico Internacional de Vida Rural* (Caracas: mimeo., 1961).

[7] Source: J.S. MacDonald, sample survey of 600 household heads in Cd. Guayana 1965, unpublished tabulations.

as an alternative to migration to Ciudad Guayana, was not feasible until a new road was opened in 1966. But Ciudad Guayana suffered a severe housing shortage, so there was rarely anything better than shanties for the accommodation of rural migrants. Only in 1966 was the first public housing for the poor and unskilled opened in the steel town.

The housing and industrialization programs were designed and administered from Caracas by remote control with little feedback over a distance of 300 air-miles. What did the Guayanese people think of these intrusions? How did they choose between old and new, social development and economic development? Was the official priority on village housing an instance of misplaced paternalism? How important was housing compared to other consumption or investment preferences? Did the generation of industrial employment override rural social development which was not accompanied by increased cash income?

Ciudad Guayana and the rural counties of Piar and Roscio provide, from 1960 to 1965, one of the rare opportunities in which "quasi-experimental" comparisons can be made in answer to these questions. Groups in three contrasting development situations can be compared: first, the migrants in the new urban development area with industrial employment, but only improvised shanty accommodations; second, the rural hinterland's people who received modern public housing, but little more than a bare agricultural livelihood; and, third, their fellow villagers who had attached themselves neither to the industrial sector nor the welfare state. This third category, some 45,000 villagers remaining without public housing at the end of the Vivienda Rural program in 1965, serves as benchmark.

The three categories provided not only real alternatives from which the village people could choose, but also they were clear alternatives: migrants in Ciudad Guayana averaged 60% more cash income than Vivienda Rural recipients, and 80% more than villagers without public housing; these differentials were not canceled out by rents in the city; migrants and nonmigrants were conscious of the disparity; and they believed that it would continue into the distant future.

To see how and why they did move among these three possibilities, interviews were taken at the end of 1965 with 200 household heads in three sample strata: 100 in Ciudad Guayana who had migrated from Piar and Roscio between 1960 and 1965; 50 who had remained in Piar and Roscio, but had received a Vivienda Rural house; and 50 residents of Piar and Roscio who had remained in traditional dwellings.[8]

---

[8] For details of sampling procedure, see Appendix II.

To identify aspirations and preferences with a basis in concrete experiences, questions were asked about the turning points in the housing history of the 200 informants. Each informant's house was classified under one of three objective categories: Vivienda Rural house; Standard private house; and Substandard private house. Table 1 shows the three sample strata cross-classified by dwelling type.

TABLE 1

House Type	*Cd. Guayana* %	*Hinterland* %
Vivienda Rural	–	50
Standard Private	31	11
Substandard Private	69	39

Note: Only differences of 10% or more are statistically significant and meaningful in all the tables.

The number of rural people in standard private houses was negligible, but nearly one-third of the city people had already moved up from shanty conditions, in no more than six years in Ciudad Guayana. For the migrant, greater employment in the modern sector and higher income had already been translated into better accommodation. Were it not for the Vivienda Rural program, only one-fifth of the villagers would have risen above shanties. Migrants to Ciudad Guayana also typically came from shanties; only 9 percent had come from Vivienda Rural houses.

Informants were asked to compare their present dwelling with their previous dwelling in terms of an overall appraisal, as demonstrated in Table 2. The risk that the passage of time would distort recollections was controlled because the samples of urban residents and Vivienda Rural occupants were drawn only from people who had migrated or moved within the interval 1960–1965.

TABLE 2

GENERAL COMPARISON OF PRESENT AND PREVIOUS DWELLING

Preference	*Cd. Guayana*		*Vivienda Rural*	*Other Rural*
	All Housing	*Substandard*		
	%	%	%	%
This house better	62	40	92	68
This house same	3	2	2	3
This house worse	36	58	6	30

Note: The column captions refer to present housing type. For Cd. Guayana residents, the previous dwelling used as reference for comparison is the last dwelling before Piar and Roscio. For Vivienda Rural occupants, the previous dwelling was private substandard.

For either urban or rural residents, a change of dwelling was an improvement, as a rule. This varied, however, among the sample strata in the direction one would expect, as Table 2 indicates. Vivienda Rural recipients stated overwhelmingly that their move was an improvement. One-third of privately housed informants, in city and country, felt that they had effected no improvement by moving. There is not much difference between one rural hut and another; and city shanties are as miserable as village huts. Villagers without government housing were, on balance, in favor of their present dwelling, as were the migrants to the city. Neither of these sample strata considered the move as advantageous as the Vivienda Rural recipients. Since so many migrants to Ciudad Guayana did achieve better housing in less than six years, this may seem inconsistent. However, the objectively modern standard houses achieved by one-third of the city residents were surrounded by appalling slums which depreciated them in the eyes of migrants from even the poorest villages. This speaks well for the Vivienda Rural program. Also the fact that only 9% of migrants to Ciudad Guayana had previously lived in Vivienda Rural houses shows that the great majority of people in Piar and Roscio actively supported the program by not abandoning it.

TABLE 3

SPECIFIC COMPARISONS OF PRESENT AND PREVIOUS DWELLING
PROPORTIONS DECLARING PRESENT BETTER

Specific Comparison	*Cd. Guayana* %	*Vivienda Rural* %	*Other Rural* %
Size	57	88	67
Floors	45	56	46
Walls	35	81	35
Roof	34	94	41
Toilet	38	67	39
Kitchen	41	69	35
Water Supply	50	46	48
Electricity	44	33	35
Rooms—No.	44	94	54
Bedrooms—No.	43	94	56

Note: For Cd. Guayana residents, the previous dwelling used as reference is the last dwelling before migrating from Piar and Roscio.

Table 3 shows that Ciudad Guayana residents were inclined to prefer the size of their present dwelling. No other item was thought to be a decided improvement. As a separate substratum, urban shanty dwellers made invidious comparisons of all ten characteristics. The Vivienda Rural recipients held that eight out of ten of their new home's characteristics were superior, especially the walls and roof, the toilet and kitchen, as well as the size and rooms. The Vivienda Rural program, however, had failed to install electricity or piped water in accordance with the official plan. This complaint is reflected in the low scores for these items. Villagers without government housing were satisfied on fewer counts. They preferred their present dwelling's size, particularly the larger rooms and larger bedrooms.

TABLE 4

PRESENT HOUSING FEATURE EVALUATION: POSITIVE
WHAT DO YOU LIKE BEST ABOUT PRESENT DWELLING?

Preferences	*Cd. Guayana* %	*Vivienda Rural* %	*Other Rural* %
Size	–	26	17
Clean-hygienic	–	26	–
Ownership	–	–	12
Site	24	–	19
Coolness	15	–	15
Everything	–	10	–

Note: Categories which were not given 10% of informants' preferences are not included.

In Table 4, the Vivienda Rural occupants were most emphatic about their preference for the size and cleanliness of their new homes. In fact the rural public housing program aimed to exclude the vermin and insects which are vectors of Chagas disease, and also to provide a less attractive habitat for malaria mosquitoes. Perhaps villagers did not all comprehend this payoff. But the houses are easy to keep clean, having cement floors, pantry, laundry, and (in theory, as well as sometimes in practice) shower and septic tank—a complex of refinements rare even in modern standard village houses. For this reason, only Vivienda Rural occupants expressed complete satisfaction in a considerable number of cases.

City residents and the other rural stratum were most satisfied with the location and coolness of their new dwelling. For city residents, location, away from the worst slums, the vice districts, and areas subject to flooding, is an important consideration which is not an issue in the low-density villages. Also, in the city it is important to be near work or near the bus and jitney cab lines. In city as well as country, however, coolness and location in the path of breezes are major considerations. Each Vivienda Rural house is built on the site of its recipient's former shanty, so the trouble with its location is that old shade trees were cut down during construction. Lack of shade compounds the poor ventilation due to the compact construction and lack of the traditional front porch.

The villagers in private housing confirmed their preferences for the independence and equity in property which they retained by refusing the offer of a Vivienda Rural house. The Vivienda Rural program gives no equity for at least five years. Ownership was not an issue in the city before 1966, because there was no urban public housing open to these migrants at that time and they rarely paid rent.

TABLE 5

PREVIOUS HOUSING FEATURE EVALUATION: POSITIVE
WHAT DO YOU LIKE BEST ABOUT PREVIOUS DWELLING?

Preferences	*Cd. Guayana* %	*Vivienda Rural* %	*Other Rural* %
Size	11	12	19
Ownership	–	12	–
Site	16	12	–
Coolness	23	26	17
Garden	13	–	10
Piped Water	–	10	–
Nothing	–	12	14

In Table 5, more invidious comparisons were made between present Vivienda Rural housing and previous dwelling than in the case of city or country residents without government housing. The only point not made by the Vivienda Rural stratum was the question of the kitchen garden because it remained the same as before construction. Both city residents and Vivienda Rural occupants emphasized the coolness of their former dwellings. The shanties of Ciudad Guayana are often badly placed to catch a breeze, have no shade trees, no open porch, and are made of hot corrugated metal sheets. The huts in the villages are made of cooler wattle-and-daub.

TABLE 6

PRESENT HOUSING FEATURE EVALUATION: NEGATIVE
WHAT DO YOU DISLIKE MOST ABOUT PRESENT DWELLING?

Criticisms	*Cd. Guayana* %	*Vivienda Rural* %	*Other Rural* %
Heat	12	–	–
Size	–	12	14
Lack of Water	22	12	14
Lack of Electricity	–	12	–
Don't dislike	–	16	19

Only Vivienda Rural occupants complained particularly about the lack of piped water because the other two sample strata were never led to believe they would receive it. They too complained again about not obtaining equity in their homes until they had paid five years' installments on the mortgage. (The fact that they had to repay only half the cost of construction without interest over thirty years was not taken into account.) Ownership, legal or de facto, is the rule among the Ciudad Guayana residents and privately housed villagers, who are practically all squatters. Ground or house rent is extremely rare in Ciudad Guayana or the villages. City residents expressed no regret at forfeiting their old village kitchen garden because there is a traditional disdain for agriculture. The land dwindles into insignificance compared to modern sector wages. Yet city residents did not commit themselves wholeheartedly to suffering the urban housing shortage and the messiness of the slums: they did not say that there were no good points about the village dwellings they left behind.

According to Table 6, Vivienda Rural occupants were more precise in complaining about their present accommodation than the other two sample strata. They singled out the small size of the public housing units and lack of water and electricity. All three sample strata complained about the lack of piped water, most strongly in Ciudad Guayana. Only there, also, were complaints about the heat emphasized. Moreover, it was only the city residents who did not state "nothing to dislike" about their present dwelling.

TABLE 7

PREVIOUS HOUSING FEATURE EVALUATION: NEGATIVE
WHAT DO YOU DISLIKE MOST ABOUT PREVIOUS DWELLING?

Criticisms	*Cd. Guayana* %	*Vivienda Rural* %	*Other Rural* %
No Ownership	–	–	14
Wattle-and-Daub	–	12	–
Lack of Water	26	14	14
Don't dislike	10	10	25

Lack of water figured again among all three sample strata in Table 7, which identifies complaints about previous dwellings. City residents laid greatest stress on the water problem in their villages, to the exclusion of any other housing problems there. Neither the migrants nor the Vivienda Rural occupants referred to problems of not owning their previous residence because this is no great issue in poor private housing. But, to the villagers still without government housing, the ambiguities of squatting and imprecise customary obligations to landlords were still grounds for invidious comparisons. Only the Vivienda Rural people disparaged the wattle-and-daub construction of their old huts. City people normally use corrugated metal sheets for their shanties, because it is quicker to erect and dismantle, but wattle-and-daub is cooler. Those living in metal shanties probably did not realize that wattle-and-daub harbors vectors of Chagas disease.

Table 8 gives the accumulated total of percentages for the number of times a housing feature was mentioned as being advantageous or disadvantageous in the informant's present or previous dwelling. These scores give a crude indication of the importance informants attached to them.

TABLE 8

FOCI OF CONCERN: CUMULATIVE SCORES FROM TABLES 4–7

Positive and Negative Preferences	*Cd. Guayana*	*Vivienda Rural*	*Other Rural*	*3 Strata Combined*
Size	11	*50*	*50*	*111*
Cleanliness-Hygiene	–	26	–	26
Ownership	–	12	26	38
Site	*40*	12	19	71
Coolness	*50*	26	32	*108*
Garden	13	–	10	23
Water	*48*	36	28	*112*
Electricity	–	12	–	12
Wattle-and-Daub	–	12	–	12

Key: In each stratum's column, opposite each housing feature, are the summed percentages from Tables 4–7. For example, Cd. Guayana residents gave the following percentages against the following percentages against the feature "Size": 0% (4), 11% (5), 0% (6) and 0% (7). Similarly, Other Rural villagers gave the following percentages against the feature "Wattle-and-Daub": 0% (4), 0% (5), 0% (6) and 0% (7). The numbers in italics are the most salient.

In Ciudad Guayana, heat-breeze-coolness and piped water supply were of top priority, followed closely by the site of a dwelling. In Vivienda Rural housing, the focus was on the size of a dwelling as it was among villagers without government housing. Altogether, piped water supply, size, and heat-breeze-coolness were outstanding concerns.

Having obtained a fairly detailed outline of the current balance of housing satisfactions, dissatisfactions, and preferences, we designed the next series of questions to ascertain the place of housing in the hierarchy of consumption and investment priorities. Informants were asked how they would expend a large imaginary windfall of Bs. 20,000 (U.S. $4,000), and a smaller one of Bs. 5,000 (U.S. $1,100). Respondents were to imagine spending all the money, in any way they wished, and given up to five free choices for expending each sum.

The responses were tabulated in: (a) a simple frequency distribution of choices; and (b) a weighted frequency distribution of choices' priorities, the extent to which particular items were given preference. In fact, (a) and (b) showed practically no difference. That is, the choices cited most often were also typically mentioned first.

TABLE 9

DISTRIBUTION OF BS. 20,000

Broad Choices	*Cd. Guayana* %	*Vivienda Rural* %	*Other Rural* %
Housing	42.9	32.0	26.8
Business	15.8	16.0	18.8
Education	10.1	12.0	10.9
Agriculture	8.5	14.4	22.8
Savings	8.1	11.2	5.9

Residents of Ciudad Guayana expressed eighteen preferences for spending their money, as shown in Table 9. "A new house" received 25% of all choices made by urban residents. "Establishing or expanding a business" received 16% of choices, and expenditure for "education," 10%.

These three items accounted for over 50% of all choices made. Adding "household furnishings" (8%), "fixing up the house" (6%), "enlarging the house" (0.4%), and "paying off the house" (1%) to the figure for a new house, nearly half of urban choices (43%) related to housing. The only other items with any piling of choices were for "agriculture" (9%), for "savings" (8%), and for "helping relatives" (5%).

The urban poor could realistically choose agricultural investments on a small scale, because the built-up areas of Ciudad Guayana are discontinuous, permitting small family plots in the slums. There is very little re-migration back to villages, and practically no buying of farmland. The city is their future, they declare, and a kitchen garden is the only sign of nostalgia for agriculture.

These choices show that the migrants aspire to a good house with a kitchen garden, or a small kiosk stocking tinned goods and soft drinks, and advancement through education. These realistic measures of independence from the fluctuations of the labor market, also reflect a desire for self-employment, since even poor Guayanese consider continual manual wage labor degrading.

The infrequency of "aid to kin" as an expenditure reflects the relative weakness of kinship and family structures, not only in the city but also in the villages. Elaborate weddings and dowries are foreign to the common folk in the Guayana. The kinship system is most informal and the *compadrazgo* system is very weak there by Latin American standards.

Rural respondents in private housing made seventeen kinds of choices. These were dissimilar to those made by the urban sample. No preference was given to "a car," "saving money to get married," "paying off debts," or "paying off the house," categories mentioned by the urban informants. They did choose expenditures not on the urban list: "health," "migration," "giving up work," and "travel."

Expenditure for "agriculture" (23%) almost tied for first place with housing among these people, partly because the traditional slash-and-burn shifting agriculture necessitates frequent moves from one minimal shelter to another and excludes more substantial houses or a shop.

"A new house" (20%) also tied with "establishing a business" (19%). These first three choices accounted for well over half (65%) of all preferences expressed.

Even when all the specific categories of expenditure for housing were aggregated, they acounted for only 27% among the villagers in traditional housing. The expenditures for business, education, savings, and helping relatives were practically the same as for urban residents. In effect, significant differences appeared only in the areas of housing and agriculture.

Rural respondents in government housing made sixteen types of choices. In contrast to urban residents as well as to other rural residents, none of this group selected "diversions" (women, gambling, drinking), "gifts to the church," or "helping relatives." Yet Vivienda Rural occupants made no choices not made by either urban residents or the other rural residents. Vivienda Rural residents selected "health" and "migration," items not chosen by urban respondents. Compared to other rural residents, Vivienda Rural residents cited "a car," "paying debts," and "paying off the house" as special choices.

The first choice for expenditure among Vivienda Rural occupants was "paying off the house" (19%). "Business" received 16% of the votes; and "agriculture," 14%. These first three choices were half of all choices made.

In this stratum less emphasis was given to new housing, although 32% of all choices involved housing. The sizable number of preferences for "paying off the house" indicates the residents' responsibility for their debts to the housing authority and willingness to remain in the Vivienda Rural house, at least until it is paid for.

Vivienda Rural experience has not increased educational aspirations. However, the beneficiaries of the welfare state chose "savings" twice as often as other rural respondents, suggesting that they have a strong orientation to the future. This may be due to the stronger family stability fostered by the housing program. In any case, these respondents are acquainted with banks, simply because of their continuing relationship with the housing program. Repeated negotiations with Vivienda Rural functionaries also add sophistication to their dealings with the outside world.

Vivienda Rural respondents chose "housing," "business," and "education" as often as other rural people. However, they scarcely chose "agriculture" more often than migrants did, showing that they too have turned their backs on farming, even modern farming. Compared to urban respondents, they laid less total stress on housing because their housing needs were being met.

Residents of Ciudad Guayana made fifteen choices for expending Bs. 5,000, as Table 10 shows. "A new house" accounted for 37%, more than twice as many as the next highest preference. "Establishing a business" and "fixing up the house" were the next most frequent items. The first three choices accounted for well over half the preferences (65%).

When all items pertaining to housing were grouped, they accounted for over half of the migrants' choices (56%). The smaller hypothetical windfall tended to limit choices to major areas since "savings," "agriculture," and "education" received few responses.

TABLE 10

DISTRIBUTION OF Bs. 5,000

Broad Choices	*Cd. Guayana* %	*Vivienda Rural* %	*Other Rural* %
Housing	55.7	50.1	23.1
Business	16.8	12.1	24.4
Agriculture	5.3	15.4	20.5

Rural residents in private housing made twelve types of choices. Principal expenditure was on "business" (24%), with "agriculture" (21%) and "new housing" (13%) coming next. These three items accounted for over half (58%) of all choices made. When all housing choices were grouped, they equaled 23%, about the same proportion as for the other two major choices.

Rural residents without government housing chose "health" and "travel," items not on the urban list. "Clothing" and "normal household expenditures," received 6% in each case. These expenditures were not mentioned when a prize of Bs. 20,000 was proposed.

Rural residents in government housing made fourteen types of choices for spending Bs. 5,000. The principal expenditure was for "paying off the house" (28%). "Agriculture" (15%) and "business" (13%) were the other main items. These three accounted for over half of all choices. All housing items together accounted for half of all choices made.

Vivienda Rural recipients chose "migration," and "enlarging the house," items not selected by urban or other rural residents. There were no choices made for "diversions," "gifts to the church," or "gifts to charity," items which appeared in the urban selections. There were no choices made for "health" or "travel," items appearing on the other rural list.

Housing was more important to urban residents than any other item, and more important to them than to rural residents. Rural residents in private housing divided their expenditure equally among three major items, with more devoted to business and agriculture (and less to housing) than either of the other groups. Vivienda Rural residents shared with urban residents a predominant interest in housing, although they focused more on paying off their house, while migrants wanted new housing.

Table 11 indicates that, for either sum, the major concerns remained housing, business, or agriculture. Savings and education lost significance when Bs. 5,000 was considered.

TABLE 11

COMPARISON OF DISPOSITION OF BS. 20,000 AND BS. 5,000

Broad Choices	*Cd. Guayana* %		*Vivienda Rural* %		*Other Rural* %	
	Bs. 20,000	*Bs. 5,000*	*Bs. 20,000*	*Bs. 5,000*	*Bs. 20,000*	*Bs. 5,000*
Housing	42.9	55.7	32.0	50.1	26.8	23.1
Business	15.8	16.8	16.0	12.1	18.8	24.4
Agriculture	8.5	5.3	14.4	15.4	22.8	20.5
Education	10.1	3.1	12.0	9.0	10.9	7.7
Savings	8.1	5.3	11.2	5.1	5.9	3.8

The most traditional rural people aspired toward enterprise in business or agriculture. The welfare state beneficiaries in Vivienda Rural housing were diverted away from such direct productive investment. Urbanization further reduced such a propensity to invest. This makes sense in a steel town centered on heavy industry with a capital-intensive commercial service sector dominated by the branches of big corporations, offering slight promise to the self-employed little man.

There was a heavy concentration of choices in a few major areas, especially with the smaller sum. So, the smaller the windfall, the greater the unallocated choices (out of a possible five). For both Bs. 20,000 and Bs. 5,000, the proportions of particular choices were about the same. This held for all three sample strata. The greatest stability of priorities was expressed by the villagers without government housing.

The only notable shift in ranking of priorities was toward concentrating more on housing with the smaller windfall in Ciudad Guayana, and among the Vivienda Rural occupants. There was no such shift among the other villagers.

The inelasticity of demand among the least modernized people was predictable. The Vivienda Rural program has partly modernized its beneficiaries' consumption preferences. The city induces great elasticity of demand. This could no doubt be demonstrated more precisely if it had been feasible to ask the respondents to monetize their hypothetical expenditures in a detailed balanced sheet, but they were imprecise about their budgets. So it is notable that qualitative information here yielded a picture of the transition from inelasticity to elasticity.

The questions on windfall spending in Tables 9, 10, and 11 show that the migrants regarded urban shanty life as much more unpleasant than rural shanty life. They therefore chose to spend overwhelmingly for a new house. Vivienda Rural occupants would spend their money as frequently on paying off their house. Only rural occupants of private housing chose to spend substantially on other items instead.

The next series of questions clarifies the alternative directions that this housing preoccupation might take: migration for housing, or the sacrifice of income for housing, or selections among the available popular housing. Informants could consider improved rural income, as well as increased urban income. But increased cash income in the Guayanese hinterland is such a remote possibility, compared to the greater urban opportunities, that rural-urban migration is synonymous with increasing cash earnings.

The Vivienda Rural house is highly standardized. So informants had to consider only one sort of house when posing public housing against increased income or migration.

Respondents were asked to make step-by-step judgments counterpoising pairs of considerations: migration versus improved housing, increased income versus city residence in bad housing, and potentially lower income versus improved rural housing. In addition, they were asked to make their own direct appraisal of the Vivienda Rural program.

Table 12 reconfirms that urban slums make bad city housing seem much worse than bad rural housing.

TABLE 12

BETTER HOUSE VERSUS HIGHER INCOME

Choice	*Cd. Guayana* %	*Vivienda Rural* %	*Other Rural* %
Better Housing	63.0	31.4	34.6
Higher Income	36.0	66.6	61.5
Undecided	1.0	2.0	3.9

Both groups of rural people selected income over housing for different reasons. Occupants of Vivienda Rural dwellings were pleased with their house, and two-thirds of them would therefore choose an increased income. Other rural residents again demonstrated their prevailing interest in investments instead of housing.

Respondents were asked whether they would migrate to the standard Vivienda Rural dwelling. In this hypothetical move, respondents were assured no loss of current income and no moving expenses.

The urban residents were most inclined to migrate for housing, according to Table 13. More than half of the Vivienda Rural occupants appeared well pleased with their house. Vivienda Rural informants prepared to migrate to another Vivienda Rural house revealed dissatisfaction with conditions other than housing.

TABLE 13

MIGRATION VERSUS REDUCED INCOME

Response	*Cd. Guayana* %	*Vivienda Rural* %	*Other Rural* %
Prepared to migrate	59.0	31.4	34.6
Not prepared to migrate	29.0	55.9	40.4
Undecided	11.0	13.7	25.0

Rural residents in private housing again showed their relative concern with aspirations other than housing. A sizable minority were undecided, however, showing the remoteness of these villagers from the "progressive" world of the welfare state and the industrialization program. Those respondents who gave a definite answer to questions were asked to explain the reasons for their decision. (See Table 13.)

TABLE 14A

REASON FOR MIGRATION FOR HOUSING

Reason	*Cd. Guayana* %	*Vivienda Rural* %	*Other Rural* %
Economic	12.7	64.0	37.5
Housing	76.2	20.0	43.7
Other	10.1	16.0	18.8

The differences for the villagers without government housing are not statistically significant (Table 14A) though they do tend to confirm that urban respondents were more preoccupied with housing; but country people in private housing were more interested in better housing than the Vivienda Rural people, who would be motivated more by employment opportunities.

TABLE 14B

REASONS FOR NONMIGRATION FOR HOUSING

Reason	*Cd. Guayana* %	*Vivienda Rural* %	*Other Rural* %
Economic	42.5	53.8	53.3
Housing	30.0	3.9	16.7
Other	27.5	42.3	30.0

Among all three sample strata in Table 14B, the economic factor was the stated reason for not migrating, contradicting the stipulated "no loss of income" clause, which was unrealistic. These people could not pretend that income might remain the same anywhere. The largest proportion of reasons based on housing was again from migrants, reflecting their negative appraisal of the Vivienda Rural houses. Only a tiny fraction of Vivienda Rural respondents stated any reasons based on housing, implying their satisfaction with the Vivienda Rural program. Other rural residents gave a higher proportion of reasons based on housing indicating that they had thought about the Vivienda Rural and rejected it because of a specific objection.

Due account must be taken of the statistical insignificance of these figures. It seems, however, that those who were not willing to migrate for housing were deterred for reasons other than negative opinions of the Vivienda Rural. Apart from the economic reasons operating as an incentive or discouragement to migration for rural residents, idiosyncratic considerations apparently supplied the intervening variable in the decision to migrate or not.

The question put in Table 13 implied a return to rural life for migrants, but only a rural-rural move for the villagers. The urban residents were therefore asked if they would have migrated at all had a Vivienda Rural house been available prior to their having left for the city. Nearly half (46%) said that they would have migrated in any case. "Poverty of the villages" was the reason given in more than half (53%) of these cases. Only 10% stated that they did not like the Vivienda Rural houses. Of the Ciudad Guayana sample, those who would not have migrated (54%) demonstrated again the urban group's great concern with housing and their disillusionment with the situation in the city. Two-thirds of the reasons for opting for a Vivienda Rural house in retrospect comprised statements like "to have had a good house," "to have had a cheap house," or "to have had my own house."

The question of whether migrants would have remained in the countryside in a Vivienda Rural house was compared to the question of remigration for a Vivienda Rural house. Undecided responses were eliminated for the comparison.

TABLE 15

MIGRATION VS. HOUSING: COMPARISON

Migrants only: *Response*	*Yes* %	*No* %
Migration despite Vivienda Rural	45.9	54.1
Remigration for Vivienda Rural	67.0	33.0

Table 15 suggests that the relative attraction of good housing increases with actual residence in the city. However, the past and future situations which migrants were called upon to imagine were not the same. The "would you migrate" question introduced the control, "if income were the same," while the "would you have stayed in the village" question had no condition attached. Interpretation is obscured by the time dimension. Staying in the country to occupy a Vivienda Rural house does mean forfeiting higher urban income, in the long run; but, in the short run, new arrivals in the city are worse off than they were back home. Many remain unemployed for months, and cannot live off kinfolk and their own gardens as they did before. By the time the migrants were interviewed, however, few of them had not passed the desperate settling-in stage.

Our questions to this point involved matters of conjecture and speculation. To relate these again to actual experiences, all of the respondents residing in urban or rural private housing were asked whether they, in fact, ever had had the opportunity to receive a Vivienda Rural dwelling. If so, why had they refused the opportunity?

TABLE 16A

OPPORTUNITY FOR VIVIENDA RURAL

Response	*Migrants* %	*Nonmigrants* %
Opportunity to receive Vivienda Rural house	22	51
No opportunity to receive Vivienda Rural house	78	49

Table 16A shows how many migrants had had the choice of improved village housing as a real alternative. Most of them, having had neither the chance to acquire good housing nor the possibilities of adequate employment in the villages, decided to leave. To the question whether migrants would have refrained from migrating if a Vivienda Rural house had been available, nearly half said they would have migrated in any case. More than half of the reasons given were based on dissatisfaction with employment opportunities in the country.

But over half of those in the country would not have migrated for housing, since the economic inducements for remaining seemed adequate to them. This is shown by the question on migration to obtain a Vivienda Rural house.

The reason given for not having taken the opportunity to occupy a Vivienda Rural house were aggregated into "economic," "housing," and "other." While these differences are not statistically significant, they do reinforce the other results, as Table 16B shows.

TABLE 16B

NONACCEPTANCE OF VIVIENDA RURAL

Reason	*Migrants* %	*Nonmigrants* %
Economic	25.0	31.0
Housing	30.0	41.9
Other	45.0	24.1

Among migrants and nonmigrants alike, the decision not to acquire a Vivienda Rural house when it was available was based more on a combination of economic and personal factors than on strong feelings against the government housing. Among nonmigrants, however, there were two important criticisms of the program: "I don't like the Vivienda Rural houses," and "I don't like the sites." This last criticism refers to the refusal of the Vivienda Rural program to scatter houses far beyond hamlets, to the disadvantage of some shifting cultivators and ranch hands. Also it refers to the weak foundations which cause many Vivienda Rural houses to develop cracks as they settle. Shanties and wattle-and-daub huts sit more lightly and, in any case, can be abandoned without much loss after site erosion.

All respondents were also asked to appraise the Vivienda Rural program directly. All were overwhelmingly in favor of the Vivienda Rural program, as Table 17 shows. Perhaps some informants were afraid to be critical, but our impressions and circumstantial evidence suggest that

TABLE 17A

APPRAISAL OF VIVIENDA RURAL HOUSES

Response	*Cd. Guayana* %	*Vivienda Rural* %	*Other Rural* %
Like them fine	76.0	90.2	57.7
Like them all right	4.0	9.8	11.5
Don't like them	14.0	0	23.1
Couldn't say	6.0	0	7.7

most were frank. Again a large fraction of the rural people in private housing were critical, but the recipients of the houses made no adverse statement at all.[9]

Those who liked the houses very much or moderately were asked why, as shown by Table 17B.

TABLE 17B

REASONS FOR LIKING THE VIVIENDA RURAL HOUSES

Reason	*Cd. Guayana* %	*Vivienda Rural* %	*Other Rural* %
The houses are easy to buy and pay for	24.0	19.2	19.1
Comfortable	21.5	19.9	18.0
Hygienic	21.0	18.5	16.9

Reasons were distributed in the same way in all three groups. Nothing was said about the construction or the layout of the Vivienda Rural houses. There were so few negative statements about the Vivienda Rural houses that no detailed proposals for improvements can be made.

CONCLUSION AND EPILOGUE

The poorer people's aspirations for two nonsubstitutable priorities, modern standard housing and industrial employment, were irreconcilable when the social and economic development programs were located in separate districts. Which did the Venezuelan Guayanese choose? Did the Vivienda Rural program slow down migration to the city?

From 1960 to 1965, 7,000 migrants went from Piar and Roscio to Ciudad Guayana, while migration beyond the steel town probably drew another 7,000 to 14,000 from the two counties. With natural increase in Piar and Roscio at 3.5% per annum, the population of the two counties went from 65,000 in 1961 to something in the order of 51,000 to 58,000 in 1966, depending on the volume of migration beyond Ciudad Guayana. As a result, approximately one-fifth of the people remaining in Piar and Roscio had Vivienda Rural houses by 1966. This is a great achievement in absolute terms, compared to the miserable huts which prevailed in use before 1960.

Nearly one-tenth of migrants to Ciudad Guayana during this period (1960–1965) had lived in Vivienda Rural houses in Piar and Roscio. There is no sign that the flow from the hinterland was not steady, year by

[9] Destructive criticism was not hidden by refusal to be interviewed. The migration survey in Cd. Guayana and the housing survey in Piar and Roscio both encountered less than 4 percent refusals.

year from 1960 to 1965. So, if one-fifth of those remaining in the villages had received public housing from 1960 to 1965, the migrants who, on average, left for the city in mid-1963, had half the chances of other people to receive public housing, that is, one in ten. This demonstrates that migration was not at all selective, in relation to the availability of modern standard housing in the villages.

This conclusion is supported by the proportion of migrants who had had the opportunity to move into a Vivienda Rural house: nearly a quarter had the chance, as opposed to half of the villagers who remained behind; nearly a tenth of the migrants had taken a Vivienda Rural house and then left for the city; up to a fifth of the nonmigrants took a Vivienda Rural house and stayed. Thus the public housing program failed to decelerate the rural exodus.

Yet the variety of consistent evidence that all three sample strata preferred Vivienda Rural houses seems to contradict this. They gave a vote of confidence to the Vivienda Rural program, but it did not stop depopulation. The divergence between actual behavior—high migration rates—and expressed attitudes—strong housing priorities—does make sense, however. The rural people migrated, even if they did have a Vivienda Rural house, because employment and cash income were far superior in the city. Moreover, a large portion of recent migrants had already built or bought modern standard houses, showing their fellows that cash could be translated into higher levels of living in the city, despite the surrounding slums.

Migration was thus the only way of balancing income against living conditions, by moving away from immediately better housing in the villages to better pay in the city—which could be applied eventually to better housing in the city. The Vivienda Rural program in isolation was no substitute for increased cash income, in the Venezuelan Guayanese view.

Criticisms of Vivienda Rural housing and alternative accommodation revealed problems unknown to the housing authorities back at headquarters in Caracas.[10] In particular, Ciudad Guayana residents emphasized the priorities of site, coolness, and piped water; Vivienda Rural occupants emphasized spaciousness alone, as did villagers without government housing. Although informants did not provide clear indications

---

[10] An ethnographic study in 1963–1965 of the city's oldest shantytown showed, in microcosm, the general lack of mutual comprehension between the residents, who did not know what the planners were doing (nor why), and the planners, who treated the city as if it did not yet have any residents. See L. Peattie, *The View From the Barrio* (Ann Arbor: University of Michigan, 1967).

about detailed improvements in design, construction, and management of public housing, they were matter-of-fact and rationalistic in weighing pros and cons.

Our surveys revealed an overall picture which was not realized by either the housing authority or the regional development authority. The villagers' and migrants' preferences should not have been ignored because they had more options than the planners had allowed for in their model-building. A large proportion of villagers without government housing preferred to stay in their own housing. The Vivienda Rural authority should not have been surprised that demand for their housing had dwindled by 1965. A large proportion of Ciudad Guayana migrants had already moved up to modern standard housing there.

The CVG's urban development plans assumed that migrants who were not immediately allocated elite public housing would remain in shanties, unless public housing at lower rents was made available to them.

Small projects for self-help housing accompanied by some basic social infrastructure were started by the CVG, without realizing that they could be fruitfully geared in with the "spontaneous" house-building that had already transformed half of shantytown's dwellings from 1960 to 1965. Since the Vivienda Rural program was too expensive to rehouse all the shanty dwellers in city and country, the preferences of the independent-minded should have been brought into play through government support for self-help. The resentment of so many villagers and migrants against paying any rent anywhere—and the open option to stay out or drop out of the modern housing sector—bode ill for public housing in the city.

Our housing and migration surveys were made at the end of the CVG's first five years, during which heavy industry and supporting public works were top priority. From 1966, however, social development was given high priority in the city. The CVG and the Vivienda Rural authorities then began to cooperate in resolving the contradiction between putting industrial employment in one place and modern standard housing outside commuter range. A new highway was built to bring half of the hinterland's population within commuting distance. The Vivienda Rural program, having run out of customers in Piar and Roscio, started constructing in the city's shantytowns. That year too, the CVG completed 1,000 low-rent row houses for the lower ranks of its steel and construction workers. In 1967, the CVG completed another mass low-rent project of small cottages, similar to the Vivienda Rural model in size, but with the addition of a veranda in accordance with the preferences found by our surveys. This was turned over to the new CVG-financed municipal housing foundation, FUNVICA.[11] It had been set up to build low-rent apartments for the manual and clerical workers with secure employment.

These were steps in the right direction, according to our findings. However, the great expansion of public housing for shantytown people ran into grave difficulties because popular attitudes had not been taken into account. The planners did not realize that the great reluctance to pay any rent was not simply due to actual inability to pay or cultural resistance to modernization. It was firmly based on two factors. First, there was the ready option to build one's own modern standard dwelling without interminable rents, foregoing the social infrastructure which went with public housing. Secondly, public housing did not give equity through time payments in the foreseeable future, so that tenants felt neither as independent as they had in their old villages, nor as responsible for upkeep as title-holders would. Moreover, the shantytowners were not involved in the slightest way in the authorities' remote-control planning, nor were they informed about the directions being taken by the various projects. Until the 1968 elections, they had practically no contact with the CVG through political parties or machine politics.

The outcome was invasions of several new public housing projects which the authorities had not been able to fill immediately with rent-paying tenants. Although many of these squatters were ejected eventually, the dwellings needed extensive repairs. The remaining squatters in the projects were a precedent for subsequent invasions. Also, one-sixth of the city's dwellings were officially empty in mid-1967—for the most part, public housing. This seems puzzling in a city, a state, and a country with high proportions of shanties—over one-third of all dwellings in Bolívar State in 1961, nearly half in Ciudad Guayana in 1965. But it does make sense on the basis of the attitudes measured by our surveys. If public housing recipients had been given immediate equity in public housing, the squatters' invasions could have been upstaged and the strong feeling for a house of one's own channeled into creating a steadier flow of mortgage repayment into a home-finance fund. Whatever the authorities did, public housing in city or village had to be heavily subsidized and it already was. Striking a compromise with the Guayanese preference for independence could have avoided further losses.

APPENDIX I: THE VIVIENDA RURAL PROGRAM

From March 1958 to December 1965, a total of 43,186 houses were constructed under the state project, Vivienda Rural (Rural Housing). There were

[11] Fundación de la Vivienda del Caroní.

2,035 Vivienda Rural houses in Roscio and Piar, of which 96 were in agricultural reform settlements. These 96 were therefore excluded from our interviews which sought to isolate the effects of improved housing alone. The houses in our areas of interest were occupied from 1960.

Assistance provided

(a) Government low-cost housing was planned for areas of from 200 to 10,000 population. Upata, the largest population center in the two counties, exceeded this maximum, but was given many government houses—perhaps because it is agricultural.

(b) Houses were sold at Bs. 5,000 (Bs.4.50 to $ U.S. 1.00) with down payment of Bs. 100 and monthly payments of Bs. 20 to 100 depending on income. Mortgage loans were for thirty years, interest free. Payments were not always collected with regularity.

(c) Houses were of cement block construction with three bedrooms, living room, kitchen, dining room, pantry, laundry, and bath.

(d) Houses were built directly by the Vivienda Rural authorities for individuals. Some were built through technical assistance self-help schemes and some as part of land reform and agricultural resettlement programs, but these were excluded from our survey.

(e) In theory, the program provided medical, educational, and home economy services, but in fact in Bolívar State these services were not provided regularly during the first five years.

Criteria of eligibility

Individuals were selected on the following bases, although many exceptions were made and fatherless families and old people were not discriminated against:

(a) Security of employment;
(b) Family composition and size;
(c) Length of time resident and working in locality;
(d) Whether there was a responsible head of household;
(e) Minimum income of Bs. 300 monthly and maximum income of Bs. 800;
(f) The willingness of the family to aid in the construction of the house.

APPENDIX II: DESIGN OF HOUSING SURVEY

A. *Urban residents.* One hundred residents of Ciudad Guayana who had come from the two hinterland districts of Roscio and Piar since the commencement of Vivienda Rural construction there were found by four methods. (1) The household sample survey of migrants in the city conducted by J. MacDonald in mid-1965 yielded household heads who had come from the southeastern districts since 1960. This survey was a two-strata sample with cluster sampling of all dwellings in the city. Its representativeness was verified by two other household surveys using different sampling procedures. (2) The personnel records of the Guri Dam which identified workers who resided in Ciudad Guayana and had been born in the hinterland. They were visited and interviewed if they had come to the city since 1960; (3) A complete census of the two largest low-income special development housing schemes for shanty dwellers. The authors are grateful to FUNVICA, the local housing authority, for including questions on year of arrival and previous residence; (4) The balance of 6 cases to make the total of 100 were found by asking the three Venezuelan interviewers to find appropriate household heads among their friends and acquaintances.

None of the interviewers nor their own families were from the hinterland. Nevertheless some slight bias may have crept in here. Altogether these last three sources were biased toward poorer and lower-middle class people, away from professionals, executives, and businessmen. The hinterland, however, produced very few people at that occupational level. Moreover, its bias away from them meant that it concentrated on the very kinds of people who were potential beneficiaries of the Vivienda Rural houses.

B. *Rural Residents.* The rural sample was drawn from five scattered population centers out of the nine in Piar and Roscio districts which had received Vivienda Rural houses, had private dwellings contiguous to or interspersed with Vivienda Rural dwellings, had no agrarian reform provisions combined with the granting of the Vivienda Rural houses, and had sent considerable numbers of migrants to Ciudad Guayana. Both types of rural informant were selected by fixed-interval sampling starting from a random point in the middle or periphery of each settlement.

David Lowenthal
American Geographical Society
New York City

POST-EMANCIPATION RACE RELATIONS: SOME CARIBBEAN AND AMERICAN PERSPECTIVES*

To compare race relations is even harder than to compare systems of slavery. However variously slavery may be defined, it is at least systematized—that is, slave trading, labor, provisioning, punishment, rebellion, and manumission are viewed as clear-cut categories, often formally codified and self-consciously compared with conditions elsewhere.[1]

In race relations none of this is true. Race itself may refer to anything from a linguistic community to a genealogically isolated population, and contexts shift through time as well as across cultures. In the narrower sense, races, as distinct from ethnic elements, are not even groups; individual behavior and self-images are not congruent with external identifications. Relationships considered "racial" may be limited to certain public or legal institutions in one society, but in another may include psychological responses in most realms of life. In short, race relations can be compared only in the context of entire social systems.[2]

Nevertheless, residents, travelers, and migrants, struck by similarities and differences, habitually compare racial conditions, often in order to justify or to condemn one situation or another. Comparative perspectives

---

* Revised from a paper read in a symposium on comparative race relations at the Southern Historical Association meeting, Louisville, Kentucky, 13 November 1970.

1 Carl N. Degler, "Slavery in Brazil and the United States: An Essay in Comparative History," *American Historical Review* 75 (1970): 1004–1028.

2 Pierre L. van den Berghe, *Race and Racism: A Comparative Perspective* (New York: John Wiley, 1967).

on interracial experience are vital elements of social history, notwithstanding the variability of racial definitions.

Assuming a general familiarity with the United States, I shall focus primarily on the Caribbean. But a caveat is necessary. The Caribbean is not one but fifty societies, and racial conditions vary greatly from island to island as well as from epoch to epoch. To generalize even about British Commonwealth societies as demographically unlike as Barbuda, inhabited solely by a thousand blacks; Anguilla, with 6,000 folk of shades from dark to light brown; Barbados, whose 10,000 whites maintain economic but not political dominance over some 40,000 middle-class colored people and 200,000 blacks; Trinidad, 40 percent of whose million are East Indian—is to do violence to reality. Population size, racial mixtures, and differences in production, land tenure, colonial status, and cultural orientation make race relations in each Caribbean society unique.[3]

There is no space to explore the differences here. For purposes of comparison with the United States, let me concentrate instead on some broad similarities within the non-Hispanic Caribbean societies, which share a general set of West Indian socioeconomic circumstances, ways of life, and—despite geographical, political, and linguistic barriers, and a fiercely competitive spirit—a mutual awareness of their resemblances.

One-to-one connections between the "severity" of any slave regime and subsequent patterns of race relations have no historical validity. But the basic differences between American and Caribbean race relations today are nonetheless rooted in their antecedent slave systems. The status of free colored people was perhaps the most crucial difference. Relatively more numerous in the West Indies, the free colored played a far more significant role in shaping West Indian than American society. The American slave states were the home of large numbers of whites, of whom only a minority were involved with slavery; the West Indies were less the home than the place of exile of much smaller white populations, practically all of whom depended on slavery. In the United States free nonwhites were a source of strain because they competed economically with working-class whites. The West Indies mainly lacked such whites, and planters and governments welcomed free colored and free black people as artisans, traders, and bulwarks against overwhelming slave numbers. In short, North American society found no place for free nonwhites, whereas they fitted easily into Caribbean social structures. Where American slave-

[3] David Lowenthal, "The Range and Variation of Caribbean Societies," *Annals New York Academy of Sciences* 83 (1960): 786–795.

owners feared the free colored as likely instigators of slave revolt, the West Indian planter welcomed them as allies against insurgent slaves.[4]

Differing views about class reinforced this distinction. In the United States, egalitarian principles required that all men be viewed as equals, blacks excepted. Slaves could easily be excluded, but free black and colored men posed an embarrassing dilemma. This dilemma was resolved by means of residential segregation, attempts at African colonization, and, ultimately, a whole system of racially discriminatory legislation.

West Indian societies were by contrast profoundly hierarchical. Like most Europeans, West Indian whites assumed that status and rewards should be ascriptive and that a stratified society was both natural and desirable. The free colored early became a middle class between the white elite and the slaves. They were accorded status and opportunity distinguishing them from slaves, without threatening the place of the ruling whites. Because West Indian whites were given to actual or temperamental absenteeism, free colored influence grew, and by the time of emancipation their numbers equalled or surpassed those of the whites. As one historian of Trinidad remarks, "They were in their time the true West Indians, and they knew it." [5] Although they eventually claimed and received full civil rights, true equality was prevented by narrow suffrage based on property and by social bias based on color—a bias internalized by nonwhites themselves.

From these presuppositions, egalitarian in the United States, hierarchical in the Caribbean, emerged several consequences important for race relations, including racial categories themselves. American whites lumped all nonwhites together as "black," a dichotomy that emancipation hardened by erasing the distinction between bond and free. Nonwhites did differentiate themselves on the basis of color, but such distinctions were relatively unimportant in the face of strict white barriers against all nonwhites. With time, black Americans came to feel themselves a unified race, regardless of apparent skin color. Thus both white and black in the United States accept and live by a strictly dichotomous classification, in which "whites" com-

---

[4] Elsa V. Goveia, *Slave Society in the British Leeward Islands at the End of the Eighteenth Century* (New Haven: Yale University Press, 1965), pp. 232–33, 258–59.

[5] James Millette, "The Civil Commission of 1802: An Account and an Explanation of an Issue in the Early Constitutional and Political History of Trinidad," *Jamaican Historical Review* 6, nos. 1 and 2 (1966): 38.

prise those whose progenitors are all European and "blacks" all the rest, however small the African share of their ancestry.

In the Caribbean, by contrast, the white minority position and the survival of a class system made gradations between white and black significant to whites as well as to nonwhites. After emancipation the free colored generally became "colored" as distinct from "black"; shade distinctions between black and colored, and among the colored, remained crucial facts of West Indian society and self-perception. In short, race in the West Indies was conceived not as a black-white dichotomy, but rather as a continuum through various degrees of color.

As their racial classifications differed, so did American and West Indian concepts of what race comprised. The American dichotomy demanded a rigid distinction based on phenotype in everyday life and on genotype as an ultimate criterion; both white and black took for granted that anyone who *looked* nonwhite was black and that anyone of nonwhite *ancestry* was black. However well-educated, well-to-do, well-connected, or light-skinned a nonwhite might be, he remained a "black." [6]

In the Caribbean color was a function not only of appearance and ancestry but also of culture, experience, and achievement. A black man who achieved eminence or power was quite generally viewed as "colored" or even as "white." White enclaves strove to maintain racial purity by excluding nonwhites, but many West Indian whites were "white" by courtesy, not by virtue of undiluted European ancestry.[7]

Passing for white was important in the West Indies, but the mechanism and social context differed from the American phenomenon. In the United States, a Negro who sought to pass would move to a remote milieu where his background was unknown. In the West Indies, the small size of the society and the limited number of white families, all genealogically well known, put such a procedure out of the question. West Indian "passing" was not the achievement of the stranger whose African ancestry no one could know; it was accomplished by the prominent figure who was accepted as white despite what everyone surmised of his ancestry. In sum, Caribbean "race" incorporated a broader range of nonphysical attributes modifying and ameliorating distinctions of color per se, whereas in the United States racial differentiation remained simple, narrow, and intransigent.[8]

---

[6] Winthrop D. Jordan, *White over Black: American Attitudes toward the Negro, 1550–1812* (Chapel Hill: University of North Carolina Press, 1968).

[7] E. Hayot, "Les gens de couleur libres du Fort-Royal, 1679–1823," *Revue Française d'Histoire d'Outre-Mer,* 106, no. 203 (1969): 127; Shelia J. Duncker, "The Free Coloured and Their Fight for Civil Rights in Jamaica, 1800–1830" (M.S. thesis, University of London, 1961), pp. 39–48.

[8] M. G. Smith, *A Framework for Caribbean Studies* (Jamaica: University College of the West Indies, Extra-Mural Dept., 1955).

These differences shaped the post-emancipation histories of the two realms. In most West Indian territories emancipation came without riot, bloodshed, or disorder, despite the planters' fears and failure to plan for the future. By contrast, civil war and great turmoil accompanied emancipation in the United States. Yet American slaveowners formed a minority of the whites, whereas the whole structure of West Indian society was slave-based. West Indian social structure was indeed the product of slavery, but slavery proved not essential to its continuance. For the planter emerged after emancipation with his prerogatives fairly intact. In the American South emancipation radically altered the plantation system, undermined planter power, and vitiated many planter values; in the West Indies the plantocracy retained system, power, and values. Many estates failed, changed hands, or were consolidated, and imperial rule later replaced local. But the shape, structure, and implicit aims of the system were substantially unaltered.

Most of the former free colored people and newly freed slaves remained mute or resigned to that continuance. Many thousand workers abandoned the estates for subsistence farming; many hundred colored professionals were discouraged by white discrimination; many missionaries and magistrates deplored planter coercion and legislative social neglect. Yet such desertions, disappointments, and protests seldom led to rebellion and never to anarchy; by and large West Indians in all walks of life accepted things as they were.

Although hierarchical in structure and European in focus, West Indian society was locally ameliorative and encouraged some social mobility. As the whites departed and nonwhite suffrage gradually broadened, as local education expanded and discriminatory barriers relaxed, colored and later black West Indians gradually moved into positions of power and prestige, in the process emulating white outlooks and attitudes. Indeed, to gain success one had to adopt colonial values. Colored middle-class accession to white elite prerequisites involved no fundamental change in the hierarchical structure nor in its sustaining values. Quite to the contrary, middle-class West Indians opposed structural change as a threat to the status they had gained or coveted.

Success, the world over, frequently weakens middle-class reform and compromises their ideals. West Indian history is unique in that middle-class achievers rarely intended fundamental change; firm believers in the system, they sought mainly to inherit white places. Social reform inspired many young West Indians, to be sure; the memoirs of West Indian men of affairs all relate how they tried to banish misery and poverty. But until recently such sentiments seldom lasted much beyond student days abroad. Once back home, radical change seemed chimerical or mischievous, and reformers became careerists.

Most West Indian leaders during the century after emancipation were men of profoundly conservative temper, at home with imperial control and at ease with imperial values—including a hierarchy based on color. Black and colored legislators, civil servants, judges, and doctors were increasingly numerous, but their values were correspondingly white. For these values, and for their subservience, willing or otherwise, to metropolitan interests, local leaders of emergent West Indian states came to be regarded as "Afro-Saxons," or "black men with white minds." [9]

As a consequence, West Indian black power movements, though they initiate the black American rhetoric, are really based on quite different premises. Black power in the West Indies is not only anti-white, it is also anti-*colored*. Black hostility toward the Caribbean light-skinned elite and middle class accords with the "white" status they have always sought and at least partially achieved. West Indian pan-Africanists have, in fact, historically rejected mulattoes as allies of whites and Europeans. Blyden, the island-born nineteenth-century advocate of Negro repatriation to Africa, openly and unremittingly detested mulattoes and urged the extension of southern American anti-miscegenation laws to forbid marriage or fornication between "genuine Negroes" and "half-castes." [10]

Garvey, Blyden's spiritual successor, spoke for a black peasantry that was leaderless because, he explained, "the educated class of my own people . . . are the bitterest enemies of their own race." [11] Black unity was the crux of Garvey's appeal. He affirmed pride in being Negro, denounced colored men who sought assimilation with whites, and taught his followers to venerate their Africanness. In Jamaica, Garvey made little headway against black apathy and self-abasement. But in the United States after 1916, Garvey's Universal Negro Improvement Association aroused a tremendous response among the darker, less-educated Negroes who seemed forgotten by the light-skinned leaders of "the Talented Tenth." [12]

---

[9] Rex Nettleford, "The African Connexion—The Significance for Jamaica," in John Hearne and Rex Nettleford, *Our Heritage*, Public Affairs in Jamaica, no. 1 (Mona, Jamaica: University of the West Indies, Department of Extra-Mural Studies, n.d.), p. 52; Rex Nettleford, "National Identity and Attitudes to Race in Jamaica," *Race* 7 (1965–66): 62.

[10] Hollis R. Lynch, *Edward Wilmot Blyden: Pan-Negro Patriot, 1832–1912* (London: Oxford University Press, 1967), pp. vii, 118, 139.

[11] Marcus Garvey to Major Robert R. Moton, 29 February 1916, Robert Russa Collection, Tuskegee Institute Archives (courtesy of Carl S. Matthews).

[12] August Meier, *Negro Thought in America, 1880–1915: Racial Ideologies in the Age of Booker T. Washington* (Ann Arbor: University of Michigan Press, 1964); Edmund David Cronon, *Black Moses: The Story of Marcus Garvey and the Universal Negro Improvement Association* (Madison: University of Wisconsin Press, 1964).

West Indian status distinctions between black and mulatto had only limited relevance, however, to Negroes in the United States. To be sure, descendants of free-colored folk of antebellum origin dominated Negro society in most American cities well into the twentieth century, and "successful" Negroes still are usually lighter than the rest. But these distinctions, unimportant to whites, were seldom formalized by blacks. The very idea of color stratification was at odds with what Negro Americans sought, and those who did not deny its existence tended to minimize its significance. Garvey's appeals to black men victimized by the West Indian color-class system alienated Americans of mixed blood as well as black Americans unwilling to regard mulattoes as their oppressors. The impassable white barrier, the strong prejudice against all nonwhites alike, then as now gave American Negroes a sense of community regardless of shade, which is still absent in the West Indies.

Both independence and the black-power movement have reactivated conflict between black and brown in the West Indies. "We have identified the mulatto with the betrayal of the Revolution," writes a Guyanese celebrant of slave insurrection; when brown men do the right thing they have "repudiated the mulatto heritage." [13] A Trinidadian notes that "today there are fewer and fewer 'red niggers' and more and more Black men of light complexion, who have healed the psychological and moral gaps in their consciousness, and understood that their salvation and identity lie in their self-identification with the Black masses." [14] West Indians of all shades have begun to wear Afro wigs, less from any sense of identification than from motives of prudence and safety. Some political leaders in the self-governing West Indies seek solidarity with the electorate by exaggerating their own "blackness"; thus Bradshaw of St. Kitts has claimed to be a full-blooded Ashanti,[15] and the lighter-skinned premier of Dominica, when not asserting Carib ancestry, emphasizes African antecedents.

Black power is "a forceful weapon for the American Negro," concedes a small-island journal, but "may be a suicidal one for the West Indian, falsifying both his inter-racial origins and his quickly deepening culture." [16] American Negro origins are, to be sure, no less "interracial" than are West Indian; it is the perception of color that differs. It is all very well to insist that "blackness" has little to do with skin color and to claim with Stokely Carmichael that Castro is really the "blackest" man in the Carib-

[13] P. H. Daly, *Revolution to Republic* (Georgetown, Guyana: Daily Chronicle, 1970), pp. 67, 69.

[14] "After the Carnival," *Embryo* (St. Augustine, Trinidad: University of the West Indies), Supplement, n.d., p. S1.

[15] V. S. Naipaul, "St. Kitts: Papa and the Power Set," *New York Review of Books* (May 8, 1969): 23.

[16] "Black Pride or Black Power," *Dominica Star* (16 November 1968): 1.

bean; but it is not easy to convince most West Indians that by analogy some of the "whitest" figures are black leaders like the despotic prime ministers of St. Kitts and Grenada.[17] And when Carmichael refers to his early life in Trinidad with pride because the school teachers and the police were black, local realities conform still less with black power, "since these figures of authority, in full complaisance to colonial policy, often used their powers not to liberate our people, but to maintain us in a condition of servility." Carmichael's naiveté "makes nonsense of black power in the West Indies where we are revolting against a black-skinned Afro-Saxon administration." [18] And so the West Indian returns to what he has always known; whether or not "Massa Day Done," in Eric William's phrase, "not all whites were Massa [and] not all Massas were white." [19]

West Indian migrants in the United States play ambivalent roles, some as freedom fighters, others as middle-class strivers, further complicating these distinctions. West Indian emigration continually drains away potential rebels, leaving behind those more prone to endure neocolonialism. "One of the reasons that the British West Indies have remained statically conservative, impoverished and without a revolutionary movement," remarks Cruse, "is that all such radicals leave home, like other ambitious locals, and go off to make revolutions somewhere else." [20] Yet most emigrants are not radical, let alone revolutionary; their goals are strongly middle-class. "We come here to work, man, not to fight the white man," [21] typifies the West Indian migrants' response to black power. By contrast with the few black militants, the average West Indian overseas is apt to resent being reminded that "the song is we shall overcome, not we shall come over." [22]

The less ambitious stay-at-home is still more passive; black West Indians are said to be "the most conformist and accommodative people in the Caribbean." [23] But the local temper is too complex to be summed up in such generalizations. It is equally true that West Indians at home share the

---

[17] "Tapia Special on the Current National Crisis," *Tapia* (Port-of-Spain), no. 6, (8 March 1970): 2.

[18] "Rt. Hon. Dead Horse, C.H.: Filling the Political Vacuum," *Tapia*, no. 7 (19 April 1970): 2.

[19] Eric Williams, *Massa Day Done: A Masterpiece of Political and Sociological Analysis* (Port-of-Spain: P.N.M. Publishing Co., 1961), p. 7.

[20] Harold Cruse, *The Crisis of the Negro Intellectual* (New York: William Morrow, 1967), p. 435.

[21] Clyde K. Picon, letter, 19 July, in *Trinidad Guardian*, 31 July 1967.

[22] Gordon K. Lewis, "Race Relations in Britain: A View from the Caribbean," *Race Today* 1 (1969): 79.

[23] Cruse, *The Crisis of the Negro Intellectual*, p. 135.

absentee spirit of those away, and "because we are all expatriates" a Trinidadian declares, all "West Indians are extremists." [24]

Sovereignty and colonialism compound these differences in racial accommodation and protest. Most West Indians have long known what black Americans are only now expressing—that they are a subjugated people like other colonials. In the Caribbean, political and racial subordination converged; in the United States, independence obscured the realities of racial subordination. Emancipation thus led to politically divergent roads. In the United States, Reconstruction with black participation under northern protection gave way to racial reaction when southern whites regained control. In the Caribbean local whites retained political control after emancipation but subsequently, fearing that continued local self-rule portended nonwhite hegemony, they relinquished power into imperial hands. The drive for racial equality in the West Indies thus fused with the drive toward self-government, culminating in local sovereignty under manhood suffrage and in the virtual eclipse of local white political power—though some colored beneficiaries of the colonial system are uneasy about independence in majority black regimes. In the United States, by contrast, racial equality and integration until recently were advanced, if at all, largely through federal intervention in state and local affairs.

Formal sovereignty has not, to be sure, lessened West Indian dependence on the Western world. Strategically subordinate to American interests, economically dominated by international corporations and foreign investors, lacking a viable culture of their own, West Indians seem condemned to perpetual subservience, to be forever, in a Trinidadian's phrase, "the Third World's third world." [25] Yet despite this subjection to external white powers, West Indians, mostly black, by and large run their internal affairs, whereas black American efforts to develop any community autonomy whatever are nullified by an all-enveloping larger society. There are certain resemblances between Jamaica or Montserrat and such all-black communities as Mound Bayou, Mississippi, or North Shreveport, Louisiana. But Mound Bayou and North Shreveport have not become general exemplars because they are utterly dependent communities in an impinging white world.[26] As for the urban ghetto, all large-scale institutions—schools, police, welfare, health, mass transit, political machines, sources of

[24] C. L. R. James, "Introduction," in Errol Hill, ed., *Caribbean Plays*, 2 (St. Augustine, Trinidad: University of the West Indies, Extra-Mural Department, 1965), p. vi.

[25] V. S. Naipaul, "Power to the Caribbean People," *New York Review of Books* 15, no. 4 (3 September 1970): 33.

[26] Harold M. Rose, "The All-Negro Town: Its Evolution and Function," *Geographical Review* 55 (1965): 362-81.

credit—"are totally controlled from outside the community and generally not even susceptible to any influence from community members." [27] Jamaicans and Montserratians are largely masters in their own houses, however heavily mortgaged their houses may be.

This is an accident of geography no less than of history. Isolation and definite boundaries give almost every West Indian island, however small, a degree of self-government and a sense of its own identity. Despite impoverishment and exploitation, West Indians feel that they are to some extent in control of their own multiracial destiny. In the United States, continentality and pervasive communications make local autonomy a chimera. Black capitalism, black political power, black culture are victims of the black minority position, for no local concentration permits blacks to control their own destiny even to the degree the 6,000 inhabitants of Anguilla enjoy.

Majority-minority differences entail still another consequence. In the United States race relations until recently did not consciously or fundamentally touch most whites. Only now do racial affairs force themselves on the attention of all Americans, and even now most whites do not directly experience the realities of racial involvement. White America remains cocooned against contact with the black ghetto. But in the Caribbean a different racial balance required from the start that most people—and all whites—be intimately involved in interracial relationships.

No West Indian is unaware, inexperienced, or unaffected by interracial contacts. Because race, class, and personal identity are all intimately linked, racial awareness suffuses every aspect of West Indian life. Although formal discrimination is absent, and segregation a thing of the past, the Caribbean is intensely racialist; race is constantly discussed, invoked, avowed to be significant. To the extent that racial distinctions are by definition invidious, West Indian societies that describe themselves as "multiracial" are far removed from paradise. But West Indians have learned through experience to cope with many racial distinctions, invidious or otherwise. In the smaller islands especially, propinquity and the need for collaboration in local affairs demands intimacy among people who see themselves as racially different. This gives them a background that makes them seem highly sophisticated by contrast with Americans, white or black.[28] One measure of this sophistication is the extraordinary prepon-

[27] Charles A. Valentine, "Blackston: Progress Report on a Community Study in Urban Afro-America," New York, 1970, mimeo., p. 73.

[28] Gloria Cumper, "In Search of a New Identity," in "Jamaica A Special Report," *The Times* (London, 26 September 1968): I; Douglas Hall, "The Colonial Legacy in Jamaica," *New World Quarterly* 4, no. 3 (High Season, 1968): 7–22.

derance of West Indians who direct black-studies programs in American universities.

As local majorities, nonwhite West Indians often contrast their lot vis-à-vis whites favorably with that of Negro Americans. "However black and dispossessed" West Indians may have been, explains a Barbadian, they never "felt the experience of being in a minority." [29] They suffer neither the ghettoization nor the sense of isolation and anomie, helplessness and powerlessness, that afflicts many black Americans. But "whiteness is only half the enemy," another West Indian adds. "Like the American Negro, the West-Indian is dispossessed. Unlike the American Negro, he has never faced that terrible white power-structure that has made black definition there possible," and as a result "he cannot relate himself to himself." [30] The West Indian obsession with differences in shade sustains an atmosphere that, if less polarizing, perpetuates other serious problems of identity and action, problems for white, colored, and minority groups as well as for black West Indians.

[29] George Lamming, "The Pleasures of Exile," *Tamarack Review*, no. 14 (Winter 1960): 40.

[30] Winston Hackett, "Identity in the Poetry of Walcott," *Moko* (Port-of-Spain) no. 8 (14 February 1969): 2.

Monsignor Bryan O. Walsh
Episcopal Vicar for Spanish-Speaking Peoples
Catholic Archdiocese of Miami

CUBAN REFUGEE CHILDREN*

During the past twelve years almost half a million Cubans have sought refuge in Miami. Among them were over 14,000 unaccompanied children between 6 and 18 years of age. This article tells for the first time the story of how the children's exodus began. It covers the period between the middle of November 1960, when we first became aware of the need, and 1 February 1961, when I met with the Secretary of the U.S. Department of Health, Education and Welfare to brief him on the plight of the unaccompanied children among the refugees. Two days later, President Kennedy announced a government aid program for Cuban refugees which included money for the care of unaccompanied children, "the most troubled group among the refugee population." [1]

About 4:30 p.m. on 26 December 1960, Pan American World Airways Flight 422 from Havana touched down at Miami International Airport. There were few passengers, if any, on that flight who did not experience a real sense of relief as they descended from the airplane. Events in Cuba were rapidly moving toward a climax and those who could were joining the increasing exodus to Miami. Two teen-agers, a Cuban brother and sister, were among the passengers. Sixto Aquino and his sister, Vivian, must have shared in the general relief, but they still had reason to be apprehensive. No friends or relatives waited for them outside the doors of U.S. Customs. They had left their parents behind not knowing when they would

---

* This article is taken from the introductory portion of the author's comprehensive study of Cuban refugee children in the United States, now in progress.

[1] *New York Times*, 4 February 1961. "Cuban Refugees," p. 1.

see them again; and they were going as aliens into a new adult world where almost everything would be strange and new, including the language. Although Sixto and his sister did not know it, they were the first of a long line of youths who would make this same trip during the following twenty-three months.

Waiting for them at the desk of U. S. Immigration was a social worker, Mrs. Louise Cooper, from Miami's Catholic Welfare Bureau. The day before, in response to a cryptic message from Cuba, Mrs. Cooper and I, as Catholic Welfare Bureau Executive Director, had begun what was to become a daily vigil at the immigration desk. Thus it was on Christmas Day 1960 that the program of the Catholic Welfare Bureau for the care and protection of unaccompanied Cuban children in the United States actually got under way.

News reporters, sworn to secrecy, would christen it Operation Pedro Pan. Before it ended it would involve thousands of families, Cuban and American, several foreign governments, numerous officials of federal and state government, well over 100 child welfare agencies, and the three major faiths in a unique effort of cooperation to help children, the innocent victims of power politics and clashing ideologies. Even though Operation Pedro Pan itself would only last less than two years, the Cuban Children's Program would go on for many years and would have a very real influence on the development of cooperative programs between government and voluntary child welfare agencies in the United States.

It is important to understand the difference between Operation Pedro Pan and the Cuban Children's Program. The Cuban Children's Program was inaugurated to provide foster care for Cuban refugee children who found themselves in the United States without the care and protection of their parents. Operation Pedro Pan was developed to help Cuban parents send their children unaccompanied to the United States to avoid Communist indoctrination. Both programs developed at the same time but, while Operation Pedro Pan terminated with the missile crisis, the Cuban Children's Program is still in operation at the time of writing. Between the 3 January 1961 break in Cuban-U.S. diplomatic relations and the October 1962 missile crisis, 14,048 Cuban students were helped by Operation Pedro Pan to enter the United States; 6,486 of them received foster care in the Cuban Children's Program either on their arrival or shortly thereafter.

Cuban refugees had begun to arrive in Miami on 1 January 1959, the morning after the fall of Batista. During the following year some 4,000 Cubans had taken refuge in Miami. Most of them had either been associated with the previous government or were of the upper class who felt threatened by the new regime. However, the increasing radicalization of the Cuban situation during the summer and autumn of 1960 caused more and more Cubans of all classes to look toward Miami. The lines of visa applicants outside the U.S. Embassy in Havana lengthened in proportion as the crisis grew more serious. By October, Cuban refugees were recognizable on the streets of Miami. The local community and state and federal authorities were being alerted to their plight by concerned people such as Miami's Bishop (now Archbishop) Coleman F. Carroll.

It is now calculated that there were 12,000 refugees in Miami in December 1961, although estimates at that time placed the figure two to three times higher. Until the missile crisis forced the end of commercial air traffic between Havana and Miami, almost 200 new refugees arrived each day.

During this same period thousands more arrived by small boat across the treacherous Straits of Florida and through such third countries as Spain, Jamaica, and Mexico. After the missile crisis in October 1962, these were the only routes available for three years until President Johnson inaugurated the Varadero Freedom Flights in December 1965, The refugee exodus then entered a new phase with the emphasis on the reunification of families. During the first months of these flights the majority of children separated from their parents in 1961-1962 were reunited with them in exile. By January 1971, it is estimated that there were 261,000 Cubans living in Miami and almost as many throughout the country.

This paper is concerned with how it all began and the first five weeks of our two programs. By the end of this time the Catholic Welfare Bureau had built up the basic organization that was necessary to administer both programs and, with this, came much more adequate record-keeping. The story of the following years is well documented in Catholic Welfare Bureau files and its extraction presents a very different type of challenge. In the beginning, however, as in every new operation, there was little time or opportunity for record-keeping in the formal sense. This paper, therefore, is the result of careful gathering of data from correspondence, minutes of meetings, and appointment books. For their own protection the names of some people still in Cuba have been purposely omitted. The story of their contributions to the program must wait for other and hopefully happier times on that island.

There is one question that is frequently, if not inevitably, raised and which merits at least some discussion at this time. It is posed in different ways. Why did Cuban parents send their children into exile alone? How could a parent do that? Why did the parents not come with them? At times this question has been asked by the children themselves, especially the younger ones as they grew older. They have also been posed by Americans who have learned of the program. To this question there are no simple answers and perhaps no one answer which covers all situations and circumstances. This Cuban phenomenon was not, however, unique or unprecedented.

In modern times many children have been separated from their parents and have found themselves in foreign lands and among strange people who differed from them in culture and often in language. The nineteen-thirties saw Jewish children smuggled out of Nazi Germany and cared for in foster homes in England and other countries. A number were later brought to the United States. The Spanish Civil War caused the evacuation of thousands of children from Spain.[2] Basque children were taken to Belgium, France, and England and cared for in special camps and schools. Children—5,000 it is said—were sent to Russia as the Republican government went down to defeat. In 1937 a ship sailed from Barcelona to Mexico with some 460 children accompanied by a number of their teachers.[3] In 1940 during the Battle of Britain approximately 1,000 British children were sent to the United States for safety.[4] With the end of World War II, and in the years following, some 5,000 war orphans were brought from Europe to new homes in the United States.

But the Spanish experience was the most important for Cuban parents. Cuba had always been close to Spain. It was the last of the Spanish American colonies to gain independence. The large Spanish migration to the island since independence had kept its ties to the motherland close and strong. As Castro and his leading followers made statement after statement, each more radical than the one before, concerning the education of the young generation, the fear of the parents mounted. It is my conviction that, as the threat of communism grew, Cuban parents were greatly influenced by the memory of the Spanish Civil War.[5] They recalled the

[2] "The first refugees (from Bilbao) to be evacuated were children, to be parcelled out among those who agreed to look after them. The CGT in France agreed to take 2,300 and the Soviet Government undertook the care of Communist children. A Basque children's relief committee in England, supported by the British branch of the Roman Church, agreed to look after 4,000 children. . . . Opinion was nevertheless so cautious in America that even a project to bring certain Basque children there was dropped as a possible breach of neutrality." Hugh Thomas, *The Spanish Civil War* (New York: Harper & Row, 1961), pp. 437, 438.

[3] Michael Kenny (Washington, D.C., Catholic University), unpublished manuscript. "From 1937–1943 they ('Los Niños de Morelia') were educated and cared for in the España-Mexico school or similar institutions entirely at the expense of the Mexican Government. See 'Los Niños de Morelia' by Vera Foulkes, Social Work Thesis presented to U.N.A.M. Mexico D.F., 1953."

[4] Kathryn Close, *Transplanted Children* (New York: The United States Committee for the Care of European Children, Inc., 1953), p. 79.

[5] "As the revolution entered its second year, it was evident that a large part of Catholic opinion, particularly among the regular clergy, was opposed to the

stories and rumors of children sent to Russia for training, and of other children held as hostages. They began to fear the same thing happening in Cuba. They saw that last refuge from indoctrination, the private school, threatened and they doubted their own ability to offset the effects of indoctrination and propaganda on their children.

During 1960 rumors that added to the panic of the parents began to circulate in Cuba and in exile circles in Miami. The principal one among these referred to the *patria potestad* or the rights of parents over their children. Purported copies of a new decree circulated throughout underground circles. According to this decree (as rumored) "all children will remain with their parents until they are three years old, after which they must be entrusted for physical and mental education to the Organización de Círculos Infantiles" (state day-care centers). Children from three to ten would live in government dormitories in their home provinces and would be permitted to visit their parents "no less than two days a month." Older children would be "assigned to the most appropriate place" and thus might never come home.[6] Spawned by this basic rumor, other stories related that children were picked up off the streets and never seen again; that orphanages, such as "Casa Beneficencia," had been emptied and all the children sent to Russia for indoctrination; that in the town of Bayamo, fifty mothers had signed a pact to kill their children rather than hand them over to Castro; etc.

Additional rumors concerning this decree preceded each major anniversary in the revolutionary calendar: 1 January 1961, 26 July 1961, 1 January 1962.[7] Although Castro himself branded the *patria potestad* docu-

---

government, and that it was hardening daily in direct proportion to the alienation of Havana from Washington. Early in the new year a document was circulated for signature among the Spanish clergy in which they reaffirmed their loyalty to Franco. The meaning of this gesture could not escape anyone in Cuba, where the memory of the Spanish civil war is more alive than anywhere else in the world outside of Spain itself. The document amounted to a condemnation of Castro on the grounds that, as the Republican government had supposedly once done in Spain, Castro now was culpably betraying the revolution to communism." Leslie Dewart, *Cuba, Church and Crisis* (London: Sheed and Ward, 1963), p. 154.

[6] *Time*, October 6, 1961. "Cuba—And Now the Children," p. 41.

[7] "We have heard, of course, from time to time of the efforts, the laws that are being drawn up to prevent any child over the age of five to leave Cuba. Last July 26th, or prior to that time, when on Fidel's great celebration we knew there were sitting on his desk laws that would do just that. There was, according to the information supplied to us by the underground, quite a controversy between two sets of Fidel's advisers, the economists and party-line Communists. The economists maintained that it was necessary to keep the flow of U.S. dollars and therefore they were for continuation of allowing people to leave. The comment of the party line, of course, as we know, is to grab on to the children. Now the deadline for this to happen is supposedly January 1st, 1962. And we just expect sooner or later it is going to happen." Testimony of Wendel N. Rollason, Director, Inter-American Affairs Commission, Miami, Florida. *U. S. Senate Hearings*, December 1961, p. 159.

ment a forgery put out by the underground and the CIA to discredit the regime, the departure of Fidelito, Castro's own twelve-year-old son, for Russia helped confirm the rumors. When the government organized the Association of Youth Rebels and Rebel Pioneers, the fear of the parents grew as they saw their children become active in these youth groups of the regime and as they began to reflect the first effects of this indoctrination. A few parroted phrases of propaganda heard on the radio were enough to put parents into a panic.

In the beginning of the children's exodus, two groups of parents seemed most affected by this fear: the small minority, generally of the middle class, who were practicing Catholics and those of the middle class who worked in foreign-owned businesses and saw their own world rapidly disappearing. In general members of the wealthy upper class had solved their problem—they were already in Miami. Consequently, although families of all classes were represented from the beginning, the majority of those interested in sending their children to the United States belonged to the middle class and had sent their children to private schools. This is evidenced in the many thousands of letters received by the Catholic Welfare Bureau from families asking for help in getting their children to the United States, and by those who succeeded in their quest. For Catholic parents, the changing attitude of the hierarchy toward the regime confirmed their fears.

> On November 21st, 1960 Monsignor Enrique Perez Serantes (the Archbishop of Santiago de Cuba who saved Castro's life after his 1953 attack on the Moncada Barracks) issued his third Pastoral on the subject (Communism in the Castro Regime), this time against those Catholics who continued to support the revolution. On December 4th, the hierarchy issued their final joint document, this time an open letter to Castro challenging him for the last time to repudiate communism, and hoping 'that the Lord may illumine you.' On December 16th Fidel Castro spoke on television and fired the last salvo in the war of words between the revolution and the Church.[8]

Another factor that influenced the decisions of a certain number of parents was that of involvement in the anti-Castro underground. In some cases it was the parents who were active and in others their teen-aged sons. The former feared that their children might be used against them by the regime either as hostages or spies.[9] The latter feared that their sons' involvement would get the whole family in trouble.

---

[8] Leslie Dewart, *Cuba, Church, and Crisis*, p. 161.

[9] "They are taking the children of underground members who have been caught and either jailed or shot and to punish the families these children are being sent deliberately, being picked and sent to Russia by way of retaliation, as a way of

By December 1960 opposition to the regime, already widespread among Catholic university students, involved the younger age groups, such as the Juventud Obrera Católica and Juventud Estudiantil Católica, and students in the various Catholic secondary schools such as Colegio de Belén and Colegio de La Salle in Havana.[10] These two types of youngsters, the underground activists and those who had received indoctrination, showed up among the unaccompanied children in Miami and presented us with special problems due to their anger against their parents for having shipped them to Miami.

Some parents had, of course, other reasons for staying in Cuba beside activity in the underground or the lack of a visa. Many stayed because they owned property which they hoped to keep as long as possible. Others remained because they expected the regime to be overthrown shortly, if not by the underground groups or exiles, perhaps by the U.S. Marines. Others were unwilling to leave because of aged or sick parents, or because a husband or brother, wife or sister was a political prisoner. There were those who stayed because they felt that it was the proper thing to do. Later, some, such as certain engineers and medical doctors, were not allowed to depart because they had special training or qualifications that were needed.

For some, the separation between parents and children was to be rather short, a few weeks or months. For the majority, it would be about three or four years. For others, it would stretch into several years and, for a few, forever. During the course of our program some parents and two children died before they could be reunited. A few parents changed their minds about the regime. Their children in exile were faced with the terrible decision of having to choose between life in the United States and a return to their parents in Cuba. One did choose to return after eight years in the United States. It was against this background of crisis and fear in an island one hundred miles from our shores that we in Miami became involved in the biggest child refugee program ever recorded in the Western Hemisphere.

Toward the end of September 1960 the staff of the Centro Híspano

---

a threat to other families of what is going to happen to their own children if they do not knuckle under. Children are paraded in front of their fathers in prison as a means of exhorting confession." Ibid., p. 160.

[10] "Student (university) opposition to the Castro regime was at first amorphous, but as the tempo of the revolution increased and the communists gained in strength, it took on definite form. Later in 1959 and throughout 1960, anti-Castro organizations established branches within the University of Havana. Among them, one known as Trinchera (The Trench), whose leaders originated from the Catholic University Association (Agrupación Católica Universitaria) soon acquired some importance. The Church provided the framework for these students' anti-communist activities, offering them a doctrinal alternative to Communism." Jaime Suchlicki, *University Students and Revolution in Cuba, 1920–1968* (Coral Gables, Florida: University of Miami Press, 1969), p. 95.

Católico became alarmed at the rapid increase in the number of newly arrived Cubans seeking assistance. This agency had been founded by Bishop Carroll in 1959 for the specific purpose of helping the Spanish-speaking newcomer adjust to life in Miami. In recent years, the number of Spanish-speaking newcomers in Miami had increased, many of them Puerto Ricans and Latin American emigrants, in marginal jobs. The social service agencies, including the Catholic Welfare Bureau, were not geared to their needs. The purpose of the Centro Híspano Católico was to provide an agency where a bilingual staff could make the Latins feel at home. Close working relationships existed between the Centro and the Catholic Welfare Bureau, although each had its own administration. When the Centro opened its doors, Cuban refugees were not a problem. The vast majority of refugees from Cuba during the first eighteen months of the Castro Regime were able to provide for themselves.[11]

Events in Cuba during the summer and fall of 1960, however, were to swell the exile exodus quickly. On 29 June the oil refineries were confiscated; 6 July the expropriation with compensation of all U.S. property in Cuba was authorized; 6 August U.S.-owned sugar mills, as well as other U.S. business concerns, were taken over by the Cuban government; 14 October the Urban Reform Law was enacted confiscating urban rental property. These events in rapid succession caused more and more people to make the decision to leave for Miami.

This led in turn to the imposition of increasing restrictions on what people leaving Cuba could take with them. More of the exiles arrived in Miami destitute for all practical purposes. The burden of assistance fell first on their own relatives and Cuban friends already established in Miami.[12] Then they turned to the Centro Híspano Católico, the only agency in the community, public or private, available to the Spanish-

---

[11] "Most Cuban refugees arriving in the United States during the first year and a half after the Castro Revolution were able to bring sizable amounts of money as they fled Cuba and upon arrival in the United States were self-supporting. Restrictions on removal of money and possessions from Cuba became increasingly severe after mid-1960. Real and personal property of refugees was confiscated. Each departing refugee was permitted to take only five U.S. dollars and items for personal use. Later no money could legally be taken from Cuba by refugees and clothing was restricted to a given number of pieces. Without funds, household goods and other essentials, refugees were in immediate need of welfare assistance upon arrival." *The Cuban Migration 1959–1960* (Miami, Florida: Research Institute for Cuba and the Caribbean; Center for Advanced International Studies, University of Miami, 1967), p. 24.

[12] "The weight of welfare assistance fell first on the local Cuban community in the Miami area. In fact, as Reverend Bryan O. Walsh, Executive Director of the Catholic Welfare Bureau of Miami, observed it was not until the support resources of the Cuban colony in the Miami area were reaching saturation that the larger community became fully aware of the Cuban refugee problem." Ibid, p. 24.

speaking newcomer. They were not eligible for medical care at Jackson Memorial Hospital; as yet there was no Cuban Refugee Emergency Center; Cuban children were not admitted to the Dade County public schools unless they paid tuition. Therefore, at this time the Centro Híspano Católico received the full impact of the exile influx.

Through a series of meetings beginning 29 September, the Bishop and the Centro Staff alerted the community to the presence of a rapidly increasing number of refugees in Miami with insufficient resources. Community leaders quickly recognized that the problem was beyond their capacity to solve and appealed to the federal government on the basis that the exiles were here because of U.S. national policy and that Miami was simply the most convenient port of entry.[13]

President Eisenhower appointed Mr. Tracy Voorhees, who had headed the Hungarian Refugee Program in 1956–1957, to look into the Miami situation, and allocated $1,000,000.00 for emergency aid. Mr. Voorhees came to Miami to evaluate the problem and recommended to the president that an emergency center be opened in Miami by the federal government. This recommendation was approved, and on 2 December 1960 the Cuban Refugee Emergency Center opened its doors in the old offices of the Dade County Board of Public Instruction on N.W. Third Avenue.

The Cuban Children's Program had its beginnings in the offices of the Catholic Welfare Bureau, 395 N.W. First Street, Miami, in late November 1960. This Bureau (now the Catholic Service Bureau), the social service agency of the Catholic Diocese of Miami, was founded in 1933 and in 1945 was licensed by the Florida State Department of Public Welfare for child welfare programs. In 1960 it was a small, multi-function child and family agency with a total staff of fifteen persons and one small group home for children, St. Joseph's Villa. During that year it had cared for about eighty dependent children in the Villa and in foster-family homes. As a member of the United Fund of Dade County, which at that time was undergoing one of its periodic financial crises, the Catholic Welfare Bureau had recently been advised to expect a thirty percent cut in its budget for 1961 due to the failure of the United Fund Appeal.

Even without the question of coping with the Cuban refugee influx, the future for all social service agencies in Miami was pretty gloomy in the fall of 1960. Public welfare agencies, always weak in Florida, were no better off than the voluntary ones. Florida had for many years competed with Mississippi for the last place among the states in per capita welfare

---

[13] Minutes, Board of Directors, Welfare Planning Council, 18 October, 1960, p. 2. Copy in files of the Catholic Welfare Bureau.

expenditure. Any additional strain on the welfare purse, whether public or private, would be catastrophic.

Into my office in the Catholic Welfare Bureau about 15 November 1960 a Cuban man brought a fifteen-year-old Cuban boy named Pedro. He asked me to provide a foster home or boarding school for him. Pedro had arrived in Miami a month earlier, sent by his parents who expected their relatives and friends to care for him, not realizing that these people could scarcely house and feed themselves. The youngster had been passed from one to another, often on a daily basis, with no one willing or able to accept responsibility for him. The effect on the boy's physical and mental well-being can easily be imagined. In his first month in the United States he had lost twenty pounds. It was a scared and hungry child that stood in my office that November afternoon.

Temporary arrangements were made for the care of the boy while the agency studied the situation. Knowing what was happening in our sister agency, the Centro Híspano Católico, we realized very quickly that Pedro was the first of many and that, as the situation in Cuba grew worse, the number of truly dependent children in Miami would increase.

It was clear to me and my staff that without outside help we could not render anything more than token assistance. We realized that the question of providing for such children within their religious heritage would be fundamental in the minds of the children themselves and of their parents. In common with the rest of the community, we saw very clearly that the only solution lay in the acceptance of financial responsibility by the federal government.

We turned for help to the Welfare Planning Council, which at that time was the community agency charged with the responsibility for identifying needs and planning for solutions in the social welfare field. Its membership included most social service agencies. Since my arrival in Miami in January 1957, I had played an active role in the work of the council, serving on many committees and study groups. The council had a Family and Child Care Division of which Mr. Robert S. Jones was the executive secretary. At my request Mr. Jones called a meeting of all the child welfare agencies in the county, both public and private. The third week of November we met at the offices of the Welfare Planning Council. Present were representatives of Dade County Welfare Department, Florida State Department of Public Welfare, Florida Children's Home Society, Children's Service Bureau, Jewish Family and Children's Service, and of course the Catholic Welfare Bureau.

At Mr. Jones' request I outlined the current situation as I saw it. The Miami area was experiencing an unprecedented influx of refugees from

Cuba. Among the refugees, there was an unknown number of unaccompanied children and there was every likelihood that the number would increase. As the child welfare agencies of the community, we were faced with the prospect of having to care for these children whose relatives or friends were unable to receive them in their homes. The agency representatives present were well aware of the fact that community leaders had already appealed to the federal government for help in meeting the needs of the refugees in general.

We discussed Mr. Voorhee's mission in Miami and I reminded them that Mr. Voorhees had directed the federal government's program for the Hungarian Free Fighters based at Camp Kilmer, New Jersey, in 1956–1957. It was from this center that the Hungarian refugees were resettled in various parts of the country. Among them were many teen-agers who were placed with families without any of the usual investigation and planning regarded as essential by child welfare agencies. In fact, the voluntary national resettlement agencies, such as Catholic Relief Services, Church World Services, and United Hebrew Immigrant Aid Society were not set up to run child welfare programs. As a result many of their placements, including some in Miami, had failed. My worry was that, unless our local agencies responded to the challenge, it was very likely that responsibility for the care of unaccompanied Cuban refugee children would be given by Mr. Voorhees to these same agencies. He had already asked them to come to Miami to help in the resettlement of the Cubans. My first concern therefore was that the program for the care of the unaccompanied children should be handled by child welfare agencies. My second concern was that the religious heritage of the child be safeguarded. This was one of the chief reasons why parents were sending their children into exile. My third concern was how a program of foster care could be funded.

There was relatively little discussion since the agency representatives present understood these concerns and, indeed, shared my convictions. At this meeting, it was agreed that a request would be made to Mr. Voorhees to include in his report to President Eisenhower recommendations for the funding of a special foster care program for the care of unaccompanied Cuban refugee children under the auspices of the Miami child welfare agencies. Three of the agencies offered to care for the children within their religious heritage. Since most Cubans were at least nominally Catholic, it was recognized that the main burden would fall on the Catholic Welfare Bureau. The Children's Service Bureau agreed to care for Protestant children and the Jewish children would go to the Jewish Family and Children's Service. Upon recommendation of this meeting, the Cuban Refugee Executive Committee, on 22 November, requested ". . . funds for foster care in institutions or family homes for children separated from their parents, who have been sent here to avoid coercive regimentation."[14]

Among the many other items included in this resolution, this was to be the *only* one calling for local expenditure of welfare funds which would be included in Mr. Voorhees' recommendations to the president.

> If it should prove necessary beyond what private charity can do, such Mutual Security Funds, ($1,000,000.00 allocated by President Eisenhower on December 2, 1960) will also be utilized for assistance to Cuban Refugee Children in extreme need.[15]

Meanwhile, other evidence of the flight of Cuban children came to the attention of the authorities. The dramatic case of two children brought to Key West Juvenile Court was symptomatic of the problem that was to mushroom into immense proportions within a very short time—that of those families without relatives or friends in Florida upon whom they could call.

> In November 1960 a Cuban mother brought her two children to Key West. She feared that they would be sent to Russia because she and her husband were actively opposed to the Castro Regime. She asked the Judge of the Juvenile Court to find a home for them. The Judge assumed jurisdiction and placed the children in foster care. The mother returned to Cuba to be with her husband and to continue her work in the counterrevolutionary movement.[16]

It was to help such families that Mr. James Baker came to Miami from Havana about the second week of December 1960. Mr. Baker was the headmaster of Ruston Academy, an American school in Havana, whose pupils were drawn from U.S. residents and upper-class Cuban families. Mr. Baker was joined in Miami by several U.S. businessmen formerly of Havana, and they set out to seek some way of providing shelter and education in Miami for those children who did not have relatives or friends here. Mr. Baker had sent one of his teachers to Miami and Washington the previous month to look over the situation. As a result of that visit, the decision had been made to open a boarding school in Miami for such children, and this was the purpose of the December trip. While looking for a suitable building for his school, Mr. Baker heard about the plans of the

---

[14] Resolution adopted by the Welfare Planning Council of Dade County, 22 November, 1960. Copy in the files of the Catholic Welfare Bureau.

[15] Voorhees, Tracy S., *Interim Report to the President on the Cuban Refugee Problem* (Washington, D.C.: Government Printing Office, 19 December, 1960), p. 10.

[16] U. S. Department of Health, Education and Welfare, *Cuba's Children in Exile,* Social Rehabilitation Service, Children's Bureau, 1967, p. 1.

Catholic Welfare Bureau to provide care for unaccompanied refugee children and came to see me on 12 December 1960.

Mr. Baker talked about his plans and told me about the fears of many of his Cuban friends for the welfare of their children. He also explained that some of these friends were active in the anti-Castro underground and were afraid that their children would be taken by the government and used as hostages.

I recall our conversation very well. I had become convinced by this time that uncoordinated and scattered efforts would only do damage to the cause. Believing also that only licensed child-placing agencies should care for unaccompanied refugee children, I thought that even the best boarding school would only be a partial solution. I pointed out to Mr. Baker that this was a job for a social agency which could plan for the total care of the child, including the legal questions of custody, which were bound to come up sooner or later. I also pointed out that some children, especially the younger ones, belonged in foster families, not in institutions. I noted that the question of religious heritage would be very important in the minds of most Cuban parents, Jewish and Protestant, perhaps even more than Catholics, if the separation should prove to be lengthy. I was also able to tell him that Mr. Voorhees had indicated that funds would be available for the care of the children. As a result Mr. Baker agreed to work with us. He would get the children out of Cuba and we would see that they were met upon arrival in Miami and that they would receive proper care. He estimated that approximately 200 children would be involved in this operation. Thus began Operation Pedro Pan, our project to fly the children out of Cuba.

Working with Mr. Baker were several members of the American Chamber of Commerce in Havana, U.S. businessmen whose properties had been taken over or confiscated by the Cuban government. These men were now in Miami waiting to see what would happen in Cuba, and they had informally reorganized the American Chamber of Commerce here. They had agreed to raise funds to help Mr. Baker in his plans. One of them was Mr. Kenneth Campbell, who later wrote:

> The idea was that American firms which had been in business in Cuba would provide the funds. Jim (Baker) and his colleagues in Cuba would make the necessary arrangements to get the children out, and the group would be responsible for caring for the children once they arrived in the United States. First funds were obtained by donations from American companies which had done business in Cuba, and I believe, from one British company. I regret not being able to recall the names of all the companies which made donations, but I know that one of

> the companies which made a substantial donation was Esso Standard Oil Company. I am sure that the British company which made a donation was the Shell Oil Company.
>
> In order to prevent the Cuban Government from tracing the source of the funds, these first donations as I recall, were paid to the Catholic Welfare Bureau, which in turn issued checks to a series of American citizens residing in the Miami area, who issued personal checks for one or more airplane fares, which were transmitted to the W. Henry Smith Agency in Havana. This was a travel agency owned and operated by H. Gilbert Smith who was Executive Secretary of the American Chamber of Commerce of Cuba during the time that I was president of the Chamber.[17]

The basic plan was as follows:

The American Embassy in Havana would be asked to grant a student visa. This would require proof that someone would be responsible for the child while in the United States and that the child was actually enrolled in a U.S. school. The Catholic Welfare Bureau attempted to meet these requirements by giving a letter to Mr. Baker for the U.S. Embassy accepting responsibility for any child designated by him and also by making arrangements to have a U.S. Immigration Form I-20 completed by a school for each child as proof of enrollment.

Mr. Baker returned to Cuba on 13 December to put the plan into motion. Before he left he made arrangements for all communications between us to go via U. S. diplomatic pouch, thanks to the cooperation of Mr. Culver Gidden, U.S. State Department Reception Center in Miami, and Mr. Daniel Braddock, Chargé d'Affairs, U.S. Embassy in Havana.

Two days later, on 15 December 1960, several members of the American Chamber of Commerce came to see me. Among them were Mr. Kenneth Campbell, Mr. Bob O'Farrell of Esso Standard, and Mr. Richard Colligan of Freeport Sulphur Company. They brought a letter from Mr. Baker and the first list of 125 names, which had come over in the diplomatic pouch that morning.

Our network of contacts was growing. By this time it included Mrs. Norma Lemberg, a former Havana resident, who was responsible for getting I-20 forms from Mrs. Agnes Ewald at Coral Gables High School, and Dr. Sergio Giquel, who relayed many messages to and from Cuba.

Mr. Baker's visit had brought a new dimension to the problem, mainly the question of children coming to us directly from Cuba, without any friends or relatives to meet them. In agreeing to work with Mr. Baker, we

---

[17] Kenneth Campbell, personal letter to Monsignor Bryan O. Walsh, July 16, 1964.

were accepting responsibility for the reception of the children right at the point of entry, Miami International Airport, and we were agreeing to provide foster care for those who had neither friends nor relatives able and willing to take them into their own homes.

The justification for this for me was simple, even though some social welfare agencies in Miami questioned our taking on this additional responsibility. Once our agencies had received the promise of government support, it seemed clear to me that our agencies were obligated to provide a well-arranged and well-planned reception for those children who would need care. Our first thought was to provide care and protection, when necessary, for the children already living here with friends and relatives. It is important to stress the *when necessary*. When separation from parents is necessary, it is always much better for a child to be with relatives or friends if at all possible. We know that even a poor family is usually better than any foster family or group care institution.

We knew only too well that as soon as word got out in Miami that we were taking children under care we would be inundated with requests. When we talked to Mr. Baker earlier that same week of December 1960, not one of us could foresee what the future would hold. Within a few short weeks the whole complexion of things would change. The U.S. Embassy would be shut down, and a series of events would be put in motion leading to the Bay of Pigs invasion on 17 April 1961. What most people saw as a short-term emergency situation in December 1960 would become a long-term possibility as hope for an early solution to the Cuban question faded.

Even before we had actually taken our first child under care, we had moved from being just the Cuban Children's Program into what would be called in time Operation Pedro Pan. After Mr. Baker's return to Cuba, there was little we could do in Miami except wait. Since funds would only be available on a reimbursement basis after the child was under care, we had nothing to work with. We had no assurance that any of Mr. Baker's children would actually be able to come, and we did not know whether any more children would come at all after 1 January. The impossibility of planning in advance became a way of life for the next several years. We never knew for the first six years of the program what the next day would bring.

In the meantime, we had children in Miami like Pedro who needed care, but because of the uncertain situation we had decided to wait until January before actually taking them under care. By that time we thought we would at least know whether or not more would be arriving. If only a few children required care, then federal funds would not be forthcoming. We were well aware that the key phrase in Mr. Voorhee's Interim Report to the President of 19 December 1960 was ". . . *if it should prove neces-*

sary beyond what private charity can do," and that we could count on federal funds only after we had exhausted our own resources.

All these agencies were very small as American social agencies go. The Catholic Welfare Bureau's one small group home for children between the ages of six and twelve, run by the Sisters of St. Joseph, had 20 children in residence at that time and nine empty beds. We had about 35 other children, mostly infants waiting for adoption placement, in foster family care. The County Welfare Department had a group of buildings vacant at their Kendall complex. These had been used for several years as a home for dependent and delinquent Negro children. Only a short time before, the county had integrated its facilities for children and thus vacated these buildings. The department offered these buildings to us for use in an emergency. They had been designed to accommodate 60 children. Eventually these became known both in Cuba and in Miami as El Campamento de Kendall, the reception center for several thousand Cuban children.

We also had another resource available without which it would have been utmost folly to attempt what we did. We knew that we could fall back on the more than 130 Catholic Charities agencies throughout the rest of the country. Thus, although we had little or nothing in the way of material and physical resources on hand, we did know that once the program got moving we had places to turn to for help. This unique capability of the Catholic Welfare Bureau was the source of our confidence in accepting the responsibility for such a program and in offering leadership to the community in what was recognized as a serious problem to be faced. History would testify that this confidence was not unfounded.

So it was that during the month of December we waited in Miami as people made preparations for the Christmas holidays. Christmas Eve was a Saturday and our offices were closed when I received word that the first of the children might be arriving the next day. The staff had dispersed for the long weekend, and I could not get in touch with our social workers. I had no idea how many children would come in the next day. Any children who came in could be taken to St. Joseph's Villa even if they had to sleep on the floor the first night. There was little else that we could do. The matter was complicated by the holidays, the shortness of time, the unknown number of children, and above all by the lack of communication with the people in Cuba. We were sure that if the authorities there got any wind of a mass movement of unaccompanied children, they would clamp down right away and ask questions afterward.

As I drove home that afternoon the enormity of the task ahead slowly dawned on me. What would we do if all 200 arrived within the next couple of days? There would not be time to gear up the program, open up the buildings at Kendall, hire the necessary staff. We could do all of these things, if we had time. Even a slow buildup over a couple of weeks would be all the time that we needed. Once we got the children moving out of Miami to agencies around the country it would become routine. As I drove home, the faith with which I had made the promise to Jim Baker was justified and God gave me a solution to the immediate problem, the first of many such answers to prayer in the months and years to come. My way home took me by Assumption Academy, a private girls' boarding school run by the Sisters of the Assumption. I had never been in the place, but I realized suddenly that the school would be empty for the holidays and that about 200 children could be accommodated there, even if they all came on the same flight. I stopped and went in to make my plea. Mother Elizabeth was most responsive and agreed to allow us to use the school, providing everyone could be out by the sixth of January. I remember her remarking that she could not refuse such a request on Christmas Eve. She did not realize that many would be teen-age boys and I did not tell her. As it turned out, we never had to place boys there and the few girls we did place there were out by 6 January.

Later that same day I went to St. Joseph's Villa to see what we could do there. We worked it out so that ten or twelve boys could be accommodated there, at least overnight. Our immediate problem was solved. We had places to take the children from the airport. Yet we were caught between two conflicting desires. On the one hand we hoped that not too many would come in at the same time or even the same day, and on the other hand we wanted to see the children get out of Cuba. Over all loomed the specter of 1 January, the second anniversary of Fidel Castro's assumption of power. There was nothing else we could do that day, except wait for the word from Cuba and for the first children to arrive.

After Christmas we could begin to implement other plans. We would request that the County Welfare Department turn over to us the facilities at Kendall. We would also begin the task of opening up a large house at 175 S.E. 15 Road, across the street from the Assumption Academy, which had been offered to us by Mr. Maurice Ferré, a Puerto Rican industrialist in Miami whose grandparents came from Cuba. This would become our first all-Cuban receiving home for teen-age boys, since we knew that neither the Sisters of the Assumption nor St. Joseph's would welcome teen-age boys. But on Christmas Day none of this could be done.

Christmas Day 1960 was as usual in Florida—warm. About 11:00 a.m. I was able to locate Mrs. Louise Cooper, one of our social workers, as she came home from Mass. I asked her to go to the airport with me to meet the two flights expected that afternoon, Pan Am's Flight 422 and National's Flight 452. By this time we ourselves had become emotionally involved in the race against the 1 January deadline. No longer were we simply a social agency concerned about a community problem. We were now sharing the worries of families we did not even know, hundreds of miles away in a life and death struggle in the Cold War. Our excitement rose as time drew near for the first of the flights to arrive.

No children were aboard.

All our anticipation, worry, planning were held in abeyance as we awaited the second flight. No children arrived that day.

We were deeply disappointed. But we did accomplish one thing that Christmas Day. We made arrangements to work with the officials of the U.S. Immigration and Naturalization Service and to involve them in identifying the unaccompanied children arriving on Cuban flights. For some twenty-two months this would be a daily contact. The officer in charge at the airport was Mr. Patrick Crowley and from him and his staff we were to receive the very finest cooperation.

The next day, 26 December, Mrs. Cooper returned to the airport vigil while I began the task of opening up Kendall and the 15th Road operations. We took possession of Mr. Ferré's house and began the struggle to get the necessary clearances from the Zoning Department, the Health Department, the Fire Department, and the Building Department, a struggle that we would repeat many times in the years to come. After much discussion, we finally convinced these public officials that we were trying to help the community and that we needed their help to solve the problems and overcome the difficulties. Often it seemed that the purpose of the applicable rules was to impede rather than to help.

Finally, we got all the necessary clearances to use Ferré's house as a reception center for teen-age boys, although the Fire Department would not allow anyone to sleep on the second floor until a fire escape was installed. We could not argue with this. I sent a man and a truck down to Camp Matecumbe, a summer youth camp owned by the Diocese of Miami in south Dade County, to borrow bunk-beds, tables, and chairs. We made arrangements for some household supplies and Mother Elizabeth of Assumption Academy agreed to allow our boys to eat lunch and supper in the school dining room. Breakfast we could handle in the house.

The 26th of December also brought several requests for placements of children already in Miami. Some of these were children on Mr. Baker's list who already had tourist visas and whose parents had decided not to wait for the student visas as time began to run out. They had been staying with friends in Miami who had put them up for a few days. At the airport, Mrs. Cooper waited for the plane from Cuba. This time her watch was not in vain. On the second flight, late in the evening, the first children arrived and she took them under care, bringing them to St. Joseph's Villa. Thus it was that Sixto Aquino and his sister, Vivian, were the first unaccompanied children actually taken under care by the agency. The waiting was over and the Cuban Children's Program and Operation Pedro Pan were under way.

No new children came on the 27th. Two came on the 28th, none on the 29th. There were six on the 30th and 12 on the 31st. All these were met at the airport and taken under care. However, none of them had a student visa, and we could not understand what was delaying the operating of Mr. Baker's plan. The mass influx that we had both feared and hoped for did not materialize.

On 29 December the first boys moved into the Ferré house, which was informally christened "Cuban Boys Home." We still were without staff as such. Mr. Raymond McGraw, a social worker with the Catholic Welfare Bureau, was drafted as temporary housefather, alternating with me while the search for houseparents went on.

The time had come to make a formal request that the government implement Mr. Voorhees' report of 19 December to President Eisenhower. As far as the Catholic Welfare Bureau was concerned, the program had already gone beyond what "private charity could do." On 29 December Mr. Jones of the Welfare Planning Council and representatives of the three voluntary child-welfare agencies and the Florida State Department of Public Welfare met with Mr. Leo C. Beebe, special assistant to Mr. Voorhees, at the Cuban Refugee Center to discuss the situation.

The Cuban Refugee Center had been opened by Mr. Voorhees on 2 December 1960 in the old administration building of the Dade County Board of Public Instruction, 223 N.W. Third Avenue. Mr. Beebe had been borrowed by Mr. Voorhees from the Ford Motor Company and was at that time acting director of the center. The results of that meeting were summarized in a letter sent by Mr. Jones to Mr. Beebe. In addition, he reported that the agencies concerned felt that the situation as it existed then fell within the terms of the commitment made by Mr. Voorhees in his Interim Report of December 19. He requested the implementation of contractual arrangements between the licensed child-welfare agencies and the federal government for the care of dependent Cuban children.

We knew that we were breaking new ground with this request. Never before had the U.S. government funded foster care of refugee children in the United States. Previous child refugee programs had been supported by private organizations, church groups, and individual donations. Nobody in Mr. Voorhees' office seemed to know how the recommendation made by him on 19 December should be implemented.

Finally, about the middle of January 1961, provision was made for the funds to be channeled to the child welfare agencies through the voluntary national resettlement agencies, such as Catholic Relief Services. It was the middle of February, however, before the first monies actually reached us, by which time we were almost $100,000 in debt. The financial base of the Cuban Children's Program was finally guaranteed on 1 March 1961 when contracts were signed between the three child welfare agencies and the Florida State Department of Public Welfare, acting as the agent of the U.S. Department of Health, Education, and Welfare. These contracts provided for the reimbursement of the agencies on a per diem per child basis at the rate of $6.50 per day for institutional care and $5.50 per day for foster care. These funds were for the care of the children in the United States. Operation Pedro Pan was funded by donations such as those referred to by Mr. Campbell in his letter.

Meanwhile, on Friday, 30 December, at about 6:30 a.m. I was awakened by a telephone call from Havana. To my surprise, the caller was Jim Baker. We had agreed not to call each other directly, since as a U.S. citizen in Cuba, he was in a very vulnerable position. He explained very briefly that the U.S. Embassy was holding up the issuance of student visas and that I was to call Mr. Frank Auerbach, of the Visa Section in the U.S. Department of State in Washington, D.C., for details of the trouble. As soon as the office opened at 9:00 a.m. I called Mr. Auerbach and told him of the call from Havana and of our keen interest in the matter. He told me that he would personally look into the matter and return my call as soon as possible.

Within a few hours Mr. Auerbach called and advised me that the U.S. government was willing to issue the two hundred student visas requested by Mr. Baker's group, with one condition: a recognized and established organization in the United States would have to assume *ultimate* responsibility for the children. The Catholic Welfare Bureau would be most acceptable to the Department of State, as it was a licensed child welfare agency. This was the only way that the visas could be issued, since the U.S. government could not accept this responsibility. Mr. Auerbach knew that our agency had been promised funds by the government; nevertheless, he had to have an unconditional statement from us accepting this responsibility. A new element was thus introduced into the problem and I was faced with the moment of decision.

The rumors were strong in Cuba and in Miami that no children would be allowed to leave Cuba after 1 January. If so, these children would have to leave Cuba within two days. There was no time for consultation. I decided to sign the required statement on my own authority and to accept the consequences if the whole thing backfired. Mr. Auerbach asked me to send him two copies of the statement, mailing one to his office and one to his home because of the holidays. He promised to authorize the visas as soon as he had one of the copies in hand. Within the hour the copies were in the mail Special Delivery.

Time was running out, but not in the way we had expected. 1 January 1961 came and went with no new law about children. Castro did not cut off the exodus of Cuban children; instead he demanded that the U.S. Embassy staff in Havana be reduced to the size of the Cuban staff in Washington, from 120 to 15 persons. This brought a quick reaction in Washington from the President and on 3 January the United States broke diplomatic relations with the Cuban government. The Embassy in Havana and the Consulates in Havana and Santiago de Cuba were shut down, leaving no place in Cuba where people could secure visas for travel to the United States. For us it seemed to mark the end of Operation Pedro Pan. No unaccompanied children arrived in Miami on 1, 2, or 3 January. Our hopes revived when four came on the fourth.

The departure of the U.S. Chargé d'Affairs was the signal for most U.S. citizens to leave also. Mr. Jim Baker and his wife arrived in Miami on 5 January. He told us that there had been delays in getting the visas for the children, due to the number of requests, the slowness of communications with Washington, and the surveillance by the secret police. Nevertheless, at the last moment, as the Embassy was being shut down and the staff were actually burning papers in the traditional manner, he was allowed to stamp twenty-five passports himself.

To all of us who met that day in the Catholic Welfare Bureau, it seemed that the hopes of Mr. Baker and his friends to help Cuban parents send their children to the U.S. were now finished, since no more visas could be given in Cuba. In the general gloom as we all shared Mr. Baker's disappointment, there were two bright spots—children could still come if they had visas since the rumored law had not materialized, and the Cuban Children's Program was in operation. We could now return to our primary responsibility—the task of developing the program for the children already in Miami who needed care. That same day, Mr. Baker became a temporary housefather at the Cuban Boys Home, in the old Ferré house on S.E. 15th Road.

THE "VISA WAIVER"

The closing of the U.S. Embassy marked the end of the first phase of the Operation Pedro Pan. Despite our disappointment, we quickly proceeded with our plans for the Cuban Children's Program to meet the needs of the many children already in Miami who we knew needed our care. We also knew that we could still expect many more children from Cuba, since a great many Cuban families had passports, with multiple entry Tourist B1 Visas. As soon as their parents knew that care was available in Miami these children would come. We had much to do. New staff had to be recruited, houseparents for the Cuban Boys Home and for Kendall, cooks and janitors, social workers, clerks and typists, and a good bookkeeper. I believe that it was at this point that we made a decision which was to be very important for the administration of the program in the future. The Cuban Children's Program became a completely separate department of the Catholic Welfare Bureau, with its own staff directly responsible to the executive director. The original purpose of this was to protect the regular program of the Catholic Welfare Bureau from being swallowed up in the new project. It also meant that the regular programs were not affected by the periodic evaluations and audits carried out by agencies of the federal government.

Mrs. Louise Cooper was the first person formally assigned to the Cuban Children's Program. We were also able to locate a Cuban man as a resident housefather at the Cuban Boys Home. This man, Angel Carrión, was to become so identified with the home that it became known as "Casa Carrión" to hundreds of Cuban youths. In a few weeks he was joined by his wife, Nina. The first houseparents at Kendall were Mr. and Mrs. Fernando Pruna. Since the vacant buildings there needed some repairs and maintenance to make them habitable, the county welfare gave us temporary use of Cottage No. 1 in their main complex. Because it was located right in the middle of their own operations close to their home for the aged, this proved less than satisfactory, and at once there were complaints that the Cuban children were noisy and undisciplined.

In the meantime Mr. Baker had not given up on his plans to help those children caught in Cuba without visas. He had organized a group of trustworthy friends in Havana to keep up the effort at that end. A plan was devised which would allow them to send children to Kingston, Jamaica, traveling on a visa granted by the British Embassy in Havana. They would then be given a visa for the United States by the Consul General in Kingston and from there come to Miami. For this we needed the cooperation of the British government and the assurancc that there would be no long wait in Kingston for the U.S. visa. We would also need a place for the children to stay at least one night there. We thought the plan worth trying, even though it would be slower and more expensive than the direct Havana to Miami route. However, it would also give the impression to the Cuban authorities that the children were going to Jamaica to school and not to the United States.

The month of January proved critical in the development of our two programs, the Cuban Children's Program and Operation Pedro Pan. Each day brought new developments. By the end of the month the programs were well under way and there would be no fundamental change, despite the fantastic growth and development, in either one. It was then that I began to keep a diary covering most of the month. Each night, when I was ready to go to bed, I used a dictaphone to record the major happenings of the day. The following chronicle is based on this record, supplemented by appointment books and other records in the files of the Catholic Welfare Bureau.

Friday, 6 January: Mr. Baker, Mrs. Cooper, and I gathered in my office at the Catholic Welfare Bureau to discuss the situation. Mr. Baker told us about the last days in Havana, the difficulties in getting visas for the children's passports. We discussed the prospect for the future and Jim Baker talked about his Jamaica plan. We decided to call Mr. Frank Auerbach, our contact at the State Department in Washington. He was interested, and since I was scheduled to be in Washington on the 8th to attend the White House Conference on the Aging as a Florida state delegate, Mr. Auerbach invited me to call him on my arrival. Since it would be Sunday, he asked that I call him at home, which I took to be another sign of his great interest in our program. Seven children came today.

Saturday, 7 January: I spent this day at the Boys Home, helping to get it organized, getting to know the youngsters. Two more children arrived at the airport.

Sunday, 8 January: I flew to Washington and upon arrival, I called Mr. Auerbach as he had asked. He made arrangements for me to meet him outside one of the side doors of the State Department at 2:00 p.m. It was a bright, cold winter afternoon, and the streets around the State Department were completely deserted. Somehow the weather, the day, the time, the happenings of the past weeks all combined to create an atmosphere of intrigue and conspiracy. Promptly at two, Mr. Auerbach drove up and we met for the first time. We entered the building and walked along deserted corridors to the office of Mr. Robert F. Hale, Director of the Visa Office, who was waiting for us. We spent about three hours discussing the possibility of bringing the children out via Jamaica on the two KLM flights a week among other possibilities. It was then that I heard for the first time the words "visa waiver." [18]

---

[18] *Hearing Before the Subcommittee to Investigate Problems Connected with Refugees and Escapees of the Committee of the Judiciary*, U.S. Senate, 87th Congress, First Session, December 6, 7, 13, 1961.

"When the United States broke off diplomatic and consular relations with Cuba on January 3, 1961, the closing of the Embassy at Havana and the Consulate

Mr. Auerbach proposed at our meeting that on the petition of the Catholic Welfare Bureau, the State Department would grant visa waivers for children coming directly from Cuba. This would enable the airlines to board them in Havana on direct flights to Miami without running the risk of a fine of $1,000 in each case for bringing a passenger to the United States without a valid visa. The question was whether the Cuban authorities would cooperate in allowing such a child to leave. This we could only find out by trying. At any rate, it offered another way of continuing Operation Pedro Pan.

The meeting ended on the following note. The State Department would take up the question of visa waivers with the Justice Department early the following morning. The matter of transit visas for Jamaica would also be discussed with the British Embassy. I was to check with the Church in Jamaica on the possibility of enlisting its help in meeting the children in Kingston, getting them to the U.S. Consulate, putting them up overnight, and then sending them on to Miami the next day. As soon as Mr. Auerbach had any news he was to call me at my hotel. He asked that I wait for the call on Monday and not attend the meetings of the White House Conference on the Aging. In Miami, two more children arrived.

Monday, 9 January: I called the Diocese of Kingston in Jamaica by telephone the first thing in the morning and talked to Father William A. Connolly, the chancellor. I told him that we needed his help for Cuban children and he thought that something could be worked out, since they had both a boys' and a girls' boarding school. He also told me that they were beginning to get some Cuban refugees. He would talk to the Bishop. I told him that as soon as I got clearance, I could fly down and discuss details with him and explain completely what we had in mind. I then called our office in Miami and asked our Supervisor of Child Welfare, Miss Rachel Erwin, to be ready to go to Jamaica with me the next day, Tuesday, 10 January. The KLM flights came in on Tuesday and Thursday and I wanted to be in Kingston on the next flight.

During the afternoon I received the call I was expecting from the

---

at Santiago shut off the means of escape for the thousands of Cubans besieging these offices for Visas. Relatives, friends, and social agencies soon began to ask the Department of State to take emergency action in behalf of these peoples.

"As a matter of sound and humanitarian national policy, and in keeping with the traditional role of the U.S. as a haven for those fleeing persecution, the Department concluded that it should ask the Department of Justice to act jointly in *waiving the visa* requirement, pursuant to Section 212 (d) (4) (A) of the Immigration and Nationality Act, in individual cases involving specific elements of unforeseen emergency." Testimony of Robert F. Hale, Director, Visa Office, Department of State.

State Department. We were given the go-ahead on both proposals. We could bring the children out by way of Kingston on British visas, and then come to Miami on visa waivers. We could also try to bring them out directly from Havana on visa waivers. We were given a very big concession regarding the visa waivers which was to make our program of distribution in Cuba much easier. This was blanket authority to issue visa waivers to all children between the ages of six and 16. For children between 16 and 18 years of age, we would have to submit their names and birthdates to Washington for prior security clearances. We could not do anything for a child under six nor for anyone over 18. All of this was verbal; we had nothing in writing.

I immediately called Miami to confirm the trip to Kingston for the next day and to let Jim Baker and Mrs. Cooper know the new possibilities we had. That same evening I flew back to Miami. Meanwhile, Mr. Baker called his contacts in Havana and told them to call on the British Embassy for help. Copies of Mr. Baker's lists were brought up to date, so that Miss Erwin could take them with her to Kingston the next day. Our flight was scheduled for 8:30 a.m. so everything had to be prepared at once. Three more children arrived today.

Tuesday, 10 January: I met Rachel Erwin at the airport and we boarded the BWIA flight for Jamaica. Rachel was rather upset when she learned that we would be flying over Cuba. She wondered how we would explain away all the lists of Cuban children we were carrying if by chance we made a forced landing. We landed safely, however, in Kingston and were met by Father Connolly, who took us to lunch at the bishop's house. There we gave them full details of our mission. Father Connolly had already talked to the principals of the two boarding schools, St. George College and Immaculate Conception College. The principal of the latter was Mother Lucy, former principal of Corpus Christi School in Miami and a blood-sister of Mother Patrina who had been with me in Homestead for several years. Bishop McEleney, the Bishop of Kingston, assured us that we would have full cooperation.

Next stop on our schedule was to return to the airport to see the arrival of the KLM flight from Havana. While we were waiting, a Cuban man came up to me and asked if I was there to meet the children from Cuba. Needless to say his question was a shock, since the whole Operation Pedro Pan was supposed to be a secret and we were trying to avoid giving the Cuban authorities the impression that there was a wide-scale organized effort to help children leave the island. We were sure that this would bring about reprisals against parents and others in Cuba who were cooperating. I tried to look innocent and told him that we were simply curious to see the flight. But by now we were beginning to feel that we were really involved in an international intrigue. We then went to see the two boarding schools where the children would stay and where we were to spend the next couple of nights, Miss Erwin at Immaculate Conception and I at St. George.

Back in Miami two more children came. We learned that the friends left behind in Havana by Mr. Baker were deliberately sending out the children in small numbers so as not to attract attention.

Wednesday, 11 January: Father Connolly, who was by now as enthusiastic and as emotionally involved in the project as we were, took us to meet the U.S. consul general and the managers of Pan American and KLM airlines. The consul general had been alerted by the Department of State and had already talked to the Jamaican officials and secured their full cooperation. By noon, we had done all we could and Father Connolly took us sightseeing for the afternoon.

Thursday, 12 January: I returned to Miami, leaving Rachel Erwin in Kingston to wait for the first children to arrive. She and Father Connolly met the KLM flight on the chance that some children might be on it, but there were none.

Friday, 13 January: After almost a week's absence, I found myself back in the office. It had been a very fruitful week—each day two or three children had arrived—and it looked as if our Operation Pedro Pan was going to continue. There were urgent problems that needed settling in Miami. We had a total of 50 children under care in three different locations—the Cuban Boys Home, St. Joseph's Villa, and Cottage No. 1 in Kendall. They were for the most part teen-age boys.

The most urgent problem was school. Since it was the middle of the year, both public and Catholic schools were refusing to enroll them unless they had previously attended American-type schools and could speak English. This posed few difficulties for those children who had been pupils of Ruston Academy and the American Dominican Academy in Havana and spoke excellent English, but many of the children had attended Cuban schools. We spent much of Friday discussing what we should do with them. Everyone was still hopeful that within a few months these children would be able to return to Cuba.

Someone suggested that we should open our own school in Miami, using Cuban teachers and following the Cuban secondary school curriculum, the bachillerato program. I knew that the Centro Híspano Católico, located in the old Gesu School building, had empty classrooms. So I made arrangements to meet with Sister Miriam, O.P., the Supervisor of Social Services, there the next morning.

Saturday, 14 January: This was a day of great activity in getting the bachillerato program of the Centro Híspano Católico organized. The following report was dictated by me that same evening and gives some idea of how quickly we were able to get things organized to meet newly identified needs. It should be remembered that all this took place in the midst of great activity in the overall Cuban refugee program.

> The problem of secondary education for Cuban refugee children in Miami has been brought to a head by the fact that the Catholic Welfare Bureau has 50 children under care as of today. We have been faced with the problem of getting these children in school; both Catholic and the public American high school systems are unable to provide them with the type of education they require. I was told last night that when these children return to Cuba they will be required to begin their secondary education all over again or at least at the point where they left off upon their arrival in this country. The American high school curriculum is of no use to them as far as continuing their Cuban education is concerned.
>
> This morning I discussed plans with Sister Miriam of the Centro Híspano Católico specifically around the possibility of establishing a Cuban secondary school at the Centro Híspano Católico. Sister's enthusiasm encouraged me and I asked about the possibility of having some of the Dominican Sisters who have lately come from Havana assigned to this work. Sister thought that there was a possibility. She told me that four classrooms are available and a science laboratory at the Centro Híspano Católico and that we could get a program going there.
>
> I talked with Jim Baker, director of Ruston Academy, about the possibility of this program and of getting Cuban teachers to set up this bachillerato. He was enthusiastic in his support. At nine o'clock this morning I called Bishop Carroll and told him of our plans and asked his approval and his help in getting the service of at least two Dominican Sisters who were experienced in this work. He promised to call Mother Emmanuel (the Provincial Superior of the Dominican Sisters of Albany, who had operated the American Dominican Academy in Havana until the break in diplomatic relations and who also had operated the Centro Híspano Católico) and ask for them.
>
> At 2:30 p.m. the Bishop called me and told me we had the go-ahead signal and that we could expect two Sisters, one of whom would be Mother Daniel and the other Sister Ana María, both of whom are in Miami at the present time. I then discussed with the Bishop the opening date and at my suggestion the date was moved up to Wednesday, 18 January instead of the following Monday which the Bishop had suggested. The report of this has been given to the *Voice* for publication and on Monday the Diocesan Superintendent of Schools, Monsignor William F.

> McKeever, the former Director of Secondary Education of the City of Havana, Dr. Ernesto Garcia Tuduri, Mr. Jim Baker, and the Sisters will meet at Centro to complete arrangements, the details and plans.[19]

The same afternoon Jim Baker and I reviewed the plans for bringing the children out of Cuba. The latest word from Havana was that the British ambassador had agreed to stamp all the children's passports with a British visa and that even the children who were to come directly to the United States would be supposedly in transit to some British possession, such as Nassau, Bahamas. This was thought to give them a better chance to leave Cuba without questions being asked, since the Cuban government was anxious to maintain friendly relations with Britain. The children would also have the visa waiver required for them to board the plane. Today was the first in eight days with no new children arriving.

My former housekeeper in Homestead, Mrs. Mary L. Larkin, agreed to come and act as housekeeper in the Cuban Boys Home, pending the arrival of the new houseparents. I talked to Rachel Erwin in Kingston. I asked her to return to Miami as she was more needed here than down there. I felt that Father Connolly would be able to handle the program at that end. She told me that they were expecting, according to KLM, the first children to arrive 17 January.

Sunday, 15 January: Today we had a long discussion with the boys at the Cuban Boys Home regarding the school they would attend. Many of them were disappointed to learn that they would go to a Cuban school, because they had heard that American high schools were easier and the course a year shorter. I told them that if they were still here in September, they would all be in an American high school. One boy, a student of Ruston, was to go to Archbishop Curley High School and some of the younger ones to Sts. Peter and Paul Elementary School. No children came today.

Monday, 16 January: I was in Tallahassee all day, but when I returned, Mr. Baker reported to me that the meeting on the bachillerato had been most fruitful and that no real difficulties stood in the way of the program. One problem concerned textbooks. Word was sent to Havana to have the children bring their textbooks with them whenever possible. There were two children on today's flight.

Tuesday, 17 January: Mr. Baker reported his first problems with discipline at the Boys Home. Last night the boys had stayed up after the usual lights out in an apparent test of authority and many had missed breakfast, going out to a restaurant without permission. Mr. Baker and

[19] Bryan O. Walsh, unpublished diary.

I talked to them and explained that we were in place of their parents and that we would have to have their cooperation. At Mr. Baker's suggestion we asked them to form a sort of Student Council who could assist the house administration in matters of this sort. They elected one of the quietest and least likely boys as their president. Baker and I discussed at length the whole question of rules and discipline, Cuban customs of child-rearing, the type and use of punishments and sanctions. I felt that this would be where our first cultural clash would occur, both in the house and in school. I was glad I had a few months the previous summer in intercultural studies at the Catholic University of Puerto Rico. It gave me at least some insight into what I could expect as well as an elementary knowledge of Spanish, which was improving rapidly. One child came today.

Wednesday, 18 January: This was registration day in the new program at the Centro, and I took several of the boys to school myself and introduced them to their new teachers. The program went well, and in addition to our own children, several children living with their parents or relatives took advantage of the opportunity offered.

We received word from Kingston that the first seven children had arrived there the previous afternoon on schedule and would be coming to Miami that same afternoon. Miss Ariela Carbonell, a new social worker aide on our rapidly growing staff, accompanied me to the airport to meet them on the 3:00 p.m. Pan Am flight. They were four girls and three boys, three of them being brothers and sisters. Our work of the previous week had not been in vain. At least seven children had managed to leave Cuba without U.S. visas and arrive in the United States. One of the girls had relatives waiting for her. Her brothers stayed with us, one for the Boys Home, and the younger one for St. Joseph's Villa. This was usually the case. Relatives and friends would take the little girls, but no one wanted teen-age boys. The other girls went to St. Joseph's Villa and the boy to our home. Two more children arrived this same night on a direct flight from Cuba.

Thursday, 19 January: The formal opening of the bachillerato program was a Mass celebrated by Monsignor McKeever at which I preached my first sermon in Spanish. Mrs. Larkin reported for duty at the Cuban Boys Home, where we now had 18 boys. This day we were also asked by two people for help in getting the children of relatives out of Cuba. We told them that we were working on a program, but that it would be several weeks before we could do anything about it. We had decided to work only with those we knew until we were sure that the system was really working. One child came today.

Friday, 20 January: The new bookkeeper for the Cuban Children's Program was hired. He was Mr. Jesús González, lately arrived from Havana, who would in time become the head of the accounting office of the Catholic Welfare Bureau and would make great contributions to the success of the program. I also attended a meeting of the Welfare Planning Council, the agency which had helped so much a month earlier in requesting federal funds for our agencies. It was now in a major crisis because of the failure of the United Fund. Its budget had been cut back so badly that it was reduced to a staff of two, the executive director and a secretary. This case illustrates the serious state of social welfare service in Miami even without the refugee influx. The manager of the Pan American office in Havana visited our office and asked help for a child. The child had a student visa but needed an I-20 immigration form to go with it.

News came today that five more children had arrived the day before in Jamaica. A letter was also received from Father Connolly assuring us that all was going very well. That end of the program seemed to be working smoothly.

One child also arrived on the direct flight. There was some excitement about the Jamaica group. Since one of the children would turn eighteen on 22 January, she had to be in the U.S. by that date, or she might face a long wait in Kingston for a regular visa. Children between six and 18 coming through Kingston on our program were still being admitted on the visa waiver. This girl was Sandra Carbonell, the sister of a Catholic Welfare Bureau social worker aide. She made it just on time, Sunday morning.

Our program was growing and I was concerned that there was no sign of any funds from the federal government despite the promises of Mr. Voorhees. On 18 January he had made his final report to President Eisenhower, who was going out of office. The new president was John F. Kennedy, and with him came a new administration which we hoped would be more responsive to the needs of the refugees. We were existing on monies borrowed from other funds for day-to-day expenses and the bills were beginning to pile up. Members of the Diocesan Chancery personnel were getting nervous, since they really doubted that we would ever receive any federal funds. The national Catholic refugee agency, Catholic Relief Services, had established its offices in the Cuban Refugee Center, and its programs for the resettlement of rcfugees was now in operation. I knew that they too were depending on federal funds. So I called the national director, Bishop Edward E. Swamstrom, for advice on how to shake loose the money. He offered to make the necessary contacts and later assured me that reimbursement would be forthcoming.

Saturday, 21 January: At Kendall we decided that we could accommodate about 100 children. We wanted to move the children out of Cottage No. 1 and we also knew that we needed more staff. Among the U.S. citizens who had come from Cuba after the break in diplomatic relations were several Ursuline nuns, who had operated the Ursuline Academy in Havana for many years. They were staying at the Assumption Academy awaiting reassignment. I talked to Mother Thomas, their Superior, and asked them to take over the Kendall operation for us. The advantages seemed great. They were accustomed to dealing with Cuban children. They spoke Spanish and yet they were Americans and therefore used to working in this country. The one difficulty was that this was the pre-Vatican II era and their rules did not allow them to work with boys. I went to the bishop for help. As always, he responded at once and went to visit Mother Thomas that same evening and brought with him Archbishop (now Cardinal) Vagnozzi, the Apostolic Delegate, who was on a short visit to Miami and greatly interested in the Cuban refugee situation. I was present. The bishop and the archbishop assured Mother Thomas that times were different and that this was an emergency situation in which they had an obligation to help the people with whom they worked for so long in Havana. We would get houseparents to assist them with the boys, but they could supervise the whole Kendall operation. The Ursulines agreed to take over Kendall.

The buildings at Kendall consisted of three separate structures, a girls' cottage, a double-wing boys' cottage, with kitchen and dining room in the middle, and a new four-classroom building with plenty of recreation area around. It was about a mile from the main complex buildings and thus suitable for an independent operation. We would not run into conflicts with the county welfare programs which included a home for the aged and a hospital in addition to the county children's home.

Sunday, 22 January: This was the busiest twenty-four hour period yet in receiving children from Cuba. Seventeen children came into Miami in the twenty-four hours ending at midnight Sunday, 11 directly from Cuba and six from Kingston. Not all the children required care. Usually about half of those arriving had some relatives or friends waiting for them. However, almost as many already in Miami were requesting care.

Monday, 23 January: Nine more children arrived directly from Cuba on visa waivers. The number of people coming to the office got bigger every day as word spread in the Cuban colony that we had a way of getting children out of Cuba. Fifteen children were taken into foster care today, the biggest number to date.

Tuesday, 24 January: We now had 24 boys in the Cuban Boys Home. Slow progress was being made by the contractor in installing the fire escape. All the boys were still sleeping downstairs. Even though we could use the upstairs during the day for recreation, it was not a very satisfactory arrangement. It would be another week before it was completed. I noticed that the boys were beginning to regard the house as their home. Only three had requested permission to visit relatives over the weekend, which was a change. The first days they could not wait to get out of the house.

The bachillerato program continued to grow. As of this date 60 children were enrolled, of whom 30 were under the care of the Catholic Welfare Bureau.

Mrs. Cooper, Mr. Baker, and I reviewed the program and we decided that Mr. Baker and a friend would take over responsibility for the airport details, meeting all the flights from Cuba and those from Kingston. Because of the necessity for secrecy, we had minimum communications with Havana and therefore we never knew what to expect. We had eight more children who needed foster care this day.

From the beginning we had known that we could rely on the Catholic agencies around the country to provide foster care for the children. In December, Philadelphia Catholic Charities had agreed to accept 40 children under 12 years of age. Mrs. Cooper reported that the first five would travel the next day. While this was a big help and the first breakthrough in sending children to other dioceses, it was a limited answer. We really needed placements for teen-age boys. But again the pattern that was to prevail for the rest of the program was already apparent. Everyone wanted little girls, and maybe little boys, but nobody wanted teen-age boys and few were willing to take them.

This same afternoon I visted Kendall to inspect the operation there in Cottage No. 1 and to see what was being done to prepare the other buildings.

Wednesday, 25 January: We had a staff conference, including the houseparents, to draw up some general policies for the many teen-agers we now had under care. Present were Sister Louis Gonzaga from St. Joseph's Villa, Mr. and Mrs. Fernando Pruna from Kendall, Mr. Jim Baker from the Cuban Boys Home, Mr. Raymond McGraw, Mrs. Cooper, and myself from the Catholic Welfare Bureau. Our problem was twofold: (1) we had rarely had a teen-ager under care before in the Catholic Welfare Bureau and we never had had them in group care; (2) we had the cultural differences and the problem of helping Cuban teen-agers adjust to life in the United States. We considered items such as allowances, school expenses, clothing, purchases, visits of relatives, and visits to relatives.

We received word that there would be a National Resettlement Conference held in Miami the following Sunday, Monday, and Tuesday to boost the resettlement process. Among those invited were Catholic Charities Directors from all over the country. This would give us an opportunity to push for foster-home placements, especially for teen-age boys.

Tonight we had our first medical emergency. One of the children who had arrived the previous week and was staying with friends in Hialeah was knocked down by an automobile and hurt. He was in Hialeah Hospital and the hospital needed medical authorization which his friends could not give. I called Judge William R. Culbreath of the Juvenile Court and he took jurisdiction, declaring the boy dependent, and gave the necessary authorization to the doctor and the hospital. This was another one for the policy manual, which was growing every day.

Thursday, 26 January: We purchased the first vehicle, a used car. At the Cuban Boys Home we noticed the first signs of difficulty within the group when one boy asked to be moved to a foster home, claiming the other boys were picking on him. Up to now the boys had been nice to each other since they all had felt themselves to be Cuban brothers suffering together in exile. Now that they were beginning to settle in, things were returning to normal "boy life." Today we took 14 children into care—all new arrivals at the airport.

Friday, 27 January: This day I spent in the office catching up on my correspondence. The rate of arrivals continued high with ten children today.

Saturday, 28 January: The Cuban Boys Home fire escape was finished today and we could now use the upstairs bedrooms. It was a short-lived relief since 13 new boys arrived this same day and we had no beds for them in Kendall. So we took them to the Boys Home where we now had a total of 42. It was clear that we had to step up our efforts to place children around the country.

Sunday, 29 January: The National Resettlement Conference got under way on this day, and the delegates were greeted by some 2,000 Cuban refugees in Dade County Auditorium. The whole effort of the conference was to convince the rest of the country that the refugees posed a national problem and that Miami needed the help of the nation in solving it.

One problem facing us was how to elicit this support for our Cuban children without breaking our secrecy on Operation Pedro Pan. During the conference we decided not to talk about the children, but to work quietly with individuals who could help, especially the Diocesan Directors of Catholic Charities, most of whom, including the Secretary of the National Conference of Catholic Charities, Monsignor John O'Grady, were in Miami for the conference. Some of the media people, newspaper reporters and the like, were beginning to get wind of what was going on. We admitted to the presence of unaccompanied Cuban children, but would say nothing about helping them get here. We did indicate that the less said about that the better, since we were convinced that any publicity would have quick repercussions in Cuba. Today was another big day at the airport with 12 more children.

Monday, 30 January: The Secretary of the U.S. Department of Health, Education and Welfare, Mr. Abraham Ribicoff, arrived in Miami to look into the Cuban refugee situation on behalf of the new president. I did not attend the public meeting because I did not want to talk publicly about the children. The secretary asked for me and asked some questions about child welfare needs and it was just as well that I was not present. I made an appointment to meet with him privately, together with Bishop Carroll and Sister Miriam from the Centro Híspano Católico.

Tuesday, 31 January: At a closed meeting of the Catholic Relief Services for their diocesan resettlement directors, I spoke at length about the need we had for foster family and group care for unaccompanied children. I stressed the need for keeping secret our participation in getting children out of Cuba.

One of the first dioceses to respond to our appeal was our neighbor and mother diocese, the Diocese of St. Augustine, Florida. I met with Father Sager and Father Lenihan to discuss turning their St. John's Youth Camp at Switzerland, Florida, into a home and school for teenage boys. Seven children came yesterday from Cuba and seven more today.

Wednesday, 1 February: I met with Secretary Ribicoff and gave him a written report of the children's program stressing our desire for no publicity. In my report I wrote:

> *Current Situation*: For the last two weeks the program has been functioning very smoothly. As of today 174 children have come in (from Cuba). Of these 53 have been and are being cared for by relatives and friends, the rest by the Catholic Welfare Bureau except for two by the Jewish Family Service. Also 15 children who arrived earlier and had been living alone in Miami have also been taken under care by the Catholic Welfare Bureau.
>
> *Arrangements for Care*: As of January 31st 120 children were under the direct care of the Catholic Welfare Bureau in

> three group homes, three boarding schools, and some foster homes. In addition 20 have been sent to the Catholic Children's Bureau, Philadelphia. It is felt that only about 120 can be cared for in Miami and therefore arrangements have been made to have the children now arriving cared for under the auspices of the Catholic Charities Bureaus throughout the country. Accommodations for more than the 510 currently on the list (Mr. Baker's) are guaranteed.

Secretary Ribicoff told me that he had asked the Children's Bureau to work with us on details of a purchase-of-care contract, which would formalize the relationship between our agencies and the federal government.

Thus it was, 39 days after the first fruitless wait at the airport on Christmas Day, the Cuban Children's Program and Operation Pedro Pan were now in full swing. We were taking care of children already in Miami; we were helping children leave Cuba directly for Miami and via Jamaica; we were placing children in foster care throughout the country; and our relationship with the federal government was about to be placed on a formal basis. Come what might our program was now on a firm foundation.

We could not read the future. We still shared the common hope that it would not be too long, maybe a year at the most, until these children could be reunited with their parents. We still were thinking in terms of a few hundred children coming from Cuba. We were pretty sure that sooner or later the Cuban authorities would discover what was going on, and put a stop to the exodus. It was too early for us to realize that all these assumptions would within a few months be proved wrong. In the meantime, however, we had a job to do. The next period would be one of expansion.

We would continue to grow in all aspects of the program during the following 21 months. We would receive more than 14,000 children at the airport. We would take 7,464 children under care. We would place them in foster care in 35 states under the auspices of 95 different child welfare agencies. We would set up three large reception centers in Miami and establish two group-care facilities for teen-age boys in Miami with a State Department of Public Welfare authorized population of 1,500 children and a total staff in Miami of 465 persons. We would do all of this before the Cuban Missile Crisis shut off commercial air traffic on 22 October, 1962.

We were able to keep all of this out of the newspaper until 9 March 1962 when the Cleveland *Plain Dealer* decided to break the spirit of cooperation and prepared a story for publication. When all efforts to suppress the story failed, we agreed to a press release giving the basic story but omitting all references to what was being done within Cuba.

Operation Pedro Pan ended with the October 1962 Missile Crisis, but the work of caring for Cuban children was to go on for many years. As this is being written we have completed ten years of operation. We have a total of 165 children under care and have been operating more or less at this same level since shortly after the Freedom Flights began on 1 December 1965. The parents of our children were given priority on these flights and within the first six months of the flights from Varadero, the majority of our children had been reunited with their parents.

Today we continue to receive new children under care. The numbers are much fewer, but the program is the same. We offer care and protection to unaccompanied Cuban refugee children and we expect to continue to do this as long as there are Cuban refugee children.

One of our recent cases was a seventeen-year-old Cuban boy, of *campesino* background, who swam five miles across Guantánamo Bay to the U.S. Naval Base in order to come to the United States. This boy was five years old when Castro took over. All he ever knew was the Castro regime. He is from the sector of the Cuban population which has been identified as one of the chief beneficiaries of the Revolution. Yet he left his family, which he dearly loves, and all that he knew. He came and his family agreed to his coming, because they knew that he would be taken care of here on his arrival.

Ten years after its inception the Cuban Children's Program continues to offer to Cuban parents and their children an alternative to Communist indoctrination, and that choice is still being made after ten years of indoctrination.

EPILOGUE

Sixto Aquino, who with his sister were the first children to come on 26 December 1960, wrote me a letter dated 12 May 1971 in which he describes those events:

> As to our feelings on December 26, Vivian and I remember being scared and sad and also to have had a sense of an adventure about to begin.
>
> After we left St. Joseph's Villa, we went to live at the home of cousins of my mother's, Mr. and Mrs. Antonio Santos of Hialeah, Fla. Vivian attended Immaculata and St. Patrick's High Schools, graduating in 1963. Since, she has attended Charron Williams Business School in Miami and the University of Maryland. She married Eduardo Latour, a professional photog-

rapher in 1967 and became the mother of a daughter, Vivian in 1969. She is expecting a second child within the month.

I graduated from St. Patrick's High School, 1965, and enrolled at Georgetown University in Washington where I obtained an A.B., Economics in 1969 and where I will shortly obtain an M.A., Economics. I am presently working for the Inter-American Development Bank.

CHRONOLOGY

1 January 1959	Castro assumes power in Cuba.
January 1959–June 1960	Gradually increasing exodus of Cuban refugees to Miami.
29 June 1960	Foreign-owned oil refineries confiscated.
6 August 1960	U.S. sugar mills seized.
September 1960	Cuban refugees noticed in Miami. Meeting at Centro Híspano Católico to discuss means of helping them.
14 October 1960	Urban Reform Law promulgated in Cuba.
October 1960	Series of community meetings to alert government officials to needs of Cuban refugees.
November 1960	Mr. Tracy Voorhees is appointed by President Eisenhower to look into Miami situation. $1,000,000.00 in Mutual Security Funds is allocated for emergency aid.
November 1960	First Cuban refugee child in need of foster care is brought to the Catholic Welfare Bureau. Cuban mother brings two children to Key West and returns to Cuba.
22 November 1960	Welfare Planning Council of Dade County adopts resolution calling for federal government to establish a federally-funded program for Cuban refugees.
2 December 1960	Cuban Refugee Center in Miami opened by U.S. government.

12 December 1960	Mr. James Baker from Havana is in Miami seeking help for unaccompanied Cuban children.
15 December 1960	First list of unaccompanied children is received in Miami from Mr. Baker.
24 December 1960	Word received that first children would arrive on 25 December.
25 December 1960	No children.
26 December 1960	First children arrived in Miami under Operation Pedro Pan.
29 December 1960	First shelter for unaccompanied Cuban refugee children in Miami is opened.
29 December 1960	The Welfare Planning Council requests funds from the federal government for the care of Cuban children.
3 January 1961	United States breaks diplomatic relations with Cuba.
9 January 1961	Visa waiver program approved by the State Department.
25 January 1961	First unaccompanied Cuban children to be relocated out of Miami left for Philadelphia.
3 February 1961	U.S. Department of Health, Education and Welfare is assigned responsibility by President Kennedy for all Cuban refugee programs.
22 October 1962	Cuban Missile Crisis. Last commercial flight between Havana and Miami—the end of Operation Pedro Pan.
1 December 1965	Freedom Flights between Varadero and Miami begin with first priority for parents of unaccompanied Cuban children already in United States.

H. Jon Rosenbaum
Department of Political Science
Wellesley College

William G. Tyler
Department of Economics
University of Florida

POLICY-MAKING FOR THE BRAZILIAN AMAZON*

Long a region seemingly immune to modernization and relegated to governmental neglect, the Brazilian Amazon has nonetheless frequently been the theme of political rhetoric. While the area has stagnated, Brazilians have continually referred to it as the "Land of Promise." [1] Now, however, it appears that Amazonia is finally to become a major government beneficiary.

An area comprising 42 percent of Brazil's territory but only about three percent of its population, a land often inaccurately portrayed as both a "Green Hell" and a "Green Paradise," the Amazon recently has been selected by President Garrastazu Médici as the site of a major development effort. Its colonization and economic development have been assigned priority status within the president's "Plan for National Integration."

The national euphoria provoked by the government's program for the Amazon perhaps can only be rivaled in recent Brazilian history by

---

* Full research for this article was conducted in Brazil where H. Jon Rosenbaum was a Guest Scholar at the Instituto Brasileiro de Relações Internaciaonais, Rio de Janeiro, during the summer of 1970. William G. Tyler was a visiting Professor of Economics at the Brazilian School of Public Administration, Getulio Vargas Foundation, Rio de Janeiro, 1966–1969.

[1] See Frances Foland, "A Profile of Amazonia: Its Possibilities for Development" in *Journal of Inter-American Studies and World Affairs* 13, No. 1 (January 1971): 62–77.

the inauguration of Brasilia's construction in the late 1950s. Once again a symbol of Brazilian grandeur has been created with which nearly the entire nation can identify.

The authors seek to be less ambitious than the development plan to be discussed in this article and attempt only to provide the reader with an overview and elementary analysis of contemporary Amazonian developments. It is our hope that this will furnish the basis for more sophisticated and detailed treatment of the topic in the future by the current writers and other social scientists.

REGIONAL ECONOMIC DEVELOPMENT AND THE BRAZILIAN AMAZON

Until lately the economic history of the Amazon region had been essentially the history of the boom and subsequent decline of the rubber economy. During the late nineteenth and early twentieth centuries expanding demand in the international rubber market expressed itself in the form of inflated rubber prices. To take advantage of the profitable opportunities afforded by surging demand and prices, the collection, processing, and exportation of Brazilian natural rubber was increased sixfold between the 1870s and the first decade of the 1900s. Since production methods did not change, this increment in output was accounted for entirely by augmentation of the labor force. It is estimated that the population of the Amazon region grew from 337,000 in 1872 to some 1,100,000 inhabitants in 1906.[2]

Given the existing health conditions and high mortality rates, it is evident that most of the population growth was due to migration, primarily from the Brazilian Northeast. The rubber boom, opulent and audacious at its apex, was brief, however. With the development of Asian supply sources, prices began to fall sharply after the end of World War I, signaling the termination of the boom and the end of an era. As rubber prices declined, those migrants that did not leave the Amazon area or die from the effects of malaria or other diseases were compelled to eke out a miserable existence from subsistence hunting, fishing, and gathering.

From the decline of the rubber economy until the recent revival of interest in the area, the Amazon region stagnated, isolated from the rest of Brazil and participating only marginally in Brazil's impressive economic growth during the past fifty years. The states of Amazonas and Pará plus the other Amazon territories had a combined per capita income

[2] Celso Furtado, *The Economic Growth of Brazil* (Berkeley, California: University of California Press, 1965), p. 143; Caio Prado Junior, *História Econômica de Brasil* (São Paulo: Editôra Brasiliense, 1965), p. 246.

in 1967 of approximately $171.[3] This compares with per capita income figures of $833 and $600 for the states of Guanabara (the former federal district containing the city of Rio de Janeiro) and São Paulo, respectively. Moreover, comparing the figures for 1947 (our earliest reliable data) with those of 1967, it can be concluded that the disparity in per capita income had increased.[4] Normally, discussions of Brazilian regional income inequality center on the more populous Northeast,[5] but the per capita income of the Amazon region exceeds that of the Northeast by a mere $10.

The physical separation of the Amazon region from the rest of Brazil has been reflected in the paucity of inter-regional linkages which has minimized the region's ability to benefit from the growth occurring in the dynamic South and Center-South. It has often been argued that regional income inequalities tend to grow in the less developed countries during the early phases of development, while during later phases there are reasons to believe that such disparities decrease.[6] The Brazilian experience seems to conform to this proposition both with respect to the Amazon region and the Northeast. Growth and spread effects emanating from the thriving Center-South have been offset by backwash or perverse spread effects and the lack of inter-regional linkages. The little internal factor mobility that has occurred has served to intensify the divergence of regional incomes. The emigration of skilled and innovative manpower from the peripheral areas is well known, and there is evidence to suggest that

---

[3] These estimates have been made using national income account data provided by the Getúlio Vargas Foundation and population projections available in Instituto Brasileiro de Geografia e Estatîstica, *Anuário Estatîstico, 1969,* vol. 30 (Rio de Janeiro: 1969).

[4] The $171 figure appears smaller still when we consider that Furtado has estimated the per capita income for all of Brazil in 1900 to be around $224. See Furtado, *The Economic Growth of Brazil,* p. 164.

[5] See Werner Baer, "Regional Inequality and Economic Growth in Brazil," *Economic Development and Cultural Change,* vol. 12, No. 3 (April, 1964); Stefan H. Robock, *Brazil's Developing Northeast: A Study of Regional Planning and Foreign Aid* (Washington, D.C.: The Brookings Institution, 1963); and Albert O. Hirschman, *Journeys Toward Progress* (New York: The Twentieth Century Fund, 1963), ch. 1.

[6] See Gunnar Myrdal, *Economic Theory and Under-Developed Regions* (London: Gerald Duckworth, 1957); Francois Perroux, "Note Sur La Nation de 'Pole de Croissance,'" *Economic Appliquee,* vol. 8, Nos. 1 and 2 (1955); and Alfred O. Hirschman, *The Strategy of Economic Development* (New Haven: Yale University Press, 1958). For an affirmative empirical test of this hypothesis see Jeffrey G. Williamson, "Regional Inequality and the Process of National Development: A Description of the Patterns," *Economic Development and Cultural Change,* vol. 13 (1965).

considerable private capital resources also have flowed from the poorer regions.[7]

If the backwash effects of growth exceed the positive spread effects, regional income disparities will increase. Government policy, of course, can influence such a situation. A central government can take measures to allocate public investment, stimulate private investment, juggle the external terms of trade, or manipulate the tax structure so as to favor the less developed region. In fact, such management has been the conscious objective of the Brazilian government in recent years with respect to the Northeast. The Superintendency for the Development of the Northeast (SUDENE) was established in 1960 for the expressed purpose of funneling economic resources into the Northeast. Public investments were increased markedly, and an elaborate system of fiscal and credit incentives was implemented to lure private investment capital to the area.[8] The Amazonian equivalent of SUDENE, named SUDAM (the Superintendency for the Development of the Amazon), was established in 1966, but only in the last few years has the Amazon attracted substantial attention and resources.

For a country to underwrite a development scheme designed to decrease regional income disparities through rapid, concerted development in the poorer regions, however, is not without its costs. Given the fact of limited economic resources, real resources can only be diverted to the poorer regions at the expense of the richer areas. Hence it is indeed quite possible that the desire to ease regional income disparities will force a country to settle for a lower rate of overall economic growth. Growth is likely to be maximized by concentrating effort at the so-called growth poles rather than by diffusing the thrust in an attempt to grow evenly. The essential economic issue is one of comparative benefits at the margin. The appropriate question for government policy-makers to ask is not whether an Amazonian development scheme will yield benefits but whether the resultant benefits to society will be greater than those stem-

---

[7] Conselho de Desenvolvimento do Nordeste, *A Policy for the Development of the Northeast* (Rio de Janeiro, 1959), p. 26. Although this well-known report deals with the Northeast, many of its findings would presumably also hold for the Amazon region.

[8] For an analysis of the investment incentive see Albert O. Hirschman, "Desenvolvimento Industrial no Nordeste Brasileiro e o Mecanismo de Crédito Fiscal do Artigo 34/18," *Revista Brasileira de Economia*, vol. 21, No. 4 (December 1967). See also David Goodman, "Industrialization and Regional Economic Development in the Brazilian Northeast," H. Jon Rosenbaum and William G. Tyler, editors, *Contemporary Brazil: Issues in Economic and Political Development* (New York: Praeger Publishers, Inc., scheduled for January, 1972).

ming from alternative uses of the economic resources involved.[9] If so, the scheme is economically justifiable; if not, other reasons must be convincingly put forth, and its cost to economic efficiency and economic development should be evaluated in terms of the noneconomic benefits. Such economic costs will be dependent upon the magnitude of the resources utilized in the scheme and the opportunity cost involved per unit of expenditure.

It is clear that noneconomic rationales can provide adequate justification for regional development schemes. The SUDENE programs in the Northeast constitute a case in point. The Northeast accounts for over 25 percent of the Brazilian population. To have distinct and growing regional income disparities with the Northeast representing such an important segment of society is socially divisive at best and conducive to separatism or civil war at worst. The population of the Amazon region, on the other hand, represents only about three percent of the total population.[10] Therefore, given the large amount of expenditures forecast (approximately $500 million in the next few years), social divisiveness in the Amazon region alone would not appear to constitute an adequate justification.

In some ways the desire to develop the Amazon can be seen as an attempt to find a new strategy for growth and economic development in Brazil. Concern has been expressed in government policy-making circles that the possibilities of further import substitution are limited and that continued growth based upon import substituting industrialization is questionable.[11] Export promotion of manufactured products, in many respects a continuation of the import substitution strategy, while receiving some government attention, does not appear to have the widespread official support necessary for its success as a strategy of growth.[12] The expansion of the internal market has been afforded much discussion among policy makers as a means of sustaining Brazil's economic development,[13] but

---

[9] In more precise economic terms, the project (or a group of projects) having the highest benefit-cost ratio should be the one selected.

[10] Population estimates have been made from data published in IBGE, *Anuário Estatístico, 1969.*

[11] See, for example, Ministério do Planejamento e Coordenação Geral, *Programa Estratégico de Desenvolvimento, 1968–1970,* Industrialização Brasileira; Diagnóstico e Perspectivas (Rio de Janeiro: January 1969).

[12] Part of the lack of confidence in the export promotion approach can be explained by the profound pessimism that many Brasilia policy-makers have concerning protectionism in the developed countries. Two recent bitter confrontations with the United States regarding soluble coffee and cotton textiles have fortified this pessimism.

[13] See Gabinete do Ministro Extraordinário para Planejamento e Coordenação

little action has been taken to accomplish such ends. A successful development strategy involving the expansion of the domestic market would imply both a redistribution of income and a massive education program. The possibility that these measures might eventually undermine the current regime's political support (although they could create new supporters) would presumably explain the government's apparent failure so far to undertake effective action to implement such a strategy.

On the other hand, the expansion of the internal economy via the opening of new areas and frontier development may not offer such problems. Indeed, opening up the interior can constitute a model of national economic development. By undertaking sizable public investment and providing incentives for private investment in the Amazon region, the government can furnish a stimulus for continued economic expansion in Brazil. Funneling economic resources for investment into the frontier area will have a growth impact. For the model to be economically efficient, one must assume that more productive investment opportunities do not exist elsewhere. It is, however, likely that they do.

Despite any economic limitations, the frontier development strategy offers some political prospect likely to be considered desirable by the present Brazilian government. The process of economic development is invariably accompanied by political change, often involving the redistribution of political power. Different strategies of economic development affect different groups in different ways. For example, by allowing and encouraging the massive participation of foreign direct investment, the import substitution and manufactured export promotion strategies can be effected in such a way as to minimize change in the political structure. A new industrial elite emerges but, to the extent that it is a foreign elite within the country, its impact on the polity is quite different than would be the case with an emergent national industrial elite. With the frontier opening development model the elite that is strengthened is essentially a military one. In the untamed hinterland it is the military that builds roads, pacifies Indians, maintains order, transports supplies, and provides a multitude of other administrative services. It is not surprising, then, to find that the Brazilian military itself is among the most vociferous advocates of the frontier development strategy.

OPERATION AMAZON

Development of the Amazon has always been one of Brazil's fondest national aspirations, but one unhappily frustrated by a lack of resources,

Econômica, *Diretrizes Gerais do Govêrno: Programa Estratégico de Desenvolvimento* (Rio de Janeiro: July 1967).

the need to deal with more urgent problems, and the paucity of government interest. Despite past promises of progress, such as those made by President Hermes da Fonseca at the turn of the century and by President Vargas in 1940, government commitment until recently has proved largely illusory. New pledges of a brighter future for the Amazon region accompanied the military's assumption of power in 1964,[14] and in 1966 President Castelo Branco announced the beginning of Operation Amazon, a coordinated attempt to realize the conquest of the Brazilian Amazon. While dramatic results were not achieved during the Castelo Branco presidency and that of Costa e Silva which followed, the administrative agency responsible for coordinating Amazonian development was reorganized with the creation of SUDAM and the city of Manaus was made a free port. Since then, the commitment to the Amazon has grown dramatically, reflecting the military's decision that, in the words of one high ranking foreign ministry official, the "first priority is the integration of Brazil and of the Amazon with Brazil." [15]

As presently constituted, Operation Amazon, embodying the frontier development strategy, is multi-dimensional. The primary institutional response has been the establishment of SUDAM, whose function is to coordinate development activities in the Amazon area. Modeled after the Northeast regional development organization SUDENE, it is charged with harmonizing the operations of the federal agencies and attracting private investment. To accomplish the latter objective, an elaborate set of fiscal and credit incentives has been instituted. Although the incentives greatly parallel those previously enacted in the populous Northeast, the effects so far have been dissimilar. Whereas in the Northeast private investments were largely made along the line of uneconomic regional import substitution in capital intensive industries, investments lured to the Amazon region by SUDAM's incentives have tended to go more for agricultural expansion and the development and processing of natural resources. Considerable progress in these endeavors has been achieved but it still remains to be seen whether SUDENE's inefficiency and mistakes in resource allocation can continue to be avoided in the Amazon region.

A second dimension of Operation Amazon has been the creation of a free port in the major city of Manaus in 1967 and its subsequent

---

[14] These resolutions are contained in Humberto de Alencar Castelo Branco, *Integração da Amazônia* (Rio de Janeiro: Imprensa Nacional, 1965).

[15] Maury Gurgel Valente, "A Amazônia Brasileira e as Outras Amazônias," in *Problemática da Amazônia* (Rio de Janeiro: Livraria-Editôra da Casa do Estudante do Brasil, 1969).

extension to several smaller Amazonian towns. Ostensibly the purpose of the free port is to stimulate economic activity in a zone by removing all taxes on imported goods.[16] As was to be expected, Manaus was soon swamped by a deluge of imported consumer goods of all sorts—ranging from television sets to ice cream, from canned fruits to Swiss watches, from Persian rugs to Japanese radios. Nearly all available data indicate that the level of economic activity in Manaus has increased dramatically. Unemployment has decreased, construction has risen sharply, and tourism has surged markedly (especially by Brazilians on shopping tours). In short, the waving of the magic policy wand has suddenly and miraculously transformed a sleepy river town once again into a booming commercial center.

Like the rubber boom preceding it, the commercial boom resulting from the creation of the free port has not been without its negative repercussions. Informants have described the closing of several recently established manufacturing enterprises that were unable to withstand the onslaught of competitive imports. In addition, it is clear that the surge of luxury imports is not destined for the impoverished economy of Manaus, and it is not surprising that Brazilian industry in the Center-South has voiced complaints about the intrusion into its markets. The Free Zone has had an economic cost in the form of adverse balance of payments effects, tax revenue losses, damages to nascent local industry, and impairment of growth in the Brazilian industrial complex in the Center-South. This cost, socialized in part, is borne largely by the Center-South, and the gains, while highly visible, contribute little to the long run growth of the Amazon region. Smuggling—whether legally sanctioned and facilitated or not—is hardly replete with favorable growth and spread effects.

The most important component of Operation Amazon consists of the trans-Amazonian highway system. While important public investments in such areas as electric energy, sanitation, and housing have been undertaken, in terms of emphasis, magnitude, and impact the most significant investments are being directed towards the creation of a highway system integrating the region and linking it to the rest of the country. The Médici administration has placed considerable emphasis on the development of transportation as an integrative and developmental instrument, and so it is also understandable that the expansion of the Amazonian transport system has been accorded preeminence in the current Amazon-

---

16 Importantly, the tax exemptions include not only any import taxes but indirect domestic taxes as well. This enables foreign imports to undercut the highly taxed Brazilian manufactured goods even if the two are produced at identical costs.

ian venture. The Decree Law of National Integration of 16 June 1970 stipulates in Article 2 that the first measure to be initiated in the Amazonian program will be the immediate construction of two highways, one linking Cuiabá and Santarém and the other, the transamazônica, uniting the Northeast with the Amazon. At the time of this writing, in November 1970, construction (having begun on 1 September 1970) was underway on both.

These roads are designed to serve as the main agents facilitating the occupation and exploitation of the Amazon. They are needed, according to Minister of Transportation Mário Andreazza, because riverine transportation has proven unequal to the task of modern colonization and has bound Amazonians to the rivers and the land directly adjacent to them. This, Andreazza contends, has isolated them and limited their horizons.[17]

The projected highways have aroused a great deal of controversy. The rapidity with which they were decided upon and begun has led to charges of improper planning, waste, and incompetence.[18] Cost estimates are inconsistent, varied, and incomplete, but some forecasts for construction alone of the transamazônica highway system range up to $100 million. It would seem that the expenditure of such large amounts of resources would merit careful study and consideration, but this has not been the case. No adequate feasibility study of the highway's costs and benefits has been made. In fact there is even considerable debate about the qualities and capacity of the soil to support the highway and sustain agricultural activity. Nevertheless, construction has begun. Obviously, elements other than economic criteria are instrumental in the making of Amazonian policy.

FACTORS INFLUENCING THE DETERMINATION OF CONTEMPORARY AMAZONIAN POLICY

Publicly the Brazilian government has credited two closely related considerations with motivating its decision to promote the accelerated development of the Amazon.[19] The first of these is linked to the Amazonian demographic reality. One of the few remaining sparsely populated areas in the world thought suitable for human habitation in great num-

---

17 Brasil, Ministério das Transportes, Departamento Nacional de Estradas de Rodagem, Mário Andreazza, *Transamazônica*, Pronunciamento feito na Câmara dos Deputados en 1° de julho de 1970, p. 6.

18 See, for example, the article by Roberto de Oliveira Campos entitled "La Rage de vouloir conclure" in the newspaper *Estado de São Paulo*, 22 Julho, 1970.

19 Brasil, Ministério do Interior, Superintêndencia do Desenvolvimento da Região Centro-Oeste, *Integração Nacional*, Dezembro/1969, p. 2. Mimeo.

bers, the Amazon is believed by the Brazilian leadership to be vulnerable to foreign seizure, gradual denationalization, or exploitation by domestic enemies.

The second attraction Amazonian development has for the president and his advisors is that it is intended to contribute significantly to the resolution of not just one (the security of the Amazon) but to two of the country's major problems. Government planners calculate that the employment and settlement of hundreds of thousands of now unemployed and underemployed Northeasterners will provide at least a partial solution to the Northeast's endemic misery, overpopulation, and hunger and to its social tensions. If all goes according to plan, Northeasterners will be the Amazon's roadbuilders and colonizers, and their agricultural output will supposedly help feed their relatives who remain behind.

In short, Amazonian development is being depicted by its proponents as benefiting the entire nation. Sponsors of the plan even argue that the relatively prosperous Center-South will also profit since the Amazon's development will lead to the expansion and strengthening of the internal market for the Center-South's industrial output.[20]

Additional but generally less well known factors have also been responsible for the importance the government has assigned to the Amazon's development. As would be expected in contemporary Brazil, military politics have been especially influential in the determination of Amazonian and other policy. Government enthusiasm for Operation Amazon certainly has not been restrained by the military, which for the most part is possessed with the notion that the Amazon must be occupied physically in order to deny it to foreign predators. In attempting to persuade the president to commit himself fully to the occupation of the Amazon a few military enthusiasts have even relied upon seemingly preposterous arguments. Some officers, for instance, have sought to exploit the tension created by the Venezuelan-Guyanese border dispute in order to emphasize the necessity for immediate Brazilian settlement of the Amazon. These officers have insinuated that if Brazil does not populate and thus control the Amazon, Venezuela may use it as an invasion route.

Other groups within the Brazilian military have boosted accelerated activity in the Amazon for purely selfish reasons. Illustrative is the case of the Army Corps of Engineers who have been especially vocal and energetic supporters of Operation Amazon. Members of the corps realize that they will be the primary military participants in the development of

---

[20] Brasil, Ministério do Interior, Superintêndencia do Desenvolvimento da Região Centro-Oeste, *Pronunciamento do Exmo. Sr. Ministro de Estado do Interior a Frente de Serviços da BRs 080/158*, p. 1. Mimeo.

the Amazon and that their stature and power within the military will therefore be fortified.

Factional rivalries have also tended to affect the Amazonian policy-making process. For example, General Albuquerque Lima, a leader of the *Linha Dura* (Hard Line) group and an admitted presidential aspirant, has charged the regime with the neglect of the Amazon, and his commitment to the Amazonian cause has attracted considerable support among younger officers. President Médici's recognition that he had to circumvent a possible threat to his administration from Albuquerque Lima and his followers may have induced the president to treat the Amazon as a particularly urgent matter.[21]

Aside from the incentive provided by the military's exhortations and machinations, the president's decision to treat the Amazon's development as a critical issue can be traced to yet other enticements. The 1970 Northeastern drought aggravated the Northeast's already high unemployment and dramatically demonstrated that a viable solution to that area's periodic crisis had still to be found. This event and its consequences provided the regime with a situation which required immediate amelioration and the obvious solution was merely to commence the construction of the Amazonian highways which were already projected. In this way the traditional massive migration to the Center-South of the unemployed, uneducated, and underqualified Northeasterners during times of drought could be redirected to the Amazon. By resettling Northeasterners in the Amazon region, Amazonian development could serve as a political and social escape valve for the government with respect to the Northeast. In addition, resettlement could allow the government to skirt the delicate issue of population control.

Finally, it is likely that President Médici estimated that advancing the Amazon's development would be a safe and popular program to undertake. Mineral deposits would probably be discovered, and although the entire region could not be occupied during his presidency, some settlement would occur. Moreover, by undertaking such an ambitious and audacious project, an effort could be made to appeal to nationalist sentiments diverting public attention away from such unpleasant topics as political repression and the torture of political prisoners and focusing it on the more positive achievements of the current administration. In some ways Operation Amazon can be interpreted as a desire by the military to legitimize itself and attain greater popularity.

---

[21] A compendium of General Albuquerque Lima's views on the Amazon is available in General Afonso Augusto de Albuquerque Lima, *A Participação do Ministério do Interior no Desenvolvimento e na Ocupação da Amazônia* (Rio de Janeiro: Imprensa do Exército, 1968), 68p.

THE POLICY-MAKING ENVIRONMENT AND THE PUBLIC MANDATE

Although the present Brazilian government is far less dependent upon public sympathy than upon the support of the military establishment, civilian approval for the intensification of the Amazon's development has coincided with the military's disposition and therefore provided the government with an unusually comfortable policy-making setting. The Amazon has been the favorite topic of frightened Brazilian nationalists who, for at least the past one hundred years,[22] have been convinced that the Amazon is coveted by others. This conviction, whether sincerely held or not, has often been the subject of demagogic oratory. Nevertheless, it is an opinion shared by less sophisticated Brazilians who also believe that Brazil must occupy the Amazon in order to deny it to others and to demonstrate that Brazil is not a petty, unimportant country but one capable of fantastic feats.

Some Brazilian nationalists tend to regard any foreign advice concerning the Amazon or foreign activity in the region as evidence of a conspiratorial plot. This has given rise, in turn, to the construction of fanciful attributive theories. While these speculations are quite varied, they are all founded on the assumption that, on a planet which presumably is becoming too small for its population and where distances have lost meaning, large unoccupied spaces will somehow tend to be utilized.

As might be expected, many of these plots have been attributed to American intriguers. Some alarmists claim that the United States is planning to employ the Amazon as a huge concentration camp for its dissident black activists.[23] Others insist that the United States wishes to possess the Amazon for its value in the event of a nuclear war.[24] It is suggested that the United States would keep the Amazon in reserve, and Americans would be evacuated to it if nuclear war was threatened, or American nuclear submarines, planes, and missiles would be secreted there thus permitting the United States to emerge and dominate the world after a nuclear cataclysm. Still other worried nationalists assert that the United

---

[22] During the 1930s, for example, some nationalists objected to the settlement of Japanese in the Amazon, and this led to the publication of the following work: Vieira Antovila Rodrigues Mourão, *O perigo amarelo no Amazônia brasileira* (Manaus: Seção de Publicidade da Interventoria do Estado de Amazonas, 1942), 135pp.

[23] This is implied in Nicia Vilela Luz, *A Amazônia para os Negros Americanos* (Rio de Janeiro: Editôra Saga, 1968), 188pp.

[24] Raimundo Rodrigues Pereira, "A última fronteira," *Veja*, 14 de outubre, 1970, p. 56.

States is to be confronted soon with a dangerous scarcity of drinking water, and the Amazon's sweet water thus will be a temptation to the American imperialists.[25]

Perhaps the greatest single outcry related to the Amazon was recently provoked by the Hudson Institute's proposal to create several "Great Lakes" in the Amazon Basin.[26] This prompted the suspicion that the United States was attempting to deceive Brazil into flooding the Amazon area in order to prevent it from ever attaining great power status.

Some nationalists recognize that overt seizure of the Amazon is unlikely but warn against the possibility of gradual denationalization and foreign economic and cultural infiltration. They predict that mineral prospecting aerial mapping, land acquisition, and religious proselytizing by American nationals will lead to the eventual loss of the Amazon, and they point to the historical precedent of Mexico's experience with Texas.[27] It is surmised that American capitalists will not be satisfied with mere participation in the development of Amazonia but will gradually take over the entire area to insure a relatively close supply of minerals for American industry and to obtain other fabulous riches from the Amazon unrestricted by Brazilian regulations.

Although the United States is usually depicted as the villain by the "frightened nationalists," the motives of other countries are distrusted also. China and India are sources of some anxiety because it is thought that they will soon need to search for areas in which to resettle their huge and still expanding populations.[28] In addition, the Amazonian colonization schemes of Brazil's neighbors, particularly those of Peru and Colombia, are viewed with apprehension. It is felt that, if these countries successfully settle their Amazonian territories while Brazil is inactive, it will become impossible to protect the Brazilian Amazon. Finally, at least one Brazilian even believes that Europe presents a danger to the Amazon. Senator Guido Mondin claims that, while at an unnamed embassy in Athens, he saw a report of a meeting of Western and Eastern European countries at which the Amazon's future was decided.[29]

International efforts to study the Amazon or to assist in its develop-

---

[25] Amália Martelli, *Amazônia: Nova Dimensão do Brasil* (Petropolis, R. J.: Editôra Vozes, Ltda., 1969), p. 132.

[26] The Hudson Institute's proposal and criticisms of it are contained in *Revista Brasileira de Política Internacional*, Ano XI, No. 41–42 (março/junho de 1968). The entire issue of this publication is devoted to the Amazon.

[27] Genival Rabelo, *Ocupação da Amazônia* (Rio de Janeiro: Edições Gernasa, 1968), p. 54.

[28] Ibid., pp. 140 and 142.

[29] Brasil, *Diário do Congresso Nacional* (Seção II), Julho 9, de 1970, p. 2549.

ment are feared, too, since international development schemes are perceived as subtle contrivances designed to undermine Brazil's sovereignty. Especially notable is the resentment caused by the birth control advice of such international organizations as the International Bank for Reconstruction and Development. It is thought that if Brazil limits its population it will be prevented from fully occupying the Amazon.[30]

REACTION TO THE AMAZONIAN POLICY

Notwithstanding the propitious policy-making environment, President Médici's program has not met with unanimous approval. While it is true that the president's general popularity has been favorably affected by his Amazonian policy,[31] Médici's Amazon plans have been criticized by a vocal minority. The disparagement and adulation provoked by the Amazon venture, however, have been due almost entirely to the government's decision to construct the two Amazonian roads. Other aspects of the Amazonian Integration Plan have received little attention. This is understandable since these roads are being proclaimed by the government itself as the most consequential aspect of the Plan.

Some of the most vituperative disapprobation has been voiced by the recently somnolent Brazilian Congress. Congressional debate was stimulated by the announcement of the government's intention to begin immediate construction of the Amazonian roads, and some Northeastern congressmen who feel that their states are being victimized have been particularly hostile. Notable have been the vehement remarks of Senator José Ermírio de Morais who has argued that the roads are without importance to the nation's development and will result in a reduction of resources available for investment in the Northeast, the exploitation of Northeastern workers, and only benefit American and other foreign economic interests.[32] Ermírio and many of his colleagues from the Northeast fear that resources originally destined for their states will now be redirected to the Amazon, and their apprehension has not been assuaged by the government's insistence that the Northeast will benefit from the

---

[30] In this context it is easy to understand the furor that raged when it was revealed that foreign Protestant missionaries had been dispensing birth control advice and devices in the Amazon.

It should be noted that undocumented accounts in this section were related to the authors in private conversations with Brazilian citizens.

[31] An opinion poll conducted in Brazil's most populous state, São Paulo, shortly after the announcement of the Amazonian plans of the current government indicated that President Médici's popularity had increased sizably. "Popularidade," *Jornal do Brasil*, Julho 23, 1970.

[32] Brasil, *Diário do Congresso Nacional* (Seção II), Julho 9, 1970, pp. 2548–2549.

construction of the Amazonian roads.[33] Some also share Ermírio's conviction that the government's Amazonian policy is not a patriotic initiative designed to prevent the Amazon from falling prey to foreign imperialists but instead is an act of connivance with the imperialists. As they see it, the highways will primarily benefit the United States Steel Company and other firms wishing to exploit Brazil's mineral reserves.[34] Other Northeastern politicians are not so specific in their criticism. Governor João Agripino of Paraíba State, for instance, has charged that the transamazônica highway (the road uniting the Northeast with the Amazon) will merely "link misery with poverty." [35]

While Northeastern politicians have been at the forefront of those attacking the Médici government's plan, perhaps because they believe the loss of funds and people to the Amazon will decrease their own power, the Amazonian roads have had other critics as well. Many congressmen, some of whom even approve of the program, have been incensed because they were not permitted to participate in the scheme's formulation. Likewise, some technocrats, such as Roberto Campos, the former minister of planning and ambassador to the United States, feel that their advice should have been sought more seriously before the plan's promulgation.[36]

The Brazilian press, while generally favorably disposed toward the regime's initiative, has offered some mild criticisms. While not questioning the inherent value of the roads, some newspapers have broached the economic issue by questioning whether Brazil can afford such an immense undertaking. The *Estado de São Paulo*, for example, has stated editorially that "It is only known that the highway will cost more than a developing country should be able to afford. If this nation has survived the financial drain caused by the Brasilia project, nothing proves that it will be capable of another gigantic financial bleeding." [37] Other newspapers, in common with technocrats such as Campos, have expressed concern that the announcement of the project was not preceded by sufficient study and debate

[33] Minister of Interior Costa Cavalcanti has emphasized that the three principal instruments of national integration are transport, colonization, and irrigation, and that the first phase of the National Integration Plan will include the irrigation of the Northeast's parched farmland. Brasil, Embaixada do Brasil, Washington, *Boletim Especial*, "Programa de Integração Nacional," No. 153, Agosto 24, 1970.

[34] Cavalcanti has also denied that the Amazon roads will pass near the United States Steel concession. Since water transport provides by far the most economic means of transport for iron ore, it is difficult to see any appreciable advantages of the roads for U.S. Steel.

[35] "Amazon Highway," *Brazil Herald*, 8 August 1970.

[36] Campos, *O Estado de São Paulo*, 22 Julho 1970.

[37] "Uma nova Brasília?" *O Estado de São Paulo*, 16 Julho 1970.

of its economic viability.[38] Commentators have also found fault with the plan's emphasis on mass migration and warned that if it is unaccompanied by enough capital and technological support, it will not contribute to the Amazon's development but will further jeopardize Brazil's security. Instead of facing a foreign threat to its Amazonian territories, Brazil could find itself confronting an Amazon separatist movement supported by frustrated colonists.

The government's revolutionary opposition has denounced the road-building project as a neo-colonialist experiment. Many former political prisoners freed in exchange for the release of diplomats kidnapped in Brazil are now in Algeria and have formed the "Front brésilien d'information" there. This group has charged that the Brazilian government has decided to construct the Amazonian roads in order to "please its imperialistic associates and at the same time to do away with an annoying nucleus of rebellion in the Northeast, caused less by the drought than by the shameless exploitation of the active population." [39]

Despite criticisms such as those just reviewed, the government's Amazonian development plans have met with warm support in many quarters. Effusive acclaim, as would be expected, has come from the paranoiac nationalists. In general, serious students of Amazonian affairs, such as Professor Arthur Cezar Reis, the former governor of Amazonas and the author of at least a dozen articles dealing with the Amazon, have welcomed President Médici's initiative.[40] Except for the displeasure of some Northeastern congressmen, as has already been mentioned, Congress has warmly praised the regime. Senator Dinarte Mariz, a Vice Leader of ARENA, the government party, expressed the dominant attitude when he enthusiastically approved the construction of the Amazonian roads and proclaimed that "this decree law represents the major and most courageous act of the Brazilian revolution in favor of the people." [41]

CONCLUSION

Operation Amazon is an integral part of the government's National Integration Plan; and, therefore, it is appropriate to ask whether or not

[38] Minister of Transportation Andrezza has stated that the project has been studied since 1967 by the National Department of Roads (DNER). "Transamazônica garantirá expansão do Nordeste," *Jornal do Brasil*, 27 Julho 1970, p. 28.

[39] Front brésilien d'information, *Bulletin*, No. 13, Septembre 1970.

[40] Orlando Mota, "Transamazônica é comprovação de nossa maióidade," *O Cruzeiro*, 28 Julho 1970, p. 85.

[41] Brasil, *Diário do Congresso Nacional* (Seção II), Junho 23, 1970, p. 2229. By "revolution" the Senator is presumably referring to the political events transpiring since 1964.

it will contribute substantially to Brazil's political integration. The answer is dependent, naturally, upon what standards are employed to measure success and upon the interpretation given the integrative concept. Definitions for the term integration abound. According to one noted authority, Professor Myron Weiner of MIT, "The term 'integration' . . . covers a vast range of human relationships and attitudes—the integration of diverse and discrete cultural loyalties and the development of a sense of nationality; the integration of political units into a common territorial framework with a government which can exercise authority; the integration of rulers and ruled; the integration of the citizen into a common political process; and, finally, the integration of individuals for purposive activities." [42]

Certainly territorial integration will be advanced as a result of the development of road transportation in the Amazon region. The government will be able to exercise political control over areas where its presence has been intermittent or nonexistent. Along the new roads will travel not only colonists but also such government agents as tax collectors, postmen, and the army. It is still unclear, however, whether development of the Amazon will further elite-mass integration in Brazil, or, for that matter, whether it will tend to reduce the political polarization which exists between the government and its revolutionary opponents.

It does seem that the Amazon's development is intended to stimulate the integration of more than just territory. Mass-elite integration may be furthered through the creation of a national development symbol which will attract wide allegiance among the masses. This has been done previously in Brazil and been successful politically, briefly reducing the antagonism between the elite and the masses. Perhaps the Amazon project is another attempt at the creation of a grandiose development goal which will appeal to national pride.

Characteristically, anticipation has been generated that the development of the Amazon will somehow solve many, if not all, of Brazil's problems. This strategy, for lack of a better phrase, may be called panacea politics. The construction of Brasilia, Mao's Great Leap Forward, and Khrushchev's Conquest of the Virgin Lands are all contemporary examples of panacea politics. Of course, promises made or implied by panacea politicians are rarely, if ever, fulfilled completely, and the danger is that repeated unsatisfactory experiences may result in an inability on the part of the elite to mobilize the masses for yet another great effort. In Brazil's case, it is still too early to determine whether the masses can be

[42] Myron Weiner, "Political Integration and Political Development," *Annals of the American Academy of Political and Social Science*, 358 (March 1965): pp. 54.

persuaded to make another gallant attempt or whether cynicism will be insurmountable.

Even if the Amazon project does contribute to the integration of the elite and the masses in Brazil, there is no guarantee that it will also lead to the dissolution of the revolutionary counter-elite. Potential mass support may be denied the counter-elite, but it is unlikely that the success of the Amazon venture will be enough to reduce the conflict and competition between the government and its political enemies. The character of the entire political system is at issue, not merely the economic development of the country. It is difficult to see how the Amazon project can assist in the integration of conflicting political values. The transfer of population to the Amazon may weaken the hold of the semi-feudal Northeastern large landholders, but the revolutionary opposition is hardly likely to believe that the government initiated Operation Amazon for that purpose.

In conclusion, if progress does come to the Amazon, new integrative problems may arise while old integrative issues are being resolved. Political and economic change is often accompanied by an increase in governmental responsibilities. The mobilized Brazilian masses who settle the Amazon will almost certainly make new demands of the government, and these may be malintegrative.

Martin S. Stabb
Department of Spanish, Italian, and Portuguese
The Pennsylvania State University
University Park, Pennsylvania

ARGENTINE LETTERS AND THE PERONATO: AN OVERVIEW*

In recent years students of contemporary Argentine letters have begun to recognize the importance of the period 1946–1955 as one of crisis, of fundamental reassessment, and of generational strife.[1] Though it would be an oversimplification to assign the cause of these trends to the political and social changes wrought by Juan D. Perón, the study of his regime—particularly as it affected cultural activity—can help put into clearer focus the confusing picture of literary groups, "generations," and *promociones* that confronts the student of recent Argentine literature.

It should be emphasized that *peronismo*, for better or for worse, was more than an exclusively political movement: its influence was also far-reaching in broad areas of popular culture, social standards, in matters of dress, speech, and in the use of leisure time. Its effects were complex, but on balance they all tended to produce a feeling of relaxation, a loosening-up of formalities and traditional practices: stuffed shirts were displaced by *descamisados*; the normal work week was frequently broken up by

* The research here reported was assisted by a grant awarded by the Joint Committee on Latin American Studies of the Social Science Research Council.

[1] See Angela B. Dellepiane, "La novela argentina desde 1950 a 1965," *Revista Iberoamericana*, Núm. 66 (julio-dic. 1968), pp. 239–244; Juan Carlos Ghiano, *La novela argentina contemporánea* (Buenos Aires: Dirección General de Relaciones Culturales, s.f.), p. 7; Noé Jitrik, *Seis novelistas argentinos de la nueva promoción* (Mendoza: Bibl. San Martín, 1959), pp. 29–30; Emir Rodríguez Monegal, *El juicio de los parricidas* (Buenos Aires: Dencalión, 1956), pp. 9, 84–85, 90. For a discussion of this generation of writers in the context of general Spanish American trends, see José J. Arrom, *Esquema generacional de las letras hispánicas* (Bogotá: Instituto Caro y Cuervo, 1963), pp. 214–217.

strikes and government encouraged vacations; formal attire was no longer required at the opera; and many of the public parks that previously had, by some unwritten law, been considered the semi-private preserve of the middle and upper classes, became crowded with picnicking workers and their families.

The relationship between literary activity and the regime may be approached in two ways. First there is the matter of the direct actions taken by Perón and his government to influence, encourage, or inhibit literary production. Secondly, there are the more subtle problems of how the *peronato*, the mood and very air of Argentina during what some writers have called *la década absurda*, affected the literary community.

Without attempting to make a detailed study of Perón's actions toward creative writers, a few highlights of his policies in this area may be noted. First of all, during the early years of his regime Perón meddled relatively little in literary activity and made few major efforts to stifle freedom of expression. By the end of the 1940s, however, the peronato began to take on an increasingly totalitarian shape. It soon became evident that such matters as the molding of Argentine reading habits would be a concern of the government.

Several new publications attest to this interest: *Argentina*, a general magazine whose first issue appeared in January of 1949, proclaimed that it was "destinada a difundir nuestro estilo de vida, en el mundo de habla española. . . ." Its staff, however, hastened to point out that although it was published by the government, "de ninguna manera es una revista oficial." [2] Among the better-known writers who collaborated on the literary sections of *Argentina* were Manuel Gálvez, Guillermo House, Arturo Cancela, and Hugo Wast. Writing on the theme "Hay que cambiar nuestras costumbres," Wast struck a chord which was to become typical of the Peronist cultural campaign: "Los diarios más importantes . . . rechazan sin apelación toda crítica formada sobre un autor argentino vivo. Si es sobre un autor extranjero, suele ser aceptado." [3] Whether this criticism was or was not justified, it is clear that the writers supporting the regime thought of themselves as champions of a national literature who were waging the good fight against the cosmopolites and *extranjerizantes* who controlled the literary pages of *La Nación* and *La Prensa*. Consistent with officialist programs, the magazine also printed several pieces in sup-

---

[2] Oscar Ivanissevich, untitled editorial, *Argentina*, Núm. 1 (enero 1949), p. 2. The author was minister of education and, shortly afterward, Rector of the University of Buenos Aires.

[3] *Argentina*, Núm. 4 (mayo, 1949), p. 11.

port of Perón's "Estatuto del Trabajador Intelectual," and in favor of the constitutional reform of 1949.

A similar publication, *Sexto Continente* "Revista de cultura para América Latina," appeared in the same year (1949). Though it did not openly acknowledge governmental support, *Sexto Continente*'s pages reveal beyond any reasonable doubt that its editors (Alicia Eguren and Armando Cascella) and contributors were working in close collaboration with the regime.[4] Like *Argentina*, the review stressed national themes in literature, attacked the political and literary positions of *La Prensa* and *La Nación*, supported Perón's pet projects (the constitutional reform, the so-called "Third Position" in foreign relations, etc.), and even attempted to provide ideological underpinning for the regime.[5] Among its contributors were Raúl Scalabrini Ortiz, J. A. García Martínez, Arturo Cancela, the philosophers M. A. Virasoro and Carlos Astrada. From the strictly literary point of view, the laudatory pieces on work by Leopoldo Marechal, Guillermo House, and Raúl Scalabrini Ortiz indicate just what kind of writing was enjoying semi-official approval.

It would be incorrect to assume, however, that *Sexto Continente* was simply a propaganda vehicle for the government. More accurately, the emphasis in the magazine was on Argentine life, history, traditions, and folklore. On occasion, its contributors would even engage in vigorous criticism of national problems and defects. Perhaps most interesting was their fresh look at certain half-forgotten districts in the Argentine hinterland. Jorge W. Abalos' novel *Shunko*, for example, is a simple and touching story of a rural teacher's struggle to educate a group of poverty-stricken Indian children in a dusty corner of Santiago del Estero. It is of some significance that, although Abalos' book had nothing in it either for or against Perón, it was a peronista publication which gave it the attention that it merited. Other evidence suggests that the marked growth of interest in regionalism and folklore in contemporary Argentine culture received much of its impetus during the Perón years.[6] To what extent this trend was a direct outgrowth of governmental policies would be difficult to determine: cer-

---

[4] An indication that the publication was subvented by the government may be seen in the fact that it sold for two pesos, a price substantially lower than that of magazines of similar size and format.

[5] See especially the articles by Armando Cascella, "Trascendencia de la tercera posición," *Sexto Continente,* Núm. 7–8 (nov.-dic. 1950), p. 21, and by Miguel Angel Virasoro, "El trabajo y la dignidad del Ser," ibid., pp. 27–41.

[6] Though I have not attempted to document this point formally, I am struck by the fact that so many Argentines associate the vogue of folk music with the Perón period. It was during the mid and late forties that one of the first popularizers of *música folklórica* of the northern interior, Atahualpa Yupanqui, began performing (and even writing on the subject) for urban audiences.

tainly it was consistent with Perón's glorification—his enemies would say courting—of the lower classes.

But the dictator's desire to incorporate all levels of Argentine society into the new era of *justicialismo* made it imperative that the higher culture as well appear to support the vague ideology of the regime. And so the universities were rapidly brought under peronista domination. This process seems to have been accelerated during the late forties and early fifties. A case in point was the University of Buenos Aires where the "reorganization" of 1949 saw the staunch Peronist, Oscar Ivanissevich named rector while he retained his earlier appointment as minister of education. The university's *Revista* was entrusted to Father Hernán Benítez, an ardent nationalist of decidedly peronista persuasion. A biographical note placed in the journal by way of introducing Benítez to the readers indicates the degree to which the regime was seeking to penetrate intellectual life. The new editor is modestly identified as, "Hernán Benítez, Director Espiritual de la Fundación 'Eva Perón' y profesor titular de Ética Justicialista en la Escuela Superior Peronista: Dicta la cátedra de perfeccionamiento filosófico en la Facultad de Filosofía y Letras de la Universidad de Buenos Aires, dirige el Instituto de Publicaciones de la misma. . . ." [7]

Along with the Peronization of the universities, two other events of the early fifties had a substantial impact on Argentine cultural life: the seizure of *La Prensa* and the dictator's support of a new association of writers friendly to the regime and opposed to the prestigious anti-Peronist "Sociedad Argentina de Escritores" (SADE). When, after a long period of harassment, *La Prensa* finally ceased publication, Perón had not only succeeded in silencing a political foe, but he had also deprived an impressive group of writers of access to one of the most widely read literary pages in Spanish America. The new government-controlled *La Prensa* appeared in November of 1951. Gone were the familiar names of literary contributors like Rafael Alberto Arrieta, Ernesto Morales, and a host of others; in their place was a new team of reviewers and critics—men who if not dyed-in-the-wool peronistas were at least on cordial terms with the regime. Some were literary figures of considerable distinction: César Tiempo, Alberto Insúa, Elias Castelnuovo, Leopoldo Marechal, Fermín Chávez, Horacio Rega Molina, and others. Yet some—and many of these appeared frequently—were shadowy, relatively unknown writers: Pablo Carvallo,[8] Eduardo Azcuy, and F. Rodolfo Álvarez, for example.

---

[7] *Revista de la Universidad de Buenos Aires*, Núm. 17 (enero-marzo 1950), p. 11.

[8] Carvallo's articles are especially interesting since they indicate early Marxist support of Perón. See "El hombre y la máquina," *La Prensa*, May 11, 1952, p. 11,

Most of the men who wrote for the pre-Peronist *La Prensa*'s literary section were also members of the independent, anti-government literary association, the SADE. Dominated by men of liberal political tendencies, supporters of the anti-Perón Partido Radical and, in some cases, of the Left, this organization was an obvious target for the dictator. Perón's efforts to destroy it, or at least to establish a parallel body more favorable to his regime were aided by the fact that a number of Argentine writers were never quite comfortable in the organization and would probably have agreed with Manuel Gálvez's view that "En la SADE existía una especie de dictadura izquierdista. . . ." [9] And so, when Arturo Cancela, backed by Marechal, Wast, Carlos Obligado, Gálvez, and others decided to form a separate association of independent writers, Perón was quick to lend his wholehearted support. The new group, the Asociación de Escritores Argentinos (ADEA), sought membership in the Peronist labor organization, the CGT, and was immediately welcomed into the fold. Perón and Eva were made honorary members, their portraits were hung in the Association's main salon,[10] and early in 1951, the membership proposed their own candidate—Manuel Gálvez—to oppose SADE's Ezequiel Martínez Estrada as the Argentine nominee for the Nobel Prize. But as the ADEA became more enmeshed in the Perón regime, what prestige it still had declined sharply; Gálvez himself wrote that by late 1951 in the group "abundaban los autores de textos escolares, y escaseaban los nombres de auténtico prestigio, casi todos de los cuales estaban en la SADE . . ." [11]

More important than these specific events was the intellectual environment which Perón's rule had created in the Argentina of the late forties and early fifties. Though there is available abundant literary and personal testimony regarding the period, partisan fervor has made any neat, objective characterization of this environment difficult, especially for Argentines themselves. Certainly the overriding personalism of the regime stands out as one of its most distinguishing features. Whether Perón be considered a thinly-disguised Fascist, a precursor of National

---

and "La herencia cultural y la clase trabajadora," *La Prensa*, June 22, 1952, p. 9. Several Argentine scholars have suggested to me that Carvallo may be the pseudonym of a better known writer, but if this is so, I have not been able to ascertain his identity.

[9] *Recuerdos de la vida literaria* IV, (Buenos Aires: Hachette, 1965): 174.

[10] According to Gálvez (*Memorias* IV: 175) the portrait of Eva was actually placed in an adjoining corridor, rather than alongside that of Perón himself in the main salon. Eva never quite forgave the organization.

[11] *Memorias* IV: 176.

Liberation type leaders along the lines of a Nasser, Sukarno, or Castro,[12] or simply another Latin American caudillo of populist tendencies, the fact remains that his was a regime in which the cult of the person overshadowed ideological concerns.

Perón's glorification of the lower classes, and the corresponding denigration of those he called the "oligarchy," is another hallmark of his regime. Yet the appeal to the proletariat had only the vaguest sort of ideological base. Justicialismo was seldom defined: for the peronistas it seemed sufficient to assert repeatedly that this new social praxis "would make Communism unnecessary." In place of theory Perón offered the workers higher wages, shorter hours, handouts, seats at the opera, inexpensive vacations, the charismatic figure of Evita, and a plethora of catchy slogans, the most important of which was "Perón cumple"; that is, "Perón delivers the goods." Of course, at the same time that he was raising workers' living standards, Perón was cooperating with industry: at least with those industrialists and businessmen whose operations fitted into his schemes for Argentine economic development and whose pocketbooks were always available to support the right causes.[13]

Though at times Perón could use force to accomplish his ends—imprisonment, torture, police brutality, and the like—his regime was infinitely less oppressive, less brutal, less bloody, and simply less dramatic than those of an Adolf Hitler or of the Stalin of the 1930s. Perhaps he was more like Mussolini, though even here the Argentine leader does not quite fit the pattern. Among other differences, Perón, though a professional soldier, seldom attempted to cast himself in a Caesarean role as did Il Duce—he had no Ethiopias and, once firmly in the saddle, he enjoyed only lukewarm support from the upper echelons of Argentina's armed forces.[14] In short, for most of the time that he controlled the country, he ruled more by dint of his personality and his understanding the Argentine people than he did by the sword.

---

[12] The view of Perón and Peronism as precursors of National Left type movements seems to have gained considerable popularity among heterodox radicals of the last decade. Juan José Hernández Arregui has been especially influential in this regard. See his *La formación de la conciencia nacional: 1930–1960* (Buenos Aires: Ediciones Hachea, 1960).

[13] An excellent and only slightly fictionalized account of Perón's shakedown of businessmen is found in Manuel Peyrou's novel *Acto y ceniza* (Buenos Aires: Emecé, 1963).

[14] Though Perón gradually lost the backing of the military elites, he established a firm base of support among the noncommissioned officers. Through special clubs for noncoms and other benefits he established himself as the sergeants' and corporals' friend. Even today some of the most ardent peronistas to whom I have talked, were noncoms during his regime.

Rather than a magic blend of rare qualities, his personality was a fortuitous combination of traits well-suited to enable their possessor to manipulate the Argentine populace with considerable ease. Perón was pragmatic, flexible, astute, and self-interested: he never made a fetish of ideology or consistency, or of personal integrity. His policies indicated, moreover, that he believed that many of these same traits were to be found in the majority of Argentines.[15] He enjoyed the material things in life and also wanted his countrymen to enjoy them. Consistent with his personality and with his view of Argentine character, Perón—following good psychological techniques—dominated the country by "reward and reinforcement" rather than by terror or sheer force. The labor syndicates that turned out en masse to cheer the *jefe's* speeches in the Plaza de Mayo might get special privileges and a better contract; the industrialist who contributed generously to the Fundación Eva Perón might be permitted to keep his factory in operation without harassment by overzealous safety inspectors, and the intellectual who publicly voiced approval of the regime might be promoted in his university post or government job. In short, much of the widespread support for the regime was simply purchased.

For many Argentines the regime—especially after 1951—presented a sorry spectacle of rampant personalism, of crass materialism, of contagious corruption, and of irrational decisions in both the economic and political spheres. Yet most of his opponents did not then and do not now *hate* the dictator. Rather, they wished to ignore him, to make believe he wasn't really there. Perón seems to have inspired in many a kind of disgust, a kind of uncomfortable feeling akin to that experienced by the fastidious housewife who discovers dust in the corners. For many a proper Argentine—proper writers included—Perón, peronismo, and his manipulation of a literate, relatively advanced nation were things to be ashamed of and to be forgotten.

Yet others, though they might have disliked the cult of the person, the erosion of democratic processes, and the crassness of the regime, felt equally uncomfortable in the anti-Perón camp. Young intellectuals—men in their early thirties or still in the university during the waning years of the peronato—found themselves in an especially ambivalent position. On the one hand, they had little in common with the narrowly nationalistic, often staunchly Catholic traditionalists who had supported Perón since the early days of his rise to power—men like Marechal, Gálvez, or Wast;

---

[15] Ernesto Sábato in his *El otro dostro del peronismo* (Buenos Aires, 1956), p. 34, supports this view: ". . . cada nación tiene también el rostro que inmanentemente se merece, pues todos somos culpables de todo, y en cada argentino había un fragmento de Perón."

on the other, they found an immense gulf between themselves and what may be called the anti-Perón literary establishment. The latter group, composed of writers like Borges, Mújica Lainez, Victoria Ocampo, and Mallea, were then in their forties or early fifties, were the leaders of the SADE, and were regular contributors to such highly regarded publications as *Sur* and *La Nación*. Politically, many were middle-of-the-road liberals, supporters of the split and in one view, the discredited Partido Radical; while some tended more toward what we now call the Old Left. But regardless of political orientation, as a group they reflected the upper bourgeois world of the Barrio Norte. From the literary standpoint they were politely cosmopolitan rather than noisily nationalistic. Their works tended to be polished, sophisticated, and often a bit foreign in flavor. Among other sins, they were inclined to use the familiar *tú* in their writing, rather than the genuinely Argentine *vos*. In the eyes of the young intellectuals, they lacked a certain intensity: most important, they appeared to suffer from a disinclination to probe the visceral realities of the nation.

The frame of mind of the new writers—a student and novelist-to-be like David Viñas, an essayist like Rodolfo Kusch, a poet and fiction writer like Alberto Vanasco, or emerging critics such as Adolfo Prieto or Noé Jitrik—is best revealed in the ephemeral literary reviews which blossomed forth in the early 1950s. These publications—*Semirrecta, Letra y Línea, Espiga, Centro, Capricornio, Las Ciento y Una,* and perhaps most important, *Contorno*—all made their appearance between late 1951 and 1953.[16] Often the same men collaborated on several of these magazines; they were further united by the bond of age since virtually all were born between 1924 and 1930. In short, they may be thought to constitute a genuine, though loosely-knit, literary generation. They have frequently spoken of themselves as such, and one critic, Emir Rodríguez Monegal, has even referred to them as *la generación de los parricidas*.[17]

The targets at which most of the new generation's attacks were directed were the writers of "uncommitted" literature: that is, those authors whom the *nueva promoción* considered to be effete, unconcerned with the national crisis, and devoted to the notion of literature as entertainment. Most of those under fire were members of what I have called the

---

[16] *Espiga* actually was started a few years earlier in Rosario, though it was moved to Buenos Aires in 1951. For further discussion of the literary reviews of the period, see Héctor René Lafleur et al., *Las revistas literarias argentinas 1893–1967*, Edición corregida y aumentada (Buenos Aires: Centro Editor de América Latina, 1968), pp. 255–287.

[17] *El juicio de los parricidas*, pp. 21–22.

Barrio Norte Establishment, and underlying much of the new generation's criticism of them was the fact that these older writers either chose to ignore the impact of the dictator or that in their simplistic rejection of the regime they failed to grasp the full significance of peronismo as a social phenomenon. A glance at what the older generation was producing during the late years of the dictatorship will help us appreciate the mood of the young Turks. Mújica Lainez, for example, was turning out a series of nostalgic evocations of the Argentine upper bourgeosie's past glories (*Aquí vivieron, La casa, Los viajeros*); Mallea was persisting in writing inward-turned novels of existential anguish and mutism (*Los enemigos del alma, Chaves*); Bioy Casares preferred fantasy and the world of dreams (*El sueño de los héroes*); Victoria Ocampo journeyed back some twenty years into the past to recapture material for her libresque memoirs (*Testimonios*); while Borges, of course, was continuing to produce his magnificent—though apparently gratuitous—*ficciones.*

Yet it may be argued that there was a very definite relationship between this kind of writing and the realities of the peronato in the sense that these works were characterized by an overriding mood of escape: escape into the past, escape into the inner world of the anguished psyche, escape into the imaginary realm of fantasy, or escape to that world of physical and spiritual amenities symbolized by Europe. To what extent this escapism may be attribued to the atmosphere created by the Perón regime, or to what extent it represents a literary trajectory which these writers might have pursued regardless of the sociopolitical circumstances, would be difficult to determine. Yet, when we read Mújica's fine description of his protagonists in *Los viajeros*—the members of a once-wealthy Argentine immigrant family desperately counting their inflation-eroded pesos preparatory to making a never-to-be realized return trip to Europe ("inseparable de la idea de lujo y señorío, así como la Argentina se enlazaba con nociones sórdidas y deprimientes"),[18] we cannot resist the temptation to interpret their mood as a reflection of the social change wrought by Perón. Similar conclusions could, I think, be drawn from many of the other works in which the theme of escape figures so prominently.

The fact that the older generation's escapism might have been interpreted as a veiled critique of Perón and his regime did not, however, impress the younger writers. Thus Borges was soundly attacked, as were Victoria Ocampo, Mújica Lainez, and Eduardo Mallea.[19] Writers on the

---

[18] *Los viajeros* (Buenos Aires: Sudamericana, 1955), p. 28.

[19] A good sampling of this sort of generational sniping may be found in the articles in the special issue of *Contorno*, Núm. 5–6 (sept. 1955), dedicated to the

other side of the political fence also came under fire—pro-Perón traditionalists like Manuel Gálvez and Leopoldo Marechal, for example.

Even more interesting than the attacks against the established writers was the expression of desperation and anguish which fill the pages of the literary reviews that the new generation was producing. As H. A. Murena wrote in *Las Ciento y Una* "nuestra vida cultural de argentinos y americanos yace herida, enferma, caída en la más miserable miseria." [20] Or as the director of *Semirrecta*, Eduardo Eggers, expressed it: "A la juventud argentina le falta sangre. Se quiere remediar este mal con transfusiones, pero inútilmente, porque su anemia no consiste en una deficiencia de glóbulos sino en falta de fuerza interior. . . . De otro modo no podría permanecer cruzada de brazos ante una situación que . . . sólo ella puede salvar. . . ." [21] Recalling that the foregoing was written during the closing years of the peronato, one might assume that the situation to which Eggers refers was simply the existence of a repressive dictatorship, and that his intent was to rally support for the overthrow of the regime.

Yet the mood of the emerging generation of writers was more complex: the situation was one of grays rather than blacks and whites, and a clear course was not readily discernible. As the same writer confessed, "Pocas veces debe haber habido generaciones jóvenes tan desprovistas de rumbos fijos, de metas, de ideales-guías." [22] At the root of the desperation felt by these young men were deep-seated feelings of guilt: self-directed guilt as well as guilt shared with writers of the older generation. Ismael Viñas expresses this aspect of the group's mood especially well in the first issue of *Contorno*: "Rebeldía, rechazo, desconcierto. Eso es lo que sentimos. El mundo, este mundo inmediato, nuestro país, nuestra ciudad, nos aprietan como algo de que somos responsables. . . . El momento por que atravesamos, de confusión y remoción . . . agrava nuestra desconcierto y nuestra sensación de culpa. Sentimos que de algún modo somos responsables por lo que los representantes del intelecto, por lo que los hombres del espíritu no han hecho. Aún más por sus omisiones que por sus actos nos sentimos culpables." [23] When the general atmosphere of the early fifties is taken into account the revolt of the younger writers—the parricides to use Rodríguez Monegal's apt term—against the older gen-

---

Argentine novel. Similar criticisms of the older generation of writers appear in *Letra y Línea*, No. 4 (julio 1954) and in *Semirrecta*, Núm. 6–7 (1953). Though it is centered on only one author, Adolfo Prieto's *Borges y la nueva generación* (Buenos Aires: Letras Universitarias, 1954) follows a similar line of attack.

[20] "Las ciento y una," *Las Ciento y Una*, No. 1 (junio 1953), p. 3.

[21] *Semirrecta*, Núm. 6–7 (1953), p. 1.

[22] Loc. cit.

[23] "La traición de los hombres honestos," *Contorno*, No. 1 (nov. 1953), p. 2.

eration becomes much more than the usual struggle of young Turks to displace the old guard. As the foregoing quotations indicate, the new writers were especially sensitive to the fact that the established men, "los representantes del intelecto," had in some way failed to understand the nature of the Argentine crisis.

Though few members of the younger literary generation supported Perón, unlike the 40- and 50-year-olds, they were acutely aware of the changes in Argentine life and culture which were taking place. As one of *Semirrecta*'s contributors noted late in 1953: "La vida nacional está atravesando una hora que puede traer un cambio fundamental en su vida social y cultural. Tiene lugar una crisis en plena evolución, cuyo carácter más esencial consiste en la desintegración de una cultura y sociedad vigente y su reemplazo por otra cuyos rasgos no percibimos con claridad." [24] A bit later, David Viñas, who was to become the most successful novelist of the nueva promoción, put the issues into even sharper focus in a memorable article written for *Contorno*. Viñas observes that the promoción of 1920—Mallea and Borges especially—reacted to Perón by longing for a return to "los tolerantes y corteses ademanes del *bon veille* [sic] *régime*." And so, he goes on, "todos se aliaban contra el Candidato Imposible estableciendo por centésima vez el reino de los Santos frente a los Abyectos, sin advertir que la *Imposibilidad* era parte de la realidad, era la *Realidad* misma, y que no cabía condenarla imponiéndole el sayo amarillo." [25]

The position of the *Contorno* group became even clearer a year and a half later. Number 7/8 of the magazine, published in July of 1956, is a revealing post-mortem of the Peronato: the lead editorial, significantly titled "Peronismo . . . ¿y lo otro?" set forth the idea that while the group never supported the dictator, neither did they support "anti-Peronism." To do so, they felt, would blind them to what was happening in the country. For one contributor Perón was a scapegoat discovered by the anti-Peronists to explain away the impotence of the Argentine nation; the same writer also notes that those who had been passively anti-Peronist were in effect supporting the oligarchs and upper bourgeoisie.[26] Ismael Viñas, while speaking warmly of "las clases populares . . . la parte sincera . . . del peronismo," points out that only those who saw the move-

---

[24] Ramón Capecchi, "Nuestra generación y la crisis, "*Semirrecta*, Núm. 6–7, (1953), p. 11.

[25] "La historia excluida: ubicación de Martínez Estrada," *Contorno*, Núm. 4 (dic. 1954), pp. 14–15.

[26] Osiris Troiani, "Examen de conciencia," *Contorno*, Núm. 7–8 (julio 1956), pp. 9–11.

ment as the advanec of the mob were pleased by Perón's fall.[27] The *Contorno* group's reaction to the simplistic anti-Perón breast-beating of the *Sur* group (as exemplified by Victoria Ocampo's comments in the first issue of the magazine to appear after the Revolución Libertadora) are sharply critical: "El Bien Absoluto, como el Mal Absoluto, existen sólo en los cuentos para miños o en las revistas de historietas." [28]

Juan José Sebreli, an outspoken leftist and one of the most articulate essayists of the *Contorno* group, presented a remarkably favorable view of the Peronato in the same issue. In his "Aventura y revolución peronista" he stresses the idea that Perón was clearly an Argentine product, that rather than an innovator, "puede decirse que ese conjunto de condiciones políticas, económicas, y sociales que es el peronismo lo inventó a Perón, encontró en él una forma de expresión y un nombre, que podía haber sido cualquier otro." Sebreli also stresses his notion of Peronism as a challenge, as a movement which invited youth to break with the stuffy traditions of the past. He even interprets Evita's *Razón de mi vida* in these terms: he suggests that the writings and life style of the dictator's famous wife represented a reaction against "los modelos de perfección que eran el padre, la maestra, y el prócer . . ." There was a certain "mad joy" in the Perón period, he tells us, a living for the moment: what Sebreli calls Argentina's "monótona vida cotidiana" was for the first time in history actually threatened; and even the wild inflation of the regime's closing years served to make people think in terms of immediate satisfaction rather than in terms of thrift and prudence. His summation is striking: "Los diez años de peronismo significaron, en suma, un desafío al imperio de las costumbres, a la majestad de los valores establecidos, de todos los clisés morales y las mórbidas inhibiciones del filisteísmo, de la hipócrita ideología de la virtud y de la explotación de la Vieja Argentina . . . Perón parecía, en sus últimos tiempos, haber concebido una teoría según la cual la humanidad entera y él inclusive tenían que divertirse . . . El peronismo demostró que es posible combinar la libertad más desenfrenada con el despotismo." [29]

That the Perón experience had a much greater effect on contemporary Argentine letters than many foreign readers would suspect or that many Argentines would admit, is further borne out by examining the works of two important writers who have remained sufficiently aloof from

[27] "Miedos, complejos y malosentendidos," *Contorno*, Núm. 7–8 (julio 1956), pp. 11–12.

[28] Rodolfo Mario Pandolfi, "17 de Octubre, trampa y salida," *Contorno*, Núm. 7–8 (Julio 1956), p. 22.

[29] Juan José Sebreli, "Aventura y revolución peronista: Testimonio," *Contorno*, Núm. 7–8 (julio 1956), pp. 45–49.

literary cliques to make their inclusion in either the established group or the younger group very difficult.

The first of these, Ernesto Sábato, was born in 1911, and hence is some fifteen or twenty years older than the men of nueva promoción. A scientist who had abandoned his profession for that of a writer, Sábato came from the middle class and was for many years a contributor to *Sur*. Even before the publication of a first novel, *El túnel* (1948), he had produced a collection of essays (*Uno y el universo*), a genre which he continued to cultivate in the fifties. Two groups of themes are of special interest in these essays. The first revolve about Sábato's notion of the masculine versus the feminine principle in life. In several articles published in *Sur* and in the lead essay of *Heterodoxia*, he speaks of "maleness" in terms of the tendency toward abstraction, rationality, and modernity; "femaleness" is associated with concreteness, the realm of instinct and the irrational. The two principles work with each other in a dialectical relationship: they may be used to explain either literary trends (Romanticism being equated with "lo femenino" and Classicism with "lo masculino") or political phenomena.[30]

A second, and closely related theme which recurs frequently in many of his essays, as well as in *El túnel*, is the awareness of a gulf which separates the abstract world of logic, order, and rationality from the real world of chance, blind instinct, and the absurd. Indeed, Sábato's steady drift away from the certainties of his youth—science and Marxism—toward a much greater appreciation of instinct and the irrational marks the trajectory of his literary career.

Despite his leftist leanings, during the period under consideration here he was essentially an uncommitted writer: what literary associations he maintained were with the *Sur* group. Though hardly an activist, he opposed Perón; moreover, he professed no great faith in the common man or in his values.[31] He was, in short, what the young revolutionaries might call a standoffish bourgeois. Yet the final years of the peronato and the period of soul-searching immediately following the dictator's overthrow did much to reshape his thinking on the nature of man, on history, and on Argentine realities.

His short essay, *El otro rostro del peronismo*, published in June of 1956, is an important document illustrating the changing image of Peronism among Argentine intellectuals. Sábato's description of the fateful night in September of 1955 following Perón's ouster is especially reveal-

---

[30] *Heterodoxia* (Buenos Aires: Emecé, 1953), p. 47.

[31] Ibid., p. 91. See also his "Sentido común" in *Uno y el universo*, 2ª. edic. (Buenos Aires: Sudamericana, 1948), pp. 178 179.

ing: "mientras los doctores, hacendados, y escritores festejábamos ruidosamente en la sala la caída del tirano, en un rincón de la antecocina vi como las dos indias que allí trabajaban tenían los ojos empapados de lágrimas." Sábato goes on to point out the complexities of the Perón experience, noting that in addition to the materialism and "base appetites" which gave the movement its impetus, "hubo un genuino fervor espiritual, una fe pararreligiosa en el conductor que les hablaba [a las masas] como a seres humanos y no como a parias . . ." [32] Earlier in the essay he explains the appeal of Peronism (and the failure of orthodox Marxism in Argentina) in terms of his theories on sex and the irrational. "Las masas," he tells us, "son femeninas" and as such are characterized by an essential irrationality. Perón grasped this truth and hence was successful in gaining mass support; the Marxists, on the other hand, persisted in trying to win the people by a rationalistic, essentially "masculine" approach and hence failed.

Several other casual remarks in the essay shed light on Sábato's literary career as well as his political thinking. When he writes of Perón's use of "la razón de la sinrazón, como sostenían Don Quijote y el Hombre del Subterráneo," one immediately thinks of the vast "underground" metaphor in his novel of 1961, *Sobre héroes y tumbas.* We also see a foreshadowing of the "flight into the interior" motif which figures so prominently in the same novel, when he contrasts the rational, European, "masculine" world of "aquellos doctos de Buenos Aires" with the irrational, indianized "feminine" realm of the interior provinces—the zone of the *cocinera india* and the *cabecita negra.* But he ends his essay on a note that bears repeating: he warns his countrymen not to accept the strictly peronista view of Argentine reality: "No incurramos ahora en el sofismo inverso . . . de que 'el pueblo argentino' era únicamente la masa de los desposeídos, y que el resto de millones de habitantes del país era una nada. . . ." [33]

Like Sábato, Ezequiel Martínez Estrada had a unique relationship to the nueva promoción, as well as an ambiguous view of the Peronato. That Martínez Estrada was one of the few if not the only writer of his generation to whom the young men of the late 1940s and early 1950s looked for direction, has been frequently pointed out: [34] that he apparently found the Argentina of Aramburu, Frondizi, and the Revolución Libertadora—not the Argentina of Perón—so unpleasant that he felt

[32] *El otro rostro del peronismo* (Buenos Aires: Imp. López, 1956), p. 43.

[33] Ibid., p. 57.

[34] See E. Rodríguez Monegal, *Parricidas*, p. 13; A. H. Murena, *El pecado original de América* (Buenos Aires: Sur, 1958), pp. 105–129; as well as *Contorno*, Núm. 4 (dic. 1954) dedicated exclusively to Martínez Estrada.

obliged to leave is a fact that is seldom noted. It would be stretching a point to say that Martínez Estrada sympathized with the Perón regime, though it may be argued that in his essays of the immediate post-Perón years (*¿Qué es esto?*, *Exhortaciones*) he looks back to the period preceding the revolution of September 1955 with an unusual degree of tolerance and comprehension. The comments of J. J. Sebreli, in the ephemeral magazine *Capricornio* (Fall, 1954) perhaps shed some light on the matter: "Martínez Estrada es uno de los pocos intelectuales argentinos—el Murena de 1948 y 1949 fue otro—quien ante las convulsiones del Terror revolucionario, no corre a refugiarse en la paz del Humanismo contrarevolucionario." [35] He then quotes Martínez Estrada directly: "Dicen que hay una atmósfera irrespirable en nuestro país. Es que se ha removido la basura con un ramo de flores." Sebreli goes on to report Martínez as saying: "Mi país estaba paralizado. Ahora anda. No sé si hacia el abismo, pero anda." [36] Recall that this comment was made in 1954, after eight years of intensive Peronization. Sebreli's final observation is that while Martínez Estrada could never quite bring himself to support any political group—the peronistas included—for a brief period he did overcome his middle-class prejudices to the extent that he could glimpse the possibility of a truly revolutionized Argentina: that the Perón experience was instrumental in opening his eyes to this possibility seems quite clear.

Yet this view of Martínez Estrada's position might be counterbalanced by a comment coming from another quarter. Victoria Ocampo, writing in the first post-Perón number of *Sur* (Fall, 1955) would include Martínez Estrada among the unilaterally anti-Perón writers of her circle: "Ultimamente Martínez Estrada me decía que habíamos sido *casi* todos cobardes (se refería, creo, a nosotros los escritores), pues hubiéramos debido hacernos matar gritando la verdad. Es cierto . . . pocos de entre nosotros han llegado al límite de extremo coraje que se necesita, en tiempos de dictadura . . ." [37] Estrada's ambivalence—if indeed both Sebreli and Ocampo have reported his views accurately—should not surprise those who are familiar with the frequent dialectical interplay of opposites which characterizes much of his work.

Perhaps Martínez Estrada's real relationship to the Argentina of 1945–1955 may be best appreciated in his excellent—and somewhat overlooked—fiction of the period (*Tres cuentos sin amor*, *Sábado de gloria* and *Marta Riquelme*). As Juan Carlos Ghiano observes "Martínez

---

[35] "Martínez Estrada o el alma encadenada," *Capricornio*, Núm. 8 (nov.-dic. 1954), p. 22.

[36] Loc. cit.

[37] *Sur*, Núm. 237 (sept.-oct. 1955), p. 7.

Estrada interpreta en sus historias un país debilitado en las resistencias morales, por consiguiente presa fácil de quienes se cubren con el lenguaje de la caridad para explotar a una sociedad enferma . . . ha escrito la obra narrativa que representa para le década 1945–55 el equivalente de lo que fue *El matadero* de Echeverría en el período de Rosas . . .[38]

To this point I have touched upon the nature of the Perón regime, some aspects of its relationship to literary activity, and the makeup of several literary circles or cliques of the period. Among the prose writers we can distinguish at least three such groups: the nationalistic, conservative peronista "Old Guard"; the liberal anti-Perón Barrio Norte Establishment associated with *Sur*, *La Nación*, and the independent *La Prensa*; and finally, the younger writers who made their debuts during the peronato. The first two groups, composed of men born between the turn of the century and World War I, had clear-cut ideas about Perón and his movement: they were either fervently for it or passionately against it. The third group—the "nueva promoción," the "parricides," the generation of 1950, or whatever one chooses to call them—were, in the main, born in the twenties: as heterodox radicals their sensitivity to what lay behind the Perón movement was far greater than that of their elders; moreover, as the regime crumbled and was replaced by one which smacked of the old days, they began to interpret peronismo in decidedly revolutionary terms.

Of course the scheme suggested here—the tripartite division of literary groups on the basis of age and sociopolitical orientation—is, like all such schemes, rudimentary, oversimplified, and incomplete. Several important groups are not included in it—for example the writers of the "Old Left," men like Álvaro Yunque, Leonidas Barletta, Elías Castelnuevo, and others. Moreover, a number of major authors do not fall neatly into any one of the three divisions. We have already noted the exceptional cases of Sábato and Martínez Estrada. Along with these writers might be added the name of Julio Cortázar, who can hardly be considered a member of the nueva promoción (he was born in 1914), but whose remarkable works began to appear in the fifties. Finally I should point out that my scheme is based on prose fiction and essays: writers who are primarily poets or dramatists have not been taken into account.

With these reservations in mind a few generalizations may be made about the group which, I believe, most clearly reflects the Argentina of Perón—the younger writers. But first—and at the risk of presenting a mere catalogue of authors—some representative names should be noted.

---

[38] *La novela argentina contemporánea*, p. 18.

Among the essayists and critics: Adolfo Prieto (1928), Juan José Sebreli (1930), Rudolfo Kusch (1922), Ismael Viñas (1926), Noé Jitrik (1928), Julio Mafud (1928), and H. A. Murena (1924); among the novelists, David Viñas (1929), Beatriz Guido (1924), Eduardo Dessein (1921), Andrés Rivera (?), Valentín Fernando (1921), Antonio Di Benedetto (1922), Alberto Rodríguez (1920), J. J. Manauta (1919), and perhaps Marta Lynch (1929).

These authors, with few exceptions, are essentially committed: committed to probing, defining, and in some cases to revolutionizing their surroundings; or, to use one of their favorite terms, their *contorno*. As a group they tend toward the Left and so it should come as no surprise that political themes figure prominently in their works. For example, David Viñas in his novels *Cayó sobre su rostro* (1955) and *Los dueños de la tierra* (1958) attacks the image of idealism, moderation, and solid bourgeois virtues which the Partido Radical had epitomized in the first half of the century. In a later novel, *Dar la cara* (1962), he explores the complex world of student micropolitics during the immediate post-Perón period. Beatriz Guido, in *Fin de fiesta* (1958), traces the career of an archtypical conservative caudillo through the turmoil of the early thirties until his death in the fateful month of October of the year 1945. Although H. A. Murena's *Las leyes de la noche* (1958) is more of a psychological-existential study of a young woman's search for identity, it contains a strong subplot centered on Perón's consolidation of popular support. On the other hand, *El precio* (1956) by Andrés Rivera is directly concerned with political matters; specifically with the manipulation of the labor movement during the dictatorship. Finally, in one of the best novels of this type, *La alfombra roja* (1962), Marta Lynch paints a fine composite picture of her protagonist Aníbal Rey—a charismatic political leader whose "moral anesthesia" made him quite capable of being "on good terms with both God and the Devil."

The theme of generational strife is perhaps as important in the work of the nueva promoción as is the political theme—moreover, the two concerns are frequently intertwined. David Viñas again is one of the best representatives of the group: his *Cayó sobre su rostro* is as much the story of conflict between father and son as it is an account of the rise of the Radicales and the fall of the Conservadores. In his *Dar la cara* generational strife becomes especially intense: newly liberated university students deplore the fact that many of their comrades continue to seek guidance from older intellectuals; as the protagonist Bernardo notes, "hace más de diez años que venimos inventando maestros en este país . . . que se mueran de una vez." [39] The theme is further developed in the same

[39] *Dar la cara* (Buenos Aires: Ed. Jamcona, 1962), p. 518.

novel when the protagonist realizes that there exists a real generation gap between himself—a thirtyish ex-student activist—and the younger militants who are just savoring their first taste of manning the barricades. The conflict between Braceritas, the finely drawn protagonist of Beatriz Guido's *Fin de fiesta*, and his vaguely antiestablishment grandson, Adolfo, provides the framework for yet another novel where political and generational strife are fused. In Valentín Fernando's *Desde esta carne* (1952) the emphasis is on the very young—in this case, teen-agers who challenge parental authority and values in no uncertain terms. As one youngster proclaims, "el sentido de una familia, de un hogar, de una dignidad, de un bienestar . . . [son] palabras huecas. No creo en todo eso . . ." [40]

And Eduardo Dessein, one of the lesser-known novelists of the nueva promoción, seems to be speaking for a goodly number of his contemporaries in his aptly titled *Su generación* (1956) when he has his principal character, a struggling artist, ask "¿Qué somos, a los treinta años? Una promesa que ya no se ha cumplido y cada día trayendo una aproximación mayor al conformismo." [41] In one of the better scenes of this rather spotty novel, the author provides an especially vivid picture of the abyss between generations when the protagonist, as he watches his father reading the daily paper, cynically observes, "Aunque no lo sabía estaba buscando trocitos supervivientes de la democracia, el liberalismo, el propreso científico, el ateísmo, la sabiduría de la Iglesia, el marxismo y la higiene . . ." [42]

Another recurrent motif in the work of the newer generation of novelists, and one which is closely related to the the matter of generational strife, is the theme of childhood and adolescence. The principal characters in novels like Viñas' *Los años despiadados* (1956), *Un dios cotidiano* (1957), Guido's *La casa del ángel* (1954), Fernando's *Desde esta carne*, or Federico Peltzer's *Tierra de nadie* (1955) are, to use Juan Carlos Ghiano's appropriate description, "niños destruídos por los adultos, contra los cuales se eleva la acusación . . . del narrador." [43] Novels of this sort probe deeply into infantile and juvenile psychology, and especially into the realm of sex. Indeed the writers of the nueva promoción—like their counterparts in other countries—may be the first literary generation to go beyond conventional restraints in their exploration of the subject. In the work of some of the more marginal members of the group,

[40] *Desde esta carne* (Buenos Aires: Sudamericana, 1952), p. 124.
[41] *Su generación* (Buenos Aires: Nova, 1956), p. 11.
[42] Ibid., p. 49.
[43] *La novela argentina contemporánea*, p. 21.

Renato Pellegrini, for example, this interest has manifested itself in two surprisingly graphic novels of life among Buenos Aires' homosexuals, *Siranger* (1957) and *Asfalto* (1964).

Though it may be argued that the theme of adolescence, along with the frank treatment of sex, are hallmarks of the literature of our times, the emphasis on these subjects in the Argentina of Perón and the years immediately following his fall appears quite significant. For one thing, in the novels noted the societal dimension of individual personal problems is almost always present; and often the political background impinges directly upon the main line of the narrative. The fight between the young Rubén—the protagonist of *Los años despiadados*—and a group of slightly older Peronista youths, or the May Day voters who destroy the statue of the angel—and with it, symbolically, the innocence of the young girl—in *La casa del ángel* are illustrative of this relationship. To make a broad generalization, the novels of the period reflect the fact that profound forces of social change had been set in motion, or at least accelerated, in Perón's Argentina: that these forces should manifest themselves in literature through an intense interest in generational strife, adolescence, and sex should come as no surprise. The importance of these themes is further underscored by the essayists of the nueva promoción; most notably by Sebreli, in his very successful *Buenos Aires, vida cotidiana y alienación* (1965).

Earlier I touched upon the theme of the rediscovery of the Argentine hinterland. It was suggested that Perón played some part in getting writers and folklorists to explore beyond the city of Buenos Aires and beyond what may be considered the conventional rural setting of Argentine letters—the eastern pampas. The dictator's motives in encouraging regionalism may have been simply to solidify his hold on the entire nation; or perhaps Perón sensed that his image as a potential leader of a Latin American "third world" made it imperative that the Europeanized, cosmopolite, picture of the nation be modified to permit intellectuals of Indian and mestizo countries to feel some kinship with the new Argentina.[44] At any rate, a number of novelists and essayists—most of whom were not peronistas—attest to this new interest in regionalism.

Considering the relative poverty of much of rural Argentina it is not surprising that the novelists of the interior should inject a strong note of social protest into their work. Thus Alberto Rodríguez's *Matar la tierra* (1952) and *Donde haya Dios* (1955) reveal the plight of farmers trying

[44] There is perhaps some significance in the fact that several non-Argentine "indigenista" writers collaborated in the peronista review *Sexto Continente*. A few pieces by José Vasconcelos and Jorge Icaza appear in the review during 1949.

to work marginally-irrigated lands in the arid wastes of Cuyo; while Juan José Manauta in *Los aventados* (1952) and *Las tierras blancas* (1956) has written novels centered about the pathetic lives of itinerant *campesinos* who eke out a bare existence on the over-eroded sterile lands of Entre Ríos. Even the city-oriented Viñas has been attracted by regional themes, as his novel of the early development of the Patagonian frontier, *Los dueños de la tierra* (1958), demonstrates. Several of these novels are, moreover, notable for their stylistic and technical excellence, qualities not always associated with regionalism. Manauta's *Las tierras blancas*, for example, employs a deceptively simple structure: an alternating interior monologue of only two characters. And Antonio Di Benedetto's *Zama* (1956) combines historical material, regionalism of the Northeast, an underlying tension of primeval forces versus the forces of man the civilizer, with a mood of mystery suggesting contemporary magical realism.

A parallel interest in the interior, especially in the indigenous cultures of Argentina, is also evident in the work of the essayists of the nueva promoción. Though there existed a rich tradition of Argentine literature devoted to the land (writings of Lugones, Rojas, Mallea), it was Martínez Estrada who acted as this group's mentor. H. A. Murena's *El pecado original de América* (1954), Rudolfo Kusch's *La ciudad mestiza* (1952), *La seducción de la barbarie* (1953), and *América profunda* (1962), and perhaps Julio Mafud's *El desarraigo argentino* (1959), all reveal his influence. Consistent with the general lines of Martínez' thought, the common denominator found in the work of these essayists is the search for a greater authenticity for both the individual and the society as a whole. In the case of Kusch this quest led to the far North of the nation where in the poverty, ignorance, and stench of the Indian he seemed to find a certain existential genuineness lacking in the "civilized" Argentina of "las buenas maneras, la perfecta constitución, el gran arte o las pomposas bibliografías . . ." [45] Mafud's emphasis is only slightly different. By probing the psychology of the *desarraigados*—the uprooted and the rootless—he believed that Argentina might gain a clearer understanding of itself. Historically, Mafud observes, the archtypical desarraigado was the Indian; in the nineteenth century it was the gaucho, while in our century it is the urban proletariat and the *cabecita negra*. That the latter term is frequently associated with the Perón period is significant.

At the risk of pressing the point, it seems clear that the experience of the peronato—the undeniable release of repressed forces for social change—led these essayists in the directions we have been analyzing. Mafud, for example, makes the point that Perón's real hold on Argen-

[45] *América profunda* (Buenos Aires: Hachette, 1962), p. 188.

tina was due, in the first place, to his awareness of the desarraigo of the masses and, secondly, to his establishing of structures designed to resolve this chronic uprootedness.[46] Kusch, following close on the heels of Martínez Estrada, suggests that Argentine social and historical realities may be viewed best as a constant struggle of "los de abajo . . . esa aposición irremediable de hediondos contra pulcros . . ." [47] Among the leaders of *los de abajo* Mafud singles out Tupac Amaru, Pumacahua, Rosas, and—as the reader has probably guessed—Perón. Yet these writers are not, strictly speaking, Peronists: they simply saw in the dictator's obvious popularity that the well-scrubbed, well-mannered, reasonable *pulcro* of Buenos Aires was only part of a reality which included illiterate speakers of Quechua in the Northwest, poverty-stricken cabecitas negras of Corrientes or the Chaco, and the masses of unpleasant-smelling workers who wept at Evita's funeral.

Jorge Luis Borges once remarked that the only word never mentioned in treatises on chess was the word "chess" itself. Until quite recently it was possible to make a similar observation about the words "Perón" or "peronismo" in studies of contemporary Argentine letters. For example, the reader of Arturo Cambours Ocampo's *El problema de las generaciones argentinas* (1963) is told that the author wishes to link literary activity to the "vivencias espirituales" of the nation, yet in the 332 pages of this study, purportedly centered on "las últimas promociones," hardly a word about Perón, peronismo, or the profound social changes of the decade 1945–1955 appears. In a much more sensible and less pretentious study, Guillermo Ara's *Los argentinos y la literatura nacional* (1966), the same omissions may be seen.

Of course Perón's rise and fall are very recent events and we perhaps should not condemn literary historians and critics for not trying to take them into consideration. It may also be argued that in the past students of Spanish American letters studied more of the socio-political periphery of literature than the literature itself, and that we are now witnessing a salutory reaction against this tendency. But even after taking all this into consideration, it is still difficult to explain the apparent lack of interest in the impact of the Perón experience upon literature. Significantly, many Argentines themselves—with the exception of the nueva promoción writers—have been the leaders in this campaign of silence. As we saw earlier, for a goodly number of Argentine writers and intellectuals Perón, peronismo, and all that these words conjure up represent an unpleasant and short-lived deviation from the "normal" trajectory of the

[46] *El desarraigo argentino* (Buenos Aires: Americalee, 1959), pp. 122–126.
[47] *América profunda*, p. 14.

nation's development. The course of events in Argentina since 1955 would suggest that on the political level such a view is untenable; and as I have tried to show here, an examination of literary activity of the period leads to a similar conclusion.

To sum up: the peronato had a profound effect on Argentine letters. Writers, whether they were old-fashioned conservatives like Gálvez or Wast, apolitical cosmopolites like Borges, or heterodox radicals like Martínez Estrada or Sábato all reflect, in one way or another, its influence. An even greater effect may be seen in the case of the younger authors—the parricides, the *enojados*, or simply the nueva promoción. For writers like Viñas, Murena, Guido, Sebreli, and the others, Perón and the peronato were inextricably linked with their own coming of age. By contrast with the men born before the First World War they were much more sensitive to the period's ambiguities and deeper implications. Their attitude toward the older generation was more than a reaction against specific literary and political positions. On a rather superficial level it may seem to be the familiar conflict of the committed writer versus the dwellers in the ivory tower; but looking a bit below the surface we see the new generation's principal attack directed toward the tendency to label, to categorize, and to place a stamp of approval or disapproval on a dynamic, and often ambiguous, reality.

John Stephen Gitlitz
Department of Political Science
University of North Carolina
Chapel Hill

IMPRESSIONS OF THE PERUVIAN AGRARIAN REFORM*

On 24 June 1969 the military government of Peru, exercising its de facto power to issue legislation by decree, promulgated a law of agrarian reform.[1] In Latin America legal norms—even radical ones—are not necessarily to be feared. Many countries have agrarian reform laws and in most of these agrarian structures have not been changing rapidly. Indeed, the previous administration in Peru had passed a mild law in 1964, but the hacienda structure of the Peruvian Andes remained virtually intact. Few feared that the new code enacted by the military would present a strong challenge to tradition.

Forty-eight hours after its promulgation opinions began to change. The government announced that interventors were being sent to eight of the largest sugar estates on the northern coast.[2] Intervention is the first step toward expropriation. The sugar estates lie at the heart of the Peruvian oligarchy: they were exempt from the 1964 legislation.[3]

---

* I am indebted to the National Science Foundation for a grant which enabled me to spend July and August 1970 in Peru in preparation for undertaking dissertation research. While in Peru I spent a number of weeks in the Andes, first near Cajamarca and then in the area of Cuzco. This paper is a summary of my impressions of the agrarian reform process after one year. It contains, therefore, a number of preliminary ideas which should not be construed as the result of systematic research.

1 The law has been translated into English. Fred L. Mann and John Huerta, *Text of Decree-Law No. 17716: Agrarian Reform Law* (Lima: Iowa-Peru Mission Program Reports T-5, 1969).

2 Julio Cotler, *Crisis política y populismo militar en el Perú* (Lima: Instituto de Estudios Peruanos, 1969), p. 51.

3 "Lands owned by industrial processors of sugar cane are exempted from expropriation up to the amount indispensable for maintaining the efficient operation of

If the government of Peru is to be appraised or considered as revolutionary as it claims, judgment must largely be formed on the basis of this agrarian reform law. Skeptics, however, immediately attributed the law to limited political aims. Hence, they argued, it would have limited effects. In response, this author would like to consider the practical application of the reform—now more than one year old. The paper is organized around political interpretations and it concentrates on political effects. I believe and I hope to show, however, that the intent of the military may have been more profound and that the effects of application have already been far greater than those so cynically envisioned. In the process I think that a number of tentative conclusions can be made. Power within Peru has been redistributed, but the military may be encountering problems in creating a new, just society. The manner in which the military leaders seem to have begun to confront these problems reveals much about the way they view the political game.

The paper is divided into three sections. In the first I present a few comments on the law itself. Then I consider its application, first to the modern agricultural regions of the Peruvian coast and next to the more traditional agricultural zones of the Andes.

THE AGRARIAN REFORM LAW

Legislation sets the parameters within which any reform must proceed, and some understanding of the processes which it envisions is required.

The new code is very similar to that of 1964, which it followed. There are only a few major differences. The 1964 version exempted from reform estates judged agro-industrial complexes, i.e., those of the most wealthy, powerful families, corporations, and even foreign firms. The 1969 law eliminates this exemption. Virtually all land is subjected to redistribution. The major exceptions are the lands of certain recognized Indian or peasant communities.[4]

---

the processing plants (Art. 38, 39 and 43)." Fred L. Mann, John Huerta, Dennis Morrissey, et al; *Preliminary Analysis: Agrarian Reform Law No. 17716* (Lima: Iowa-Peru Mission Program Reports T-4, 1970), p. 109.

[4] Ibid., pp. 62–63. During the second decade of this century usurpation of Indian lands reached scandalous levels. In a number of areas desperate peasants revolted. Although they were bloodily suppressed, they gave impetus to the creation of a new legal entity, the indigenous community. Once peasant communities were officially recognized as such, they obtained inalienable right to their land. For more detailed analysis of these events see Edward Dew, *Politics in the Altiplano* (Austin: University of Texas Press, 1969), p. 29. The present law reflects this earlier precedent.

There is, however, a legal minimum to which any owner is entitled, providing that he privately owns and works his land. The reform can only expropriate excess beyond that minimum, which varies somewhat according to region.[5] There are certain conditions under which the minimum can be denied: (1) if the land is contiguous to a peasant community lacking land, it can be taken; (2) if the owner-operator has violated Peruvian labor laws, the minimum can be expropriated.[6] Although these exceptions appear innocent, they probably would include most of the larger estates, particularly those in the Andes, whose owners have long been known to disregard labor legislation. For example, few have paid legal minimum wages.[7]

The process through which land may be expropriated occurs basically in three steps. An area must first be declared an Agrarian Reform Zone.[8] Once an area has been so declared, land within it is subject to affectation (*afectación*), roughly expropriation.[9] At this point the government assumes management and administration of the property. The landowner will receive payment in cash and bonds redeemable over a period of twenty to thirty years. There are major benefits if the landowner plans to invest these funds.[10]

---

[5]

Region	*Type of Exploitation*	*Basic Exemption*
coast	irrigated, cultivated	150 hectares
	dry farmed	300 hectares
	natural pasture	1,500 hectares
mountains	irrigated, cultivated	15–55 hectares
	dry farmed	30–110 hectares
	natural pastures	sufficient for 5000 sheep

This table is expanded in Mann, et al, *Preliminary Analysis*, p. 57c.

[6] Ibid., p. 42.

[7] Lack of respect for labor laws has characterized landowners throughout Latin America. For an excellent discussion of this point see Solon L. Barraclough and Arthur L. Domike, "*Agrarian Structure in Seven Latin American Countries*," in Rodolfo Stravenhagen, *Agrarian Problems and Peasant Movements in Latin America* (Garden City, New York: Doubleday and Company, Inc., 1970), pp. 74–78.

[8] The entire process is summarized in detail in Mann, et al; *Preliminary Analysis*, pp. 461c. This is the normal procedure. Under certain circumstances land can be taken more rapidly. For example, peasant communities are entitled to allotment up to a prescribed minimum without awaiting such declaration (ibid., p. 43). Also, where there have been previously serious peasant-owner difficulties land can be taken prior to creation of a Zone (ibid, p. 42).

[9] "The term is defined in the Law as: a restriction on the right of rural property imposed expressly and specifically for agrarian reform purposes, being applicable to all or any part of a holding, for its expropriation by the State and subsequent transfer to peasants duly qualified under the Law." Mann. et al; *Preliminary Analysis*, p. 16.

[10] Ibid., pp. 79–83. "If the bondholder supplies, in cash, one-half of the capital necessary to finance a duly qualified industrial enterprise, the State Developing

In the final step, adjudication, lands are redistributed to the new owners. Three basic forms of exploitation are envisioned. (1) Private ownership is allowed, although officially and probably effectively discouraged. In no case are private plots to be distributed below a minimum size known as the family farm units. This varies according to region.[11] (2) Recognized peasant communities will be allowed to continue communal ownership of the land. It is hoped, however, that these will be modernized and converted into the third form of ownership, cooperatives. (3) Cooperatives are viewed as vital, and it is hoped that these will facilitate economies of scale while serving as market, technical aid, and credit mechanisms.[12]

The law also establishes complex procedures at each of these stages. There is ample room for appeal and there is ample room for bureaucratic red tape, particularly when there is little or no real interest in application. Therefore we must turn our attention to the manner in which the law has indeed been applied.

AGRARIAN REFORM ON THE PERUVIAN COAST

Agricultural structures in Peru can be divided into two clearly defined though interrelated zones: the mountains and the coast. Mountain agriculture is traditional, poor and unproductive, and semi-feudal. Coastal agriculture, on the other hand, is relatively modern, relatively productive, and relatively prosperous. The coast is an area of large estates, of huge fields of cotton and sugarcane, two export products which alone accounted for just under twenty percent of foreign exchange earnings in 1965.[13] Although there is considerable variation, some of the estates employ in production the newest technology and the most modern machinery. They have large, stable labor forces. Unlike labor in the mountains, the coastal workers are Spanish speaking and relatively literate. They receive cash wages and often have written contracts.[14] Indeed, it was on the coast

---

Banks must accept bonds at 100% of their value for supplying the other one-half of such capital (Art. 181). A 'duly qualified enterprise' is not defined but apparently refers to those approved by the Industrial Bank." Ibid., p. 83.

[11] At no point is the family farm unit to be less than three hectares. It may be larger. Ibid., pp. 71a–72.

[12] Ibid., pp. 66–72.

[13] Exports of mineral products, largely dominated by foreign investors, accounted for over fifty-five percent. Exports of fish meal and related products, produced by domestic and foreign firms, contributed twenty-five percent. Banco Central de Reserva del Perú, *Cuentas Nacionales del Perú: 1950–1965* (Lima: Banco Central de Reserva del Peru, 1966), pp. 48–49.

[14] Pontificia Universidad Católica del Perú, Departmento de Ciencias Sociales; *La reforma agraria en dos complejos agro-industriales: Cayalti y Tuman* (Lima; Pontificia Universidad Católica del Perú, Departamento de Ciencias Sociales, 1970), pp. 15–23.

that the first rural labor syndicates were organized, and most estates are effectively and actively organized, largely under the control of the American Popular Revolutionary Alliance (APRA) of Víctor Raúl Haya de la Torre.

Under the new law the earliest, and to date most extensive, agrarian reform efforts have affected the coast. Indeed, for a considerable period it appeared that the coast would be the only area seriously affected and that the military was uninterested in assuming the burden of extending reform to the mountains. This led political pundits to argue that the reform was not seriously motivated by any truly revolutionary social ethic or morality. Rather it was a purely political move, designed to weaken severely two of the nation's strongest power contenders, the oligarchy and the APRA, which, in unholy alliance, had dominated and made a farce out of politics during the Belaúnde Terry era.

I feel that this is too narrow an interpretation, that the intention of the military government was and is far more sincere, generous, and social. I would not, however, preclude a political motivation—a motive which might to some extent dictate priorities. Let us consider, therefore, how the reform has actually affected the oligarchy and the APRA.

The nature of the oligarchy, an idea of the extent of its economic power, and the ease with which its base can be attacked may all be seen in one example. Within days of the promulgation of the law of 26 June, nine estates had been intervened.[15] The largest of these was the Hacienda Pomalca, property of the de la Piedra family.[16] It covered roughly 143,000 hectares, although most of this was desert land. It employed about 4,200 workers, and accounted for eleven percent of the total area devoted to the cultivation of sugarcane in Peru.[17] All together the nine estates, representing seven families and one foreign firm, occupied fifty-nine percent of the area cultivated with sugarcane.[18]

Agriculture is—or rather was—not the only source of wealth for the oligarchy. The prominent families had used foreign exchange earnings to expand, principally into two areas. First, they dominated the import-export sector of the economy.[19] Second, they had joined with

---

[15] Specifically, the government had sent agents to "act as inspectors and approve or disapprove transactions." The process of affectation did not begin until two months later. Mann, et al; *Preliminary Analysis*, p. 58.

[16] Julio de la Piedra was a prominent senator in the APRA-Odriísta Coalition which confronted Belaúnde.

[17] Mann, et al; *Preliminary Analysis*, p. 8.

[18] Ibid., p. 8.

[19] Francois Bourricaud, "Structure and Function of the Peruvian Oligarchy," *Studies in Comparative International Development*, Volume II, No. 2, passim.

foreign sources to control the flow of capital and credit within Peru. They were prominent on the directorates of banks, credit agencies, and insurance companies.[20] This combination had given them a dominent hold over the Peruvian economy.[21] They have also been directly politically active. They have served in both houses of Congress, been dominant in political parties, and organized what has been for years perhaps the most important pressure group in Peruvian politics, the National Agrarian Society (SNA). One member of the SNA served in the Prado government as prime minister.[22]

Thus the agrarian reform, by cutting the land base from underneath the oligarchs, has deprived them of their traditional source of wealth. How have they reacted? At best, we can only say that to date their opposition has varied. Perhaps it can most accurately be described as having been confused, fearful, and to some extent ambivalent.

The reform was not foreseen, and it came far too quickly for opposition to solidify. By the time the oligarchy could react it was presented with a *fait accompli.* As a result, protest was largely ineffectual. As far as I can tell, it was limited mainly to strident newspaper advertisements proclaiming the approaching demise of Peruvian agriculture as a result of the reform. Only one family attempted to interfere directly with the activities of a ministerial interventor on its estate. The government responded by accelerating the process of intervention and by police occupation of the hacienda.[23]

With their preponderant control of urban wealth the families might have seriously hurt the government but, although they undoubtedly have done some damage, they have lacked the unity to undertake decisive action. The estates were the original source of oligarchic wealth, but the economic empires of the oligarchy are today much larger, and in 1969 the oligarchy did not depend on agriculture alone. Indeed, a number of

---

[20] For example, the above seven families had investments in at least eleven different banks, credit agencies or insurance companies. Carlos Malpica Santisteban, *Los dueños del Perú* (Lima: Ediciones Ensayos Sociales, 1968), pp. 71–106 passim.

[21] This is in contrast to many Latin American countries where the two sectors, agriculture and financial, have developed separately. In some, for example Brazil, conflict between the sectors has been politically important. In Peru, however, the two have been united through much of this century. Only recently has there developed an independent urban class, based primarily on immigrant involvement in commerce and consumer oriented industry. As a result, the position of the oligarchy had probably been weakened somewhat.

[22] Pedro Beltrán, director of *La Prensa*, one of Peru's two leading daily newspapers, was appointed prime minister in June 1959. At the same time he held the position of minister of the treasury. Fredrick B. Pike, *The Modern History of Peru* (London: Weidenfeld and Nicolson, 1967), p. 297.

[23] Mann, et al., *Preliminary Analysis*, p. 46.

estates in recent years had proven less and less profitable. Some were deeply in debt. As a result, there were instances in which owners were quite happy to see reform. They cooperated extensively with the workers from the ministry of agriculture and seemed most concerned only to obtain the best remuneration possible.[24]

This is not to imply that there is no serious conflict between the military government and the oligarchic families. There is, and it seems at the moment to be very bitter. Rather I wish to imply that the truly powerful families could, and may have been willing to, have lived with the agrarian reform. The most serious contention has occurred, and continues to occur, on the urban front.

The earliest interpretations of agrarian reform were, as mentioned, twofold. On the one hand, the reform was a political weapon against the oligarchy. On the other, it was aimed at weakening severely the APRA. I have already mentioned that coastal agriculture employs a large, salaried work force, that this force had been highly organized since the early 1930s, and that it has formed one of the most important bases of the APRA's "solid North." [25]

In addition it should be noted that, whereas the military leaders have been traditionally allied with the oligarchy, and therefore their current position surprised many, the military hostility toward the APRA has been one of the constants of Peruvian politics for almost forty years.[26]

This analysis argues that the military hoped, through the agrarian reform, not only to eliminate one set of lower-class demands but also to sidetrack the APRA-controlled labor union structures. Thus, the reform would envision turning the estates over to worker-owned-and-managed cooperatives. It would be hoped that these would remain under government control, or under the control of pro-government leaders. At the same time, worker-owned cooperatives would make syndical grievance structures superfluous. Although such action might not weaken inbred

---

[24] A number of points included here and throughout the paper come from persons in responsible positions who understandably would probably wish to remain anonymous. I hope that the reader will accept my belief that these sources are relatively reliable.

[25] For a lengthy discussion of the relationship between the growth of the APRA and the syndical struggles on the estates, see Peter Klaren, *La formación de las haciendas azucareras y los origenes del APRA* (Lima: Moncloa-Campodonico, 1970).

[26] This famous feud began with the abortive 1931 APRA uprising in Trujillo in which a number of officers were killed. The military responded with a wholesale slaughter of Apristas, and the APRA has never been forgiven. Fear of an APRA victory in the elections which were to have been held in 1969 is often quoted as a cause of the 1969 coup. For an easily readable although thoroughly biased account of the genesis of this feud, see Pike, *The Modern History of Peru*, Chapters 8, 9, and 10.

partisan loyalties, it would present a severe blow to the APRA control of local structures.

If this is indeed what the new government wished to accomplish—and many in the APRA feel that it is—then the success of the effort to date is highly problematical. This can be seen through a consideration of a number of somewhat related factors.

On the estates the response from the workers to the reform seems to have been, on the whole, favorable. The only detailed study I have seen shows that the peasants in general had and have high expectations of what the reform will bring, although their knowledge of the reform is highly inadequate.[27] This stems from a number of causes in addition to simple peasant ignorance. At least during the first year of application government efforts toward structuring worker-ministry communications were highly disorganized, even though a number of means were employed. There was some reliance on propaganda—posters, pamphlets, etc. This, however, was limited generally to efforts immediately prior to the visit of functionaries to the estates.

The government did institute a number of basic cooperative courses. Although these proved to be the most effective channel of communications, according to the above mentioned study, they did not reach the vast majority of workers. They failed, almost totally, to touch the workers' families. Thirdly, the government did organize a series of radio programs on the reform. These, however, were too esoteric and were scheduled at inconvenient hours. As a result, they received very little attention. Many, including numerous worker leaders, were unaware of the programs. Similarly, lecturers visited the estates at various times. Again, most were too abstruse and attendance was sparse. Finally, the emerging cooperatives were encouraged to publish newsletters. These, however, seem to have had very limited circulation.[28]

Thus, efforts at developing an effective program of communications were inadequate. Moreover, propaganda was not the only area slighted due to ministerial inattention. As far as I can tell, there were few if any attempts to create at developing any form of base level organization to support either the reform or the government.

By the end of the first year cooperatives had been formed on many of the estates, and elections had been held to fill the directorates. The APRA, however, won control of a surprising number. It even won victories on some estates where it had not succeeded in controlling or orga-

---

[27] Pontificia Universidad Católica, *La reforma agraria.*
[28] Ibid., pp. 45–49.

nizing unions in the past.[29] Whether or not as a direct result, the military government has since decided to change the pattern by which cooperatives are being turned over to worker control. Boards of directors were increased in size by including governmental appointees. The APRA was thus denied a controlling majority.

Meanwhile, the beginnings of a much more active program of propaganda and organization can be seen. Within the ministry of agriculture divisions charged with the task of propaganda and training have become much more active. Radio seems to be much more effectively utilized, although I know of no studies which have demonstrated this point. The government also announced and for a short period emphasized the formation of the so-called Committees for the Defense of the Revolution.[30] Apparently the intention was to build a mass base for the government around local cells developed at places of residence and work. In April 1970, the press was full of announcements of committee formation. Exactly what the committees were intended to do was never clear, at least to me. Moreover, the organizational wave seemed to pass rapidly, and it appears today that few additional committees are being formed.[31]

More specific anti-APRA activities, following the old precedent of cooptation or elimination, may also have been developing. On the other hand, there have been efforts at winning over to the cause of reform numerous middle-level Aprista leaders. At the same time, there has been considerable harassment of those leaders and activists who refused to cooperate. A number are now in jail.[32]

This then seems to be the point to which agrarian reform seems to have advanced on the Peruvian coast. If summarizing now seems abrupt, it is because the process has not yet drawn to a close. Nevertheless, with some hesitation we can draw a number of conclusions. Whatever interpretation one chooses to accept—social or political—it cannot be denied that already there has been a tremendous effect. The process of redistribution has advanced considerably. Most of the major sugar producing

[29] Unfortunately I do not have precise information on the numbers involved. This account was first discussed with me by Apristas themselves. I later heard very similar arguments from other sources.

[30] The committees were organized independently of the ministry of agriculture.

[31] According to rumor, the choice of name was not entirely felicitous. Leftist militants rapidly became active in organization efforts, and there was danger that they might gain control of the committees. When the cabinet was confronted with this situation, it was decided to deemphasize and limit the range of the organizations. In Peru today such gossip is incessant and frequently inciting. Indeed, it is often the only source of information but it should always be taken with a grain of salt.

[32] Several Apristas mentioned to me that harassment had increased following elections.

areas have been affected, as have many of the cotton estates. In most of these holdings at least the foundation of cooperative structures has been laid. And in a number of cases the land has already been adjudicated; that is, management and ownership have been turned over to the former agricultural wage laborers.[33]

It remains to consider the political effects to date of reform on the coast. On the one hand, the rural land power base of the oligarchy has been eliminated quite successfully, and, in the city, attempts to limit the power resulting from the traditional concentration of tremendous economic wealth are continuing, in spite of loud and international furor. On the other hand, the success of the effort against APRA is at least debatable. Nationally, the APRA leadership seems weaker, definitely confused, and on the defensive, but it is hardly eliminated. Past experience has shown how dangerous it is to predict APRA's demise. At the local level, Aprista organization remains relatively strong and somewhat independent, but it is possible that central APRA authority over the local branches may be weaker than before. It seems to this observer that the question of APRA organization and its control, if it does survive may continue to be central to Peruvian history in the near future.

On another plane, the nature of government-worker relations is still not clear. Although the workers quite openly, obviously, and strongly support the reform, they have not yet been welded into a cohesive political force to support the reform and the government when needed. Except for the earlier ineffectual Committees for Defense of the Revolution, it is only recently that the regime has appeared to move in this direction. In his 3 October 1970 speech, marking the second anniversary of the Revolution, President Velasco seemed to hint at the formation of a political party following some form of corporatist model of organization.[34]

Finally, unlike the Mexican, Bolivian, or even to some extent the Cuban agrarian reforms, control and action in Peru have been initiated and dictated from above. Until now there has been little if any real participation from below. The reform has been throughout a centralized administrative effort, and it has shown once again that aversion to participation in partisan politics which Huntington found characteristic of military governments throughout the developing world.[35]

---

[33] A number of estates were given over to the cooperatives to mark the first anniversary of the law. For example, workers received ownership of the estates of Cayaltí, Tumán, and Laredo. Title was given personally by the minister of agriculture, General Jorge Barandiarán Pagador, *El Comercio* (Lima), 25 June 1970, p. 4.

[34] *Oiga* (Lima), No. 394, 8 October 1970, pp. 8–9.

[35] Samuel P. Huntington, *Political Order in Changing Societies* (New Haven: Yale University Press, 1968), pp. 243–244.

AGRARIAN REFORM IN THE PERUVIAN ANDES

In some ways the traditional landowners of the Andes have enjoyed an even more powerful position than those of the coast. Concentration of land ownership is great. One hundred and eighty-one proprietors own over sixty percent of the cultivated land. One million laborers possess no land whatsoever.[36] Moreover, the peasant is in many ways far more primitive than the coastal laborer. The Andean Indian is often an isolated human being in both physical and geographic senses. He has had little contact with the outside world. Often he does not speak Spanish, is illiterate, and is totally unskilled in any but the most primitive of agricultural techniques. The hacienda peasants often live in almost slave-like conditions and relationships to the landlords that statistical charts and generalizations are unable to portray adequately in terms of human feelings and realities.

In contrast, however, to the nearly absolute power wielded by traditional landlords on their estates, their political power varies greatly both in nature and in force from that exercised by their coastal counterparts. Consequently, the Andean hacendados do not belong to what has been designated as the oligarchy or, at best, sit only on the periphery of that elite. Therefore, if one accepts the argument that the agrarian reform was designed to serve anti-oligarchical and anti-APRA ends, it would be logical to expect a minimum of action in the mountain areas in contrast to the coast.

The basis of this difference is largely economic: this area's contribution to the national economy is not very great. Mountain agriculture is not particularly productive and, in fact, since the decline of the wool export boom early this century, the mountain estates have produced little of export value. As a result, Andean landowners have exercised considerably less powerful a hold over Peruvian economy, with an attendant loss of political power. Moreover, there are indications that this power has been declining in recent years. Presidents since Odría, who came to power in 1948, seem to have felt far less obligation to repress peasant demands than have earlier executives.[37]

The argument of political expediency can be extended, nevertheless, to explain certain phases of agrarian reform in the mountain zones. To understand this, one must review some recent events in the Peruvian Andes. Traditionally, the Indian has accepted his lot although there

---

[36] Ministry of Agriculture, *Perú: tierra sin patrones* (Lima: Ministry of Agriculture, 1970), p. 7.

[37] LaMond F. Tullis, *Lord and Peasant in Peru: A Paradigm of Political and Social Change* (Cambridge: Harvard University Press, 1970), p. 67.

have been sporadic, isolated, and bloodily repressed outbreaks throughout Peruvian history. During the late 1950s and early 1960s, however, manifestations of peasant discontent became far more widespread. These included at least three guerrilla outbreaks, none very successful.[38]

Much more important than these, however, have been extensive land invasions, common throughout the country but particularly concentrated in the south. An owner would arise in the morning, look out over his lands, and see anywhere from a few hundred to a few thousand peasants—men, women, children, and their animals—sitting and waiting. The response of the owners varied. Sometimes they gave in to the peasants, fleeing and abandoning their land or agreeing to yield some portion of it. Sometimes the reaction was more bloody. Abelardo Luna, for example, resided in a flat valley about one hour's ride north of Cuzco. Upon finding his land occupied he fled to that city and requested that the mayor, who happened to be his son-in-law, send help. Aid was sent and the serfs were evicted with considerable force.[39]

Three important points can be drawn from the invasion movement of the 1960s. First, one of the primary bases of traditional power in the mountains was this intimate contact between landowners and local authorities. Many of the latter were often virtually named by the former. Often these two were, as in the Luna example, related. This close identification has created, and continues to create, problems for the administration of reform.

Second, the peasant unrest had been one of the motivations for passing the 1964 agrarian reform law.

Third, the political interpretation of agrarian reform in the Andean region argues that redistribution and tenure change will proceed only in those areas where the peasants have been active in expressing their discontent, either through spectacular manifestations or through an ongoing

[38] Two of these actions, those of Luis de la Puente Uceda near Cuzco and of Héctor Béjar near Ayacucho, can properly be called guerrilla uprisings. However, the participation of peasants in either of these is questionable. At most, there was a minimum of peasant support. The third, the movement led by Hugo Blanco in the Valley of la Convención near Cuzco, was almost totally a peasant phenomenon. It was, however, principally syndicalist in nature and only assumed guerrilla aspects in response to police pressure. Three accounts of these movements, all of them interesting although sprinkled with liberal amounts of imagination are Gonzalo Añi Castillo, *Historia secreta de las guerrillas* (Lima: Ediciones Más Allá, 1967) Hector Bejar, *Perú 1965: una experiencia guerrillera* (Lima: Compodonico Ediciones, S.A., 1969), and Victor Vilanueva, *Hugo Blanco y la rebelión campesina* (Lima: Editorial Juan Mejía Baca, 1967).

[39] Hugo Neira, *Los Andes: tierra o muerte* (Santiago: Editorial ZYX, 1968), p. 138, tells part of this story. Other details were related to me by various agrarian reform personnel in the department of Cuzco, August 1970.

process of organization. Agrarian reform, therefore, is nothing but a palliative and, once the regions have been pacified, little more will be done.

Does evidence support this argument? Early government activity did give credence to it. After affectation on the coast the military did begin to move ınto the mountain areas fairly quickly, but government action began primarily in those areas affected by the unrest of the 1960s. For example, Luna's estate was located in the Pampa de Anta, one of the zones in which peasant activity reached a peak of intensity. The Pampa is now a showcase reform project, and Luna's estate house complex is now the administrative headquarters.[40]

Thus to some extent the argument that there may indeed have been a political motivation to the reform or, at least, to priorities of application can be supported. Now (December 1970), however, reform appears to have moved considerably beyond this point. Throughout most of the mountains, even in those regions most removed from peasant activities of the last decade, activity has begun. In Cajamarco, for example, most of the preliminary studies, such as those involving compilation of land titles, were well underway although, as far as I know, no land had actually been affected by the end of 1970. Moreover, although much remains to be done, estates throughout the Andes have already been affected. Whatever its motivation, the reform is extensive and is producing tremendous shifts of power and major social effects. The arguments of the skeptics may not yet have been disproven, but to a large extent they have already been shown to be irrelevant.

Nevertheless, the reform is not yet by far a total social revolution. In examining the events in the Andes, we find that, just as on the coast, the government has shown an aversion to partisan politics, an unwillingness to allow decisions to be made at a local level by those affected, and a reluctance to become involved in the work of political mobilization.

Propaganda efforts have once again been greatly limited. In wandering through the mountain zones, for example, I saw very few posters, slogans, etc., which might have drawn peasant attention to the reform. This was just as true in the showcase area of the Pampa de Anta as in the virtually untouched region of Cajamarca.[41] Indeed, it was my per-

---

[40] Even the law gives some support to this political interpretation. It states that land in zones of earlier unrest can be affected prior to declaration of an Agrarian Reform Zone. Mann, et al; *Preliminary Analysis*, pp. 23–24.

[41] Colorful pop-art posters advertising the reform have been prepared by the ministry of agriculture. One, for example, shows a peasant lady in indigenous dress, with an infant on her back, holding an axe, and proclaiming, "We are free. The Revolution is giving us land." However, these seem to have had their widest circulation in Lima. The only copies I saw in the highlands were inside Agrarian Reform Offices.

sonal impression that the only formal organization more or less constantly publicizing the alternatives presented by the new legislation throughout the regions I visited was the Church. Individual clerics and laymen associated with the Church devoted considerable effort to discussing new developments with the peasants. In at least one area they have mimeographed simple, illustrated pamphlets expounding basic points. I would hesitate, however, to suggest that this represents organized policy rather than individual predilection.

As far as I know, the only area in which the government had attempted a serious organizational effort on behalf of the reform by August 1970, was the Pampa de Anta. My impression is that the activity there is regarded as a pilot project which, if successful, will be extended to other areas. It aims to form a new, local leadership cadre capable of managing and defending reform-created cooperatives. Although individuals involved in the political uprisings of the past decade are not being excluded from the new leadership, there is an effort to bypass the more radical leaders. The project seems to be proceeding through selection of groups of potential leaders and instruction of these via short lecture courses.[42]

Agrarian reform in the Andes has thus been evolving through limited affectation and widespread studies in preparation for more extensive affectation. That no more has been accomplished after one year of intense propaganda in Lima is probably less due to lack of serious political concern than to the large number of problems and considerable opposition which the reform in the mountains has been encountering.

Landlord reaction, as on the coast, was not uniform. A few Andean owners seem quite willing to work for change. Others have attempted in many ways to oppose the reform. The latter apparently predominate, and opposition has probably been somewhat more effective than on the coast. There are a number of possible reasons. Landowners had more time to react before the process reached them. They were more powerful within their own milieu. Relations between owners and local officials, as has been indicated, were and often still are quite intimate. Whereas on the coast labor has long been actively and effectively organized, there are few, if any, large nationally powerful groups with real interest in mountain land reform. Finally, the national government has probably, at least until now, given somewhat lower priority to Andean reform than to other programs.

Opposition has taken numerous forms. There have been widespread

---

[42] Personal interviews with personnel of the Ministry of Agriculture and the Oficina Nacional de Cooperatives (ONDECOOP) connected with the Pampa de Anta project. Lima and Cuzco, August 1970. I was also under the impression that these programs were largely under civilian control.

efforts to turn the peasant against the reform or at least to make him distrust reform personnel. Traditionally, intimate contacts between government and peasant have taken one of two forms: military service or local official repression, both generally hated and feared by the peasantry. The socialization of centuries has inbred a suspicion of anything related to governmental authority. Landowners, aided by general ignorance of the reform, have been able to exploit this mistrust with considerable success.

Landowners in the Cuzco area, for example, have been known to call their peasants together in the estate complex square on Sunday after church. There they have discussed the meaning of agrarian reform. They have asserted that land would be given only to those who agreed to work for the state, produce would be gathered by the state for distribution, work would be done under the eyes of the police, with whips, peasants would have to work for the state without pay for twenty years, and those who did not work would be sent to the jungles, etc. Government employees working in the zone have reported that such discussions have increased peasant distrust. In some cases peasants have hidden from the reform workers or have given them false information, hoping that the reform would therefore not reach them.[43]

There are reports that owners have also taken to harassing peasant leaders who might attempt to speed up introduction of the reform or to enforce enactments unfavorable to the owner. The national daily *Expreso* printed the following account of a statement by peasant leaders on an estate in the department of Lima: "They emphasized that the landowners are resorting to false denunciations in order to have peasant leaders jailed, and they indicated, lamentably, that the police have worked against these laborers." [44]

Finally, estate owners have also resorted to the classic strategy of those threatened with the loss of land through government reform—that of parceling the land through private initiative.[45] Apparently throughout the Peruvian highlands *patrones* have come to the conclusion that it would be better to sell most of their land prior to the arrival of the reform, thus

---

[43] Roca Wallparimachi, "Labor de los hacendados en la Pampa de Anta para crear resistencia a la aplicación de la reforma agraria," report presented to the 39th Congress of Americanists, Lima, 8 August 1970.

[44] *Expreso* (Lima), 22 August 1970, p. 16.

[45] The law allows private parceling only with the approval of the Agrarian Reform Agency. Mann, et al; *Preliminary Analysis*, p. 126. Needless to say, many have undertaken to divide their lands without such permission. One bureaucrat complained to me that this activity was widespread in this area but that he lacked power to enforce the law. I have encountered numerous other examples, but I know no studies analyzing the exact extent of violation.

obtaining three advantages. First, they hope in this way to be able to choose the land to form that minimum which they will be allowed to keep. Naturally they choose the best. Second, although the reform stipulates that owners be paid for their land, it bases this payment on earlier assessments made by the owners themselves for taxation purposes and these are notoriously low in comparison with the true value of the land. Moreover, it postulates payment largely in bonds, in which landowners have little confidence. Private parceling, on the other hand, allows the hacendados to receive immediate payment in cash, and often, by playing on peasant ignorance of the law, to obtain a considerably higher price. Third, by selling to peasants the worst land, often on steep mountain slopes or far too high for productive agriculture, and by selling them amounts smaller than the minimum family unit, the patrón ensures that the peasant will not be able to support himself and his family on his new plot and must continue to seek outside employment, hopefully for low wages, from the landowner.

Opposition has not been limited to landowners. There is some evidence that, within the government itself, the reform is encountering problems due to bureaucratic inertia as well as personnel problems from those who, if not entirely opposed to change, at least hope to profit from it. Although a new government can replace some key officials, even a revolution cannot hope to change a bureaucracy overnight. To a large extent it must live with those who staff the lower level positions. Often these are officials of local origin who through the years have come to identify with local status hierarchies and have developed intimate contacts, even family ties, with the landholding elite of that area. Local bureaucrats, therefore, often feel that they have much to lose and little to gain in enforcing a rapid reform.

As yet there have been no detailed studies of the dimensions of this problem. Dramatic events such as that reported in the citation from *Expreso* are probably much less important than everyday lack of enthusiasm. President Velasco himself has alluded to this difficulty at least once.[46]

To give some idea of the nature of the problem, I will relate two anecdotes I heard while in the mountains. First, I was told of one local official who ordered all those under him to do only what was specifically required of them. In particular, they were not to speak of the reform or to publicize it to the peasantry any more than absolutely necessary. Sec-

[46] He alluded to this in his speech of 3 October 1970. *Oiga* (Lima), No. 394, 8 October 1970, pp. 8–9.

ond, I heard of one office in which engineers carrying out the preliminary studies prior to affectation were charging for their services.[47]

Landowner opposition and bureaucratic bungling are formidable obstacles to any rapid reform. They are, however, eventually soluble. Unfortunately, the land reform is encountering still other problems that may in the long run prove much more difficult, if not impossible, to resolve.

First, under the process of affectation peasant communities are ceded top priority for redistribution. Where a peasant community lacks land, it is entitled to make up the legal minimum immediately from those privately held lands which border it. It is entitled to these even before the declaration of an Agrarian Reform Zone. Meanwhile, according to the law, no community lands can be affected. But what is to happen in a region where there are nothing but traditional peasant communities, all lacking land? There are many such areas within the mountain zones.

At some point land has to be adjudicated, either to private ownership, to cooperatives, or to peasant communities. This is undeniably desired by the mass of peasants. It is likely to become more difficult, however, when the process of adjudication is brought down to the level of individual cases. Whether land goes to private ownership, cooperatives, or community, a time will come when peasants will have to be assigned individual plots. Given the tremendous diversity of land even within small areas, it will be almost impossible to make these plots equal in anything more than the most arbitrary sense. Therefore, the size and location of the allotments eventually distributed is likely to have a major effect on the new, evolving social hierarchy. This alone will probably create conflict.

Unfortunately, redistribution will not occur in a vacuum. Peasant society is not undifferentiated. Wealth in terms of amount of land possessed and consequent social status have not been equal on estate, community, or private farm in the past. Estate owners have long had their favorite peasants, and often these have been rewarded with larger plots or higher pay. Within the limits of their abject poverty, they have consequently enjoyed higher status.

Reform, as a result, is likely to encounter a problem. If assigned plots through reform are to be equal, those who enjoyed relatively higher positions under the traditional system will not be entirely happy. If, on the other hand, concessions are made and old status lines followed, those who remain on the bottom will be discontented. Whichever alternative is

[47] I cannot vouch for the truth of these. They should be taken with that grain of salt sprinkled on all rumors.

chosen, the process of redistribution is likely to encounter, and even give birth to, tensions and oppositions within the peasant villages.[48]

However, even these problems pale before another far more serious and perhaps truly insoluble difficulty. In the final analysis, today in Peru there is just not enough land. Someone will have to be left out, or the basic family unit will have to be made too small. There is no reason to elaborate extensive and complicated calculations, but it is worth repeating briefly the conclusions of the Iowa-Peru mission study. At best, given the conditions envisioned by the Decree-Law, approximately 1,400,000 hectares will become available for redistribution. The total sum is likely to be near this, although certain loopholes may in the end leave it somewhat reduced.

It must also be remembered that much of this land is far from productive. Allowing for an average minimum family farm unit of three hectares and setting as a goal bringing all those presently possessing more than one hectare but less than three up to that level, the reform will be able to benefit approximately 650,000 families. No land will remain to be given to all those families possessing some land but less than one hectare (about 300,000) or those presently possessing no land whatsoever (about 350,000). Thus an equal number of families, 650,000, will not benefit from the reform.[49]

CONCLUSIONS

In Peru agrarian reform is already a reality. On the coast, most land has been affected and much has been adjudicated. Whether one argues that the reform is a by-product of purely political ends or that

---

[48] Numerous previous reforms have shown this. Two examples will suffice. (1) Pararín is a peasant community traditionally possessing highlands above the Pativilca Valley. In the early 1960s, however, the *comuneros* invaded valley lands and successfully established control over a fairly extensive area. They then requested aid from the Universidad Agraria to establish a cooperative. Immediately, however, discussion broke down over the issue of status and land distribution. Although a compromise was reached and a cooperative was established, bitter feelings remained. The cooperative has since broken apart. (Personal interview with César Benavides, Lima, August 1970.) (2) The village of Yanamarca bordering the Mantaro Valley struggled for years to obtain land titles. After the 1964 law it achieved success. Personnel from the ministry of agriculture then arrived and attempted to establish a cooperative. However, those opposing equal distribution soon withdrew. At various times this upper status faction attempted to gain control of the cooperative in elections, to intransigently oppose it, or to form their own cooperative. The process of redistribution was greatly hampered, and at one point the two factions, threatening to invade each other's lands, actually came to blows. Rodrigo Sánchez, *Reforma agraria y cooperativa en Yanamarca* (Lima: Instituto de Estudios Peruanos, 1970).

[49] Mann, et al; *Preliminary Analysis*, pp. 136–144.

it has resulted from the profound social conscience of a new military, it has already had widespread social effects. Hence the argument is largely irrelevant.

In the Andes the reform is advancing, rapidly or slowly according to one's perspective, although it has not been as thorough as on the coast. It has made considerable progress in zones affected by peasant unrest during the 1960s. It is more than beginning to advance in other areas. Does this imply that the political interpretation offered by the skeptics has some validity? I think not, although it should be allowed that, given a broader social goal, the military government has not been unaware of where it was likely to encounter political opposition and has assigned priority to moves to counter that opposition.

A more accurate explanation for slower advance in the mountain areas, while admitting lower priority, must also recognize the much greater complexity of the problem in that region and the greater difficulties of movement. Landlord opposition appears to have been more effective. The bureaucracy appears less effectively committed and controlled. The national government's authority has never been absolute in the more backward Andean regions. At the same time the mass of the population is generally more ignorant and passive. Finally, the greater social and economic complexity of the problem in the mountains presents numerous additional difficulties.

If, on the one hand, an examination of the reform process allows us to make some tentative comments on the military's social conscience, it also enables us to observe in action the military's conception of politics. Throughout, the agrarian reform has been an exercise in rule from the top down. There has been virtually no participation in decision-making by the concerned sectors. At the same time the officers have not seen fit, at least as yet, to mobilize the peasantry which they say they are benefiting. There has been no serious effort to develop a powerful political force capable of carrying through the reform, defending it against its detractors, or supporting the military government itself. There have been, however, some hints that the government is beginning to see this lack and to move to correct it.

Thus, the Peruvian military government has undertaken a profound reform. It has undertaken to effect this change on its own, independent of, and in spite of, other political forces. To date it has been successful.

Georg Maier
Department of Government and Public Affairs
Southern Illinois University at Edwardsville
Edwardsville, Illinois

PRESIDENTIAL SUCCESSION IN ECUADOR, 1830-1970

Introduction

An article[1] by Professors Richard B. Gray and Frederick R. Kirwin entitled "Presidential Succession in Chile: 1817–1966" and subsequent correspondence with one of the coauthors encouraged me to write a similar study on Ecuador. In researching the available material on the subject I can well appreciate the reasons for the great lack of comparative data on the Latin American presidency and the need for additional studies on this subject.

Of the few sources available on Ecuador's presidents no two provide exactly the same information. This pertains to biographical data as well as to time served in the executive office. There is even disagreement as to who served at a given time. Some of these discrepancies are the result of the turbulent events of the first three decades of Ecuador's republican history during which the country attempted to make strides toward the establishment of a national identity.

In these three decades there emerged numerous local caudillos each claiming to be or being identified as the nation's chief executive. To complicate the picture further, there was the case of General Luis Urdaneta who proceeded to reincorporate Ecuador into the *Unión Grancolombiana* in the name of the liberator Simón Bolívar but without having consulted him. The incumbent president, Juan José Flores, unable to stop Urdaneta's advance, attempted to reason with him. Flores proposed to send a delega-

[1] Richard B. Gray and Frederick R. Kirwin, "Presidential Succession in Chile: 1817–1966," *Journal of Inter-American Studies* 11 (1969): 144–59.

tion to Bolívar to find out whether he was actually interested in governing the nation. Urdaneta agreed, but before the message reached Bolívar, the latter had died at Santa Marta, Colombia. Nevertheless, some sources list Bolívar as president of the nation.[2]

The large number of presidents in the twentieth century also can be considered as peculiar to Ecuador's political culture. The citing of examples may best illustrate this situation.

The 1960 presidential election was won by José María Velasco Ibarra who was to assume office on 1 September of that year. On the previous day, 31 August, the incumbent Camilo Ponce Enríquez handed over the reins of government to his vice-president, Francisco Illingworth. For our purposes, it is unimportant whether this was done because Ponce Enríquez wanted to assure Illingworth of a presidential pension or because, as it is claimed, he could not stand the sight of Velasco Ibarra, to whom he would have to hand over the reins of government on the next day. Of importance, however, are the possibilities that arise out of such an event when a listing of Ecuador's chief executives is compiled. Should Illingworth be included in that list since he was president of the nation for one day? Or, for that matter, should Ponce Enríquez's term be considered as not completed since it fell one day short of being such?

Another case occurred on 7 November 1961, after President Velasco Ibarra was overthrown by the armed forces. The latter designated the president of the Senate, Camilo Gallegos Toledo, as his successor. On the same day, the nation's vice president, and constitutional successor to the presidency, Carlos Julio Arosemena Monroy, was sworn in by Congress. Thus, on the same day Ecuador had two governments. By 9 November, the Congress, with support from the air force, convinced the rest of the military that the vice president should be allowed to take over.

An Ecuadorian source lists Gallegos Toledo as the nation's chief executive for the two-day period—7–9 November—and Arosemena's term starting with the latter date.[3] Again the problem arises whether a) Gallegos Toledo should be listed for the two days inasmuch as he was not the constitutional successor, b) two chief executives should be listed for the two days, or c) Arosemena alone should be listed beginning with 7 November.

Such incidents, while not necessarily common, are not isolated either.

---

[2] See George I. Blanksten, *Ecuador Constitutions and Caudillos* (Berkeley: University of California Press, 1951), p. 10; or Manuel A. Yépez, *Capítulos-Apuntes Varios: 1830–1942* (Quito: Talleres Gráficos Nacionales, 1945), p. 403.

[3] Federico E. Trabucco, *Síntesis Histórica de la República del Ecuador* (Quito: Editorial Santo Domingo, 1968), pp. 13, 690.

Only the circumstances surrounding these incidents may differ. Invariably, a value judgment has to be made when a compilation of Ecuador's chief executives is undertaken. The information provided in this article will, therefore, reflect a certain bias. It is hoped that this point of view will not greatly alter the main purpose of this study which is to investigate the objectives of Professors Gray and Kirwin as set forth in their article on the Chilean presidents.[4] These are: (1) to identify by name every individual who has occupied the office of president, and to compile a biographical profile of each; (2) to provide an accurate chronology of his dates in office; (3) to examine his accession to the presidency by election or other means, and the manner in which he left the office; and (4) to construct modest theories of political stability or instability in Ecuador as they apply to presidential change. Emphasis has also been placed in evaluating these objectives in light of Ecuador's political culture.

The same broad criteria are likewise observed in defining the term president as being "the person on the top of the government hierarchy who performs the function of chief of state, head of state, or chief executive." This includes elected and nonelected president, vice-president serving as acting president, and interim president. The only departure is in the listing of governing juntas as "provisional governments" because of the difficulty in defining who the dominant member was or, for that matter, what "dominant" implies.[5] Also, more emphasis is given to the constitutional requirements surrounding the presidency because of the comparatively large number of constitutions and their impact on presidential succession.

BIOGRAPHICAL DATA (See Appendix A)

Biographical information on Ecuador's presidents was in some cases difficult to obtain and often contradictory. Some information was available, however, for each of the elected presidents and all but a few of the nonelected presidents. Whenever possible, the data were double checked.

The biographical data tend to support certain contentions generally made by historians and political scientists in their treatment of Ecuador's political history.

These contentions are:

(1) "Ecuadorian national politics frequently represents the spectacle of a struggle for power between the Sierra and the Coast."

---

[4] Gray, "Presidential Succession," p. 145.

[5] The four-man military junta that ruled the country between 1963 and 1966 may serve as an example. Ramón Castro Jijón was considered the titular head and Marcos Gándara Enríquez the most influential and powerful. Publicly, however, great stress was placed by the four men on their desire to be considered of an equal status.

(2) "The Story of Ecuador is a tale of two cities."

(3) "Traditionally, the Sierra has been Ecuador's stronghold of social and political conservatism. . . . Social and political liberalism . . . has for the most part been centered in the Coast."

(4) "Historians generally refer to the period before 1895 as the era of Conservative rule, and to the years between 1895 and 1944 as the period of Radical-Liberal rule." [6]

When these contentions are compared to the actual accession of individuals to the presidency, however, we can come to the following conclusions:

At no time has one region dominated the other for an extended period. The dominance of the two regions is attributable to the fact that practically all the people live there and because of their overwhelming socioeconomic importance as compared to the rest of Ecuador's national territory.

In writing about Brazil's republican period (1889–1930) Professor Peterson states that "two states stood out above all others in strength throughout almost all the years of the republic, Sáo Paulo and Minas Gerais, and they contrived to control the selection of the president of the republic. Working together they could control the elections. The result was that they rotated the office of president of the republic between their outgoing governors during most of the years of the republic." [7]

The Brazilian situation is neither comparable to the relationship of the Sierra to the Coast nor, for that matter, to the two cities: Quito and Guayaquil. Of the fifty Ecuadorian presidents, data on birthplaces were available for forty-nine. Of these, all but three (foreign-born) were born in the Coast or Sierra. Of the remaining forty-six, fifteen came from Quito, seventeen from Guayaquil, and fourteen were born in the provinces. These fourteen, of whom Eloy Alfaro, Leonidas Plaza Gutiérrez, and Isidro Ayora are the most prominent, ruled for thirty-nine out of the 140-year republican period.

Further evidence that no "contriving" took place between the two regions or the two cities in respect to the control of presidential selection can only be stated in form of hypothesis: there is little historical evidence that a president born in one of these regions or cities favored his birthplace over the other and no evidence that one region or city wanted its candidate elected because the outgoing president came from the other region or city.

---

[6] Blanksten, *Ecuador Constitutions*, pp. 21, 23, 28, 60, 161.

[7] Phyllis Peterson, "Brazil, Revolution or Reaction," in Martin C. Needler, *Political Systems of Latin America*, 2nd ed. (New York: Van Nostrand Reinhold Co., 1970), p. 525.

The third contention, i.e., that the Sierra is the conservative and the Coast the radical-liberal stronghold, is also only partially valid on the basis of presidential accession. If carried to its logical conclusion, it would be assumed that conservative presidents come from the Sierra, and liberal presidents from the Coast. Gabriel García Moreno, for example, who ruled the nation directly or indirectly for a period of sixteen years (1859–75) and is considered the most prominent conservative president, was born in Guayaquil. Generals José María Urbina and Ignacio de Veintimilla, two prominent nineteenth-century liberals who governed for about ten years, were born in Ambato and Quito respectively.

Finally, the contention that the conservative era lasted from 1830 to 1895 and the radical liberal era from 1895 to 1944 is again misleading when viewed on the basis of the presidential birthplaces. Of the eighteen presidents during the so-called conservative era, eight were born in the Sierra, eight in the Coast, one was foreign-born, and for one the data was not available. The eight presidents from the Coast ruled about twenty-eight years (43% of the time). During the radical-liberal era (1895–1944) fourteen presidents were from the Sierra and ten from the Coast. The fourteen presidents from the Sierra ruled for a period of fifteen years (31% of the time).

Thus, regardless of the period involved, there is no indication that presidents were recruited predominantly from one region, one city, or one party. If the Sierra and the Coast appear favored, it is because more than 95% of the population lives there. If the cities of Quito and Guayaquil appear overrepresented, it is because together they have over 20% of the total population. Finally, if the Conservative and Radical-Liberal parties show the greatest number of accessions to the presidency it is because they were the only two parties with any sizable following until 1944, with the Socialist party playing the role of a third party from 1926 on.

Ecuadorian presidents show a strong record of higher education, and formal educational qualifications show increasing improvement as time has progressed. With the exception of Juan José Flores, whose educational training was marginal at best, all Ecuadorian presidents had at least some form of secondary training. Those who pursued a military career from an early age (Flores, Urbina, Veintimilla, Alfaro, Plaza Gutiérrez) had the least formal education.

The educational record of the elected presidents is particularly impressive. Of the thirty elected presidents, eighteen (60%) had a university education, with fifteen (50%) holding doctoral degrees (thirteen in jurisprudence and two in medicine). The degrees were primarily received from the two public universities in Quito and Guayaquil. University training abroad is sporadic and more frequent in the last decades (Velasco Ibarra, Arosemena Tola, Plaza Lasso, Ponce Enríquez). Of the fifty individuals who occupied the presidency in either an elected or nonelected capacity, thirty-nine (78%) had university training and twenty-five (50%) held doctoral degrees (twenty-two in law and three in medicine).

Not only have Ecuadorian presidents occupied public office prior to their assumption of the presidency, but they have continued in public life afterwards. Several have been elected to Congress or become governors; many others have pursued a diplomatic career. In Ecuador it is not customary for a president, once having served his term of office, to retire from public life.

The thirty elected presidents have served a total of thirty-nine terms of which fifteen (38%) were completed. Twice in Ecuador's history (1912–24, 1948–60) three presidents have been able to complete their terms of office in succession. Only one of five reelected presidents has been able to complete two terms and that was Leonidas Plaza Gutiérrez (1901–05, 1912–16). In addition to the completed terms, there were two presidents (Emilio Estrada and Aurelio Mosquera Narváez) who died while in office, one (Gabriel García Moreno), who was assassinated, and two (Carlos Julio Arosemena Tola, Otto Arosemena Gómez), who were only elected on an interim basis. Seventeen were either forced to resign or were overthrown, and one (Juan de Dios Martínez Mera) was impeached by Congress.

The military's contribution of men to the presidency is also noteworthy but shows a rapid decline as time has progressed. Of the fifty presidents, eleven (22%) had pursued a military career. Only seven (14%) of these were elected. The last military man to be elected to the presidency was Leonidas Plaza Gutiérrez in 1912.

The average Ecuadorian president is fifty-two years of age at the time of his entry into office. The age range is considerable, Juan José Flores was barely thirty years old and José María Velasco Ibarra was past seventy-five when elected for a fifth term in 1968.

An overwhelming majority of Ecuador's presidents had direct government experience before becoming presidents. Congress has been the single largest source from which presidents have been drawn. It is also noteworthy that presidents-to-be have enjoyed a leadership position in Congress, i.e., presidents of constituent conventions, or presidents or vice-presidents of either house of Congress. Since these are elective offices, a successful candidate can be considered as enjoying a considerable amount of prestige among his fellow congressmen. Thirty-seven (74%) of Ecuador's presidents served in Congress and twenty-three (46%) held leadership positions in it. The record in election to congressional leadership is held by Alfredo Baquerizo Moreno who was president of the Senate on eight occasions.

The biographical data show a certain trend in presidential qualifications. The typical Ecuadorian president is fifty-two years old, a lawyer, born either in Quito or Guayaquil, and has attended his hometown university. He has extensive public experience having served as governor or in either or both houses of Congress, where he enjoyed a position of leadership. The educational preparation and public service also reflect the socio-economic background of the presidential candidates. With the exception of presidents who rose to power as a result of their military exploits and a few interim presidents, the heads of state have generally been recruited from the upper sector of Ecuadorian society, which makes up about two percent of the population.[8] This small group, where the *apellido* (family name) is of the utmost importance, has effectively controlled the economic and political life of the country.

THE ELECTED PRESIDENCY (See Appendix B)

For purposes of convenience in this study, an "elected president" is anyone who was either directly or indirectly elected to his post. In the 140 years of Ecuador's republican history, thirty-nine elected presidents have served about 109 years (78% of the time). In fact, they have served 120 years (87% of the time) if the nonelected years of their service are included. Elected presidents have been the rule, but a closer examination of how some came to be elected or the methods used to elect them does not reveal, in my judgment, adherence to constitutional methods.

Too often in Ecuador's history strong men have come to power by overthrowing the existing government. They have then proceeded to legalize their position by convoking a constituent convention which was charged with drafting a new fundamental law and electing them to a full constitutional term. The two most prominent figures in nineteenth-century Ecuadorian politics, Gabriel García Moreno and Eloy Alfaro, serve as excellent examples. Together they served about twenty years in the presidency. Each served two terms which began on a nonelected basis. On each occasion they convoked a constituent convention which drafted new constitutions (1861, 1869, 1897, 1906) and proceeded to elect them to the presidency. It is interesting to note that all four of the constitutions called for direct popular election of the president yet these two strongmen pre-

[8] Georg Maier, *The Ecuadorian Presidential Election of June 2, 1968: An Analysis* (Washington: Institute for the Comparative Study of Political Systems, 1969), p. 6.

ferred to have the convention delegates elect them. The question here arises whether presidents elected under such circumstances can be considered constitutional presidents since their accession originally was not in accordance with constitutional provisions.

In only one case has a strongman taken over the reins of government and convoked a constituent convention without "forcing" the latter to "elect" him. This was Alberto Enríquez Gallo who assumed power in 1937 and convoked the 1938 constituent convention, which subsequently elected Aurelio Mosquera Narváez to the presidency.

García Moreno and Alfaro are, to be sure, only the most prominent individuals to use such "irregular" election practices. Juan José Flores (1830, 1843), Diego Noboa (1851), José María Urbina (1852), Ignacio de Veintimilla (1878), José María Plácido Caamaño (1883), Isidro Ayora (1929), and José María Velasco Ibarra (1944) were elected under similar circumstances. The above may help explain the reason for the writing of at least twelve of Ecuador's sixteen constitutions.

There are still others (Carlos Julio Arosemena Tola and Otto Arosemena Gómez) who have been elected by Congress on an interim basis. In both cases the interim presidents were elected to fill out an uncompleted term when constitutional successors were not available. Here again we are dealing with so-called elected presidents, not with constitutional presidents.

Finally, there is the nominal election of Aurelio Mosquera Narváez, on 10 August 1938, which deserves special attention because of the nature of the circumstances surrounding his ascent to office.[9] The fifty-three delegates to the 1938 constituent convention were ideologically split between nineteen liberals, fourteen conservatives, and twenty socialists. There were two prominent presidential candidates: the Liberal Carlos Alberto Arroyo del Río and the Socialist Alberto Enríquez Gallo. The Conservative delegates, unable to come up with a viable candidate and unwilling to support either of the two candidates, left the session. This left it up to the Liberals and Socialists to make the final selection. After deliberating deep into the night, both candidates were rejected—Arroyo del Río for representing foreign companies in a legal capacity, and General Enríquez Gallo for having assumed dictatorial powers the year before. At this point, someone advanced the name of Aurelio Mosquera Narváez and everyone seemed relieved if not pleased that the deadlock had finally been broken. A delegation was immediately sent to Mosquera's house—this was at 3 A.M.—to convey the good news to him. He was awakened and told that

[9] Julio C. Troncoso, *Odio y Sangre* (Quito: Editorial "Fray Jodoco Ricke," 1959), pp. 98–99.

he was urgently needed at the presidential palace which he was to occupy. Mosquera's initial reaction was that he was having a bad dream. Finally, convinced of the seriousness of the matter, he dressed and left—to become another of Ecuador's elected presidents.

Thus, of a total of thirty-nine elected presidents, only twenty-three were elected in accordance with constitutional procedure, i.e., by the election method provided in the constitution then in force. Of these twenty-three, one president (Juan José Flores) was elected by Congress, one (Francisco Robles) by an electoral college composed of popularly elected provincial assemblies, and the rest by direct popular vote.

If the number of constitutionally elected presidents were reduced to those who were elected in a more or less free atmosphere, i.e., when a candidate was not imposed on the electorate or when wholesale fraud in the manipulation of votes did not occur, only eight would qualify. One of these elections took place in the nineteenth century, when Antonio Borrero became president in 1875. The other seven were José María Velasco Ibarra, 1934, 1952, 1960, 1968; Carlos Alberto Arroyo del Río, 1940; Galo Plaza Lasso, 1948; and Camilo Ponce Enríquez in 1956.

As the above shows, there is a great discrepancy between an elected, a constitutionally elected, and a constitutionally and democratically elected president. The trend in Ecuador is definitely toward the last alternative. In fact, the 1968 presidential election was a model of a free and honest election.[10]

THE NONELECTED PRESIDENCY

The major observation that can be made about nonelected presidents in Ecuador is that, while they have been abundant, none has served for any appreciable length of time. A second characteristic is the comparatively large number of provisional juntas of which only the last (11 July 1963–29 March 1966) was purely military in its composition.

In the 140-year period under discussion there have been no fewer than thirty-eight nonelected presidents, and seven collegially-headed juntas, serving thirty-one years (22% of the total time). Also grouped into the nonelected category are two constitutional successors to the presidency who assumed the office as a result of the death of the incumbent.

The longest term of nonelected incumbency occurred in 1926, when Isidro Ayora took over as provisional president and ruled for a three-year period. Second in length—two years, nine months—was the government of the military junta which overthrew Carlos Julio Arosemena Monroy

---

10 Maier, *The Ecuadorian Presidential Election*, p. 63.

in 1963. Generally speaking, however, nonelected presidents have served for very short periods. At least six individual presidents and one provisional junta served for less than a month each. The plural provisional government of 1944 served the shortest period of time, which was four days. On the average, nonelected governments in Ecuador have existed for a period of seven months. This in itself indicates that extended dictatorships are not the norm in Ecuador.

There have been fourteen nonelected presidents who also served on an elected basis. The majority of these came into office on a nonelected basis and subsequently legitimized their power by getting themselves elected without any interruption in office. In only two cases do the elected and nonelected terms of a president not coincide, nor is there any meaningful connection between the two terms. Carlos Alberto Arroyo del Río was interim president in 1939 for one month and was elected to the presidency a year later with two other interim presidents serving in the meanwhile. The case of Alfredo Baquerizo Moreno may be considered as somewhat unusual as he was elected to the presidency in 1916 and then served as interim president in 1931. This is but one example of the tendency of Ecuadorian presidents to continue in public life after having already served in the highest national office.

Aside from the fact that nonelected presidents are on the average somewhat younger (51.5 years) than their elected counterparts, there is no meaningful difference between them in regards to birthplace, educational background, or exposure to public life. Of the eleven military men who have occupied the presidency, three served only in an elected capacity, four only in a nonelected capacity, and an additional four in both.

CONSTITUTIONAL QUALIFICATIONS FOR THE PRESIDENCY

If Latin Americans are indeed the most experienced constitution makers in the world,[11] then some of the credit should go to Ecuador. With sixteen constitutions in its republican history, the nation ranks fifth in number of constitutions among the twenty Latin American republics.[12] The majority (eleven) of these constitutions date back to the nineteenth century.[13]

Most Latin American constitutions were drafted by one of three main bodies:[14] the constituent convention, congress, or the nation's chief

---

[11] Alexander T. Edelman, *Latin American Government and Politics*, rev. ed. (Homewood, Il.: The Dorsey Press, 1969), p. 387.

[12] Ibid., p. 388.

[13] The dates of Ecuador's constitutions are: 1830, 1835, 1843, 1845, 1851, 1852, 1861, 1869, 1878, 1884, 1897, 1906, 1929, 1945, 1946, and 1967.

[14] Edelman, *Latin American Government*, pp. 385–87.

executive. The Ecuadorian experience shows only the employment of conventions in the drafting of constitutions. Constituent conventions were responsible for the drafting of fifteen constitutions. One, the 1869 constitution, was the work of a national convention that had been convoked by Gabriel García Moreno for the purpose of providing a democratic semblance to his illegal assumption of power. Subsequently, this national convention drafted the constitution under Garcia Moreno's guidance.

Constituent conventions are generally considered to be the most democratic bodies to draft a new constitution, assuming that the convention delegates were democratically elected and not handpicked by the individual responsible for convoking such an assembly. This is true of the post-World-War-II conventions in Ecuador. Prior to that time, however, and especially during the nineteenth century, the delegates served as mouthpieces of the individual who convoked the convention rather than as representatives of the electorate. The general trend was for a strongman to assume power on a nonconstitutional basis. He then proceeded to convoke a constituent convention whose members had the dual duty of drafting a new constitution and electing the strongman to the presidency, thereby legitimizing his regime. As mentioned before, there were eleven such incidents in the nineteenth century and two in the twentieth century, accounting in part for the comparatively large number of such national charters.

While these constitutions serve primarily to legalize a caudillo's way to power, they also reflect his personal likes and dislikes. Seldom do the constitutions reflect the nation's history, its customs, its ideas and values. The following is a comparison of Ecuador's constitutions with respect to presidential qualifications.

A general agreement exists in all constitutions on the subject of citizenship. The majority (eleven) consider only individuals born on Ecuadorian soil (*jus solis*) as qualified for the presidency, and an additional three also include the offspring of Ecuadorian citizens born elsewhere (*jus sanguinis*). The first and third constitutions (1830 and 1843), drafted under the auspices of General Juan José Flores, deserve special mention on this subject because the latter was a Venezuelan citizen. The 1830 constitution requires native birth but also includes citizens of *Gran Colombia* who were in the service of the nation before it became a republic. The 1843 constitution, drafted after Flores had already acquired citizenship, makes no distinction between native-born and naturalized citizens. Thus, in both cases, the constitution served to accommodate the person responsible for the supervision of its drafting.

The age requirement is thirty years in two constitutions, thirty-five years in seven constitutions, and fifty years in the other seven. The 1830 constitution calls for an age limit of thirty years, again designed to accommodate General Flores who had barely reached that age when the constituent convention swore him in as the nation's first president.

Only two constitutions mention residency as a requirement for election. The 1843 constitution calls for a six-year, and the 1929 constitution for a five-year residency in Ecuador prior to the election. This requirement has proven unpopular in modern days if for no other reason than the difficulty of its enforcement. It would appear difficult to disqualify a genuinely popular leader or a caudillo on such a ground, inviting them to assume power on a nonconstitutional basis and drafting but another constitution. One may wonder what course the political career of José María Velasco Ibarra would have taken had such a requirement existed in the more recent constitutions. The career of Velasco Ibarra dates back to 1934 when he was first elected to the presidency. Since then, he has been president on five occasions but has always preferred to live in self-imposed exile whenever his term ended. The ownership of wealth, either as property or as a certain yearly income, is a qualification which no longer exists. It was popular in the nineteenth century and was included in the first nine constitutions. Since the 1884 constitution, however, this requirement is not mentioned.

The method of presidential election has undergone three fundamental changes. The early constitutions called for an indirect election of the president by either Congress or a special convention convoked for such purpose. The sixth constitution (1852) provided for a popularly elected electoral assembly which was to be responsible for the election of the president. Only one president, Francisco Robles, was elected by this method. Beginning with the seventh constitution (1861) presidential election is to be conducted by a direct popular vote. As previously mentioned, presidents were not always elected in accordance with this constitutional requirement.

All constitutions, with the exception of two, provide for a four-year presidential term. That of 1843 called for an eight-year term and the 1869 constitution for a six-year term. These two constitutions were attempts by Flores and García Moreno, respectively, to prolong their terms of office, but neither succeeded since Flores was overthrown and García Moreno assassinated. Antonio Borrero, the only other president to be elected under the 1869 constitution, was ousted from office after having served one year.

A president seeking reelection has to wait out either one term (twelve constitutions) or two terms (four constitutions). Reelection is not uncommon with five presidents having been elected to office on more than one occasion. José María Velasco Ibarra holds the record with five elected terms.

Of the sixteen constitutions, ten provide for the office of a vice-president and the rest do not. In the twentieth century only the last two (1946, 1967) call for a vice-president. The office appears ideal for Ecuador's regional politics since it allows for a balancing of the ticket. This balancing act has been scrupulously employed, especially since the promulgation of the 1946 constitution. Since vice-presidents are elected separately, however, the regional balance has not always been maintained, nor, for that matter, have the two offices always been occupied by members of the same party. Twice, in 1958 and 1968, vice-presidents have come from a different party than their elected presidents. Regardless of party affiliation or regional balance, vice-presidents have proved troublesome and there is a general tendency to look at the office with suspicion.

The constitution currently in force dates back to 1967. It was drafted by convention delegates who were popularly elected in a free election and all the political spheres were represented. The content again, however, is more representative of the previous constitutions than a realistic reflection of Ecuador's political culture. In the 1968 presidential campaign, the conservative candidate Camilo Ponce Enríquez already attacked the constitution calling the document unrealistic.[15] Under the present constitution a president must be a native born citizen, forty years of age or over, and in full exercise of his political rights. He is elected by direct popular vote for a four-year term and has to stay out of the presidency one term before becoming eligible for reelection. The constitution also provides for the office of a vice-president who must meet the same requirements.

Any discussion of constitutional qualifications for the presidency should include a realistic evaluation of such qualifications in light of Ecuador's political culture. Two case studies may provide some understanding of their importance or, better, insignificance.

The first incident occurred in 1932 surrounding the election of Neptalí Bonifaz to the presidency. The conservative Bonifaz won the popular election but a liberal-dominated legislature attempted to disqualify him. The pretext that he was born in Peru, and thus ineligible for the office, was used in an attempt to keep him from assuming office. The outcome was the infamous and bloody "Four-Days War," which resulted in the victory of the liberal elements and Bonifaz was prevented from taking office. How questionable the charge was is reflected by the vote of the 1929 constituent convention when Isidro Ayora was elected president

[15] Maier, *The Ecuadorian Presidential Election*, p. 60.

but Neptalí Bonifaz received six votes.[16] No one contested his candidacy or qualifications then but, he did not win either.

The second incident occurred in 1933 when Juan de Dios Martínez Mera was elected president, again facing a belligerent Congress. Since there was no doubt about his constitutional qualifications, Martínez Mera was twice asked to resign but refused. A military insurrection proved equally unsuccessful. Congress then proceeded to censure his cabinet both individually and collectively. Martínez Mera appointed new ministers. Finally, the Chamber of Deputies formally accused the president of having attempted to overthrow the government and institute a dictatorship. The Senate then proceeded to impeach him and instructed his minister of interior to assume the office on an interim basis. Lacking decisive support, Martínez Mera had to abide by the Congressional decision.[17]

While both these incidents are relics of the past and unlikely to be repeated, they demonstrate a weakness of constitutional requirements in the face of political reality. If the constitutional requirements do not fit a powerful president, he either serves on an extra-legal basis or rewrites the constitution to fit his purpose. If, on the other hand, the elected president is not sufficiently powerful he can be ousted either through violent means or be disqualified on the basis of trumped-up charges ostensibly justified within the constitutional context. Thus, even the constitutional requirements for the presidency are subject to tampering if a powerful sector within the political system objects to them. Whether this is democratic, legal, or right is a question which misses the point. It is merely another characteristic of Ecuador's political culture.

PRESIDENTIAL SUCCESSION (See Appendix C)

Ecuador has experienced eighty-four governmental turnovers in a period of one-hundred and forty years or an average of one in about every one-and-a-half years. These changes of government are identified as either stable or nonstable and the only criteria employed to distinguish between these two categories is an election. If an election took place, regardless of whether it was constitutional or democratic, or neither, the change is considered stable. Any other change, i.e., natural death, assassination, resignation, or overthrow of the incumbent is considered nonstable.

To identify a stable change as one which is peaceful, nonforced, and constitutional and a nonstable change as nonpeaceful, forced (either open or covert), and nonconstitutional[18] would be nearly impossible given the

[16] Yépez, *Capítulos-Apuntes Varios*, p. 343.
[17] Troncoso, *Odio y Sangre*, pp. 89–91.
[18] Gray, *Presidential Succession in Chile*, p. 149.

nature of Ecuadorian political culture. I have stated before that a change is not necessarily constitutional if an election took place since many Ecuadorian presidents have chosen their own method of election rather than the current constitutional method. Furthermore, with so many changes having taken place, it is a sheer impossibility to detect either open and especially covert force. Even in the case of the few democratically conducted constitutional elections in Ecuador, people lost their lives during the election campaigns. Consequently, such elections ought to be considered nonstable if the above criteria were employed.

The great number of presidential changes should be considered as an integral part of Ecuador's political culture. A thorough study of the country's history leaves one with the definite impression that Ecuadorians have nothing against governmental changes. What they do object to and have managed to combat effectively are dictatorships. To fend off or defeat dictatorships the electorate has shown little concern over the constitutional provisions involving change. In discussing the forceful abdication in 1931 of General Luis Larrea Alba, who had proclaimed himself dictator, and his replacement by Alfredo Baquerizo Moreno, the authoritative historian Alfonso Rumazo Gonzáles notes:

> Was the Constitution saved? Was the new head of state constitutional? Or is it that the facts have greater weight than constitutions, in which case one deduces the insufficiency of the already outmoded constitutional law? [19]

Thus, if the change is for the better, Rumazo Gonzáles is arguing, its constitutionality ceases to be of importance. Nor, for that matter, is political stability as defined by the constitution a factor.

The pattern of numerous presidential changes in Ecuador seems often to be duplicated in present-day Italy or during the Fourth Republic in France. In the two European countries, these changes can occur within constitutional context, but in Ecuador they cannot. Thus, it may be argued, Ecuador suffers more from unrealistic constitutions than unconstitutional presidential changes. Were the constitutions to reflect more realistically the nation's political culture, the frequent presidential changes would not be interpreted as political instability, but rather as a major characteristic of Ecuadorian politics, which they actually appear to be.

If presidential succession in the nineteenth and twentieth centuries is separately discussed, one finds that in the same period of time there is a

[19] "Se salvó la Constitución? Fue constitucional el nuevo Mandatario? O es que los hechos son superiores a las constituciones, en cuyo caso se podrá deducir la deficiencia del ya envejecido derecho constitucional?" See Alfonso Rumazo González, *Gobernantes del Ecuador* (Quito: Editorial Bolívar, 1932), p. 240.

remarkable difference in the number of presidents as well as changes. In the nineteenth century (1830–1901)[20] there were a total of twenty-five presidents and juntas and thirty-six government turnovers. In the twentieth century (1901–1970) there were a total of forty-four presidents and juntas, and forty-eight government turnovers. Despite the much larger number of presidents and turnovers in the twentieth century, the political climate was much healthier. With the exception of Eloy Alfaro, who also ruled in the nineteenth century, no single Ecuadorian president could remotely compare with some of his nineteenth-century counterparts. The absolute dictatorial control over the nation which was enjoyed by Juan José Flores, José María Urbina, Gabriel García Moreno, Ignacio de Veintimilla, or Eloy Alfaro was never duplicated in the twentieth century. With the assassination of Eloy Alfaro in 1911, the last of the dictators left the political scene.

Thus, an Ecuadorian would view the twentieth century republican experience as the more stable and democratic—not because changes occurred within a constitutional context, but because the presidents in power ruled in a more or less democratic fashion. Besides, as many Ecuadorians have stated to me, the more changes that occur, the greater the number of people to get a share of the pie. This, they claim, is real democracy.

An analysis of presidential succession in Ecuador reveals that few ousted presidents were victims of power struggles. The reason for the inability of elected presidents to serve out their terms of office was probably best stated by Antonio Borrero after his victory in the 1875 election. A tremendous crowd greeted him in one of the main plazas of Quito. Upon seeing this multitude, Borrero turned to his trusted friend, Dr. Federico Malo, and whispered in his ear: "And, will there be jobs for so many people?" "I doubt it, Sir," answered Dr. Malo. Borrero is supposed to have replied, "Then I know what is awaiting me!" [21] Borrero was not wrong. Within a few months conservatives and liberals turned against him, accusing him of having betrayed them and proving to him what all Ecuadorian presidents should know: political popularity is nothing more than a misunderstanding. With the same facility with which the people embrace a leader and help him reach the pinnacle of political power, they repudiate and overthrow him.[22] Antonio Borrero served for only one year before he became a victim of his country's political culture.

A second factor causing rapid changes is the inability of Ecuador's presidents to govern effectively. There is a favorite Ecuadorian saying that

[20] The year 1901 is used because Eloy Alfaro terminated his term of office, which had begun in 1895, in that year.

[21] Troncoso, *Odio y Sangre*, pp. 39–40.

[22] Idem.

the country's presidents are not overthrown but rather that they overthrow themselves. Instead of leading, they are led. The able student of Ecuadorian politics Alfredo Pareja Diezcanseco refers, for example, to Ecuador's perennial president José María Velasco Ibarra as the "leader led." [23]

This apparent inability to govern effectively seems more a reflection of Ecuador's political culture than of the personalities of the nation's presidents. None of the numerous political parties enjoys a sufficient national following nor has a sound enough program on which a president can depend for continued support. *Personalismo* is still the strongest tie that binds the people to the nation's chief executive. But the force of personal magnetism is difficult to sustain for an extended period of time. This has prompted presidents to concentrate their efforts on short-term projects that will be identified with them; which also provides a way by which political supporters can be repaid through the award of contracts, jobs, and other kickbacks. When the money runs out these favors are discontinued. The one-time friends turn against their benefactor and the "political orgy" is over.[24] The ineffectiveness of a president in governing, therefore, is often related to the lack of funds necessary to sustain his personalismo and keep him in office. All too frequently and quickly the money runs out and so does the president.

The above observations on the practical aspects of Ecuadorian politics are intended to show that the characteristics of presidential succession in a given country can be viewed realistically when that country's political culture is appreciated. This should be taken into account when a cross-national survey is conducted. While certain conclusions can be drawn in comparing the average age of presidents or their educational and public records, no conclusion on presidential succession is meaningful without an appreciation of each country's political culture. Surely, the Ecuadorian experience is a demonstration of the proposition that the concept of "stable" or "democratic" presidential succession as established in one political culture cannot be applied to all others with equal validity.

APPENDIX A

(1) COMPARATIVE DATA ON THE PRESIDENTS OF ECUADOR

Period covered	140	years (1830–1970)
Number of presidents	50	(and seven collegially-headed juntas)

---

[23] Alfredo Pareja Diezcanseco, "Teoría y Práctica del Conductor Conducido," *Combate* 4 no. 20 (1962): 9–23.

[24] In the 1939 presidential election campaign, the liberal candidate, Carlos Alberto Arroyo del Río affirmed that the hour of "political orgy" was over in Ecuador. See Maier, *The Ecuadorian Presidential Election*, p. 25.

Average age on entering office	52
Previous experience	
Lawyers	25 (50%)
Physicians	3 (6%)
Military	11 (22%)
Served in Cabinet	26 (52%)
Served in Congress	37 (74%)
Held leadership position in Congress	23 (46%)
State governors	11 (22%)
No major civilian governmental experience	2 (4%)
Elected presidents*	39
Time in office	109 years (78% of total time)
Number with more than one elected term	5
Average years in office	2.5 years
Terms completed	15 (38%)
Average age entering office	52.5 years
Served in Congress and/or Cabinet	25 (86%)
Nonelected presidents**	38 (and seven collegially-headed juntas)
Time in office	31 years (22% of total time)
Average years in office	7 months
Number also elected president	14
Average age entering office	51.5 years
Served in Congress and/or Cabinet	22 (56%)

*Fourteen presidents in Ecuador served both as elected and nonelected presidents, and are included in both categories for the statistical analysis.

** This does not include Jose María Velasco Ibarra's assumption of dictatorial power on 22 June 1970.

(2) BIOGRAPHIES OF PRESIDENTS OF ECUADOR*

(Chronological Order by First Term)

Juan José Flores

b. 19 July 1800, Puerto Cabello (Venezuela).

d. 1 October 1864, on board the "Sinyrk."

* In addition to the sources cited in the footnotes, the following works have been useful in compiling this data:

Arboleda, R. Gustavo. *Diccionario Biográfico de la República del Ecuador.* Quito: Tipografía de la Escuela de Artes y Oficios, 1910.

Destruge, Camilo. *Album Biográfico Ecuatoriano.* Guayaquil: Tipografía "El Vigilante," 1904.

Hilton, Ronald. *Who's Who in Latin America.* Part III. Stanford, California: Stanford University Press, 1951.

Lara Cruz, Alfredo, ed. *Galería Histórica Biográfica: 1830–1960.* Quito: Imprenta Adrentina, 1960.

Education: no formal education
Occupation: military career; governor of Pasto Province, 1823; general, 1829; chief of staff of the armed forces, 1835; president of the Senate, 1837.
Presidency: (1) nonelected, age 30, interim president;
(2) elected (constituent convention), age 30, 1 term, term interrupted by various individuals who enjoyed regional control.
(3) elected (constituent convention), age 39, 1 term, term ended constitutionally.
(4) nonelected, age 43, interim president until constituent convention was called together.
(5) elected (constituent convention), age 43, 1 term, overthrown.

Vicente Rocafuerte
b. 1 May 1783, Guayaquil.
d. 16 May 1847, Lima, Peru.
Education: Colegio de los Nobles, Madrid; completed his studies in Paris.
Occupation: Educator, writer, politician; elected to Cortes in Spain, 1812; *Jefe Supremo* of Guayaquil, 1830; deputy from Pichincha Province, 1834; governor of Guayas Province, 1839–42; deputy from Pichincha Province 1843; president of the National Convention, 1845–46; president of the Senate, 1846; diplomat in Peru, Bolivia, Chile, 1846.
Presidency: (1) nonelected (elected by a provisional assembly), age 51;
(2) elected (constituent assembly), age 52; 1 term, term ended constitutionally.

Vicente Ramón Roca
b. 2 September 1792, Guayaquil.
d. 23 February 1858, Guayaquil.
Education: privately educated
Occupation: politician; chief of police in Guayaquil, 1829; deputy at the Riobamba Convention, 1830; perfect of Guayaquil, 1831, 1834; vice-president of Congress, 1833; governor of Guayas Province, 1835; senator from Guayas Province, 1837–39; member of the provisional governing junta, 6 March 1845–7 December 1845.
Presidency: elected (constituent assembly), age 53, 1 term, term ended constitutionally.

Pérez Merchant, Braulio. *Diccionario Biográfico del Ecuador*. Quito: Escuela de Artes y Oficios, 1928.
Quién es Quién en Guayaquil. Guayaquil: Artes Gráficas Senefelder, 1967.
Quién es Quién en Quito. Guayaquil: Artes Gráficas Senefelder, 1966–67.
Rolando, Carlos A. "Los Presidentes del Ecuador," *Boletín del Centro do Investigaciones Históricas* 4, nos. 4–6 (Guayaquíl, 1963): 234–46.
Rumazo Gonzáles, Alfonso, *Gobernantes del Ecuador*. Quito: Editorial Bolívar, 1932.
Tobar Donoso, Julio. *Monografías Históricas*. Quito: Editorial Ecuatoriana, 1937.

Manuel de Ascásubi

b. December 1804, Quito,

d. 25 December 1876.

Education: unknown.

Occupation: military career, rank of colonel, politician; substitute senator from Chimborazo Province, 1846; governor of Imbarura and Pichincha Provinces; vice-president of the Republic, 1847; minister of war, minister of interior.

Presidency: (1) nonelected, age 45, made office after Congress could not decide on a successor to Vincente Ramón Roca.

(2) nonelected, age 71, replaced Francisco Javier Leon who had taken over after the assassination of Gabriel Garciá Moreno.

Diego Noboa

b. 15 April 1789, Guayaquil,

d. 3 November 1870, Guayaquil.

Education: Colegio San Luis, Quito.

Occupation: public official, politician; treasurer of Guayas Province, 1820–22; intendant of department of Guayaquil, 1827; minister in Peru, 1831; president of the Senate, 1839; member of the governing junta, 6 March 1845–7 December 1845; president of the Senate, 1848; president of the junta of Guayas Province, 1863.

Presidency: (1) nonelected, age 61, (convoked constituent convention);

(2) elected (constituent convention), age 62, 1 term, overthrown by General José María Urbina.

José María Urbina

b. 19 March 1808, Ambato,

d. 4 September 1891, Guayaquil.

Education: Naval School.

Occupation: military career, politician; colonel, 1835; deputy from Loja Province, 1843; governor of Manabí Province, 1845; deputy from Pichincha Province, 1846; president of the Chamber of Deputies, 1849; civil and military chief of Guayaquil, 1850; deputy from Guayas Province, 1850; deputy from Guayas Province to 1878 constituent convention; minister in Chile, 1879; chief of staff, 1880.

Presidency: (1) nonelected, age 43, overthrew President Diego Noboa.

(2) elected (constituent convention), age 44, 1 term, term ended constitutionally.

Francisco Robles

b. 5 May 1811, Guayaquil,

d. 11 March 1893, Guayaquil.

Education: Naval College.

Occupation: military career, politician; captain of a frigate, 1845; military commander and governor of Guayas Province, 1847; brigadier general, 1851; deputy from Manabí Province, 1852; governor of Guayas Province, 1854–56; major general, 1876.

Presidency: elected (constituent convention), age 45, 1 term, overthrown.

Gabriel García Moreno

b. 24 December 1821, Guayaquil,

d. 6 August 1875, Quito.

Education: J. D. Central University of Quito, 1844.

Occupation: lawyer, politician; governor of Guayas Province, 1847; senator from Guayas Province, 1853; rector, Central University of Quito, 1857; senator from Pichincha and Tungurahua Province, 1857; member of governing junta, 1 May 1859–17 January 1860; civil and military chief of Imbabura Province, 1868; minister of the Treasury, 1869.

Presidency: (1) nonelected, age 39, convoked constituent convention;
(2) elected (constituent convention), age 40, 1 term, term ended constitutionally;
(3) nonelected, age 48, took over after the overthrow of President Javier Espinosa;
(4) elected (constituent convention), age 48, 1 term, assassinated.

Jerónimo Carrión

b. 1804, Loja

d. 5 May 1873.

Education: Unknown.

Occupation: politician; governor of Azuay Province, 1845–47; deputy from Loja Province, 1845 and 1852; senator from Loja Province, 1847–49; vice-president of the Republic, 1859; major general of the Chilean army, 1866.

Presidency: elected, 1 term, age 61, first president to be elected by direct popular suffrage, overthrown and replaced by his vice-president, Pedro José de Arteta.

Pedro José de Arteta

b. March 1797, Quito,

d. 24 August 1873, Quito.

Education: J. D. University of St. Thomas, Quito.

Occupation: lawyer, politician; rector of the University of St. Thomas, 1830; secretary of the constituent convention of 1830; minister of interior and foreign relations, 1836; vice-president of constituent convention of 1843; deputy from Pichincha Province to constituent convention of 1861; vice-president of the Republic, 1867; deputy from Pichincha to constituent convention of 1878. President of both chambers of Congress.

Presidency: nonelected, age 70, succeeded Jeronimo Carrión after the latter's forceful abdiction.

Javier Espinosa

b. 1815, Quito,

d. 4 September 1870.

Education: J. D. University of Quito, 1838.

Occupation: lawyer, politician; consul in Lima, 1849; district attorney of the Supreme Court, 1865.

Presidency: elected (popular), age 53, 1 term, overthrown by Gabriel García Moreno.

Francisco Javier León

b.

d. 10 August 1880.

Education: J. D.
Occupation: lawyer, politician; minister of interior, 1873; minister of foreign relations; vice-president of the Republic, 1869.
Presidency: nonelected, completed term of Gabriel García Moreno who was assassinated.

Antonio Borrero
b. 28 October 1827, Cuenca,
d. 9 October 1911.
Education: J. D. University of Cuenca, 1856.
Occupation: lawyer, politician; vice-president of the Republic, 1863; secretary of the bishopric Cuenca, 1872; minister of the superior Court in Azuay Province, 1874; governor of Azuay Province, 1888–92.
Presidency: elected (popular), age 48, 1 term, overthrown by General Ignacio de Veintimilla.

Ignacio de Veintimilla
b. 31 July 1828, Quito,
d. 19 July 1908, Quito.
Education: Colegio Militar, Quito.
Occupation: military career, politician; minister of war, 1865–67; inspector of the army, 1866; brigadier general, 1867; commanding general of Guayaquil.
Presidency: (1) nonelected, age 48, overthrew President Antonio Borrero;
(2) elected (constituent convention), age 50, 1 term, proclaimed dictatorship;
(3) nonelected, age 54, overthrown.

José María Plácido Caamaño
b. 5 October 1838, Guayaquil,
d. 31 December 1901, Sevilla (Spain).
Education: J. D. Central University of Quito.
Occupation: lawyer, politician, general; commander of the 2nd Division, 1883; member of Provisional Government, 9 July 1883–9 February 1884; minister plenipotentiary to the United States, 1888; governor of Guayas Province, 1888–1895.
Presidency: elected (constituent convention), age 46, 1 term, term ended constitutionally.

Antonio Flores Jijón
b. 23 October 1833, Quito,
d. 30 August 1915, Geneva.
Education: J. D. Central University of Quito, 1855.
Occupation: lawyer, politician; diplomatic carrier (Colombia, France, England, Vatican, Peru, Spain), 1863–1885; vice-president of the Chamber of Deputies, 1867; deputy from Pichincha Province, 1883–84.
Presidency: elected (popular), age 55, 1 term, term ended constitutionally. Flores Jijón was in Europe at the time of his election. Pedro José Cevallos, his vice-president, served until his return.

Luis Cordero
b. 6 April 1833, Cuenca,
d. 30 January 1912, Cuenca.
Education: J. D. University of Quito.
Occupation: lawyer, politician; political chief of Cuenca, 1876; member of the provisional junta, 9 July 1883–9 February 1884; senator from Azuay Province and president of the Senate, 1885; senator from the provinces of Bolívar and Azuay, 1892; minister in Chile, 1910; rector of the University of Azuay, 1911.
Presidency: elected (popular), age 59, 1 term, abdicated after liberal uprising and succeeded by his vice-president, Vicente Lucio Salazar.

Vicente Lucio Salazar
b. 20 December 1832, Quito,
d. 1896, Quito.
Education: J. D.
Occupation: lawyer, politician; secretary of the Ecuadorian Legation in Colombia; deputy from Pichincha Province and president of that Chamber, 1896; minister of the Treasury, 1883; president of the Senate, 1892; vice-president of the Republic, 1895.
Presidency: nonelected, age 62, took over from the incumbent Luis Cordero who was forced to resign.

Eloy Alfaro
b. 25 June 1842, Montecristi, (Manabí Province),
d. 28 January 1912, Quito.
Education: private.
Occupation: military career, politician; civil and military chief of Esmeraldas Province, 1880; brigadier general, 1884; lieutenant general, 1895.
Presidency: (1) nonelected, age 53, liberal revolution.
(2) elected (constituent convention), age 55, 1 term, term ended constitutionally.
(3) nonelected, age 63, headed revolution which overthrew President Lizardo García.
(4) elected, (constituent convention), age 65, 1 term, overthrown.

Leonidas Plaza Gutiérrez
b. 18 April 1865, Charapotó (Manabí Province),
d. 18 September 1932, Huigra.
Education: military.
Occupation: military career, politician; sergeant major, 1884; major general in Costa Rica, 1893; governor of Azuay Province, 1896; commander in chief of the coastal provinces and of the coastal army, 1900; deputy from Tungurahua Province and president of the Chamber of Deputies, 1900–1901; minister of finance, 1911; deputy from Esmeraldas Province, 1911; chief of staff of the armed forces, 1911–12.
Presidency: (1) elected (popular), age 36, 1 term, term ended constitutionally.

(2) elected (popular), age 47, 1 term, term ended constitutionally.

Lizardo García

b. 26 April 1842, Guayaquil,

d.

Education: Secondary education.

Occupation: banker, merchant, member and cofounder of the Chamber of Commerce in Guayaquil, 1889–1905; minister of the Treasury, 1895; senator from Guayas Province, 1898–1904; vice-president of the Senate 1898; manager of the Bank of Commerce and Agriculture in Guayaquil, 1903.

Presidency: elected (popular), age 63, 1 term, overthrown by General Eloy Alfaro.

Carlos Freile Zaldumbide

b.

d.

Education:

Occupation: gentleman farmer, politician; minister of public instruction, 1896; deputy from Pichincha Province and president of the constituent convention, 1906; president of the Senate, 1911.

Presidency: nonelected, twice,

(1) succeeded Eloy Alfaro after the latter was forced out of office;

(2) succeeded Emilio Estrada after the latter's death and was himself overthrown. In both cases he was president of the Senate, i.e., the first in line of succession since the 1906 constitution did not provide for a vice-president.

Emilio Estrada

b. 28 May 1855, Quito,

d. 21 December 1911, Quito.

Education: Colegio Rocafuerte, Guayaquil, 1869.

Occupation: industrialist, politician; governor of Guayas Province, 1895, 1909, and 1910; vice-president of the Chamber of Deputies, 1899–1900; fiscal inspector of consulates, 1906;

Presidency: elected (popular), age 56, 1 term, died in office.

Francisco Andrade Marín

b.

d. Quito.

Education: J. D. Central University of Quito.

Occupation: lawyer, politician; member of the Municipal Council of Quito, member of the Council of State, deputy from Manabí Province to the 1883 constituent convention; minister of public works 1892; minister of the Treasury; president of the Chamber of Deputies, 1911.

Presidency: nonelected, succeeded Carlos Freile Zaldumbide in his position of president of the Chamber of Deputies, called for elections which were won by Leonidas Plaza Gutiérrez.

Alfredo Baquerizo Moreno

b. 28 September 1859, Guayaquil,

d. 20 March 1951.

Education: J. D., 1884.

Occupation: lawyer, politician; secretary to minister of the Superior Court in Guayaquil, 1894–1901; director of the Public Library and mayor of Guayaquil 1890–96; minister of foreign relations, 1902–12; minister in Cuba and ambassador to Peru 1903–1907; vice-president of the Republic, 1903–06; senator from Guayas Province and president of the Senate, 1912–1916.

Presidency: (1) elected (popular), age 57, 1 term, term ended constitutionally.

(2) nonelected, age 72, took over from General Luis Larrea Alba whose desire to rule as a dictator was not acceptable to the people.

José Luis Tamayo

b. 29 July 1858, Guayaquil,

d. 8 July 1947.

Education: J. D. 1886.

Occupation: lawyer, politician; civil and military chief of Manabí Province, 1895; undersecretary of foreign relations, minister of interior; president of the Chamber of Deputies 1898–99; senator from Esmeraldas Province, 1902–05.

Presidency: elected (popular), age 62, 1 term, term ended constitutionally.

Gonzalo S. Córdova

b. 15 July 1863, Cuenca,

d. 13 April 1928, Valparaíso (Chile).

Education: J. D. University of Cuenca.

Occupation: lawyer, politician; deputy from Cañar Province, 1892, 1896–97; governor of Cañar, 1898–1902; minister of interior, 1903–06; senator from Carchi Province and vice-president of the senate, 1912; minister in Chile, Argentina, and the United States, 1911–13; minister in Venezuela, 1922.

Presidency: elected (popular), age 61, 1 term, overthrown by revolution.

Isidro Ayora

b. 31 August 1879, Loja,

d.

Education: M. D. Central University of Quito, 1905.

Occupation: doctor, educator, politician: professor at Central University of Quito, 1912; rector of the same University, 1925; minister of social security, 1926; member of the provisional junta, 10 January 1926–31 March 1926.

Presidency: (1) nonelected, age 47, convoked constituent convention,

(2) elected (constituent convention), age 50, 1 term, abdicated in favor of General Luis Larrea Alba.

Luis Larrea Alba
b. 25 October 1894, Guayaquil,
d.
Education: Military Academy in Quito and Santiago, Chile.
Occupation: military career, politician, military attache in Italy and Peru; intendant general of the police in Guayas Province, deputy from El Oro Province to the 1928 constituent convention; minister of national defense; founder of the Ecuadorian Socialist Revolutionary Vanguard.
Presidency: nonelected, are 37, took over after the overthrow of Isidro Ayora and was forced out of office after attempting to institute a dictatorship.

Carlos Freile Larrea
b. 1892, Quito
d.
Education: City and Guilds of London Institute, degree in civil engineering.
Occupation: civil engineer, gentleman farmer, politician; president of the Guayaquil and Quito Railway Company; president of the Chamber of Agriculture (Zone I); minister of public works, 1939; minister plenipotentiary to Great Britain.
Presidency: nonelected, age 40, took over after the resignation of Alfredo Baquerizo Moreno; was, in turn, overthrown and replaced by Alberto Guerrero Martínez after having occupied the presidency for five days.

Alberto Guerrero Martínez
b. Guayaquil,
d.
Education: J. D. University of Guayaquil.
Occupation: lawyer, politician; deputy from Los Ríos Province, 1914; senator, president of the Senate 1923–24.
Presidency: nonelected, took over after the "Four Days War" and prepared for elections.

Juan de Diós Martínez Mera
b. 9 March 1875, Guayaquil,
d.
Education: medicine, law, University of Guayaquil, no degree.
Occupation: lawyer, politician: secretary of the Guayaquil Council; vice-rector of the Colegio Vicente Rocafuerte; president of the Chamber of Deputies, minister of the treasury.
Presidency: elected, (popular), age 57, 1 term, was impeached by Congress.

Abelardo Montalvo
b.
d.
Education: J. D. University of Quito.
Occupation: lawyer, politician; deputy and senator from Pichincha Province, deputy to the constituent convention of 1906; professor of law at Central University; rector of the Colegio Nacional Mejia.

Presidency: nonelected, replaced Juan de Dios Martínez Mera when the latter was impeached; stayed on until the popular election of José María Velasco Ibarra.

José María Velasco Ibarra

b. 19 March 1893, Quito,

d.

Education: J. D. University of Quito

Occupation: lawyer, university professor, politician; deputy from Pichincha Province, 1932; president of the Chamber of Deputies, 1933.

Presidency: (1) elected (popular), age 41, 1 term, resigned.

(2) nonelected, age 51, ushered in by revolution.

(3) elected, (constituent convention), age 52, 1 term, proclaimed dictatorship.

(4) nonelected (assumed dictatorial powers), age 53, overthrown.

(5) elected (popular), age 59, 1 term, term ended constitutionally.

(6) elected (popular), age 67, 1 term, overthrown.

(7) elected (popular), age 75, 1 term, currently in office.

Antonio Pons

b.

d.

Education: M. D.

Occupation: doctor, politician; minister of interior, 1934.

Presidency: nonelected, replaced José María Velasco Ibarra in 1935 and handed over the reins of government to the military after having been in office for about a month.

Federico Páez

b. 6 June 1876, Quito,

d.

Education: Ecole Superieur des Mines (Paris), 1895–97; Ecoles des Hautes Etudes Sociales (Brussels), 1900.

Occupation: civil engineer, politician; civil engineer in Quito and Guayaquil, 1913–18; deputy from Pichincha Province 1916–18; senator 1932–35; minister of public works, 1935; professor of geophysics in Costa Rica, 1940–1943.

Presidency: nonelected, age 59, put in power by the armed forces; ruled as a dictator and relinquished power to General Alberto Enríquez Gallo.

Alberto Enríquez Gallo

b. 24 July 1895, Tanicuchi (León Province),

d. 13 July 1962, Quito.

Education: Colegio Militar "Eloy Alfaro," Quito, 1912.

Occupation: military career, rose to rank of general, 1937; minister of defense, 1935; unsuccessful presidential candidate of a Liberal-Socialist coalition in 1948.

Presidency: nonelected, age 42, took over from Federico Páez who resigned; abdicated in favor of Manuel María Borrero after having convoked the constituent convention of 1938.

Manuel María Borreo
b. 1886, Cuenca,
d. 1966, Quito
Education: J. D.
Occupation: author, lawyer, politician; minister of the Superior Court in Quito; deputy from Azuay Province; Ecuadorian consul in Valparaíso (Chile); governor of Azuay Province; minister of the Supreme Court.
Presidency: nonelected, age 52, interim president for less than three months.

Aurelio Mosquera Narváez
b. 2 August 1883, Quito,
d. 17 November 1939.
Education: M. D. Central University of Quito, 1906.
Occupation: doctor, politician; university professor 1907–1912, deputy from Pichincha Province, 1914–5 and 1928–9; deputy from same province and vice-president of the Chamber of Deputies 1930–1931; vice-president of the Senate, 1935.
Presidency: elected (constituent convention), age 55, 1 term, died in office.

Carlos Alberto Arroyo del Río
b. 27 November 1893, Guayaquil,
d.
Education: J. D. University of Guayaquil, 1914.
Occupation: lawyer, politician; secretary of the Guayaquil Municipal Council, 1917–18; deputy from Guayas Province, 1922–23, president of that Chamber, 1923, president of the Senate, 1939.
Presidency: (1) nonelected, age 46, took over after the death of President Aurelio Mosquera Narváez, left office to campaign in the forth coming elections.
(2) elected, (popular), age 47, 1 term, was overthrown.

Andrés F. Córdova Nieto
b. 8 May 1892, Cañar,
d.
Education: J. D. University of Azuay (Cuenca), 1919.
Occupation: lawyer, politician; deputy from Azuay Province, 1922–25, 1934–35, 1939–40; professor of civil law, University of Azuay, 1925–43; dean of that Law School, 1939–43; senator from Azuay Province, 1930–31; president of Chamber of Deputies, 1939–40; member of constituent convention, 1967.
Presidency: nonelected, age 41, replaced interim president, Carlos Alberto Arroyo del Río who resigned in order to run in the 1940 presidential election.

Julio E. Moreno
b. 20 October 1880, Quito,
d.
Education: law, Central University of Quito, no degree.
Occupation: lawyer, politician; member of 1929 constituent convention; minister of interior, 1926–30; president of the Senate, 1939.

Presidency: nonelected, age 51, took over from Andres F. Córdova Nieto for less than a month until elections were held.

Carlos Mancheno Cajas
- b. 1902, Riobamba,
- d.
- Education: military education.
- Occupation: military career, rank of colonel; minister of national defense, 1947.
- Presidency: nonelected, age 45, overthrew Jose María Velasco Ibarra and resigned after a few days due to lack of support by the armed forces.

Mariano Suárez Veintimilla
- b. 6 June 1897, Otavalo
- d.
- Education: Central University of Quito, law.
- Occupation: lawyer, politician; deputy from Pichincha Province on several occasions; vice-president of that Chamber; president of the constituent assembly, 1946–47; vice-president of the Republic, 1946–47; minister of agriculture and the treasury.
- Presidency: nonelected, age 50, took over after Carlos Mancheno Cajas was forced out of office and was in turn replaced by Carlos Julio Arosemena Tola, who was elected by a special convention.

Carlos Julio Arosemena Tola
- b. 1894, Guayaquil,
- d. 20 February 1952, Guayaquil.
- Education: Cornell University (U.S.A.)
- Occupation: banker, politician.
- Presidency: elected, (Special Congressional Convention), interim president who took over after the resignation of Mariano Suárez Veintimilla and served until elections could be called.

Galo Plaza Lasso
- b. 17 February 1906, New York,
- d.
- Education: University of Maryland, 1929, Georgetown School of Foreign Affairs, 1930.
- Occupation: gentleman farmer, politician, diplomat; civil attache, Ecuadorian legislation in Washington, 1929; member of Quito Municipal Council, 1937; minister of national defense, 1938–40; ambassador to the United States, 1944–46; senator from Pichincha Province, 1946; U.N. representative in Cyprus, 1964; secretary general of the OAS, 1967.

Camilo Ponce Enríquez
- b. 31 January 1912, Quito,
- d.
- Education: J. D. Central University of Quito, 1938.
- Occupation: lawyer, politician; minister of foreign relations, 1952; minister of public works, of interior, 1952; head of and founder of the Social Christian Movement, 1951.
- Presidency: elected (popular), age 44, 1 term, term ended constitutionally.

Carlos Julio Arosemena Monroy
b. 24 August 1919, Guayaquil,
d.
Education: J. D. University of Guayaquil, 1945.
Occupation: lawyer, politician; counsellor in Ecuadorian embassy in Washington, 1945–46; deputy from Guayas Province, 1952 and 1958; president of the Chamber of Deputies; vice-president of the Republic, 1960–61; deputy from Guayas Province to the constituent convention of 1967; deputy from Guayas Province, 1968.
Presidency: nonelected, age 42, succeeded Jose María Velasco Ibarra in 1961, after he was overthrown; was himself overthrown in 1963 by a military junta.

Clemente Yerovi Indaburo
b. August 1904, Barcelona (Spain),
d.
Education: Colegio 'San Gabriel" (Quito), some university training.
Occupation: economist, banker; president of the Chamber of Agriculture Guayaquil; director of the Central Bank of Ecuador, minister of economics, 1948, director of the National Development Bank, senator; Ecuadorian ambassador to the European Common Market.
Presidency: nonelected, age 62, was appointed by Ecuador's political party leaders after the abdication of the governing military junta.

Otto Arosemena Gómez
b. 19 July 1925, Guayaquil,
d.
Education: J. D. University of Guayaquil.
Occupation: lawyer, politician; president of the Provincial Electoral Tribunal (Guayas Province), deputy from Guayas Province, president of Chamber of Deputies, functional senator for commerce (representing the coastal provinces); vice-president of the Senate.
Presidency: elected (constituent convention), age 41, for an interim period until elections could be held.

APPENDIX B

ELECTION DATA ON ECUADOR'S ELECTED PRESIDENTS

Chief Executive	*Actual Method of Election*	*Constitutional Method of Election*	*Term for which elected*	*Completed Term*
Juan José Flores	Const. Convention (1830)	Congress or Nat'l Assembly	4 yrs.	No
Vicente Rocafuerte	Const. Convention (1835)	– . –	– . –	Yes
Juan José Flores	Congress	– . –	– . –	Yes
Juan José Flores	Const. Convention (1843)	– . –	8 yrs.	No
Vicente Ramón Roca	Const. Convention (1845)	– . –	4 yrs.	Yes
Diego Noboa	Const. Convention (1851)	– . –	4 yrs.	No
José M. Urbina	Const. Convention (1852)	indirect, popular (Electoral Assembly)	4 yrs.	Yes
Francisco Robles	indirect, popular (Electoral Assembly)	– . –	4 yrs.	No
Gabriel García M.	Const. Convention (1861)	direct, popular	4 yrs.	Yes
Jerónimo Carrión	direct, popular	– . –	4 yrs.	No
Javier Espinosa	– . –	– . –	4 yrs.	No
Gabriel García M.	Nat'l Convention (1869)	– . –	6 yrs.	No
Antonio Borrero	direct, popular	– . –	6 yrs.	No
Ignacio de Veintimilla	Const. Convention (1878)	– . –	4 yrs.	No

APPENDIX B—Continued

Chief Executive	*Actual Method of Election*	*Constitutional Method of Election*	*Term for which elected*	*Completed Term*
José M. Plácido Caamaño	direct, popular	– . –	4 yrs.	Yes
Antonio Flores Jijón	– . –	– . –	4 yrs.	Yes
Luis Cordero Crespo	– . –	– . –	4 yrs.	No
Eloy Alfaro	Const. Convention (1897)	– . –	4 yrs.	Yes
Leonidas Plaza Gutiérrez	direct, popular	– . –	4 yrs.	Yes
Lizardo García	– . –	– . –	4 yrs.	No
Eloy Alfaro	Const. Convention (1906)	– . –	4 yrs.	No
Emilio Estrada	direct, popular	– . –	4 yrs.	No
Leonidas Plaza Gutiérrez	– . –	– . –	4 yrs.	Yes
Alfredo Baquerizo Moreno	– . –	– . –	4 yrs.	Yes
José Luis Tamayo	– . –	– . –	4 yrs.	Yes
Gonzalo S. Córdova	– . –	– . –	4 yrs.	No
Isidro Ayora	Const. Convention (1929)	– . –	4 yrs.	No
Juan de Diós Martínez Mera	direct, popular	– . –	4 yrs.	No

José M. Velasco Ibarra	– . –	– . –	4 yrs.	No
Aurelio Mosquera Narváez	Const. Convention (1938)	– . –	4 yrs.	No
Carlos Alberto Arroyo del Río	direct, popular	– . –	4 yrs.	No
José M. Velasco Ibarra	Const. Convention (1945)	– . –	4 yrs.	No
Carlos Julio Arosemena Tola	Congress	– . –	interim period	......
Galo Plaza Lasso	direct, popular	– . –	4 yrs.	Yes
José M. Velasco Ibarra	– . –	– . –	4 yrs.	Yes
Camilo Ponce Enríquez	– . –	– . –	4 yrs.	Yes
José M. Velasco Ibarra	– . –	– . –	4 yrs.	No
Otto Arosemena Gomez	Const. Convention (1967)	– . –	interim period	......
José M. Velasco Ibarra	direct, popular	– . –	4 yrs.	No

APPENDIX C

PRESIDENTIAL TERMS IN ECUADOR

CLASSIFIED BY STABLE (S) OR NONSTABLE (NS) CHANGE*

	Took Office	*Left Office*
Juan José Flores[1]	13 May 1830 (NS)	21 Sept. 1830 (S)
	22 Sept. 1830 (S)	10 Sept. 1834 (NS)
Vicente Rocafuerte[1, 2]	10 Sept. 1834 (NS)	8 Aug. 1835 (S)
	9 Aug. 1835 (S)	30 Jan. 1839 (S)
Juan José Flores[1, 2]	31 Jan. 1839 (S)	15 Jan. 1843 (S)
	16 Jan. 1843 (NS)	31 March 1843 (S)
	1 Feb. 1843 (S)	6 March 1845 (NS)
Provisional Junta (3 men)	6 March 1845 (NS)	7 Dec. 1845 (S)
Vicente Ramón Roca[2]	8 Dec. 1845 (S)	15 Oct. 1849 (S)
Manuel de Ascásubi	15 Oct. 1849 (NS)	20 Feb. 1850 (NS)
Diego Noboa[1]	20 Feb. 1850 (NS)	25 Feb. 1851 (S)
	26 Feb 1851 (S)	17 July 1851 (NS)
José María Urbina[1, 2]	17 July 1851 (NS)	6 Sept. 1852 (S)
	7 Sept. 1852 (S)	31 Aug. 1856 (S)
Francisco Robles	1 Sept. 1856 (S)	1 May 1859 (NS)
Provisional Junta (3 men)	1 May 1859 (NS)	17 Jan. 1860 (NS)
Gabriel García Moreno[1, 2]	17 Jan. 1860 (NS)	1 April 1861 (S)
	2 April 1861 (S)	6 Sept. 1865 (S)
Jerónimo Carrión	7 Sept. 1865 (S)	5 Nov. 1867 (NS)
Pedro José de Arteta	5 Nov. 1867 (NS)	19 Jan. 1868 (S)
Javier Espinosa	20 Jan. 1868 (S)	18 Jan. 1869 (NS)
Gabriel García Moreno[1]	18 Jan. 1869 (NS)	31 July 1869 (S)
	1 Aug. 1869 (S)	6 Aug. 1875 (NS)
Francisco Javier León	6 Aug. 1875 (NS)	19 Aug. 1875 (NS)
Manuel de Ascásubi	19 Aug. 1875 (NS)	8 Dec. 1875 (S)
Antonio Borrero	9 Dec. 1875 (S)	18 Dec. 1876 (NS)
Ignacio de Veintimilla[1]	18 Dec. 1876 (NS)	20 April 1878 (S)
	21 April 1878 (S)	26 March 1882 (NS)
	26 March 1882 (NS)	9 July 1883 (NS)
Provisional Junta (5 men)	9 July 1883 (NS)	9 Feb. 1884 (S)
José María Placido Caamaño[2]	10 Feb. 1884 (S)	30 June 1888 (S)
Antonio Flores Jijón	1 July 1888 (S)	31 Aug. 1892 (S)
Luis Cordero	1 Sept. 1892 (S)	15 April 1895 (NS)
Vicente Lucio Salazar	15 April 1895 (NS)	5 June 1895 (NS)
Eloy Alfaro[1, 2]	5 June 1895 (NS)	16 Jan. 1897 (S)
	17 Jan. 1897 (S)	31 Aug. 1901 (S)
Leonidas Plaza Gutiérrez[2]	1 Sept. 1901 (S)	31 Aug. 1905 (S)
Lizardo García	1 Sept. 1905 (S)	16 Jan. 1906 (NS)
Eloy Alfaro[1]	16 Jan. 1906 (NS)	31 Dec. 1907 (S)
	1 Jan. 1908 (S)	11 Aug. 1911 (NS)
Carlos Freile Zaldumbide	11 Aug 1911 (NS)	31 Aug. 1911 (S)
Emilio Estrada	1 Sept. 1911 (S)	21 Dec. 1911 (NS)
Carlos Freile Zaldumbide	21 Dec. 1911 (NS)	5 March 1912 (NS)
Francisco Andrade Marín	5 March 1912 (NS)	31 Aug. 1912 (S)

	Took Office	*Left Office*
Leonidas Plaza Gutiérrez[2]	1 Sept. 1912 (S)	31 Aug. 1916 (S)
Alfredo Baquerizo Moreno[2]	1 Sept 1916 (S)	31 Aug. 1920 (S)
José Luis Tamayo[2]	1 Sept. 1920 (S)	31 Aug. 1924 (S)
Gonzalo S. Córdova	1 Sept. 1924 (S)	9 July 1925 (NS)
Provisional Junta (7 men)	9 July 1925 (NS)	10 Jan. 1926 (NS)
Provisional Junta (6 men)	10 Jan. 1926 (NS)	31 March 1926 (NS)
Isidro Ayora[1]	31 March 1926 (NS)	16 April 1929 (S)
	17 April 1929 (S)	24 Aug. 1931 (NS)
Luis Larrea Alba	24 Aug. 1931 (NS)	15 Oct. 1931 (NS)
Alfredo Baquerizo Moreno	15 Oct. 1931 (NS)	28 Aug. 1932 (NS)
Carlos Freile Larrea	28 Aug. 1932 (NS)	2 Sept. 1932 (NS)
Alberto Guerrero Martínez	2 Sept. 1932 (NS)	4 Dec. 1932 (S)
Juan de Diós Martínez Mera	5 Dec. 1932 (S)	17 Oct. 1933 (NS)
Abelardo Montalvo	17 Oct. 1933 (NS)	31 Aug. 1934 (S)
José María Velasco Ibarra	1 Sept. 1934 (S)	20 Aug. 1935 (NS)
Antonio Pons	20 Aug. 1935 (NS)	26 Sept. 1935 (NS)
Federico Páez	26 Sept. 1935 (NS)	22 Oct. 1937 (NS)
Alberto Enríquez Gallo	22 Oct. 1937 (NS)	10 Aug. 1938 (NS)
Manuel María Borrero	10 Aug. 1938 (NS)	2 Dec. 1938 (NS)
Aurelio Mosquera Narváez	2 Dec. 1938 (S)	17 Nov. 1939 (NS)
Carlos Alberto Arroyo del Río	17 Nov. 1939 (NS)	10 Dec. 1939 (NS)
Andrés F. Córdova Nieto	10 Dec. 1939 (NS)	10 Aug. 1940 (NS)
Julio E. Moreno	10 Aug. 1940 (NS)	31 Aug. 1940 (S)
Carlos Alberto Arroyo del Río	1 Sept. 1940 (S)	28 May, 1944 (NS)
Provisional Junta (plural)	28 May 1944 (NS)	31 May 1944 (NS)
José María Velasco Ibarra[1]	31 May 1944 (NS)	9 Aug. 1944 (S)
	10 Aug. 1944 (S)	30 March 1946 (NS)
	30 March 1946 (NS)	23 Aug. 1947 (NS)
Carlos Mancheno Cajas	23 Aug. 1947 (NS)	2 Sept. 1947 (NS)
Mariano Suárez Veintimilla	2 Sept. 1947 (NS)	17 Sept. 1947 (S)
Carlos Julio Arosemena Tola[3]	18 Sept. 1947 (S)	31 Aug. 1948 (S)
Galo Plaza Lasso[2]	1 Sept. 1948 (S)	31 Aug. 1952 (S)
José María Velasco Ibarra[2]	1 Sept. 1952 (S)	31 Aug. 1956 (S)
Camilo Ponce Enríquez[2]	1 Sept. 1956 (S)	31 Aug. 1960 (S)
José María Velasco Ibarra	1 Sept. 1960 (S)	9 Nov. 1961 (NS)
Carlos Julio Arosemena Monroy	9 Nov. 1961 (NS)	11 July 1963 (NS)
Provisional Junta (4 men)	11 July 1963 (NS)	29 March 1966 (NS)
Clemente Yerovi Indaburo	29 March 1966 (NS)	15 Nov. 1966 (S)
Otto Arosemena Gómez[3]	16 Nov. 1966 (S)	31 Aug. 1968 (S)
José María Velasco Ibarra	1 Sept. 1968 (S)	21 June 1970 (NS)
José María Velasco Ibarra	21 June 1970 (NS)	

* This table does not include regional rulers nor vice-presidents who assumed office temporarily because the incumbent was either out of the country or physically handicapped.

[1] These individuals either assumed office as nonelected presidents and were later elected with no interruption in office, or they proclaimed a dictatorship after having been constitutionally elected, or both.

[2] Completed their constitutional term of office.

[3] Were elected for an interim period by Congress until elections could be held.

ROBERT E. MCNICOLL

NUEVAS CORRIENTES

Latin America: Coming of Age?

A revolutionary change in the shape of inter-American relations has taken place in the last few years. The most casual observer is aware of this fact but it is difficult to assess the effects of the changes and to determine the prevailing tendency for the future. Fidel Castro's takeover of Cuba in 1959 appeared for a while to be just another Latin American "revolution" but it soon developed into a major threat to United States hegemony, confirmed by the ensuing missile crisis which marked the entry of another great power into the Western Hemisphere, a major zone of United States influence. Nothing in the Americas has been the same since then, although the effects of Castro's regime on other American States continue to be debated with more heat than light. Results tend to reflect previously established positions on the nature both of Castro's government and that of the states influenced by his activities.

Naturally, the attitude of the United States toward its Western Hemisphere role is an important factor in determining what happens and there have been significant changes here, too. The most dramatic, of course, was the assassination of President John F. Kennedy in 1963. Kennedy, as standard bearer for the Alliance for Progress, and personally tremendously popular in Latin America, may have represented the last chance for a cooperative effort with Latin America to help it to develop but also to keep it closely allied with the United States. Kennedy's phrase to describe the Alliance may be taken as its epitaph as well as his own: "a vast cooperative effort, unparalleled in magnitude and nobility of purpose, to satisfy the basic needs of the American people for homes, work and land, health and school. . . ."

Despite Johnson's pledge to continue the Alliance as a living memorial to Kennedy, the spirit had gone out of it, or perhaps its time had passed. Overshadowing the continuing efforts was the effect on Latin America of actions like the Dominican intervention culminating in a "Johnson Doctrine" which, though consistent with the whole process of Cold War diplomacy, did not arouse the enthusiasm of the Latin American partners. In 1968 a new administration was elected which has produced the policy of the "low profile." Whatever it means, it does not mean United States initiative in determining events in the Western Hemisphere but rather a reaction to events in which minimum United States interests are considered rather than action in defense of vague ideological principles. It is a policy that may encourage the development of Latin American self-sufficiency and may tend to destroy the old habit of Latin American countries looking first to the United States before making up their own minds. The policy appears to favor multilateral and international agency dealings with Latin America rather than the very intimate binational relations that have been typical of inter-American affairs.

The actions of Latin American states have given many opportunities for trying out the new policy. The Peruvian military took over in October 1968, in an apparently authentic revolution of a new type. Not only did it take over U.S. properties but it entered into negotiation with the other members of the Andean subgroup of the Latin American Free Trade Association (LAFTA) to establish principles regulating foreign investments in all the Andean countries in a manner to protect nationalistic interests. Relations were established with members of the Socialist bloc and loans, sales, and technical agreements made.

Despite considerable furor in certain U.S. and Latin American sectors, the United States government followed a low-key procedure in negotiations, refraining from applying the Hickenlooper amendment, and continuing military aid. Even the sensitive sugar quota was only slightly cut despite the requests of W. R. Grace that part of the payments be held back to guarantee payment for expropriated sugar properties. The wisdom of the procedures will be questioned for a long time, but it does appear that the more forceful alternatives would have been counterproductive. Responsible and adult or not, the moves of the Peruvian state have been accepted on a basis of equality and the United States appears as only another state instead of the erstwhile Colossus.

With the minor questions of the 200-mile limit of territorial waters in which the Pacific coast nations were joined by giant Brazil, there came in 1970 another epochal change—the election of Salvador Allende in Chile. Not only is the election the first victory by an avowed Marxist, but the Communist-dominated front that elected Allende has a program that would bring to an end American investments in Chile and the present anti-Castro alignment of the Organization of American States. Allende has already received authority to take over the billion-dollar copper mines of U.S. interests and has renewed relations with Cuba with a visit from Castro planned for the future.

Again, the U.S. reaction was proper, mild, and completely legal, although President Nixon did omit to send the *pro forma* congratulations to Allende on his election as indicated by protocol.

A number of different factors appear to be working to establish a new basis of equality among American states. The OAS itself, under the direction of Galo Plaza, is attempting to adjust itself to a "polycentrist" situation and make itself the mechanism for the channeling of European money into New World development. Secretary-General Plaza announced on 2 August 1971 that he had interviewed authorities of West Germany, Belgium, France, the Holy See, Netherlands, Spain, Switzerland, and the United Kingdom in support of European trade with and investment in the Latin American countries. In the interviews with President Heinemann of West Germany, Plaza reportedly stressed the interest of Latin America in greater scientific and technical exchange with Germany. Another aspect of these new relations between the OAS and Europe is the establishment of an OAS office in Europe, first set up in Geneva but with plans to move to Brussels. (*Alliance for Progress Weekly Newsletter*, 2 August 1971)

All these present and indicated future changes would appear to make the OAS merely a regional office of the UN instead of the United States bureau it once was in the days of Secretary-General Leo S. Rowe.

This one-world type of development has considerable backing everywhere and does not compare with the even greater danger of close alignment between Latin American states and the Cold War opponents of the United States.

The United States is confronted with a Latin America in which a number of countries oppose former United States policy on inter-American unity and openly solicit the aid and the cooperation of non-American countries which have been Cold War enemies of the United States. Is this a sign of coming of age or merely of opportunism? Before considering the Latin American attitude toward this, let it be mentioned that this development is one approved by many North American students of international relations. If the United States is to be a real world power there should be no regional or parochial interests to interfere with this development. The United States is no more concerned with Chile than with Vietnam. If Latin American states can find their place in the world community and cease to be a special care to the United States, all the better. It may be debated whether the OAS is of more value to the United States than to the Latin American nations. While no one wishes to see our opponents gain power at our expense, many would be happy to see Latin American countries form part of the Third World and no longer act as rebellious wards of the United States. And, as of this moment, are we quite sure of which nations are our opponents and which are our unconditional friends?

As far as the attitude of Latin Americans is concerned, I feel that the greatest problem for the United States lies in their conviction that their development requires a socialistic internal organization and that economic cooperation with the United States is harmful to them. This conviction has been shaping up a long time in the economic thinking of people like Raúl Prebisch and is perhaps most clearly expressed in some of Celso Furtado's sentences. It constitutes an alternative and opposing theory to that of the Alliance of Progress and, to the extent it is accepted by Latin American governments, would negate the possibility of the line of development governing policies in the Sixties:

> "Spheres of influence" no longer have any significance to the superpowers from the point of view of military security. And, as they relate to the underdeveloped world, the spheres of influence should be interpreted as systems of economic domination which in turn reduce the underdeveloped countries' ability to adapt their own structures to the requirements of a policy of national development. . . .
>
> The hegemony which the United States exercises in Latin America constitutes a serious obstacle to the development of the majority of the countries in the region, since it inordinately reinforces the anachronistic power structures. (Celso Furtado, *Obstacles to Development in Latin America*, Garden City, N.Y., 1970, p. 65)

This theory is widely accepted in Latin American intellectual and government circles and represents a much more serious barrier to relations between the United States and Latin America than the romantic theories of Rodó and Rubén Dario at the beginning of the century. The conflict of economic theories has been joined for a number of years and the names of people like Raúl Prebisch and Celso Furtado fill the conversations of all those who are concerned with this basic conflict, so closely related to the political developments.

In retrospect, it will no doubt appear paradoxical that the United

States on becoming one of the two great superpowers in the world should at the same time lose its position of dominance in its home zone of traditional preeminence.

Whether this new situation will really be better for the Latin American states, or not, remains to be seen. If they are, in fact, coming of age as a result of developments beyond their shores as well as within their boundaries, this status of majority entitles them to make their own errors.

THE PERUVIAN REVOLUTION

Despite the economic aims of the Peruvian revolution which are easy to understand in view of the foregoing, the real nature of the inner direction of the military group is hard to calibrate. No doubt the Soviet authorities also have their difficulties in understanding the thrust of the movement. A well-trained technocratic group which has lost confidence in civilian politicians is driving for economic and nationalistic aims which are generally supported and make sense from any ideological point of view. The difficulty for the movement's future—in addition to short-term difficulties such as shortage of meat and the impatience of groups that need housing—is the problem of organizing a mass group that will second the efforts of the regime.

The Velasco government has not shown great ability in doing this although every effort is being made to establish a dialogue with the public. The problems of communication are well stated in Carlos Delgado in *OIGA* (2 July 1971, p. 13):

> Uno de los riesgos inevitables de todo proceso revolucionario que de veras abre nuevas perspectivas para la acción trasformadora de la sociedad, consiste en que no suele ser comprendido en su real significación, aun por muchos de quienes dicen respaldarlo. Más aún, a veces algunos de los propios actores del proceso parecen incapaces de captar su sentido verdadero.
>
> La revolución peruana no podía constituir excepción a esta regla, sobre todo por tratarse de un proceso de tan alta y completa singularidad, de un fenómeno políticosocial que de manera tan categórica escapa a todos los esquemas y, por tanto, resulta ser inasible para quienes intentan apreciarla utilizando un instrumental interpretativo surgido de otro momento histórico y, en consecuencia, de otra realidad.
>
> Existen dos ejemplos muy claros que ponen de relieve esta situación. Uno, el más reciente, lo constituye la gran mayoría de comentarios referentes al inicio de la política de movilización social del gobierno revolucionario. En medio de las distorsionadas interpretaciones publicadas últimamente en periódicos que dicen estar identificados con la revolución peruana, destaca la

falaz e irresponsable afirmación de que hasta hoy el pueblo no ha podido participar en el proceso revolucionario. Este planteamiento elemental sugiere, con toda claridad, que hasta el momento no han existido formas de participación popular y que todas ellas se darán únicamente a partir de hoy.

Un comentario así revela incompresión total de lo que la revolución peruana representa. En esencia, las trasformaciones estructurales iniciadas hace dos años y medio suponen necesariamente, formas de participación. La trasferencia de poder efectivo que conlleva, por ejemplo, la reforma agraria, significa alteración profunda e irreversible de la estructura de poder tradicional en el campo. Y esto tiene un significado político y social de incalculable importancia para toda la sociedad peruana. Al implicar modificación sustantiva de la posición de los grupos campesinos en la estructura de poder, la reforma agraria es, en esencia, una forma fundamental de movilización social. Al adquirir las inmensas propiedades de los antiguos latifundistas, los campesinos organizados cooperativamente están ya desde hace dos años participando en el proceso de la revolución, es decir, en el esfuerzo creador de una nueva sociedad.

. . . .

Es preciso desterrar la falacia de que el desarrollo económico sólo puede expresarse en formas empresariales capitalistas La revolución peruana aspira a un desarrollo económico que fundamentalmente descanse en nuevas formas empresariales de carácter social capaces de garantizar la participación plena de los trabajadores en la propiedad y las decisiones de la empresa. Lo anterior implica que los mecanismos de financiación estatal deberán orientarse cada vez más decididamente al estímulo y al impulso de las nuevas formas empresariales inherentes a la opción no capitalista y no comunista del proceso revolucionario peruano.

En esta perspectiva, la comunidad laboral demuestra ser una expresión revolucionaria de deforma de la empresa capitalista propia de un sistema económico cuyo futuro desarrollo, para ser consecuente con la orientación fundamental de la Revolución habrá de responder a una concepción autogestionaria, cooperativista, comunitaria, de directo control de los trabajadores peruanos sobre la riqueza que crea su trabajo.

In the search for popular understanding and support, President Velasco highlighted the government's interest in his July 28 speech commemorating the one-hundred and fiftieth anniversary of Peruvian independence: (*OIGA*, 30 July 1971, p. 19.)

El presidente aclaró que la reciente creación de un sistema nacional de apoyo a la movilización social no debe ser entendida ni como el comienzo de la participación popular —la que en realidad, según dijo, comenzó desde el momento mismo en que

> empezo el proceso revolucionario— ni como el propósito de formar un partido político. Aún más, la movilización social, tal como la entiende el gobierno revolucionario, excede ampliamente los criterios exclusivamente políticos porque comprende todas aquellas facetas de la vida humana en que el ciudadano peruano puede y debe intervenir con capacidad de elección y decisión. "La participación popular", añadió, "tiene diversos planos de realización, distintas manifestaciones y, por tanto, múltiples formas de expresión.

If an immediate problem is popular support, a longer-lasting and more vital problem is economics. In addition to the agrarian reform, measures to repatriate Peruvian assets and control the loss of foreign exchange by useless travel and expenditure by private citizens, the government still referred to pressures derived from the policies "de las potencias hegemónicas" and the lack of understanding of other nations as obstacles in attaining a better economic status. Minister of Economics Francisco Morales Bermúdez was still able to present an impressive balance for the year 1970, completed in June of 1971.

The figures given showed that the cost of living which had increased 16% in 1966 and 19% in 1968 had only increased 6% in 1969 and 5% in 1970. The export goal of 966 million dollars had been passed to reach 1,032 million dollars. At the same time imports did not exceed 705 million dollars. From Argentina (*Analisis*, 15 June 1971, p. 27) it was reported:

> De acuerdo a la explicación de Morales Bermúdez, esos hechos se inscriben dentro de los objetivos que el gobierno se había trazado para 1970: 1) Continuar el proceso de reactivación económica interna: 2) Iniciar un agresivo proceso de capitalización ampliando la capacidad productiva de la economía con énfasis en el proceso de reforma agraria y 3) Reducir los niveles de desempleo y subempleo.

While there is a close correlation between economic solvency and political success, the relation is not absolute, as is shown by cases like Cuba's. When a change of economic structure is under way high political morale may compensate for unimpressive economic attainments. Peru's case is an interesting study to show whether a definite "Third World" nation can combine economic and political expertise sufficiently well to continue in its stated course.

A Review Article by
Roy J. Hensley*

BOOKS

TWO APPROACHES TO ECONOMIC DEVELOPMENT

Papanek, Gustav F., ed. *Development Policy.: Theory and Practice.* Cambridge: Harvard University Press, 1968. Dedication statement, preface, tables, figures, index. xiv, 367 pp. $12.50.

Phillips, Hiram S. *Guide for Development: Institution-Building and Reform.* New York: Frederick A. Praeger, 1969. Preface, note to preface, acknowledgments, list of figures and table, bibliography. xvii, 282 pp. $15.00.

The role of rich countries in assisting poor countries to initiate and sustain economic development has been undergoing extensive reassessment as the 1960s Decade of Development has ended. The number, sweep, and variety of major, new examinations of the nature of the development problem and what now needs to be done about it, as well as what now can be done about it, exceeds anything we have had in the past.[1] Much has been learned in the post-

* Professor of Economics, University of Miami.

[1] The most celebrated official study is: *Partners in Development,* A Report of the Commission on International Development, Lester B. Pearson, Chairman (New York: Frederick A. Praeger, 1969). A selection of other, more or less global, assessments is: *Report of the U. N. Committee for Development Planning,* Professor Jan Tinbergen, Chairman, January, 1970; Sir Robert Jackson, *A Study of the Capacity of the United National Development System* (Geneva, 1969); Raul Prebisch, *Transformation and Development: The Great Task of Latin America,* A Report presented to the Inter-American Development Bank, April 1970; Graham Jones, *The Role of Science and Technology in Developing Countries,* Published for the International Council of Scientific Unions (New York: Oxford University Press, 1971); *U.S. Foreign Assistance in the 1971's: A New Approach,* Report of the Task Force on International Development, Rudolph A. Peterson, Chairman, March, 1970; Jagdish N. Bhagwati, *Amount and Sharing of Aid* (Washington, D.C.: Overseas Development Council, 1970); Robert E. Asher, *Development Assistance in the Seventies* (Washington, D.C.: The Brookings Institution, 1970); and Gunnar Myrdal, *Asian Drama: An Inquiry into the Poverty of Nations,* Vols. I–III (New York: Pantheon, 1968).

Many of these assessments with their policy recommendations tend to support positions taken in reports presented by the Secretary-General of the United Nations Committee on Trade and Development to the two sessions of that organization:

World War II period about the development process; but the level of our ignorance continues to be high. Perhaps the problem is growing more rapidly than our understanding of how to deal with it. For example, recent recognition of and emphasis on the ecological implications of worldwide industrialization poses problems not yet comprehended, much less incorporated into our analytical and policy propositions. Certainly we are still groping for meaningful, general theory and policy to explain and promote development.[2] In fact, though it is often said that development consists of socioeconomic-political transformation, we have not yet agreed exactly what this means.[3] Presumably, the goal is to improve the well-being of the general population in these, and perhaps other, dimensions. But as Enke expresses it, the "difficulty is to decide what the 'output' is that is to be increased; GNP, foreign exchange, or jobs, for instance. . . ." [4] All of these measures, along with many others frequently mentioned or used, seem to be both means and ends—they may be desired for their own sake as well as for their ability to produce other states that enhance well-being.

After over two decades of concern, it is disheartening to know so little about what is surely the central issue of our times. Yet in some ways the record suggests we are doing better than our state of knowledge would indicate. If one accepts growth rates in real product as a surrogate, however imperfect, for economic development, there has been general improvement. The system is moving in the right direction. A recent study estimates an average weighted rate of growth in real per capita income for all non-Communist less developed countries of 1.9 percent per year for the period 1955–1965.[5] The authors term this "one of the most striking economic facts of the two postwar decades." [6] Variation among country rates was wide—from below zero to more than 12 percent—and population growth rates were increasing. Thus, aside from questions about the nature and completeness of the data, there are no assurances here that growth will be sustained and accelerated to provide mean-

Towards a New Trade Policy for Development (1964) and *Towards a Global Strategy of Development* (1968). For a specific comparison of the Pearson Commission report and UNCTAD proposals see David H. Pollock, "Pearson and UNCTAD: A Comparison," *International Development Review*, XII, No. 4, 1970, pp. 14–21.

[2] See the survey articles of Stephen Enke, "Economists and Development: Rediscovering Old Truths," *Journal of Economic Literature*, VII (December, 1969), pp. 1125–1139, and Bruce F. Johnston, "Agriculture and Structural Transformation in Developing Countries: A Survey of Research," *Ibid.*, VIII (June, 1970), pp. 369–404.

[3] Irma Adelman and Cynthia Taft Morris rank 74 countries in terms of 41 social, political, and economic indicators in *Society, Politics, & Economic Development: A Quantitative Approach* (Baltimore: The Johns Hopkins Press, 1967).

[4] Op. cit., p. 1131.

[5] Everett E. Hagen and Oli Hawrylyshyn, "Analysis of World Income and Growth, 1955–1965," *Economis Development and Cultural Change*, XVIII, No. 1, Part II (October, 1969), pp. 46–48. Communist less-developed countries grew at 6.3 percent per capita for the first half of the period; data were not available for the second half.

[6] Ibid., p. 46.

ingful increases in various dimensions of living and to provide some "catching up" with the more developed countries. During the same period, 1955–1965, the non-Communist more developed countries were estimated to have an average real per capita growth rate of 2.8 percent per year; the rate for more developed Communist Europe was estimated to be 4.0 percent.[7]

Regardless of the state of our knowledge regarding developmental content and processes, there seems to be widespread agreement that more must be done through a set of global strategies that while they utilize the knowledge we have they also generate additional understanding. This is echoed over and over again in the major assessments previously cited. The role of the developed countries in formulating and executing these strategies will depend heavily on their experience in the last decade or two trying to understand and promote development.

The two books listed here are records of attempts to understand and to generalize from different experiences in promoting economic development. In the Papanek volume we have firsthand experience of economic advisors working out of a prestigious United States educational institution, bringing youth, enthusiasm, and the latest training to presumably receptive administrations in some of the quite promising developing country situations in the world. The Harvard Development Advisory Service, said to be conceived by Professor Edward S. Mason, is financed by the Ford Foundation, the World Bank, the United Nations, and recipient governments. It provides teams of advisors to assist with the analysis and formulation of policy for development programs in less developed countries. The ten papers (plus an editor's evaluation chapter) printed here were selected from seventeen chosen for discussion at a conference of development advisors, country experts, and others. Additional conferences and publications are planned at irregular intervals in the future.

The papers deal with Advisory Service Work in Africa (Liberia), Asia Pakistan), and Latin America (Argentina and Colombia). Their unifying theme is "the actual applications of economic theory and analytical techniques to important government policy issues, showing the lessons learned as a result of that application" (p. vii). Thus, in purpose at least, we see an effort here to utilize the knowledge we have and to generate new knowledge in the process.

The first group of papers, Part I, is concerned with general planning and development strategy. Wouter Tims describes a growth model that evolved in the preparation of Pakistan's Third Five Year Plan. A vehicle was needed to select a feasible growth target for Pakistan's economy, both in overall terms and in sectoral terms, at that point in its history. Tims emphasizes that the model, a version of a two-gap formulation relating investment to domestic savings and exports to demand for imports, provided a means for making consistent projections for each of various alternative assumptions. Thus policymakers were made more aware of the implications of their prospective decisions, and in particular, they were made to see the limits to feasible policies.

---

[7] Ibid., pp. 47–48.

Tims' discussion of how this model was developed and used demonstrates the mixture of induction and deduction involved in problem solution—in this instance, as Papanek expresses it, "cooperation between discipline—and problem—oriented economists" (p. 355).

In the second chapter Alfred H. Conrad discusses some of the important questions involved in the building and application of econometric models for development planning. He uses as examples the Tims growth model for Pakistan, the Maynard-van Rijckeghem stability model for Argentina (described in Chapter 7), and a preliminary two-gap model of the Liberian economy (an appendix to Chapter 2). Conrad stresses that, despite conceptual and data problems, econometric models provide a means for indicating "the trade-offs among the several objectives that must somehow be reconciled in the planning process" (p. 41). He feels the models for Pakistan and Argentina, which were implemented, were successful in creating a setting for continuous revision of objectives and policy.

David Felix examines import substitution in Chapter 3. He concentrates on the question: "Why does ISI (import-substituting industrialization) in time lose its power to sustain a GNP growth rate in excess of the growth in the capacity to import, irrespective of whether the import capacity is reduced by excessive reliance on ISI?" (p. 59). Argentina is taken as a case example. ISI has been a popular growth strategy in Latin America. The Economics Commission for Latin America (ECLA), a strong advocate earlier, now finds, however, "that ISI has lost its effectiveness in the more industrialized Latin American countries, so that their growth rate has become closely tied to growth of the capacity to import. . . ." (p. 68). Felix extends ECLA's explanation to make a still stronger case for the likelihood of decreasing growth effects from ISI. He suggests that as ISI takes place production and demand shifts occur which limit further reduction of imports and reduce the inducement to investment. At the same time an industrial cost-price structure emerges which makes it difficult to enlarge the capacity to import by industrial exports. Argentine data tend to support these hypotheses, though one gets the feeling at times that the data may have been stretched beyond their limits. Certainly this is an impressive effort, however, to assess how import substitution has influenced growth.

The final paper in the first group is "Imports, Investment, and Growth—Colombia," by John Sheahan. This is an attempt to explain why Colombia failed to achieve its potential during the 1950s and the first half of the 1960s. Colombia is compared to Argentina and Chile: "these countries managed to advance a considerable distance toward industrialization without developing their exports at the rate necessary to balance rising import requirements of new industries focused on domestic markets" (p. 114). Sheahan does not find that Colombia promoted import substitution too fast, but the resulting structure of production absorbed so much foreign exchange that necessary imports of capital goods for further expansion were impossible. This sounds very similar to the explanations of ECLA and Professor Felix; it would be interesting to see Felix's Argentine analysis applied to Colombia. Perhaps ISI did proceed too fast and too far in Colombia.

The remaining papers are concerned with somewhat more specific questions. Part II consists of three papers analyzing problems of inflation: "Exchange-Rate Systems in Conditions of Continuing Inflation—Lessons from Colombian Experience" by Harold B. Dunkerley; "Exchange Policy—Argentina" by Richard D. Mallon; and "Stabilization Policy in an Inflationary Economy—Argentina" by Geoffrey Maynard and Willy van Rijckeghem. These are all concerned with short-term policies, though as Dunkerley suggests early in his paper, inflation, with accompanying balance of payments difficulties, is likely to be continuous in countries attempting to promote more rapid growth.

Both Argentina and Colombia have had persistent inflation, balance of payments problems, and increasingly high debt-service charges. Stabilization efforts have often involved devaluation and other exchange rate system modifications; results have been mixed, at best. Both countries' recent experiences are detailed and suggestions are made to try to achieve better price and growth performance. In particular, fixed rate systems with frequent devaluations, given past history and the expectations which now seem to prevail, are not expected to be very effective. As previously mentioned, Maynard and van Rijckeghem present a short-term stabilization model for Argentina, which Professor Conrad praises, feeling it permits "choice of policy and the definition of the objectives to proceed together. . . ." (p. 49).

Part III contains a single paper on fiscal policy, "Sales Taxation and Development Planning—Colombia," by Richard M. Bird. Papanek comments on the lack of field research in the fiscal policy area and the difficulties of generalizing regarding appropriate policies. A general sales tax was enacted in Colombia in 1963 (effective in 1965) to cope with a government revenue crisis. Bird is primarily interested in analyzing the effects of the tax for the allocation of resources, distribtuion of income, production, consumption, and the balance of payments. He traces each of these through and concludes that other tax measures would have been preferable to the general sales tax with differential rates for Colombia at that point in its history. Bird concludes that tax changes to meet short-run revenue problems without adequate consideration for their long-run development consequences are not advisable. Developing country decision-makers, those with sales taxes and those likely to get them, should find Colombia's experience useful.

Part IV also contains a single paper, "Lessons in Agricultural Development—Pakistan," by Walter P. Falcon and Carl H. Gotsch. During the Second Plan, 1960/61–1964/65, the agricultural sector in both East and West Pakistan shifted from general stagnation to strong growth. For West Pakistan the sources of growth are principally water, fertilizer, improved seed, plant protection, improved cultural practices, and interaction effects. East Pakistan experienced a similar increase in agricultural output; this was attributed to an extension of area, fertilizer, plant protection, improved seeds, and more extensive irrigation and drainage facilities. Falcon and Gotsch feel these physical changes were possible because of an active government program to disseminate information and new and better inputs and to improve opportunities for the agricultural population to benefit from increased output. They discuss, in detail, all that was done and conclude that there may be a good deal of value to other developing countries in Pakistan's agricultural experience which culminated in the period of their Second Plan.

Part V contains the final Development Advisor paper, "Wages and Labor Scarcity—Liberia," by R. S. Weckstein. Labor surplus conditions have usually been considered typical of developing countries, so analysis has focused on this kind of situation. Currently there is heightened concern about projected increases in unemployment and underemployment.[8] Weckstein assesses the experience of Liberia, which in many ways can be considered a labor-scarce economy. The country has a small, slowly growing population that has not yet shown strong desires to shift from traditional occupations. Real wage rates have been rising. Weckstein suggests some possible explanations and what it may mean for further development. He thinks labor-scarce conditions will become more common as countries successfully move toward development.

Papanek's summary evaluation chapter makes up Part VI of the book. He stresses the interaction between theory and practice which is provided in the experience of this group of Development Advisors. In the process of applying and testing theoretical propositions new and better propositions are emerging, presumably to the benefit of all.

Overall, these studies constitute a very useful work for all who are concerned with improving the condition of the world's poor countries. They advance understanding of both development objectives and policies by intensively examining particular units of experience and then raising questions about their general applicability. I would mention two criticisms: (1) The detail reported sometimes seems excessive. (2) Attention is devoted almost exclusively to economic questions. Papanek does note, in his concluding chapter, that in an ultimate sense political and social factors govern, but in a proximate sense economic questions have significant influence. As an economist, one can agree with this, but still wish for fewer pages of economic detail and more recognition of other forces. Recall that development is thought to be socioecomonic-political transformation.

The second book is based on experience also. Phillips states that it is an effort to synthesize fifteen years of experience in foreign assistance activities . . . in predecessor organizations of what is now known as the Agency for International Development" (p. xi). The work "is intended as a practical guide for individuals and organizations engaged in effecting changes in the developing countries, and especially those concerned with the development of institutions contributing to economic growth, social development and nation-building" (p. vii). Phillips notes that development is a complex process which we do not fully understand, but that institutions are being built and countries are changing. He

[8] See Johnston, op. cit., p. 386.

presents his experience in working in these processes, particularly in regard to "institutions engaged in program administration, education, and training, and the social and political environment essential for their success" (p. viii).

The book is organized in three parts: Part I has seven chapters describing and analyzing, quite superficially, institutions and change (institutions are specific entities working in the development process). Part II, in four chapters, presents some selected examples of institutions and their role in development. Part III consists of a single chapter of policy recommendations. Each of these parts will be considered somewhat further, in turn.

Initially, Phillips emphasizes four key inputs that enable institutions to develop and thrive: leadership with some commitment to development; indiduals with development-oriented education or experience and a cause; outside assistance; and resources for development. These inputs contribute to a number of critical elements in the change process. Finally, out of a great deal of rambling, repetitious discussion twenty elements of institution-building are said to be identified. Then Part I ends with fourteen elements to use in evaluating results. Phillips is commendably modest, often stressing the tentative nature of his suggestions, but this does not add any more substance to his rambling catalog of factors, problems, and recommendations which are frequently summarized in box diagrams filled with connecting arrows.

Four cases are presented in Part II. They are: (1) land reform in Taiwan; (2) corn production in Asia; (3) tax modernization in Chile; and (4) fiscal management in Thailand. These are very brief, fragmented treatments that provide little in the way of understanding or generalization.

The recommendations chapter in Part III includes a variety of proposals to create a more favorable environment for development, to increase capacity to carry out programs, and to train people to function more effectively. All of this, with numerous sublists and categories, is presented in the same fragmented fashion.

Overall, the book is a superficial, disjointed treatment which many people are likely to find difficult to finish.

In these two books we have quite different examples of how theory and practice can interact to advance understanding of objectives and policies. Both should be examined to see what different results may come out of sets of experience that have some similarity.

BOOK REVIEWS

Smith, Peter H. *Politics and Beef in Argentina: Patterns of Conflict and Change*. New York and London: Columbia University Press, 1969. Acknowledgments, introduction, bibliography and sources, index. x, 292 pp. $10.00.

In *Politics and Beef in Argentina*, Peter Smith has provided a worthwhile volume for the person with a general interest in Argentina, an essential source for the Argentine historian, and a valuable case study for the development specialist. It will be appreciated most by those readers who have a familiarity with standard histories of Argentina and can recognize its novelty.

Professor Smith seeks to explain the transformation of Argentina from a country controlled by a landowning elite around the turn of the century to a nation in which urban workers held the power some half century later. He uses the social, economic, and political conflicts experienced by and within the beef industry as a medium to demonstrate how the change transpired.

A central theme is the refutation of the standard argument that political change and national development occurred as a result of the challenge to the rural aristocracy by the urban middle class. Professor Smith asserts that ". . . the notion that political modernization is typified by class-oriented urban-rural conflict needs to be tested against the possibility that the process might be characterized, instead, by the development of intra-class conflict within the rural sector."

He examines this hypothesis at length by analyzing the activities of five interest groups (the first three upper class, and second two urban and lower class) related to the beef industry: (1) packinghouse managers, (2) breeders, (3) fatteners, (4) consumers in Buenos Aires, and (5) packinghouse workers. The interactions among these groups and between these groups and representatives of other sectors (e.g., wheat producers, labor leaders, and industrialists) are traced from the period in which Argentina emerged as a major beef produer to the early Peron years.

It is shown that the dominant forces in the growth and development of political parties and the consequent opening-up of the political system were intra-upper class, rural conflicts. Since many of the legislators had interests in the beef industry, disputes between breeders, fatteners, and packers found ready voices. Once beef production for export assumed a dominant role in the economy, and given the fact that the law-makers had strong and divided interests in beef questions, the older system of *acuerdo* (i.e., informal agreements by the inner circle of the executive branch and a puppet-like Congress) was no longer possible.

From 1912 when the Saenz Pena law broadened the popular political base until the late 1930s when the system was closed again, Congress was a sounding board for the politics of beef. During this period, however, the system primarily served the interests of the breeders, fatteners, and packers at the expense of workers and consumers. Even the Radical Party and President Yrigoyen sided with the upper class rather than the lower and middle sectors as is often alleged.

Beef producers were so successful in organizing and getting their interests represented (partially to fight each other) that they effectively excluded the lower classes from the decision-making process. Urban workers were never strong enough to precipitate an authentic urban-rural battle.

Not until the Peron years did a truly urban-rural conflict emerge. This was *not* brought about, however, by the efforts of a modernizing middle class (they had usually identified with the ruling group); rather, it resulted from the rural reaction to Peron's ability to capitalize on previously ignored lower class demands.

There are three important by-products for the development specialist which emerge from Professor Smith's argument. First, he establishes that broadly-based modernization does not necessarily follow socioeconomic change. In fact, if those responsible for change are well enough organized, economic growth can retard political development by effectively excluding the lower and/or middle classes.

Second, development can be very selective. Growth in economic indicators such as production, exports, and gross product per capita does not necessarily represent improving conditions for the majority of the citizens of a country.

Third, analyses of countries should include the possibility of retrogression. The Argentine example demonstrates that a country can "take-off" only to return to a relatively stagnant state.

None of these contentions is new, but seldom does one find such a detailed case in which they can be examined.

It is difficult to find a major weakness of the book. One might argue that it does not give a complete picture of the history of Argentina over the period, but it is claimed only that "the results are more suggestive than definitive" and that studies of other sectors are also needed. Most readers will not be able to challenge the analysis since Professor Smith probably knows as much about the "politics of beef" as anyone.

Surely, some historians will argue with his interpretation of facts and perhaps with his refutation of the "middle class thesis." It is difficult, however, not to appreciate the effort which must have been necessary to research the many primary and secondary sources which are cited, but which, incidentally, do not get in the reader's way.

FRED MILLER
Assistant Professor of Economics
Oregon State University

Schuh, G. Edward, in Collaboration with Alves, Eliseu Roberto, *The Agricultural Development of Brazil.* New York: Frederick A. Praeger, 1970. Foreword by Lowell S. Hardin, xxxiii, 456 pp., $18.50.

This book is the sixth in a special Praeger series of "bench mark studies" on agricultural development in Latin America. The other volumes report studies on Uruguay, Mexico, Argentina, Peru, and Venezuela.

The objectives of the Brazilian study are to:

(1) Determine, for recent years, changes which have taken place in agricultural output and food consumption;

(2) Determine those factors associated with the above changes and identify major strengths and weaknesses of the agricultural sector;

(3) Predict some of the variables affecting agriculture in the next decade; and,

(4) Array, in order of priority, means of improving the agricultural sector.

The authors find that food and fiber output in Brazil has expanded *pari-passu* with demand. They regret, however, that agriculture has not made a more significant contribution to overall development, particularly given the vast potential of this sector. It is quickly added that because output has kept pace with demand, it does not mean that quality of diets has been adequate. The nutrition level of the lower income class has been below minimal requirements.

Most of the increase in output is attributed to new lands which have been brought under cultivation rather than to increases in productivity. The slow rate of growth in output per unit of land and labor is one of the major weaknesses of Brazilian agriculture, as seen by the authors.

Causes of this weakness include an inadequate "educational and research infrastructure" for agriculture. But in this respect Schuh and Alves are optimistic about some recent developments, including the strengthening of such institutions as the Escola Superior de Agricultura at Viçosa, Minas Gerais. On the other hand, they are critical of the development of the extension service, indicating that more emphasis has been placed on "fomento" (or the practice of providing technical assistance in the form of physical labor and inputs at less than comparable market costs) rather than building extension a la U.S.A. They further suggest that there have been too many organizations and agencies, often with conflicting goals, dealing with Brazilian agriculture.

Other weaknesses include inadequate budget support for agriculture and obstreperous government policy. In this latter regard, overevaluation of the currency, limitation of exports, the establishment of price ceilings for foodstuffs, and the promotion of rapid industrialization at agriculture's sacrifice are singled out, although little evidence is presented to show how and why these policies have inhibited agriculture.

Schuh and Alves rely heavily on studies from the Fundação Getúlio Vargas (FGV) to project supply and demand for agricultural commodities in 1970 and 1975. Chapter 9, in fact, contains 34 tables taken directly from studies by the FGV. The sum and substance of this chapter is that Brazil has not been in the past a food crisis country and that it will not be in the future. It is suggested that there will be little difficulty in supplying food and fiber to meet the effective demand. Again, at this point, however, the authors suggest that the agricultural sector has the potential to do a great deal more than simply meet effective demand and, in fact, could do so if appropriate measures were undertaken.

These measures are summarized in the final chapter and include:

(1) Strengthening agricultural research;

(2) Increasing investment in rural people;

(3) Developing supply industries for modern agricultural inputs; and

(4) Strengthening the labor market infrastructure.

Other measures including improving credit policy, improving transportation in the rural sector, and rationalizing government policy are recommended, but these means are of "secondary importance" vis-à-vis the above list.

Despite what some other observers (including T. Lynn Smith and, more recently, personnel of the Inter-American Agricultural Development Committee and the Land Tenure Center) have said on the subject, Schuh and Alves place little emphasis on land reform. In fact, they avoid even using such standard terminology as *minifúndio* and *latifúndio* because they feel these concepts are too "emotion-laden" (p. 143). Nor do they attempt to reconcile, in any detailed analysis, their views with those of the above researchers. The authors, in fact, suggest that large units may be large of necessity, because soil productivity is low. They are not convinced that data which show a low productivity per hectare on large units and a high productivity per hectare for small ones are sufficient justification for breaking up the former. They feel that, "The problem which gives rise to the demand for land reform is basically a labor-market problem, and reflects in large part the low value attached to agricultural labor" (p. 416). Thus, low wages among agricultural workers, they indicate, have causes which are much more fundamental than the distribution of land. They recommend policy designed to "valorize labor" and create employment alternatives to ameliorate land tenure problems. Schuh and Alves say little about the political and social power vested in land—a problem that other researchers feel must be attacked as a pre-condition for rural development.

My principal criticism of the book is that the final recommendations are not strongly supported by the preceeding data and analysis. Also, the study says little that is new about Brazilian agriculture. Notwithstanding these weaknesses, the book brings together, in one convenient reference, a wealth of data and basic descriptive material and is recommended to those students of Brazil with an interest in agriculture and economic development.

L. HARLAN DAVIS
Assistant Professor of Agricultural Economics
University of Georgia

Dulles, John W. F. *Unrest in Brazil: Political-Military Crises, 1955–1964.* Austin: The University of Texas Press, 1970. Introduction, sources of material, appendix, glossary, index. xv, 449 pp. $10.00.

The big prize in South America is Brazil. Whoever controls Brazil will dominate South America. If revolutionary Marxists manage to obtain the upper hand Latin American events will be predictably chaotic. Should the capitalist multi-national corporation gain complete control, then a new set of circumstances will appear that clearly indicate a crash course between the United States and Brazil sooner or later. If past history gives us any indication Brazil will probably disappoint both Marxists and imperialists and come up with an economic-political mix which will frustrate analysts on both side of the political spectrum.

Brazil seems to resist neat categories. Books, monographs, and research articles tend to tell us more about the people writing them than they do about the nation being described. This certainly is the impression I received from reading *Unrest In Brazil*.

John W. F. Dulles, a mining engineer by training, is also the son of the late Secretary of State. Both of these points are important to keep in mind when reading *Unrest in Brazil*. This is a strange book. The facts about the period are there, but so many unselective bits of information appear that one gets the impression that Mr. Dulles has indiscriminately scooped up every piece of data available without differentiating between important items and those that are trivial and trite. There is too much respectful reporting of who said what and when and not enough "why?"

Brazilian specialists and those familiar with the terrain will read this book with care and gingerly pick out the nuggets that Dulles has dredged up. But the beginner should be warned that all that glitters is not gold.

Nonetheless the book is a valuable piece of work. It provides a frame of reference and pinpoints actors on the Brazilian political stage. Most everyone is there. The book is a great help for anyone trying to reconstruct the period and obtain a grasp of the complex forces at work.

I would argue with the last sentence of the introduction. Dulles writes: "It is hoped that this book's account of the political-military crisis during the ten year period will throw some light on the role played by the military while civilians governed Brazil and will be of help to readers who seek to appraise that role." Civilians never really governed Brazil. From 1891 to 1964 civilian politicians performed within a military frame of reference, some more successfully than others, but all had to reach understandings with Brazil's military.

The book is divided into eight chapters and a one-page epilogue which appears to be an attempt to keep the material as current as possible. It reports an incident in 1966 which now appears to be a relatively trivial event involving an attempted political agreement of Carlos Lacerda with Juscelino Kubitschek and João Goulart. An eleven-page appendix follows and briefly describes the Brazilian political party system with heavy emphasis on the activities of the Communist Party. There is a twenty-page bibliography which also lists the numerous interviews Dulles had with political figures when he visited Brazil. There are twenty eight pages of photographs.

Chapter I covers the election of 1955 by setting the scene with the August 1954 suicide of Vargas and the assumption of the presidential office by Vice President Café Filho. The jockeying of the various candidates for the 1955 presidential election is skillfully described. There is a curious statement by Dulles that after the election alliances were negotiated with Ademar de Barros (PSP) and Plínio Salgado's (PRP) by Juscelino Kubitschek. Dulles writes that Plinio's price for support of the president-elect was a promise that the forthcoming administration would not recognize the Soviet Union or grant legality to the Communist Party. This statement is footnoted by an interview with Plínio Salgado in Brasília, October 14, 1965, one of five different interviews Dulles had that day. Two things worry me about this type of information. One

—it simply does not seem likely that Kubitschek needed Salgado's help to the extent of making such a binding agreement which was never corroborated by Kubitschek. Second—Plíno Salgado's public statements and published memoirs of events indicate a tendency to inflate his own importance. Salgado has been proven wrong too many times for me to accept this statement at face value. There is no similar follow-up by Dulles on the alleged alliance negotiated between Ademar de Barros and Kubitschek.

In a book aimed at explaining the role of the military there is the puzzling omission of the death of Estillac Leal, a nationalist general in April 1955. Even the popular magazine *Time* felt this event important enough to publish a relatively long story about it.

Chapter II covers the two coups of November 1955 which enabled Kubitschek to take office behind the protection of General Henrique Lott, the strong man of the regime. The material holds up well in this chapter.

Chapter III treats the Kubitschek years, 1956–1959, and though the period is one of the most difficult to pull together, I again got the impression that the right questions were not being asked. The role of the Military Club does not come into focus nor is inflation and the wave of strikes that accompanied the final years of the Kubitschek administration described adequately.

Chapter IV describes the Jánio Quadros administration and his flight from Brasília. Quadros wrote later in *História do Povo Brasileiro*, Vol. VI (1968), his reasons for resigning. It compares well with what Dulles has written. Goulart is handled in Chapters V and VI. The deterioration is selectively pinpointed. Goulart emerges as singularly inept politician unable to control the men around him especially his charismatic brother-in-law Leonel Brizola. Another odd omission is the skipping over the role of the author along with Herbert Hoover, Jr., in the negotiations with the Brazilian government on behalf of the Hanna corporation attempt to acquire iron deposits in Brazil. This is indeed too much modesty and would have been a valuable addition to our knowledge of the incident.

Chapter VII reports on the events of 1964 and opens with a description of the fatal political rally of March 13, which most observers feel is the dividing line in the collapse of the Goulart administration. One must again be careful of Dulles' unqualified statement that CGT leaders were in charge of all the arrangements for this mass meeting, as other sources indicate this was not necessarily true. Chapter VIII details the events of the military movement of April 1964. Over one hundred books have been written in Brazil all presenting the "true" story and all of course illustrating a different aspect of the revolution. Dulles presents a relatively clear-cut picture of the event. Nothing is mentioned concerning the role or non-role of the United States in the revolution.

The Dulles book is useful for students of Brazilian affairs and if used carefully is a welcome addition to the growing list of books on the nation.

JORDAN M. YOUNG
Associate Professor of Social Science
Pace College

Hartog, J. *Curaçao, From Social Dependence to Autonomy.* Aruba, Netherlands Antilles: De Wit, Inc. Appendix, table of contents. xi, 424 pp. $16.00.

This volume, one of a series of five dealing with the Netherlands Antilles, is a welcome addition to the English-speaking reader's scanty knowledge of the Antilles. The author has utilized a wide range of archival resources to present data on most aspects of Curaçaon life including such items as dress and diet.

Dr. Hartog has presented a factual account of the events on the island of Curaçao from prehistoric times through the period of independence in 1954. Although the author states that the "new volume" is offered to the foreign reader, the fact that the work is oriented toward the local, and overwhelmingly lay public, is indicated not only by his approach but also by his constant reference to "our Island." The specific identification of historic figures as relatives of individuals now residing on Curaçao adds to this impression. Perhaps part of the "chatty" feeling which one draws from this work may be due to the English translation, which at some points is rather weak.

The author has failed almost completely to integrate or place the factual material into a total social context. Dr. Hartog introduces the last chapter with the statement that he is dealing only with facts without attempting an interpretation due to the unavailability of numerous records and lack of sufficient perspective, as if interpretation has been attempted in the preceding chapters. In addition there are several instances in which the organization results in some confusion for the reader. For example a topic may be presented with the principal discussion on page 27 while the reader must wait until page 35 before the supporting material is revealed. It is noted that on page 58 the evacuation of 402 Indians to the mainland is explained by the fact that the Dutch commander felt that the Indians were "entirely popish and not to be trusted," and in league with the Spaniards. Further the Commander felt that provisions would run short! However it is only on page 94 that the religious factor is clearly stressed as one of the "first" reasons for the evacuation. In other instances there is no clarification of the points presented. Statements are made to the effect that the remaining resident Indians were "annoyed" and the administration was "deceived" by the Indians; yet the specific circumstances causing these attitudes are never revealed. There is no attempt to explain Indian reaction other than by general reference to continued Spanish "inciting" Indians against the Dutch.

Curaçao can be considered an example of one type of segmented society depending on the definition utilized. However, due to the lack of any general consolidating statement as well as in-depth discussion, little or no understanding of the complex societal relationships can be drawn from the isolated facts. It is primarily during the remarks on church groups that one obtains some idea of these inter-relationships. For example various churches cater to single ethnic or racial groups while others cater to several as indicated by the fact that various languages may be utilized within a single church service.

Perhaps the most important omission involves data which would indicate the roles played by mulattos and Negroes in Curaçaon society since emancipation. In regard to the relation between Curaçaon society and slavery, the author states at one point "the slave trade, slavery and its abolition, will be dealt with in a separate chapter because they are unconnected with general historic developments" (p. 120). Subsequently Dr. Hartog presents very vital factual information on the operation of slavery on the island so that some idea of the relationships between the white citizenry versus the free Negro, mulatto, and the enslaved is obtained for that period. Judging from his presentation, however, persons of African descent appear to cease to exist after emancipation. Naturally an omission of this type might be construed to mean that as a group the neglected element was consequently integrated into the society as a whole. One is deterred from drawing this conclusion by a series of statements which occur throughout the book refering to "coloured" Curaçaons, "white and colored," and divisions along racial lines of certain Dutch Protestant churches in the past. During a discussion of the franchise in the late 1890s, it is stated that Hamelberg faced a problem in determining its basis; for if the property basis were too narrow the Jewish groups would be "given a disproportionate influence," if it were wide " 'supremacy would practically be in the hands of the blacks and coloured persons' for there was in these groups already a fairly large number of well to do people" (p. 405). This is virtually the only statement in the book which gives a clue to the possible adjustments of blacks and coloreds on the island after emancipation. The tendency, which is prevalent among Europeans and those of European descent, to consider the slave period as the only one in which persons of African descent are worthy of note (especially when they continue to be present in large numbers and are essentially isolated from the dominant group) has contributed to unnecessary feelings of inferiority on the parts of most persons of African descent and to the feelings of inate superiority on the part of the caucasoid elements. This approach is now considerably outdated, as well as out of place in any work of supposed scientific or historical value.

Nevertheless, due to the documentation, this work is of considerable value not only to the Curaçaon residents but to those interested in general Caribbean development, as apparently few authors have shown interest in the history of the Netherlands Antilles whether they wrote in Dutch or English. Consequently the volume contributes to knowledge of the Netherlands Antilles as well as the Caribbean in general.

VERA GREEN
Assistant Professor of Anthropology
University of Houston

Slater, Jerome. *Intervention and Negotiation, The United States and the Dominican Republic.* New York, Evanston, and London: Harper & Row, Publishers, 1970. Foreword by Hans J. Morgenthau, preface, notes, bibliography, index, illustrations. xviii, 254 pp. $7.95.

When United States troops landed in the Dominican Republic in April 1965 some observers foresaw a "Johnson Corollary" to the Monroe Doctrine to the effect that intervention in the domestic affairs of Caribbean nations was justified in order to prevent the spread of Communism. Critics of what many considered a precipitate and unwise action were vociferous in their condemnation of the affair, and piecemeal defenses of the administration policy failed to quiet the uproar. Now, with the perspective of some five years, the author of this work has set out to analyze "the full range of U.S. policy in the Dominican revolution from the military intervention of April, 1965, to the withdrawal of United States troops in September, 1966."

Events in Cuba led Washington to adopt a new policy toward Latin American dictatorships and exert pressure for more liberal governments and the institution of economic and social reforms, and OAS support was secured for sanctions against Trujillo in the Dominican Republic. These efforts continued after the dictator's assassination as the Kennedy administration strove to insure a democratic regime, and the election of Juan Bosch was widely heralded as ushering in a new era in Dominican affairs with the promise of significant reforms, although the United States Ambassador, John Bartlow Martin, was less optimistic about the new president and his Partido Revolucionario Dominicano (PRD). Finally, as even the State Department became disillusioned over the new government, a military group led by Colonel Elías Wessin y Wessin took control. The author contends that while Bosch was not the most astute politician, "the crucial reason for Bosch's downfall was that he meant what he said about ruling by democratic methods, respecting the civil liberties of leftist opponents, and effecting major political, economic, and social changes."

During the next eighteen months Donald Reid Cabral emerged as leader of the junta, but he failed to secure popular support and even antagonized the military. The revolution began in April 1965 as a coup, with the original participants being "a rather mixed bag" of liberals, reactionaries, and less reputable opportunists. Yet the uprising gained popular support, the PRD began to dominate, and it became clear that success would mean a return of Bosch to the presidency. At this point, and apparently with the urging of U.S. Embassy officials, the military under the leadership of Wessin y Wessin decided to oppose the rebellion. While United States officials distrusted Bosch and the PRD, "by far the more important factor in the decision to intervene was the embassy's specific assessment, reached almost at the outset, that there was a significant degree of Communist participation in the revolution." At this point the author begins a day-by-day and almost hour-by-hour account of the events that followed.

As the fighting continued and it appeared that the revolutionists were on the verge of victory, Ambassador W. Tapley Bennett on April 28, at the request of one member of the governing triumvirate, advised Washington to provide United States troops, and the first contingent arrived at San Isidro that night. "There is not the slightest doubt," says the author, "that the primary, indeed the overwhelming factor in the U.S. decision to intervene was the belief in both the embassy and the State Department that the apparently imminent constitutionalist victory would pose an unacceptable risk of a Communist takeover." Washington, however, in attempting to justify the intervention, exaggerated the number of Communists or Castroites in the revolutionary group and their degree of influence, thereby casting further doubts on the validity of the operation. Yet the author does not question United States intentions so much as he does the intervention itself, for he rejects the contention that Washington was motivated by a desire to prevent reform by supporting a reactionary military oligarchy that would provide stability. Although there is no clear evidence that United States troops participated in the fighting, they did prevent the rebel forces from uniting and allowed Wessin to destroy the weakened segments. The Washington authorities began a series of moves designed to restore a damaged reputation, bring respectability to the operation, and prepare for a restoration of constitutional government. The Organization of American States sought through the Special Committee of the Tenth Meeting of Consultation to arrange for a political settlement, but this committee "was almost a total disaster," and "the real power to arrange a settlement continued to remain in the hands of the United States." After a succession of Washington emissaries had failed to achieve a solution, Ellsworth Bunker arrived on the scene as chairman of an OAS ad hoc committee with wide authority. Dominating the negotiations, Bunker finally brought about agreement among the various factions on a Provisional Government under Héctor García-Godoy pending the outcome of elections. This interim government survived a number of crises as García-Godoy and Bunker worked closely together to establish a foundation for free elections and acceptance of the outcome by all groups. The United States was committed to scrupulous neutrality and went to great lengths to demonstrate its impartiality, and the author maintains that "the issue of fraud or deliberately rigged elections can be dismissed as unfounded." The new government of Joaquin Balaguer instituted a number of programs and the gross national product rose seven percent in 1969, but at the time of writing the Dominican Republic was "again on the edge of a new explosion."

The author takes great pains to explain the reasons for United States policies, i.e., first to understand, then to judge, and his judgments are very critical. Substantial errors were made in the pre-intervention period by not supporting particular groups at crucial times; the military intervention was a mistake because of the "predictably enormous political and moral costs," and the venture would not have been justified even if the revolution had been "*unmistakably* Communist;" domestic considerations and worldwide responsibilities played an unwarranted role in the decision to intervene; and serious errors were made in the post-intervention period when opportunities were lost to effect the "really sweeping military reform" essential for political and social change. Rejected are parallels with the Vietnam war and the Soviet invasion of Czechoslovakia, as are charges that the Dominican affair reflects an antiliberal or counterrevolutionary policy on the part of the United States.

There are perils involved in the writing of what some call "instant history," accounts produced so close to the events that relevant documents are not available. In this book the author has supplemented published materials, official and unofficial, by interviews with a number of participants, some of whom he is not allowed to identify. When taking issue with existing works the author is careful to indicate the other points of view, and he obviously strives to be fair and even-handed in his treatment of other interpretations as he does in dealing with the issues. Still his own position is clear, and he does not hesitate to draw his own conclusions. Whether, as contended, "Along with the war in Vietnam, the U.S. intervention in the Dominican revolution of 1965 has come to represent in the United States and all over the world the bankruptcy of recent American foreign policy" is another question. How many examples does one need for a generalization of this sort?

RAYMOND G. O'CONNOR
Professor of History
University of Miami

Tebeau, Charlton W. *A History of Florida.* Coral Gables, Florida: University of Miami Press, 1971. Illustrations, index. xii, 502 pp. $12.50.

This handsome, profusely illustrated, and delightfully readable volume is a credit to its author, "Super-Prof" Tebeau, and to the University of Miami Press. It is also a reward to Dr. Tebeau's multitude of ex-students and friends. Florida's history is longer than that of any other state, and the 18-page Selected Bibliography attests to its attraction for writers as well as to the author's diligence. This is a book worth owning for layman and scholar, history buff and serious student.

Beginning with a sketch of "Natural Endowments and First Inhabitants," Dr. Tebeau moves on to "Discovery and Exploration." The early explorers of the historical period were, of course, Spaniards, most of them unlucky. Juan Ponce de León, Lucas Vásquez de Allyón, Pánfilo de Narváez, Hernando de Soto, and a number of Jesuit priests paid with their lives for their curiosity about the strange and enchanting land. Tristán de Luna and Angel de Villafañe also failed in attempts to establish settlements there, and by this time Spaniards were convinced that the land could not be colonized. To Philip II it was a rude shock, therefore, to learn that French Protestants had actually founded a settlement on the Florida coast. On September 8, 1565, able Pedro Menéndez de Avilés founded St. Augustine and soon destroyed the French colony. Twenty-one years later Sir Francis Drake paid St. Augustine an unwelcome visit, for he landed 1,000 men and burned the village and its orange groves. St. Augustine was rebuilt, and it remained a key outpost along the homeward route of Spanish galleons.

"International Rivalry in Florida, 1670–1763" concerns the triangular struggle among Spanish, English, and French for the Southeast and for control of the Indian tribes of the region. Charleston was founded in 1670, the same year that Spain was forced to acknowledge Britain's rights to her coastal colonies. Robert Searles' attack on St. Augustine in 1668 had alerted Spaniards to the impending danger, and in 1672 work began on the Castillo de San Marcos, the massive coquina-built fort that still stands in St. Augustine. At the same time the French were working their way down the Mississippi valley from Canada, and they added a new element of rivalry to the Gulf region, causing the Spaniards to resume their efforts to found a settlement at Pensacola.

Step by step Dr. Tebeau continues his synthesis through the British period (1763–1784), the second Spanish period (1784–1821), the rise of Anglo-American pressure, and devious schemes for acquiring Florida before the final cession in the Adams-Onís Treaty. The territorial era, early statehood, and the costly Seminole War include many intriguing events of Florida history. Florida became a state in 1845, and it had grown considerably in population and wealth by the time it seceded from the Union in 1861.

The remaining 265 pages of text are devoted to the Civil War in Florida, Reconstruction, the Bourbon era, the Spanish-American-Cuban War, and on to the present. In the second half of the twentieth century Florida's growth has been constant. It was accelerated in recent years by the space exploration programs at Cape Kennedy, and a substantial increase in tourism is anticipated when the Florida Disney World opens in October of this year. It is perhaps appropriate that a history of this remarkable state should begin with a description of the natural world and conclude with one of the Disney World.

DONALD E. WORCESTER
Professor of History
Texas Christian University

Borah, Woodrow and Cook, Sherburne F. *The Population of the Mixteca Alta, 1520–1960.* Berkeley: University of California Press, 1968. Notes, map, tables. 89 pp. $3.00.

This is the most recent monograph co-authored by Woodrow Borah and Sherburne F. Cook on the fascinating problem of the Indian population of Mexico. It differs from their previous studies in two respects. First, the geographical area examined is relatively small; it comprises only the Mixteca Alta, 5,000 square miles of rugged terrain west of the city of Oaxaca. Second, the period investigated is extensive; it spans Mexico from pre-Conquest times to the census of 1960. The authors assert: "So far as we know, ours is the first attempt to examine the movement of population for a relatively restricted region in Mexico. It is, we hope, a demonstration of the kind of intensive local research which could be carried out for many areas of Mexico through exhaustive (and exhausting) study of the great variety of sources available" (p. 3).

This is an excellent suggestion. It implies that our present knowledge of the population history of Mexico is inadequate and that before further generalizations about the total population curve can be made, more serious local investigations should be completed. Borah and Cook's comprehension of the ecological and ethnological aspects of the Mixteca Alta over a period of more than four centuries demonstrates the type of knowledge required for such a study. The authors' use of a wide time span unfortunately weakens the real value of their local research. The period is so lengthy that they fail to analyze the composition and characteristics of the population at a given historical moment. They ignore, for example, the variables of birth, mortality, and migration that are the dynamic factors of population change. Vital statistics may be scarce; there are, however, enough nineteenth- and twentieth-century demographic data to make some reasonable generalizations. For the sixteenth century the paucity of reliable statistical data is a severe handicap. A few church registers, nevertheless, undoubtedly remain that would contain records of baptisms, marriages, deaths, or even entire lists of *confesantes*. These are most likely to be found in the Archivo Arzobispal in Oaxaca or in one of the many impressive sixteenth- and seventeenth-century churches that Borah and Cook vividly describe. Even one or two such volumes dated as late as the middle of the sixteenth century would be extremely useful in delineating major post-Conquest demographic patterns.

The techniques that Borah and Cook use in this study are more advanced than in their previous studies. Their expression of change as the ratio of the population to a base figure (Cook and Lesley Byrd Simpson, 1948) and the mean percentage change per year (1960) is dropped in favor of an "annual depletion rate" formula:

$$r = \frac{\frac{Na-Nb}{t}}{Na} \times 100$$

where t=time; Na=population at the earlier date; and Nb=the population at the later date. For the Mixteca Alta the authors calculate the rate for several periods: 1532–1548, 1560–1569, 1569–1579, 1579–1590, 1569–1590, and 1590–1600. These rates are then plotted on a graph against the mean year of each period. From the graph they conclude that the depletion rate remained a steady −4.5% per year from 1532 to about 1575; that the rate decreased sharply after 1575, an indication that demographic recovery had begun; that the decline reached full force by the 1530s; and that the decline probably ended between 1595 and 1620.

Shortcomings in the Borah-Cook methodology should be noted. The depletion rate, for instance, is based on a sample group of towns for each period. It is based, furthermore, on the mean rate of the rates for each village, not the mean depletion rate of the total sample population. A group of small towns with a large change could therefore create an abnormally high rate even though the mean of the total is low. Since Borah and Cook did not publish their findings for each town, it is impossible to check the accuracy of the stated rate. The graph they constructed of the depletion rate is sharply rounded off between 1575 and 1595. The result gives an annual depletion rate of less than one percent for 1595, while the actual plotted figure is nearer three percent. The one percent depletion rate is in line with their assumption that demographic recovery was strong after 1575. The rounded off graph, however, fails to represent the true erratic nature of the depletion rate. Counts taken shortly after severe epidemics are low. With a high birth rate, the population can increase sharply within ten years. The true rate, thus, is cyclical. Borah and Cook also do not present adequate documentation to prove that the population reached its perigee between 1600 and 1620.

After experimentation with ratios (1948), the "equation for the radioactive disintegration of an element or the die-away curve of a laboratory population" (1957), and the logarithm of the logarithm of the population (1960), they finally used the common formula to represent continuous population change long utilized by demographers: $P_2 = P_1e^{-kt}$. They employed this formula with the base population of 1569, which they considered nearly exact, and a *k* of −.045 to estimate the population of 1532 and 1520. These figures were correlated with others to give a 1520 estimate of 600,000–700,000. With the same formula they calculated the 1590 population: 57,000. They concluded the low, perhaps 20,000, was reached between 1600 and 1620 and assume that after this period continuous upward change occurred.

The weaker aspects of this study are evident in the authors' two page survey of the Mixteca Alta region from 1882 to 1960: inadequate examination of the dynamics of population growth; incomplete examination of the errors in census statistics; and insufficient study of the influence of *mestizaje*. The value of this monograph, and many of the past works of Borah and Cook, is that they tend to stimulate further research. The authors themselves note that their monograph is not exhaustive, when they conclude: "All these phenomena deserve further examination, but not in this paper" (p. 62). Let us hope they focus their talents on the same subject in the future.

NOBLE DAVID COOK
University of Bridgeport

Wauchope, Robert, gen. ed. *Handbook of Middle American Indians.* (Vol. 6, *Social Anthropology.* Manning Nash, ed.). (Vols. 6 and 7, Evon Z. Vogt, ed.). Austin: University of Texas Press, 1967 and 1969. Vol. 6: viii, 597 pp. $15.00. Vols. 7 and 8: viii, 965 pp. $15.00.

When one can no longer travel through some parts of Mexico or Guatemala without meeting several anthropologists in each village, some type of "population control" on the part of anthropologists is clearly needed. Anthropology is faced with its own pollution crisis in the mountains of mediocre or redundant publications. It is only with periodic stock-takings such as the handbook under review that one can determine how far knowledge has progressed. The pollution crisis is reflected in the fact that this long-awaited handbook is several years behind schedule. Some papers in the volumes under review were written several years ago, and it is not always clear up to what time a particular paper attempts to summarize research. For instance, the chapter on population utilizes 1950 census data.

The volume on social anthropology includes an introduction by the editor and twenty-five topical summaries. As in any work of this type, some topics have been slighted or omitted. For instance, the chapter by Romney includes a great deal of excellent and unpublished material on kinship terminology, but neglects most other aspects of kinship. The excellent paper by Edmonson on "Games, Gossip and Humor" in fact fails to discuss the role of gossip in social relations.

Two papers on ethnic and communal relations by Julio de la Fuente and Eric Wolf are especially noteworthy. The former summarizes very well the wide variety of relationships between Indians and non-Indians ranging from decidedly friendly relations to openly violent contacts. Eric Wolf rightly considers the market as the most important institution in respect to the integration of communities, while the extra-market commercial network links lower to higher levels of integration. He also sees the tendency of factions to become political parties on the state level as perhaps the most effective means of undermining the autonomy of a community.

The chapters on "Agricultural Systems" by Angel Palerm and on "Settlement Patterns" by William Sanders are thorough and provide numerous insights. Several papers deal with social change using a variety of approaches. In his paper on urbanization, Arden King questions the view that Indian urban migrants are victims of poverty, that Indian village life is superior to urban life, and that life in cities is detrimental to Indians. He puts forth the provocative belief that Indians probably suffer less maladjustment and dismay than has been theorized, provided the economic opportunities are present.

While the approach of the volume on social anthropology is comparative, the approach of the volumes on ethnology is in the style of gazeteer summaries by area or linguistic groupings. This approach is based upon an ethnographic outline devised by Evon Vogt which insures comparable coverage for different areas of Middle America by means of regional introductions and ethnographic summaries of contemporary Indian cultures. These volumes are therefore more valuable for reference than for reading. Sections dealing with distribution, history, and bibliography are very useful, but sections dealing with social structure or the character of the peoples generally fail to provide integrated analyses indicating the essential features. Maps of distribution of each ethnic group are generally adequate, but a composite map for all of Middle America would have been more useful.

The photographs in all three volumes are interesting, especially those in the last two volumes which include many that were previously unpublished. The publication of volume six in a less expensive format for a wider audience would be welcome.

ALAIN Y. DESSAINT
Lecturer in Anthropology
University of Hawaii

BOOKS RECEIVED

General and Regional Latin America

Chilcote, Ronald H., ed. *Revolution and Structural Change in Latin America: A Bibliography on Ideology, Development, and the Radical Left (1930–1965).* (Hoover Institution Press, Bibliographical Series, 40. Vol. II. Cuba and Venezuela) Stanford, California: Hoover Institution Press, 1970. Author index, periodical index. 603 pp.

Dyer, John M. *Guidelines to Operating in Latin America.* Miami, Florida: Field Research Projects, 1970. Foreword, illustrations. xi, 73 pp.

Kantor, Harry. *Patterns of Politics and Political Systems in Latin America.* Chicago: Rand McNally and Company, 1969. Preface, A Note on the Study of Comparative Government, epilogue, index. xiii, 742 pp.

Kennedy, Paul P. *The Middle Beat, A Correspondent's View of Mexico, Guatemala, and El Salvador.* New York: Teachers College Press, 1971. Introduction, preface, index. xix, 235 pp. $8.50.

Martz, John D., ed. *The Dynamics of Change in Latin American Politics.* (Second Edition) Englewood Cliffs, New Jersey: Prentice-Hall, Inc., 1971. Preface, introduction, list of contributors. x, 395 pp.

Rabinovitz, Francine F. and Trueblood, Felicity M., eds. *Latin American Urban Research.* Beverly Hills, California: Sage Publications, Inc., 1971. Introduction, bibliography, appendix. 352 pp. $15.00.

Worcester, Donald and Schaeffer, Wendell G. *The Growth and Culture of Latin America.* (Second Edition) New York, London and Toronto: Oxford University Press, 1971. Preface, glossary, index. xxi, 1,146 pp. $20.00.

Zimmerman, Irene. *Current National Bibliographies of Latin America.* Gainesville: Center for Latin American Studies, University of Florida, 1971. Introduction, appendix, bibliography, index. x, 139 pp. $7.00.

Countries of Latin America

Brazil

Hower, Alfred and Preto-Rodas, Richard A., eds. *Crônicas Brasileiras.* Gainesville, Florida: University of Florida Press, 1971. Introduction, vocabulary. xiii, 224 pp. $5.00.

Hunter, John M. *Economic Aspects of Higher Education in Brazil.* (Monograph Series, No. 5) East Lansing, Michigan: Latin American Studies Center, Michigan State University, 1971. iv, 84 pp.

Johnson, Allen W. *Sharecroppers of the Sertão: Economics and Dependence* on a *Brazilian Plantation*. Stanford, California: Stanford University Press, 1971. Introduction, glossary, bibliography, index. 153 pp. $6.50.

Love, Joseph L. *Rio Grande do Sul and Brazilian Regionalism, 1882–1930*. Stanford, California: Stanford University Press, 1971. Preface, notes, glossary, note on sources, index. xv, 311 pp. $10.00.

Schmitter, Philippe C. *Interest Conflict and Political Change in Brazil*. Stanford, California: Stanford University Press, 1971. Figures and tables, glossary of Brazilian terms, index. xvi, 499 pp. $15.00.

Schneider, Ronald M. *The Political System of Brazil: Emergence of a "Modernizing" Authoritarian Regime, 1964–1970*. New York and London: Columbia University Press, 1971. Appendixes, essay on sources, index of names, index of subjects. xviii, 431 pp. $13.50.

Shirley, Robert W. *The End of Tradition, Culture Change and Development in the Município of Cunha, São Paulo, Brazil*. New York and London: Columbia University Press, 1971. Preface, glossary, bibliography, index. xi, 304 pp. $10.00.

Wagley, Charles. *An Introduction to Brazil*. (revised ed.) New York: Columbia University Press, 1971. Preface, selected bibliography, index. xv, 341 pp. $11.00.

Caribbean Region

Reckford, Barry. *¿Does Fidel Eat More Than Your Father?* New York and Washington: Praeger Publishers, 1971. Introduction. 191 pp. $5.95.

Rueda, Manuel, ed. *Adivinanzas Dominicanas*. Santo Domingo: Editora del Caribe, 1970. Índice general. 461 pp.

Colombia

Dow, J. Kamal. *Colombia's Foreign Trade and Economic Integration in Latin America*. Gainesville: University of Florida Press, 1971. Tables, introduction, bibliography. ix, 84 pp. $5.00.

Ecuador

Gibson, Charles R. *Foreign Trade in the Economic Development of Small Nations: The Case of Ecuador*. (Praeger Special Studies in International Economics and Development.) New York, Washington and London: Praeger Publishers, 1971. Preface, list of tables, list of figures, appendix, bibliography. xxii, 352 pp. $17.50.

Mexico

Alisky, Marvin. *Guide to the Government of the Mexican State of Sonora*. Tempe, Arizona: Center for Latin American Studies, Arizona State University, 1971. Preface, introduction. 48 pp. $1.00.

Bazant, Juan. *Los Bienes de la Inglesia en México (1856–1875)*. Guanajuato: El Colegio de México, 1971. Prefacio, introducción, índice onomástico, índice analítico. xiii, 364 pp.

Brading, D. A. *Miners and Merchants in Bourbon Mexico, 1763–1810*. (Cambridge Latin American Studies, No. 10). New York and London: Cambridge University Press, 1971. Tables and figures, preface, abbreviations, measures and money, glossary, appendixes, maps, index. xvii, 382 pp. $16.50.

Cheetham, Sir Nicolas. *Mexico: A Short History*. New York: Thomas Y. Crowell Co., 1971. Preface, list of illustrations, list of maps, bibliographical note, index. 302 pp. $7.50.

Galarza, Ernesto. *Barrio Boy*. Indiana: University of Notre Dame Press, 1971. Preface, glossary. vii, 275 pp. $7.95.

Quirk, Robert E. *Mexico*. (*The Modern Nations in Historical Perspective*, Robert W. Winks, gen. ed.) Englewood Cliffs, New Jersey: Prentice-Hall, Inc., 1971. Bibliographical essay, index. viii, 152 pp.

Sawatzky, Harry Leonard. *They Sought a Country: Mennonite Colonization in Mexico*. Berkeley, California: University of California Press, 1971. Appendix, bibliography, index. xi, 387 pp. $11.50.

Wilkie, Raymond. *San Miguel: A Mexican Collective Ejido*. Stanford, California: Stanford University Press, 1971. Introduction, references, index. xvii, 190 pp. $7.50.

Nicaragua

Walker, Thomas W. *The Christian Democratic Movement in Nicaragua*. Tucson, Arizona: The University of Arizona Press, 1970. Introduction, sources. 70 pp.

Peru

Hilliker, Grant. *The Politics of Reform in Peru: The Aprista and Other Mass Parties of Latin America*. Baltimore, Maryland: The Johns Hopkins Press, 1971. Preface, note on sources, appendices, index, figures, tables, xv, 201 pp. $10.00.

Stephens, Richard H. *Wealth and Power in Peru*. Metuchen, New Jersey: The Scarecrow Press, Inc., 1971. Introduction by Harold L. Lasswell, preface, author's introduction, appendixes, selected annotated bibliography, index. ix, 219 pp. $5.00.

Venezuela

Powell, John Duncan. *Political Mobilization of the Venezuelan Peasant*. Cambridge, Massachusetts: Harvard University Press, 1971. Introduction, notes, index. 259 pp. $8.50.

INTER-AMERICAN RELATIONS

Gil, Federico G. *Latin American-United States Relations*. New York, Chicago, San Francisco, Atlanta: Harcourt Brace Jovanovich, Inc., 1971. Preface, index. x, 339 pp. $3.95.

Mellander, G. A. *The United States in Panamenian Politics: The Intriguing Formative Years*. Danville, Illinois: The Interstate Printers and Publishers, Inc., 1971. Bibliography, index. 215 pp. $7.95.

Ulloa, Berta. *La Revolución Intervenida: Relaciones Diplomáticas entre México y Estados Unidos (1910–1914)*. Guanajuato, México: El Colegio de México, 1971. Índice general, obras citadas, índice analítico, índice de ilustraciones, ix, 394 pp.

MISCELLANEOUS

Aldridge, Owen A., ed. *The Ibero-American Enlightenment.* Urbans and London: University of Illinois Press, 1971. Introduction, contributors. x, 335 pp. $10.00.

Carpentier, Alejo. *The Kingdom of This World.* (Translated from the Spanish by Harriet de Onís.) New York: Collier Books, 1971. $1.50.

Day, Mark. *Forty Acres: Cesar Chavez and the Farm Workers.* New York, Washington and London: Praeger Publishers, 1971. Introduction by Cesar Chavez, a personal prologue, appendix, suggested readings, illustrations. 222 pp. $6.95.

Moquin, Wayne, ed. *A Documentary History of the Mexican Americans.* New York: Praeger Publishers, 1971. Editor's preface, introduction by Feliciano Rivera, list of illustrations, index. xiv, 399 pp. $13.50.

Pérez, José Joaquín. *Obra Poética.* Santo Domingo: Universidad Nacional Pedro Enrique Ureña, 1970. Indice, 352 pp.

Rhodes, Robert L., ed. *Imperialism and Underdevelopment.* New York: Monthly Review Press, 1971. Introduction, bibliography. xii, 416 pp. $11.95.

Rostow, W. W. *Politics and the Stages of Growth.* New York and London: Cambridge University Press, 1971. Preface, introduction, notes, index, appendix. xiii, 410 pp. $9.50.

Sable, Martin H. *Latin-American Studies in the Non-Western World and Eastern Europe.* Metuchen, New Jersey: Scarecrow Press, 1970. Preface, author index, subject index. xxiii, 701 pp. $15.00.

AUTHOR INDEX

Author	Title	No.	Pages
Bode, Barbara	The Image of Christ in Spanish America as a Model for Suffering	2	246–257
Cochrane, James D.	The Movement for Regional Arms Control in Latin America	1	1–17
Foland, Frances M.	A Profile of Amazonia	1	62–77
Fringer, Katherine	The Contribution of Capistrano de Abreu to Brazilian Historiography	2	258–278
Gitlitz, John S.	Impressions of the Peruvian Agrarian Reform	3–4	456–474
Hicks, Frederic	Interpersonal Relationship and Caudillismo in Paraguay	1	89–111
Hodge, John E.	Juan M. Thome, Argentine Astronomer from the Quaker State	2	215–229
Lamb, Ursula	Units of One and the Visible Event	1	131–135
Leslie, John C.	The International Air Transport Association: Some Historical Notes	3–4	319–341
Lovatón, Ramón Lugo	La Virgen de las Mercedes en la Isla de Santo Domingo	1	53–63
Lowenthal, David	Post-Emancipation Race Relations: Some Caribbean and American Perspectives	3–4	367–377
MacDonald, John S.	Jobs and Housing: Alternative Developments in the Venezuelan Guayana	3–4	342–366
MacDonald, Leatrice D.	Jobs and Housing: Alternative Developments in the Venezuelan Guayana	3–4	342–366
Machado, Manuel A., Jr.	La Ganadería americana: una propuesta para la historia comparativa	2	159–165
Maier, Georg	Presidential Succession in Ecuador: 1860–1968	3–4	475–509
Mullen, Edward J.	*Contemporáneos* in Mexican Intellectual History, 1928–1931	1	121–130
Nett, Emily M.	The Functional Elites of Quito	1	112–120
Pardo, Marta Eugenia	The Image of Christ in Spanish America as a Model for Suffering	2	246–257

AUTHOR	TITLE	NO.	PAGES
Petersen, John H.	Student Political Activism in Guatemala	1	78–88
Pincus, Joseph	Interim Adjustment Policy in the CACM	2	182–196
Raine, Philip	The Catholic Church in Brazil	2	279–295
Richardson, Miles	The Image of Christ in Spanish America as a Model for Suffering	2	246–257
Rosenbaum, H. Jon	Policy-Making for the Brazilian Amazon	3–4	416–433
Rutan, Gérard F.	Provincial Participation in Canadian Foreign Relations	2	230–245
Smith, Peter Seaborn	Bolivian Oil and Brazilian Economic Nationalism	2	166–181
Solberg, Carl	Rural Unrest and Agrarian Policy in Argentina, 1912–1930	1	18–52
Stabb, Martin S.	Argentine Letters and the Peronato: An Overview	3–4	434–455
Stinson, Hugh B.	The Movement for Regional Arms Control in Latin America	1	1–17
Tyler, William G.	Policy-Making for the Brazilian Amazon	3–4	416–433
Villamil, José A.	Situación demográfica de Guatemala y sus efectos socioeconómicos	2	197–214
Walsh, Bryan O.	Cuban Refugee Children	3–4	378–415

TITLE INDEX

TITLE	AUTHOR	NO.	PAGES
Argentine Letters and the Peronato: An Overview	Martin S. Stabb	3–4	434–455
Bolivian Oil and Brazilian Economic Nationalism	Peter Seaborn Smith	2	166–181
The Catholic Church in Brazil	Philip Raine	2	279–295
Contemporáneos in Mexican Intellectual History, 1928–1931	Edward J. Mullen	1	121–130
The Contribution of Capistrano de Abreu to Brazilian Historiography	Katherine Fringer	2	258–278
Cuban Refugee Children	Bryan O. Walsh	3–4	378–415
The Functional Elites of Quito	Emily M. Nett	1	112–120
La Ganadería americana: una propuesta para la historia comparativa	Manuel A. Machado, Jr.	2	159–165
The Image of Christ in Spanish America as a Model for Suffering	Miles Richardson, Marta Eugenia Pardo, and Barbara Bode	2	246–257
Impressions of the Peruvian Agrarian Reform	John S. Gitlitz	3–4	456–474
Interim Adjustment Policy in the CACM	Joseph Pincus	2	182–196
International Air Transport Association: Some Historical Notes	John C. Leslie	3–4	319–341
Interpersonal Relationship and Caudillismo in Paraguay	Frederic Hicks	1	89–111
Jobs and Housing: Alternative Developments in the Venezuelan Guayana	John S. MacDonald and Leatrice D. MacDonald	3–4	342–366
John M. Thome, Argentine Astronomer from the Quaker State	John E. Hodge	2	215–299
The Movement for Regional Arms Control in Latin America	Hugh B. Stinson and James D. Cochrane	1	1–17
Policy-Making for the Brazilian Amazon	H. Jon Rosenbaum and William G. Tyler	3–4	416–433
Post-Emancipation Race Relations: Some Caribbean and American Perspectives	David Lowenthal	3–4	367–377

TITLE	AUTHOR	NO.	PAGES
Presidential Succession in Ecuador, 1860–1968	Georg Maier	3–4	475–509
A Profile of Amazonia	Frances M. Foland	1	62–77
Provincial Participation in Canadian Foreign Relations	Gérard F. Rutan	2	230–245
Rural Unrest and Agrarian Policy in Argentina, 1912–1930	Carl Solberg	1	18–52
Situación demográfica de Guatemala y sus efectos socio-económicos	José A. Villamil	2	197–214
Student Political Activism in Guatemala	John H. Petersen	1	78–88
Units of One and the Visible Event	Ursula Lamb	1	131–135
La Virgen de las Mercedes en la Isla de Santo Domingo	Ramón Lugo Lovatón	1	53–61

BOOK SECTION INDEX

Author	Title	No.	Pages
Alisky, Marvin	*Uruguay: A Contemporary Survey*. Reviewed by Elman R. Service	2	311–312
Borah, Woodrow and Cook, Sherburne F.	*The Population of the Mixteca Alta, 1520–1960*. Reviewed by Noble David Cook.	3–4	535–537
Corten, André and Coren, Andrée	*Cambio Social en Santo Domingo*. Reviewed by Nancie Solien Gonzalez	1	149–150
Dean, Warren	*The Industrialization of Sáo Paulo, 1880–1945*. Reviewed by Sidney M. Greenfield	2	300–303
Dulles, John W. F.	*Unrest in Brazil: Political-Military Crises, 1955–1964*. Reviewed by Jordan M. Young.	3–4	527–529
Gonzalez, Nancie L.	*The Spanish-Americans of New Mexico: A Heritage of Pride*. Reviewed by Celia S. Heller	2	308–311
Grieb, Kenneth J.	*The United States and Huerta*. Reviewed by Raymond G. O'Connor	1	150–151
Hartog, J.	*Curação, From Social Dependence to Autonomy*. Reviewed by Vera Green.	3–4	530–531
Moreno, Francisco José	*Legitimacy and Stability in Latin America: A Study of Chilean Political Culture*. Reviewed by James D. Cochrane	1	146–148
Papanek, Gustav F.	*Development Policy: Theory and Practice*. Reviewed by Roy J. Hensley.	3–4	517–523
Petras, James	*Political and Social Forces in Chilean Development*. Reviewed by Paul E. Sigmund	1	151–154
Phillips, Hiram S.	*Guide for Development: Institution-Building and Reform*. Reviewed by Roy J. Hensley.	3–4	517–523
Pineda, Virginia G Gutiérrez de.	*Familia y Cultura en Colombia*. Reviewed by Aaron Lipman	2	305–306
Schuh, G. Edward	*The Agricultural Development of Brazil*. Reviewed by L. Harlan Davis.	3–4	525–527

AUTHOR	TITLE	NO.	PAGES
Sierra, Justo	*The Political Evolution of the Mexican People.* Reviewed by Robert L. Bidwell	2	306–308
Slater, Jerome	*Intervention and Negotiation, the United States and the Dominican Republic.* Reviewed by Raymond G. O'Connor.	3–4	531–534
Smith, Peter H.	*Politics and Beef in Argentina: Patterns of Conflict and Change.* Reviewed by Fred Miller.	3–4	523–525
Stein, Stanley J. and Barbara H.	*The Colonial Heritage of Latin America. Essays on Economic Dependence in Perspective.* Reviewed by Donald E. Worcester	2	303–305
Tebeau, Charlton W.	*A History of Florida.* Reviewed by Donald E. Worcester.	3–4	534–535
Wauchope, Robert	*Handbook of Middle American Indians.* Reviewed by Alain Y. Dessaint.	3–4	537–538
Wiarda, Howard J.	*Dictatorship and Development: The Methods of Control in Trujillo's Dominican Republic.* Reviewed by Manuel Ortega	1	141–146

GREAT SEAL UNIVERSITY OF MIAMI
CORAL GABLES FLORIDA 1925